# OBJECT-ORIENTED PROGRAMMING IN C++

## 2ND EDITION

## Richard Johnsonbaugh
## Martin Kalin
**DePaul University**

*An Alan R. Apt Book*

Prentice Hall
Upper Saddle River, NJ 07458

**Library of Congress Cataloging-in-Publication Data**

Johnsonbaugh, Richard,
    Object-Oriented Programming in C++ / by Richard Johnsonbaugh and
Martin Kalin. – 2nd ed.
    p.     cm.
    Includes bibliographical references and index.
    ISBN  0–13–015885–2
    1. C++ (Computer programming language).  2. Application software–Development
    I. Kalin, Martin  II. Title.

Publisher: *Alan Apt*
Senior acquisitions editor: *Petra Recter*
Editorial/production supervision: *Scott Disanno*
Editor-in-chief: *Marcia Horton*
Executive managing editor: *Vince O'Brien*
Managing editor: *Eileen Clark*
Copyediting: *Patricia Johnsonbaugh*
Creative director: *Amy Rosen*
Art director: *Heather Scott*
Cover art: *Marjory Dressler*
Assistant to art director: *John Christiana*
Assistant vice-president of production and manufacturing: *David W. Riccardi*
Manufacturing buyer: *Pat Brown*
Composition: *PreTEX, Inc.*

© 2000, 1996 by Prentice Hall, Inc.
Pearson Higher Education
Upper Saddle River, New Jersey 07458

The author and publisher of this book have used their best efforts in preparing this book. These efforts include the research, development, and testing of the theory and programs in the book to determine their effectiveness. The author and publisher make no warranty of any kind, expressed or implied, with regard to these programs or the documentation contained in this book. The author and publisher shall not be liable in any event for incidental or consequential damages in connection with, or arising out of, the furnishing, performance, or use of these programs.

Printed in the United States of America

10  9  8  7  6  5  4  3  2  1

**ISBN   0-13-015885-2**

Prentice-Hall International (UK) Limited, *London*
Prentice-Hall of Australia Pty. Limited, *Sydney*
Prentice-Hall Canada Inc., *Toronto*
Prentice-Hall Hispanoamericana, S.A., *Mexico*
Prentice-Hall of India Private Limited, *New Delhi*
Prentice-Hall of Japan, Inc., *Tokyo*
Prentice-Hall (Singapore) Pte. Ltd., *Singapore*
Editora Prentice-Hall do Brasil, Ltda., *Rio de Janeiro*

**TRADEMARK INFORMATION**

IBM is a registered trademark of International Business Machines Corporation

Unix is a trademark of Bell Laboratories

Borland C++ is a registered trademark of Borland International, Inc.

SUN refers to Sun Microsystems, a registered trademark of SUN Microsystems, Inc.

Microsoft, MS DOS, and Windows are either registered trademarks or trademarks of Microsoft, Inc.

CodeWarrior is a trademark of Metrowerks

# The JK Computer Science and Mathematics Series

## Published by Prentice Hall

---

E. Gose, S. Jost, and R. Johnsonbaugh, **Pattern Recognition and Image Analysis**, 1996.

R. Johnsonbaugh and M. Kalin, **Applications Programming in ANSI C**, 3rd ed., 1996.

R. Johnsonbaugh and M. Kalin, **Applications Programming in C++**, 1999.

R. Johnsonbaugh and M. Kalin, **C for Scientists and Engineers**, 1997.

R. Johnsonbaugh, **Discrete Mathematics**, 4th ed., 1997.

R. Johnsonbaugh and M. Kalin, **Object-Oriented Programming in C++**, 2nd ed., 2000.

# Preface

This book is based on C++ courses given by the authors at DePaul University and can be used for self-study or for a course on object-oriented programming in C++. We assume no prior knowledge of C++, but we do assume knowledge of C. Coverage of C at the level provided in R. Johnsonbaugh and M. Kalin, *Applications Programming in ANSI C*, 3rd ed. (Upper Saddle River, N.J.: Prentice Hall, 1996) provides sufficient background for this book. The book and its supplements—a CD-ROM containing Microsoft's C++ compiler, an *Instructor's Guide*, and a World Wide Web site—provide a comprehensive support system to help the reader master C++. In this book, as in our other C and C++ books, we make extensive use of examples, figures, self-study exercises, sample applications, lists of common programming errors, and programming exercises. We strive for clarity throughout the book and also illustrate a variety of good programming practices.

This book treats object-oriented principles (see Chapter 1); emphasizes sound programming practices; introduces templates and the standard template library (see Chapter 7); presents in depth the C++ input/output class hierarchy (Chapter 8); features major, useful examples (e.g., a stack class, Sections 3.2 and 7.2; and a random access file class, Section 8.6); and introduces object-oriented programming in the Microsoft Foundation Classes in Chapter 9.

The C++ language presented here is based on the approved standard. As such it contains the latest additions and changes to the language including

- The logical type **bool**.
- The **string** class.
- New-style headers.
- Namespaces and the namespace **std**.
- New-style casts.
- STL (Standard Template Library).
- Exception handling.
- Run-time type identification.
- The operator **new[ ]**.
- The template input/output classes.
- The **stringstream** classes.

## Overview

During the 1980s and early 1990s, C became the language of choice for many applications and systems programmers. Most major software available for personal computers was written in C: spreadsheets, word processors, databases, communications packages, statistical software, graphics packages, and so on. Virtually all software written for the UNIX environment was likewise written in C, and many mainframe systems meant to be ported from one platform to another were also coded in C. In the early 1980s, Bjarne Stroustrup of AT&T Bell Labs developed C++ as an extension of C that supports object-oriented programming, a type of programming that is well suited to the large, complex software systems now written for all platforms, from the cheapest personal computers to the most expensive mainframes. C++ also corrects some shortcomings in C, which C++ includes as a subset, and it supports abstract data types and generic functions through templates.

C++ is a highly complex language. Fortunately, most C++ programmers can benefit from its power without mastering each and every one of its features. We focus on the most useful aspects of the language, but we place some of the more esoteric and specialized parts of the language in end-of-chapter sections labeled *C++ Postscript*. We focus on *using* C++ to write practical programs based on sound design techniques, rather than on tricks and surprises in C++.

# About This Book

This book includes

- Examples and exercises that cover a wide range of applications.
- Motivating real-world applications.
- A broad variety of programming exercises. The book contains over 100 programming exercises.
- End-of-chapter lists of common programming errors.
- Coverage of STL (the Standard Template Library) (Chapter 7).
- Discussion of the standard C++ input/output class library (Chapter 8).
- Coverage of object-oriented programming in the Microsoft Foundation Classes (Chapter 9).
- Exercises at the ends of sections so that readers can check their mastery of the sections. The book contains over 500 such exercises. Answers to the odd-numbered section exercises are given in the back of the book, and answers to the even-numbered section exercises are given in the *Instructor's Guide*.
- Figures to facilitate the learning process.
- The latest changes and additions to the C++ language.
- Major data structures, including stacks (Sections 3.2 and 7.2) and files (Section 8.6), implemented in C++.
- Understandable code. We have opted for clarity rather than subterfuges based on obscure C++ features.
- Microsoft's Visual C++ student compiler.

# Changes from the First Edition

- Recent changes and additions to C++ are incorporated throughout the book.

- Namespaces are introduced earlier (Section 2.1) because namespace **std** is needed for the new-style headers.

- Exception handling is also introduced earlier (Section 2.8).

- An entire chapter is devoted to polymorphism (Chapter 5).

- Inheritance (Chapter 4) and polymorphism (Chapter 5) are introduced earlier to underscore their importance to the object-oriented programming paradigm. Operator overloading therefore comes later (Chapter 6).

- Run-time type identification is integrated into the main body of the text (Section 5.5).

- An entire chapter (Chapter 7) is devoted to templates and the standard template library.

- Chapter 8 (Chapter 7 in the first edition) on the C++ input/output class hierarchy is considerably revised to incorporate significant changes to this hierarchy.

- Chapter 9 is added to cover object-oriented programming in the Microsoft Foundation Classes.

- Some of the more recondite parts of the language are reserved for *C++ Postscript* sections at ends of chapters.

- The number of worked examples has been increased to nearly 300.

- The number of exercises has been increased to over 500.

- We have extensively revised the sample applications.

- The figures are boxed to separate them visually from the text.

- A World Wide Web site has been established to provide up-to-date support for the book.

- Microsoft's Visual C++ student compiler is included on a CD-ROM.

## Organization of the Book

Chapter 1 introduces key concepts associated with object-oriented design and programming: classes, abstract data types, objects, encapsulation, the client/server model, message passing, inheritance, polymorphism, and others. The chapter contrasts object-oriented design with top-down functional decomposition and offers examples to illustrate the differences between the approaches.

Important changes and additions to C++ are detailed in Chapter 2. Chapter 2 also introduces namespaces, type **string**, the **new** and **delete** operators, exception handling, and basic C++ input/output. The reader can begin using these important C++ features right away.

Chapter 3 covers the basics of classes so that the reader can begin using classes at once. The chapter explains how to declare classes; how to write constructors, destructors, and other methods; **static** data members and methods; and pointers to objects. Chapter 3 relies heavily on examples to explain how classes may be used to implement abstract data types and to meet the object-oriented goal of encapsulation.

Inheritance (including multiple inheritance) is the topic of Chapter 4. Through examples and sample applications (e.g., a sequence hierarchy), the chapter illustrates basic programming techniques.

Polymorphism is covered in Chapter 5. Section 5.1 carefully explains the distinction between run-time and compile-time binding. Sections 5.4 and 5.5 explain abstract base classes and run-time type identification.

Chapter 6 is devoted to operator overloading. The chapter shows how to overload common operators (e.g., **+**, **/**) as well as the subscript, function call, memory management, preincrement, and postincrement operators among others. Many examples and sample applications highlight the power of operator overloading.

Templates and STL (standard template library) are explained in Chapter 7. A template stack class (Section 7.2) shows templates in action, and a sample application (stock performance reports in Section 7.4) demonstrates how to use STL.

Chapter 8 serves several purposes. First, the chapter examines the C++ input/output library in detail so that the interested reader can exploit the powerful classes contained therein. This treatment culminates in a sample application that builds a random access file class through inheritance from a system file class. Second, the chapter uses the input/output library as a major, sophisticated example of object-oriented design realized in C++. Third, the hierarchy provides an excellent example of the use of templates. Chapter 8 pays close attention to manipulators, which are powerful ways to do sophisticated input/output in C++. We believe that Chapter 8 offers an unrivaled examination of C++'s input/output.

Chapter 9 covers object-oriented programming in the Microsoft Foundation Classes (MFC). We clarify the relationship between MFC and the Win32 Applications Programmer Interface, Microsoft's C libraries for accessing systems services. We also introduce the basic concepts and constructs of event-driven programming. The chapter focuses on object persistence through serialization and interapplication communication under Microsoft's Common Object Model. We provide two sample applications together with an overview of MFC and Visual C++.

Two appendices are provided for reference. Appendix A contains the ASCII table. Appendix B contains a list of some of the most useful C++ functions and class methods. We describe the parameters and return values, the header to include, and what the function or method does.

We rely heavily on short examples, figures, and tables to illustrate specific points about the syntax and semantics of C++. From our experience teaching C++ and other languages, we are convinced that no single method is appropriate for clarifying every aspect about a language.

Most of our students agree with us that learning and using C++ is exciting. We have tried to incorporate this view by using engaging examples, sample applications, programming exercises, and short segments of code.

## Chapter Structure

The basic chapter organization is as follows:

Contents

Overview

Section

Section Exercises

Section

Section Exercises

$\vdots$

C++ Postscript

Common Programming Errors

Programming Exercises

In every chapter except 1 and 2, several sections are devoted to sample applications. Each of these sections contains a statement of a problem, sample input and output, a solution to the problem, and a well-documented implementation of a solution to the problem in C++. Most of these sections conclude with an extended discussion.

The sample applications include the following:

- A stack class (Sections 3.2 and 7.2)

- Tracking films (Sections 4.3 and 5.2)

- A sequence hierarchy (Section 4.6)

- A complex number class (Section 6.2)

- An associative array (Section 6.8)

- Stock performance reports (Section 7.4)

- A random access file class (Section 8.6)

- Interapplication communication under Microsoft's Common Object Model (Section 9.5)

The *C++ Postscript* sections discuss less-used parts of the language and give additional technical details about certain parts of the language.

The *Common Programming Errors* sections highlight those aspects of the language that are easily misunderstood.

The book contains over 100 programming exercises drawn from a wide variety of applications.

## Examples

The book contains nearly 300 examples, which clarify particular facets of C++ for the reader and show the purpose of various C++ features. A box ■ marks the end of each example.

## Exercises

The book contains over 500 section review exercises, the answers to which are short answers, code segments, and, in a few cases, entire programs. These exercises are suitable as homework problems or as self-tests. The answers to the odd-numbered exercises are given in the back of the book, and the answers to the even-numbered exercises are given in the *Instructor's Guide*. Our experience in teaching C++ has convinced us of the importance of these exercises.

The applications covered in the programming exercises at the ends of the chapters include the following:

- Simulation (Programming Exercise 2.9)

- Queues (Programming Exercises 3.8 and 7.4)

- Process synchronization (Programming Exercise 3.10)

- Databases (Programming Exercise 3.15)

- Local area networks (Programming Exercises 3.17 and 6.7)

- Array hierarchy (Programming Exercise 4.4)

- Dating services (Programming Exercise 5.10)

- Iterators (Programming Exercises 7.6, 7.7, and 7.8)

- Scheduling (Programming Exercise 7.14)

- An indexed file class (Programming Exercise 8.5)

- A dialog-based application with a graphical-user interface for a system administrator (Programming Exercise 9.9)

Not every reader will be interested in all of these applications; however, we think that it is important to show the variety of problems that C++ can address.

# CD-ROM

The book comes with a CD-ROM that has the Student Edition of the current release of Microsoft's Visual C++ Integrated Development Environment, which includes a C++ compiler, a debugger and class browser, help facilities, the Microsoft Foundation Classes and the ActiveX Template Library, and many other resources for applications development. All of our sample applications, including the Microsoft-specific applications of Chapter 9, may be compiled and run under Visual C++.

## Instructor Supplement

An *Instructor's Guide* is available from the publisher at no cost to adopters of this book. The *Instructor's Guide* contains solutions to even-numbered section exercises, sample syllabi, and transparency masters.

## World Wide Web Site

The World Wide Web site

```
http://condor.depaul.edu/~mkalin
```

contains the source code, header files, and data files for all of the book's sample applications; the source code for some of the longer examples; sample syllabi; transparencies; a sample chapter; information about using Microsoft Visual C++; additional technical details about the Microsoft Foundation Classes; and an errata list.

# Acknowledgments

We thank the following reviewers: Adair Dingle, Seattle University; Rex Jaeschke, independent consultant; Glenn Lancaster, DePaul University; and Winnie Y. Yu, Southern Connecticut State University.

We are again grateful to our friendly copy editor, Patricia Johnsonbaugh, for checking numerous details and suggesting changes that improved the book.

We are indebted to the School of Computer Science, Telecommunications and Information Systems at DePaul University and its dean, Helmut Epp, for providing time and encouragement for the development of this book.

We received consistent support from the people at Prentice Hall. Special thanks go to Alan R. Apt, publisher; Petra Recter, senior acquisitions editor; and Scott Disanno, production editor.

R.J.
M.K.

# Brief Table of Contents

1 OBJECT-ORIENTED PROGRAMMING   1

2 FROM C TO C++   21

3 CLASSES   98

4 INHERITANCE   175

5 POLYMORPHISM   229

6 OPERATOR OVERLOADING   285

7 TEMPLATES AND THE STANDARD TEMPLATE LIBRARY   340

8 THE C++ INPUT/OUTPUT CLASS HIERARCHY   402

9 OBJECT-ORIENTED PROGRAMMING IN THE MICROSOFT FOUNDATION CLASSES   479

A ASCII TABLE   527

B SELECTED C++ FUNCTIONS AND METHODS   531

HINTS AND SOLUTIONS TO ODD-NUMBERED EXERCISES   574

INDEX   601

# Contents

**Preface   v**

## 1 OBJECT-ORIENTED PROGRAMMING   1

**1.1**   Object-Oriented and Procedural Programming   2
Relationships   4
**1.2**   Classes and Abstract Data Types   5
Information Hiding   5
Encapsulation   6
Abstract Data Types   6
**1.3**   The Client/Server Model and Message Passing   9
The Client/Server Model   9
Message Passing and Method Invocation   10
**1.4**   Inheritance and Polymorphism   12
Inheritance   12
Polymorphism   13
Polymorphism and Recursion   14
**1.5**   Interfaces and Components   17
Component Technology   19

## 2 FROM C TO C++   21

**2.1**   Namespaces   22
**2.2**   Introduction to C++ Input/Output   27
Manipulators   29
Mixing C and C++ Input/Output   34
**2.3**   Files   35
Testing Whether Files Are Open   37
**2.4**   C++ Features   38
Casts   38
**static_cast**   38
**const_cast**   39
**reinterpret_cast**   40
**dynamic_cast**   40
Constants   40
The Data Type **bool**   40
Enumerated Types   41
Defining Variables   42
Structures   43

**2.5** The Type **string**  44
Defining **string** Variables  45
Conversion to C-Style Strings  45
String Length  45
Writing and Reading **string**s  45
Assignment  47
Concatenation  48
Modifying Strings  48
Extracting a Substring  51
Searching  51
Comparing Strings  53
**2.6** Functions  56
Prototypes  56
The **main** Function  57
References  57
Call by Reference  58
Return by Reference  59
Inline Functions  62
Default Arguments  63
Overloading Functions  64
Function Signatures  65
**2.7** The **new** and **delete** Operators  70
**2.8** Exception Handling  73
C++ Postscript  78
Keywords  78
Unnamed Namespaces  78
Anonymous Unions  78
The Member Selector Operators  79
Common Programming Errors  83
Programming Exercises  93

# 3 CLASSES  98

**3.1** Classes and Objects  99
Class Declarations  99
Information Hiding in C++  100
The Member Selector Operator  101
Class Scope  103
The Difference between the Keywords **class** and **struct**  103
Defining Class Methods  104
Using Classes in a Program  106
**3.2** Sample Application: A Stack Class  109
**3.3** Efficiency and Robustness Issues for Classes and Objects  112
Passing and Returning Objects by Reference  113
Object References as **const** Parameters  113
**const** Methods  114

Overloading Methods to Handle Two Types of Strings    116

**3.4**    Sample Application: A Time Stamp Class    117

**3.5**    Constructors and the Destructor    124

Constructors    124

Arrays of Class Objects and the Default Constructor    127

Restricting Object Creation Through Constructors    127

The Copy Constructor    129

Defining a Copy Constructor    129

Disabling Passing and Returning by Value for Class Objects    135

Convert Constructors    136

The Convert Constructor and Implicit Type Conversion    137

Constructor Initializers    138

Constructors and the Operators **new** and **new[ ]**    139

The Destructor    139

**3.6**    Sample Application: A Task Class    145

**3.7**    Class Data Members and Methods    151

**static** Variables Defined Inside Methods    155

**3.8**    Pointers to Objects    157

The Pointer Constant **this**    159

Common Programming Errors    161

Programming Exercises    169


**4    INHERITANCE    175**

**4.1**    Introduction    176

**4.2**    Basic Concepts and Syntax    178

**private** Members in Inheritance    180

Adjusting Access    181

Name Hiding    182

Indirect Inheritance    183

**4.3**    Sample Application: Tracking Films    185

**4.4**    **protected** Members    190

**4.5**    Constructors and Destructors Under Inheritance    195

Constructors Under Inheritance    195

Derived Class Constructor Rules    198

Destructors Under Inheritance    202

**4.6**    Sample Application: A Sequence Hierarchy    205

**4.7**    Multiple Inheritance    216

Inheritance and Access    217

Virtual Base Classes    218

C++ Postscript    221

**protected** Inheritance    221

**private** Inheritance    222

Common Programming Errors    223

Programming Exercises    226

# 5 POLYMORPHISM 229

**5.1** Run-Time versus Compile-Time Binding in C++ 230
Requirements for C++ Polymorphism 231
Inheriting **virtual** Methods 235
Run-Time Binding and the Vtable 236
Constructors and the Destructor 237
**virtual** Destructors 237
Object Methods and Class Methods 240
**5.2** Sample Application: Tracking Films Revisited 242
**5.3** Name Overloading, Name Overriding, and Name Hiding 252
Name Overloading 252
Name Overriding 253
Name Hiding 255
Name Sharing in C++ Programming 257
**5.4** Abstract Base Classes 260
Abstract Base Classes and Pure **virtual** Methods 260
Restrictions on Pure Functions 262
Uses of Abstract Base Classes 262
Microsoft's **IUnknown** Interface 263
**5.5** Run-Time Type Identification 265
The **dynamic_cast** Operator 265
The Rules for **dynamic_cast**s 271
Summary of **dynamic_cast** and **static_cast** 272
The **typeid** Operator 272
Extending RTTI 274
C++ Postscript 275
Strong and Weak Polymorphism 275
Common Programming Errors 276
Programming Exercises 280

# 6 OPERATOR OVERLOADING 285

**6.1** Basic Operator Overloading 286
Operator Precedence and Syntax 289
**6.2** Sample Application: A Complex Number Class 291
**6.3** Operator Overloading Using Top-Level Functions 296
**6.4** **friend** Functions 302
**6.5** Overloading the Input and Output Operators 305
**6.6** Overloading the Assignment Operator 307
**6.7** Overloading Some Special Operators 311
Overloading the Subscript Operator 312
Overloading the Function Call Operator 315
Overloading the Increment and Decrement Operators 318
Type Conversions 321
**6.8** Sample Application: An Associative Array 324

**6.9**   Memory Management Operators   329
C++ Postscript   334
**friend** Classes   334
Common Programming Errors   335
Programming Exercises   338

# 7   TEMPLATES AND THE STANDARD TEMPLATE LIBRARY   340

**7.1**   Template Basics   341
Template Instantiations   345
Template Classes in a Parameter List   347
Function-Style Parameters   348
**7.2**   Sample Application: A Template Stack Class   351
Assertions   358
**7.3**   The Standard Template Library   359
Containers, Algorithms, and Iterators   360
Reasons for Using STL   360
Container Basics   362
Basic Sequential Containers: **vector**, **deque**, and **list**   363
Efficiency of **vector**s, **deque**s, and **list**s   367
Basic Associative Containers: **set**, **multiset**, **map**, and **multimap**   367
Container Adaptors   370
Other Containers   372
Algorithms   377
Other STL Constructs   382
**7.4**   Sample Application: Stock Performance Reports   385
C++ Postscript   394
Template Classes and Inheritance   394
Common Programming Errors   395
Programming Exercises   397

# 8   THE C++ INPUT/OUTPUT CLASS HIERARCHY   402

**8.1**   Overview   403
Templates   407
**8.2**   The Classes **ios_base** and **basic_ios**   408
**ios_base**   408
**basic_ios**   414
Exceptions   416
**8.3**   The High-Level Input/Output Classes   419
**basic_istream**   419
**basic_ostream**   424
**basic_iostream**   426
**8.4**   Manipulators   428
**8.5**   The File Input/Output Classes   432
**basic_ofstream**   433

**basic_ifstream**  434

**basic_fstream**  436

8.6  Sample Application: A Random Access File Class  438

8.7  The Character Stream Input/Output Classes  457

**basic_ostringstream**  457

**basic_istringstream**  458

**basic_stringstream**  460

8.8  Sample Application: A High-Level Copy Function  461

8.9  The Buffer Classes  463

**basic_streambuf**  463

**basic_filebuf**  465

**basic_stringbuf**  472

C++ Postscript  474

Common Programming Errors  475

Programming Exercises  477

# 9  OBJECT-ORIENTED PROGRAMMING IN THE MICROSOFT FOUNDATION CLASSES  479

9.1  Windows Programming in MFC  481

Code Generators for MFC Programming  482

9.2  The Document/View Architecture in MFC  483

Document Serialization  486

9.3  Sample Application: Document Serialization  489

9.4  The Common Object Model  503

Changeable Servers and Unchangeable Interfaces  505

The Interface Hierarchy  505

The **IDispatch** Interface  506

Types of COM Applications  507

VC++ Support for COM  508

COM and OLE  508

9.5  Sample Application: An Automation Server and Controller  510

The Challenge of Reference Counting  522

C++ Postscript  523

Acronyms Used in Chapter 9  523

Programming Exercises  524

## APPENDICES

A  ASCII TABLE  527

B  SELECTED C++ FUNCTIONS AND METHODS  531

HINTS AND SOLUTIONS TO ODD-NUMBERED EXERCISES  573

INDEX  601

# OBJECT-ORIENTED PROGRAMMING

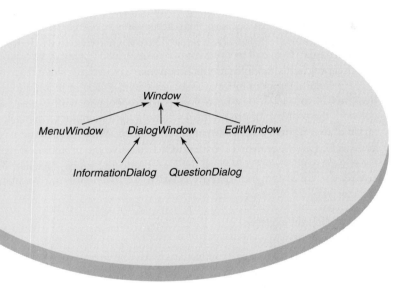

1.1 Object-Oriented and
Procedural Programming

1.2 Classes and Abstract Data
Types

1.3 The Client/Server Model
and Message Passing

1.4 Inheritance and
Polymorphism

1.5 Interfaces and Components

**C**++ is a hybrid language that can be used simply as an extended and improved standard C, which is a procedural language. C++ also can be used as an object-oriented language that has distinctive programming constructs not found in C and other procedural languages. This chapter discusses the basic concepts, advantages, and programming techniques associated with object-oriented programming. Subsequent chapters then explore the details of object-oriented programming in C++.

## 1.1 OBJECT-ORIENTED AND PROCEDURAL PROGRAMMING

Programs consist of **modules**, which are parts that can be designed, coded, and tested separately and then assembled to form a program. C++ descended from C, which is a **procedural language** because its modules are procedures. Procedural languages are sometimes called **imperative languages** because their procedures are sequences of imperative statements such as assignment statements, tests, and procedure invocations. In C++ as in C, a *function* is a procedure. C++ can be used simply as improved C, that is, as a procedural language in which a program's modules are its functions.

Procedural programming is associated with a design technique known as **top-down design**. In top-down design, a *problem* is associated with a *procedure*. For example, consider the problem of producing a schedule for a manufacturing task such as building an automobile. We label the problem *MainProblem*. We intend to use a procedural language such as C, Pascal, or even procedural C++ to solve the problem. If we choose procedural C++, we assign *MainProblem* to the C++ procedure **main**. Because *MainProblem* is too complex to solve straightforwardly in **main**, we *decompose* the problem into subproblems such as

- Building the chassis.
- Building the engine.
- Building the drivetrain.
- Assembling the already built components.
- Inspecting the components and their assembly.

We assign each *subproblem* to a *subprocedure*, which is a function that **main** invokes. Just as the problem *MainProblem* decomposes into various subproblems, so the procedure **main** decomposes into various subprocedures to handle the subproblems. The subprograms may be further decomposed, of course; this decomposition is then mirrored by a decomposition of the subprocedures (see Figure 1.1.1). This process of **top-down, functional decomposition** continues until a subproblem is straightforward enough that the corresponding subprocedure can solve it. If a procedural C++ program is written in a highly modular style, its primitive procedures (that is, functions) tend to be very simple and short, consisting even of a single statement (for example, the **return** of some value).

Top-down design has the appeal of being intuitive and orderly. Many complex problems continue to be solved using this design technique. Yet the technique has drawbacks,

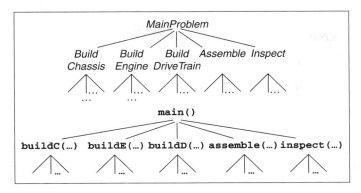

**FIGURE 1.1.1** Problem and procedure decomposition.

especially with respect to what is known euphemistically as **software maintenance**, which deals with the testing, debugging, and upgrading of software systems. Experienced programmers know that the most difficult task is not writing a program in the first place, but rather *changing* it afterwards because the program is flawed ("infected by bugs"), the program's requirements change, the program needs to execute more efficiently, and so on. Suppose that we need to change significantly the program that solves *MainProblem*. The change is so significant that we need to change **main**. In particular, suppose that **main** must now pass an additional argument to *each* of the subprocedures that it invokes, and that each of these must pass this additional argument to their subprocedures, and so on until the change has rippled throughout the entire hierarchy sketched in Figure 1.1.1. This phenomenon is known as **cascading changes**: a change in a procedure such as **main** cascades or ripples down to its subprocedures and to their subprocedures and so on until the change impacts much if not all of the decomposition hierarchy. The threat of cascaded changes can take the fun out of maintenance programming!

**Object-oriented programming** is an alternative to procedural programming. The design technique associated with object-oriented programming is **object-oriented design**. Object-oriented programming and object-oriented design are meant to address major problems associated with procedural programming and top-down design, problems such as cascading changes. In an object-oriented program, the modules are **classes** rather than procedures.

In object-oriented design, a **class** is a collection of **objects**. For example, the class *Human* is a collection of objects, that is, human beings such as you, me, and Mary Leakey. Objects in a class share **properties**, **features**, or **attributes**. Humans, for instance, share the properties of being *featherless*, *bipedal*, and *risible*. In an object-oriented language such as C++, a class is a *data type* and variables of this type can be defined in the usual manner. For example, if **Human** is a user-defined data type in C++, we can define a variable such as **maryLeakey** to represent the object—that is, the person—Mary Leakey who belongs to the class of human beings.[†] A variable of type **Human** can have **member variables** or

---

[†] Whenever the term *class* is used to designate a collection of objects, we italicize the name. For example, the class *Human* is a collection of human beings. Whenever the term *class* is used to designate a data type, we use a monospace typeface. For example, the class **Human** might be a C++ data type.

**fields** to represent properties or features distinctive of human beings. In C++, these member variables or fields are called **data members**. For example, the C++ class **Human** might have an **int** data member **feetCount** with its value set to 2 to represent that humans, including Mary Leakey, are bipedal.

A class such as *Human* has actions or processes associated with it. For instance, humans *eat*, *laugh*, *work*, *tango*, and so on. For convenience, we call such actions or processes *operations*. The operations associated with classes are represented by procedures. For example, if the C++ class **Human** is to model human objects such as Mary Leakey, the class needs a procedure—that is, a function—that represents how humans tango; such a procedure might show a video sequence that has two humans doing the tango. In C++, the functions that belong to a class are called **function members**. In object-oriented languages generally, such functions are called **methods**. We use both terms throughout the book. Classes as data types must combine variables (C++ data members) and procedures (C++ function members) in appropriate ways so that these data types can be used to model entities such as humans, automobiles, neutron stars, and Nordic ski teams. From a programming standpoint, a class as a data type is thus an aggregation of member variables and procedures that enables the class to model objects.

Object-oriented design is the design counterpart of object-oriented programming. Object-oriented design focuses on classes, which are the main programming modules in object-oriented languages. Classes are designed so that they model the entities with which a program deals. Consider again the task of building a scheduling system for manufacturing automobiles. We first need to design classes such as *Automobile*, *Engine*, *Worker*, and *PaintMachine* to represent things such as automobiles, their engines, and the workers and machines involved in the manufacturing process. Each class must model the properties and operations of the entities that the class is to represent. Class design is as challenging and creative as the object-oriented programming that depends upon it.

## Relationships

Relationships among classes and between objects and the classes to which they belong are also of interest in object-oriented design and programming. Such relationships are of different types. For instance, there is a *has a* (that is, *has property*) relationship between an *Automobile* class and an *Engine* class: an *Automobile has an Engine*. By contrast, there is an *is a* (that is, *is a subclass of*) relationship between a *PaintMachine* class and a *Machine* class: a *PaintMachine is a (subclass of a) Machine*. Between an object and a class there is an *instance of* or *belongs to* relationship: *Mary Leakey is an instance of a Human*. For more on object-oriented design, see J. Rumbaugh, et al., *Object-Oriented Modeling and Design*, (Englewood Cliffs, N.J.: Prentice Hall, 1991) or G. Booch, *Object Oriented Analysis and Design With Applications*, 2nd ed., (Reading, Mass.: Addison-Wesley, 1994).

## EXERCISES

1. What are program modules?
2. In a procedural language, what is the basic program module?
3. In an object-oriented language, what is the basic program module?
4. Is C++ a procedural or an object-oriented language?

5. In the context of top-down functional decomposition, what are cascading changes?

6. In the context of top-down functional decomposition, what is a primitive subproblem?

7. What does software maintenance deal with?

8. In object-oriented design, what are classes meant to represent?

9. What is a class in a programming language?

10. In a programming language class such as **Human**, how are human properties such as age and gender typically represented?

11. In a programming language class such as **Human**, how are human operations such as eating and working represented?

12. Design a class *Student* with several properties and operations.

13. Give an example, different from the ones in Section 1.1, of a *has a* relationship between two classes.

14. Give an example, different from the ones in Section 1.1, of an *is a* relationship between two classes.

15. Given an example, different from the ones in Section 1.1, of a *belongs to* relationship between an object and a class.

## 1.2 CLASSES AND ABSTRACT DATA TYPES

A class is a powerful object-oriented programming construct that directly supports the design, implementation, and use of an abstract data type. We begin with an overview of the class as a programming construct and then we explain what an abstract data type is and how a class supports it. We also emphasize the advantage to the programmer of using abstract data types rather than primitive built-in data types.

### Information Hiding

Consider the challenge of designing modern software products such as browsers, word processors, databases, spreadsheets, and data communications packages. These products undergo rapid development cycles in which a new and perhaps significantly different version replaces an older version. How can users survive such changes? For one thing, the products try to maintain a consistent **interface**. Consider your word processor. From one version to the next, it still supports commands that allow you to *Open* a document, *Save* a document, *Print* a document, *Copy* a document, *Format* a document in some special way, perform a *Spell Check* on the document, and the like. The word processor's *interface* is the functionality made available to the user through commands such as the ones just listed. We say that the interface is **public** to underscore that it is visible to the user. What is typically *not* public in a modern software product is the underlying **implementation**. An experienced programmer might be able to *guess* how the word processor is implemented, but the vendor deliberately hides these details from the user. For one thing, the product would be too hard to use if the user had to know thousands of technical details. For another, the vendor may be in the process of fixing known bugs and would like to leave them hidden until the fix is implemented as a patch or even a new version. We say that the implementation is **private** to underscore that it is *not* visible to the user. The implementation is *hidden* from the user, whereas the interface is *exposed* to the user. A goal of modern software design is thus to keep a product's public interface constant so that users remain fluent in the product even as its *private* implementation improves or otherwise changes.

In an object-oriented language, a class is a *module that supports information hiding*. In a C++ class, we can use keywords such as `public` and `private` to control access to the class's properties and operations. We can use the keyword `public` to expose the class's interface and the keyword `private` to hide its implementation. To use C++ as an object-oriented language is thus to use classes, a programming construct that directly supports information hiding. Object-oriented languages thus have, in the class, a programming construct well suited to building modern software systems.

## Encapsulation

In procedural programming, the modules are procedures, and data are manipulated by procedures. The standard mechanism for this style of data manipulation is passing arguments to and returning a value from a function. In object-oriented programming, the modules are classes. Data and the procedures to manipulate the data can be **encapsulated** or contained within a class. Imagine a `String` class—that is, data type—that can be used to create strings, concatenate them, change the characters they contain, check whether a given character occurs in a `String`, and so on. The `String` class would have data members (variables) to represent the characters in a `String` and, perhaps, such other information as a `String`'s length. Such variables are encapsulated within the class in the sense that every `String` object has the variables specified in the `String` class. A `String` class also would have function members (methods) to manipulate its data members. For example, the `String` class presumably would have a method to create a new `String` object, another method to copy one `String` object to another, another method to check whether a `String` object contains a specified character, and so on. Methods, like data members, also are encapsulated within the class. A method is thus a function encapsulated in a class. A top-level function, such as a C++ program's `main`, is *not* encapsulated in any class.

A typical role of the class's encapsulated data members is to support its encapsulated methods. The encapsulated data members are typically hidden so that they provide behind-the-scenes support for the exposed encapsulated methods. For example, a `String` class might have a public `Length` method that gives the `String`'s length. The `String` class might support this public method with a private data member `len` that records the `String`'s length.

## Abstract Data Types

The concepts of information hiding and encapsulation relate closely to that of an **abstract data type**. Suppose that our goal is to build a `WordProcessor` class that has the functionality of a modern word processor. To make the class easy to use, we distinguish sharply between a public interface consisting of high-level operations such as `Save` and `Print` and a private implementation consisting of low-level details in support of the public interface. In this case, our class is an **abstract data type**. A data type is *abstract* if it exposes in its public interface only high-level operations and hides all low-level implementation details. C++

supports classes, which enable information hiding; and information hiding—specifically, the hiding of low-level implementation details—is the key to creating abstract data types. Further, an obvious way to deliver the required functionality in an abstract data type is to encapsulate the appropriate functions as class methods.

**EXAMPLE 1.2.1.** Suppose that we define a **Stack** class whose public interface consists of methods to

- Insert an object into a **Stack** if the **Stack** is not full. Such an operation is known as a *push*.
- Remove the most recently inserted object from a **Stack** if the **Stack** is not empty. Such an operation is known as a *pop*.
- Inspect the most recently inserted object, if any, but without removing it. Such an object occupies the *top* of a **Stack**.

A **Stack** is called a **LIFO (Last In, First Out) list** because insertions and deletions occur at the same end, known as the *top*. Figure 1.2.1 shows a **Stack** of letters in three states. In the left subfigure, the **Stack** is empty. The middle subfigure shows the **Stack** after the operations **push(A)** and **push(B)** have occurred. Because **B** was inserted last, it is at the top. The right subfigure shows the **Stack** after a **pop** operation, which removes **B**. After **B** has been removed, **A** is at the top.

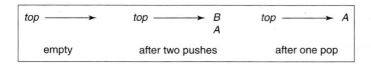

**FIGURE 1.2.1** A **Stack** in three states.

The **Stack** operations are high-level in that they require no knowledge of the **Stack**'s underlying implementation. Accordingly, the **Stack** as described is an abstract data type. ∎

Abstract data types spare the programmer the job of learning implementation details. The term *abstract* underscores precisely this point: a data type is abstract if it allows the user to abstract from—that is, to ignore—its low-level, implementation details. Further, abstract data types can be studied formally to reveal important properties about them. For example, the **Stack** described previously cannot overflow or underflow because pushes occur only if a **Stack** is not full, and pops occur only if a **Stack** is not empty. At least one successful push therefore precedes the first successful pop. The number of objects on a **Stack** equals the total number of pushes minus the total number of pops. If, after the first push, the total number of pushes always exceeds the total number of pops, a **Stack** is empty only before the first **push**, but never thereafter.

The use of abstract data types promotes program reliability and robustness. For example, suppose that we write an application that requires precise integer arithmetic. If we use low-level, built-in data types such as **int** or **long**, *we* need to attend carefully to implementation details such as an **int**'s range. In C++ as in C, an **int**'s range may vary from one system to another. Suppose that, on a given system, an **int**'s maximum value is 2,147,483,647. It is again *we* who must be careful, in our coding, not to perform arithmetic computations that exceed this maximum ("integer overflow"). Contrast this situation with one in which we use the abstract data type **Integer**. We now can focus on the integer computations that our program requires without concern for implementation details such as range. (An **Integer** class that implemented an abstract data type would typically extend indefinitely the range of built-in types such as **int** or **long**.) If an **Integer** operation did cause an integer overflow, the **Integer** type itself would provide clearly specified exception-handling so that the results would not be system-dependent.

Abstract data types can be implemented in procedural languages such as C and Pascal, but these languages provide little direct support for abstract data types. By contrast, the class construct of object-oriented languages provides direct support for abstract data types through information hiding and encapsulation. An object-oriented language such as C++ is the tool of choice for building abstract data types. Abstract data types, in turn, are the data types of choice in modern programming.

## EXERCISES

1. What is a class method?

2. What is a class interface?

3. What is a class implementation?

4. Explain why a class's interface is said to be *public*.

5. Explain why a class's implementation is said to be *private*.

6. How does a class support information hiding?

7. Does a class encapsulate both its data members and its methods?

8. Could a data member be either public or private?

9. Could a method be either public or private?

10. What advantages result from keeping a class's implementation details private?

11. What is an abstract data type?

12. Clarify what the term *abstract* means in the phrase *abstract data type*.

13. Suppose that we implement a **Stack** class so that pushes cannot occur on a full **Stack** and pops cannot occur on an empty **Stack**. Show that, at any time, the total number of elements on the **Stack** equals the total number of pushes minus the total number of pops.

14. What is the advantage to the programmer of using an abstract data type such as **Integer** rather than a built-in data type such as **int**?

# 1.3 THE CLIENT/SERVER MODEL AND MESSAGE PASSING

Well-designed programs have similarities in style regardless of whether the programs are based upon a procedural, an object-oriented, or some other model. For example, such programs tend to be modular and to have a flow of control that is clear. Nonetheless, well-designed object-oriented programs have distinctive stylistic features that incorporate key object-oriented constructs such as information hiding and encapsulation. In this section, we sketch some stylistic features of object-oriented programs.

## The Client/Server Model

Object-oriented programming is based on a **client/server model** of computing. This model explains the emphasis placed on information hiding in object-oriented programming. For example, the C++ standard library has a **string** class (see Section 2.5) whose public interface includes methods to create and destroy **string**s, concatenate them, search them for characters, and so on. The **string** class is a provider of services for string processing. The **string** class is a server of **string** objects that provide string-processing functionality. A C++ program that uses the **string** class is a *client*. A client requests services from a **string** object by invoking one of its methods, which is characterized as sending a **message** to the object. For example, the code segment

```
string s1 = "The Day the Music Died";
int n = s1.length();
```

first creates and initializes a **string** object **s1**. The code segment then sends a message to **s1** to request its length, that is, the number of characters in *The Day the Music Died*. The code segment occurs in a program that acts as a *client* of the **string** object **s1**, a server. We pass a message to a server such as **s1** by invoking one of its methods, that is, one of the functions encapsulated in **s1** as a **string** object.

A good server provides services with a minimum of effort on the client's part. In particular, the client should *not* be required to know *how* the server provides the services. The server's implementation details should be hidden from the client. The client should need to know *only* the server's interface, which typically consists of methods that the client can invoke. Such methods send messages to the server, which are requests for services. The server may send data back to the client, perform actions that the client requests, and so on. Good servers practice information hiding so that clients find them easy to use. For example, to get a **string**'s length, a client needs to know only the method **length**. The client does not need to know whether a **string** object stores the length in an encapsulated variable, whose value is returned; whether the **length** method, on each invocation, counts the number of cells in an array until encountering a null terminator; or whether some other technique is used to determine the length.

Information hiding also promotes server robustness. For example, suppose that a **string**'s interface consists of well-designed and thoroughly tested methods, with all implementation details hidden. In particular, assume that we test the public **string** methods **m₁**, **m₂**,...,**mₙ** until we are confident that no sequence of invocations can "break" a **string** server, that is, cause the **string** server to behave in some inappropriate way. Because a client has access only to these exposed methods and not to the **string**'s underlying implementation, we can be confident that client manipulation of **string** objects cannot "break" such objects. The robustness of a **string** server obviously contributes to the overall robustness of an application that uses such servers.

## Message Passing and Method Invocation

A program designed and implemented under the object-oriented model tends to have a distinct coding style. In an object-oriented program, classes and objects behave as servers, and modules that use classes and objects, such as functions in a C++ program, behave as clients. Clients request services in a distinctive manner, which we explore in this subsection.

**EXAMPLE 1.3.1.** A bookie has a computer file of bets on football games. A record such as

**A1Y4CBDL+2810/04/9850,000**

is formatted as follows:

- The first four characters identify a bettor. In this example, **A1Y4** identifies the bettor.
- The next four characters identify the two teams, with each team identified by two characters. In this example, the teams are the Chicago Bears (**CB**) and the Detroit Lions (**DL**). Because **CB** occurs *first*, the bet is that the Bears will beat the Lions.
- The next three characters give the point spread. The first of the three characters is either **+** or **−**, which indicates whether the first of the two teams listed (in this case, the Chicago Bears) is giving (**+**) or getting (**−**) points. The string **+28** thus means that the Chicago Bears are giving 28 points. **A1Y4**'s bet is that the Bears will beat the Lions by more than 28 points.
- The next eight characters, in this example **10/04/98**, represent the date on which the game is played. In this case, the date is October 4, 1998.
- The remaining characters represent the amount of the bet, in this case $50,000.

The bookie's data file does not comply with the so-called Year 2000 Standard because, in a date, a year is represented by two rather than four characters (for example, **98** instead of **1998**). The bookie therefore allowed one of his customers to pay off debts by writing a C++ program that would take the current data file *bets.dat* as input and produce the data file *y2kCompliantBets.dat* as output. All dates in *bets.dat* are 20th century rather than 21st century dates. Figure 1.3.1 shows how the program was coded in object-oriented C++.

Within **main**, there is one call to the top-level function **getline** but all other calls involve the message-passing style of method invocation. This style promotes code readability. For example, calls such as

```cpp
#include <string>
#include <fstream>
using namespace std;
int main() {
  // Open input and output streams
  const int dInd = 17; // index for insertion
  ifstream in;
  ofstream out;
  string buffer;
  in.open( "bets.dat" );
  out.open( "y2kCompliantBets.dat" );
  // Convert 2-field dates such as "98" to
  // 4-field dates such as "1998"
  while ( getline( in, buffer ) ) {
    buffer.insert( dInd, "19" );
    out << buffer << '\n';
  }
  in.close();
  out.close();
  return 0;
}
```

**FIGURE 1.3.1**  C++ program to bring a bookie's data file into year 2000 compliance.

```cpp
in.open( "bets.dat" );
out.open( "y2kCompliantBets.dat" );
//...
in.close();
out.close();
```

are easy to understand even without documentation because **in** and **out** are input and output streams, respectively. Given that **buffer** is a **string**, the meaning of

```cpp
buffer.insert( dInd, "19" );
```

is likewise clear. Nonetheless, even object-oriented programs require explicit documentation!

The call to the **string** method **insert** also underscores the benefit of information hiding. The **insert** method clearly must reconstruct the **string** by moving current characters to make room for the newly inserted ones. Exactly how this is done is an implementation detail hidden from the client. The client benefits from *not* having to know such implementation details; instead, the client simply sends the appropriately parameterized **insert** message to the **string** object, which then delivers the service by attending to low-level, implementation details.  ∎

Because a well-designed class exposes only what a client absolutely needs to request services, such a class's interface usually consists exclusively of high-level methods. A class's data members typically constitute the class's low-level support of these high-level methods. Client code therefore tends to be correspondingly high-level, as the program in Figure 1.3.1 illustrates. The message-passing style also underscores that classes and objects behave as servers whose interfaces are, in effect, a publication of the services provided. If services are hard and cumbersome to request, a class and its objects cannot expect many clients. So a well-designed class is precisely one that delivers appropriate services in a clear, straightforward manner.

## EXERCISES

1. Briefly describe how the client/server model relates to object-oriented programming.

2. If a class or an object is a server, what acts as the client?

3. In an object-oriented program, why do clients typically request services from a class by invoking its methods rather than by accessing its data members?

4. How does a client request service from a class or an object?

5. Explain the relationship between message passing and method invocation.

6. How does information hiding contribute to a server's robustness?

7. Explain why a well-designed class's interface typically exposes the class's services as *high-level* methods.

8. Does the message-passing style of object-oriented programming eliminate the need for documentation in object-oriented programs?

## 1.4 INHERITANCE AND POLYMORPHISM

Classes can be stand-alone or they can occur in **inheritance hierarchies**, which consist of parent/child relationships among classes. Inheritance is a convenient and efficient way to *specialize* or *extend* a parent class by creating a child class. For example, given the class **Window**, we could specialize it through inheritance by deriving a child **MenuWindow** class. Inheritance also allows the designer to combine features of classes in a common parent. For example, given the classes **Car**, **Motorcycle**, and **Truck**, we could combine their shared features in a common parent class called **Vehicle**.

Polymorphism is a powerful feature of object-oriented programming that exploits the potential of inheritance hierarchies. We go into the details of polymorphism after further clarifying inheritance.

## Inheritance

Inheritance supports a form of **code reuse**, which we explain through an earlier example. Suppose that we build a **Window** class to represent windows that appear on a computer's screen. The **Window** class has data members to represent a window's width and height, its *x* and *y* screen coordinates, its background and foreground colors, its border width, its style (e.g., framed), and so forth. We encapsulate appropriate methods to provide functionality for creating and destroying windows, moving them, resizing and reshaping them, changing their properties (e.g., background color), and so on. Once the **Window** class is built, we decide to refine or specialize it by building a **MenuWindow** subclass that inherits the **Window** data members and methods but then adds some of its own. For example, the **MenuWindow** subclass has data members and methods to support lists of menu items, user choices of menu items, and so on. Other subclasses are possible. Figure 1.4.1 illustrates a possible inheritance hierarchy with **Window** as the parent class. The arrows point from the children to the parent.

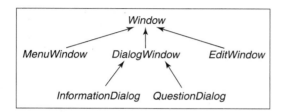

**FIGURE 1.4.1**  An inheritance hierarchy.

Different object-oriented languages support different types of inheritance. All such languages support at least **single inheritance** in which a child class has exactly one parent. Under a single-inheritance system, for example, the child class **SportsCar** might have **Car** as its single parent class. Some languages, including C++, support **multiple inheritance** in which a child class may have multiple parents. Under a multiple-inheritance system, the child class **SportsCar** might have **Car** and **Toy** as parent classes. Whether the inheritance is single or multiple, a child class can inherit data members and methods from each parent. The code segment

```
class Sportscar : public Car {
   // Sportscar members
};
```

shows the C++ code in which a **Sportscar** class is derived from a **Car** class. The colon **:** represents inheritance and means *is derived from* or *is a subclass of.* The keyword **public** signifies one type of C++ inheritance. For now, we intend to illustrate only the basic syntax.

How to design and exploit inheritance hierarchies are central issues in object-oriented design and programming. Chapter 4 explains the details of C++ inheritance.

## Polymorphism

The term *polymorphism* is derived from Greek and means *having many forms.* In an object-oriented language, there can be *many methods with the same signature.*[†] In Figure 1.4.1,

---

[†] A function's signature consists of its name together with the number and types of its parameters. For example, if a base class method and a derived class method are both named **m** and each has a single **int** parameter, they have the same signature. A function's return type is not part of its signature.

an appropriate **Window** method is **display**, which displays the **Window** on the screen; yet different types of windows display themselves differently. For example, a **MenuWindow** presumably displays a list of choices when it displays itself, whereas a **MessageWindow** may show only a single string. So there should be various *forms* or versions of the **display** method, presumably a separate one for each class in the **Window** hierarchy. Nonetheless, it is easier on the client (that is, the user of the **Window** hierarchy) to send a *single* display message to any type of **Window**. For example, regardless of whether pointer **w** points to a **MenuWindow** or a **MessageWindow**, we should be able to execute

```
w->display();
```

If **w** happens to point to a **MenuWindow**, then this class's **display** method should be invoked. If **w** happens to point to a **MessageWindow**, then this class's **display** method should be invoked. The system, not the client, should determine the type to which **w** points and, from the type, determine which version of **display** to invoke. In this example, **display** is thus a **polymorphic method**.

In general, polymorphic methods belong to classes in an inheritance hierarchy. It is common for each class in the hierarchy, from the parent class throughout all of the child classes, to provide its own appropriate version of a polymorphic method. In the context of polymorphism, a child class is said to **override** a parent's method of the same signature if the child class provides its own definition of this method. For example, if **MenuWindow** provides its own definition of the **display** method, then **MenuWindow** overrides the **display** method available in its parent class **Window**.

## Polymorphism and Recursion

Mastering polymorphism is central to becoming adept at object-oriented programming. Polymorphism has diverse uses. In this subsection, we single out one use to underscore how object-oriented languages offer alternatives to their procedural counterparts in solving certain types of problems.

**EXAMPLE 1.4.1.**   Consider the problem of printing each element in a list. Suppose that the list $L$ is

$$(n_1, (n_2, n_3, n_4), n_5)$$

$L$ has three elements: the first element is the node $n_1$, the second element is the sublist $(n_2, n_3, n_4)$ consisting of three nodes, and the third element is the node $n_5$. In a procedural language such as C, a function to print lists like $L$—that is, lists that may contain nested sublists to an arbitrary level—would likely be recursive. Figure 1.4.2 shows what the C function might look like, with **Element** as a structure to represent list elements. An **Element** structure contains information about whether a structure variable represents a simple node or a nested sublist. For example, the structure member **isNode** is set to 1, if the element is a simple node rather than a sublist, and to 0, if the element is a sublist. If an **Element** is a sublist, the member **firstElement** points to the first **Element** in the nested sublist. Although short, the function in Figure 1.4.2 has complex logic. Recursive functions are notoriously hard to write precisely because they typically require complex, difficult logic.

```
void printList( Element* e ) {
   if ( e == NULL )   /* an Element? */
     return;            /* base case 1: if not, return */
   else if ( e->isNode )  /* node or sublist? */
     printNode( e ); /* base case 2: if node, just print */
   else { /* else recursively invoke printList */
     Element* temp = e->firstElement;
     while ( temp != NULL ) {
       printList( temp ); /** recurse **/
       temp = temp->nextElement;
     }
   }
}
```

**FIGURE 1.4.2** Using recursion to handle nested sublists in C.

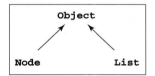

**FIGURE 1.4.3** Classes **Object**, **Node**, and **List** in a hierarchy.

Now consider the class hierarchy depicted in Figure 1.4.3, which has **Object** as a parent class and **Node** and **List** as two of its child classes. A list's elements may be objects that belong to any class in the **Object** hierarchy; in particular, a list may contain any mix of simple **Node**s and sub**List**s nested to arbitrary levels. Assume that the classes **Object**, **List**, and **Node** all have a polymorphic **print** method, which behaves appropriately for each class. For example, the **print** method for a **Node** simply prints the node's contents, whereas the **print** method for a **List** iterates through the list and invokes each element's own **print** method, thereby causing all the **List**'s elements to be printed, including elements that happen to be sub**List**s. Figure 1.4.4 shows the C++ code for the **List**'s polymorphic **print** method. The syntax **List::print** contains the **scope resolution operator**, which is the double colon **::**. To the left is the C++ class name, in this case **List**; to the right is the method name, in this case **print**. The scope resolution operator is needed because there may be many **print** methods with the same signature. Also, the method contains the keyword **const**, which signals that the method does not change the value of any data member of the associated object (see Chapter 3). We assume that the C++ **List** class has methods **HasMoreElements** and **NextElement**, which can be used to iterate through a **List**'s elements, whether these be simple nodes or nested sublists. Method **HasMoreElements** returns a **bool**ean value: **true**, if there are still more elements in the list to process, and **false**, if the iteration has already processed each element. Method **NextElement** returns, as a pointer to an **Object**, the list's next element.

```
void List::print() const {
    Object* obj;  // each element is in Object hierarchy
    while ( HasMoreElements() ) {
      obj = NextElement(); // Node or subList
      obj->print();         // polymorphic print
    }
}
```

**FIGURE 1.4.4** The polymorphic **print** method for the **List** class.

The variable **obj** is of type **Object***, where **Object** is the parent class for **Node** and **List**. Accordingly, **obj** can point to an object of any class within the **Object** hierarchy. When the polymorphic **print** method is invoked in the statement

```
obj->print();
```

the system first determines the type to which **obj** points, in this case, whether **obj** points to a **Node** or a **List** object. Once the system determines this type, the system then invokes the appropriate **print** method, in this case either **Node::print** or **List::print**. Whenever **obj** points to a nested sub**List**, the effect is the same as recursion in that **List::print** is invoked from within its own body. Yet the syntax remains straightforward rather than complex because the recursion is implicit rather than explicit. The main point is that the system, not the programmer, determines which **print** method to invoke. Contrast this approach with the recursive C function in Figure 1.4.2. In that case, the programmer must determine whether the current list element is a node or a nested sublist. In the polymorphic version, this determination is left to the system, which simplifies the code. ■

The logic of **List::print** in Figure 1.4.4 is considerably simpler than the recursive logic of **printList** in Figure 1.4.2. The contrast illustrates how polymorphism can be used, in an object-oriented language, to perform tasks that require explicitly recursive or otherwise complex logic in procedural languages. Polymorphism has other uses as well, which Chapter 5 covers in detail. A key challenge of class and hierarchy design is to provide classes in the hierarchy with the appropriate polymorphic methods, that is, with methods that simplify the task of writing client programs.

It should be emphasized that object-oriented constructs such as polymorphism do not eliminate complexity from programs. Complex problems require complex programs, regardless of the language used. Yet object-oriented constructs do allow the programmer to *distribute* a program's complexity in ways not available in traditional, procedural languages. In the case of **List::print**, for example, polymorphism allows us to delegate to the system the task of determining whether to invoke **Node::print** or **List::print** during each loop iteration. This delegation simplifies the code, which nonetheless performs the same complex task as its recursive C counterpart.

## EXERCISES

1. Give an example of single inheritance.

2. Give an example of multiple inheritance.

3. Does C++ support multiple inheritance?

4. Briefly describe what polymorphism is and why it is so powerful a programming technique.

5. What does it mean for a child class to *override* a method available in a parent class?

6. Do polymorphic methods have the same signature?

7. What is the relationship between inheritance and polymorphism?

8. Briefly sketch how the system determines which polymorphic method to invoke when control reaches the method invocation.

## 1.5 INTERFACES AND COMPONENTS

The distinction between the exposed and the hidden is central to object-oriented programming. A well-designed class typically exposes high-level methods and perhaps some data members. (For example, a `Color` class might have a public data member that represents a particular color such as red.) For simplicity, however, we assume a design model in which a class's public part consists of high-level methods and its private part consists of low-level methods and data members in support of these high-level methods. Recall that a class's interface consists of what it exposes and that its implementation consists of what it hides.

Some object-oriented languages (for example, Java) have *interface* as a reserved word but C++ does not. However, C++ has a construct called an **abstract base class** that can be used to specify an interface as a collection of public, high-level methods.[†]

**EXAMPLE 1.5.1.** Suppose that we are designing classes to support input and output operations on files. Presumably the classes would be in a hierarchy to promote code reuse. Assume, further, that we agree that every class in the hierarchy should define this set of methods:

- `Open`. Opens a named file.

- `Close`. Closes a file previously opened.

- `Rewind`. Sets the file's internal position marker to the beginning.

---

[†] Although an abstract base class can be used to specify an interface, this construct has broader uses in C++. Chapter 7 goes into detail.

```
// abstract base class used as an interface specification
class StdFile {
public:
    virtual void Open( const char* name, int mode ) = 0;
    virtual public void Close() = 0;
    virtual void Rewind() = 0;
};
```

**FIGURE 1.5.1** An abstract base class used as an interface.

There likely would be other methods as well, for example, a method to rename a file. Some methods might be parameterized. For example, **Open** might take at least two arguments: the name of the file to open, and the mode—input or output—in which to open the named file.

Figure 1.5.1 shows the C++ code for an abstract base class with these methods. For now, we can ignore the keyword **virtual** and the syntax **= 0** that follows each function's declaration. Chapter 7 covers these details. The important point is that **StdFile** declares but does not define the three methods **Open**, **Close**, and **Rewind**. In C++ as in C, to *declare* a function is to give its name, return type, and parameter types. To *define* a function is to provide its body, that is, the statements that perform whatever operations are appropriate for the function. In C++ as in C, function definitions always occur between a left brace, **{**, and a matching right brace, **}**. For example, the code segment

```
void f(); // declaration
```

*declares* the method **f**, whereas the code segment

```
void f() { /* f's body */ } // definition
```

defines this method. So the methods in the **StdFile** class are declared but not defined.

■

Now suppose that we create an **InputFile** class, an **OutputFile** class, a **RandomFile** class, and whatever additional input/output classes are appropriate. We can use the C++ compiler to enforce the requirement that each such class *define* the methods declared in the **StdFile** interface.

**EXAMPLE 1.5.2.** The code segment

```
class OutputFile : public StdFile {
  //*** definitions for Open, Close, and Rewind
  //     together with other methods, member variables, etc.
};
//**** This variable definition is possible only if
//      OutputFile defines Open, Close, and Rewind
OutputFile out1;
```

derives class **OutputFile** from class **StdFile** and defines an object **out1** of type **OutputFile**. If **Outfile** does not *define* each of the methods declared in **StdFile**, the compiler is required to issue a fatal error message at the definition of variable **out1**. By deriving **OutputFile** from the abstract base class **StdFile**, we in effect ensure that a client can invoke the methods **Open**, **Close**, and **Rewind** on any **OutputFile** object.                                                                    ■

Interfaces, if well built and shared among classes, are a convenience to programmers. Learning a shared interface allows a programmer to request services, using the *same* methods, from a variety of classes. A shared interface is thus a form of polymorphism suited to component technology. Figure 1.5.2 depicts the situation in which several classes implement the **StdFile** interface. To invoke a method declared in an interface, the programmer should not need to know how the method is actually defined in a class. In effect, a method's definition is an implementation detail that could remain hidden. The method's declaration should be sufficient for the programmer to request services by invoking the method. The art of designing high-level, programmer-friendly interfaces is to populate them with methods whose functionality is clear from the declaration together with whatever additional documentation might be appropriate.

```
class InputFile : public StdFile {
  //*** definitions for Open, Close, and Rewind
  //     together with other methods, member variables, etc.
};
class OutputFile : public StdFile {
  //*** definitions for Open, Close, and Rewind
  //     together with other methods, member variables, etc.
};
class RandomFile : public StdFile {
  //*** definitions for Open, Close, and Rewind
  //     together with other methods, member variables, etc.
};
```

**FIGURE 1.5.2** Several classes implementing the **StdFile** interface of Figure 1.5.1.

## Component Technology

A software **component** is a prebuilt part that can be combined with other such parts to build an application. A component is placed in a **container**, a software construct designed to integrate components by handling communications among them. The container and its components then constitute the application. A software component is analogous to a hardware component such as a disk drive or printer; and the container is analogous to a computer bus, which integrates components by enabling them to communicate with one another. Calendar components, browser components, e-mail components, database access components, and many others are already available.

A software component is typically delivered as a binary file and, therefore, its contents are hidden from the programmer who uses it. If the component is well constructed, the user need not know even the language in which it is written. To be usable, however, a component must expose at least one interface; a component typically exposes several interfaces. From the user's viewpoint, then, a component is the *back end* of some front-end interface. A programmer manipulates a component precisely through the methods exposed in its interfaces.

Components play a central role in modern software architecture. They have become a mainstay in Windows, UNIX, and other contemporary systems. Under Windows, for example, even large applications such as *Word* and *Excel* can act as components in some other application. A component extends the object-oriented concept of an object as a provider of services exposed in a high-level interface as a collection of methods. Chapter 9 examines component technology using the Microsoft Foundation Classes.

## EXERCISES

1. Does an interface contain function definitions or declarations?

2. With respect to an interface, is it true that a function's *definition* is an implementation detail hidden from the client?

3. Is *interface* a keyword in C++?

4. What C++ construct can be used to specify an interface?

5. An abstract base class is a C++ data type. Can variables of this type be defined?

6. What is a software component?

7. What is a container in component technology?

8. How are applications built using component technology?

9. A component may be described as the *back end* of the interfaces that it supports. Clarify what this term means.

10. Explain why a component is useless to clients if it does not expose any interfaces.

11. If a component is well designed, must a client know the programming language in which it is written?

12. Is a component typically delivered as a binary or a text file?

# CHAPTER
# 2

# FROM C TO C++

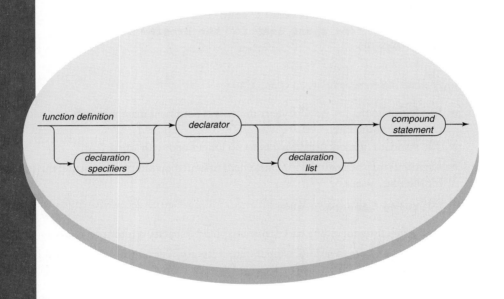

2.1 Namespaces

2.2 Introduction to C++ Input/Output

2.3 Files

2.4 C++ Features

2.5 The Type **string**

2.6 Functions

2.7 The **new** and **delete** Operators

2.8 Exception Handling

C++ Postscript

Common Programming Errors

Programming Exercises

**B**ecause C++ contains standard (ANSI) C as a subset, most standard C programs are also C++ programs. Nevertheless, C++ programmers replace parts of C with their improved C++ counterparts and make extensive use of the object-oriented extensions.

The simple C++ program

```
// This program outputs the message
//
//     C++: one small step for the program,
//     one giant leap for the programmer
//
// to the screen
#include <iostream>
using namespace std;

int main() {
   cout << "C++: one small step for the program,\n"
        << "one giant leap for the programmer\n";
   return 0;
}
```

shows some differences between C and C++:

- In addition to the `/* */` C-style comments, a comment may begin with `//` and extend to the end of the line.
- The standard headers (e.g., *iostream*) no longer end with "dot h."
- Identifiers may be confined to *namespaces* to limit their rampant exposure; this accounts for the line

      ```
      using namespace std;
      ```

- Every function, including **main**, must explicitly specify a return type.
- There is an alternative to C's input/output library (e.g., **cout** may be used instead of **printf**).

In this chapter, we discuss some differences between C and C++; we introduce some extensions to C found in C++; and we introduce the C++ input/output library.

## 2.1 NAMESPACES

C++ provides **namespaces** to prevent name conflicts. For example, if each of two libraries has an identifier **cout** and an application tried to use both libraries, a name conflict would result. Such name conflicts are a potential problem in large applications involving several programmers, who must be careful to find unique names for identifiers. We will routinely use the namespace **std**, which covers the standard C++ definitions, declarations, and so on for the standard C++ library.

**EXAMPLE 2.1.1.** Suppose that two libraries have a variable named `inflag`. If each vendor enclosed the variable within a namespace, an application could use both libraries at once. The syntax for enclosing a definition in a namespace is

```
namespace mfc { // vendor 1's namespace
   int inflag;  // vendor 1's inflag
   //...
} // no closing semicolon required
namespace owl { // vendor 2's namespace
   int inflag;  // vendor 2's inflag
   //...
} // no closing semicolon required
```

A namespace begins with the keyword **namespace** and generally is followed by a name such as **mfc** or **owl** that identifies the namespace. (The C++ Postscript explains unnamed namespaces and lists all C++ keywords.) An opening and a closing brace mark where the namespace begins and ends. ∎

Whatever can be declared or defined outside a namespace can be declared or defined inside one as well; hence, function declarations and definitions, variable definitions, **type-def**s, and the like all may occur inside a namespace.

A namespace can be used to disambiguate a name that otherwise would cause a conflict.

**EXAMPLE 2.1.2.** Given the namespaces of Example 2.1.1, the code segment

```
mfc::inflag = 3;     // mfc's inflag
owl::inflag = -823; // owl's inflag
```

uses **mfc**'s **inflag** and then **owl**'s **inflag**. The **scope resolution operator** `::` occurs between the namespace name (e.g., **owl**) and the variable (e.g., **inflag**). C++ operators and their precedence are given in Figure 2.1.1. ∎

**EXAMPLE 2.1.3.** We simplify Example 2.1.2 with a **using declaration** that lets us use **inflag** as shorthand for **mfc::inflag**. The code segment

```
using mfc::inflag;  // using declaration for mfc::inflag
inflag = 3;          // mfc::inflag
owl::inflag = -823; // namespace name needed
```

illustrates a using declaration. After the declaration, we can drop **mfc::** and simply use **inflag** to reference **mfc::inflag**. However, to reference **owl**'s **inflag**, we must use the full name **owl::inflag**.

A using declaration applies to a *single* item in the namespace. For example, suppose that the **mfc** namespace includes not only **inflag**, but a function **g**

```
namespace mfc {    // vendor 1's namespace
   int inflag;     // vendor 1's inflag
   void g( int ); // vendor 1's g
   //...
}
```

| Description | Operator | Associates from the | Precedence |
|---|---|---|---|
| Scope resolution | `::` | left | High |
| Function call | `()` | left | (Evaluated first) |
| Array subscript | `[ ]` | left | |
| Class indirection | `->` | left | |
| Member selector | `.` | left | |
| Postincr/postdecr | `++ --` | left | |
| Cast operators | `static_cast` | left | |
| | `const_cast` | left | |
| | `dynamic_cast` | left | |
| | `reinterpret_cast` | left | |
| Size in bytes | `sizeof` | right | |
| Preincr/predecr | `++ --` | right | |
| One's complement | `~` | right | |
| Unary not | `!` | right | |
| Address | `&` | right | |
| Dereference | `*` | right | |
| Unary plus | `+` | right | |
| Unary minus | `-` | right | |
| Storage allocation (single cell) | `new` | right | |
| Storage allocation (array) | `new[ ]` | right | |
| Free storage (single cell) | `delete` | right | |
| Free storage (array) | `delete[ ]` | right | |
| Member object selector | `.*` | left | |
| Member pointer selector | `->*` | left | |
| Multiplication | `*` | left | |
| Division | `/` | left | |
| Modulus | `%` | left | |
| Addition | `+` | left | |
| Subtraction | `-` | left | |
| Left shift | `<<` | left | |
| Right shift | `>>` | left | |
| Less than | `<` | left | |
| Less than or equal to | `<=` | left | |
| Greater than | `>` | left | |
| Greater than or equal to | `>=` | left | |
| Equal | `==` | left | |
| Not equal | `!=` | left | |
| Bitwise and | `&` | left | |
| Bitwise exclusive or | `^` | left | |
| Bitwise inclusive or | `\|` | left | |
| Logical and | `&&` | left | |
| Logical or | `\|\|` | left | |
| Conditional | `? :` | right | |
| Assignment | `= %= += -=` | right | |
| | `*= /= >>= <<=` | | |
| | `&= ^= !=` | | |
| Throw exception | `throw` | right | (Evaluated last) |
| Comma | `,` | left | Low |

**FIGURE 2.1.1** Precedence of C++ operators (operators between horizontal lines have the same precedence).

The using declaration for **mfc::inflag**

```
using mfc::inflag;
```

does *not* cover **mfc::g**. To invoke **g**, we need to use the full name

```
mfc::g( 8 );   // ok, full name
```

or introduce a using declaration that covers **g** in particular

```
using mfc::g; // using declaration for g
g( 8 );       // ok
```
■

**EXAMPLE 2.1.4.**  The code segment

```
using namespace mfc; // using directive
inflag = 21;         // mfc::inflag
g( -66 );            // mfc::g
owl::inflag = 341;   // full name needed
```

illustrates a **using directive**, which is equivalent to a using declaration for each item in a namespace. Note that the keyword **namespace** occurs in a using *directive*, which covers *all* identifiers in a namespace. This keyword does *not* occur in a using *declaration*, which covers *one* item in a namespace.  ■

**EXAMPLE 2.1.5.**  The code segment

```
using std; //***** ERROR: missing "namespace" *****
```

contains an error. The syntax for using an entire namespace (using directive) is

```
using namespace std;
```

The syntax for using a particular item in a namespace (using declaration) is

```
using std::cout;
```
■

Our programs typically include the using directive

```
using namespace std;
```

This using directive covers all the identifiers in C++'s **std** namespace, which includes all of the standard libraries.

**EXAMPLE 2.1.6.**  The code segment

```
#include <iostream>
using namespace std;
```

shows a typical use of a using directive with a standard header in a C++ program. The header *iostream* is included. The variables, functions, and so on in *iostream* are in the namespace **std**. Because it would be tedious to prefix each use of the variables, functions, and so on in *iostream* with **std::**, the using directive

```
using namespace std;
```

permits us to use the names in *iostream* without adding **std::** to each name.  ■

The standard C++ headers such as *iostream* do *not* end with a "dot h" as do the standard C headers such as *stdio.h*, although a particular C++ implementation may supply separate, nonstandard "dot h" headers. The definitions, declarations, and so on in nonstandard C++ "dot h" headers typically are *not* placed in namespaces. The standard C header files (e.g., *stdlib.h*) have been renamed: *.h* is dropped and a *c* is prefixed. Thus *stdlib.h* becomes *cstdlib*, *ctype.h* becomes *cctype*, and so on.

## EXERCISES

**1.** What purpose does a namespace serve?

**2.** Does a namespace require a semicolon after its closing brace?

**3.** Explain the error:

```
namespace foo {
  void showDate( int, int );
  //...
}
namespace bar {
  void showDate( int );
  //...
}
using foo::showDate;
showDate( 23 );
```

**4.** Given

```
namespace myLib {
  int Baz;
  //...
}
using myLib::Baz;
using namespace myLib;
```

indicate which is the using declaration and which is the using directive.

**5.** Explain the error:

```
namespace myLib {
   void Baz( int, int );
}
using namespace Baz;
```

**6.** Explain the error:

```
namespace myLib {
   //...
}
using myLib;
```

**7.** What is the C++ name of the C header *math.h*?

## 2.2 INTRODUCTION TO C++ INPUT/OUTPUT

C++ provides an alternative to C's input/output library. Although the programmer still can use the C input/output library, the new input/output library provides an easier-to-use, extensible, and more flexible system. In this section we present sufficient basic information so that the reader can start using certain of these features. We defer an extended discussion of C++ input/output to Chapter 8.

In C++, input to a program is treated as a stream of consecutive bytes from the keyboard, a disk file, or some other source. Output from a program is treated as a stream of consecutive bytes to a video display, a disk file, or some other destination. Thus C++ input/output is called **stream input/output** (see Figure 2.2.1).

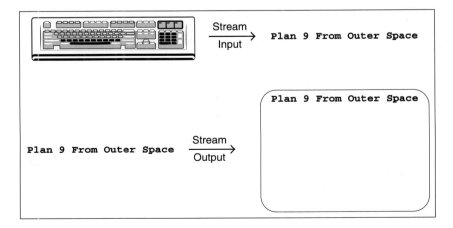

**FIGURE 2.2.1** Stream input/output.

The header *iostream* must be included to use the C++ standard input and output variables and functions as well as manipulators with no arguments. The variable **cin** refers to the standard input, **cout** refers to the standard output, and **cerr** refers to the standard error. Although the default destinations are the same (the video display), output using **cout** is typically buffered, whereas output using **cerr** is typically *not* buffered. The variables **cin**, **cout**, and **cerr** in C++ are the more powerful and flexible counterparts of **stdin**, **stdout**, and **stderr** in C.

The operator **>>** is used for input and **<<** is used for output. Both operators recognize the data type supplied, so no format string (like that required for **printf** or **scanf**) is necessary.

**EXAMPLE 2.2.1.**   If **x** is a **float**, the statement

```
cin >> x;
```

reads a **float** value from the standard input and stores it in **x**. The input is converted to **float** because the variable **x** is of type **float**. If **len** is of type **long**, the statement

```
cout << len;
```

writes the value of **len** to the standard output. The output is converted from **long** because the variable **len** is of type **long**.                                                                ∎

The next example shows how multiple variables may be read or written in a single statement.

**EXAMPLE 2.2.2.**   The following program prompts the user for an **int** and a **float** and then writes the values to the standard output.

```
#include <iostream>
using namespace std;

int main() {
   int id;
   float av;
   cout << "Enter the id and the average: ";
   cin >> id >> av;
   cout << "Id " << id << '\n'
        << "Average " << av << '\n';
   return 0;
}
```

The operators **>>** and **<<** associate from the left; so in the statement

```
cin >> id >> av;
```

first a value is read into **id**, and then a value is read into **av**. Similarly, in the statement

```
cout << "Id " << id << '\n'
     << "Average " << av << '\n';
```

first **Id** followed by a blank is written, then the value of **id** is written, then a newline is written, and so on.                                                                ∎

The default action of the input operator `>>` is to skip white space before reading the next input item. The situation is similar to that of the C library function **scanf**, except that even if the variable is of type **char**, the operator `>>` skips white space before reading the character. In the next subsection, we will discuss how to change the default action of skipping white space.

Where a true or false value is expected (e.g., in a **while** statement), an expression such as

```
cin >> val
```

is converted to true, if a value is read into **val,** and false, otherwise.

**EXAMPLE 2.2.3.**   The program

```
#include <iostream>
using namespace std;
int main() {
   int val, sum = 0;
   cout << "Enter next number: ";
   while ( cin >> val ) {
      sum += val;
      cout << "Enter next number: ";
   }
   cout << "Sum of all values: " << sum << '\n';
   return 0;
}
```

reads values from the standard input until the user signals end-of-file. It then writes the sum of all of the values read.   ■

## Manipulators

Input and output can be formatted using **manipulators** (see Figure 2.2.2). Except for **setw**, a manipulator permanently changes the state of the stream to which it is applied. In the case of **setw**, its effect lasts only for the next input or output operation. For example, placing the manipulator **hex** in the output stream causes all subsequent output of **short**s, **int**s, and **long**s to be written in hexadecimal. To use manipulators without arguments (e.g., **hex**, **endl**), the header *iostream* must be included. Manipulators with arguments (e.g., **setfill**, **setw**) require the header *iomanip*.

The manipulator **endl** outputs a newline and flushes the buffer.

**EXAMPLE 2.2.4.**   The output of the code segment

```
int i = 4, j = 6, k = 8;
char c = '!';
cout << i << c << endl
     << j << c << '\n'
     << k << c << endl;
```

| Manipulator | Effect |
|---|---|
| `dec` | Input or output in decimal |
| `endl` | Write newline and flush output stream |
| `fixed` | Use fixed notation for floating-point numbers: `d.ddd` |
| `flush` | Flush output stream |
| `hex` | Input or output in hexadecimal |
| `left` | Left-justify |
| `oct` | Input or output in octal |
| `right` | Right-justify |
| `scientific` | Use scientific notation for floating-point numbers: `d.dddEdd` |
| `setfill( c )` | Make `c` the fill character |
| `setprecision( n )` | Set floating-point precision to `n` |
| `setw( n )` | Set field width to `n` |
| `showpoint` | Always print decimal point and trailing zeros |
| `noshowpoint` | Don't print trailing zeros. Drop decimal point, if possible. |
| `showpos` | Use `+` with nonnegative numbers |
| `noshowpos` | Don't use `+` with nonnegative numbers |
| `skipws` | Skip white space before input |
| `noskipws` | Don't skip white space before input |
| `ws` | Remove white space |

**FIGURE 2.2.2** Some C++ manipulators.

is

```
4!
6!
8!
```

∎

The manipulators **dec**, **hex**, and **oct** may be used to read or write integer data in decimal, hexadecimal, or octal.

**EXAMPLE 2.2.5.**  The output of the code segment

```
int i = 91;
cout << "i = " << i << " (decimal)\n";
cout << "i = " << oct << i << " (octal)\n";
cout << "i = " << hex << i << " (hexadecimal)\n";
cout << "i = " << dec << i << " (decimal)\n";
```

is

```
i = 91 (decimal)
i = 133 (octal)
i = 5b (hexadecimal)
i = 91 (decimal)
```

If **dec** were omitted from the last line

```
int i = 91;
cout << "i = " << i << " (decimal)\n";
cout << "i = " << oct << i << " (octal)\n";
cout << "i = " << hex << i << " (hexadecimal)\n";
cout << "i = " << i << " (hexadecimal)\n";
```

the last output would again be in hexadecimal

```
i = 91 (decimal)
i = 133 (octal)
i = 5b (hexadecimal)
i = 5b (hexadecimal)
```

because once the status of **cout** is changed by using a manipulator (other than **setw**), the status remains in effect until changed again. ∎

The field width may be set by using the manipulator **setw**. If the field width is less than the number of columns required to write the item, the item is written anyway. For example, to write the integer 3572, four columns are needed. If the field width is less than 4, the integer is written anyway (in four columns). If the field width is greater than 4, the item is right-justified with blanks added at the left to fill out the specified number of columns. As we shall see, the programmer can specify left justification and can change the fill character. The default value for the field width is zero. Thus, by default, each data item is written in the minimum number of columns. After an item is written, the field width reverts to zero. So, if several items are to be written with a particular field width, the field width must be set before each item is written.

The following examples show *typical* behavior of manipulators, but there are differences among systems.

**EXAMPLE 2.2.6.**  The following code segment prints the numbers 1, 10, 100, and 1000 right-justified in a field of width 6:

```
for ( i = 1; i <= 1000; i *= 10 )
    cout << setw( 6 ) << i << '\n';
```

The output is

```
     1
    10
   100
  1000
```

The manipulator **setw** must be used as shown. For example, the output of the code segment

```
cout << setw( 6 );
for ( i = 1; i <= 1000; i *= 10 )
   cout << i << '\n';
```

is

```
     1
10
100
1000
```

After the field width is set to 6 and **1** is output, the field width reverts to its default value of zero. Thus only the first line is output in a field of size 6. ■

The manipulator **setfill** is used to specify a particular fill character, which is then used to fill the extra space when the field width is larger than the item to be output.

**EXAMPLE 2.2.7.** The following code segment prints the values 1, 10, 100, and 1000 right-justified in a field of width 6. The asterisk is used to fill the extra columns:

```
cout << setfill( '*' );
for ( i = 1; i <= 1000; i *= 10 )
   cout << setw( 6 ) << i << '\n';
```

The output is

```
*****1
****10
***100
**1000
```

Notice that once the fill character is set, it remains in effect until it is changed. ■

The manipulator **setprecision** is used to specify the number of digits of precision of floating-point numbers. The default precision is 6.

**EXAMPLE 2.2.8.** The code segment

```
float a = 1.05, b = 10.15, c = 200.87;
cout << setfill( '*' ) << setprecision( 2 );
cout << setw( 10 ) << a << '\n';
cout << setw( 10 ) << b << '\n';
cout << setw( 10 ) << c << '\n';
```

prints the values, 1.05, 10.15, and 200.87, right-justified in a field of width 10. The asterisk is used to fill the extra columns. The output is

```
******1.05
*****10.15
****200.87
```

■

The manipulators **left** and **right** may be used to left- or right-justify output in its field.

**EXAMPLE 2.2.9.** The following code segment prints names, left-justified in a field of width 10, and numbers, right-justified in a field of width 6:

```
int a = 5, b = 43, c = 104;
cout << left << setw( 10 ) << "Karen"
     << right << setw( 6 ) << a << '\n';
cout << left << setw( 10 ) << "Ben"
     << right << setw( 6 ) << b << '\n';
cout << left << setw( 10 ) << "Patricia"
     << right << setw( 6 ) << c << '\n';
```

The output is

```
Karen          5
Ben           43
Patricia     104
```

The **showpoint** manipulator forces a decimal point to be output as well as all trailing zeros. By default, floating-point numbers are printed in either fixed or scientific (i.e., exponential) notation, whichever takes the least number of columns. Scientific notation can be specified using the **scientific** manipulator, and fixed notation can be specified using the **fixed** manipulator.

**EXAMPLE 2.2.10.** The code segment

```
float a = 5, b = 43.3, c = 10304.31;
cout << showpoint << fixed << setprecision( 2 );
cout << setw( 8 ) << a << '\n';
cout << setw( 8 ) << b << '\n';
cout << setw( 8 ) << c << '\n';
```

prints three floating-point numbers in a field of width 8. The precision is set to 2. The decimal point and trailing zeros are printed because of the **showpoint** manipulator. The **fixed** manipulator forces the output to appear in fixed notation. The output is

```
    5.00
   43.30
10304.31
```

If the **showpoint** and **fixed** manipulators are not used,

```
float a = 5, b = 43.3, c = 10304.31;
cout << setprecision( 2 );
cout << setw( 8 ) << a << '\n';
cout << setw( 8 ) << b << '\n';
cout << setw( 8 ) << c << '\n';
```

the output is

```
       5
    43.3
 1.03e+04
```

because, by default, floating-point numbers are output in the minimum amount of space. This means dropping trailing zeros and the decimal point for numbers of the form $x$.000000 and using either fixed or scientific notation, whichever is shortest. ∎

After using the **showpoint** manipulator, its effect can be canceled by using the **noshowpoint** manipulator. Similarly, forcing a plus sign to be printed can be canceled by using the **noshowpos** manipulator and skipping white space before input can be disabled by using the **noskipws** manipulator.

**EXAMPLE 2.2.11.** The following program copies the standard input to the standard output, a character at a time. *All* characters are copied, including white space.

```
#include <iostream>
using namespace std;
int main() {
   char c;
   cin >> noskipws;
   while ( cin >> c )
      cout << c;
   return 0;
}
```
∎

## Mixing C and C++ Input/Output

Using the C input/output library functions (**printf** and the like) and the C++ class library (**cout** and the like) in the same program can cause problems because reads and writes from the two libraries are not automatically synchronized. If the two libraries are mixed, the function

```
ios::sync_with_stdio()
```

should be invoked before doing any input or output. The function call does the synchronization required for intermixing C and C++ input/output.

### EXERCISES

1. Write a statement that uses **cin** to read a **short** value into **i** and a **long double** value into **x**.

2. Write a statement that uses **cout** to write the values read in Exercise 1.

3. Write a statement to set the field width on **cout** to 12.

**4.** Write a statement to set the fill character on **cout** to the digit zero.

**5.** Write a statement to set the precision on **cout** to zero.

**6.** Write a statement to set left-justification on **cout**.

**7.** Write a statement to set right-justification and use + with nonnegative numbers on **cout**.

**8.** Write a statement to disable printing the decimal point and trailing zeros on **cout**.

**9.** Write a program that writes a hexadecimal dump of the standard input. Write 25 hexadecimal values per line. Separate the values with one space. Use **setfill** to write a single digit hexadecimal value *h* as **0***h*.

**10.** Write a code segment that first outputs the line

```
Sun  Mon  Tue  Wed  Thu  Fri  Sat
```

(there are two spaces between the days) and then prints the dates, right-aligned under the days. Assume that the variable **day** specifies the starting day: 0 is Sunday, 1 is Monday, and so on. Assume that the variable **stop** specifies the last date. For example, if **day** is 2 and **stop** is 31, the output is

```
Sun  Mon  Tue  Wed  Thu  Fri  Sat
                1    2    3    4    5
  6    7    8    9   10   11   12
 13   14   15   16   17   18   19
 20   21   22   23   24   25   26
 27   28   29   30   31
```

## 2.3 FILES

It is possible to read from and write to (disk) files. The technique is to replace **cin** by a variable associated with an input file and to replace **cout** by a variable associated with an output file. We include the header *fstream* to use files. The operator **>>** is used for input in the same way that it is used with **cin**, and **<<** is used for output in the same way that it is used with **cout**.

**EXAMPLE 2.3.1.** The program in Figure 2.3.1 reads incomes from the file *income.in* until end-of-file and writes the income and tax to the file *tax.out*.

The program in Figure 2.3.1 reads from and writes to files, so we must include *fstream*. We do not need to include *iostream* because we do not write to the standard output or read from the standard input.

We must define a variable of type **ifstream** to read from a file, and we must define a variable of type **ofstream** to write to a file:

```
ifstream infile;
ofstream outfile;
```

```
// This program repeatedly reads an income from
// the file income.in until end-of file.  Income
// under 6000 greenbacks is taxed at 30 percent,
// and income greater than or equal to 6000
// greenbacks is taxed at 60 percent.  After
// reading each income, the program prints the
// income and tax.
#include <fstream>
using namespace std;
const int cutoff = 6000;
const float rate1 = 0.3;
const float rate2 = 0.6;
int main() {
   ifstream infile;
   ofstream outfile;
   int income, tax;
   infile.open( "income.in" );
   outfile.open( "tax.out" );
   while ( infile >> income ) {
      if ( income < cutoff )
         tax = rate1 * income;
      else
         tax = rate2 * income;
      outfile << "Income = " << income
              << " greenbacks\n"
              << "Tax = " << tax
              << " greenbacks\n";
   }
   infile.close();
   outfile.close();
   return 0;
}
```

**FIGURE 2.3.1** A program that reads from and writes to files.

After defining these variables, we open the files and associate each variable with the actual file to be read or written:

```
infile.open( "income.in" );
outfile.open( "tax.out" );
```

We explain this syntax in the next section (see Example 2.4.10.) Thereafter in the program, the files are referenced by using the variables **infile** and **outfile**.

The program then uses a **while** loop, with condition

```
infile >> income
```

to read incomes, compute taxes, and write the results to the output file. As long as there are values in the input file to read, the expression

```
infile >> income
```

is converted to true. When end-of-file is reached, the expression is converted to false. After the **while** loop, we close the files:

```
infile.close();
outfile.close();
```

If the variables **infile** and **outfile** go out of existence normally, as happens when the program terminates normally, the files will automatically be closed. However, it is good programming practice to close files when they are no longer used.

The values in the file *income.in* may be entered in any desired format. All that is required is for at least one white space to separate consecutive values. By default, **<<** assumes that white space delimits the data. For example, *income.in* might be

```
2214 10500 31010
```

In this case, after the program terminates, the file *tax.out* is

```
Income = 2214 greenbacks
Tax = 664 greenbacks
Income = 10500 greenbacks
Tax = 6299 greenbacks
Income = 31010 greenbacks
Tax = 18605 greenbacks
```

■

## Testing Whether Files Are Open

After opening a file, it is a good idea to check whether the file was successfully opened. After

```
ifstream infile;
infile.open( "scores.dat" );
```

if the file *scores.dat* has been successfully opened, the expression in the **if** statement

```
if ( infile )
   //...
```

is converted to true. If the file cannot be opened, the expression is converted to false. Similarly, if the file *scores.dat* has been successfully opened, the expression in the **if** statement

```
if ( !infile )
   //...
```

is converted to false. If the file cannot be opened, the expression is converted to true.

**EXAMPLE 2.3.2.** The following code segment attempts to open the file *scores.dat*. If the file is not successfully opened, an informative message is output and the program is terminated.

```
ifstream infile;
infile.open( "scores.dat" );
if ( !infile ) {
   cerr << "Unable to open scores.dat\n";
   exit( 0 );
}
```

The function **exit** requires the header *cstdlib*.                                    ■

## EXERCISES

1. Write a program that reads lengths (assumed to be in yards) from the file *yard.in* until end-of-file, converts the lengths to feet and inches, and outputs the original and converted lengths to the file *length.out*. Check whether the files were successfully opened.

2. Write a program that reads integers from the file *data.in* until end-of-file and outputs the sum of all of the integers to the file *int.out*. Check whether the files were successfully opened.

## 2.4 C++ FEATURES

In this section, we list additional C++ features.

## Casts

C++ adds four new casts:

**static_cast   const_cast   dynamic_cast   reinterpret_cast**

We discuss each in turn.

## static_cast

The cast **static_cast** is the most commonly used cast. It is used to convert one data type to another and handles all "reasonable" casts, for example, converting **int** to **float**. The other casts are special-purpose casts.

**EXAMPLE 2.4.1.** The C cast

```
average = ( float ) hits / ( float ) at_bats;
```

becomes

```
average = static_cast<float>(hits)
            / static_cast<float>(at_bats);
```

The type to convert to (**float** in this example) is placed in angle brackets, and the expression whose value is to be converted (**hits** and **at_bats** in this example) follows in parentheses.  ∎

## const_cast

As the name implies, **const_cast** is used to cast away **const**ness. More precisely, it is used to cast a pointer to a **const** object to a pointer to a non**const** object.

**EXAMPLE 2.4.2.** The program in Figure 2.4.1 shows how to use **const_cast**. When the function **find** locates the value 4 in the array **a**, it returns the address of the cell that holds 4 as a pointer to **const**. In **main**, the array **a** is not **const**; thus, in **main**, **const** can be safely cast away.  ∎

```cpp
#include <iostream>
using namespace std;

const int* find( int val, const int* t, int n );

int main() {
   int a[ ] = { 2, 4, 6 };
   int* ptr;
   ptr = const_cast<int*>(find( 4, a, 3 ));
   if ( ptr == 0 )
      cout << "not found\n";
   else
      cout << "found; value = " << *ptr << '\n';
   return 0;
}

const int* find( int val, const int* t, int n ) {
   int i;
   for ( i = 0; i < n; i++ )
      if ( t[ i ] == val )
         return &t[ i ];
   return 0; // not found
}
```

**FIGURE 2.4.1** A program that uses **const_cast**.

## reinterpret_cast

The cast **reinterpret_cast** is used to convert a pointer of one type to a pointer of another type, to convert from a pointer type to an integer type, and to convert an integer type to a pointer type. Because the effect is implementation dependent, **reinterpret_cast** should be used with caution.

**EXAMPLE 2.4.3.** In the code segment

```
int i;
float f = -6.9072;
unsigned char* p = reinterpret_cast<unsigned char*>(&f);
cout << hex; // print bytes of f in hex
for ( i = 0; i < sizeof( float ); i++ )
    cout << static_cast<int>(p[ i ]) << '\n';
```

**reinterpret_cast** is used to convert from type pointer to **float** to type pointer to **unsigned char**. ∎

## dynamic_cast

The cast **dynamic_cast** is used for casting across or within inheritance hierarchies. We postpone the details until Section 5.5.

## Constants

In C++, unlike in C, a **const** variable can be used anywhere a constant can appear, for example, as an array size and as an expression in a **case** label.

**EXAMPLE 2.4.4.** We may define a **float** array of size 100 by writing

```
const int Size = 100;
float a[ Size ];
```
∎

## The Data Type bool

In C, *true* is represented by nonzero, and *false* by zero. C++ added the integer type **bool** to represent the **bool**ean values **true** and **false**, which are new keywords. All relational, equality, and logical operators now produce a result of type **bool**, not **int**. Integer and pointer expressions are still permitted where a **bool** value is expected. For example

```
int val;
cin << val;
if ( val ) {
    //...
}
```

is still valid; if **val** is nonzero, the condition is considered **true**, but if **val** is zero, the condition is considered **false**.

By default, when **bool** expressions are output, **true** is output as 1, and **false** is output as zero. The manipulator **boolalpha** may be used to read and write **bool** expressions as **true** and **false**. The manipulator **noboolalpha** may be used to read and write **bool** expressions as 1 and 0.

**EXAMPLE 2.4.5.**  The output of the code segment

```
bool flag;
flag = ( 3 < 5 );
cout << flag << '\n';
cout << boolalpha << flag << '\n';
```

is

```
1
true
```
■

## Enumerated Types

In C, we declare[†] an enumerated type such as

```
enum marital_status { single, married };
```

and then define variables of type **enum martial_type** as, for example,

```
/***** C syntax *****/
enum marital_status person1, person2;
```

In C++, by contrast, **marital_status** without the keyword **enum** is a type. Accordingly, we can define variables as in this code segment:

```
//***** C++ syntax *****
marital_status person1, person2;
```

**EXAMPLE 2.4.6.**  After declaring the anonymous **enum**

```
enum { MinSize = 0, MaxSize = 1000 };
```

we can use **MinSize** and **MaxSize** as constants, for example,

```
int minval = MinSize, arr[ MaxSize ];
```

Indeed, one of the main uses of anonymous **enum**s is to define constants.  ■

---

[†] In C or C++, we use the term "define" to refer to a statement that allocates storage for a variable or to refer to the header and body of a function. We use the term "declare" to refer to the description of a data type.

## Defining Variables

In a C function, definitions and declarations must occur at the beginning of a block. In C++, definitions and declarations may occur anywhere in a block, except that they must appear prior to the point at which they are first used.

**EXAMPLE 2.4.7.** The code segment

```
void reverse_and_print ( int a[ ], int size ) {
   int i;
   // fill the array
   for ( i = 0; i < size; i++ )
      a[ i ] = 2 * i;
   // reverse the data in the array
   int temp;
   for ( i = 0; i < size / 2; i++ ) {
      temp = a[ i ];
      a[ i ] = a[ size - 1 - i ];
      a[ size - 1 - i ] = temp;
   }
   // print the array
   for ( i = 0; i < size; i++ )
      cout << a[ i ] << '\n';
}
```

shows how one can define variables within the block that delimits the body of the function **reverse_and_print**.

The variable **temp** is defined just before it is needed in the second **for** loop:

```
int temp;
for ( i = 0; i < size / 2; i++ ) {
```
■

A variable can be defined in a **for** loop. Its scope is the body of the **for** loop.

**EXAMPLE 2.4.8.** The function of Example 2.4.7 could be rewritten

```
void reverse_and_print ( int a[ ], size ) {
   for ( int i = 0; i < size; i++ )
      a[ i ] = 2 * i;
   int temp;
   for ( int i = 0; i < size / 2; i++ ) {
      temp = a[ i ];
      a[ i ] = a[ size - 1 - i ];
      a[ size - 1 - i ] = temp;
   }
   for ( int i = 0; i < size; i++ )
      cout << a[ i ] << '\n';
}
```

Notice that variable **i** is defined in each **for** loop because, when a variable is defined in a **for** loop, its scope is the body of the **for** loop. ■

## Structures

C++ has modified C's version of **struct**. A minor change is that "**struct**" need not be included as part of the type.

**EXAMPLE 2.4.9.**   Given the declaration

```
struct Point {
   double x, y;
};
```

we may create variables by writing

```
Point p1, p2;
```
■

A much more significant extension to C's **struct** is that, in addition to data members, in C++ a **struct** can contain functions. A construct that contains data members and functions is called a *class*; we explore this concept in detail in the remainder of the book. (C++ also allows the use of the keyword **class** in place of **struct**.) Here we illustrate the syntax for dealing with **struct**s and classes.

**EXAMPLE 2.4.10.**   The declaration

```
struct Point {
   double x, y;
   void setVal( double, double );
};
```

illustrates the syntax for declaring a **struct** that contains data members (**x** and **y**) and a function (**setVal**). (The function **setVal** is defined elsewhere. In Section 3.1, we explain how to define such functions.)

The member selector operator is used with **struct** member functions just as it is with data members. For example, after defining a variable of type **Point**

```
Point p;
```

we can use the member selector operator to reference **p**'s data members

```
p.x = 3.14159;
p.y = 0.0;
```

as well as to invoke **p**'s member function

```
p.setVal( 4.11, -13.090 );
```
■

**EXAMPLE 2.4.11.**   To handle input files, we define a variable of type **ifstream** (see Section 2.3):

```
ifstream infile;
```

Because the variable **infile** is a class-type variable, we use the *member selector operator* to invoke functions within the class:

```
infile.open( "stocks.in" );
// process file
infile.close();
```                                                                    ■

## EXERCISES

1. The variable **val** is of type **long**. Write an expression that casts it to **double**.

2. The variable **s** is of type **const char\***. Write an expression that casts it to **char\***.

3. Given the declaration

```
enum good_jobs { tinker, tailor, soldier, spy };
```

define two variables of this enumerated type.

4. Write a complete program to read up to 100 **float**s from the standard input, compute the average of the numbers read, and then print each number and its absolute difference from the average. Define variables near the point at which they are first used.

5. What is the error?

```
void reverse_and_print( int a[ ], int size ) {
    for ( int i = 0; i < size; i++ )
        a[ i ] = 2 * i;
    int temp;
    for ( i = 0; i < size / 2; i++ ) {
        temp = a[ i ];
        a[ i ] = a[ size - 1 - i ];
        a[ size - 1 - i ] = temp;
    }
    for ( i = 0; i < size; i++ )
        cout << a[ i ] << '\n';
}
```

# 2.5 THE TYPE string

C++ furnishes the type **string** as an alternative to C's null-terminated arrays of **char**. Use of type **string** requires the header *string*. By using **string**, the programmer does not have to be concerned about storage allocation or about handling the annoying null terminator. Instead, the system handles storage allocation and is responsible for the internal representation of the string.

## Defining string Variables

The statements

```
#include <string>
using namespace std;
string s1;
string s2 = "Bravo";
string s3 = s2;
string s4( 10, 'x' );
```

illustrate ways to define **string** variables. Variable **s1** is defined without an initializing value; by default, it is set to the null string. Variable **s2**'s initializing value is the C-style string **"Bravo"**. Variable **s3** is initialized to **s2**; thus, both **s2** and **s3** represent the string *Bravo*. Variable **s4** is initialized to the string consisting of **10 x**'s; thus, **s4** represents the string *xxxxxxxxxx*.

## Conversion to C-Style Strings

There are contexts in which a C-style string (null-terminated array of **char**) is required. For example, when we open a file, the file name must be a C-style string. The function **c_str** returns a pointer to a **const** null-terminated array of **char** that represents the string.

**EXAMPLE 2.5.1.**   If the **string** variable **filename** holds the name of an input file, the file can be opened by executing

```
string filename = "infile.dat";
ifstream infile;
infile.open( filename.c_str() );
```
∎

## String Length

The function **length** returns the length of a string.

**EXAMPLE 2.5.2.**   The output of the code segment

```
string s = "Ed Wood";
cout << "Length = " << s.length() << '\n';
```

is **Length = 7**.
∎

## Writing and Reading strings

Operator **<<** can be used for output of **string**s.

**EXAMPLE 2.5.3.**  The output of the code segment

```
string s1;
string s2 = "Bravo";
string s3 = s2;
string s4( 10, 'x' );
cout << s1 << '\n'
        << s2 << '\n'
        << s3 << '\n'
        << s4 << '\n';
```

is

```
Bravo
Bravo
xxxxxxxxxx
```

(The first line of output is blank.)                                  ■

Operator **>>** can be used for input of **string**s.  The default action is to skip white space and then read and store characters until end-of-file or another white-space character is read. No white space is stored.

**EXAMPLE 2.5.4.**  Given

```
string s;
cout << "Enter a string: ";
cin >> s;
```

if we type

```
Ed Wood
```

**s** represents the string *Ed*.

Notice that after the definition, **s** represents the null string whose length is 0. After reading the string *Ed*, its new length is 2. The system automatically provides sufficient storage to represent the string of length 2.                                  ■

The function **getline** is used to read a line into a variable of type **string**.[†] The first argument is the input stream and the second argument is a variable of type **string**. It reads characters from the input stream, storing them in the **string** variable until

- End-of-file is reached.

---

[†] In some versions of Microsoft Visual C++, **getline** does not work correctly.

- A newline is read, in which case the newline is removed from the stream but it is *not* stored in the variable.

- The maximum allowable size for a string is reached (typically 4,294,967,295).

If **getline** reads no characters, it returns a value that evaluates to **false**. This condition can be used to terminate a program that reads to end-of-file.

**EXAMPLE 2.5.5.** The program in Figure 2.5.1 outputs a double-spaced copy of the input. ∎

```
#include <iostream>
#include <fstream>
#include <string>
using namespace std;
int main() {
    string buff;
    ifstream infile;
    ofstream outfile;
    cout << "Input file name: ";
    cin  >> buff;
    infile.open( buff.c_str() );
    cout << "Output file name: ";
    cin  >> buff;
    outfile.open( buff.c_str() );
    while ( getline( infile, buff ) )
        outfile << buff << "\n\n";
    infile.close();
    outfile.close();
    return 0;
}
```

**FIGURE 2.5.1** A program to demonstrate the use of **getline**. The program outputs a double-spaced copy of the input.

## Assignment

The assignment operator = can be used to perform string assignments. The left-hand side must be a **string**; the right-hand side can be a **string**, a C-style string, or a **char**.

**EXAMPLE 2.5.6.** The output of the code segment

```
string s1, s2;
s1 = "Ray Dennis Steckler";
s2 = s1;
cout << s1 << '\n';
cout << s2 << '\n';
```

is

```
Ray Dennis Steckler
Ray Dennis Steckler
```

■

## Concatenation

Operators **+** and **+=** can be used to perform string concatenation. Both the left and right operands of **+** can be **string**s; or one can be a **string** and the other a C-style string; or one can be a **string** and the other a **char**. The left-hand side of **+=** must be a **string**; the right-hand side can be a **string**, a C-style string, or a **char**.

**EXAMPLE 2.5.7.** The output of the code segment

```
string s1 = "Atlas ", s2 = "King", s3;
s3 = s1 + s2;
cout << s1 << '\n';
cout << s2 << '\n';
cout << s3 << '\n';
s1 += s2;
cout << s1 << '\n';
cout << s2 << '\n';
```

is

```
Atlas
King
Atlas King
Atlas King
King
```

■

## Modifying Strings

The function **erase** removes a substring from a string. The first argument gives the index where the substring to be removed begins, and the second argument gives the length of the substring. As usual, the index of the first character is 0. If the second argument is omitted, **erase** removes all characters, beginning at the index specified, to the end of the string. If both arguments are omitted, **erase** removes all characters, leaving the null string.

**EXAMPLE 2.5.8.**   The output of the code segment

```
string s = "Ray Dennis Steckler";
s.erase( 4, 7 );
cout << s << '\n';
```

is

```
Ray Steckler
```

The arguments 4 and 7 specify the substring beginning at index 4 of length 7: **Dennis** and the following blank.                                                                            ∎

In Section 2.8, we show how to use exception handling to check whether the first argument to **erase** is out-of-bounds.  If the first argument is in-bounds, the length of the string removed is the smaller of

- The value of the second argument.
- The string's length minus the value of the first argument.

The function **insert** inserts a string at a specified position.  The first argument gives the index where the insertion begins, and the second argument is the string to be inserted. The second argument can be a **string** or a C-style string.

**EXAMPLE 2.5.9.**   The output of the code segment

```
string s1 = "Ray Steckler";
string s2 = "Dennis ";
s1.insert( 4, s2 );
cout << s1 << '\n';
cout << s2 << '\n';
```

is

```
Ray Dennis Steckler
Dennis
```

The argument 4 references the character **S**; thus, **Dennis**, followed by a blank, is inserted after the blank in **s1**.                                                                  ∎

We can use exception handling to detect an out-of-bounds argument to **insert**.

The function **replace** replaces a substring with a specified string.  The first argument gives the index of the first character of the substring that is to be replaced, the second argument tells how many characters are in this substring, and the third argument is the string that replaces the substring.  The second argument can be a **string** or a C-style string.

**EXAMPLE 2.5.10.**   The output of the code segment

```
string s1 = "Ray Dennis Steckler";
string s2 = "Fran";
s1.replace( 4, 6, s2 );
cout << s1 << '\n';
cout << s2 << '\n';
```

is

```
Ray Fran Steckler
Fran
```

The arguments 4 and 6 specify the substring beginning at index 4 of length 6: the substring **Dennis**. This substring is replaced by **Fran**.   ■

We can use exception handling to detect an out-of-bounds argument to **replace**. If the first argument is in-bounds, the length of the string replaced is the smaller of

- The value of the second argument.

- The string's length minus the value of the first argument.

The function **swap** swaps two strings.

**EXAMPLE 2.5.11.**   The output of the code segment

```
string s1 = "Ray Dennis Steckler";
string s2 = "Ed Wood";
s1.swap( s2 );
cout << s1 << '\n';
cout << s2 << '\n';
```

is

```
Ed Wood
Ray Dennis Steckler
```
   ■

The operator **[ ]** can be used to reference a character at a specified index.

**EXAMPLE 2.5.12.**   The output of the code segment

```
string s = "Nan";
cout << s[ 1 ] << '\n';
s[ 0 ] = 'J';
cout << s << '\n';
```

is

```
a
Jan
```
■

## Extracting a Substring

The function **substr** returns a substring. The first argument is the index of the first character of the substring, and the second argument is the length of the substring.

**EXAMPLE 2.5.13.**   The output of the code segment

```
string s1 = "Ray Dennis Steckler";
string s2;
s2 = s1.substr( 4, 6 );
cout << s1 << '\n';
cout << s2 << '\n';
```

is

```
Ray Dennis Steckler
Dennis
```
■

We can use exception handling to detect an out-of-bounds argument to **substr**. If the first argument is in-bounds, the length of the substring is the smaller of

- The value of the second argument.
- The string's length minus the value of the first argument.

## Searching

The function **find** is used to search a string for a substring. The syntax is

```
s1.find( s2, ind )
```

If **s2** is a substring of **s1** at index **ind** or higher, **find** returns the smallest index $\geq$ **ind** where **s2** begins. If **s2** is not found, **find** returns "plus infinity," typically 4,294,967,295. If a second argument is not supplied, it defaults to zero. The argument **s2** can be a **string**, a C-style string, or a **char**.

**EXAMPLE 2.5.14.** The output of the code segment

```
string s1 = "Ray Dennis Steckler";
string s2 = "Dennis";
string s3 = "Ed Wood";
int f;
f = s1.find( s2 );
if ( f < s1.length() )
   cout << "Found at index: " << f << '\n';
else
   cout << "Not found\n";
f = s1.find( s3 );
if ( f < s1.length() )
   cout << "Found at index: " << f << '\n';
else
   cout << "Not found\n";
```

is

```
Found at index: 4
Not found
```
■

The function **rfind** is similar to **find**. It returns the largest index $\leq$ **ind** where **s2** begins, or "plus infinity," if **s2** is not found. If a second argument is not supplied, it defaults to "plus infinity."

The function **find_first_of**, which is invoked as

```
s1.find_first_of( s2 )
```

returns the index of the first character in **s1** that is also in **s2**; if unsuccessful, it returns "plus infinity." The argument **s2** can be a **string**, a C-style string, or a **char**. The function **find_first_not_of**, which is invoked similarly to **find_first_of**, returns the index of the first character in **s1** that is not in **s2**; if unsuccessful, it returns "plus infinity."

**EXAMPLE 2.5.15.** The output of the code segment

```
string s1 = "Abby";
string s2 = "bx";
cout << s1.find_first_of( s2 ) << '\n';
cout << s1.find_first_not_of( s2 ) << '\n';
```

is

```
1
0
```
■

## Comparing Strings

The operators ==, !=, <, <=, >, and >= can be used for string comparison. The left- and right-hand sides can both be **string**s, or one can be a **string** and the other a C-style string.

**EXAMPLE 2.5.16.**  The output of the code segment

```
string s1 = "panorama";
string s2 = "panda";
if ( s1 == s2 )
   cout << "Equals\n";
else
   cout << "Not equal\n";
if ( s1 != s2 )
   cout << "Not equal\n";
else
   cout << "Equals\n";
if ( s1 < s2 )
   cout << "Less than\n";
else
   cout << "Not less than\n";
if ( s1  > s2 )
   cout << "Greater than\n";
else
   cout << "Not greater than\n";
```

is

```
Not equal
Not equal
Not less than
Greater than
```

■

### EXERCISES

1. Define **string**s t1 and t2. Initialize t1 to *David Letterman* and t2 to the null string.

2. Write a statement that writes the lengths of the strings of Exercise 1 to the standard output.

3. Write a complete program that reads all of the lines in the file *text.in* into an array of **string**. The program then writes the lines in reverse order to the file *text.out*. Assume that there are at most 1000 lines in the file *text.in*.

In Exercises 4–35, tell whether the code is correct or not.  If there is an error, explain the problem.  If there is no error, show what is output.  Assume that "plus infinity" is 4,294,967,295.

```
 4. string s;
    s = "C++ is great fun!";
    cout << s << '\n';

 5. string s1 = "C++ is great fun!";
    char s2[ 30 ];
    s2 = s1;
    cout << s2 << '\n';

 6. string s;
    s = "C++ ";
    s += "is great fun!";
    cout << s << '\n';

 7. string s = "C++ is great fun", t;
    t = s + "!";
    cout << t << '\n';

 8. string s = "C++ is great fun", t;
    t = s + '\n';
    cout << t;

 9. string s;
    s = "C++ is great fun" + '\n';
    cout << s;

10. string s = "Charles Foster Kane";
    s.erase( 7, 7 );
    cout << s << '\n';

11. string s = "Charles Foster Kane";
    s.erase( 7, 1000 );
    cout << s << '\n';

12. string s = "Charles Foster Kane";
    s.erase( 1000, 1000 );
    cout << s << '\n';

13. string s = "Charles Foster Kane";
    s.erase( 7 );
    cout << s << '\n';

14. string s = "Charles Foster Kane";
    s.erase();
    cout << s << '\n';

15. string s = "Foster Kane";
    s.insert( 0, "Charles " );
    cout << s << '\n';
```

```
16. string s = "Windows 95";
    s.replace( 8, 2, "98" );
    cout << s << '\n';

17. string s = "Windows 95";
    s.replace( 8, 1000, "98" );
    cout << s << '\n';

18. string s[ 4 ];
    s[ 0 ] = "OS/MVS";
    s[ 1 ] = "UNIX";
    s[ 2 ] = "Solaris";
    s[ 3 ] = "Windows NT";
    int i;
    for ( i = 0; i < 2; i++ )
        s[ i ].swap( s[ 3 - i ] );
    for ( i = 0; i < 4; i++ )
        cout << s[ i ] << '\n';

19. string s = "Windows 95";
    for ( int i = 0; i < s.length(); i++ )
        s[ i ] = toupper( s[ i ] );
    cout << s << '\n';

20. string s1 = "Ray Dennis Steckler", s2;
    s2 = s1.substr( 4, 1000 );
    cout << s2 << '\n';

21. string s = "John Beresford Tipton";
    cout << s.find( 'e' ) << '\n';

22. string s = "John Beresford Tipton";
    cout << s.find( 'e', 7 ) << '\n';

23. string s = "John Beresford Tipton";
    cout << s.find( 'e', 12 ) << '\n';

24. string s = "John Beresford Tipton";
    cout << s.find( 'e', 1000 ) << '\n';

25. string s = "John Beresford Tipton";
    cout << s.rfind( 'e' ) << '\n';

26. string s = "John Beresford Tipton";
    cout << s.rfind( 'e', 7 ) << '\n';

27. string s = "John Beresford Tipton";
    cout << s.rfind( 'e', 12 ) << '\n';

28. string s = "John Beresford Tipton";
    cout << s.rfind( 'e', 1000 ) << '\n';
```

29. ```cpp
    string s = "John Beresford Tipton";
    cout <<s.find_first_of( "ei" ) << '\n';
    ```

30. ```cpp
    string s = "John Beresford Tipton";
    cout << s.find_first_of( "ABC" ) << '\n';
    ```

31. ```cpp
    string s = "John Beresford Tipton";
    cout << s.find_first_not_of( "JohnBeresfordTipton" ) << '\n';
    ```

32. ```cpp
    string s = "John Beresford Tipton";
    cout << s.find_first_not_of( "John Beresford Tipton" ) << '\n';
    ```

33. ```cpp
    string s1 = "John Beresford Tipton";
    string s2 = "John Bear";
    if ( s1 <= s2 )
       cout << "less than or equal\n";
    else
       cout << "not less than or equal\n";
    ```

34. ```cpp
    string s = "John Beresford Tipton";
    if ( s >= "John Bear" )
       cout << "greater than or equal\n";
    else
       cout << "not greater than or equal\n";
    ```

35. ```cpp
    if ( "John Beresford Tipton" == "John Bear" )
       cout << "equal\n";
    else
       cout << "not equal\n";
    ```

36. Write a complete program that reads lines until end-of-file from the file *names.in*, sorts them, and then writes the sorted list of names to the file *names.srt*. Use *insertion sort*, which, for $i = 1$ to the last index, assumes that the entries in the sublist at indexes 0 through $i - 1$ are sorted and then inserts the item at index $i$ at the correct position in the sorted sublist. Use an array of **string**.

## 2.6 FUNCTIONS

In this section, we highlight some of the ways that C++ has extended C functions.

### Prototypes

**Function prototype** refers to the style of declaring functions and writing function headers in which the data types of the parameters are included in the parentheses. For example, the function

```cpp
char grade( int exam1, int exam2, float exam1_weight ) {
   //... grade's body
}
```
```

is written in prototype form. In C++, prototypes are required and every function must be declared prior to being used. A return type *must* be specified; a missing return type does *not* default to `int` as is the case in C. In C++, a function that has no parameters can have an empty parameter list. In C, such a function prototype must have the keyword **void** between the parentheses that delimit the parameter list. As examples:

```
int print( void ) { /* C style */
    //... print's body
}
int print() { // C++ style
    //... print's body
}
```

## The `main` Function

Every program should contain a function called **main**. Since the system does not declare a prototype for **main**, its type is implementation dependent. However, C++ requires that every implementation support both

```
int main() {
    //... main's body
}
```

and

```
int main( int argc, char* argv[ ] ) {
    //... main's body
}
```

As in C, in the latter form, **argc** is the number of arguments passed to the program, and **argv[ 0 ]** through **argv[ argc - 1 ]** are the addresses of the passed arguments. Other definitions of **main** such as

```
void main() {
    //... main's body
}
```

need not be supported by a particular implementation.

The **return** statement

```
return status;
```

in **main** terminates the **main** function and thus the program as a whole and returns the value *status* to the invoking process. The status value 0 is used to signal normal termination. (Some operating systems use other status values for other purposes.)

## References

A **reference**, signaled by the ampersand **&**, provides an alternative name for storage.

**EXAMPLE 2.6.1.** The code

```
int x;
int& ref = x;
```

creates one **int** cell with two names, **x** and **ref**. For example, either

```
x = 3;
```

or

```
ref = 3;
```

stores the value 3 in the **int** cell.                                                                          ■

References operate somewhat like pointers except that no dereferencing is required. For example, we could obtain the effect of the code in Example 2.6.1 by replacing **ref** with a pointer. In this case, to store a value in the **int** cell using the pointer, a dereference would be required. As we will see in the next subsections, references are particularly useful in passing arguments to and returning values from functions.

## Call by Reference

If we designate a parameter as a reference parameter using the ampersand **&**, we obtain **call by reference** in which the reference parameter refers to the actual argument passed to the function and *not* to a *copy* of the argument. The default calling convention in C++, like C, remains call by value.

**EXAMPLE 2.6.2.** In the program

```
#include <iostream>
using namespace std;

void swap( int&, int& );

int main() {
   int i = 7, j = -3;
   swap( i, j );
   cout << "i = " << i << '\n'
        << "j = " << j << '\n';
   return 0;
}
void swap( int& a, int& b ) {
   int t;
   t = a;
   a = b;
   b = t;
}
```

the prototype

```
void swap( int&, int& );
```

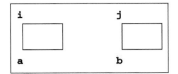

**FIGURE 2.6.1** Passing arguments by reference.

specifies that the arguments to **swap** are passed by reference. After **swap** is invoked, the names **a** and **b** in **swap**'s body refer directly to the storage in **main** named **i** and **j** (see Figure 2.6.1). The function **swap** works not with copies of **i** and **j** but directly with **i** and **j**. The output of the program is

```
i = -3
j = 7
```

■

**EXAMPLE 2.6.3.** The function **print_row**

```
void print_row( ofstream& out, char c, int n ) {
   for ( int i = 0; i < n; i++ )
      out << c;
   out << '\n';
}
```

writes the character **c**, **n** times, followed by a newline to the file associated with the variable **out**. As shown, the variable **out** is passed by reference

```
ofstream& out
```

In fact, the variable **out** must *not* be passed by value. To write to a file, the variable **out** must be changed because it must keep track of details such as formatting information (field width, whether to skip white space, etc.) and where in the buffer to write the next output. ■

## Return by Reference

By default in C++, when a function returns a value

**return** *expression*;

*expression* is evaluated and its value is copied into temporary storage, which the invoking function can then access. We call this method of returning a value **return by value**.

**EXAMPLE 2.6.4.** When the function

```
int val1() {
   //...
   return i;
}
```

is invoked, the value **i** is copied into temporary storage, which the invoking function can then access.

If the function **val1** is invoked as

```
j = val1();
```

the value **i** is copied into temporary storage and then copied into **j** (see Figure 2.6.2).   ∎

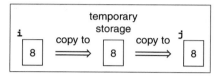

**FIGURE 2.6.2**  Return by value.

An alternative to return by value is **return by reference**, in which the value returned is *not* copied into temporary storage. Rather the actual cell in the **return** statement is made available to the invoking function. Return by reference is signaled by appending an ampersand to the return type.

**EXAMPLE 2.6.5.**   Because the return type **int&** in the function

```
int& val2() {
    //...
    return i;
}
```

has an ampersand, it returns its value by reference. When the **return** statement is executed, the cell **i** is made available to the invoking function.

If the function **val2** is invoked as

```
j = val2();
```

the value in **i** is copied into **j** (see Figure 2.6.3). Unlike return by value, this is the only copy that takes place.   ∎

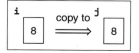

**FIGURE 2.6.3**  Return by reference.

**EXAMPLE 2.6.6.** The following function can be used by programmers who like arrays that begin at 1. The function takes an index **i** into an **int** array **a**, with 1 as the index of the first cell, translates it into a C++ index that begins at 0 (by subtracting 1), and returns by reference the value in the array:

```
int& new_index( int a[ ], int i ) {
   return a[ i - 1 ];
}
```

The return designation **int&** signals that the function is returning an **int** by reference. The cell **a[ i - 1 ]**, not a copy, is returned. The function **new_index** could be invoked as

```
val = new_index( a, 8 );
```
∎

One advantage of using return by reference is that a function that returns a value by reference can be used on the left side of an assignment statement. For example, the following is a valid invocation of the function **new_index** of Example 2.6.6:

```
new_index( a, 8 ) = -16;
```

In this case, the value $-16$ is stored in the eighth cell of **a**.

Since a function that uses return by reference returns an actual cell, it is important that the cell remain in existence after the function returns.

**EXAMPLE 2.6.7.** The function

```
int& f() {
   int i;
   //...
   // ***** ERROR: i goes out of existence
   return i;
}
```

contains an error. When **f** returns **i**, **i** goes out of existence. Thus the invoking function cannot access the cell **i** that is returned.

There is *no* error if return by value is used:

```
int f() {
   int i;
   //...
   return i; // OK
}
```

Here the value of **i** is copied into temporary storage to which the invoking function has access.
∎

## Inline Functions

The keyword **inline** can be used in a function declaration to request that a function be expanded "inline," that is, that each occurrence of a call of the function be replaced with the code that implements the function. The compiler, for various reasons, may not be able to honor the request. The situation is analogous to a macro expansion. When the preprocessor expands a macro, it replaces each occurrence of the macro with the macro's definition. When a macro is expanded or when a function is expanded inline and the program is run, the overhead of a function call is avoided so that the program may execute more efficiently. A disadvantage of using macros or inline functions is that if the expansions are large or there are many expansions, the size of the executable image can become quite large.

Unlike a macro that is expanded by the preprocessor, an inline function is expanded (i.e., translated) by the compiler. When the preprocessor expands a macro, it simply does text substitution without regard to the semantics of the code. On the other hand, when the compiler expands an inline function, it takes into account the semantics. For this reason, inline functions are generally preferable to macros.

An inline function is visible from the point at which it is declared to the end of the file.

Example 2.6.8 shows how the program of Example 2.6.2 would be written with **swap** changed to an inline function.

**EXAMPLE 2.6.8.**  Consider the program

```
#include <iostream>
using namespace std;

inline void swap( int&, int& );

int main() {
   int i = 7, j = -3;
   swap( i, j );
   cout << "i = " << i << '\n'
        << "j = " << j << '\n';
   return 0;
}
void swap( int& a, int& b ) {
   int t;
   t = a;
   a = b;
   b = t;
}
```

Notice that the keyword **inline** occurs in the function's declaration but not in the function's definition. Assuming that the compiler honors the request to expand **swap** inline, no function call occurs at the line

```
swap( i, j );
```

Because **swap** is an inline function, the compiler replaces the line

```
swap( i, j );
```

with the code that implements **swap**.  ∎

# Default Arguments

C++ allows the programmer to specify default values as constants for function parameters in the function's declaration. If arguments are missing in the invocation of the function, the default values are used.

**EXAMPLE 2.6.9.**  The function declaration

```
void f( int val,
        float s = 12.6,
        char t = '\n',
        string msg = "Error" );
```

has default values for the parameters **s**, **t**, and **msg** but no default value for the parameter **val**.

Valid invocations of **f** are

```
f( 14, 48.3, '\t', "OK" );
f( 14, 48.3, '\t' );
f( 14, 48.3 );
f( 14 );
```

In the invocation

```
f( 14, 48.3, '\t', "OK" );
```

arguments are supplied for all of the parameters. Therefore, the initial values of the parameters are

```
val = 14,    s = 48.3,    t = '\t',    msg = "OK"
```

In the invocation

```
f( 14, 48.3, '\t' );
```

no argument is supplied for the parameter **msg**. Therefore, the default value **"Error"** is used. The initial values of the parameters are

```
val = 14,    s = 48.3,    t = '\t',    msg = "Error"
```

Similarly in the invocation

```
f( 14, 48.3 );
```

the initial values of the parameters are

```
val = 14,    s = 48.3,    t = '\n',    msg = "Error"
```

In the invocation

```
f( 14 );
```

the initial values of the parameters are

```
val = 14,    s = 12.6,    t = '\n',    msg = "Error"
```

It is an error to invoke **f** as

```
f();
```

because no default value is supplied for the first parameter.  ∎

Example 2.6.9 shows that one can supply default values for some parameters but not for others. However, *all* of the parameters without default values must come first in the parameter list and then be followed by *all* of the parameters with default values.

**EXAMPLE 2.6.10.** The function declaration

```
// ***** ERROR: Invalid mix of default
// and nondefault values ***
void g( int val = 0,
        float s,  // ***** ERROR
        char t = '\n',
        string msg = "Error" );
```

is invalid because the parameter **val** with a default value is followed by the parameter **s** without a default value. ∎

## Overloading Functions

C++ permits identically named functions within the same scope if they can be distinguished by the number and type of parameters. If there are multiple definitions of a function **f**, **f** is said to be **overloaded**. The compiler determines which version of an overloaded function to invoke by choosing from among the identically named functions the one function whose parameters best match the arguments supplied. The precise rules for determining which function is the "best match" are complicated; however, an *exact* match is always the best match.

**EXAMPLE 2.6.11.** The program shown in Figure 2.6.4 overloads the function **print**. When the statement

```
print( x );
```

is executed, the function

```
void print( int a ) {
   cout << a << '\n';
}
```

is invoked because the argument is of type **int**. However, when the statement

```
print( y );
```

is executed, the function

```
void print( double a ) {
   cout << showpoint
        << a << '\n';
}
```

is invoked because the argument is of type **double**. ∎

```
#include <iostream>
#include <iomanip>
using namespace std;
void print( int a );
void print( double a );

int main() {
    int x = 8;
    double y = 8;
    print( x );
    print( y );
    return 0;
}
void print( int a ) {
    cout << a << '\n';
}
void print( double a ) {
    cout << showpoint
         << a << '\n';
}
```

**FIGURE 2.6.4** Overloading the function `print`.

**EXAMPLE 2.6.12.** The mathematics function `sqrt` is overloaded to support the three floating-point data types:

```
float sqrt( float );
double sqrt( double );
long double sqrt( long double );
```

If a `float` argument is passed, the value of the square root is returned as a `float`. If a `double` argument is passed, the value of the square root is returned as a `double`. If a `long double` argument is passed, the value of the square root is returned as a `long double`. The other mathematics functions (e.g., `sin`) are similarly overloaded. ∎

Overloaded functions are used to give a common name to similar behavior on different data types. In Example 2.6.11, "print" is a common name for similar behavior on different data types. From the point of view of the user, there is a single function `print` that prints different data types.

## Function Signatures

C++ requires that overloaded functions have distinct **signatures**. A function's signature consists of

- Its name.
- The number, data types, and order of its arguments.

To be distinct, functions must have distinct signatures.

**EXAMPLE 2.6.13.** The functions

```
void f();
void g();
```

have distinct signatures because they have distinct names. ∎

**EXAMPLE 2.6.14.** The functions

```
void f();
void f( int );
```

have distinct signatures despite sharing a name. The number of arguments distinguishes the *two* functions named **f**. ∎

**EXAMPLE 2.6.15.** The functions

```
void p( double );
void p( unsigned );
```

have distinct signatures because the data types of their single arguments differ. ∎

**EXAMPLE 2.6.16.** The functions

```
void m( double, int );
void m( int, double );
```

have distinct signatures because the order of their two arguments differs, even though each function expects one **double** and one **int** argument. ∎

The return type is *not* part of a function's signature. Therefore, functions cannot be distinguished by return type alone.

**EXAMPLE 2.6.17.** The functions

```
int s( int );
double s( int ); // ***** ERROR: not distinct from s above
```

are not distinct and the compiler should issue an error message to that effect. ∎

## EXERCISES

Which of the definitions in Exercises 1–5 are required to be portable?

1. ```
   int main() {
        //... main's body
   }
   ```

2. ```
   int main( int argc, char* argv[ ], char* envp[ ] ) {
        //... main's body
   }
   ```

3. ```
   main() {
        //... main's body
   }
   ```

4. ```
   void main() {
        //... main's body
   }
   ```

5. ```
   int main( void ) {
        //... main's body
   }
   ```

6. Write a function **upper** that is passed a **string** argument by reference and converts the lowercase letters to uppercase. Characters that are not lowercase letters are unchanged.

7. What is the output?

   ```
   #include <iostream>
   using namespace std;

   struct Point {
       int x, y;
   };
   void move( Point q ) {
       q.x--;
       q.y++;
   }
   int main() {
       Point p;
       p.x = 5;
       p.y = -12;
       move( p );
       cout << "p.x = " << p.x << '\n';
       cout << "p.y = " << p.y << '\n';
       return 0;
   }
   ```
   ```

8. What is the output?

```cpp
#include <iostream>
using namespace std;

struct Point {
    int x, y;
};
void move( Point& q ) {
    q.x--;
    q.y++;
}
int main() {
    Point p;
    p.x = 5;
    p.y = -12;
    move( p );
    cout << "p.x = " << p.x << '\n';
    cout << "p.y = " << p.y << '\n';
    return 0;
}
```

9. What is the output?

```cpp
#include <iostream>
using namespace std;

struct Point {
    int *x, *y;
};
void move( Point q ) {
    --*q.x;
    ++*q.y;
}
int main() {
    Point p;
    int a = 5, b = -12;
    p.x = &a;
    p.y = &b;
    move( p );
    cout << "*p.x = " << *p.x << '\n';
    cout << "*p.y = " << *p.y << '\n';
    return 0;
}
```

**10.** What is the output?

```
#include <iostream>
using namespace std;

struct Point {
    int *x, *y;
};
void move( Point& q ) {
    --*q.x;
    ++*q.y;
}
int main() {
    Point p;
    int a = 5, b = -12;
    p.x = &a;
    p.y = &b;
    move( p );
    cout << "*p.x = " << *p.x << '\n';
    cout << "*p.y = " << *p.y << '\n';
    return 0;
}
```

**11.** Find and correct the error:

```
void print( ofstream fp, int i ) {
    fp << i << '\n';
}
```

**12.** Show examples of valid invocations with different numbers of arguments of the function whose declaration is

```
void getstr( string& buff, int size = 1, char term = '\n' );
```

**13.** Further overload the function **print** of Example 2.6.11 by writing a version that has one **char** parameter **c**. This version prints the ASCII value of **c**.

**14.** Further overload the function **print** of Example 2.6.11 by writing a version that has a **char** parameter **c** and an **int** parameter **n**. This version prints **n** **c**'s followed by a newline.

**15.** What is the error?

```
#include <iostream>
#include <string>
using namespace std;

void print( int count, int i = 0 ) {
    for ( int j = 0; j < count; j++ )
        cout << i << '\n';
}
```

```
        void print( int count, const char* s = "Beavis" ) {
           for ( int j = 0; j < count; j++ )
              cout << s << '\n';
        }
        int main() {
           print( 10 );
           return 0;
        }
```

16. Find the error:

```
        int& dbl( int i ) {
           int j = 2 * i;
           return j;
        }
```

## 2.7 THE new AND delete OPERATORS

The **new**, **new[ ]**, **delete**, and **delete[ ]** operators are used to allocate and free storage dynamically (i.e., while the program is running). The operator **new** allocates a single cell; **new[ ]** allocates an array; **delete** frees a single cell allocated by **new**; and **delete[ ]** frees an array allocated by **new[ ]**. These operators work much like the C library functions **malloc**, **calloc**, and **free**. Unlike the C functions, however, **new**, **new[ ]**, **delete**, and **delete[ ]** are built-in *operators* rather than library functions. Finally, **new** and **delete** are keywords.

The **new** operator is used to allocate storage dynamically.  The basic syntax is the keyword **new** followed by a type.  For example,

```
    new int
```

requests storage for one **int**. If **new** is successful in allocating the storage, the value of the expression

```
    new int
```

is a pointer to the allocated storage.  In Section 2.8, we explain what happens if the requested storage cannot be allocated.  Given

```
    int* int_ptr;
```

a typical statement to allocate storage is

```
    int_ptr = new int;
```

The **new** operator infers the return type and the number of bytes to allocate from the type of storage requested.

The **new[ ]** operator is used to allocate an array dynamically. For example, the code segment

```
    int_ptr = new int[ 50 ];
```

requests an array of 50 `int` cells. If **new** succeeds in allocating the array, the first cell's address is stored in `int_ptr`.

The **delete** operator is used to free storage allocated by **new**. If `int_ptr` points to a single `int` cell allocated by **new**, we can release this storage by writing

```
delete int_ptr;
```

The **delete[ ]** operator is used to free storage allocated by **new[ ]**. If `int_ptr` points to an array of `int` cells allocated by **new[ ]**, we can release this storage by writing

```
delete[ ] int_ptr;
```

**EXAMPLE 2.7.1.**    The program in Figure 2.7.1 constructs a linked list using storage cells allocated dynamically. After constructing the list, the program prints the contents of the cells and then steps through the list and frees the allocated nodes. ■

```cpp
#include <iostream>
#include <string>
using namespace std;

struct Elephant {
    string name;
    Elephant* next;
};

void      print_elephants( const Elephant* ptr );
Elephant* get_elephants();
void      free_list( const Elephant* ptr );

int main() {
    Elephant* start;
    start = get_elephants();
    print_elephants( start );
    free_list( start );
    return 0;
}

//   get_elephants dynamically allocates storage
//   for nodes.  It builds the linked list and
//   stores user-supplied names in the name
//   member of the nodes.  It returns a pointer
//   to the first such node.
```

**FIGURE 2.7.1** Constructing a linked list using dynamic storage allocation.

```
Elephant* get_elephants() {
   Elephant *current, *first;
   int response;
   // allocate first node
   current = first = new Elephant;
   // store name of first Elephant
   cout << "\nNAME: ";
   cin >> current -> name;
   // prompt user about another Elephant
   cout << "\nAdd another? (1 == yes, 0 == no): ";
   cin >> response;
   // Add Elephants to list until user signals halt.
   while ( response == 1 ) {
      // allocate another Elephant node
      current = current -> next = new Elephant;
      // store name of next Elephant
      cout << "\nNAME: ";
      cin >> current -> name;
      // prompt user about another Elephant
      cout << "\nAdd another? (1 == yes, 0 == no): ";
      cin >> response;
   }
   // set link field in last node to 0
   current -> next = 0;
   return first;
}

//   print_elephants steps through the linked
//   list pointed to by ptr and prints the name
//   member in each node as well as the position
//   of the node in the list
void print_elephants( const Elephant* ptr ) {
   int count = 1;
   cout << "\n\n\n";
   while ( ptr != 0 ) {
      cout << "Elephant number " << count++
           << " is " << ptr -> name << '\n';
      ptr = ptr -> next;
   }
}
//   free_list steps through the linked list pointed
//   to by ptr and frees each node in the list
```

**FIGURE 2.7.1** Continued.

```
void free_list( const Elephant* ptr ) {
   const Elephant* temp_ptr;
   while ( ptr != 0 ) {
      temp_ptr = ptr -> next;
      delete ptr;
      ptr = temp_ptr;
   }
}
```

**FIGURE 2.7.1** Continued.

The operators **new**, **new[ ]**, **delete**, and **delete[ ]** should be used together and not intermixed with C storage management functions such as **malloc**, **calloc**, and **free**. We recommend *not* using the C storage management functions in C++ programs because the C functions, unlike **new**, **new[ ]**, **delete**, and **delete[ ]**, do not interact properly with certain important parts of C++ such as constructors and destructors (see Section 3.5).

## EXERCISES

1. Write a statement to allocate one cell of type **double** and store its address in the pointer **dbl_ptr**.

2. Write a definition for the variable **dbl_ptr** of Exercise 1.

3. Write a statement to free the storage allocated in Exercise 1.

4. Write a statement to allocate an array of 100 cells of type pointer to **int** and store the address of the first cell in the pointer **ptr**.

5. Write a definition for the variable **ptr** of Exercise 4.

6. Write a statement to free the storage allocated in Exercise 4.

7. Change Example 2.7.1 so that the user can choose to supply no names.

## 2.8 EXCEPTION HANDLING

An **exception** is a run-time error caused by some abnormal condition, for example, an out-of-bounds index or **new**'s inability to allocate requested storage. In C++, a function **f** can recognize conditions that identify exceptions and then signal that an exception has occurred. This signaling process is called **throwing an exception** (**throw** is a keyword). Once thrown, an exception can be *caught* or handled by a function that invokes **f** by using a **catch** block (**catch** is a keyword). A **catch** block is an exception handler that occurs after a **try** block, which is used to indicate interest in exceptions (**try** is a keyword). The general form used in a function **g** that invokes a function that might throw an exception is

```
void g() {
  //...
  //*** signal willingness to handle exceptions
  //    that may occur when this block executes
  try {
    f(); // code that may throw exceptions
  }
  //**** exception handlers
  catch( int x ) {
    // code to handle a thrown int
  }
  catch( char s ) {
    // code to handle a thrown char
  }
  //*** other catch blocks
  //...
}
```

The **catch** blocks may occur in any order. The critical requirement is that the **catch**ers come *after* the **try** block in which the exceptions might be thrown. Matching of exceptions and catchers is by type. If **f** throws an **int** exception, it is caught in **g** by the **int catch** block; if **f** throws a **char** exception, it is caught in **g** by the **char catch** block; and so on. If **f** does not throw an exception, execution resumes immediately after the **catch** blocks. A **catch** block may have a parameter (as shown in the preceding example) or simply be entered because of the type of exception thrown (as in the following examples).

**EXAMPLE 2.8.1.** The function **erase**, used with type **string** (see Section 2.5), throws an exception of type **out_of_range** if its first argument, which is an index into the string, is out-of-bounds (**out_of_range** is a system-defined type). Code that uses **erase** could test for an out-of-bounds index as follows:

```
string s;
int index, len;
// process s
while ( true ) {
  cout << "Enter index and length to erase: ";
  cin >> index >> len;
  try { // code that might raise an exception
    s.erase( index, len );
  }
  catch( out_of_range ) {
    continue;
  }
  break;
}
```

After the statements

```
cout << "Enter index and length to erase: ";
cin >> index >> len;
```

execute, the statement

```
s.erase( index, len );
```

in the **try** block executes. If **index** is in-bounds, execution resumes with the **break** statement, and the **while** loop terminates. If **index** is out-of-bounds, **erase** throws an exception of type **out_of_range**, which is caught by the **catch** block. In this latter case, the **continue** statement in the **catch** block executes, and the **while** loop executes again; the user is prompted for a valid **index**. In this example, the **catch** block has no parameters; it is entered simply because of the type of exception (**out_of_range**) thrown.  ■

The functions **insert**, **replace**, and **substr**, used with type **string**, also throw an **out_of_range** exception if the first argument is out-of-bounds.

**EXAMPLE 2.8.2.**   If either **new** or **new[ ]** is unable to allocate requested storage, it throws an exception of type **bad_alloc**. A function that uses **new** or **new[ ]** could test for failure to allocate storage as follows

```
int* ptr;
// code just before new is used goes here
try { // code that might raise an exception
   ptr = new int;
}
catch( bad_alloc ) {
   cerr << "new: unable to allocate storage...aborting\n";
   exit( EXIT_FAILURE );
}
// code if no bad_alloc exception goes here
```

The constant **EXIT_FAILURE** is defined in the header *cstdlib*.  ■

The following example shows how a function throws an exception.

**EXAMPLE 2.8.3.**   Given the definitions and declaration

```
const int MaxSize = 1000;
float arr[ MaxSize ];
enum out_of_bounds { underflow, overflow };
```

the following function attempts to access an element in **arr**

```
float& access( int i ) {
   if ( i < 0 )
      throw underflow;
   if ( i >= MaxSize )
      throw overflow;
   return arr[ i ];
}
```

A function that calls **access** can test for underflow or overflow by checking for an exception:

```
void g() {
   //...
   try {
      val = access( k );
   }
   catch( out_of_bounds t ) {
      if ( t == underflow ) {
         cerr << "arr: underflow...aborting\n";
         exit( EXIT_FAILURE );
      }
      if ( t == overflow ) {
         cerr << "arr: overflow...aborting\n";
         exit( EXIT_FAILURE );
      }
   }
   //...
}
```

If the function **access** of Example 2.8.3 were to throw an exception of, say, type **string**, **g**'s **catch** block would not handle the exception because this **catch**er expects an **int**. In general, if a function throws an exception but there is no **catch**er to handle it, the system handles the exception by invoking the function **unexpected**. In effect, **unexpected** is the default handler for exceptions not caught by user-supplied **catch** blocks. The function **unexpected** typically displays an error message and aborts the program.

An exception can be rethrown by using **throw** with no argument.

**EXAMPLE 2.8.4.**   The code segment

```
string s;
int index, len;
//...
try {
   s.erase( index, len );
}
```

```
catch( out_of_range ) {
    cerr << "erase: out of range\n";
    throw; // rethrow exception
}
```

illustrates a rethrown exception. After printing a message, the **catch** block rethrows the exception; the exception thrown is the original type—**out-of-range** in this case. ∎

In C, an exception is typically signaled by the return value of the invoked function. For example, in C, if **malloc** fails to allocate storage, it returns **NULL** (0). The problem with this method of signaling exceptions is that the invoking function *must* test the return value. If it does *not* test the return value, program execution continues—possibly with disastrous results. In C++, when a function throws an exception, the exception is handled—even if the invoking function does not use **try** and **catch** blocks. In the latter case, the system default handler, **unexpected**, executes.

Assertions, discussed in Section 7.2, provide another means of dealing with exceptions. Conditions are introduced that *must* be satisfied in order for the code to be correct. If a condition fails, the code is incorrect and the program terminates with a message. Assertions do not permit the program to attempt to recover from a violation and continue executing. Assertions are intended for debugging, whereas exception handling is for dealing with run-time problems.

C++ through the header *csignal* provides yet another method of dealing with certain kinds of exceptions [see, e.g., R. Johnsonbaugh and M. Kalin: *Applications Programming in ANSI C*, 3rd ed., (New York: Prentice Hall, 1996), Section 11.2]. Signals can be used to handle exceptions such as keyboard interrupts that are external to the program (such exceptions are called *asynchronous exceptions*). Throwing and catching exceptions handles only exceptions that result from executing the C++ code itself (such exceptions are called *synchronous exceptions*).

## EXERCISES

1. Show **try** and **catch** blocks that check for an out-of-bounds index in the function **replace** used by type **string**.

2. Show **try** and **catch** blocks that check for an out-of-bounds index in the function **substr** used by type **string**.

3. Show **try** and **catch** blocks that check for **new[  ]**'s inability to allocate storage.

4. Rewrite the linked list program of Example 2.7.1 so that it checks whether **new** succeeds in allocating storage.

5. What happens if a function throws an exception and no **catch** blocks are provided?

6. Explain the error:

```
try {
    int* ptr = new int;
}
```

```
catch( bad_alloc ) {
   cerr << "new: unable to allocate storage...aborting\n";
   exit( EXIT_FAILURE );
}
*ptr = 8;
```

## C++ POSTSCRIPT

## Keywords

The C++ keywords are

| | | | | |
|---|---|---|---|---|
| and | continue | goto | public | try |
| and_eq | default | if | register | typedef |
| asm | delete | inline | reinterpret_cast | typeid |
| auto | do | int | return | typename |
| bitand | double | long | short | union |
| bitor | dynamic_cast | mutable | signed | unsigned |
| bool | else | namespace | sizeof | using |
| break | enum | new | static | virtual |
| case | explicit | not | static_cast | void |
| catch | export | not_eq | struct | volatile |
| char | extern | operator | switch | wchar_t |
| class | false | or | template | while |
| compl | float | or_eq | this | xor |
| const | for | private | throw | xor_eq |
| const_cast | friend | protected | true | |

## Unnamed Namespaces

In C, to prevent a top-level function (i.e., a function not contained in a class) from being visible outside its containing file, we can declare it **static**. The preferred C++ way is to place such a function in an *unnamed namespace*.

**EXAMPLE.** The unnamed namespace

```
// Occurs in file F1.cpp
namespace { // unnamed namespace
   void g() { cout << "g\n"; }
}
```

contains a definition for **g**. Only functions defined in the same file as **g**, *F1.cpp*, are able to invoke **g**. ∎

## Anonymous Unions

C++ allows anonymous unions, that is, unions without tags.

**EXAMPLE.** The union

```
union {
    int i;
    float x;
};
```

is anonymous. The members can be used as ordinary variables:

```
i = 10;
x = -3827.34;
```

Within the same scope, no other variables with the same names as an anonymous union's members are allowed, and no variables whose type is that of an anonymous union can be defined. ■

## The Member Selector Operators

C++ supports pointers that can point *only* to members of a class. The **member object selector operator** `.*` and **member pointer selector operator** `->*` are used to dereference such a pointer and thereby access the class member to which it points.

**EXAMPLE.** The code segment

```
struct C {
    int    x;
    float y;
    float z;
};

int main() {
    // define a local float variable
    float f;

    // define a pointer to int
    int* i_ptr;

    // define two C variables
    C c1, c2;

    // define a pointer to a float
    // member of C
    float C::*f_ptr;

    // make f_ptr point to C member y
    // (Note that the assignment does not
    // specify a C object, e.g., c1 or c2.)
    f_ptr = &C::y;

    // set c1.y to 3.14
    c1.*f_ptr = 3.14;
```

```
// set c2.y to 2.01
c2.*f_ptr = 2.01;

// make f_ptr point to C member z
f_ptr = &C::z;

// set c1.z to -999.99
c1.*f_ptr = -999.99;

// make f_ptr point again to C member y
f_ptr = &C::y;

// reset c1.y
c1.*f_ptr = -777.77;

// ***** ERROR: x is not a float
//        member of C
f_ptr = &C::x;

// ***** ERROR: f is not a member
//        of C, period
f_ptr = &f;

// ok -- i_ptr can hold the address of
// any int and C::x is public, hence
// visible in main
i_ptr = &c1.x; // c1.x is an int
//...
}
```

illustrates the syntax for defining and using a pointer to a class member. The syntax

```
c1.*f_ptr = 3.14;
```

says: Access the member (`.`) by dereferencing the pointer to the member (`*`). The pointer definition

```
// define a pointer to a float
// member of C
float C::*f_ptr;
```

does *not* say that **f_ptr** is a pointer to a **float**, but rather that **f_ptr** is a pointer to a **float** member of **C**. An error thus occurs if we try to assign to **f_ptr** the address of local **float**variable **f**, which is *not* a **C** member:

```
// ***** ERROR: f is not a member
//        of C, period
f_ptr = &f;
```

A different error occurs when we try to make **f_ptr** point to data member **x**, which is an **int** rather than a **float** member of **C**. Once defined, **f_ptr** may point to either **y** or **z**, as both members are **float**s.

Finally, a pointer that is *not* class specific may be used to access data members. In our example, **i_ptr** of type **int\*** can be assigned the address of **c1.x** because **c1.x** is an **int**.  ■

Pointers to class objects may be used in combination with pointers to class members. Such a combination requires use of the member pointer selector operator **->***.

**EXAMPLE.**   We expand the preceding example to illustrate the access to a class member through two pointers—a pointer to a class object and a pointer to its **float** data members:

```
struct C {
    int    x;
    float y;
    float z;
};

int main() {
    // define two C objects
    C c1, c2;

    // define a pointer to C
    C* c_ptr;

    // define a pointer to a float
    // member of C
    float C::*f_ptr;

    // make c_ptr point to c1
    c_ptr = &c1;

    // make f_ptr point to z
    f_ptr = &C::z;

    // set c1.z to 123.321
    c_ptr ->* f_ptr = 123.321;

    // make c_ptr point to c2
    c_ptr = &c2;

    // set c2.z to 987.789
    c_ptr ->* f_ptr = 987.789;

    // make f_ptr point to y
    f_ptr = &C::y;

    // set c2.y to -111.99
    c_ptr ->* f_ptr = -111.99;
    //...
}
```

Pointer **c_ptr** is of type **C*** and so can hold the address of either **c1** or **c2**. Pointer **f_ptr** is again of type "pointer to **float** member of **C**" and so can hold the address of either **C::y** or **C::z**. In an expression such as

```
// set c2.y to -111.99
c_ptr ->* f_ptr = -111.99;
```

the operator `->*` may be viewed as performing two tasks. First, the arrow `->` gives us access to the class object, in this case `c2`, by dereferencing `c_ptr`. Second, the star `*` gives us access to a particular data member, in this case `c2.y`, by dereferencing `f_ptr`. The syntax `->*` thus says: Access the member through the pointer to the object (`->`) by dereferencing the pointer to the member (`*`). The white space on each side of `->*` is optional. We could have written

```
// set c2.y to -111.99
c_ptr->*f_ptr = -111.99;
```
■

A pointer to a class function follows the same syntax as that illustrated in the preceding examples for pointers to class data members.

**EXAMPLE.** The following program shows how to define and use pointers to class methods:

```
struct C {
    int x;
    short f( int );
    short g( int );
};

//...

int main() {
    short s;
    C c;

    // pointer to method with one int
    // parameter that returns type short
    short ( C::*meth_ptr )( int );

    // make meth_ptr point to method f
    meth_ptr = &C::f;

    // invoke method f for object c
    s = ( c.*meth_ptr )( 8 );

    // pointer to object c
    C* ptr = &c;

    // invoke method f for object c through ptr
    s = ( ptr ->* meth_ptr )( 9 );

    // make meth_ptr point to method g
    meth_ptr = &C::g;

    // invoke method g for object c in two ways
    s = ( c.*meth_ptr )( 10 );
    s = ( ptr ->* meth_ptr )( 11 );
    //...
}
```
■

## COMMON PROGRAMMING ERRORS

1. It is an error to use the keyword **namespace** in a *using declaration*, which applies to a *single* item in a namespace:

```
namespace gar {
    void f() {/* f's body */}
    int x;
}
using namespace gar::f(); //***** ERROR: "namespace" used
```

The correct syntax is

```
namespace gar {
    void f() {/* f's body */}
    int x;
}
using gar::f();
```

2. It is an error to omit the keyword **namespace** from a *using directive*, which applies to *all* items in a namespace:

```
#include <iostream>
using std; //***** ERROR: "namespace" missing
```

The correct syntax is

```
#include <iostream>
using namespace std;
```

3. In the absence of a using declaration or a using directive, it is an error to reference an item in a namespace without the namespace's name:

```
#include <iostream>
int main() {
    //***** ERROR: should be std::cout
    cout << "Amazin' Mets\n";
    //...
}
```

A using declaration for **cout** or a using directive for **std** would obviate the need for the full name **std::cout**.

4. To provide a proper interface to the keyboard and video display commands, the line

```
#include <iostream>
```

must appear before any keyboard input and video display output commands are used.

5. In order to use standard features as shown in this chapter, the line

```
using namespace std;
```

must follow the **#include**d headers. Thus a program might begin

```
#include <iostream>
using namespace std;
```

6. It is an error to use an old-style, "dot h," header with **using namespace std;**:

```
// ***** ERROR: wrong header for namespace std
#include <iostream.h>
using namespace std;
```

The error is corrected by omitting **.h**

```
#include <iostream>
using namespace std; // Correct
```

or, if an old-style header is to be used, by omitting **using namespace std;**

```
#include <iostream.h> // Correct
```

7. The *right* shift operator **>>** is used for input:

```
cin >> x; // ***** CORRECT *****
cin << x; // ***** ERROR *****
```

8. The *left* shift operator **<<** is used for output:

```
cout << x; // ***** CORRECT *****
cout >> x; // ***** ERROR *****
```

9. Only one value can be read after **>>** in a **cin** statement. For example, the correct way to read a value into the variable **x** and then the next value into the variable **y** is

```
cin >> x >> y;
```

*not*

```
cin >> x, y; // ***** ERROR *****
```

or

```
cin >> x y; // ***** ERROR *****
```

10. Only one expression can be output after **<<** in a **cout** statement. For example, the correct way to output the value of the variable **x** followed by the value of the variable **y** is

```
cout << x << y;
```

*not*

```
cout << x, y; // ***** ERROR *****
```

or

```
cout << x y; // ***** ERROR *****
```

**11.** The operator `<<` is evaluated before the relational, equality, logical, and assignment operators. For this reason, the statement

```
int n = 3, m = 2;
// ***** ERROR: << evaluated before <
cout << n < m << '\n';
```

contains an error. The error can be corrected by inserting parentheses:

```
int n = 3, m = 2;
cout << ( n < m ) << '\n'; // correct
```

**12.** To use manipulators with arguments, the header *iomanip* must be included.

**13.** After a manipulator is placed into the stream, *all* subsequent input or output is formatted accordingly except for the field width, which reverts to zero after a string or number is printed. Do *not* assume that at the end of a statement all input/output reverts to default settings. For example, in the following code, the input is written in decimal and then in hexadecimal twice:

```
int n = 100;
cout << n << '\n';
cout << hex << n << '\n';
cout << n << '\n'; // still hex
```

**14.** Mixing the C and C++ input/output facilities may produce unexpected results unless the function

```
ios::sync_with_stdio()
```

is invoked. As examples, the code

```
#include <cstdio>
#include <iostream>
using namespace std;

int main() {
   int a = 2, b = 5;

   // ***** RISKY *****
   printf( "%d  ", a );
   cout << b << '\n';
   return 0;
}
```

is risky; but

```
#include <cstdio>
#include <iostream>
using namespace std;
```

```
int main() {
    int a = 2, b = 5;

    // ***** OK *****
    ios::sync_with_stdio();
    printf( "%d  ", a );
    cout << b << '\n';
    return 0;
}
```

is valid.

**15.** To use files, the header *fstream* must be included.

**16.** In a C++ cast, the cast data type is enclosed in angle brackets rather than parentheses:

```
static_cast(int)(26) //***** ERROR
static_cast<int>(26) // Correct
```

**17.** In a C++ cast, the cast expression is enclosed in parentheses rather than angle brackets:

```
static_cast<int><26> //***** ERROR
static_cast<int>(26) // Correct
```

**18.** The scope of a variable defined in a **for** loop is the body of the loop. For this reason, the code segment

```
string str;
//...
for ( int i = 0; i < 100; i++ ) {
    cin >> str;
    if ( str == "BadData" )
        break;
}
// ***** ERROR: i out of scope
cout << "break on: " << i << '\n';
```

contains an error. The error may be corrected by defining **i** before the **for** loop:

```
int i;
for ( i = 0; i < 100; i++ ) {
    cin >> str;
    if ( str == "BadData" )
        break;
}
// OK
cout << "break on: " << i << '\n';
```

**19.** To use type **string**, the header *string* must be included.

**20.** The function **open** expects a C-style string. For this reason, the following contains an error:

```
string s = "myfile.dat";
ifstream infile;
// ***** ERROR: s is wrong type for open
infile.open( s );
```

The error may be corrected by supplying a C-style string

```
ifstream infile;
infile.open( "myfile.dat" ); // OK
```

or by using the function **c_str** to convert type **string** to a C-style string

```
string s = "myfile.dat";
ifstream infile;
infile.open( s.c_str() ); // OK
```

**21.** When a **string** is read with **>>**, characters delimited by white space are stored. Do *not* assume that an entire line is read. For example, given

```
string s;
cout << "Enter a string: ";
cin >> s;
```

if we type

```
Ed Wood
```

**s** represents the string *Ed*. To read an entire line, use **getline**.

**22.** The assignment operator can be used for type **string**. Whereas the right-hand side can be a **string**, a C-style string, or a **char**, the left-hand side must be a **string**:

```
string s1, s2 = "W. C. Fields";
char s3[ ] = "Mel Brooks";
s1 = s2; // OK
s1 = s3; // OK
s1 = '!'; // OK

// ***** ERROR: Can't assign string to char array
s3 = s2;
```

**23.** Operator **+=** can be used for string concatenation. Whereas the right-hand side can be a **string**, a C-style string, or a **char**, the left-hand side must be a **string**:

```
string s1, s2 = "W. C.";
char s3[ 30 ] = "Mel";
s1 += s2; // OK
s1 += " Fields"; // OK
s1 += '!'; // OK

// ***** ERROR: Can't concatenate to char array
s3 += " Brooks";
```

**24.** Operator **+** can be used for string concatenation. Both the left and right operands of **+** can be **string**s; or one can be a **string** and the other a C-style string; or one can be a **string** and the other a **char**:

```
string s1,
       s2 = "W. C. ",
       s3 = "Fields";
s1 = s2 + s3; // OK
s1 = s2 + "Fields"; // OK
s1 = 'W' + s3; // OK
s1 = "W. C. " + "Fields"; // ***** ERROR
```

In the last statement, no concatenation is attempted! The C-style strings evaluate to the addresses of their first characters. The system attempts to add these addresses, which is invalid.

**25.** It is an error for the first argument to any of the **string** functions—**erase**, **insert**, **replace**, and **substr**—to have a value greater than or equal to the length of the string:

```
string s = "My Mother, the Car";
// ***** ERROR: index 18 is out-of-bounds
s.erase( 18 );
```

Such an out-of-bounds error will typically cause the program to terminate, although exception handling can be used to handle the error.

**26.** It is invalid to invoke an undeclared function:

```
#include <iostream>
using namespace std;
int main() {
   int i = 1, j = 3;
   // ***** ERROR: swap not declared *****
   swap( i, j );
   cout << "i = " << i << '\n';
   return 0;
}

void swap( int& a, int& b ) {
   int t;
   t = a;
   a = b;
   b = t;
}
```

This error can be corrected by defining, and implicitly declaring, **swap** before **main**

```
#include <iostream>
using namespace std;
```

```
void swap( int& a, int& b ) {
    int t;
    t = a;
    a = b;
    b = t;
}

int main() {
    //... main's body
}
```

or declaring **swap** before or in **main**

```
#include <iostream>
using namespace std;

void swap( int&, int& );

int main() {
    //... main's body
}
```

27. Since it is invalid to invoke an undeclared function, each system function *must* be declared. Typically, system functions are declared by including standard headers such as *iostream*, which contain the required function declarations.

```
#include <iostream>
using namespace std;

int main() {
    // ***** ERROR: sqrt not declared
    cout << "Square root of 5 = " << sqrt( 5 ) << '\n';
    return 0;
}
```

is invalid since **sqrt** is not declared. This error can be corrected by including *cmath*, which contains a declaration of **sqrt**.

28. It is an error to interpret the function declaration

```
int f();
```

as giving no information about **f**'s parameters. In fact, the declaration states that **f** has no parameters. For this reason, the following is an error:

```
int f();

int main() {
    //...
    // ***** ERROR: call does not match declaration *****
    i = f( 6 );
    //...
}
```

**29.** It is an error not to specify a return type:

```
f( int ); // ***** ERROR: no return type *****
int main() {
   //... main's body
}
```

If **f** returns an **int**, the declaration can be corrected by writing

```
int f( int ); // OK
int main() {
   //... main's body
}
```

**30.** The only definitions of **main** that are required to be portable are

```
int main() {
   //... main's body
}
```

and

```
int main( int argc, char* argv[ ] ) {
   //... main's body
}
```

Thus definitions such as

```
// ***** ERROR: nonportable definition of main
void main() {
   //... main's body
}
```

may not work in some implementations.

**31.** Since a function that uses return by reference returns an actual cell, the cell must remain in existence after the function returns. The function

```
int& f() {
   int i;
   //...
   // ***** ERROR: i goes out of existence
   return i;
}
```

contains an error. When **f** returns **i**, **i** goes out of existence. Thus the invoking function cannot access the cell **i** that is returned. There is *no* error if return by value is used:

```
int f() {
   int i;
   //...
   // OK
   return i;
}
```

Here the value of **i** is copied into temporary storage to which the invoking function has access.

**32.** The keyword **inline** is used in a function *declaration*, not in a function definition. For this reason, the following contains an error:

```
void swap( int&, int& );

int main() {
    //...
    // ***** ERROR: no definition of swap
    swap( i, j );
    //...
}
inline void swap( int& a, int& b ) {
    //... inline's body
}
```

Here the inline **swap** is visible from its definition to the end of the file, so it is *not* visible in **main**. For this reason, the compiler will complain that it cannot find a **swap** for **main** to call.

The error is corrected by writing

```
inline void swap( int&, int& );

int main() {
    //...
    swap( i, j ); // OK
    //...
}

void swap( int& a, int& b ) {
    //... swap's body
}
```

**33.** Default arguments are supplied in a function *declaration*, not in a function definition. For this reason, the following contains an error:

```
void print( int, int );

int main() {
    //...
    // ***** ERROR: no definition of print()
    print();
    //...
}

void print( int a = 3, int b = 8 ) {
    //... print's body
}
```

Here the *declaration* tells **main** that **print** has two **int** arguments. When **main** tries to invoke **print** with no arguments, an error results.

The error is corrected by writing

```
void print( int = 3, int = 8 );

int main() {
   //...
   print(); // OK
   //...
}
void print( int a, int b ) {
   //... print's body
}
```

34. All the parameters without default values must come first in the parameter list and then be followed by all the parameters with default values. For this reason, the following is an invalid function declaration:

```
// ***** ERROR: Invalid ordering of parameters with
//                 default values *****
int f( float x = 1.3, int i, char c = '\n' );
```

The error can be corrected by omitting the default value for **x** or by adding a default value for **i**.

35. If a parameter does not have a default value, an argument must be supplied when the function is invoked. For example, if the declaration of **f** is

```
int f( float x, int i, char c = '\n' );
```

valid invocations of **f** are

```
// ***** VALID *****
f( 93.6, 0, '\t' );
f( 93.6, 0 );
```

but

```
// ***** ERROR: f must have 2 or 3 arguments *****
f( 93.6 );
```

is invalid.

**36.** The return type is *not* part of a function's signature. The functions

```
int s( int );
double s( int ); // ***** ERROR: not distinct from s above
```

are not distinct.

**37.** To free a single cell allocated by **new**, use **delete**, *not* **delete[ ]**. As examples,

```
float_ptr = new float;
delete[ ] float_ptr; // ***** ERROR *****
delete float_ptr; // ***** CORRECT *****
```

**38.** To free an array allocated by **new[ ]**, use **delete[ ]**, *not* **delete**. As examples,

```
float_ptr = new float[ 100 ];
delete float_ptr; // ***** ERROR *****
delete[ ] float_ptr; // ***** CORRECT *****
```

**39.** It is bad programming practice not to **delete** a dynamically created object *before* the object is inaccessible:

```
struct C {
  //...
};
void f() {
   C* p = new C; // dynamically create a C object
   //... use it
} //****** ERROR: should delete the object!
```

Once control exits **f**, the object to which **p** points can no longer be accessed. Therefore, storage for this object should be freed:

```
void f() {
   C* p = new C; // dynamically create a C object
   //... use it
   delete p;      // delete it
}
```

## PROGRAMMING EXERCISES

In these programming exercises, use the C++ extensions discussed in this chapter wherever possible. As examples, use C++ comments (**//**) rather than C comments (**/* */**), and use the C++ input/output library.

**2.1.** Write a program that reads integers from the standard input until the end of the file and then prints the largest and smallest values.

**2.2.** Write a program that echoes the standard input to the standard output, except that each tab is replaced by the appropriate number of spaces. Assume that tabs are set every 8 columns, unless the user specifies a different tab setting on the command line.

**2.3.** Write a function **dbl** that takes an **int** argument and multiplies it by 2. Pass the argument by reference. *Example*:

```
int x = 6;
dbl( x );
cout << x; // output is 12
```

Write a **main** function that invokes **dbl** to demonstrate that **dbl** is working properly.

**2.4.** The structure

```
struct twodim {
    int r;
    int c;
    float* a;
};
```

represents a two-dimensional array of **float**s with **r** rows and **c** columns as a one-dimensional array **a** of **r*c float**s. Write functions **main**, **val**, **get_twodim**, and **free_twodim**.

The function **get_twodim** is passed an argument of type **twodim** by reference and **int** values **row** and **col** by value. The function **get_twodim** sets **r** to **row**, **c** to **col**, and dynamically allocates an array of **r*c float** cells and stores the address of the first cell in **a**.

The function **val** receives arguments **i** and **j** by value and **x** by reference. It returns the value **x.a[ i*r + j ]** by reference.

The function **free_twodim** receives an argument of type **twodim** by reference and deletes the storage to which **a** points.

The function **main** invokes **get_twodim** to create a two-dimensional array of size $3 \times 4$. For all **i** and **j**, **main** then stores the value **2.5*i*j** in cell **i,j** by repeatedly invoking the function **val**. It then uses **cout** to print the values just stored by repeatedly invoking **val**. Finally, **main** invokes **free_twodim** to free the storage to which **a** points.

**2.5.** Write a function **print_str** that works as follows. If **print_str** is invoked with one argument **s** of type **string**, it prints **s** or the first 10 characters in **s**, whichever is shortest. If **print_str** is invoked with two arguments—**s**, a **string**, and **n**, an **int**—it prints **s** or the first **n** characters in **s**, whichever is shortest.

Write a **main** function that invokes **print_str** several times to demonstrate that **print_str** is working properly.

**2.6.** Given

```
struct numeric {
    long a[ 10 ];
};
```

write a function **print** which, when invoked with a **numeric** argument, prints the 10 **long**s in **a** one per line but, when invoked with a **string** argument, simply prints the **string**.

**2.7.** Add a function **reverse_elephant** to the program of Example 2.7.1, which receives a linked list, reverses the order of the nodes in the list, and returns the address of the first node in the reversed list. Modify **main** so that it invokes **reverse_elephant** several times to demonstrate that **reverse_elephant** is working properly.

**2.8.** This programming exercise is derived from an example attributed to Mitchell Feigenbaum and adapted by John Allen Paulos in *Beyond Numeracy* (New York: Alfred A. Knopf, 1990).

Consider the deceptively simple formula

$$\texttt{NextYr} = \texttt{Rate} * \texttt{CurrentYr} * \left(1 - \frac{\texttt{CurrentYr}}{\texttt{1000000}}\right)$$

that calculates next year's population of, say, waxwings on the basis of the current population and the growth rate. The variable **Rate** controls the growth rate and takes on values between 0 and 4. The variable **CurrentYr** gives the current value of the waxwing population and is assumed to have a value between 0 and 1,000,000. The variable **NextYr** gives the value of the waxwing population one year later. The formula guarantees that **NextYr** will also have a value between 0 and 1,000,000. For example, if **CurrentYr** is 100,000 and **Rate** is 2.6, **NextYr** is 234,000.

Now suppose that we initialize **CurrentYr** to 100,000 and **Rate** to 2.6 and compute the waxwing population 25 years hence by solving for **NextYr**, setting **CurrentYr** to **NextYr**, solving again for **NextYr**, and so on for 25 iterations. The waxwing population turns out to be roughly 615,385. We get the same result if we initialize **CurrentYr** to, say, 900,000 but leave **Rate** set to 2.6. In fact, the population stabilizes at roughly 615,385 for any value of **CurrentYr** so long as **Rate** is 2.6! For some values of **Rate**, the population oscillates. For example, if **Rate** is 3.14, after about 40 years the waxwing population takes on this pattern from one year to the next: 538,007 to 780,464 to 538,007 to 780,464, and so on indefinitely. For **Rate** equal to approximately 3.57, however, the population does not stabilize or oscillate but rather varies randomly from one year to the next.

Write a program that prompts the user for **Rate**, an initial **CurrentYr**, and a number of iterations. On each iteration, the program prints the year and the current waxwing population.

**2.9.** Simulate the Monty Hall puzzle, which gets its name from the host of the television game show "Let's Make a Deal." The puzzle involves a game played as follows. A contestant picks one of three doors; behind one of the doors is a car, and behind the other two are goats. After the contestant picks a door, the host opens an unpicked door that hides a goat. (Because there are two goats, the host can open a door that hides a goat no matter which door the contestant first picks.) The host then gives the contestant the option of abandoning the picked door in favor of the still closed and unpicked door. The puzzle is to determine which of three strategies the contestant should follow:

- Always stay with the door initially picked.

- Randomly stay or switch (e.g., by flipping a coin to decide).

- Always switch to the unpicked and unopened door.

The user should be prompted as to which strategy he or she wishes to follow as well as for how many times the game should be played. Use a random number generator to place the car at the start and to simulate the contestant's initial pick. If the contestant follows the second strategy, use a random number generator to determine whether the contestant stays or switches. The program should print the number of games played and the percentage of games won. (A game is won if the contestant gets the car.) Before running the simulation, try to determine whether any of the three strategies is better than the others. You then can use the simulator to test your answer. The results may surprise you. (For a technical discussion of this puzzle, see L. Gillman, "The car and the goats," *Amer. Math. Mo.* 99 (1992): 3–7.)

**2.10.** This programming exercise is based on Lewis Carroll's system for encoding and decoding text. We assume ASCII representation of characters. The encoding and decoding use the following table:

|     | bl | !  | "  | #  | ... | \| | }  | ~  |
|-----|----|----|----|----|-----|----|----|----|
| bl  | bl | !  | "  | #  | ... | \| | }  | ~  |
| !   | !  | "  | #  | $  | ... | }  | ~  | bl |
| "   | "  | #  | $  | %  | ... | ~  | bl | !  |
| #   | #  | $  | %  | &  | ... | bl | !  | "  |
| ⋮   |    |    |    |    | ⋮   |    |    |    |
| \|  | \| | }  | ~  | bl | ... | y  | z  | {  |
| }   | }  | ~  | bl | !  | ... | z  | {  | \| |
| ~   | ~  | bl | !  | "  | ... | {  | \| | }  |

Across the top and along the side we list, in order, the (printable) ASCII characters blank (**bl**) through ~ (see Appendix A). The first row inside the table is identical to the list across the top. Thereafter, each row is the same as the previous row, except that each character is shifted one position to the left, and the last character of a row is the first character of the preceding row.

To encode text, a string, called a *code string*, is chosen arbitrarily. To illustrate the encoding method, we assume that the code string is **Walrus** and the text to encode is

```
Meet me in St. Louis
```

Characters other than blank through ~ are not altered. We write the code string, repeated as often as necessary, on top of the text to be encoded:

```
WalrusWalrusWalrusWa
Meet me in St. Louis
```

The pairs of characters **WM**, **ae**, **le**, . . . , one on top of the other, are used as indexes into the preceding table. The encoded text results from finding the entries in the table that correspond to these pairs. The entry in row **W** and column **M** is **%**, so the first character of the encoded text is **%**. The entry in row **a** and column **e** is **G**; the entry in row **1** and column **e** is **R**; and so on. Thus the text is encoded as

```
%GRgua=aVauGLol?eiAU
```

To decode text, we reverse this process.

Write a program that repeatedly prompts the user to encode text, decode text, or quit. If the user chooses to either encode or decode text, he or she is prompted for a code string, a file to encode or decode, and an output file.

# CHAPTER

# 3

# CLASSES

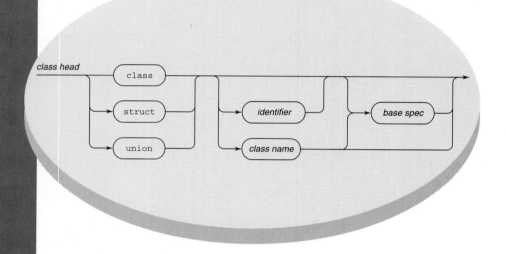

class head

3.1 Classes and Objects

3.2 Sample Application: A Stack Class

3.3 Efficiency and Robustness Issues for Classes and Objects

3.4 Sample Application: A Time Stamp Class

3.5 Constructors and the Destructor

3.6 Sample Application: A Task Class

3.7 Class Data Members and Methods

3.8 Pointers to Objects

Common Programming Errors

Programming Exercises

T his chapter examines the foundations of object-oriented programming in C++. Because object-oriented programming in any language begins with classes, we begin with the C++ syntax for declaring a class.

## 3.1  CLASSES AND OBJECTS

### Class Declarations

In C++, a class is a data type. Standard C++ has built-in classes such as **string**, and programmers can extend the language by creating their own class data types. A **class declaration** creates a class as a data type. The declaration describes the data members and methods encapsulated in the class.

**EXAMPLE 3.1.1.**   The class declaration

```
class Human {
   //... data members and methods go here
};
```

creates the class **Human**. The declaration *describes* the data members and methods that characterize a **Human**.

In the declaration, the term **class** is a keyword. The term **Human** is sometimes called the **class tag**; the tag is the identifier or name of the data type created by the declaration. Note that a semicolon follows the closing brace in the class declaration; the semicolon is required.

Given our declaration of **Human**, the statement

```
Human maryLeakey; // create an object
```

defines a variable **maryLeakey** of type **Human**. Just as the statement

```
int x; // built-in type int
```

defines an **int** variable, so

```
Human maryLeakey; // user-defined type Human
```

defines a **Human** variable. In C++, a variable of a *class* data type such as **Human** is an **object** in the sense of *object*-oriented programming.  ∎

A class declaration must come *before* the definition of any class objects. In Example 3.1.1, the declaration of **Human** therefore comes before the definition of **maryLeakey** as a **Human** object. By the way, note that the keyword **class** is *not* required in *defining* objects. Given the class declaration for **Human** in Example 3.1.1, the definitions

```
Human maryLeakey; // usual style
class Human fred; //*** legal but unusual style
```

both define **Human** objects.

Given the declaration of **Human** in Example 3.1.1, we can define either stand-alone **Human** objects such as **maryLeakey** or arrays of **Human** objects.

**EXAMPLE 3.1.2.**   Given the declaration of class **Human** in Example 3.1.1, the code segment

```
Human latvians[ 3600000 ];
```

defines an array **latvians** that has 3,600,000 elements, each of type **Human**.   ■

The C++ class extends the C **struct**ure. Indeed, the keyword **struct**, when used in C++, creates a *class*.

**EXAMPLE 3.1.3.**   The class declaration

```
struct Human {
   //... data members and methods go here
};
```

creates the class **Human**, even though the keyword **struct** is used instead of the keyword **class**.   ■

Although either of the keywords **class** and **struct** may be used to declare a C++ class, the two do differ significantly with respect to the default *information hiding* that the class supports.

## Information Hiding in C++

The C++ keyword **private** can be used to *hide* class data members and methods, and the keyword **public** can be used to *expose* class data members and methods. (C++ also has the keyword **protected** for information hiding; see Chapter 4.) In the spirit of object-oriented design, we can use **private** to hide the class *implementation* and **public** to expose the class *interface*.

**EXAMPLE 3.1.4.**   The class declaration

```
class Person {
public:
   void     setAge( unsigned n );
   unsigned getAge() const;
private:
   unsigned age;
};
```

creates a **Person** class whose interface consists of two **public** methods, **setAge** and **getAge**, and whose implementation consists of an **unsigned** data member **age**. A colon **:** follows the keywords **private** and **public**. The keyword **public** occurs first in our example, although the example could have been written as

```
class Person {
private:
   unsigned age;
public:
   void     setAge( unsigned n );
   unsigned getAge() const;
};
```

or even as

```
class Person {
public:
   void     setAge( unsigned n );
private:
   unsigned age;
public:
   unsigned getAge() const;
};
```

The last version is not good style but shows that the **private** and **public** class members may be intermixed within the class declaration.

The keyword **const** in the declaration of **getAge** signals that this method, unlike method **setAge**, does not change the value of any **Person** data member, in this case the **unsigned** data member **age**. A later subsection pursues the details of **const** methods. For now, the basic syntax and the underlying idea are important.

Clients of the **Person** class can request services by invoking the **setAge** and **getAge** methods, which are **public**; but clients have no access to the implementation data member **age**, which is **private**. The next example shows how the methods can be invoked.

Our *class* declaration contains *method declarations* for **setAge** and **getAge**. The method declarations provide the function prototypes for the methods. The two methods need to be *defined*, but we have not yet provided the definitions. We do so shortly. ■

## The Member Selector Operator

Access to any class member, whether data member or method, is supported by the **member selector operator .** and the **class indirection operator ->**.

**EXAMPLE 3.1.5.**   The code segment

```
class Person {
public:
   void     setAge( unsigned n );
   unsigned getAge() const;
```

```
    private:
       unsigned age;
    };
    int main() {
       Person boxer;
       boxer.setAge( 27 );
       //... remainder of main's body
    }
```

illustrates the use of `.` to select members. In **main** we first define **boxer** as a **Person** object and then invoke its **setAge** method

```
    boxer.setAge( 27 );
```

The member selector operator occurs *between* the class object **boxer** and the class member, in this case the method **setAge**. ∎

The member selector operator is used to access either data members or methods. However, recall that a client has access only to a class's **public** members, whether they be data members or methods.

**EXAMPLE 3.1.6.**   The program

```
    #include <iostream>
    using namespace std;
    class Person {
    public:
       void       setAge( unsigned n );
       unsigned getAge() const;
    private:
       unsigned age;
    };
    int main() {
       Person boxer;
       boxer.setAge( 27 );
       cout << boxer.age << '\n'; //*** ERROR: age is private
       return 0;
    }
```

contains an error because **main** tries to access **age**, a **private** data member in the **Person** class. Only **Person** methods such as **setAge** and **getAge** have access to its **private** members.[†] ∎

---

[†] To be precise, **private** members can be accessed only by class methods or **friend** functions, which are explained in Chapter 6.

## Class Scope

A class's **private** members have **class scope**; that is, **private** members can be accessed *only* by class methods.

**EXAMPLE 3.1.7.**   The class declaration

```
class C {
public:
   void m();   // public scope
private:
   char d;     // class scope (private scope)
};
```

gives data member **d** class scope because **d** is **private**. By contrast, method **m** has what we call *public scope* because, as a **public** member, it can be accessed from outside the class.  ∎

In C++, class scope is the *default* for members when the class is declared with the keyword **class**. In this case, members default to **private** if the keywords **public** or **protected** (see Chapter 4) are not used.

**EXAMPLE 3.1.8.**   The class declaration

```
class Z {
  int x;
};
```

is equivalent to

```
class Z {
private:
  int x;
};
```

In the first case, **x** defaults to **private**. In the second case, **x** occurs in a region of the declaration explicitly labeled **private**.  ∎

Our style is to put the **public** members first inside a declaration because this forces us then to use the label **private**, which adds clarity to the declaration. Besides, the **public** members constitute the class's interface and, in this sense, deserve to come first.

The principle of information hiding encourages us to give the class's implementation, particularly its data members, class scope. Restricting data members to class scope is likewise a key step in designing classes as abstract data types.

## The Difference between the Keywords **class** and **struct**

Recall that classes may be created using either of the keywords **class** or **struct**. If **class** is used, then all members default to **private**. If **struct** is used, then all members default to **public**.

**EXAMPLE 3.1.9.**   In the declaration

```
class C {
  int x;
  void m();
};
```

data member **x** and method **m** default to **private**. By contrast, in the declaration

```
struct C {
  int x;
  void m();
};
```

both default to **public**. Whichever keyword is used, objects of type **C** may be defined in the usual way:

```
C c1, c2, c_array[ 100 ];
```
■

**EXAMPLE 3.1.10.**   The declaration

```
class C {
    int x;   // private by default
public:
    void setX( int X ); // public
};
```

is equivalent to

```
struct C {
    void setX( int X ); // public by default
private:
    int x;
};
```

in that each declaration makes **x** a **private** data member and **m** a **public** method.
■

Our examples typically use **class** to emphasize the object-oriented principle of information hiding: a class's members default to **private** unless they are explicitly selected as part of its **public** interface.

## Defining Class Methods

Some earlier examples use the class declaration

```
class Person {
public:
    void     setAge( unsigned n );
    unsigned getAge() const;
private:
    unsigned age;
};
```

which *declares* but does not *define* the methods **setAge** and **getAge**. Class methods may be defined in two ways:

- A method may be *declared inside* the class declaration but *defined outside* the class declaration.

- A method may be *defined inside* the class declaration. Such a definition is said to be **inline**, a C++ keyword. An **inline** definition also serves as a declaration.

We use two examples to clarify the distinction.

**EXAMPLE 3.1.11.** The code segment

```
class Person {
public:
   void     setAge( unsigned n );
   unsigned getAge() const;
private:
   unsigned age;
};
// define Person's setAge
void Person::setAge( unsigned n ) {
   age = n;
}
// define Person's getAge
unsigned Person::getAge() const {
   return age;
}
```

declares **Person** methods inside the class declaration and then defines the methods outside the class declaration. The definitions use the scope resolution operator **::** because many classes other than **Person** might have methods named **setAge** and **getAge**. In addition, there might be top-level functions with these names.  ∎

**EXAMPLE 3.1.12.** The code segment

```
class Person {
public:
   void     setAge( unsigned n ) { age = n; }
   unsigned getAge() const { return age; }
private:
   unsigned age;
};
```

defines **Person**'s methods inside the class declaration. The methods are therefore **inline**.

An inline definition recommends to the compiler that the method's body be placed wherever the method is invoked so that a function call does not occur in the translated code. For example, if the compiler heeds the recommendation to make **setAge** inline, then a code segment such as

```
Person singer;
singer.setAge( 33 ); // compiler: please make inline!
```

would be translated so that the code for **setAge**'s body would be placed where the call to **setAge** occurs.                                                                    ■

A function may be defined inline even if its definition occurs *outside* the class declaration by using the keyword **inline** in a method declaration.

**EXAMPLE 3.1.13.**   In the code segment

```
class Person {
public:
    inline void     setAge( unsigned n );
    inline unsigned getAge() const;
private:
    unsigned age;
};
// define Person's setAge
void Person::setAge( unsigned n ) {
    age = n;
}
// define Person's getAge
unsigned Person::getAge() const {
    return age;
}
```

the methods **setAge** and **getAge** are still inline, although they are defined *outside* the class declaration. The reason is that the keyword **inline** occurs in the *declaration* for each method.                                                                    ■

## Using Classes in a Program

Classes are created to be used ultimately in programs. Before a class can be used in a program, its declaration must be visible to any functions that are meant to use the class. Figure 3.1.1 shows a complete program that uses the **Person** class. For clarity, we put the class declaration, which includes **inline** method definitions, and **main** in the same file. The program is quite simple, consisting only of the top-level function **main**; but it illustrates

```
#include <iostream>
using namespace std;
class Person {
public:
   void      setAge( unsigned n ) { age = n; }
   unsigned getAge() const { return age; }
private:
   unsigned age;
};
int main() {
   Person p;                // create a single Person
   Person stooges[ 3 ]; // create an array of Persons
   p.setAge( 12 );      // set p's name
   // set the stooges' ages
   stooges[ 0 ].setAge( 45 );
   stooges[ 1 ].setAge( 46 );
   stooges[ 2 ].setAge( 44 );
   // print four ages
   cout << p.getAge() << '\n';
   for ( int i = 0; i < 3; i++ )
      cout << stooges[ i ].getAge() << '\n';
   return 0;
}
```

**FIGURE 3.1.1**  A complete program using a class.

the key features in any program using a class: the class declaration, object definitions, and client requests for services.

A class declaration can be placed in a header file, which is then **#include**d wherever needed. We could amend the program in Figure 3.1.1 by placing the declaration for the **Person** class in the file *person.h* and the code for **main** in the file *testClient.cpp*. If the **Person** methods were defined *outside* the class declaration, these definitions typically would *not* be placed in the header file *person.h* because this header might be **#include**d in several other files, which would generate the error of multiple definitions for the methods. Instead, the method definitions typically would be placed in an **implementation file** such as *person.cpp*.

## EXERCISES

**1.** Explain the error in this class declaration:

```
class Person {
  // data and function members
}
```

**2.** Given the class declaration

```
class Airplane {
  // data members and methods
};
```

define an object of type **Airplane** and an array of such objects.

**3.** In the class

```
class Person {
  unsigned age;
  // other data members, and methods
};
```

is **age** a **private** or a **public** data member?

**4.** In the class

```
class Person {
  unsigned age;
  unsigned getAge() const;
  // other data members and methods
};
```

is **getAge** a **private** or a **public** method?

**5.** In a class declared with the keyword **class**, do members default to **public** or **private**?

**6.** Given the class declaration

```
class Circus {
public:
  unsigned getHeadCount() const;
  // other methods, and data members
};
```

create a **Circus** object and invoke its **getHeadCount** method.

**7.** Can any method be defined inside the class declaration?

**8.** Can any method be defined outside the class declaration?

**9.** Explain the error

```
class Circus {
public:
  unsigned getHeadCount() const;
  // other methods, and data members
};
unsigned getHeadCount() const {
   // function body
}
```

in this attempt to define method **getHeadCount** outside the class declaration.

10. If a method is defined inside the class declaration, is it automatically inline even if the keyword **inline** is not used?

11. Give an example of how the keyword **inline** is used to declare as inline a method defined outside the class declaration.

12. Why are class declarations commonly placed in header files?

# 3.2 SAMPLE APPLICATION: A STACK CLASS

### Problem

Create a **Stack** class that supports pushes and pops of **int**s.

### Sample Output

The test client in Figure 3.2.1 creates a **Stack** object and then invokes all of the **public** methods in its interface.

```
#include "stack.h" // header for Stack class
int main() {
   Stack s1;
   s1.init(); // required for correct performance
   s1.push( 9 );
   s1.push( 4 );
   s1.dump(); // 4 9
   cout << "Popping " << s1.pop() << '\n';
   s1.dump(); // 9
   s1.push( 8 );
   s1.dump(); // 8 9
   s1.pop(); s1.pop();
   s1.dump(); // empty
   s1.pop();  // still empty
   s1.dump(); // ditto
   s1.push( 3 );
   s1.push( 5 );
   s1.dump(); // 5 3
   // push two too many to test
   for ( unsigned i = 0; i < Stack::MaxStack; i++ )
     s1.push( 1 );
   s1.dump(); // 1 1 1 5 3
   return 0;
};
```

**FIGURE 3.2.1** A sample client for the **Stack** class.

The output for test client is

```
Stack contents, top to bottom:
        4
        9
Popping 4
Stack contents, top to bottom:
        9
Stack contents, top to bottom:
        8
        9
Stack contents, top to bottom:
*** Stack operation failure: Empty stack.  Popping dummy value.
Stack contents, top to bottom:
Stack contents, top to bottom:
        5
        3
*** Stack operation failure: Full stack.  Can't push.
*** Stack operation failure: Full stack.  Can't push.
Stack contents, top to bottom:
        1
        1
        1
        5
        3
```

## Solution

The **Stack** class's **public** interface consists of methods to initialize a **Stack** object, to check whether a **Stack** is empty or full, to push integers onto a **Stack**, to pop integers off a **Stack**, and to print a **Stack** to the standard output without removing any elements. A **private** method to print error messages and three data members make up the **private** implementation that supports the **Stack** interface. The class implements the standard functionality of a stack as an abstract data type.

## C++ Implementation

```
//**** file: stack.h
#include <iostream>
using namespace std;
class Stack {
```

```
public:
   enum { MaxStack = 5 };
   void init() { top = -1; }
   void push( int n ) {
      if ( isFull() ) {
         errMsg( "Full stack.  Can't push." );
         return;
      }
      arr[ ++top ] = n;
   }
   int pop() {
      if ( isEmpty() ) {
         errMsg( "Empty stack.  Popping dummy value." );
         return dummy_val;
      }
      return arr[ top-- ];
   }
   bool isEmpty() { return top < 0; }
   bool isFull() { return top >= MaxStack - 1; }
   void dump() {
      cout << "Stack contents, top to bottom:\n";
      for ( int i = top; i >= 0; i-- )
         cout << '\t' << arr[ i ] << '\n';
   }
private:
   void errMsg( const char* msg ) const {
      cerr << "\n*** Stack operation failure: " << msg << '\n';
   }
   int top;
   int arr[ MaxStack ];
   int dummy_val;
};
```

### Discussion

The **Stack** class encapsulates six high-level, **public** methods that constitute its interface:

- **init** initializes the **private** data member **top** so that **push**es and **pop**s work correctly. This is the first method that should be invoked after a **Stack** is created. Calling **init** on any **Stack**, including one with elements, has the effect of emptying the **Stack**. In Section 3.5, we show how a method such as **init** can be invoked automatically whenever a **Stack** is created. In this version of **Stack**, however, the *client* is responsible for invoking **init**.

- **push** inserts a new integer at the **top**. The method contributes to **Stack** robustness by first checking whether the **Stack** is full. If so, **push** does *not* insert an element.

- **pop** removes the integer at the **top**. The method contributes to **Stack** robustness by first checking whether the **Stack** is empty. If so, **pop** does not remove an element but instead returns an arbitrary integer value.

- **isFull** checks whether a **Stack** is full. Method **push** invokes **isFull** to determine whether a **Stack** has room for an insertion. If a **Stack** is full, **push** prints an error message before returning. If a **Stack** is not full, **push** inserts its integer parameter at the **top**.

- **isEmpty** checks whether a **Stack** is empty. Method **pop** invokes **isEmpty** to determine whether a **Stack** has elements to pop. If a **Stack** is empty, **pop** returns an arbitrary integer value. If a **Stack** is not empty, **pop** returns the **top** element.

- **dump** prints the **Stack**'s contents, from top to bottom, to the standard output. The method does not remove elements.

The **Stack** class also encapsulates, as data members, a **private** array of integers and the **private** integer **top**, which serves as an array index. The array can hold up to **MaxStack** elements. We make **MaxStack** an **enum** in the **public** section of the **Stack** class so that **MaxStack** is visible wherever **Stack** is visible. To reference **MaxStack**, we need the scope resolution operator: **Stack::MaxStack**. The class's **private** implementation also includes the method **errMsg**, which prints an error message to the standard error. This method is invoked whenever a **push** cannot occur because of a full **Stack**, or a **pop** cannot occur because of an empty **Stack**. The **private** data members and method hide implementation details from **Stack** clients. These implementation details are essential to the correct functioning of the methods in the **Stack**'s interface. Because we want a **Stack** to be an abstract data type, we hide the implementation details by making them **private**.

### *Program Development*

The **Stack** class provides services to client applications. How do we test whether the class provides the services as described in the class and method declarations? We write a **test client**, also called a **test driver** or simply **driver**. Figure 3.2.1 is our test client for the **Stack**. The client invokes all the methods in the **Stack**'s interface and tries to break the **Stack** by **pop**ping from an empty **Stack** and **push**ing onto a full **Stack**. Whenever a class is designed, a test driver should be provided that checks whether the class delivers the advertised functionality. Testing is a critical part of implementing any class.

## EXERCISES

1. Offer a reason for making all the **Stack** methods **inline**.
2. Write a method **getTop** that returns a **Stack**'s top element without removing the element from the **Stack**.

## 3.3 EFFICIENCY AND ROBUSTNESS ISSUES FOR CLASSES AND OBJECTS

Classes and objects make up the core of object-oriented programming in C++. These programming constructs are powerful but potentially inefficient. This section introduces ways in which the programmer can exploit the power of classes and objects in efficient ways. Later sections illustrate and refine the ideas introduced here. We also highlight the tradeoff between efficiency and robustness in class design.

## Passing and Returning Objects by Reference

Objects, like other variables, may be passed by reference to functions. Objects also may be returned by reference. Objects should be passed or returned by reference unless there are compelling reasons to pass or return them by value. Passing or returning by value can be especially inefficient in the case of objects. Recall that the object passed or returned by value must be *copied* and the data may be large, which thus wastes storage. The copying itself takes time, which is saved whenever an object is passed or returned by reference rather than by value. Moreover, passing and returning an object by reference is easier, at the syntax level, than passing and returning a pointer to an object. For this reason, references to objects are better than pointers to objects when either could be used as function arguments or return values.

**EXAMPLE 3.3.1.** The program in Figure 3.3.1 illustrates passing and returning objects by reference. Object **c1** is passed by reference rather than value from **main** to **f**, which means that **f** changes **c1** rather than a *copy* of **c1** by setting the parameter's name. Function **g** returns by reference the local **static** object **c3** after setting its name. It is important that **g** return by reference a **static** rather than an **auto** object. If **c3** were **auto**, then **g** would return to its invoker (in this example, **main**) a reference to a *nonexistent object*:

```
C& g() {
   C c3; //**** caution: auto, not static
   c3.set( 123 );
   return c3;
} //***** ERROR: c3 goes out of existence when g exits!
```

In general, local **auto** variables should not be returned by reference. ∎

## Object References as const Parameters

In the class declaration

```
class C {
public:
   void setName( const string& n ) { name = n; }
   //... other public members
private:
   string name;
};
```

```cpp
#include <iostream>
using namespace std;
class C {
public:
   void set( int n ) { num = n; }
   int get() const { return num; }
private:
   int num;
};
void f( C& );
C& g();
int main() {
  C c1, c2;
  f( c1 );  // pass by reference
  c2 = g(); // return by reference
  cout << c2.get() << '\n';
  return 0;
}
void f( C& c ) {
  c.set( -999 );
  cout << c.get() << '\n';
}
C& g() {
  static C c3; // NB: static, not auto
  c3.set( 123 );
  return c3;
}
```

**FIGURE 3.3.1** Passing and returning objects by reference.

method **setName**'s **string** parameter **n** is marked as **const** to signal that **setName** does not change **n** but only assigns **n** to the data member **name**. In general, if an object is passed by reference to a function **f** that does not change the object's state by setting any of its data members, then **f**'s parameter should be marked **const**. Marking the parameter as **const** safeguards against unwanted write operations with the parameter as a target and also encourages compiler optimization.

## const Methods

A method should be marked **const** if the method does not change an object's data members either directly or indirectly (that is, by invoking other methods that change the object's state).

**EXAMPLE 3.3.2.**   In the class

```
class C {
public:
   void set( int n ) { num = n; }
   int get() const { return num; }
private:
   int num;
};
```

the method **get** is marked as **const** because **get** does not change the value of any **C** data member. The **const** occurs between the method's argument list and its body.

Method **get** is a *read-only* method because **get** does not alter any data member, for example, by assigning it a value. Marking a method as **const** prevents unintended write operations on data members and also encourages compiler optimization.

Method **set** cannot be marked **const** because it alters the object's state by assigning a value to data member **num**. If **set** were erroneously marked **const**, the compiler would generate a fatal error.　■

A **const** method can invoke only other **const** methods because a **const** method is not allowed to alter an object's state either directly or *indirectly*, that is, by invoking some non**const** method.

**EXAMPLE 3.3.3.**   Class **C**

```
class C {
public:
   void m1( int x ) const {
     m2( x ); //**** ERROR: m2 not const
   }
   void m2( int x ) { dm = x; }
private:
   int dm;
};
```

contains an error. Because **m1** is marked as **const**, **m1** cannot invoke the non**const** method **m2**. The compiler's fatal error is appropriate. Were **m1** allowed to invoke the non**const** method **m2**, then **m1** would *indirectly* alter the object's state because **m2** assigns a value to data member **dm**.　■

**EXAMPLE 3.3.4.**   The class

```
class C {
public:
   void set( const string& n ) { name = n; }
   const string& get() const { return name; }
private:
   string name;
};
```

illustrates three uses of **const**. In method **set**, the **string** parameter **n** is marked as **const** because **set** does not change **n**. The method **get** returns a **const** reference to the data member **name**. In this case, the **const** signals that the returned reference to **name** should *not* be used to alter **name**. Method **get** itself is marked as **const** because **get** does not change the single **C** data member **name**.  ∎

## Overloading Methods to Handle Two Types of Strings

The class

```
class C {
public:
   void set( const string& n ) { name = n; }
   void set( const char* n ) { name = n; }
   const string& get() const { return name; }
private:
   string name;
};
```

overloads the **set** method. One overload has the prototype

```
void C::set( const string& n );
```

and would be invoked in a code segment such as

```
C c1;
string s1( "Who's Afraid of Virginia Woolf?" );
c1.set( s1 ); // string argument
```

This overload is used whenever a **string** is passed to the **set** method. The other overload has the prototype

```
void C::set( const char* n );
```

and would be invoked in a code segment such as

```
C c1;
c1.set( "What, me worry?" ); // const char*
```

This overload is used whenever a C-style string (that is, a null-terminated array of **char**) is passed to the **set** method. The overloads are convenient for clients, who can invoke a method such as **set** with either a **string** or a **const char\*** argument.

## EXERCISES

1. Why should objects be passed and returned by reference unless there are compelling reasons to pass and return them by value?

2. Why should an **auto** object never be returned by reference?

3. Given that **C** is a class and **f** is a top-level function, explain the difference between

```
void f( C& c ) { /*...*/ }
```

and

```
void f( const C& c ) { /*...*/ }
```

4. What does the class designer signal by marking a method as **const**?

5. Explain the error:

```
#include <string>
using namespace std;
class C {
public:
   void set( const string& s ) const { setAux( s ); }
private:
   void setAux( const string& s ) { dm = s; }
   string dm;
};
```

6. For a method that expects a string argument, why is it common to provide one overload to handle **string** and another to handle **const char\*** arguments?

# 3.4  SAMPLE APPLICATION: A TIME STAMP CLASS

### Problem

A **time stamp** is a value that represents an instant in time. A time stamp can be used to record when an event occurs. In a business, for example, we might use one time stamp to record when an invoice is received and another time stamp to record when the corresponding payment is sent.

Create a **TimeStamp** class that can be used to

- Set a time stamp to record when an event occurs.
- Print a time stamp as an integer.
- Print a time stamp as a string.
- Decompose a time stamp into a year, a month, a day, an hour, a minute, and a second so that these can be printed separately.

The class's public interface should include methods to provide these services.

The **TimeStamp** class should be suitable as a *utility class* for other classes. For example, an **Invoice** class might have two data members of type **TimeStamp**—one to record when the **Invoice** was sent and another to record when it was paid:

```
class Invoice {
public:
   //...
private:
   TimeStamp timeSent;
   TimeStamp timeReceived;
   //...
};
```

### Sample Output

Figure 3.4.1 shows the output for the test client of Figure 3.4.2, which creates a **TimeStamp** object named **ts** and then tests its methods. Each output section shows the **TimeStamp** as an integer and as a string. The string representation is then divided into substrings, which represent the year, the month, the day of the week, the hour, the minute, and the second.

```
Testing methods:
901076250
Tue Jul 21 19:57:30 1998
1998
Jul
Tue
19
57
30

Testing methods:
901276250
Fri Jul 24 03:30:50 1998
1998
Jul
Fri
03
30
50

Testing methods:
900776250
Sat Jul 18 08:37:30 1998
1998
Jul
Sat
08
37
30

Testing methods:
901076250
Tue Jul 21 19:57:30 1998
1998
Jul
Tue
19
57
30
```

**FIGURE 3.4.1** Output of the test client in Figure 3.4.2.

```
#include "TimeStamp.h" // declaration for TimeStamp
// test client for TimeStamp class
void dumpTS( const TimeStamp& );
int main() {
   TimeStamp ts;
   time_t now = time( 0 );
   // tests
   ts.set();                    // default arg
   dumpTS( ts );
   ts.set( now + 200000 ); // user-supplied arg 1
   dumpTS( ts );
   ts.set( now - 300000 ); // user-supplied arg 2
   dumpTS( ts );
   ts.set( -999 ); // bogus arg, resets to current time
   dumpTS( ts );
   return 0;
}
void dumpTS( const TimeStamp& ts ) {
   cout << "\nTesting methods:\n";
   cout << '\t' << ts.get() << '\n';
   cout << '\t' << ts.getAsString() << '\n';
   cout << '\t' << ts.getYear() << '\n';
   cout << '\t' << ts.getMonth() << '\n';
   cout << '\t' << ts.getDay() << '\n';
   cout << '\t' << ts.getHour() << '\n';
   cout << '\t' << ts.getMinute() << '\n';
   cout << '\t' << ts.getSecond() << '\n';
}
```

**FIGURE 3.4.2** Test client for the **TimeStamp** class.

### Solution

Our **TimeStamp** class leverages code from C++'s standard library. In particular, we use two functions whose prototypes are in the header *ctime*: **time** and **ctime**. The library function **time** returns the current time as an arithmetic type.[†] We provide methods to set a **TimeStamp** to the current time or to a user-specified time. There is also a method that returns a **TimeStamp** as an integer. The library function **ctime** converts a return value from **time** into a human-readable string (e.g., *Mon Apr 1 11:45:07 1999*). We provide a method that returns such a string, but we also provide methods that decompose the string into substrings. For example, the method **getYear** would select *1999* from our sample string and return it as a string; the method **getHour** would select *11* and return it as a string.

---

[†] On many systems, the library function **time** returns an integer that represents the elapsed seconds from a predetermined instant (e.g., midnight on January 1, 1970) to the present instant.

Our **TimeStamp** class incorporates functionality already provided in a procedural library but does so in an object-oriented style with the benefits of information hiding and encapsulation. Such a class is called a **thin wrapper** to underscore that the class does not provide radically new functionality but rather packages in an object-oriented style the functionality already provided in a procedural library. Details of our implementation are given in the Discussion section.

## C++ Implementation

```
#include <iostream>
#include <ctime>
#include <string>
using namespace std;
class TimeStamp {
public:
   void set( long s = 0 ) {
      if ( s <= 0 )
         stamp = time( 0 );
      else
         stamp = s;
   }
   time_t get() const { return stamp; }
   string getAsString() const { return extract( 0, 24 ); }
   string getYear() const { return extract( 20, 4 ); }
   string getMonth() const { return extract( 4, 3 ); }
   string getDay() const { return extract( 0, 3 ); }
   string getHour() const { return extract( 11, 2 ); }
   string getMinute() const { return extract( 14, 2 ); }
   string getSecond() const { return extract( 17, 2 ); }
private:
   string extract( int offset, int count ) const {
     string timeString = ctime( &stamp );
     return timeString.substr( offset, count );
   }
   time_t stamp;
};
```

## Discussion

We begin with two top-level functions declared in the header *ctime* because our **Time-Stamp** class uses these functions. The prototype for the function **time** is

```
time_t time( time_t* ptr );
```

The data type **time_t** is an arithmetic type, which could be a standard arithmetic type such as **long** or a nonstandard arithmetic type suited for a particular system. In any case, the function returns a value that represents the current time. The argument to **time** may be either the address of a **time_t** variable or 0 (**NULL**). If the argument is a **time_t** variable, the current time is stored in the variable.

The prototype for **ctime** is

```
char* ctime( const time_t* ptr );
```

The function expects the address of a **time_t** variable, typically a variable whose value has been set by a previous call to **time**. Function **ctime** returns the time as a C-style string. On our system, for example, the code segment

```
time_t now = time( 0 );
cout << now << '\n'
     << ctime( &now ) << '\n';
```

outputs

```
901075140
Tue Jul 21 19:39:21 1998
```

The string returned by **ctime** is actually

```
Tue Jul 21 19:39:21 1998\n
```

so that the last character is a newline **\n**. The string is always formatted as follows:

- The first three characters represent the day, e.g., **Tue**.
- The fourth character is a blank.
- The fifth through seventh characters represent the month, e.g., **Jul**.
- The eighth character is a blank.
- The ninth and tenth characters represent the day of the month, e.g., **21**.
- The 11th character is a blank.
- The 12th and 13th characters represent the hour, going from **00** (midnight) through **23** (11 P.M.).
- The 14th character is a colon.
- The 15th and 16th characters represent the minute, going from **00** through **59**.
- The 17th character is a colon.
- The 18th and 19th characters represent the second, going from **00** through **59**.
- The 20th character is a blank.
- The 21st through 24th characters represent the year, e.g., **1999**.
- The 25th character is a newline.
- The 26th character is a null terminator.

We use this information to extract parts of the returned string. For example, the method

```
string TimeStamp::getYear() const {
   return extract( 20, 4 );
}
```

invokes **private** method **extract** with two arguments, which together specify a substring in the string representation of the **TimeStamp**. Method **extract** does the work:

```
string extract( int offset, int count ) const {
  string timeString = ctime( &stamp );
  return timeString.substr( offset, count );
}
```

This **private** method, meant to be invoked only by the class's **public** methods, first invokes **ctime** on the **private** data member **stamp**, a **time_t** variable that stores an arithmetic value representing the time. Method **extract** invokes **ctime** each time to regenerate a string representation of the time and then returns the appropriate substring. To return the year, for example, **extract** returns the substring that starts at position 20 and has 4 characters.

Once a **TimeStamp** object has been defined in a code segment such as

```
int main() {
   TimeStamp ts; // define a TimeStamp object
   //...
}
```

its **set** method may be invoked with either zero arguments or one argument

```
TimeStamp ts1, ts2;
ts1.set();                      // argument defaults to 0
ts2.set( time( 0 ) + 1000 ); // now + 1,000 ticks
```

because **set**'s prototype has a default value for the parameter

```
class TimeStamp {
public:
   void set( long s = 0 ) {
      if ( s <= 0 )
        stamp = time( 0 );
      else
        stamp = s;
   }
   //...
};
```

Method **set** checks whether the user supplied a parameter and sets **stamp** to the user-supplied value if the parameter is greater than 0. Otherwise, **set** uses the current time, obtained by a call to the library function **time**. The parameter **s** is of type **signed long** so that we can trap a negative integer passed as an argument

```
TimeStamp ts;
ts.set( -999 );  // bad TimeStamp value
```

In this invocation, **ts**'s **stamp** would be set to the current time rather than to −999, as we do not accept negative values as legal times.

The remaining **public** methods such as **get**, **getAsString**, **getYear**, and the like return the time stamp string or a substring thereof to the invoker. In the code segment

```
TimeStamp ts;
ts.set();                          // set to current time
cout << ts.get() << '\n'           // output as integer
     << ts.getAsString() << '\n';  // output as string
     << ts.getMonth() << '\n'      // output month only
     << ts.getYear() << '\n';      // output year only
```

the call to **get** returns the time stamp as an integer. The remaining calls return as a string either the entire time stamp string or a substring of it.

### Program Development

We tested the **TimeStamp** class with several sample runs. On our system, one test run produced the output shown in Figure 3.4.1. The test client makes four calls to **TimeStamp**'s **set** method. The first call tests whether **set** can be called with no arguments. Because the method's declaration has a single argument with a default value of 0, this call should work. The second call invokes **set** with an argument that represents a future time. The third call invokes **set** with an argument that represents a past time. The fourth and last call invokes **set** with an illegal argument, namely, a negative integer. After each call to **set**, we test the other eight methods to see if they return the proper values. From the output we can determine whether the various **get** methods work as they should.

## EXERCISES

1. Explain why the **TimeStamp** class is known as a *thin wrapper*.

2. Explain how the **TimeStamp** class practices information hiding.

3. What functionality does the **TimeStamp** class encapsulate?

4. The **TimeStamp** class overloads the **public** method **set** so that it may be invoked with no arguments or with a single argument. Summarize how each overloaded function works.

5. Why is the **extract** method made **private** rather than **public**?

6. Write another client to test whether the **TimeStamp** class delivers the advertised functionality.

## 3.5 CONSTRUCTORS AND THE DESTRUCTOR

Class methods typically are invoked *by name*.

**EXAMPLE 3.5.1.** Assume that `Window` is a class defined in the header *windows.h*. The code segment

```
#include "windows.h" // class Windows, etc.
int main() {
   Window mainWin;    // create a Window object
   mainWin.show();    // invoke show method
   //...
}
```

creates a `Window` object `mainWin` and then invokes its `show` method by name

```
mainWin.show(); // invoke show by name
```

∎

Some methods need not be invoked explicitly by name, for the compiler invokes them automatically. **Class constructors** and the **class destructor** typically are invoked automatically *by the compiler* rather than by the programmer. We examine the constructors first.

### Constructors

A **constructor** is a method whose name is the same as the class name. A suitable constructor is invoked automatically whenever an instance of the class is created, for example, whenever a variable of the class type is defined.

**EXAMPLE 3.5.2.** The code segment

```
class Person {
public:
   Person(); // constructor
   Person( const string& n ); // constructor
   Person( const char* n );   // constructor
   void setName( const string& n );
   void setName( const char* n );
   const string& getName() const;
private:
   string name;
};
```

declares a class `Person` that has a `private` data member and six `public` methods. Three of the methods are the constructors

```
Person(); // constructor
Person( const string& n ); // constructor
Person( const char* n );   // constructor
```

These methods have the same name as the class, **Person**, and have *no return type*. A constructor must *not* have a return type. So, for example, the declaration

```
void Person(); //***** ERROR: no return type!
```

is an error.                                                                           ■

As Example 3.5.2 shows, a class may have more than one constructor. Class constructors thus can be *overloaded*. However, each constructor must have a distinct signature (see Section 2.6). In Example 3.5.2, the three constructors have distinct signatures: the first expects no arguments, the second expects a **const string** reference, and the third expects a C-style string (that is, a **const char\***).

**EXAMPLE 3.5.3.**   The code segment

```
#include "Person.h" // class declaration
int main() {
   Person anonymous;          // default constructor
   Person jc( "J. Coltrane" ); // parameterized constructor
   //...
}
```

illustrates how two constructors for the class of Example 3.5.2 can be invoked. The definition of **anonymous** causes the **default constructor** to be invoked. The default constructor is a constructor that can be invoked with no arguments. All other constructors are known generically as **parameterized constructors**. The definition of **jc**

```
Person jc( "J. Coltrane" );
```

makes it look as if **jc** were a function that expected a single argument. Instead, **jc** is a *variable* of type **Person**. The syntax signals the compiler that the appropriate parameterized constructor in the **Person** class should be invoked with the argument **"J. Coltrane"** to initialize the storage for the variable **jc**.               ■

As the name suggests, a *constructor* is a method called when an object is first *constructed*, that is, created. A constructor provides a class with a special method that is invoked automatically whenever an object is created. In short, the programmer need not remember to invoke a constructor. Constructors are used to initialize data members and to do any other processing appropriate to an object's creation. Constructors are particularly useful in making classes *robust*.

**EXAMPLE 3.5.4.**   The **Stack** class of Section 3.2 does not have constructors. For a **Stack** to work properly, however, its **top** must be initialized to −1. Although the version in Section 3.2 provides the **init** method to perform this initialization, the programmer may forget to invoke **init** after creating a **Stack** object. In the code segment

```
#include "Stack.h"
int main() {
   Stack s1;
   s1.push( 89 ); //*** Trouble: top not initialized!
   //...
}
```

**top**'s value is not properly initialized and, therefore, is indeterminate. We can fix the problem by adding a default constructor

```
class Stack {
   Stack() { init(); } // ensures initialization
   //...
};
```

that invokes **init** for us. When a **Stack** object such as **s1** is defined, the compiler invokes its default constructor, which in turn invokes **init**. ∎

A constructor is distinctive because it has the same name as the class and no return type. Otherwise, a constructor may do anything that other functions do: contain assignments, tests, loops, function calls, and the like. Also, constructors may be defined inside or outside class declarations.

**EXAMPLE 3.5.5.**   In the code segment

```
class Person {
public:
   Person() { name = "Unknown"; }
   Person( const string& n );
   Person( const char* n );
   void setName( const string& n );
   void setName( const char* n );
   const string& getName() const;
private:
   string name;
};
Person::Person( const string& n ) {
   name = n;
}
Person::Person( const char* n ) {
   name = n;
}
```

we define the default constructor **inline**, but we define the parameterized constructors outside the declaration. ∎

## Arrays of Class Objects and the Default Constructor

If C is a class, we can define arrays of C objects, and the arrays may be of any dimension. If C has a default constructor, the default constructor is invoked for each C object in the array.

**EXAMPLE 3.5.6.** The code segment

```
#include <iostream>
using namespace std;
unsigned count = 0;
class C {
public:
    C() { cout << "Creating C" << ++count << '\n'; }
};
C ar[ 1000 ];
```

produces the output

```
Creating C1
Creating C2
...
Creating C999
Creating C1000
```

The default constructor is invoked automatically for *each* of the 1,000 C objects in the array **ar**. ∎

## Restricting Object Creation Through Constructors

Suppose that we have an **Emp**loyee class with a data member that represents an employee's unique identification number

```
class Emp {
private:
    unsigned id; // unique id number
    //...
};
```

and that we want to prevent an **Emp** object from being created without initializing **id**. In short, we want to disallow a definition such as

```
Emp elvis; // undesirable--no id specified
```

**EXAMPLE 3.5.7.** The code segment

```
class Emp {
public:
   Emp( unsigned ID ) { id = ID; }
   unsigned id; // unique id number
private:
   Emp(); //**** declared private for emphasis
   //...
};
int main() {
   Emp elvis; //***** ERROR: Emp() is private
   Emp cher( 111222333 ); // OK, Emp( unsigned ) is public
   //...
}
```

generates an error at the definition of **elvis**. Creating object **elvis** would require the compiler to invoke **Emp**'s default constructor in **main**, but **Emp**'s default constructor is **private** and so inaccessible in **main**. The creation of **cher** is legal because **Emp**'s parameterized constructor is **public** and, therefore, accessible in **main**.

We declare **Emp**'s default constructor in the **private** region for emphasis—to underscore that **Emp**loyees must be constructed with an identification number. Yet even if we changed **Emp**'s declaration to

```
class Emp {
public:
   Emp( unsigned ID ) { id = ID; }
   unsigned id; // unique id number
private:
   //...
};
```

by eliminating the declaration of **Emp**'s default constructor, the variable definition

```
Emp elvis; //***** ERROR: no public default constructor
```

would remain an error because **Emp** does *not* have a **public** default constructor. The compiler provides a **public** default constructor for a class with two exceptions:

- If a class explicitly declares *any* constructor, the compiler does *not* provide a **public** default constructor. In this case, the programmer must provide a **public** default constructor if desired.
- If a class declares a non**public** default constructor, the compiler does *not* provide a **public** default constructor.

So, in the first **Emp** declaration, the compiler does not provide a **public** default constructor because the class declares a constructor *and* a non**public** default constructor. In the second **Emp** declaration, the compiler does not provide a **public** default constructor because the class declares a constructor. ∎

C++ programmers often make selected constructors `private` and others `public` to ensure that objects are properly initialized when created. A `private` constructor, like any `private` method, has *class scope* and therefore cannot be invoked outside the class.

## The Copy Constructor

Up to now we have divided constructors into two groups: the *default constructor*, which is invoked with *no* arguments, and the *parameterized constructors*, which must be invoked with arguments. Among the parameterized constructors, however, two kinds are important enough to have special names: **copy** and **convert constructors**.[†] We examine the copy constructor in this subsection and convert constructors in a later subsection.

The copy constructor creates a new object as a copy of another object. Two common prototypes for the copy constructor are

```
Person( Person& ); //***** Note: Person reference
```

and

```
Person( const Person& ); //***** Note: Person reference
```

In each case, the parameter type is a *reference*. Accordingly, the prototype

```
Person( Person ); //***** ERROR: illegal constructor
```

is in error.

A copy constructor may have more than one parameter but all parameters beyond the first must have default values. For example, the prototype

```
Person( const Person& p, bool married = false );
```

declares a copy constructor.

If the user does not provide a copy constructor, the compiler does. The compiler's version copies each data member from the source to the corresponding data member in the target.

**EXAMPLE 3.5.8.**    The code segment

```
Person orig( "Dawn Upshaw" ); // create a Person object
Person clone( orig );          // clone it
```

illustrates the copy constructor. Assuming that the compiler's copy constructor is used, objects `orig` and `clone`, although distinct, now have data members that are member for member identical.    ■

## Defining a Copy Constructor

The class author typically defines a copy constructor for a class *whose data members include a pointer to dynamically allocated storage*.[‡]

---

[†] Officially, the *convert* constructor is called the *converting* constructor.

[‡] Class authors typically overload the assignment operator = for a class if they define a copy constructor (see Section 3.5.6).

**EXAMPLE 3.5.9.** The program in Figure 3.5.1 defines an object **d1** of type **Namelist**. When the statement

```
#include <iostream>
#include <string>
using namespace std;

class Namelist {
public:
   Namelist() { size = 0; p = 0; }
   Namelist( const string [ ], int );
   void set( const string&, int );
   void set( const char*, int );
   void dump() const;
private:
   int size;
   string* p;
};
Namelist::Namelist( const string s[ ], int si ) {
   p = new string[ size = si ];
   for ( int i = 0; i < size; i++ )
      p[ i ] = s[ i ];
}
void Namelist::set( const string& s, int i ) {
   p[ i ] = s;
}
void Namelist::set( const char* s, int i ) {
   p[ i ] = s;
}
void Namelist::dump() const {
   for ( int i = 0; i < size; i++ )
      cout << p[ i ] << '\n';
}
int main() {
   string list[ ] = { "Lab", "Husky", "Collie" };
   Namelist d1( list, 3 );
   d1.dump(); // Lab, Husky, Collie
   Namelist d2( d1 );
   d2.dump(); // Lab, Husky, Collie
   d2.set( "Great Dane", 1 );
   d2.dump(); // Lab, Great Dane, Collie
   d1.dump(); // ***** Caution: Lab, Great Dane, Collie
   return 0;
}
```

**FIGURE 3.5.1** Using the compiler version of the copy constructor.

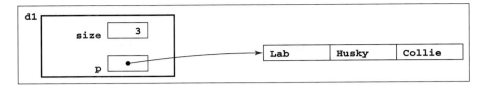

**FIGURE 3.5.2**  After the statement `Namelist d1( list, 3 );` executes.

```
Namelist d1( list, 3 );
```

executes, the constructor allocates storage to which **d1**'s member **p** points.  Then the contents of **list** are copied into this storage (see Figure 3.5.2).  Thus when the statement

```
d1.dump();
```

executes

```
Lab
Husky
Collie
```

is output.

Class **Namelist** does *not* define a copy constructor, which means that the compiler-supplied version is used in **d2**'s definition:

```
Namelist d2( d1 );   // compiler-supplied copy constructor
```

The compiler-supplied copy constructor copies the values of **d1**'s data members to **d2**'s data members (see Figure 3.5.3).  Thus the first call to **d2.dump()** prints

```
Lab
Husky
Collie
```

The statement

```
d2.set( "Great Dane", 1 );
```

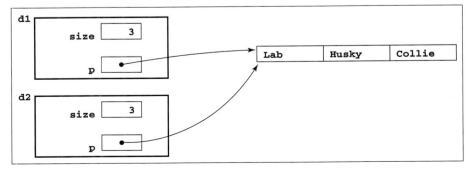

**FIGURE 3.5.3**  After the compiler-supplied copy constructor copies the values of **d1**'s data members to **d2**'s data members.

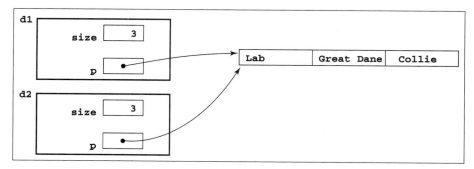

**FIGURE 3.5.4** After copying *Great Dane* into the second cell of the allocated storage to which **d2.p** points.

copies *Great Dane* into the second cell of the allocated storage to which **d2.p** points (see Figure 3.5.4). Thus when the statement

```
d2.dump();
```

executes, the output is

```
Lab
Great Dane
Collie
```

When the statement

```
d1.dump();
```

executes, because **d1.p** points to the same storage as **d2.p**, the output is also

```
Lab
Great Dane
Collie
```

This output occurs despite the fact that **d1** never invoked its **set** method! This is a subtle error. We presumably want the definition

```
Namelist d2( d1 );
```

to result in **d2**'s having its *own copy* of the strings, not sharing a copy with **d1**. But the compiler's copy constructor simply copies **d1.p** into **d2.p** and **d1.size** into **d2.size** so that both pointers point to the same storage.  ■

The program in Figure 3.5.1 illustrates the danger of using the compiler's version of the copy constructor.

**EXAMPLE 3.5.10.**  The program in Figure 3.5.5 amends the program in Figure 3.5.1 by providing a programmer-written copy constructor. In the revision, the definition

```
#include <iostream>
#include <string>
using namespace std;

class Namelist {
public:
   Namelist() { size = 0; p = 0; }
   Namelist( const string [ ], int );
   Namelist( const Namelist& );
   void set( const string&, int );
   void set( const char*, int );
   void dump() const;
private:
   int size;
   string* p;
   void copyIntoP( const Namelist& );
};

Namelist::Namelist( const string s[ ], int si ) {
   p = new string[ size = si ];
   for ( int i = 0; i < size; i++ )
      p[ i ] = s[ i ];
}
Namelist::Namelist( const Namelist& d ) {
   p = 0;
   copyIntoP( d );
}
void Namelist::copyIntoP( const Namelist& d ) {
   delete[ ] p;
   if ( d.p != 0 ) {
      p = new string[ size = d.size ];
      for ( int i = 0; i < size; i++ )
         p[ i ] = d.p[ i ];
   }
   else {
      p = 0;
      size = 0;
   }
}
void Namelist::set( const string& s, int i ) {
   p[ i ] = s;
}
void Namelist::set( const char* s, int i ) {
   p[ i ] = s;
}
```

**FIGURE 3.5.5** A version of the program in Figure 3.5.1 with a programmer-written copy constructor.

```
void Namelist::dump() const {
   for ( int i = 0; i < size; i++ )
      cout << p[ i ] << '\n';
}
int main() {
   string list[ ] = { "Lab", "Husky", "Collie" };
   Namelist d1( list, 3 );
   d1.dump(); // Lab, Husky, Collie
   Namelist d2( d1 );
   d2.dump(); // Lab, Husky, Collie
   d2.set( "Great Dane", 1 );
   d2.dump(); // Lab, Great Dane, Collie
   d1.dump(); // Lab, Husky, Collie
   return 0;
}
```

**FIGURE 3.5.5** Continued.

```
Namelist d2( d1 );
```

uses *our* version of the copy constructor, which does *not* simply copy **d1**'s data members into **d2**'s data members. Instead, our version ensures that **d1.p** and **d2.p** point to *different* storage, although the storage holds the same strings (see Figure 3.5.6).

The revised program's copy constructor

```
Namelist::Namelist( const Namelist& d ) {
   p = 0;
   copyIntoP( d );
}
```

first sets **p** to zero and then invokes the **private** method **copyIntoP** to do the work:

```
void Namelist::copyIntoP( const Namelist& d ) {
   delete[ ] p;
   if ( d.p != 0 ) {
      p = new string[ size = d.size ];
      for ( int i = 0; i < size; i++ )
         p[ i ] = d.p[ i ];
   }
   else {
      p = 0;
      size = 0;
   }
}
```

Since **p** is set to zero, the statement

```
delete[ ] p;
```

does nothing. If **d.p** is nonzero, we dynamically allocate enough storage to hold the data to which **d.p** points and copy the data into the allocated storage. If **d.p** is zero, the object being copied does not point to storage. In this case, we simply set **p** and **size** to zero.

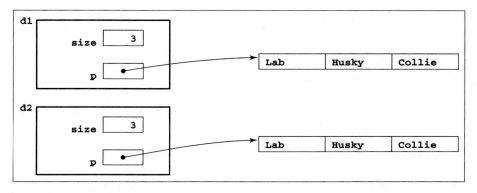

**FIGURE 3.5.6** **d1.p** and **d2.p** point to distinct copies of the same strings.

Our copy constructor, unlike the compiler-supplied version, thus ensures that the new object and the object being copied have *their own copies* of the same data (see Figure 3.5.6). ■

## Disabling Passing and Returning by Value for Class Objects

A class designer may wish to disable copying of class objects, including the copying that occurs whenever a class object is passed or returned by value. For example, authors of C++ windows classes typically disable copying of windows objects because such objects are generally large. In this subsection, we focus on the programming technique that disables copying, in particular the passing and returning of objects by value.

If the copy constructor is **private**, top-level functions and methods in other classes cannot pass or return class objects by value precisely because this requires a call to the copy constructor.

**EXAMPLE 3.5.11.**  In the code segment

```
class C {
public:
   C();
private:
   C( C& );
}
void f( C ); //*** call by value
C g();       //*** return by value
```

```
int main() {
   C c1, c2;
   f( c1 );  //***** ERROR: C( C& ) is private!
   c2 = g(); //***** ERROR: C( C& ) is private!
   //...
}
void f( C cObj ) { /*...*/ }
C g() { /*...*/ }
```

we place **C**'s copy constructor declaration in the class declaration's **private** region. Therefore, the compiler issues a fatal error on the call to **f** in **main** because we attempt to pass **c1** *by value*. We must amend **f** so that it expects a **C** reference:

```
void f( C& cObj ) { /*...*/ } // ok, call by reference
```

The compiler likewise issues a fatal error on the call to **g** in **main** because **g** returns a **C** object by value, which again requires that **C**'s copy constructor be **public** rather than **private**. We must amend **g** so that it returns a **C** reference:

```
C& g() { /*...*/ } // ok, return by reference
```
■

## Convert Constructors

A convert constructor for class **C** is a one-argument constructor used to convert a non-**C** type, such as an **int** or a **string**, to a **C** object. We have seen a convert constructor already.

**EXAMPLE 3.5.12.** The class

```
class Person {
public:
   Person() { name = "Unknown"; } // default
   Person( const string& n ) { name = n; } // convert
   Person( const char* n ) { name = n; }   // convert
   //...
private:
   string name;
};
int main() {
   Person soprano( "Dawn Upshaw" );
   //...
}
```

has a default constructor and two convert constructors, one of which converts a string constant such as **"Dawn Upshaw"** into a **Person** object such as **soprano**. ■

## The Convert Constructor and Implicit Type Conversion

A convert constructor can be used as an alternative to function overloading. Suppose that function **f** expects a **Person** object as an argument

```
void f( Person p ); // declaration
```

but that the programmer invokes **f** with a **string** such as

```
string s = "Turandot";
f( s ); // string, not Person
```

If the **Person** class has this convert constructor

```
Person( string s ); // convert constructor
```

then the *compiler* invokes the convert constructor on the **string** object **s** so that a **Person** object is available as **f**'s expected argument. The **Person** convert constructor thereby supports an **implicit type conversion**; that is, the constructor converts a **string** to a **Person**. The conversion is implicit in that the compiler performs it; the programmer does not need to provide an explicit cast.

The implicit type conversion from a string constant to a **string** is convenient for the programmer. However, an application may need to *disable* implicit type conversions of the sort just illustrated. Implicit type conversions may lead to unforeseen—and very subtle and hard to detect—errors. The keyword **explicit** may be used to disable implicit type conversions by a convert constructor.

**EXAMPLE 3.5.13.** The code segment

```
class Person {
public:
    // convert constructor marked as explicit
    explicit Person( const string& n ) { name = n; }
    //...
};
void f( Person s ) { /* note: f expects a Person... */ }
int main() {
    Person p( "foo" ); // convert constructor used
    f( p ); // ok, p is a Person
    string b = "bar";
    f( b ); //***** ERROR: no implicit type conversion
    return 0;
}
```

illustrates the syntax and use of **explicit**. The first call to **f** is valid because its argument **p** is a **Person**. The second call is invalid because its argument is a **string**, not a **Person**. Because the **Person** convert constructor has been marked **explicit**, it cannot be used to convert **b** to a **Person** in order to match **f**'s prototype. The result is a fatal compile-time error rather than a run-time error, which might have subtle but serious consequences. ∎

## Constructor Initializers

Consider the class

```
class C {
public:
   C() {
     x = 0; // OK, x not const
     c = 0; //***** ERROR: c is const
   }
private:
   int x;         // nonconst data member
   const int c; // const data member
};
```

that has a constructor to initialize its two data members. The problem is that data member **c** is **const** and, therefore, cannot be the target of an assignment operation. The solution is to use a **constructor initializer**.[†]

> **EXAMPLE 3.5.14.**   The code segment
>
> ```
> class C {
> public:
>    C() : c( 0 ) { x = -1; }
> private:
>    int x;
>    const int c; // const data member
> };
> ```
>
> illustrates a constructor initializer. In this case, the **const** data member **c** is initialized. The constructor's initialization section is introduced by a colon **:** followed by members and their initializing values in parentheses. In our example, only **c** is initialized and its value, 0, is enclosed in parentheses after its name. This is the *only* way to initialize a **const** data member such as **c**.  ∎

Constructor initialization is legal only in constructors. Any data member may be initialized in a constructor's initialization section. Of course, **const** data members cannot be initialized in any other way.

> **EXAMPLE 3.5.15.**   We amend Example 3.5.14
>
> ```
> class C {
> public:
>    C() : c( 0 ), x( -1 ) { } // empty body
> private:
>    int x;
>    const int c; // const data member
> };
> ```

---

[†] The official name for *constructor initializer* is *ctor initializer*.

by initializing both **const** member **c** and non**const** member **x**. Initialization occurs in the order in which the members are declared. In this example, data member **x** occurs first and data member **c** occurs second in the class declaration. Therefore, **x** is initialized *first* in the constructor initialization.

Our default constructor's body is now empty because the initializations do the required work. This programming style is common. ∎

## Constructors and the Operators **new** and **new[ ]**

The C++ operators **new** and **new[ ]** have advantages over the C functions **malloc** and **calloc** with respect to dynamic storage allocation for class objects. In particular, use of **new** and **new[ ]** ensures that the appropriate constructor will be invoked, whereas use of **malloc** and **calloc** does not.

**EXAMPLE 3.5.16.**   In the code segment

```
#include <cstdlib> // for malloc and calloc
class Emp {
public:
   Emp() { /*...*/ }
   Emp( const char* name ) { /*...*/ }
   //...
};
int main() {
   Emp* elvis = new Emp();                  // default
   Emp* cher = new Emp( "Cher" );           // convert
   Emp* lotsOfEmps = new Emp[ 1000 ];   // default
   Emp* foo = malloc( sizeof( Emp ) ); // no constructor
   //...
}
```

the default constructor initializes the single **Emp** cell to which **elvis** points because **new** is used. The default constructor also initializes 1,000 **Emp** cells to which **lotsOfEmps** points because **new[ ]** is used. The convert constructor initializes the **Emp** cell to which **cher** points because **new** is again used. However, no constructor initializes the cell to which **foo** points because this storage is allocated through the C function **malloc** rather than through the C++ operators **new** and **new[ ]**. ∎

## The Destructor

A constructor is automatically invoked whenever an object belonging to a class is created. The **destructor** is automatically invoked whenever an object belonging to a class is destroyed, for example, when a variable of the class type goes out of scope or when dynamically allocated storage of the class type is **delete**d. The destructor, like the constructors, is a method. For class **c**, the destructor's prototype is

```
~C();
```

White space can occur between ~ and the class name. The destructor takes no arguments so there can be only one destructor per class. The destructor, like the constructors, has no return type. The destructor declaration

```
void ~C();   //***** ERROR: no return type!
```

is therefore in error.

**EXAMPLE 3.5.17.**   The output for the program in Figure 3.5.7 is

```
hortense constructing
anonymous constructing.
foo constructing

foo destructing.
anonymous destructing.
anonymous constructing.
anonymous destructing.
hortense destructing.
```

At line 1, a **c** object is created

```
C c0( "hortense" ); // parameterized constructor
```

and the convert constructor is invoked automatically. Object **c0** exists from the time of its creation until right before **main** exits at line 7. *Before* **main** exits, **c0**'s destructor is invoked automatically, which outputs a message to that effect.

Lines 2 and 3 create objects **c1** and **c2**. For **c1**, the default constructor is invoked; for **c2**, the convert constructor is invoked. Lines 2 and 3 occur *inside* a block. Objects **c1** and **c2** exist only within the block. Therefore, right before the block exits at line 4, **c1**'s destructor and **c2**'s destructor are automatically invoked.

Line 5 dynamically allocates a **c** object using **new** and stores its address in **ptr** whose type is **C***. Because **new** is used, the default constructor is invoked automatically on the storage to which **ptr** points. At line 6, **ptr** is **delete**d, which automatically invokes the destructor on the storage to which **ptr** points. ∎

```
#include <iostream>
#include <string>
using namespace std;
class C {
public:
  C() { // default constructor
     name = "anonymous";
     cout << name << " constructing.\n";
  }
  C( const char* n ) { // parameterized constructor
     name = n;
     cout << name << " constructing.\n";
  }
  ~C() { cout << name << " destructing.\n"; }
private:
  string name;
};
int main() {
/* 1 */ C c0( "hortense" ); // parameterized constructor
        {
/* 2 */   C c1; // default constructor
/* 3 */   C c2( "foo" ); // parameterized constructor
          cout << '\n';
/* 4 */ } // c1 and c2 destructors called
/* 5 */ C* ptr = new C(); // default constructor
/* 6 */ delete ptr;  // destructor for the ptr object
/* 7 */ return 0; // c0 destructor called
}
```

**FIGURE 3.5.7** Constructor and destructor calls.

The class destructor typically does whatever clean up operations are appropriate when an object is destroyed, just as the class constructors typically do whatever operations are appropriate when an object is created. We recommend that every class with data members have at least a default constructor to handle initializations. Other constructors and the destructor should be added as needed.

## EXERCISES

**1.** Explain the error:

```
class C {
public:
   c(); // default constructor
   //...
};
```

**2.** Explain the error:

```
class Z {
public:
    void Z(); // default constructor
    //...
};
```

**3.** Can a class's constructors be overloaded?

**4.** Can a class constructor be **private**?

**5.** Must a class constructor be defined outside the class declaration?

**6.** In the class declaration

```
class C {
public:
  C();
  C( int );
  //...
};
```

indicate which constructor is the *default* constructor.

**7.** Explain the error:

```
class K {
private:
    K();
};
int main() {
    K k1;
    return 0;
}
```

**8.** In the code segment

```
class C {
public:
    C() { /*...*/ }
};
C array[ 500 ];
```

how many times is **C**'s default constructor invoked?

**9.** Explain the error:

```
class R {
public:
  R( R arg ); // copy constructor
};
```

**10.** What is the purpose of the copy constructor?

**11.** Write a code segment that illustrates how the copy constructor might be used.

**12.** If the class author does not provide a copy constructor, does the compiler provide one?

**13.** What is the output?

```
#include <iostream>
using namespace std;
class C {
public:
    C() { p = new int; }
    void set( int a ) { *p = a; }
    int get() const { return *p; }
private:
    int* p;
};
int main() {
  C c1, c2;
  c1.set( 1 );
  cout << c1.get() << '\n';
  c2 = c1;
  c2.set( -999 );
  cout << c1.get() << '\n';
  return 0;
}
```

**14.** When should a class author define a copy constructor for the class?

**15.** What is a convert constructor?

**16.** Declare a class **c** with two convert constructors.

**17.** Does the following program contain any errors?

```
class C {
public:
    C( int x ) {
     // method's body
    }
};
void g( C );
int main() {
    g( 999 );
    return 0;
}
void g( C arg ) {
    // function's body
}
```

**18.** Explain the error:

```
class Foo {
public:
  explicit Foo( int arg ) {
    // constructor's body
  }
};
void g( Foo f ) {
  // g's body
}
int main() {
    Foo f1;
    g( f1 );
    g( -999 );
    return 0;
}
```

**19.** Explain the error:

```
class C {
  C( int a ) { c = a; }
private:
  const int c;
};
```

**20.** For the class

```
class C {
public:
    // public methods
private:
    const int c;
};
```

define a convert constructor that expects an **int** argument and initializes data member **c** to this argument's value.

**21.** Explain the error:

```
class Z {
public:
  Z( int a ) : c( a ), x( -5 ) { }
  void f( int a ) : c( a ) { }
private:
  const int c;
  int x;
};
```

**22.** Explain the error:

```
class A {
public:
  void ~A();
};
```

**23.** What is the output?

```
#include <iostream>
using namespace std;
class Z {
public:
  Z( unsigned a ) : id( a ) {
    cout << id << " created\n";
  }
  ~Z() {
    cout << id << " destroyed\n";
  }
private:
  unsigned id;
};
int main() {
  Z z1( 1 ), z2( 2 ), z3( 3 );
  return 0;
}
```

# 3.6 SAMPLE APPLICATION: A TASK CLASS

## Problem

Create a **Task** class that represents a task to be scheduled. In addition to a required identifying *name*, a **Task** has a *start time*, *finish time*, and a *duration*. The public interface
should provide methods for accessing these **Task** properties. When a **Task** is destroyed, a
record describing it should be written to a log file.

## Sample Output

The output file for the test client in Figure 3.6.1 is

```
ID: Eat pizzas and drink beer
  ST: Wed Jul 22 13:34:13 1998
  FT: Wed Jul 22 15:34:13 1998
  DU: 7200
ID: Open beer
  ST: Wed Jul 22 13:34:10 1998
  FT: Wed Jul 22 13:34:12 1998
  DU: 2
```

```
#include "Task.h" //*** Task class
int main() {
  time_t now = time( 0 );
  Task t1( "Defrost pizzas" ),
       t2( "Open beer" ),
       t3( "Eat pizzas and drink beer" );
  t1.setST( now );
  t1.setFT( now + 3600 );        // an hour from now
  t2.setST( t1.getFT() );        // when pizzas defrosted
  t2.setFT( t2.getST() + 2 );    // fast work
  t3.setST( t2.getFT() + 1 );    // slight delay
  t3.setFT( t3.getST() + 7200 ); // leisure meal
  return 0;
}
```

**FIGURE 3.6.1** Test client for the **Task** class.

```
ID: Defrost pizzas
  ST: Wed Jul 22 12:34:10 1998
  FT: Wed Jul 22 13:34:10 1998
  DU: 3600
```

Each output block begins with a **Task**'s identifying name, for example, **Defrost piz-zas**. Next comes the **Task**'s start and finish times as strings. The last entry is the **Task**'s duration as an integer, which is the start time as an integer subtracted from the finish time as an integer. The **Defrost pizzas** task has a duration of 3,600 time units, whereas the **Open beer** task has a duration of only two time units. The output file reverses the order in which the **Task**s occur. For example, **Defrost pizzas** is listed last but occurs first. The output file reflects the order in which the **Task** destructors execute. The **Task** named **Defrost pizzas** is created first and *destroyed last* in our sample client, which accounts for its position in the log file. The Discussion explains how the programmer can control the log file's output.

### *Solution*

We use the **Task** constructors to ensure that a **Task** has an identifying name, represented as a **string**. To represent a **Task**'s start and finish times, we leverage the **TimeStamp** class (see Section 3.4). In particular, a **Task** has two **private TimeStamp** data members, one to represent a start time and another to represent a finish time. Instead of storing a **Task**'s duration in a data member, we compute the duration as needed by using the library function **difftime**, which returns the difference between two **time_t** values. For logging **Task** data to a file, we use an **ofstream** object opened in **app**end mode.

## C++ Implementation

```cpp
#include "TimeStamp.h" //*** for TimeStamp class
#include <iostream>
#include <ctime>
#include <fstream>
#include <string>
using namespace std;

class Task {
public:
   // constructors-destructor
   Task( const string& ID ) {
      setID( ID );
      logFile = "log.dat";
      setST();
      ft = st; // no duration yet
   }
   Task( const char* ID ) {
      setID( ID );
      logFile = "log.dat";
      setST();
      ft = st; // no duration yet
   }

   ~Task() { logToFile(); }
   // set-get methods
   void setST( time_t ST = 0 ) { st.set( ST ); }
   time_t getST() const { return st.get(); }
   string getStrST() const { return st.getAsString(); }
   void setFT( time_t FT = 0 ) { ft.set( FT ); }
   time_t getFT() const { return ft.get(); }
   string getStrFT() const { return ft.getAsString(); }
   void setID( const string& ID ) { id = ID; }
   void setID( const char* ID ) { id = ID; }
   string getID() const { return id; }
   double getDU() const { return difftime( getFT(), getST() ); }
```

```cpp
   void logToFile() {
      // set finish if duration still 0
      if ( getFT() == getST() )
        setFT();
      // log the Task's vital statistics
      ofstream outfile( logFile.c_str(), ios::app );
      outfile << "\nID: " << id << '\n';
      outfile << "  ST: " << getStrST();
      outfile << "  FT: " << getStrFT();
      outfile << "  DU: " << getDU();
      outfile << '\n';
      outfile.close(); //*** just to be safe!
   }

private:
   Task(); // default constructor explicitly hidden
   TimeStamp  st;
   TimeStamp  ft;
   string     id;
   string     logFile;
};
```

### Discussion

The **Task** class has two data members of type **TimeStamp**, which means that the class declaration for **TimeStamp** and the code that implements **TimeStamp** methods *must* be part of any program that uses the **Task** class. The **Task** class has four **private** data members: **st**, a **TimeStamp** that represents the **Task**'s start time; **ft**, a **TimeStamp** that represents the **Task**'s finish time; **id**, a **string** that represents the **Task**'s name; and **logFile**, the name of the file to which information about the **Task** is logged. There are **public** methods to **set** and **get** the data members **st**, **ft**, and **id**.

The **Task** class declares three constructors, a default constructor and convert constructors that expect the **Task**'s name as an argument. We want to disallow uninitialized definitions of **Task** objects such as

```cpp
Task takeExam; // no name provided!
```

To emphasize this point, we declare the default constructor in the **private** section

```cpp
class Task {
public:
   //...
private:
   Task(); // default constructor hidden for emphasis
   //...
};
```

Because we define other constructors, the compiler in any case would *not* provide a **public** default constructor. The important point is that a **Task** object cannot be created without a **string** or C-style string argument:

```
int main() {
   Task takeExam1; //*** ERROR: default constructor not public!
   Task takeExam2( "trouble" ); // ok, public convert constr
   //...
}
```

The **public** convert constructors take a single argument, which is the **Task**'s identifying name. The **string&** convert constructor initializes all data members:

```
Task( const string& ID ) {
   setID( ID );
   logFile = "log.dat";
   setST();
   ft = st; // no duration yet
}
```

The constructor calls the **Task** method **setID** to initialize the **Task**'s identifying string and the method **setST** to initialize the starting time to the *current* time. Method **setST** invokes the **TimeStamp** method **set**, which in turn invokes the library function **time**. After setting the start time to the current time, we set the **Task**'s finish time to its start time so that the two coincide. Because *duration* is the difference between *finish* and *start* times, duration is 0 when a **Task** is first created.

We want the **char\*** convert constructor to construct a **Task** in exactly the same way as the **string&** convert constructor. The two constructors differ only in that one expects a C-style string and the other a **string** as the **Task**'s identifying name.

By using **TimeStamp**s to represent a **Task**'s start and finish times, we can leverage the functionality of the **TimeStamp** class. For example, the **Task** class has methods to set and get the start and the finish time:

```
void setFT( time_t FT ) {
   ft.set( FT );
}
time_t getFT() {
   return ft.get();
}
```

Because **ft** is a **TimeStamp**, we delegate the setting and getting to the underlying **TimeStamp** methods **set** and **get**. This is an example of code reuse and wrapping: our **Task** class has methods such as **getFT** that are thin wrappers around **TimeStamp** methods, which do the actual work.

There is **public** method for logging **Task** data to a file. If **t1** is a **Task**, then

```
t1.logToFile()
```

may be invoked whenever desired. The method

```
void logToFile() {
   // set finish if duration still 0
   if ( getFT() == getST() )
     setFT();
   // log the Task's vital statistics
   ofstream outfile( logFile.c_str(), ios::app );
   outfile << "\nID: " << id << '\n';
   outfile << "  ST: " << getStrST();
   outfile << "  FT: " << getStrFT();
   outfile << "  DU: " << getDU();
   outfile << '\n';
   outfile.close(); //*** just to be safe!
}
```

does the work. Normally we would not make this method **inline** because of its relative complexity. Nonetheless, it is a convenience to client applications that all **Task** methods are defined inside the class declaration.

In method **logToFile**'s body, the **if** statement checks whether a **Task**'s finish time is different from its start time. If not, **logToFile** sets the **Task**'s finish time to the current time. In Chapter 2, we invoked **ofstream**'s **open** method to open a file. Here we use the constructor

```
ofstream outfile( logFile.c_str(), ios::app );
```

instead of a separate call to **open**

```
ofstream outfile;
outfile.open( logFile.c_str(), ios::app );
```

For **ofstream**s, the constructor and the **open** method are overloaded. Here we use the two-argument constructor. The first argument is the file's name as a null-terminated array of **char**, that is, a C-style string. The **string** method **c_str** converts the **string** into a C-style string. The second argument **ios::app** is the **mode** in which the file named **logFile** is opened, in this case *append* mode. When a file is opened in append mode, new records are written at the *end*. Figure 3.6.2 lists the modes and their meanings.

In method **logToFile**, the scope of **ofstream** object **outfile** is **logToFile**'s body. Therefore, **outfile**'s destructor is invoked automatically when control exits **logToFile**'s body. The **ofstream** destructor closes the output stream if it is open. Nonetheless, we explicitly invoke the **close** method to underscore that the output stream is closed after each invocation of **logToFile**.

Because the programmer may forget to invoke a **Task**'s **logToFile** method before the **Task** is destroyed, the **Task** class has a destructor that invokes **logToFile**. The destructor thus ensures that the **Task**'s data is logged. In the code segment

| Name | Purpose |
|---|---|
| `in` | Open for reading |
| `out` | Open for writing |
| `ate` | Open and move to end-of-stream |
| `app` | Open for appending |
| `trunc` | Truncate the stream if it already exists |
| `binary` | Open as a binary stream |

**FIGURE 3.6.2** Mode flags.

```
int main() {
   Task t1( "foo" );
   {
     Task t2( "bar" );
     //...
   } // t2's destructor invoked
   return 0; // t1's destructor invoked
}
```

`t2`'s destructor is invoked when control exits the block and `t2` goes out of scope. The destructor for `t1` is invoked when `main` exits with the `return` statement.

### EXERCISES

1. What change in behavior results if the mode is changed from `ios::app` to `ios::out` in the `logToFile` method?

2. Write a test driver for the `Task` class to test whether its `public` methods work as intended.

## 3.7 CLASS DATA MEMBERS AND METHODS

So far we have seen data members and methods associated with individual *objects*. For example, for the `Task` class of Section 3.6, the definitions

```
Task t1( "clean flotsam" );   // create a Task
Task t2( "purge jetsam" );    // create another
```

create two `Task` objects, *each* with its own data members `id`, `st`, `ft`, and `logFile`. C++ also supports members associated with *the class itself* rather than with objects that belong to the class. We call these **class members** as opposed to **object members** or **instance members**. The keyword `static` is used to create a *class* member.

**EXAMPLE 3.7.1.**   The declaration

```
class Task {
public:
    //...
private:
    static unsigned n; // count of Task objects
    //...
};
```

shows the syntax. The **Task** class now contains a data member **n** associated with the class **Task** itself rather than with particular **Task** objects. Because data member **n** is **static**, there is *one* **unsigned** variable for the entire class, not one **unsigned** variable **n** per **Task** object. Figure 3.7.1 illustrates for class **C**, which has a non**static** data member **x** and a **static** data member **s**.

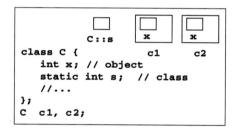

**FIGURE 3.7.1** Class versus object or instance data member.

We might use **n** to keep track of how many **Task** objects currently exist. To do so, we could amend the **string&** parameterized constructor and the **const char\*** constructor and the destructor as follows:

```
Task( const string& ID ) {
    setID( ID );
    logFile = "log.dat";
    setST();
    ft = st; // no duration yet
    n++; // another Task created
}
~Task() {
    logToFile();
    n--; // another Task destroyed
}
```

Assuming that **static** data member **n** is initialized to zero, **n** would keep a running count of **Task** objects. ∎

A **static** *data member* may be *declared* inside the class declaration, as Example 3.7.1 shows. However, such a **static** data member still must be *defined*.

**EXAMPLE 3.7.2.**  The code segment

```
class Task {
public:
   //...
private:
   static unsigned n; // count of Task objects
   //...
};
unsigned Task::n = 0; // define static data member
```

amends Example 3.7.1 by adding a *definition* for **static** data member **n**. A **static** data member declared inside the class declaration must be *defined outside all blocks*, as we show here. Note that the data member's name is **Task::n** and not **n**. Although we initialize **Task::n** to zero, this is not required. Any variable defined outside all blocks is initialized automatically to zero unless the programmer supplies a different initial value. ∎

A **static** data member does *not* affect the **sizeof** a class or an object of this class type.

**EXAMPLE 3.7.3.**  Given the code segment

```
class C {
   unsigned long dm1;
   double dm2;
};
C c1;
```

the expressions **sizeof( C )** and **sizeof( c1 )** evaluate to 16 on our system. If we change the class declaration to

```
class C {
   unsigned long dm1;
   double dm2;
   static unsigned long dm3; // does not impact sizeof( C )
   static double dm4;        // does not impact sizeof( C )
};
```

the two **sizeof** expressions still evaluate to 16 because **static** data members do not affect the **sizeof** a class and its objects. ∎

In addition to **static** data members, a class may have **static** methods. A **static** method can access *only* other **static** members, whether these be data members or function members.

**EXAMPLE 3.7.4.**   The declaration

```
class Task {
public:
   static unsigned getN() const { return n; }
   //...
private:
   static unsigned n; // count of Task objects
   //...
};
```

now includes an inline definition for the **static** method **getN**. As Example 3.7.1 shows, an *object* or *instance* method, including constructors and destructors, may access a **static** data member such as **n**. As the current example shows, a **static** method may access a **static** data member. The difference is that a **static** method may access *only* **static** members. Therefore, the code segment

```
class Task {
public:
   static unsigned getN() {
      setST();        //***** ERROR: not static!
      st = time( 0 ); //***** ERROR: not static!
      return n;       // ok, n is static
   }
   //...
};
```

contains two errors. The **static** method **getN** may access only **static** members, whether data members or methods; but **setST** and **st** are not **static**. By the way, a **static** method, like any other method, can be defined either **inline** or outside the class declaration. ∎

Suppose that **C** is a class with a **static** data member **sVar** and a **static** method **sMeth**, both **public**:

```
class C {
public:
   static int  sVar;
   static void sMeth();
   //...
};
```

There are different ways to access the **static** members, through either **C** objects or *directly* through the class **C**.

**EXAMPLE 3.7.5.**   Given that **sVar** and **sMeth** are **static** and **public** members of **C**, the code segment

```
int main() {
   C c1;
   c1.sMeth(); // through an object
   C::sMeth(); // directly and preferred
   unsigned x = c1.sVar; // through an object
   unsigned y = C::sVar; // directly and preferred
   //...
}
```

shows the two different ways to access the **static** members. Of course, information hiding recommends against **public** data members. We make **sVar public** only to illustrate the syntax.

The *preferred* way to access a **static** member is directly through the class. After all, a **static** member is associated with the class itself rather than with objects of the class type.   ∎

Assuming that

- Object **c** belongs to class **C**.
- Method **om** is an object (i.e., non**static**) method in **C**.
- Method **cm** is a class (i.e., **static**) method in **C**.

the following table summarizes the differences:

| Method Type | Has Access To | Legal Invocations |
|---|---|---|
| Object | Object and class members | `c.om()` |
| Class | Class members only | `C::cm()`, `c.cm()` |

## **static** Variables Defined Inside Methods

A local variable in a *method* can be **static**. In this case, the method has *one* underlying cell shared by *all* objects in the class when they invoke the method.

**EXAMPLE 3.7.6.**   The code

```
class C {
public:
   void m();   // object method
private;
   int x;      // object data member
};
void C::m() {
   static int s = 0; //***** Caution: 1 copy for all objects
   cout << ++s << '\n';
}
```

```
int main() {
  C c1, c2;
  c1.m();    // outputs 1
  c2.m();    // outputs 2
  c1.m();    // outputs 3
  return 0;
}
```

defines a **static** variable **s** inside method **m**'s body. Because **s** is defined inside a block, it has block scope and, therefore, is accessible only inside **m**, which increments **s** each time that it is called. Because **m** is a **C** method, its **static** local variable is shared by *all* **C** objects. By contrast, each **C** object has its *own* copy of non**static** data member **x**. Every invocation of **m** accesses the *same* underlying cell for **s**. So, in **main**, the first invocation **c1.m()** increments **s** from 0 to 1. The invocation **c2.m()** increments **s** from 1 to 2. The second invocation **c1.m()** increments **s** from 2 to 3. ∎

## EXERCISES

1. What is the difference between an *object data member* and a *class data member*?

2. Declare a class **C** with a **static** data member of type **int**.

3. Explain the error:

```
#include <iostream>
using namespace std;
class C {
public:
    void f() { cout << ++x << '\n'; }
private:
    static int x;
};
int main() {
  C c1;
  c1.f();
  return 0;
}
```

4. Explain the error:

```
class C {
public:
    static void s() { ++x; }
private:
    int x;
};
```

**5.** What is the output?

```
class Z {
public:
   void f() {
     static int s = 0;
     cout << ++s << '\n';
   }
};
int main() {
   Z z1, z2;
   z1.f();
   z2.f();
   z1.f();
   return 0;
}
```

## 3.8 POINTERS TO OBJECTS

Pointers to dynamically allocated objects occur frequently in C++ applications. Accordingly, we review the topic in this section.

The member selector operator **.** is used with an object or an object reference to access an object's members.

**EXAMPLE 3.8.1.**   The code segment

```
class C {
public:
  void m() { /*...*/ }
};
void f( C& ); // pass by reference
int main() {
   C c1;
   c1.m();   // object
   f( c1 );
   //...
}
void f( C& c ) {
   c.m();    // object reference
}
```

reviews the syntax of the member selector operator by showing it in use with the object **c1** and the object reference **c**. In both cases, the member selector operator is used to invoke the object's method **m**.  ∎

The member selector operator may be used *only* with objects and object references. Access to an object's members through a *pointer* requires the **class indirection operator**, which consists of the *minus sign* - followed by the *greater than sign* >.

**EXAMPLE 3.8.2.**  We amend Example 3.8.1

```
class C {
public:
  void m() { /*...*/ }
};
void f( C* ); // pass a pointer
int main() {
   C c1;
   c1.m();   // object
   f( &c1 ); // address of object
   //...
}
void f( C* p ) {
   p->m();  // pointer to C object
}
```

by passing **f** a *pointer* to **c1** rather than a reference to **c1**. In **f**, the class indirection operator occurs *between* the pointer **p** to the object (in this case, **c1**) and the member being accessed (in this case, method **m**). Because **f** receives a pointer to rather than a reference to **c1**, the member selection operator cannot be used with the pointer to invoke **m**:

```
void f( C* p ) {
   p.m();   //**** ERROR: p not an object or object reference
   p->m(); // correct: p a pointer to a C object
}
```

White space may not occur between the two symbols that make up the class indirection operator, although white space can occur on either side of the operator:

```
void f( C* p ) {
   p->m();    // ok
   p -> m();  // ok
   p-> m();   // ok, though peculiar
   p ->m();   // ditto
   p- >m();   //***** ERROR: white space between - and >
}
```

■

Pointers to objects typically are used in two contexts in C++. First, pointers to objects may be passed as arguments to functions or returned by functions. Example 3.8.2 illustrates this context by passing a pointer to **f**. Second, objects may be created dynamically by using the **new** and **new[ ]** operators, which return a pointer to the dynamically allocated storage.

In forthcoming chapters, our examples involve a mix of objects, object references, and pointers to objects. In these examples, we discuss the reasons behind the mix. For now, our concern is to review the syntax of the class indirection operator. For accessing an object's members:

- The member selector operator **.** is used exclusively with *objects* and *object references*.
- The class indirection operator **->** is used exclusively with *object pointers*.

## The Pointer Constant `this`

The pointer **this** can be used inside a method to access the object associated with the method's invocation (**this** is a keyword).

**EXAMPLE 3.8.3.** In the class declaration

```
class C {
public:
  C() { x = 0; }
private:
  int x;
};
```

the constructor initializes the **private** data member **x** to zero. The constructor could be rewritten

```
class C {
public:
  C() { this->x = 0; } // how this can be used
private:
  int x;
};
```

We rewrite the constructor only to illustrate the syntax of using **this**. If we create a **C** object

```
C c1; // C::C() invoked
```

**this** points to **c1** in the constructor call. In more technical terms, **this** has **&c1** as its value. ■

A class often has **public** methods to access **private** data members. For example, the **Task** class of Section 3.6 has the methods **setID** and **getID** to access the **private** member **id** that represents a **Task**'s identifying name. One version's definition is

```
void setID( const string& ID ) { id = ID; }
```

We give the parameter the name **ID** in uppercase to avoid a name conflict with the data member's name **id**. However, some C++ programmers prefer to give parameters in methods such as **setID** the *same* name as the data member to be accessed, and they avoid a name conflict by using **this**. In such a style, **setID** would be written

```
void setID( const string& id ) { this->id = id; }
```

The expression **this->id** accesses the object's *data member* named **id**. The name **id** by itself is the parameter. ∎

**EXAMPLE 3.8.4.** Suppose that we design a **File** class with a **copy** method whose definition begins as follows:

```
void File::copy( File& dest ) {
   if ( this == &dest ) // can't copy File to itself
     return;
   // otherwise, copy this File to dest
   //...
}
```

The **if** statement traps an invocation such as

```
f1.copy( f1 );
```

in which **f1** is a **File** object whose **copy** method is invoked with **f1** itself as the argument. The **if** statement's test in the **copy** method prevents the undesirable effect of copying a **File** to itself. Specifically, the **if** statement checks whether **this** and **&dest** point to the *same object*. Such checks are common in C++ methods. ∎

The pointer **this** is a *constant* and, therefore, cannot be the target of an assignment, increment, or decrement operation. Further, **this** is available only in non**static** methods.

**EXAMPLE 3.8.5.** The class declaration

```
class C {
public:
  void m( const C& obj ) {
    this = &obj; //***** ERROR: this is a constant
    //...
  }
  static void s() {
    this->count = 0; //***** ERROR: static method!
  }
private:
  static int count;
};
```

contains two errors. In method **m**, we erroneously try to assign a value to **this**, which is a constant. In the **static** method **s**, we erroneously try to access **this**. ∎

## EXERCISES

**1.** What is the error?

```
#include <iostream>
using namespace std;
class C {
public:
    void m() { cout << "C::m\n"; }
};
void g( C* );
int main() {
    C c1;
    g( &c1 );
    //...
}
void g( C* p ) {
    p.m();
}
```

**2.** What is the error?

```
class C {
public:
  void m() { /*...*/ }
};
int main() {
  C c1;
  C* p;
  p = &c1;
  p - >m();
  //...
}
```

**3.** Explain when the member selector operator **.** is used with objects.

**4.** Explain when the class indirection operator **->** is used with objects.

## COMMON PROGRAMMING ERRORS

**1.** It is an error to omit the closing semicolon in a class declaration:

```
class C {
  //...
}  //***** ERROR: no semicolon
```

The correct syntax is

```
class C {
  //...
};
```

2. The declaration for class **C** must occur *before* objects of type **C** are defined:

```
C c1, c2; //***** ERROR: class C not yet declared
class C {
  //...
}; // must go before definitions of c1 and c2
```

For this reason, it is common to put class declarations in headers that can be **#include**d wherever needed:

```
#include "classDecs.h" // including one for class C
C c1, c2; // ok
```

3. It is an error to access a non**public** class member in a function that is neither a method nor a **friend**:

```
class C {
public:
  void m() { /*...*/ }
private:
  int x;
};
int main() {
  C c1;
  c1.m();   // ok, m is public in C
  c1.x = 3; //***** ERROR: x is private in C
  //...
}
```

4. It is an error to treat a class *method* as a top-level function:

```
class C {
public:
  void m() { /*...*/ }
  //...
};
int main() {
  C c1;
  m();     //***** ERROR: m is a method
  c1.m(); // ok
  //...
}
```

**5.** It is an error to omit the member selector operator when accessing an object's members:

```
class C {
public:
  void m() { /*...*/ }
  //...
};
int main() {
   C c1;
   c1m();  //***** ERROR: member selector operator missing
   c1.m(); // ok
   //...
}
```

**6.** It is an error to use the keyword **inline** outside a class declaration. If an **inline** method is to be *defined* outside the class declaration, then the keyword **inline** is used *only in the declaration*:

```
class C {
public:
  inline void m(); // declaration is ok
  //...
};
// definition of C::m
inline void C::m() { //***** ERROR: inline occurs in
  //...                //***** declaration, not definition
}
```

**7.** If a class has no constructors, it is an error to assume that object members are initialized when the object is defined:

```
class C {
public:
  int getS() const { return s; }
private:
  int s;
};
int main() {
  C c1;
  cout << c1.getS() //***** Caution: arbitrary value printed
       << '\n';
  //...
}
```

A default constructor

```
class C {
public:
  int getS() const { return s; }
  C() { s = -1; } // s is initialized
```

```
private:
  int s;
};
int main() {
  C c1;
  cout << c1.getS() << '\n'; // ok
  //...
}
```

could be used to ensure that **c1**'s member **s** is initialized appropriately.

8. It is an error to show a return type, even **void**, for a constructor in its declaration or definition:

```
class C {
public:
  void C();    //***** ERROR: no return type allowed
  int C( C& ); //***** ERROR: no return type allowed
};
void C::C() { //***** ERROR: no return type allowed
  //...
}
```

The correct syntax is

```
class C {
public:
  C();
};
C::C() {
  //...
}
```

9. It is an error to show a return type, even **void**, for a destructor in its declaration or definition:

```
class C {
public:
  void ~C();  //***** ERROR: no return type allowed!
};
void C::~C() { //***** ERROR: no return type allowed!
  //...
}
```

The correct syntax is

```
class C {
public:
  ~C();
};
C::~C() {
  //...
}
```

**10.** It is illegal for a destructor to have an argument:

```
class C {
public:
   ~C( int );   //***** ERROR: no args allowed
};
C::~C( int ) { //***** ERROR: no args allowed
   //...
}
```

The correct syntax is

```
class C {
public:
   ~C();
   //...
};
C::~C() {
   //...
}
```

Because a destructor takes no arguments, there can be only one destructor per class. Constructors, by contrast, can be many in number because arguments can be used to give each a distinct signature.

**11.** It is an error for a class **C** constructor to have a single argument of type **C**:

```
class C {
public:
   C( C obj ); //***** ERROR: single parameter can't be a C
   C( C obj, int n ); // ok, two parameters
   //...
};
```

The *copy* constructor does have one **C** parameter, but it is a *reference*:

```
class C {
public:
   C( C& obj ); // ok
   //...
};
```

**12.** It is an error to set a **const** data member's value through an assignment operation, even in a constructor:

```
class C {
public:
   C() { c = 0; } //***** ERROR: c is const!
private:
   const int c; // const data member
};
```

A **const** member must be initialized in a constructor's initialization section:

```
class C {
public:
   C() : c( 0 ) { } // ok
private:
   const int c; // const data member
};
```

13. It is an error to invoke an *object method* as if it were a *class method*, that is, a **static** method:

```
class C {
public:
   void m() { /*...*/ }        // nonstatic: object method
   static void s() { /*...*/ } // static: class method
   //...
};
int main() {
   C c1;
   c1.m();    // ok
   c1.s();    // ok
   C::s();    // ok, s is static
   C::m();    //***** ERROR: m is not static
   //...
}
```

14. If a **static** data member is declared inside the class's declaration, it is an error not to define the **static** data member outside all blocks:

```
class C {
   static int x; // declared
   //...
};
int main() {
   int C::x; //***** ERROR: defined inside a block!
   //...
}
```

The correct definition is

```
class C {
public:
   static int x; // declared
   //...
};
int C::x;  // define static data member
int main() {
   //...
}
```

Even if **x** were **private**, it would be defined the same way.

**15.** It is an error to use the member selector operator **.** with a *pointer* to an object. The code segment

```
class C {
public:
   void m() { /*...*/ }
};
int main() {
  C c1;     // define a C object
  C* p;     // define a pointer to a C object
  p = &c1; // p points to c1
  p.m();    //***** ERROR: member selector operator illegal!
  c1.m();  // ok, c1 is an object
  //...
}
```

illustrates. The member selector operator **.** may be used only with an *object* or an *object reference*. The class indirection operator **->** is used with pointers to objects to access their members. The preceding error can be corrected by writing

```
p->m(); // ok, p a pointer to an object
```

**16.** It is an error to use the class indirection operator **->** with a class object or object reference. The code segment

```
class C {
public:
  void m() { /*...*/ }
};
int main() {
  C c1;
  c1->m(); //***** ERROR: c1 is an object, not a pointer
  //...
}
void f( C& r ) {
  r->m(); //***** ERROR: r is a reference, not a pointer
}
```

illustrates the error with object **c1** and object reference **r**. In both cases, the member selector operator **.** should be used:

```
class C {
public:
  void m() { /*...*/ }
};
```

```
int main() {
  C c1;
  c1.m(); // ok
  //...
}
void f( C& r ) {
  r.m(); // ok
}
```

**17.** It is an error to have white space between the two symbols that make up the class indirection operator `->`:

```
class C {
public:
    void m() { /*...*/ }
};
int main() {
  C c1;     // define a C object
  C* p;     // define a pointer to a C object
  p = &c1; // p points to c1
  p->m();     // ok
  p -> m();   // ok
  p-> m();    // ok
  p ->m();    // ok
  p- >m();    //***** ERROR: white space between - and >
  //...
}
```

**18.** The pointer **this** is a *constant*. It is therefore an error for **this** to occur as the target of an assignment, increment, or decrement operation.

**19.** It is an error to use **this** inside a **static** method.

**20.** It is an error for a **const** method to change a data member's value through, for example, an assignment expression.

**21.** It is an error for a **const** method to invoke a non**const** method.

**22.** If function **f** has an object parameter **obj** marked as **const**, it is an error for **f** to invoke any non**const** method of **obj** because such a method could alter **obj**'s state.

## PROGRAMMING EXERCISES

**3.1.** Implement a `Car` class that includes data members to represent a car's make (e.g., Honda), model (e.g., Civic), production year, and price. The class interface includes methods that provide appropriate access to the data members (e.g., a method to set the car's model or to get its price). In addition, the class should have a method

```
void compare( const Car& ) const;
```

that compares a `Car` against another using whatever criteria seem appropriate. The `compare` method prints a short report of its comparison.

**3.2.** An International Standard Book Number (ISBN) is a code of 10 characters separated by dashes such as 0–670–82162–4. An ISBN consists of four parts: a group code, a publisher code, a code that uniquely identifies the book among the publisher's offerings, and a check character. For the ISBN 0–670–82162–4, the group code is 0, which identifies the book as one from an English-speaking country. The publisher code 670 identifies the book as a Viking Press publication. The code 82162 uniquely identifies the book among the Viking Press publications (Homer: *The Odyssey*, translated by Robert Fagles). The check character is computed as follows:

1. Compute the sum of the first digit plus two times the second digit plus three times the third digit... plus nine times the ninth digit.
2. Compute the remainder of this sum divided by 11. If the remainder is 10, the last character is X. Otherwise, the last character is the remainder.

For example, the sum for ISBN 0–670–82162–4 is

$$0 + 2 \times 6 + 3 \times 7 + 4 \times 0 + 5 \times 8 + 6 \times 2 + 7 \times 1 + 8 \times 6 + 9 \times 2 = 158$$

The remainder when 158 is divided by 11 is 4, the last character in the ISBN. Implement a class to represent an ISBN. The class should have methods to set and get the ISBN as a string and to check whether the ISBN is valid.

**3.3.** Implement a `Book` class that represents pertinent information about a book, including the book's title, author, publisher, city, date of publication, and price. The class should include the data member

```
ISBN isbnNum;
```

where `ISBN` is the class implemented in Programming Exercise 3.2.

**3.4.** Implement a `Calendar` class. The public interface consists of methods that enable the user to

- Specify a start year such as 1776 or 1900.
- Specify a duration such as 1 year or 100 years.
- Specify generic holidays such as Tuesdays.
- Specify specific holidays such as the third Thursday in November.
- Specify a month-year such as July-1776, which results in a display of the calendar for the specified month-year.

Holidays should be marked so that they can be readily recognized whenever the calendar for a month-year is displayed.

**3.5.** Implement a **CollegeStudent** class with appropriate data members such as **name**, **year**, **expectedGrad**, **major**, **minor**, **GPA**, **coursesAndGrades**, **maritalStatus**, and the like. The class should have at least a half-dozen methods in its public interface. For example, there should be a method to compute **GPA** from **coursesAndGrades** and to determine whether the **GPA** merits honors or probation. There also should be methods to display a **CollegeStudent**'s current course load and to print remaining required courses.

**3.6.** Implement a **Deck** class that represents a deck of 52 cards. The public interface should include methods to shuffle, deal, display hands, do pairwise comparisons of cards (e.g., a Queen beats a Jack), and the like. To simulate shuffling, you can use a random number generator such as the library function **rand**.

**3.7.** Implement a **Profession** class with data members such as **name**, **title**, **credentials**, **education**, and **avgIncome**. The public interface should include methods that compare **Profession**s across the data members. The class should have at least a dozen data members and a dozen methods.

**3.8.** A **queue** is a list of zero or more elements. An element is added to a queue at its **rear**; an element is removed from a queue at its **front**. If a queue is **empty**, a removal operation is illegal. If a queue is **full**, then an add operation is illegal. Implement a **Queue** class for character strings.

**3.9.** A **deque** is a list of zero or more elements with insertions and deletions at either end, its front or its rear. Implement a **Deque** class whose elements are character strings.

**3.10.** A **semaphore** is a mechanism widely used in computer systems to enforce synchronization constraints on shared resources. For example, a semaphore might be used to ensure that two processes cannot use a printer at the same time. The semaphore mechanism first grants exclusive access to one process and then to the other so that the printer does not receive a garbled mix from the two processes. Implement a **Semaphore** class that enforces synchronization on files so that a process is assured exclusive access to a file. The public interface consists of methods that *set* a semaphore for a specified file, that *release* a semaphore protecting a specified file, and that *test* whether a semaphore is currently protecting a specified file.

**3.11.** Implement an interactive **Calculator** class that accepts as input an arithmetic expression such as

```
25 / 5 + 4
```

and then evaluates the expression, printing the value. In this example, the output would be

```
9
```

There should be methods to validate the input expression. For example, if the user inputs

```
25 / 5 +
```

then the output should be an error message such as

```
ERROR: operator-operand imbalance.
```

**3.12.** Implement a **Set** class, where a **set** is an unordered collection of zero or more elements with no duplicates. For this exercise, the elements should be **int**s. The public interface consists of methods to

- Create a `Set`.

- Add a new element to a `Set`.

- Remove an element from a `Set`.

- Enumerate the elements in the `Set`.

- Compute the **intersection** of two `Set`s `S1` and `S2`, that is, the set of elements that belong to both `S1` and `S2`.

- Compute the **union** of two `Set`s `S1` and `S2`, that is, the set of elements that belong to `S1` or `S2` or both.

- Compute the **difference** of two `Set`s `S1` and `S2`, that is, the set of elements that belong to `S1` but not to `S2`.

**3.13.** Implement a `Bag` class. A **bag** is like a set except that a bag may have duplicates. For this exercise, the bag's elements should be `int`s. The public interface should support the counterpart operations given in Programming Exercise 3.12 for sets.

**3.14.** Create a `Spaceship` class suitable for simulation. One of the constructors should allow the user to specify the `Spaceship`'s initial position in 3-dimensional space, its trajectory, its velocity, its rate of acceleration, and its target, which is another `Spaceship`. The simulation should track a `Spaceship`'s movement every clock tick (e.g., every second), printing such relevant data as the `Spaceship`'s identity, its trajectory, and so forth. If you have access to a graphics package, add graphics to the simulation.

**3.15.** Implement a `Database` class where a `Database` is a collection of *tables*, which in turn are made up of *rows* and *columns*. For example, the employee table

| Employee ID | Last Name | Department | Boss |
| --- | --- | --- | --- |
| 111–11–1234 | Cruz | ACC | Werdel |
| 213–44–5649 | Johnstone | MIS | Michaels |
| 321–88–7895 | Elders | FIN | Bierski |

has three records, each of which has four fields (*Employee ID*, *Last Name*, *Department*, and *Boss*). The public interface should allow a user to

- Create a table.

- Change a table's structure by adding or removing fields.

- Delete a table.

- Add records to a table.

- Remove records from a table.

- Retrieve information from one or more tables using a suitable query language.

**3.16.** Implement a **BankTransaction** class that allows the user to

- Open an account.

- Close an account.

- Add funds to an already open account.

- Remove funds from an already open account.

- Transfer funds from one open account to another.

- Request a report on one or more open accounts.

There should be no upper bound on the number of accounts that a user may open. The class also should contain a method that automatically issues a warning if an account is overdrawn.

**3.17.** Introduce appropriate classes to simulate the behavior of a **local area network**, hereafter **LAN**. The network consists of **nodes**, which may be devices such as personal computers, workstations, FAX machines, telecommunications switches, and so forth. A LAN's principal job is to support data communications among its nodes. The user of the simulation should, at a minimum, be able to

- Enumerate the nodes currently on the LAN.

- Add a new node to the LAN.

- Remove a node from the LAN.

- Configure a LAN by specifying which nodes are directly connected.

- Specify packet size, which is the size in bytes of a message sent from one node to another.

- Send a packet from one specified node to another.

- Broadcast a packet from one node to all others.

- Track LAN statistics such as the average time it takes a packet to reach the most distant node on the LAN.

**3.18.** Implement a **Schedule** class that produces a conflict-free, maximum-size subset of activities given an input set of activities together with the start and finish times for each activity. The conflict-free subset, together with the start and finish times, is a schedule. The schedule is conflict-free when, given any two distinct activities, one finishes before the other starts. For example, given the input set

| Activity | Start Time | Finish Time |
|----------|-----------|-------------|
| A1 | 6 | 10 |
| A2 | 1 | 5 |
| A3 | 1 | 6 |
| A4 | 9 | 12 |
| A5 | 5 | 7 |
| A6 | 6 | 14 |
| A7 | 3 | 7 |
| A8 | 10 | 14 |
| A9 | 13 | 16 |

an optimal **Schedule** is

| Activity | Start Time | Finish Time |
|----------|-----------|-------------|
| A2 | 1 | 5 |
| A5 | 5 | 7 |
| A4 | 9 | 12 |
| A9 | 13 | 16 |

Given the input set, it is impossible to produce a **Schedule** of five or more nonconflicting activities. The public interface should include methods for creating, destroying, revising, and combining **Schedule**s. *Hint*: Iterate through the activities, picking in each iteration the activity with the minimum finish time that does not conflict with any previously selected activity for the **Schedule**.

**3.19.** Implement a **SymbolTable** class. A **symbol table** lists all identifiers (e.g., function and variable names) in a program's source code together with pertinent information such as the identifier's data type, its role within the program (e.g., whether the identifier is a function name, variable name, or a label), and its position in a source code file (e.g., a line number designating the line in which the identifier occurs). The public interface should allow the user to specify one or more source files from which the **SymbolTable** is to be built. There also should be methods for displaying and editing a **SymbolTable**.

**3.20.** Implement a **RegExp** class to represent **regular expressions**, which are used in pattern matching. A regular expression is a character string that consists of ordinary and special characters. For example, the regular expression

        **aRgT**

matches only other strings with exactly these four characters in this order. Regular expressions are more interesting and useful when they include special characters such as these:

| *Special Character* | *What It Matches* |
|---|---|
| **.** | Any character. |
| **[<list>]** | Any character in **list**. For instance, |
| | **[aBc]** matches **a**, **B**, or **c**. |
| **[^<list>]** | Any character not in **list**. |
| **[<X>-<Y>]** | Any character in range **X** to **Y**. For instance, |
| | **[a-c]** matches **a**, **b**, or **c**. |
| **\*** | Zero or more occurrences of the preceding **RegExp**. |
| | For instance, **ab\*** matches **ab**, **abb**, **abbb**, etc. |

The class's interface should include methods to create and destroy **RegExp**s as well as to match **RegExp**s against other strings.

**3.21.** Implement a **Date** class to represent a date such as *Wednesday, March 21, 2001*. The class should have constructors to set a **Date** to the current date or to a user specified **Date**; to move forward *n* **Date**s, where *n* is 1, 2, . . . ; to move backward *n* **Date**s, where *n* is 1, 2, . . . ; to print a **Date** as a whole or a part (e.g., only the month); and to print all the dates from one **Date** (e.g., *Wednesday, March 21, 2001*) to another (e.g., *Monday, October 1, 2001*).

**3.22.** Implement an **Emp**loyee class. The class should restrict construction to **Emp**loyees with an identifier such as a social security number. The class should represent **Emp**loyee properties or features such as *last name, first name, marital status, home address, home phone number, salary, office, office phone number, title(s), current projects*, and the like. The class interface should include methods to access and, where appropriate, to change **Emp**loyee properties.

**3.23.** Implement a **Product** class. The class should allow construction of **Product**s with only a name; with a name and price; and with a name, price, and shelf life in days. A **Product** also has a manufacturer; a description; flags to signal whether the **Product** is fragile or edible; and an availability date, which indicates when the **Product** will first be available for consumer purchase. Add at least three other features to the class implementation. The class interface should include methods to access the implementation.

**3.24.** Implement a **Pair** class for **int**egers:

```
class Pair {
public:
    // appropriate methods
private:
    int first;
    int second;
};
```

The class interface should include methods to create **Pair**s, to set and to get each element in the **Pair**, and to swap the elements so that, after the swap, the first element becomes the second, and the second becomes the first.

# CHAPTER

# 4

# INHERITANCE

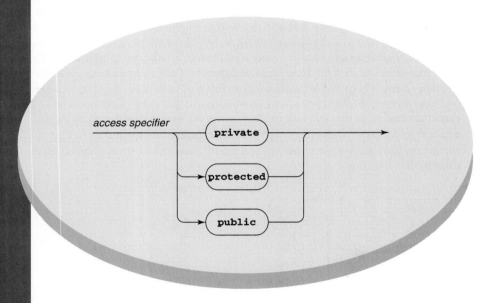

4.1 Introduction

4.2 Basic Concepts and Syntax

4.3 Sample Application: Tracking Films

4.4 `protected` Members

4.5 Constructors and Destructors Under Inheritance

4.6 Sample Application: A Sequence Hierarchy

4.7 Multiple Inheritance

C++ Postscript

Common Programming Errors

Programming Exercises

**I**n C++, we can build a new class by deriving the new class from an already existing class. The mechanism for this derivation is **inheritance**, and the derived class is said to be **inherited** from the original class. In this chapter, we introduce inheritance, and in the remainder of the book, we show how inheritance and **virtual** methods (the topic of Chapter 5) form the heart of object-oriented programming and give it power and expressiveness.

## 4.1  INTRODUCTION

Suppose that a class **Student** has already been designed and implemented and that a new application needs a class **GradStudent**. Since a **GradStudent** is a **Student**, rather than build the class **GradStudent** from scratch, we can add to the class **Student** whatever data and methods it needs to become a **GradStudent**. For example, class **GradStudent** might need additional data members to describe particular departmental exams that only graduate students must take and pass, as well as methods to store and retrieve these data. The resulting class **GradStudent** is said to be **inherited** from the class **Student**. The new class **GradStudent** is called a **derived class** or a **subclass** of **Student**. The original class **Student** is called the **base class** or **superclass** of **GradStudent**. The derived class **GradStudent** inherits all of the data and methods from the existing class **Student** (except for constructors, the destructor, and an overload of the assignment operator). A derived class thus has all of the data and methods (with the exceptions noted) of its base class, in addition to added data and methods. Such a derivation is depicted as in Figure 4.1.1. As shown, the base class is placed above the derived class, and an arrow points from the derived class to the base class.

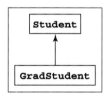

**FIGURE 4.1.1**  Class **GradStudent** is derived from class **Student**.

Inheritance promotes code reuse because the code in the base class is inherited by the subclass and thus need not be rewritten. By reusing code, we reduce the amount of code to be created. Furthermore, if the code inherited from the base class is correct, it will also be correct in the derived class. If the code were rewritten, bugs might inadvertently be introduced. For example, when class **GradStudent** is inherited from class **Student**, the code in **Student** need not be rewritten for the **GradStudent** class. Furthermore, assuming that the code for the **Student** class is correct, the part of **GradStudent** inherited from **Student** will be correct in the **GradStudent** class.

Inheritance also provides a mechanism to express the natural relationships among the components of a program. For example, a **GradStudent** *is a* **Student** and this *is a* relationship is precisely mirrored in the code through the inheritance mechanism.

Inheritance is required for *polymorphism* in which the particular method to invoke depends on the class to which the object belongs, but the class to which the object belongs is not known until the program is executing. This very powerful technique is thoroughly examined in Chapter 5.

Besides the *is a* relationship present in inheritance (e.g., a **GradStudent** *is a* **Student**), we can think of a derived class as a specialized version of the base class. For example, in Figure 4.1.2, the base class **Pen** models a pen that can draw in black ink. The derived class **CPen** models a pen that can draw in several colors, including black. A **CPen** is a **Pen** (both can draw). Furthermore, a **CPen** is a specialized version of **Pen**.

**FIGURE 4.1.2** Class **CPen** is derived from class **Pen**.

A derived class can itself serve as a base class for another class. For example, in Figure 4.1.3 class **Car** is derived from class **Vehicle**, and class **Coupe**, in turn, is derived from class **Car**. We call a relationship such as that in Figure 4.1.3 a **class hierarchy**. Notice that a **Coupe** *is a* **Car**, which, in turn, *is a* **Vehicle**. Notice also that as we move down the hierarchy, each class is a specialized version of its base class.

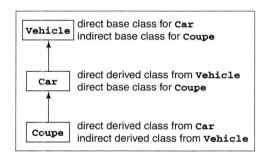

**FIGURE 4.1.3** A class hierarchy.

C++ also supports **multiple inheritance**, in which a derived class can have multiple base classes. We discuss multiple inheritance in Section 4.7.

Classes directly support the creation of abstract data types. Inheritance extends that support by promoting the derivation of new abstract data types from already existing ones. Object-oriented languages thus provide programmers with the tools for programming with abstract data types. Graphics packages, such as *Windows* and *Motif*, illustrate the point. In *Motif*, for example, there is an extended class hierarchy in which each class represents an abstract data type such as windows, fonts, and geometrical drawings. The user knows only the *public interface* to such classes, where such an interface comprises the methods that are used to create, manipulate, and destroy instances of an abstract data type. Implementation details are hidden from the user, who is all the better off by being spared the very details that cause programming tedium and error. In effect, a package such as *Motif* is a library of abstract data types presented as an object-oriented graphics toolkit.

## EXERCISES

1. Draw a class hierarchy in which a base class has multiple derived classes.

2. Explain the relationship among the terms *superclass*, *subclass*, *base class*, and *derived class*.

3. Give examples of data members and methods that might be added when a class **Employee** is derived from the class **Person**. (**Person** contains methods for entering and retrieving information such as name, address, city, and state.)

4. Show a class hierarchy that might be used to track customers and accounts at a bank.

## 4.2 BASIC CONCEPTS AND SYNTAX

To derive class **DC** from class **BC**, we write

```
// BC is the base class; DC is the derived class
class DC : public BC {
   //...
};
```

Except for

```
: public BC
```

the preceding declaration looks like an ordinary class declaration. The keyword **public** indicates that the derivation is public, and **BC** indicates that class **DC** is derived from class **BC**. In public inheritance, the **public** members in the base class are **public** in the derived class.

The C++ Postscript section at the end of this chapter discusses the other types of inheritance, in which the keyword **public** is omitted or replaced by either **private** or **protected**. In particular, if **public** is omitted

```
// BC is the base class; DC is the derived class
class DC : BC { // **** Caution: default inheritance is private
   //...
};
```

the inheritance defaults to **private**. We use only **public** inheritance in our examples.

**EXAMPLE 4.2.1.**   The code segment

```
class Pen {
public:
    enum ink { Off, On };
    void set_status( ink );
    void set_location( int, int );
private:
    int x;
    int y;
    ink status;
};
```

declares a class **Pen**. If **p** is an object of type **Pen**, the statement

```
p.set_location( x, y );
```

positions **p** at the location whose coordinates are (**x,y**). The statement

```
p.set_status( Pen::On );
```

turns the ink in the **Pen** on, and the statement

```
p.set_status( Pen::Off );
```

turns the ink in the **Pen** off.

Now suppose that our hardware is upgraded so that we have a colored pen. Rather than declare a brand new class to describe the colored pen, we can derive a colored pen class from the pen class:

```
class CPen : public Pen {
public:
    void set_color( int );
private:
    int color;
};
```

The class **CPen** inherits all of the data members and methods from the class **Pen** (see Figure 4.2.1). The declaration of class **CPen** adds the data member **color** and the method **set_color**. Colors are coded as integers, so when the method **set_color** is invoked and a value is passed to a **CPen** object, the member **color** is set to this value.

Because of the keyword **public** in the line

```
class CPen : public Pen {
```

the methods **set_status** and **set_location**, which are **public** in **Pen**, are also **public** in **CPen** and so can be invoked on an object of type **CPen** anywhere in the program.                                                                                     ■

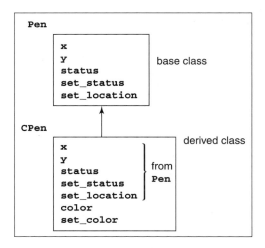

**FIGURE 4.2.1** Deriving one class from another.

## `private` Members in Inheritance

Each **private** member in a base class is visible only in the base class. In particular, a **private** member of a base class is *not* visible in a derived class. A **private** member of a base class *is* inherited by the derived class, but it is not visible in the derived class. In Example 4.2.1, data members **x**, **y**, and **status** are inherited by **CPen** from **Pen** even though they are *not* visible in **CPen**. Whenever an object of type **CPen** is created, storage for **x**, **y**, and **status** is allocated. Although a **private** member of a base class cannot be directly accessed in a derived class, it might be indirectly accessed through a derived method as the following example shows.

**EXAMPLE 4.2.2.**    Given the class declarations

```
class Point {
public:
   void set_x( int x1 ) { x = x1; }
   void set_y( int y1 ) { y = y1; }
   int get_x() const { return x; }
   int get_y() const { return y; }
private:
   int x;
   int y;
};

class Intense_point : public Point {
public:
   void set_intensity( int i ) { intensity = i; }
   int get_intensity() const { return intensity; }
private:
   int intensity;
};
```

the members of the derived class **Intense_point** are

| Member | Access Status in Intense_point | How Obtained |
|---|---|---|
| x | Not accessible | From class Point |
| y | Not accessible | From class Point |
| set_x | public | From class Point |
| set_y | public | From class Point |
| get_x | public | From class Point |
| get_y | public | From class Point |
| intensity | private | Added by class Intense_point |
| set_intensity | public | Added by class Intense_point |
| get_intensity | public | Added by class Intense_point |

Class **Intense_point** inherits data members **x** and **y**, which are visible only in class **Point**. Nevertheless, class **Intense_point** can indirectly access these data members through the methods **set_x**, **set_y**, **get_x**, and **get_y**, which *are* visible in **Intense_point**.  ∎

## Adjusting Access

The access status of an inherited member can be changed with a using declaration. For example, a **public** member in a base class that would normally be inherited as **public** in a derived class can be made **private** (or **protected**; see Section 4.4) with a using declaration.

**EXAMPLE 4.2.3.**  In the declaration

```
class BC { // base class
public:
   void set_x( float a ) { x = a; }
private:
   float x;
};

class DC : public BC { // derived class
public:
   void set_y( float b ) { y = b; }
private:
   float y;
};
```

**set_x** and **set_y** are **public** in DC. Method **set_x** could be made **private** in DC with a using declaration:

```
class BC { // base class
public:
  void set_x( float a ) { x = a; }
private:
  float x;
};

class DC : public BC { // derived class
public:
  void set_y( float b ) { y = b; }
private:
  float y;
  using BC::set_x;
};
```

Now an attempt to invoke **set_x** on a **DC** object is an error:

```
int main() {
  DC d;
  d.set_y( 4.31 ); // OK
  d.set_x( -8.03 ); // ***** ERROR: set_x is private in DC
  //...
}
```

Adjusting a **public** method in a base class to **private** status in a derived class, as shown in Example 4.2.3, disables use of the method outside the derived class. For example, if a class of sorted items is derived from a class of unsorted items, certain methods in the base class of unsorted items may not make sense in the derived class of sorted items. A base class method that inserts any item anywhere in an unsorted list should not be used, in general, to insert in a sorted list. Such a method could be disabled outside the derived class with a using declaration.

## Name Hiding

If a derived class adds a data member with the same name as a data member in the base class, the local data member **hides** the inherited data member. Similarly, if a derived class adds a method with the same name in the base class, the added method hides the base class's method.

**EXAMPLE 4.2.4.** In the code segment

```
class BC { // base class
public:
  void h( float ); // BC::h
};
```

```
class DC : public BC { // derived class
public:
  void h( char [ ] );  // ***** DANGER: hides BC::h
};

int main() {
   DC d1;
   d1.h( "Boffo!" ); // DC::h, not BC::h
   d1.h( 707.7 ); // ***** ERROR: DC::h hides BC::h
   d1.BC::h( 707.7 ); // OK: invokes BC::h
   //...
}
```

class **DC** inherits method **h** from **BC**. However, **DC** also has a local method named **h**, which means that the local method hides the inherited method. The error occurs because method **DC::h** expects a **char [ ]** argument rather than a **float** argument. The inherited **BC::h**, which does expect a **char [ ]** argument, is hidden in **d** by **DC::h** and so must be invoked with the scope resolution operator.  ∎

## Indirect Inheritance

Data members and methods may traverse several inheritance links as they are included from a base to a derived class. For example, suppose that **BC** is **DC1**'s base class and that **DC1** is **DC2**'s base class (see Figure 4.2.2). In this case, **DC2** inherits **DC1**'s data members and methods—including whatever data members and methods **DC1** inherits from **BC**. Inheritance thus may be either direct (to a derived class from a direct base class) or indirect (to a derived class from an indirect base class).

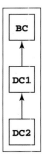

**FIGURE 4.2.2** Indirect inheritance.

**EXAMPLE 4.2.5.**   In the code segment

```
// direct base class for Cat,
// indirect base class for HouseCat
class Animal {
public:
    string species;
    float lifeExpectancy;
    bool  warmBlooded_P;
};

// direct derived class from Animal,
// direct base class for HouseCat
class Cat : public Animal {
public:
    string range[ 100 ];
    float favoritePrey[ 100 ][ 100 ];
};

// indirect derived class from Animal,
// direct derived class from Cat
class HouseCat : public Cat {
public:
    string toys[ 10000 ];
    string catPsychiatrist;
    string catDentist;
    string catDoctor;
    string apparentOwner;
};
```

**HouseCat** has 10 data members: five are added, two are inherited directly from **Cat**, and three are inherited indirectly from **Animal** by way of **Cat**. The inherited data members remain **public** in **HouseCat**.   ∎

## EXERCISES

**1.** In the code segment

```
class A {
    int x;
};

class B : public A {
    int y;
};
B b1;
```

how many data members does **b1** have?

2. Explain the error:

```
class A {
private:
    int x;
};

class B : public A {
public:
    void f() { y = x; }
private:
    int y;
};
```

3. Draw an inheritance hierarchy in which **P** has a direct inheritance link to base class **Q** and an indirect inheritance link to base class **R**.

4. Draw a class hierarchy that is at least five deep. Label each base class with its direct and indirect derived classes, and label each derived class with its direct and indirect base classes.

# 4.3 SAMPLE APPLICATION: TRACKING FILMS

### Problem

Develop an inheritance hierarchy to track films, including specialized films such as foreign films and directors' cuts (versions updated by the director after the initial release). Since every film has a title, director, time, and quality (0 to 4 stars), first implement a base class **Film** with data members to hold the common information, methods to store information in the data members, and a method to output the data.

Next derive a class **DirectorCut** from **Film**. Add data members to hold the revised time and the changes, methods to store the added information in the data members, and a method to output the data.

Finally derive a class **ForeignFilm** from **Film**. Add a data member to hold the language, a method to store the language in the data member, and a method to output the data.

### Sample Output

The output of the **main** function in Figure 4.3.1 is

```
Film--
Title: Rear Window
Director: Alfred Hitchcock
Time: 112 mins
Quality: ****
```

```
DirectorCut--
Title: Jail Bait
Director: Ed Wood
Time: 70 mins
Quality: **
Revised time: 72 mins
Changes: Extra footage not in original included

ForeignFilm--
Title: Jules and Jim
Director: Francois Truffaut
Time: 104 mins
Quality: ****
Language: French
```

### Solution

Class **Film** has four **private** data members:

| Data Member | Type | Purpose |
|---|---|---|
| title | string | Hold a title |
| director | string | Hold a director |
| time | int | Hold a time in minutes |
| quality | int | 0 stars (bad) to 4 stars (tops) |

Class **Film** has six **public** methods to copy data passed into the data members. For example, method **store_title** should have a parameter of type **const string&** that copies the value passed into data member **title**. An overloaded version of **store_title** should have a parameter of type **const char\*** that also copies the value passed into data member **title**. In this way, the title can be passed as a **string** or as a null-terminated array of **char**.

Class **Film** should also have a method **output** that outputs the values of the four data members.

Since class **DirectorCut** is derived from class **Film**, **DirectorCut** inherits **Film**'s data members and methods. We will add two **private** data members to **DirectorCut** to hold the revised time and changes and add **public** methods to copy data passed into the data members. For example, method **store_rev_time** copies the revised time into data member **rev_time**. Class **DirectorCut** will have its own method **output** that outputs the values of the six data members—four inherited from **Film** and two that were added. **DirectorCut**'s method **output** will hide **Film**'s method **output** because they have the same name.

Similarly, class **ForeignFilm** is derived from class **Film** and so inherits **Film**'s data members and methods. We will add a **private** data member to **ForeignFilm** to hold the film's language and **public** methods to copy data passed into the data member. Class **ForeignFilm** will also have its own method **output** that outputs the values of its data members.

```
int main() {
   Film f;
   f.store_title( "Rear Window" );
   f.store_director( "Alfred Hitchcock" );
   f.store_time( 112 );
   f.store_quality( 4 );
   cout << "Film--\n";
   f.output();
   cout << '\n';

   DirectorCut d;
   d.store_title( "Jail Bait" );
   d.store_director( "Ed Wood" );
   d.store_time( 70 );
   d.store_quality( 2 );
   d.store_rev_time( 72 );
   d.store_changes( "Extra footage not in original included" );
   cout << "DirectorCut--\n";
   d.output();
   cout << '\n';

   ForeignFilm ff;
   ff.store_title( "Jules and Jim" );
   ff.store_director( "Francois Truffaut" );
   ff.store_time( 104 );
   ff.store_quality( 4 );
   ff.store_language( "French" );
   cout << "ForeignFilm--\n";
   ff.output();

   return 0;
}
```

**FIGURE 4.3.1** A test client for the `Film–DirectorCut–ForeignFilm` hierarchy.

## C++ Implementation

```
class Film {
public:
   void store_title( const string& t ) { title = t; }
   void store_title( const char* t ) { title = t; }
   void store_director( const string& d ) { director = d; }
   void store_director( const char* d ) { director = d; }
   void store_time( int t ) { time = t; }
   void store_quality( int q ) { quality = q; }
   void output() const;
```

```
private:
    string title;
    string director;
    int time; // in minutes
    int quality; // 0 (bad) to 4 (tops)
};

void Film::output() const {
    cout << "Title: " << title << '\n';
    cout << "Director: " << director << '\n';
    cout << "Time: " << time << " mins" << '\n';
    cout << "Quality: ";
    for ( int i = 0; i < quality; i++ )
        cout << '*';
    cout << '\n';
}

class DirectorCut : public Film {
public:
    void store_rev_time( int t) { rev_time = t; }
    void store_changes( const string& s) { changes = s; }
    void store_changes( const char* s) { changes = s; }
    void output() const;
private:
    int rev_time;
    string changes;
};

void DirectorCut::output() const {
    Film::output();
    cout << "Revised time: " << rev_time << " mins\n";
    cout << "Changes: " << changes << '\n';
}

class ForeignFilm : public Film {
public:
    void store_language( const string& l) { language = l; }
    void store_language( const char* l ) { language = l; }
    void output() const;
private:
    string language;
};

void ForeignFilm::output() const {
    Film::output();
    cout << "Language: " << language << '\n';
}
```

### *Discussion*

Class **Film** has four **private** data members and six **public** methods to copy data passed into the data members. In one version, the parameters of **store_title** and **store_director** are of type **const string&**, and in the other version, the parameters are of type **const char\***. In this way, the title can be passed as a **string** or as a null-terminated array of **char**.

Method **output** prints the title, director, time, and quality (expressed as a number of asterisks), each suitably annotated

```
void Film::output() const {
   cout << "Title: " << title << '\n';
   cout << "Director: " << director << '\n';
   cout << "Time: " << time << " mins" << '\n';
   cout << "Quality: ";
   for ( int i = 0; i < quality; i++ )
      cout << '*';
   cout << '\n';
}
```

Class **DirectorCut** is publicly derived from **Film**

```
class DirectorCut : public Film {
   //...
};
```

and so inherits **Film**'s data members and methods. Since the methods **store_title**, **store_director**, **store_time**, and **store_quality** are **public** in **Film**, they are also **public** in **DirectorCut**. **Film**'s **private** members, **title**, **director**, **time**, and **quality**, are visible *only* in **Film**; in particular, they are *not* visible in **DirectorCut**. However, these data members can be indirectly accessed through the **public** methods **store_title**, **store_director**, **store_time**, and **store_quality**.

 **DirectorCut** adds two **private** data members, **rev_time** and **changes**, and **public** methods to copy data passed into the data members.

 Like the base class **Film**, **DirectorCut** has a method named **output**. **DirectorCut**'s **output** thus hides **Film**'s **output**. In **DirectorCut**'s **output**, we first invoke **Film**'s **output**

```
Film::output();
```

to output the title, director, time, and quality. We could *not* write

```
cout << "Title: " << title << '\n';
```

because **title** is not visible in **DirectorCut**. Method **output** concludes by writing the revised time and the changes.

 We omit a detailed discussion of class **ForeignFilm** because it is implemented similarly to **DirectorCut**.

### Program Development

One customary reason to use a class hierarchy is to provide a common interface. In our application, each class has **store**-methods to put data into the objects, and each has a method named **output** to output data. Thus each of our classes does have a common interface.

To develop a class hierarchy, the classes themselves must first be identified and their methods specified. In coding the hierarchy, it is best to first write the code for the base class; then, debug and test it. After the base class is working properly, we would code, debug, and test each derived class. In our example, we would first code, debug, and test class **Film**. Each of **Film**'s methods should be coded and tested one-by-one. After **Film** is coded correctly, we could code, debug, and test derived class **DirectorCut**. Each of the methods added by **DirectorCut** should be coded and tested one-by-one. The methods inherited from **Film** should be tested in **DirectorCut**. After **Film** and **DirectorCut** are coded correctly, we would code, debug, and test derived class **ForeignFilm**. Each of the methods added by **ForeignFilm** should be coded and tested one-by-one, and the methods inherited from **Film** should be tested.

## 4.4 protected MEMBERS

Besides **private** and **public** members, C++ provides **protected** members. In the absence of inheritance, a **protected** member is just like a **private** member; it is visible only within the class. In public inheritance, a **protected** member differs from a **private** member in that a **protected** member in the base class is **protected** in the derived class. Thus when a derived class inherits a **protected** member from a base class, that **protected** member *is* visible in the derived class.

**EXAMPLE 4.4.1.**   In the declarations

```
class BC { // base class
public:
   void set_x( int a ) { x = a; }
protected:
   int get_x() const { return x; }
private:
   int x;
};

class DC : public BC {
public:
   void add2() { int c = get_x(); set_x( c + 2 ); }
};
```

class **DC** is derived from base class **BC**. The members of the derived class **DC** are

| Member | Access Status in DC | How Obtained |
|--------|---------------------|--------------|
| set_x | public | From class **BC** |
| get_x | protected | From class **BC** |
| x | Not accessible | From class **BC** |
| add2 | public | Added by class **DC** |

In the code

```
int main() {
   DC d;
   d.set_x( 3 ); // OK -- set_x is public in DC

   // ***** ERROR: get_x is protected in DC
   cout << d.get_x() << '\n';

   d.x = 77; // ***** ERROR: x is private in BC
   d.add2(); // OK -- add2 is public in DC
   //...
}
```

**main** can access the **public** members **set_x** and **add2** of **DC** but not the **protected** member **get_x**, which is visible only within the class hierarchy. Within class **DC**, it is legal to access **get_x**:

```
void add2() { int c = get_x(); set_x( c + 2 ); }
```

It is also an error to try to access **x** outside of **BC**. In particular, **x** cannot be accessed even in **DC**:

```
class DC : public BC {
   //...
   // ***** ERROR: x is accessible only within BC
   void add3() { x += 3; }
   //...
};
```
■

A derived class may access **protected** members that it *inherits* from a base class. In other words, these **protected** members are visible in the derived class. Yet a derived class may *not* access **protected** members of a base class *object*, that is, an object that belongs to the base class but *not* to the derived class.

**EXAMPLE 4.4.2.**   In the code segment

```
class BC { // base class
protected:
   int get_w() const;
   //...
};
```

```
class DC : public BC { // derived class
public:
    // get_w belongs to DC because it is inherited from BC
    void get_val() const { return get_w(); }
    // ***** ERROR: b.get_w not visible in DC since b.get_w is
    // a member of BC, not DC
    void base_w( const BC& b ) const
        { cout << b.get_w() << '\n'; }
};
```

the reference to **get_w** in class **DC**

```
void get_val() const { return get_w(); }
```

is legal because **get_w** is **DC**'s member, which is inherited from **BC**. It is visible in **DC** because it is **protected** in **BC**. The reference to **b.get_w** in class **DC**

```
void base_w( const BC& b ) const
    { cout << b.get_w() << '\n'; }
```

is illegal because this **get_w** is **BC**'s member and it is visible only in **BC**. In other words, **b.get_w** is a member of a **BC** object that is *not* a **DC** object.  ■

A **private** member is inherited but *not* visible in a derived class. Except for a **friend** function (see Section 6.4), only methods of a class can access a **private** member of that class. A **protected** member is inherited *and* visible in a derived class. Thus a **protected** member can be visible throughout the class hierarchy. Except for a **friend** function, only methods within the class hierarchy can access a **protected** member. By making a member of a class **public**, we make the member visible wherever the class is visible.

**EXAMPLE 4.4.3.** Figure 4.4.1 shows the status of the variables for the declarations

```
class BC {
public:
    void init_x() { x = 0; }
protected:
    int get_x() const { return x; }
private:
    int x;
};
class DC : public BC {
public:
    void g() { init_x(); cout << get_x() << '\n'; }
};
```
■

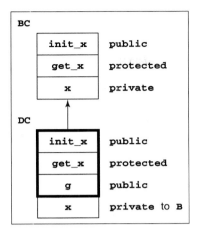

**FIGURE 4.4.1** The status of members for the declarations of Example 4.4.3.

In general, **protected** data should be avoided.  Data that might be **protected** can usually be made **private** and made accessible by **protected** accessors.  More complex data members (e.g., arrays) are sometimes better declared **protected** instead of supplying complicated accessors.  Using **private** data members promotes data hiding.  There are other advantages as well.  For example, a class with **private** data members and **protected** accessors can be completely reimplemented without disturbing the interface, that is, the **protected** and **public** member functions.

**EXAMPLE 4.4.4.**    A better design for the class

```
class BC {
   //...
protected:
   int y;
};
```

is

```
class BC {
   //...
protected:
   int get_y() const { return y; }
   void set_y( int a ) { y = a; }
private:
   int y;
};
```  ∎

## EXERCISES

1. Explain the difference between **private** and **protected** with respect to a class's data members and methods.

2. Contrast the advantages and disadvantages of **protected** and **private** data members and methods.

3. Contrast the advantages and disadvantages of **protected** and **public** data members and methods.

4. In the code segment

```
class BC { // base class
private:
    int x;
protected:
    int get_x() const;
};

class DC : public BC { // derived class
    int num3;
};
DC d1;
```

how many data members does **d1** have?

5. Explain the error:

```
class A {
protected:
    void set_x( int a ) { x = a; }
private:
    int x;
};

int main() {
    A a1;
    a1.set_x( 4 );
    //...
}
```

6. Explain the error:

```
class A {
protected:
    void set_x( int a ) { x = a; }
private:
    int x;
};

class B : public A {
public:
    void f( A& a ) { a.set_x( 5 ); }
};
```

**7.** Write the body of **init**, which initializes **DC**'s members.

```
class BC { // base class
protected:
   void set1( int a ) { num1 = a; }
   void set2( int a ) { num2 = a; }
private:
   int num1;
   int num2;
};
class DC : public BC { // derived class
public:
   void init( int, int, int );
private:
   int num3;
};
void DC::init( int n1, int n2, int n3 ) {
   //...
}
```

## 4.5 CONSTRUCTORS AND DESTRUCTORS UNDER INHERITANCE

### Constructors Under Inheritance

A derived class is a specialization of a base class. An object in a derived class inherits characteristics from the base class but also has characteristics that are specific to the derived class (see Figure 4.5.1). For this reason, a base class constructor (if any) is invoked when a derived class object is created. The base class constructor handles initialization and other matters for the "from the base class" part of the object. If the derived class has a constructor of its own, this constructor can handle the "added by derived class" part of the object.

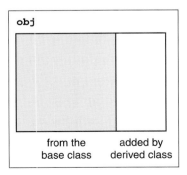

**FIGURE 4.5.1** A derived class as a specialization of a base class.

**EXAMPLE 4.5.1.**   In the code segment

```
class BC {  // base class
public:
   BC() { x = y = -1; } // base constructor
protected:
   int get_x() const { return x; }
   int get_y() const { return y; }
private:
   int x;
   int y;
};

class DC : public BC { // derived class
public:
   void write() const { cout << get_x() * get_y() << '\n'; }
};

int main() {
   DC d1;        // d1.BC() invoked
   d1.write(); // 1 written to standard output
   //...
}
```

**BC**'s default constructor is invoked when **d1** is defined because **DC** is derived from **BC**. The constructor initializes **x** and **y** to **-1**. Note that **d1** inherits its only data members from **BC**.  ∎

Base class constructors are often sufficient for the derived class. Sometimes, however, it makes sense for a derived class to have its own constructors. A constructor specific to a derived class may invoke a base class constructor, if one exists.

**EXAMPLE 4.5.2.**   The code segment

```
class Animal {
public:
   Animal() { species = "Animal"; }
   Animal( const char* s ) { species = s; }
private:
   string species;
};
class Primate: public Animal {
public:
   Primate() : Animal( "Primate" ) { }
   Primate( int n ) : Animal( "Primate" )
      { heart_cham = n; }
private:
   int heart_cham;
};
```

```
Animal slug;              // Animal()
Animal tweety( "canary" ); // Animal( const char* )
Primate godzilla;         // Primate()
Primate human( 4 );       // Primate( int )
```

has four constructors: two for base class **Animal** and two for derived class **Primate**.

The two **Primate** constructors invoke a base class **Animal** constructor in their initialization sections:

```
Primate() : Animal( "Primate" ) { }
Primate( int n ) : Animal( "Primate" )
   { heart_cham = n; }
```

The syntax indicates that each **Primate** constructor invokes an **Animal** constructor *before* executing its own body. For instance, the default **Primate** constructor invokes the base class constructor **Animal( const char* )** before executing its own body, which happens to be empty. In the case of the **Primate** constructor with one argument, the body contains an assignment of **n** to **heart_cham**. ∎

In a deep inheritance hierarchy, creation of an object belonging to a derived class may have a domino effect with respect to constructor invocation.

**EXAMPLE 4.5.3.**  In the code segment

```
class Animal {
public:
   Animal() { species = "Animal"; }
   Animal( const char* s ) { species = s; }
private:
   string species;
};
class Primate: public Animal {
public:
   Primate() : Animal( "Primate" ) { }
   Primate( int n ) : Animal( "Primate" )
      { heart_cham = n; }
private:
   int heart_cham;
};
class Human : public Primate {
public:
   Human() : Primate() { }
   Human( int c ) : Primate( c ) { }
};

Human jill();    // Human()
Human fred( 4 ); // Human( int )
```

the inheritance hierarchy is now three deep. **Human** inherits **heart_cham** directly from **Primate** and **species** indirectly from **Animal** by way of **Primate**. Each of the **Human** constructors invokes a direct base class **Primate** constructor before executing an empty body. The **Primate** constructor, in turn, invokes an **Animal** constructor before executing its own body. The effect is that the bodies of the constructors are executed in a top-down order, where **Animal** is at the top, **Primate** in the middle, and **Human** at the bottom of the inheritance hierarchy (see Figure 4.5.2). ■

```
Animal::Animal( ... )   body executes first
                │
                ▼
Primate::Primate( ... )   body executes second
                │
                ▼
  Human::Human( ... )   body executes third
```

FIGURE 4.5.2 Constructor body execution in the **Animal-Primate-Human** hierarchy.

## Derived Class Constructor Rules

If a base class has constructors *but no default constructor*, then a derived class constructor *must* explicitly invoke some base class constructor.

**EXAMPLE 4.5.4.**   The code segment

```
// BC has constructors but no
// default constructor
class BC { // base class
public:
  BC( int a ) { x = a; y = 999; }
  BC( int a1, int a2 ) { x = a1; y = a2; }
private:
  int x;
  int y;
};

// DC has a constructor (any constructor
// will do for the example)
class DC : public BC { // derived class
public:
  // ***** ERROR: DC( int ) must explicitly
  //        invoke a BC constructor
  DC( int n ) { z = n; }
private:
  int z;
};
```

is in error because **BC** does not have a *default* constructor and **DC**'s constructor does *not* explicitly invoke a **BC** constructor. We can correct the error in two ways: by having **DC**'s constructor explicitly invoke, in its initialization section, one of **BC**'s constructors or by giving **BC** a default constructor (see Figure 4.5.3).

There is rarely a good reason for a base class not to have a default constructor. Giving a base class a default constructor avoids the problem and still allows a derived class constructor to invoke any base class constructor. Accordingly, we recommend that every base class have a default constructor. ∎

Suppose that a base class has a default constructor and that a derived class has constructors, none of which explicitly invokes a base class constructor. In this case, the base class default constructor is invoked automatically whenever a derived class object is created.

**EXAMPLE 4.5.5.** The output for the code segment

```
class BC { // base class
public:
  BC() { cout << "BC::BC() executes...\n"; }
private:
  int x;
};

class DC : public BC { // derived class
public:
  DC() { cout << "DC::DC() executes...\n"; }
private:
  int y;
};

int main() {
  DC d;
  //...
}
```

is

```
BC::BC() executes...
DC::DC() executes...
```

It is legal but unnecessary for **DC**'s constructor to invoke **BC**'s default constructor explicitly:

```
// legal but unnecessary
DC() : BC() { /* constructor body /* }
```
∎

```
// approach 1: have DC's constructor explicitly
// invoke one of BC's constructors
class BC { // base class
public:
  BC( int a ) { x = a; y = 999; }
  BC( int a1, int a2 ) { x = a1; y = a2; }
private:
  int x;
  int y;
};

// DC's constructor explicitly invokes a
// BC constructor in its initialization section
class DC : public BC { // derived class
public:
  // ok: DC( int ) explicitly invokes BC( int, int )
  DC( int n ) : BC( n, n + 1 ) { z = n; }
private:
  int z;
};

// approach 2: give BC a default constructor
class BC { // base class
public:
  BC() { x = 1; y = 2; } // default
  BC( int a ) { x = a; y = 999; }
  BC( int a1, int a2 ) { x = a1; y = a2; }
private:
  int x;
  int y;
};

// DC's constructor need not invoke a BC
// constructor because BC how has a
// default constructor
class DC : public BC { // derived class
public:
  // ok: BC has a default constructor
  DC( int n ) { z = n; }
private:
  int z;
};
```

**FIGURE 4.5.3** Constructor interaction in an inheritance hierarchy. In the first approach, the derived class constructor explicitly invokes one of the base class's constructors. In the second approach, the derived class constructor implicitly invokes the base class's default constructor.

We now summarize the rules, using **DC** as a class derived from **BC**.

- If **DC** has constructors but **BC** has no constructors, then the appropriate **DC** constructor executes automatically whenever a **DC** object is created.
- If **DC** has no constructors but **BC** has constructors, then **BC** must have a default constructor so that **BC**'s default constructor can execute automatically whenever a **DC** object is created.
- If **DC** has constructors and **BC** has a default constructor, then **BC**'s default constructor executes automatically whenever a **DC** object is created unless the appropriate **DC** constructor *explicitly* invokes, in its initialization section, some other **BC** constructor.
- If **DC** and **BC** have constructors but **BC** has no default constructor, then each **DC** constructor must explicitly invoke, in its initialization section, a **BC** constructor, which then executes when a **DC** object is created.

It makes sense that the creation of a derived class object should cause some base class constructor, if any, to execute. A derived class constructor may depend upon actions from a base class constructor. For example, the derived class may depend upon the base class constructor to perform some data member initializations. Also, a derived class object is a specialization of a base class object, which means that the body of a base class constructor, if the class has constructors, should execute *first* when a derived class object is created. The body of a more specialized constructor, which is the local derived class constructor, then can handle any special details.

**EXAMPLE 4.5.6.** In the code segment

```
class Team {   // base class
public:
   Team( int len = 100 ) {
      names = new string[ maxno = len ];
   }
protected:
   string* names;
   int      maxno;
   //...
};

class BaseballTeam : public Team { // derived class
public:
   BaseballTeam( const string s[ ], int si ) : Team( si ) {
      for ( int i = 0; i < si; i++ )
         names[ i ] = s[ i ];
   }
   //...
};
```

**BaseballTeam**'s two-parameter constructor is called when a **BaseballTeam** object is created with two arguments: an array of **string** and the number of elements in the array. This constructor first invokes **Team**'s constructor, which allocates storage for an array of type **string**. The copy occurs in **BaseballTeam**'s body. It is therefore imperative that **Team**'s constructor be invoked before the body of **BaseballTeam**'s constructor executes. ∎

## Destructors Under Inheritance

Constructor bodies in an inheritance hierarchy execute in a

* base class to derived class

order. Destructor bodies in an inheritance hierarchy execute in a

* derived class to base class

order. So the destructor bodies execute in the reverse order of the constructor bodies.

**EXAMPLE 4.5.7.** The output of the code segment

```
class BC {
public:
    BC() { cout << "BC's constructor\n"; }
    ~BC() { cout << "BC's destructor\n"; }
};

class DC : public BC {
public:
    DC() : BC() { cout << "DC's constructor\n"; }
    ~DC() { cout << "DC's destructor\n"; }
};

int main() {
    DC d;
    return 0;
}
```

is

```
BC's constructor
DC's constructor
DC's destructor
BC's destructor
```
∎

A destructor often frees storage allocated by a constructor. By firing in the reverse order of constructors, destructors ensure that the most recently allocated storage is the first storage to be freed.

**EXAMPLE 4.5.8.** The output of the program in Figure 4.5.4 is

```
BC allocates 3 bytes
DC allocates 5 bytes
DC frees 5 bytes
BC frees 3 bytes
```

DC's five bytes are allocated *after* BC's three bytes, and DC's five bytes are freed *before* BC's three bytes. Note that the storage allocated by BC's constructor is freed by BC's destructor and that the storage allocated by DC's constructor is freed by DC's destructor. ∎

```cpp
class BC { // base class
public:
  BC() {
    sBC = new char[ 3 ];
    cout << "BC allocates 3 bytes\n";
  }

  ~BC() {
    delete[ ] sBC;
    cout << "BC frees 3 bytes\n";
  }
private:
  char* sBC;
};

class DC : public BC { // derived class
public:
  DC() : BC() {
    sDC = new char[ 5 ];
    cout << "DC allocates 5 bytes\n";
  }

  ~DC() {
    delete[ ] sDC;
    cout << "DC frees 5 bytes\n";
  }
private:
  char* sDC;
};

int main() {
  DC d1;
  return 0;
}
```

**FIGURE 4.5.4** Destructors freeing storage allocated by constructors.

Unlike constructors, a destructor never explicitly invokes another destructor. Since each class has at most one destructor, it is unambiguous which destructor, if any, should execute.

## EXERCISES

**1.** Explain the error:

```
class BC {
public:
   BC( int a ) { x = a; }
private:
   int x;
};

class DC : public BC {
public:
   DC() { /* constructor body */ }
   //...
};
```

**2.** In Example 4.5.3, the default constructor for **Human** explicitly invokes the default constructor for **Primate** but does not explicitly invoke the default constructor for **Animal**. Why not?

**3.** What is the output?

```
class BC {
public:
   BC() { cout << "BC constructor\n"; }
   ~BC() { cout << "BC destructor\n"; }
};

class DC1 : public BC {
public:
   DC1() : BC() { cout << "DC1 constructor\n"; }
   ~DC1() { cout << "DC1 destructor\n"; }
};

class DC2 : public DC1 {
public:
   DC2() : DC1() { cout << "DC2 constructor\n"; }
   ~DC2() { cout << "DC2 destructor\n"; }
};

int main() {
   BC b;
   DC1 d1;
   DC2 d2;
   return 0;
}
```

**4.** Is it mandatory that a derived class have a constructor?

**5.** Is it mandatory that a base class have a constructor?

**6.** Is it mandatory that a derived class have a destructor?

**7.** Is it mandatory that a base class have a destructor?

**8.** Is it possible for a derived class to have a constructor but its base class not to have a constructor?

**9.** Suppose that base class **BC** has two constructors, the default constructor **BC::BC()** and the constructor **BC::BC( int )**. **DC** is derived from **BC** and has a single constructor, **DC::DC( int )**. Must **DC** invoke *both* of **BC**'s constructors before executing its own body?

**10.** C++ requires that when a derived class object is created, a base class constructor, if one exists, be invoked. Explain the reasoning behind this rule.

**11.** Extend the class hierarchy of Example 4.5.3 at least two more levels, writing constructors for each of the additional classes.

**12.** Must a derived class destructor invoke a base class destructor if one exists?

## 4.6 SAMPLE APPLICATION: A SEQUENCE HIERARCHY

### Problem

Develop an inheritance hierarchy to handle sequences of strings and sorted sequences of strings. A **sequence** is a list in which there is a first element, a second element, and so on. For example, in the sequence

    Abby George Ben

**Abby** is the first member, **George** is the second member, and **Ben** is the third member. This sequence is considered *distinct* from the sequence

    George Ben Abby

because, for example, the first member, **George**, is different from the first member, **Abby**, of the first sequence.

A **sorted sequence** is a sequence in which the elements are in *sorted* (ascending) order. For example, the sequence

    Abby Ben George

is a sorted sequence because the elements are in sorted order. The sequence

    Abby George Ben

is *not* a *sorted* sequence because **Ben** should *precede* **George** in sorted order.

Class **Sequence** has data members

- To hold strings.
- To hold a file name.
- To hold the index of the last string.
- To handle input and output files.

Class **Sequence** has **public** methods to

- Add a string at a designated position.
- Delete a string at a designated position.
- To output the sequence.

Class **Sequence** also has a default constructor, a one-parameter **const char\*** constructor, and a destructor.

The default constructor

- Sets the index of the last string to −1 to indicate that no strings are in the sequence.

The one-parameter **const char\*** constructor

- Sets the index of the last string to −1 to indicate that no strings are in the sequence.
- Copies the file name passed into the data member that holds a file name.
- Attempts to open the file for input. If the file cannot be opened, the constructor simply returns.
- Reads the sequence from the file until end-of-file or until storage is exhausted, whichever occurs first.
- Closes the file.

The destructor

- Returns if the file name is the null string.
- Opens the file for output.
- Writes the sequence to the file.
- Closes the file.

Since a sorted sequence is a sequence, class **SortedSeq** is derived from class **Sequence**. Class **SortedSeq** adds no data members but rather inherits its data members from **Sequence**.

Class **SortedSeq** provides its own method to add an element to the sequence. This method has one parameter—the item to add. It does need a parameter to indicate where to add the item; it is added at the index consistent with the sorted order.

Class **SortedSeq** has a method **sort** to sort a sequence. Since this method is used internally only, it is **protected**.

Class **SortedSeq** has a default constructor and a one-parameter **const char\*** constructor. **SortedSeq** has no destructor; instead it uses **Sequence**'s destructor.

The default constructor invokes **Sequence**'s default constructor. The one-parameter **const char\*** constructor invokes **Sequence**'s one-parameter constructor and then sorts the sequence that was input.

### Sample Input/Output

The first session shows the class **Sequence** in action using the test client of Figure 4.6.1. The file *test.dat* does not exist; thus the sequence is initially empty. When **main** finishes executing and the **Sequence** object **items** is destroyed, the **Sequence** destructor writes the sequence created to the file *test.dat*.

```
Sequence output:

1 -- add
2 -- delete
3 -- quit
1

item to add: George
add where? 0
item added

Sequence output:
0  George

1 -- add
2 -- delete
3 -- quit
1

item to add: Ben
add where? 1
item added

Sequence output:
0  George
1  Ben

1 -- add
2 -- delete
3 -- quit
1

item to add: Abby
add where? 0
item added

Sequence output:
0  Abby
1  George
2  Ben

1 -- add
2 -- delete
3 -- quit
2

where to delete: 1
item deleted

Sequence output:
0  Abby
1  Ben
```

```
1 -- add
2 -- delete
3 -- quit
1

item to add: Pat
add where? 0
item added

Sequence output:
0   Pat
1   Abby
2   Ben

1 -- add
2 -- delete
3 -- quit
3
```

The next session shows the class **SortedSeq** in action using the test client of Figure 4.6.2, where the **SortedSeq** object is created using the constructor whose argument is the name of the file created by the preceding **Sequence** session.

```
SortedSeq output:
0   Abby
1   Ben
2   Pat

1 -- add
2 -- delete
3 -- quit
1

item to add: Doris
item added

SortedSeq output:
0   Abby
1   Ben
2   Doris
3   Pat

1 -- add
2 -- delete
3 -- quit
2

where to delete: 1
item deleted

SortedSeq output:
0   Abby
1   Doris
2   Pat
```

```
1 -- add
2 -- delete
3 -- quit
3
```

```
int main() {
    string inbuff, where;
    int wh;
    Sequence items( "test.dat" );
    while ( true ) {
        cout << "\nSequence output: \n";
        items.output();
        cout << "\n1 -- add\n"
             << "2 -- delete\n"
             << "3 -- quit\n";
        getline( cin, inbuff );
        if ( inbuff == "1" ) {
            cout << "\nitem to add: ";
            getline( cin, inbuff );
            cout << "add where? ";
            getline( cin, where );
            wh = atoi( where.c_str() );
            if ( items.addS( wh, inbuff ) )
                cout << "item added\n";
            else
                cout << "item not added\n";
        }
        else if ( inbuff == "2" ) {
            cout << "\nwhere to delete: ";
            getline( cin, where );
            wh = atoi( where.c_str() );
            if ( items.del( wh ) )
                cout << "item deleted\n";
            else
                cout << "item not deleted\n";
        }
        else if ( inbuff == "3" )
            break;
    }
    return 0;
}
```

**FIGURE 4.6.1** A test client for the **Sequence** class.

```
int main() {
   string inbuff, where;
   int wh;
   SortedSeq sortitems( "test.dat" );
   while ( true ) {
      cout << "\nSortedSeq output: \n";
      sortitems.output();
      cout << "\n1 -- add\n"
           << "2 -- delete\n"
           << "3 -- quit\n";
      getline( cin, inbuff );
      if ( inbuff == "1" ) {
         cout << "\nitem to add: ";
         getline( cin, inbuff );
         if ( sortitems.addSS( inbuff ) )
            cout << "item added\n";
         else
            cout << "item not added\n";
      }
      else if ( inbuff == "2" ) {
         cout << "\nwhere to delete: ";
         getline( cin, where );
         wh = atoi( where.c_str() );
         if ( sortitems.del( wh ) )
            cout << "item deleted\n";
         else
            cout << "item not deleted\n";
      }
      else if ( inbuff == "3" )
         break;
   }
   return 0;
}
```

**FIGURE 4.6.2** A test client for the **SortedSeq** class.

### Solution

In class **Sequence**, we use an array of **string** to hold the strings in the sequence. A **string** member holds the file name, and an **int** member holds the index of the last element in the sequence. The constructors therefore initialize this latter member to −1.

The member **addS** attempts to add an element to the sequence at the specified index. If successful, **addS** returns **true**; otherwise, it returns **false**. The method could fail to add an element if the index specified is illegal or if the storage provided is full. Therefore **addS** returns a **bool**.

Similarly, the member **del** attempts to delete an element at the specified index. If successful, **del** returns **true**; otherwise, it returns **false**. The method could fail to delete an element if the index specified is illegal. Therefore **del** also returns a **bool**.

The method **output** steps through the array of **string** and prints each string together with its index.

Class **SortedSeq** is publicly derived from class **Sequence**. Class **SortedSeq** inherits its data members from **Sequence**.

**SortedSeq**'s **addSS** locates the index, defined by the sorted order, at which to add the item. It then invokes **addS** to insert the item.

**SortedSeq**'s **sort** method uses **insertion sort** to sort the sequence. The logic is explained in the Discussion section.

## C++ Implementation

```
class Sequence {
public:
    bool addS( int, const string& );
    bool del( int );
    void output() const;
    Sequence() : last( -1 ) { }
    Sequence( const char* );
    ~Sequence();
protected:
    enum { MaxStr = 50 };
    string s[ MaxStr ];
    int last;
private:
    string filename;
    ifstream in;
    ofstream out;
};

bool Sequence::addS( int pos, const string& entry ) {
    if ( last == MaxStr - 1
          || pos < 0
          || pos > last + 1 )
        return false;
    for ( int i = last; i >= pos; i-- )
        s[ i + 1 ] = s[ i ];
    s[ pos ] = entry;
    last++;
    return true;
}
```

```
bool Sequence::del( int pos ) {
   if ( pos < 0 || pos > last )
      return false;
   for ( int i = pos; i < last; i++ )
      s[ i ] = s[ i + 1 ];
   last--;
   return true;
}

void Sequence::output() const {
   for ( int i = 0; i <= last; i++ )
      cout << i << "  " << s[ i ] << '\n';
}

Sequence::Sequence( const char* fname ) {
   last = -1;
   filename = fname;
   in.open( fname );
   if ( !in )
      return;
   while ( last < MaxStr - 1 && getline( in, s[ last + 1 ] ) )
      last++;
   in.close();
}

Sequence::~Sequence() {
   if ( filename == "" )
      return;
   out.open( filename.c_str() );
   for ( int i = 0; i <= last; i++ )
      out << s[ i ] << '\n';
   out.close();
}

class SortedSeq : public Sequence {
public:
   bool addSS( const string& );
   SortedSeq() { }
   SortedSeq( const char* );
protected:
   void sort();
private:
   using Sequence::addS;
};
```

```
void SortedSeq::sort() {
   string temp;
   int i, j;
   for ( i = 0; i <= last - 1; i++ ) {
      temp = s[ i + 1 ];
      for ( j = i; j >= 0; j-- )
         if ( temp < s[ j ] )
            s[ j + 1 ] = s[ j ];
         else
            break;
      s[ j + 1 ] = temp;
   }
}

bool SortedSeq::addSS( const string& entry ) {
   int i;
   for ( i = 0; i <= last; i++ )
      if ( entry <= s[ i ] )
         break;
   return addS( i, entry );
}

SortedSeq::SortedSeq( const char* fname ) : Sequence( fname ) {
   sort();
}
```

### Discussion

**Sequence**'s array data member and end marker

```
string s[ MaxStr ];
int last;
```

are **protected**, so that they are visible in classes such as **SortedSeq** publicly derived from **Sequence** but *not* outside the class hierarchy. The array **s** is used to hold the strings that make up the sequence. Data members

```
string filename;
ifstream in;
ofstream out;
```

are **private** to promote data hiding. These data members need *not* be directly accessed by any derived classes.

The default constructor sets **last** to **-1** to indicate that the sequence is empty.

Method **addS** first checks whether the array **s** is full

```
last == MaxStr - 1
```

or whether the requested index is out of bounds

```
pos < 0 || pos > last + 1
```

If either condition is **true**, **addS** returns **false**. Otherwise, **addS** moves strings up, beginning at the end, to make room for the added item

```
for ( int i = last; i >= pos; i-- )
   s[ i + 1 ] = s[ i ];
```

stores the item at index **pos**, updates **last**, and returns **true**

```
s[ pos ] = entry;
last++;
return true;
```

Method **del** checks whether the requested index is out of bounds

```
pos < 0 || pos > last
```

If **pos** is out of bounds, **del** returns **false**. Otherwise, **del** moves each item after **pos** down one

```
for ( int i = pos; i < last; i++ )
   s[ i ] = s[ i + 1 ];
```

updates **last**, and returns **true**

```
last--;
return true;
```

The one-parameter constructor receives a file name

```
Sequence::Sequence( const char* )
```

It then sets **last** to **-1** to indicate that the sequence is empty, copies **fname** to **filename**, and tries to open the file

```
last = -1;
filename = fname;
in.open( fname );
```

If the file cannot be opened, the constructor simply returns

```
if ( !in )
   return;
```

Otherwise, it reads the file until end-of-file or until the storage is exhausted and closes the file

```
while ( last < MaxStr - 1 && getline( in, s[ last + 1 ] ) )
   last++;
in.close();
```

The destructor first checks whether **filename** is the null string; if it is the null string, it simply returns

```
if ( filename == "" )
   return;
```

Otherwise, it opens the file for output, writes the strings to the file, and closes the file

```
out.open( filename.c_str() );
for ( int i = 0; i <= last; i++ )
   out << s[ i ] << '\n';
out.close();
```

Class **SortedSeq** is publicly derived from **Sequence**

```
class SortedSeq : public Sequence {
   //...
};
```

The default constructor simply invokes **Sequence**'s default constructor.

**SortedSeq** has a method **addSS** to add an item. It first finds the correct place in which to insert the item to be added

```
for ( i = 0; i <= last; i++ )
   if ( entry <= s[ i ] )
      break;
```

and then adds it by invoking **addS**

```
return addS( i, entry );
```

Inherited method **addS** is **public** in the base class **Sequence** and would normally be **public** in the derived class **SortedSeq** as well. However, **addS** should *not* be used in **SortedSeq**. Data can be added at *any* specified location using **addS**, which might lead to an unsorted list. To prohibit use of **addS** in **SortedSeq**, we declare it **private**

```
class SortedSeq : public Sequence {
   //...
private:
   using Sequence::addS;
};
```

The method **sort** is used internally (by the one-parameter constructor) and so is **protected**. Thus, **sort** is visible throughout the class hierarchy but not outside the hierarchy. The logic of **sort** is that of insertion sort. It assumes that

```
s[ 0 ],s[ 1 ],...,s[ i ]
```

is sorted. It then places **s[ i + 1 ]** in the correct position in this list. To do so, it first copies **s[ i + 1 ]** into **temp**

```
temp = s[ i + 1 ];
```

It then compares **temp** with **s[ j ]**, for **j** = **i**. If

```
temp < s[ j ]
```

it moves **s[ j ]** to the next position

```
s[ j + 1 ] = s[ j ];
```

and repeats after decrementing **j**. If

```
temp < s[ j ]
```

is **false**, the correct position for **temp** has been found and **temp** is copied into that position

```
s[ j + 1 ] = temp;
```

The one-parameter constructor first invokes **Sequence**'s one-parameter constructor, which sets **last** to **-1**, copies **fname** to **filename**, tries to open the file, reads the file until end-of-file if the file was successfully opened, and closes the file. It then sorts the sequence by invoking method **sort**.

## 4.7 MULTIPLE INHERITANCE

In **single inheritance**, a derived class has a single base class. In **multiple inheritance**, a derived class has multiple base classes (see Figure 4.7.1). In technical jargon, a hierarchy with only single inheritance is a **tree**, whereas a hierarchy with multiple inheritance is a **graph**.

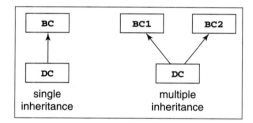

**FIGURE 4.7.1** Single versus multiple inheritance.

In a single inheritance hierarchy, a derived class typically represents a *specialization* of its base class. Because classes are user-defined data types in C++, such a derived class is a specialization or refinement of the more general data type that its base class represents. In a multiple inheritance hierarchy, a derived class typically represents a *combination* of its base classes.

**EXAMPLE 4.7.1.** In the multiple inheritance hierarchy

```
// Popup menu class -- no scroll bars
class PopupMenu {
private:
   int  menuChoices;
   Win* menuSubWins;
   //...
};
```

```
// Scrolled window class -- not a popup
class ScrollWin : public Win {
private:
  Widget horizontalSB;
  Widget verticalSB;
  //...
};

// Combination of popup and scrolled
class ScrollPopupMenu :
  public PopupMenu, public ScrollWin {
  //...
};
```

a **ScrollPopupMenu** combines a **PopupMenu** and a **ScrollWin** to form a new class that inherits features from each of its base classes. ∎

**EXAMPLE 4.7.2.**   In the multiple inheritance hierarchy

```
class Input {
  //...
};

class Output {
  //...
};

class InOutput :
    public Input, public Output { // input-output
  //...
};
```

**InOutput** is a class that supports input and output operations. It combines **Input**, which we assume supports only input operations, and **Output**, which we assume supports only output operations. ∎

## Inheritance and Access

The rules of inheritance and access do *not* change from a single to a multiple inheritance hierarchy. A derived class inherits data members and methods from *all* its base classes.

Multiple inheritance increases opportunities for name conflicts. The conflict can occur between the derived class and one of the base classes or between the base classes themselves. It is up to the programmer to resolve the conflict.

**EXAMPLE 4.7.3.**   In the code segment

```
class BC1 { // base class 1
private:
  int x;
```

```
protected:
  void set_x( int a ) { x = a; }
  //...
};

class BC2 { // base class 2
private:
  int x;
protected:
  void set_x( int a ) { x = a; }
  //...
};

class DC : public BC1, public BC2 { // derived class
private:
  int x;
protected:
  void set_x( int a ) { x = a; }
  //...
};

void tester() {
  DC d1;
  d1.set_x( 999 );        // local set_x
  d1.BC1::set_x( 111 ); // inherited from BC1
  d1.BC2::set_x( 222 ); // inherited from BC2
  //...
}
```

class **DC** has three methods named **set_x**: one is inherited from **BC1**, one is inherited from **BC2**, and one is added. The local **set_x** hides the inherited **BC1::set_x** and **BC2::set_x**. Further, **BC1** and **BC2** each has a method named **set_x**. The only way to resolve these conflicts is to use the scope resolution operator in referencing either of the inherited **set_x**'s. ■

## Virtual Base Classes

Multiple inheritance hierarchies can be complex, which may lead to the situation in which a derived class inherits multiple times from the *same* indirect base class.

**EXAMPLE 4.7.4.** In the code segment

```
class BC { // base class
  int x;
  //...
};

class DC1 : public BC { // path 1 through DC1
  //...
};
```

```
class DC2 : public BC { // path 2 through DC2
  //...
};

class Z : public DC1, public DC2 { // x comes twice
  //...
};
```

**Z** inherits **x** twice from **BC**: once through **DC1** and again through **DC2** (see Figure 4.7.2). This is wasteful and confusing. We correct the problem by changing **DC1** and **DC2** into **virtual** base classes for **Z**:

```
class BC { // base class
  int x;
  //...
};

class DC1 : virtual public BC { // path 1 through DC1
  //...
};

class DC2 : virtual public BC { // path 2 through DC2
  //...
};

class Z : public DC1, public DC2 { // x comes once
  //...
};
```

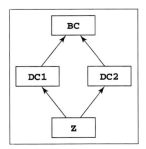

**FIGURE 4.7.2** The need for **virtual** inheritance.

There is now a single copy of **x** in **Z**. By making **DC1** and **DC2** into **virtual** base classes for **Z**, we tell them in effect to send to **Z** only one copy of whatever they inherit from their own common ancestor **B**. ∎

## EXERCISES

1. Explain the difference between using inheritance (1) to *specialize* or *refine* a class or data type and (2) to *combine* classes or data types. Which type of inheritance is best suited for each of (1) and (2)?

2. How many data members does **R** have?

```
class P {
private:
   int x;
   int y;
};

class Q {
private:
   float a;
   float b;
};

class R : public P, public Q {
public:
   void f() { /* f's body */ }
};
```

3. Write code to assign values to each of **R**'s data members.

```
class P {
protected:
   int x;
   int y;
};
class Q {
protected:
   float a;
   float b;
};
class R : public P, public Q {
public:
   void assign() { /* assign's body */ }
};
```

4. How many copies of **x** does **DC** inherit?

```
class BC {
private:
   int x;
};
```

```
class BC1 : public BC {
private:
  float y;
};

class BC2 : public BC {
  float z;
};

class DC : public BC1, public BC2 {
  //...
};
```

5. How many copies of **x** does **DC** inherit?

```
class BC {
private:
  int x;
};

class BC1 : virtual public BC {
private:
  float y;
};

class BC2 : virtual public BC {
private:
  float z;
};

class DC : public BC1, public BC2 {
  //...
};
```

## C++ POSTSCRIPT

## protected Inheritance

In a **protected** derivation

- Each **public** member in the base class is **protected** in the derived class.
- Each **protected** member in the base class is **protected** in the derived class.
- Each **private** member in the base class is visible only in the base class.

**EXAMPLE.** In the code segment

```
class BC { // base class
public:
    int get_x() const;
protected:
    void set_x( int );
private:
    int z;
};

class DC : protected BC { // protected derived class
private:
    int y;
public:
    void set_y();
};
```

class DC is derived from the base class BC. The derivation is **protected**. The members of the derived class DC are

| Member | Access Status in DC | How Obtained |
|--------|---------------------|--------------|
| get_x | protected | From class BC |
| set_x | protected | From class BC |
| z | Not accessible | From class BC |
| y | private | Added by class DC |
| set_y | public | Added by class DC |

## private Inheritance

In a **private** derivation

- Each **public** member in the base class is **private** in the derived class.
- Each **protected** member in the base class is **private** in the derived class.
- Each **private** member in the base class is visible only in the base class.

**EXAMPLE.** In the code segment

```
class BC { // base class
public:
    int get_x() const;
protected:
    void set_x( int );
private:
    int x;
};
```

```
class DC : private BC { // private derived class
private:
    int y;
public:
    void set_y( int );
};
```

class **DC** is derived from the base class **BC**. The derivation is **private**. The members of the derived class **DC** are

| Member | Access Status in DC | How Obtained |
|--------|---------------------|--------------|
| get_x | private | From class **BC** |
| set_x | private | From class **BC** |
| x | Not accessible | From class **BC** |
| y | private | Added by class **DC** |
| set_y | public | Added by class **DC** |

**EXAMPLE.**   In a derivation, **private** inheritance is the default; thus, the declaration of class **DC** in the preceding example is equivalent to

```
class DC : BC { // private (default) derived class
private:
    int y;
public:
    void set_y( int );
};
```

## COMMON PROGRAMMING ERRORS

1. In a derivation, **private** inheritance is the default, so to obtain **public** inheritance, the keyword **public** *must* be specified. For example, in the following code segment

```
class BC { // base class
    //...
};

// Caution: public not specified so inheritance
// is private
class DC : BC {
    //...
};
```

the inheritance is **private**; that is, the preceding code segment is equivalent to

```
class BC { // base class
   //...
};

class DC : private BC {
   //...
};
```

To obtain **public** inheritance, use the keyword **public**:

```
class BC { // base class
   //...
};

class DC : public BC { // public inheritance
   //...
};
```

2. It is an error to access a **protected** member outside its class hierarchy except through a **friend** function. For example,

```
class BC { // base class
protected:
   void set_x( int );
   //...
};

class DC : public BC { // derived class
public:
   void f() { set_x( 0 ); } // OK: set_x is protected in DC
   //...
};
int main() {
   BC c1;
   c1.set_x( 0 ); // ***** ERROR: set_x is protected in BC
   //...
}
```

contains an error because **set_x** is accessible only to **BC**'s methods and **friend**s and to methods and **friend**s of certain classes, such as **DC**, that are derived from **BC**.

3. It is an error to access a **private** member outside its class except through a **friend** function. For example,

```
class BC { // base class
private:
   int x;
};
```

```
class DC : public BC { // derived class
public:
   // ***** ERROR: x not visible in DC
   int f() const { return x; }
};
```

contains an error because **x** is accessible only to **BC**'s methods and **friend**s. Member **x** is not even accessible in classes derived from **BC**.

4. If a base class has constructors but no default constructor, then a derived class constructor *must* explicitly invoke a base class constructor in its initialization section:

```
class BC {
public:
   // constructors -- but no default constructor
   BC( int a ) { x = a; z = -1; }
   BC( int a1, int a2 ) { x = a1; z = a2; }
private:
   int x, z;
};

class DC1 : public BC {
public:
   // **** ERROR: DC1( int ) must explicitly invoke
   // one of BC's constructors
   DC1( int a ) { y = a; }
private:
   int y;
};

class DC2 : public BC {
public:
   // ok -- DC2 explicitly invokes a BC
   // constructor in its initialization section
   DC2( int a ) : BC( a ) { y = a; }
private:
   int y;
};
```

5. If a derived class has a method with the same name as a base class method, then the derived class's method *hides* the base class method. It is therefore an error to invoke the base class method:

```
class BC { // base class
public:
   void f( double );
   //...
};
```

```
class DC : public BC { // derived class
public:
   void f( char [ ] ); // CAUTION -- hides BC::f
   //...
};

int main() {
   DC d;
   // ***** ERROR: DC::f, which hides BC::f,
   // expects a character array, not a double
   d.f( 3.14 );
   //...
}
```

## PROGRAMMING EXERCISES

**4.1.** Derive an additional class **Documentary** from class **Film** of Section 4.3. Add appropriate data members and methods, including a method to output the data. Implement a test client to test the hierarchy.

**4.2.** Derive a class **RevSortedSeq** from class **Sequence** of Section 4.6. **RevSortedSeq** is just like **SortedSeq** except that the strings are sorted in *reverse* alphabetical order. Implement a test client to test the hierarchy.

**4.3.** Implement a **Library** hierarchy with at least a dozen classes. For purposes of the exercise, consider a *library* to be a collection of literary or artistic materials that is not for sale. In addition to the constructors and destructors, the classes should include methods that describe the classes much in the way that a human librarian might describe a class or subclass of materials among the library's holdings.

**4.4.** Implement an integer array hierarchy in which the base class represents a one-dimensional array and the derived classes represent different multidimensional arrays. The base class uses a one-dimensional array to store the integers

```
class intArray { // base class
public:
// interface
protected:
   int ar[ MaxArray ];
   int n; // element count
   // rest of implementation
};
```

and each derived class uses the inherited array to store its integers. A **Matrix** class could add a data member **rowCount** to store the number of rows and a data member **colCount** to store the number of columns. The data could be stored in **ar** by rows: row 1 first, then row 2, and so on.

Each class defines its own print method. For example, **intArray**'s print method might include the statement

```
// print elements on one line, separated by blanks
for ( int i = 0; i < n; i++ )
   cout << ar[ i ] << ' ';
```

whereas **Matrix**'s print method might include the statements

```
// print elements with each row on one line
for ( int row = 0; row < rowCount; row++ ) {
   for ( int col = 0; col < colCount; col++ )
      cout << ar[ col + row * colCount ] << ' ';
   cout << '\n';
}
```

Other classes that might be included in the hierarchy are **Array3D**, which could be directly derived from **intArray**, and **SquareMatrix**, which could be derived from **Matrix**. After creating the classes, write a test client for the hierarchy.

**4.5.** Implement a **CardGame** class that represents an ordinary 52-card deck with four suits (hearts, clubs, diamonds, and spades) and 13 cards per suit: ace, king, queen, jack, 10, . . . , 2. Represent the deck in any convenient way. Derive a **Bridge** class that includes a method **deal** to divide the deck into four 13-card hands. Derive a **Poker** class that includes a method **deal** to divide the deck into a specified number (between 2 and 7, inclusive) of 5-card hands. After creating the classes, write a test client for the hierarchy.

**4.6.** Implement a **Vehicle** class that includes data members to represent a vehicle's make, model, production year, and price. The class interface includes methods that provide appropriate access to the data members. Derive a **Car** class (see Programming Exercise 3.1) and a **Truck** class from **Vehicle**. Each of these derived classes should add appropriate data members and methods. Also, derive two classes from **Car** that represent particular cars and two classes from **Truck** that represent particular trucks. Implement a test client to test the hierarchy. Propose other classes to derive from **Vehicle**.

**4.7.** Derive classes **Reference**, **Fiction**, and **Periodical** from class **Book** of Programming Exercise 3.3. Add appropriate data members and methods to each of these classes. Implement a test client to test the hierarchy.

**4.8.** Implement a **Person** class that includes data members to represent name, address, and identification number. The class interface includes methods that provide appropriate access to the data members. Derive a **CollegeStudent** class (see Programming Exercise 3.5) and a **Professor** class from **Person**. Each of these derived classes should add appropriate data members and methods. Implement a test client to test the hierarchy. Propose classes to derive from **CollegeStudent** and **Professor**. What data members and methods might these derived classes add?

**4.9.** Derive classes **CEO**, **Actor**, and **Telemarketer** from class **Profession** of Programming Exercise 3.7. Add appropriate data members and methods to each of these classes. Implement a test client to test the hierarchy.

**4.10.** Implement an **AbsCollection** class that includes an array to represent **int**s, an **int** member **last**, whose value is the index of the last item stored in the array, and a method to enumerate the elements stored in the array. Derive a **Set** class (see Programming Exercise 3.12) and a **Bag** class (see Programming Exercise 3.13) from **AbsCollection**. Each of these derived classes should add appropriate data members and methods. Implement a test client to test the hierarchy. Propose other classes to derive from **AbsCollection**. What data members and methods might these derived classes add?

**4.11.** Derive classes **Manager**, **HourlyWorker**, and **Consultant** from class **Emp** of Programming Exercise 3.22. Also derive at least one class from each of **Manager**, **HourlyWorker**, and **Consultant**. For example, **Officer** could be a class derived from **Manager**. Each subclass should represent information that distinguishes it. For example, an **HourlyWorker** has an hourly wage and overtime rate, but an **Officer** has neither of these. A methods to each of these classes. Implement a test client to test the hierarchy.

**4.12.** Derive classes **Fruit**, **Dairy**, and **Meat**, appropriate for a grocery chain, from class **Product** of Programming Exercise 3.23. Also, derive classes from each of **Fruit**, **Dairy**, and **Meat**. (For example, **Milk** and **Butter** might be derived from **Dairy**.)

Include any reasonable data members and methods. For example, suppose that the chain changes prices on products monthly, based on supply and demand, and that the percentage change depends on the particular product. For example, in a given month, the price of ice cream might decrease 0.5 percent, whereas the price of beef might increase 6 percent. Assume that every product has **supply** and **demand** data members whose values are one of the qualitative values **low**, **medium**, or **high**. Include a method that computes a product's price change based on its values of **supply** and **demand**. Implement a test client to test the hierarchy.

# CHAPTER

# 5

# POLYMORPHISM

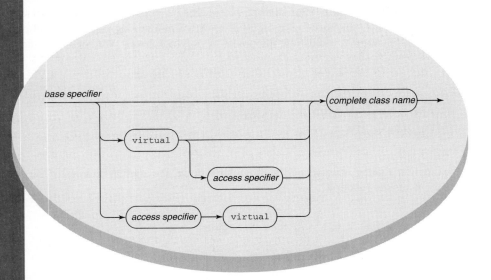

5.1 Run-Time versus Compile-Time Binding in C++

5.2 Sample Application: Tracking Films Revisited

5.3 Name Overloading, Name Overriding, and Name Hiding

5.4 Abstract Base Classes

5.5 Run-Time Type Identification

C++ Postscript

Common Programming Errors

Programming Exercises

T his chapter examines a powerful feature of object-oriented languages known as **polymorphism**. In technical terms, polymorphism is the *run-time binding* of a function's name to the code that implements the function. When a C++ program executes, the code that implements each of its component functions resides someplace in the computer's storage system. The *starting address* at which a function's code resides is the function's **entry point**. For example, a C++ program has a top-level function called **main**. Function **main**'s entry point is the address in the computer's storage system at which the executable code for **main** begins. So polymorphism is the run-time binding of a function's name to its entry point.

From the programmer's standpoint, polymorphism is a powerful tool. Imagine a hierarchy with **Window** as its base class and with 20 or so derived classes; and suppose that each class in the hierarchy has a polymorphic **close** method, which not only closes the **Window** on the screen but also does whatever background cleanup operations are appropriate for a particular type of **Window**. Assume, further, that all of the **close** methods have the same signature. The programmer can invoke a window's **close** method but without knowing exactly which **Window** type or subtype is involved. The programmer needs to remember only one method signature to invoke 20 or so different methods. Through examples and a sample application, we illustrate the power of polymorphism. We begin with a technical overview.

## 5.1 RUN-TIME VERSUS COMPILE-TIME BINDING IN C++

A function's name is associated with an entry point, the starting address of the code that implements the function.

**EXAMPLE 5.1.1.**   In the code segment

```
#include <iostream>
using namespace std;
void sayHi();
int main() {
   sayHi();
   return 0;
}
void sayHi() {
   cout << "Hello, cruel world!" << endl;
}
```

the function name **sayHi** is associated with a function body that consists of the statement

```
cout << "Hello, cruel world!" << endl;
```

The compiler binds any call to **sayHi**, such as the one in **main**, to the code that implements **sayHi**, in this case a single **cout** statement. We say that **compile-time binding** occurs for **sayHi** because the *compiler* determines what code is to be executed whenever **sayHi** is invoked. In more technical language, the compiler binds any invocation of **sayHi** to **sayHi**'s entry point. ∎

Compile-time binding has been in effect throughout our examples so far. The alternative is **run-time binding**, that is, the binding of a function's name to an entry point when the program is *running*, not when the program is being compiled. A function is *polymorphic* if its binding occurs at run time rather than compile time. In *pure* object-oriented languages such as Smalltalk, *all* functions are polymorphic. In a hybrid language such as C++, functions may be either polymorphic (bound at run time) or nonpolymorphic (bound at compile time). In particular, C++ allows only selected *methods* to be polymorphic.

## Requirements for C++ Polymorphism

Polymorphism in C++ has three requirements:

- There must be an *inheritance hierarchy*.
- The classes in the hierarchy must have a **virtual** method with the same signature (**virtual** is a keyword).
- There must be either a pointer or a reference to a base class. The pointer or reference is used to invoke a **virtual** method.

**EXAMPLE 5.1.2.**    The program in Figure 5.1.1 illustrates polymorphism and its three requirements in C++.

- There is an inheritance hierarchy with **TradesPerson** as the base class for two derived classes, **Tinker** and **Tailor**.
- There is a **virtual** method named **sayHi**; it is defined three times, once for each class in the hierarchy.
- There is a pointer **p** to a base class. In this example, **p** is of type **TradesPerson\***. The pointer **p** is used to invoke the **virtual** method **sayHi**.

In **main**, we prompt the user for an integer identifier of a class. If the user enters 1, we assign the address of a dynamically allocated **TradesPerson** to **p**. If the user enters 2, we assign the address of a dynamically allocated **Tinker** to **p**. If the user enters 3, we assign the address of a dynamically allocated **Tailor** to **p**. No cast is needed in assigning **p** the address of either a **Tinker** or a **Tailor** because a pointer to a *base class* may point to any base class or derived class object. We then use **p** to invoke one of the three **virtual** methods:

```
p->sayHi();  //**** run-time binding in effect
```

Because **sayHi** is **virtual**, the system binds its invocation at *run time*. If **p** points to a **TradesPerson**, the system binds the call to **TradesPerson::sayHi**. If **p** points to a **Tinker**, the system binds the call to **Tinker::sayHi**. If **p** points to a **Tailor**, the system binds the call to **Tailor::sayHi**. In a sample run, we entered 2 and the output therefore was

```cpp
#include <iostream>
using namespace std;
class TradesPerson { // base class
public:
   virtual void sayHi() { cout << "Just hi." << endl; }
};
class Tinker : public TradesPerson { // derived class 1
public:
   virtual void sayHi() { cout << "Hi, I tinker." << endl; }
};
class Tailor : public TradesPerson { // derived class 2
public:
   virtual void sayHi() { cout << "Hi, I tailor." << endl; }
};
int main() {
   TradesPerson* p; // pointer to base class
   int which;
   // prompt user for a number:
   // *** 1 == TradesPerson
   //     2 == Tinker
   //     3 == Tailor
   do {
     cout << "1 == TradesPerson, 2 == Tinker, 3 == Tailor ";
     cin >> which;
   } while ( which < 1 || which > 3 );
   // set pointer p depending on user choice
   switch ( which ) {
   case 1: p = new TradesPerson; break;
   case 2: p = new Tinker; break;
   case 3: p = new Tailor; break;
   }
   // invoke the sayHi method via the pointer
   p->sayHi(); //**** run-time binding in effect
   delete p;   //**** free the dynamically allocated storage
   return 0;
}
```

**FIGURE 5.1.1** Polymorphism (run-time binding) in C++.

```
Hi, I tinker.
```

In another sample run, we entered 3 and the output therefore was

```
Hi, I tailor.
```

**EXAMPLE 5.1.3.**   The program in Figure 5.1.2 defines an array of 10 pointers to the base class **TradesPerson**

```
TradesPerson* ptrs[ 10 ];
```

and then dynamically creates 10 objects:

```
// randomly create TradesPersons, Tinkers, and Tailors
for ( i = 0; i < 10; i++ ) {
  which = 1 + rand() % 3;
  switch ( which ) {
  case 1: ptrs[ i ] = new TradesPerson; break;
  case 2: ptrs[ i ] = new Tinker; break;
  case 3: ptrs[ i ] = new Tailor; break;
  }
}
```

A randomly generated integer determines whether we dynamically create a **TradesPerson**, a **Tinker**, or a **Tailor**. Next we iterate through the array, invoking each object's polymorphic **sayHi** method:

```
// polymorphically invoke the sayHi methods
for ( i = 0; i < 10; i++ ) {
  ptrs[ i ]->sayHi();
  delete ptrs[ i ]; // release the storage
}
```

After invoking an object's **sayHi** method, we release the object's dynamically allocated storage with the **delete** operator.

We seed the random number generator with a call to **srand**

```
srand( time( 0 ) );
```

so that the program does not generate the same random numbers each time it is run; hence, the program can generate different outputs on different runs. ∎

The programs in Figures 5.1.1 and 5.1.2 use the keyword **virtual** in all three versions of **sayHi**. This is good practice but not a requirement. If a *base class* method is declared **virtual**, then any derived class method with the same signature is automatically **virtual**, even if such a method is not explicitly declared **virtual**. For example, we could amend the program in Figure 5.1.1 by not explicitly declaring **Tinker::sayHi** to be **virtual**:

```
class TradesPerson {
public:
   virtual void sayHi() { cout << "Just hi." << endl; }
};
class Tinker : public TradesPerson {
public:
   void sayHi() { cout << "Hi, I tinker." << endl; }
};
//...
```

Nonetheless, **Tinker::sayHi** is still **virtual** because it has the same signature as **TradesPerson::sayHi**, the base class version that is declared **virtual**.

```
#include <iostream>
#include <cstdlib>
#include <ctime>
using namespace std;
class TradesPerson { // base class
public:
   virtual void sayHi() { cout << "Just hi." << endl; }
};
class Tinker : public TradesPerson { // derived class 1
public:
   virtual void sayHi() { cout << "Hi, I tinker." << endl; }
};
class Tailor : public TradesPerson { // derived class 2
public:
   virtual void sayHi() { cout << "Hi, I tailor." << endl; }
};

int main() {
   srand( time( 0 ) );
   TradesPerson* ptrs[ 10 ]; // pointers to base class
   unsigned which, i;
   // randomly create TradesPersons, Tinkers, and Tailors
   for ( i = 0; i < 10; i++ ) {
     which = 1 + rand() % 3;
     switch ( which ) {
     case 1: ptrs[ i ] = new TradesPerson; break;
     case 2: ptrs[ i ] = new Tinker; break;
     case 3: ptrs[ i ] = new Tailor; break;
     }
   }
   // polymorphically invoke the sayHi methods
   for ( i = 0; i < 10; i++ ) {
     ptrs[ i ]->sayHi();
     delete ptrs[ i ]; // release the storage
   }
   return 0;
}
```

**FIGURE 5.1.2** Using an array of pointers to illustrate polymorphism.

If the keyword **virtual** does *not* occur in the derived class declarations of **sayHi**, a reader of a derived class would have to look at the base class declaration of **sayHi** to determine that a derived class version is also **virtual**. This inconvenience can be avoided simply by declaring all derived class versions as **virtual**.

If a **virtual** method is defined outside the class declaration, then the keyword **virtual** occurs only in the method's *declaration*, not in its definition.

**EXAMPLE 5.1.4.**   In the code segment

```
class C {
public:
  virtual void m();  // declaration--"virtual" occurs
//...
};
void C::m() { // definition--"virtual" does not occur
  //...
}
```

**virtual** method **m** is defined outside the class declaration. Therefore, the keyword **virtual** occurs only in its declaration.  ∎

C++ allows only *methods* to be **virtual**. A top-level function cannot be **virtual**.

**EXAMPLE 5.1.5.**   The code segment

```
virtual void f(); //****** ERROR: not a method!
int main() {
  //...
}
```

contains an error because it declares **f**, a top-level function rather than a method, to be **virtual**.  ∎

## Inheriting **virtual** Methods

A **virtual** method, like a regular method, can be inherited by a derived class from a base class.

**EXAMPLE 5.1.6.**   In the code segment

```
class TradesPerson {
public:
  virtual void sayHi() { cout << "Just hi." << endl; }
};
class Tinker : public TradesPerson {
  //**** remove Tinker::sayHi
};
int main() {
  Tinker t1;
  t1.sayHi(); //*** inherited sayHi
  //...
}
```

the output is

```
Just hi.
```

Because class **Tinker** does not provide its own definition for **sayHi**, it inherits the definition from its base class **TradesPerson**.  ∎

## Run-Time Binding and the Vtable

C++ uses a **vtable** (virtual **table**) to implement the run-time binding of **virtual** methods. Although a vtable's implementation is system-dependent, its purpose is to support a run-time lookup that allows the system to bind a function's name to a particular entry point. The programmer can use **virtual** methods without understanding how the vtable works or even that it exists. Nonetheless, a basic understanding of the vtable illustrates that polymorphism incurs an overhead in storage and machine cycles.

**EXAMPLE 5.1.7.** Suppose that our application uses the inheritance hierarchy

```
class B { // base class
public:
    virtual void m1() { /*...*/ } // 1st virtual method
    virtual void m2() { /*...*/ } // 2nd virtual method
};
class D : public B { // derived class
public:
    virtual void m1() { /*...*/ } // override m1
};
```

Assuming that **m1** and **m2** are our application's only **virtual** methods, here is a conceptual representation of the vtable, with the sample entry points given in hexadecimal:

| **virtual** | *MethodSample Entry Point* |
|---|---|
| B::m1 | 0x7723 |
| B::m2 | 0x23b4 |
| D::m1 | 0x99a7 |
| D::m2 | 0x23b4 |

There is a separate vtable entry for *each* **virtual** method in the application. However, **B::m2** and **D::m2** have the same entry point (0x23b4) because derived class **D** does not override **virtual** method **m2** but rather uses the version inherited from its base class **B**.

When our application executes a code segment such as

```
int main() {
    B   b1;    // base class object
    D   d1;    // derived class object
    B* p;      // pointer to base class
    //...      // p is set to b1's or d1's address
    p->m1(); //*** vtable lookup for run-time binding
    //...
}
```

the system needs to bind the function call

```
p->m1(); //*** vtable lookup for run-time binding
```

to an entry point. The system first determines where **p** points. If **p** points to the **B** object **b1**, then the system looks in the vtable for **B::m1**'s entry point. If **p** points to the **D** object **d1**, then the system looks in the vtable for **D::m1**'s entry point. Once the vtable lookup is done, the appropriate function body is executed. ∎

A program that uses run-time binding incurs a performance penalty. The penalty in space is the amount of storage needed for the vtable. The penalty in time is the amount of time needed for vtable lookups. Pure object-oriented languages incur a relatively heavy performance penalty because *all* functions are bound at run time. In C++, by contrast, the programmer can be selective in using run-time binding (that is, **virtual** methods) and, in this way, enjoy the benefits of run-time binding without incurring a heavy performance penalty.

## Constructors and the Destructor

A constructor cannot be **virtual**. A destructor can be **virtual**.

**EXAMPLE 5.1.8.** The code segment

```
class C {
public:
    virtual C();        //***** ERROR: constructor
    virtual C( int ); //***** ERROR: constructor
    virtual ~C();       // ok, destructor
    virtual void m(); // ok, regular method
};
```

contains two errors because it declares the default and convert constructors as **virtual**. However, a destructor may be **virtual**. ∎

## virtual Destructors

We illustrate the need for **virtual** destructors with an example.

**EXAMPLE 5.1.9.** The program in Figure 5.1.3 has a base class **A** whose constructor dynamically allocates five bytes and whose destructor frees this storage so that it does not become inaccessible.

Derived class **z** has a constructor that dynamically allocates 5,000 bytes and a destructor that frees this storage so that it does not become inaccessible. We have **main** invoke **f** three times:

```
void f() {
    A* ptr;          // pointer to base class
    ptr = new Z(); // points to derived class object
    delete ptr; // ~A() fires but not ~Z()
} //***** Caution: 5,000 bytes of inaccessible storage
```

```
#include <iostream>
using namespace std;
class A { // base case
public:
   A() {
      cout << endl << "A() firing" << endl;
      p = new char[ 5 ];   // allocate 5 bytes
   }
   ~A() {
      cout << "~A() firing" << endl;
      delete[ ] p;          // free 5 bytes
   }
private:
   char* p;
};
class Z : public A {
public:
   Z() {
      cout << "Z() firing" << endl;
      q = new char[ 5000 ];   // allocate 5,000 bytes
   }
   ~Z() {
      cout << "~Z() firing" << endl;
      delete[ ] q;            // free 5,000 bytes
   }
private:
   char* q;
};
void f();
int main() {
   for ( unsigned i = 0; i < 3; i++ )
      f();
   return 0;
}
void f() {
   A* ptr;          // pointer to base class
   ptr = new Z(); // points to derived class object
   delete ptr; // ~A() fires but not ~Z()
} //***** Caution: 5,000 bytes of inaccessible storage
```

**FIGURE 5.1.3** Program to show the need for **virtual** destructors.

The constructors and destructors in **A** and **Z** print trace messages. The output is

```
A() firing
Z() firing
```

```
~A() firing

A() firing
Z() firing
~A() firing

A() firing
Z() firing
~A() firing
```

Note that only **A**'s destructor fires when **f** is invoked. Pointer **ptr** is of type **A\***, although we have it point to a derived class object:

```
ptr = new Z(); // points to derived class object
```

The call to **new** causes the constructors **A()** and **Z()** to fire. (Because **Z**'s default constructor does not explicitly invoke an **A** constructor, the compiler ensures that **A**'s *default* constructor is invoked.) When we invoke **delete** on **ptr**, however, only **~A()** fires—despite the fact that **ptr** points to a **Z** object. Because the destructors are *not* **virtual**, compile-time binding is in effect. The compiler uses **ptr**'s data type **A\*** to determine which destructor to call. Therefore, only **~A()** is called. Because **~Z()** is not called, the 5,000 bytes allocated by **Z()** are *not* freed. So 5,000 bytes of inaccessible storage are generated each time that **f** is called.  ■

**EXAMPLE 5.1.10.**    The problem with the program in Figure 5.1.3 can be fixed by making the destructors **virtual**:

```
class A { // base case
public:
   //...
   virtual ~A() { //***** virtual destructor
     cout << "~A() firing" << endl;
     delete[ ] p;        // free 5 bytes
   }
   //...
};
```

By making the base class destructor **~A()** **virtual**, we thereby make derived class destructor **~Z()** **virtual** as well. For code clarity, we should put the keyword **virtual** in **~Z()**'s declaration, but **~Z()** is still **virtual** even if we fail to do so. With this change, the output becomes

```
A() firing
Z() firing
~Z() firing
~A() firing

A() firing
Z() firing
~Z() firing
~A() firing
```

```
A() firing
Z() firing
~Z() firing
~A() firing
```

Because the destructors are **virtual**, *run-time* binding is in effect when the object to which **ptr** points is destroyed. Because **ptr** points to a **Z** object, **~Z()** is called. Recall that destructors fire *bottom to top*, which explains why **~A()** is then called as well. By making the destructors **virtual**, we thus prevent **f** from creating inaccessible storage.
∎

If a base class has a data member that points to dynamically allocated storage and a destructor to free such storage, the destructor should be made **virtual** to ensure that polymorphism is at work as derived classes are added. In commercial libraries such as the Microsoft Foundation Classes, destructors are typically **virtual** to prevent the kind of storage leakage illustrated by the program in Figure 5.1.3.

## Object Methods and Class Methods

Only a non**static** method may be **virtual**. In different words, only an *object* as opposed to a *class* method can be **virtual** (see Section 3.7).

**EXAMPLE 5.1.11.**    The code segment

```
class C {
public:
   static virtual void f(); //*** ERROR: static and virtual
   static void g();   // ok, not virtual
   virtual void h(); // ok, not static
};
```

contains an error because it tries to make a method both **static** and **virtual**.    ∎

## EXERCISES

1. Explain what a function's entry point is.
2. Explain the difference between compile-time and run-time binding.
3. What are three requirements for polymorphism in a C++ program?
4. Is every C++ function automatically polymorphic?
5. Explain the error:

```
#include <iostream>
using namespace std;
virtual void hi();
int main() {
   hi();
   return 0;
}
```

```cpp
// Reads revised time and changes.
void DirectorCut::input( ifstream& fin ) {
   Film::input( fin );
   string inbuff;
   getline( fin, inbuff );
   store_rev_time( atoi( inbuff.c_str() ) );
   getline( fin, inbuff );
   store_changes( inbuff );
}

// Writes revised time and changes.
void DirectorCut::output() {
   Film::output();
   cout << "Revised time: " << rev_time << endl;
   cout << "Changes: " << changes << endl;
}

class ForeignFilm : public Film {
public:
   ForeignFilm() { store_language(); }
   void store_language( const string& l ) { language = l; }
   void store_language( const char* l = "" ) { language = l; }
   virtual void output();
   virtual void input( ifstream& );
private:
   string language;
};

// Reads language.
void ForeignFilm::input( ifstream& fin ) {
   Film::input( fin );
   string inbuff;
   getline( fin, inbuff );
   store_language( inbuff );
}

// Writes language.
void ForeignFilm::output() {
   Film::output();
   cout << "Language: " << language << endl;
}

// class method: Film::read_input
// Reads data from an input file, dynamically creating the
// appropriate Film object for each record group.  For instance,
// a ForeignFilm object is dynamically created if the data
// represent a foreign film rather than a regular film or a
// director's cut.  Pointers to dynamically created objects are
// stored in the array films of size n.  Returns true to signal
```

```
    // success and false to signal failure.
    bool Film::read_input( const char* file, Film* films[ ], int n ) {
        string inbuff;
        ifstream fin( file );
        if ( !fin )  // opened successfully?
          return false; // if not, return false

        // Read until end-of-file.  Records fall into
        // groups.  1st record in each group is a string
        // that represents a Film type:
        //    "Film", "ForeignFilm", "DirectorCut", etc.
        // After reading type record, dynamically create
        // an object of the type (e.g., a ForeignFilm object),
        // place it in the array films, and invoke its
        // input method.
        int next = 0;
        while ( getline( fin, inbuff ) && next < n ) {
            if ( inbuff == "Film" )
              films[ next ] = new Film();            // regular film
            else if ( inbuff == "ForeignFilm" )
              films[ next ] = new ForeignFilm(); // foreign film
            else if ( inbuff == "DirectorCut" )
              films[ next ] = new DirectorCut(); // director's cut
            else //**** error condition: unrecognized film type
              continue;
            films[ next++ ]->input( fin ); // polymorphic method
        }
        fin.close();
        return true;
    }
```

### Discussion

We use the same data members from the original application. All data members remain **private**. Our first significant change is to add default constructors to handle data member initializations. For example, the default constructor for **Film**

```
    Film::Film() {
        store_title();
        store_director();
        store_time();
        store_quality();
    }
```

invokes methods to set the **Film**'s title, director, running time, and quality. For robustness, these methods all have default arguments. For example, the default argument for **store_title** is the empty string; the default time for **store_time** is 0. The other default constructors take the same approach towards their local data members.

To initiate input from a disk file, we use the **static** method **read_input**, which is declared in **Film**:

```
class Film {
public:
   //...
   // class methods
   static bool read_input( const char*, Film*[ ], int );
private:
   //...
};
```

This method's arguments are the name of the input file, an array of pointers to dynamically created objects in the **Film** hierarchy, and the array's size, respectively. The method returns **false** if it fails to open the input file; otherwise, it returns **true**. This allows a client, such as our **main**, to test for failure:

```
int main() {
   const unsigned n = 5;
   Film* films[ n ];
   // attempt to read input file and create objects
   if ( !Film::read_input( "films.dat", films, n ) ) {
     cerr << "Unable to read file Film.dat.  Exiting."
          << endl;
     exit( EXIT_FAILURE );
   }
   //...
```

If **read_input** opens the input file, it uses **getline** to read records from the file. The loop

```
int next = 0;
while ( getline( fin, inbuff ) && next < n ) {
   if ( inbuff == "Film" )
     films[ next ] = new Film();          // regular film
   else if ( inbuff == "ForeignFilm" )
     films[ next ] = new ForeignFilm(); // foreign film
   else if ( inbuff == "DirectorCut" )
     films[ next ] = new DirectorCut(); // director's cut
   else //**** error condition: unrecognized film type
     continue;
   films[ next++ ]->input( fin ); // polymorphic method
}
```

halts if **getline** reaches the end of the input file or if the array of **Film** pointers is filled. The input file's records are divided into groups: the first record of each signals whether the following records are for a **Film**, **ForeignFilm**, or **DirectorCut** object. After reading the record that identifies the group, we use an **if** construct to determine its type. If the record is for, say, a **ForeignFilm** object, then we dynamically create such an object and store its address in array **films**:

```
else if ( inbuff == "ForeignFilm" )
  films[ next ] = new ForeignFilm(); // ForeignFilm object
```

We have similar statements for **Film** and **DirectorCut** objects. We then invoke the newly created object's **input** method

```
films[ next++ ]->input( fin ); // polymorphic method
```

We also update **next**, which serves as index into array **films**. The invocation of **input** is polymorphic. Which **input** method is invoked depends on the type of the newly created object. For example, if we just created a **ForeignFilm** object, then **ForeignFilm::input** is invoked. Note that the system, not the programmer, determines the appropriate method to call. This eases the programming burden by shifting a significant part of the load to the system.

The polymorphic **input** methods are designed to read data into *local* data members. For example, **Film::input** reads data only into **Film** data members. In similar fashion, **DirectorCut::input** reads data only into **DirectorCut** data members. Because **ForeignFilm** and **DirectorCut** are derived classes with **Film** as their base class, **ForeignFilm** and **DirectorCut** inherit **Film**'s data members. Therefore, each derived class's **input** *first* invokes **Film::input** to handle its inherited data members and then reads data into its own local data members. For example, **DirectorCut::input** begins as follows:

```
void DirectorCut::input( ifstream& fin ) {
   Film::input( fin );
   //...
}
```

The polymorphic versions of **input** work very much like their original, non**virtual** counterparts in that each derived class's **input** method invokes its inherited base class method. The big difference has to do with how an **input** method is invoked. In the original application, the *programmer* explicitly invokes either **Film::input**, **ForeignFilm::input**, or **DirectorCut::input**. In the polymorphic revision, the *system* automatically invokes the appropriate **input** method for a dynamically created object. This frees the programmer from the task of determining exactly which **input** method to invoke. As the class hierarchy grows, the benefit to the programmer increases.

The polymorphic versions of **output** are identical, in internal structure, to their non**virtual** counterparts in the original application. Again the big difference has to do with who determines which **output** method to invoke. In the original application, this task falls to the programmer. In the revision, this task falls to the system.

### Program Development

Real-world applications are rarely, if ever, finished products. Such applications typically undergo constant change: bugs must be fixed, new functionality must be added to meet new requirements, application performance must be streamlined, and so on. Application design plays a major role in determining how hard it will be to make required changes. We focus here on one example.

Suppose that, over time, the **Film** hierarchy expands by several hundred new classes. Several benefits result from having the **input** and **output** methods be polymorphic and from making each class's **input** and **output** methods responsible for *local* data members only. Consider first the required changes to our application on the input side. The class method **readInput** would be changed, but in a straightforward manner. Each new class would require an **else if** in the style

```
   else if ( inbuff == "ForeignFilm" )
     films[ next ] = new ForeignFilm(); // ForeignFilm object
```

No other change to **readInput** would be required because the appropriate **input** method is invoked polymorphically:

```
   films[ next++ ]->input( fin ); // polymorphic method
```

If each class's **input** method is responsible only for its own local data members, it can first call its base class's **input** method; and if this base class has a base class itself, the process continues straightforwardly. This design mimics the calling sequence of constructors in an inheritance hierarchy (see Section 4.5). Input complexity is manageable because the labor is distributed among different **input** methods, each responsible for only its own local data members. As new classes are added to the hierarchy, their authors need to focus only on a class's local data members in overriding **input**. The inherited data members are handled somewhere up the hierarchy by **input** methods that likewise focus on their own local data members. If an error occurs during **input** and the input file is correctly formatted, then the error can be traced to a specific class's **input** method. The design thus makes the application easier to write and to manage. The overall application also should gain robustness from this modular design.

On the output side, our application's test driver would not need to change at all. The **output** methods are invoked polymorphically from within a **for** loop:

```
   // output to the standard output
   for ( unsigned i = 0; i < n; i++ )
     films[ i ]->output(); // polymorphic output
```

This loop works the same for any mix of objects dynamically created from the input, and it works the same whether **n** is 3 or 3,000,000.

## EXERCISES

1. Remove all occurrences of **virtual** from the sample application, recompile, and run the program using the same input file as before. What happens when the input and output methods are not **virtual**?

2. Our application uses the class method **readInput** to handle such basic input tasks as opening the file and creating objects to hold data in the input file. Why is a class method more appropriate than a top-level function for these tasks?

## 5.3 NAME OVERLOADING, NAME OVERRIDING, AND NAME HIDING

We describe a function as *polymorphic* only if it is bound at *run time*. In C++, only **virtual** methods are bound at run time; hence, only **virtual** methods are truly polymorphic. C++ has constructs that *resemble* run-time binding but are quite distinct from it. Accordingly, we use this section to distinguish sharply between compile-time and run-time constructs in C++.

### Name Overloading

Top-level functions can share a name if they have different signatures. Methods in the same class can share a name if they have different signatures. In either case, this is known as *name overloading*. Name overloading always involves *compile-time* binding, regardless of whether methods or top-level functions are involved.

**EXAMPLE 5.3.1.** In the code segment

```
class C {
public:
   C() { /*...*/ }          // default constructor
   C( int x ) { /*...*/ }   // convert constructor
};
void f( double d ) { /*...*/ }
void f( char c ) { /*...*/ }
int main() {
   C c1;          // default constructor called
   C c2( 26 ); // convert constructor called
   f( 3.14 );  // f( double ) called
   f( 'Z' );   // f( char ) called
   //...
}
```

there are two top-level functions named **f** and two constructors named **c**. Invocations of all four functions involve *compile-time* binding. The compiler uses the *signatures* to do the bindings. Because **c1** is created with no initial value, the compiler invokes the default constructor. Because **c2** is created with an initial integer value, the compiler invokes the convert constructor.

In similar fashion, the compiler binds the invocation

```
f( 3.14 );
```

to the function named **f** that expects a single **double** argument. The compiler binds the invocation

```
f( 'Z' );
```

to the function named **f** that expects a single **char** argument.                ■

Compile-time binding is always at work in name overloading. In this respect, over-loaded functions—whether methods or top-level functions—differ sharply from **virtual** methods, which are bound at run-time.

## Name Overriding

Suppose that base class **B** has a method **m** and its derived class **D** also has a method **m** with the *same* signature. If the methods are **virtual**, run-time binding is at work in any invocation of **m** through pointers or references. If the methods are **virtual**, the derived class method **D::m** *overrides* the base class method **B::m**. If the methods are *not* **virtual**, compile-time binding is at work in *any* invocation of **m**.

**EXAMPLE 5.3.2.** The output for the code segment

```
#include <iostream>
using namespace std;
class B {  // base class
public:
  void m() { cout << "B::m" << endl; }
};
class D : public B { // derived class
public:
  void m() { cout << "D::m" << endl; }
};
int main() {
  B* p;        // pointer to base class
  p = new D; // create a D object
  p->m();      // invoke m
  return 0;
}
```

is

```
B::m
```

Note that **p** points to a **D** object, not to a **B** object. Further, **p** is used to invoke **m**. This *looks* like run-time binding, but it is not because **m** is not **virtual**—and only **virtual** methods are bound at run time in C++. The compiler uses **p**'s data type **B\*** to bind the call to **B::m**. Recall that **D** inherits **m** from **B**. It just so happens that **D** has a *local* method named **m** with the same signature as the *inherited* method **m**. The compiler uses **p**'s data type to bind the call

```
p->m();
```

to the *inherited* **m**. The call is thus shorthand for

```
p->B::m();
```

**EXAMPLE 5.3.3.** We amend the program in Figure 5.1.1 by removing the keyword **virtual** and making no other changes (see Figure 5.3.1).

```
#include <iostream>
using namespace std;
class TradesPerson { // base class
public:
   void sayHi() { cout << "Just hi." << endl; }
};
class Tinker : public TradesPerson { // derived class 1
public:
   void sayHi() { cout << "Hi, I tinker." << endl; }
};
class Tailor : public TradesPerson { // derived class 2
public:
   void sayHi() { cout << "Hi, I tailor." << endl; }
};

int main() {
   TradesPerson* p; // pointer to base class
   int which;
   // prompt user for a number:
   // *** 1 == TradesPerson
   //     2 == Tinker
   //     3 == Tailor
   do {
     cout << "1 == TradesPerson, 2 == Tinker, 3 == Tailor ";
     cin >> which;
   } while ( which < 1 || which > 3 );
   // set pointer p depending on user choice
   switch ( which ) {
   case 1: p = new TradesPerson; break;
   case 2: p = new Tinker; break;
   case 3: p = new Tailor; break;
   }
   // invoke the sayHi method via the pointer
   p->sayHi(); //**** run-time binding in effect
   delete p;   //**** free the dynamically allocated storage
   return 0;
}
```

**FIGURE 5.3.1** Compile-time binding in the **TradesPerson** hierarchy.

The user again enters an integer used in a **switch** statement to create a single object: a **TradesPerson** object if the user enters 1, a **Tinker** object if the user enters 2, and a **Tailor** object if the user enters 3. Pointer **p** holds the address of the dynamically created object, and **p** is used to invoke the object's **sayHi** method:

```
p->sayHi();
```

Regardless of whether **p** points to a **TradesPerson** object, a **Tinker** object, or a **Tailor** object, **TradesPerson::sayHi** is always invoked and, therefore, the output is always

```
Just hi.
```

Suppose, for example, that the user enters 2 for **Tinker**. In this case, the statement

```
p = new Tinker;
```

results in **p**'s pointing to a dynamically created **Tinker** object. Then the function call

```
p->sayHi();
```

executes. Because **sayHi** is *not* **virtual**, *compile-time* binding is in effect. Because **p**'s data type is **TradesPerson\***, the compiler binds the call

```
p->sayHi();
```

to **TradesPerson::sayHi**. Note that **Tinker** has **TradesPerson** as its base class; hence, **Tinker** inherits **TradesPerson::sayHi** so that the **Tinker** object to which **p** points has a **TradesPerson::sayHi** method in addition to its **Tinker::sayHi**. If **sayHi** were a **virtual** method as in Figure 5.1.2, then *run-time* binding would be in effect. At run time, the system would determine *the type of object* to which **p** points and would then invoke that object's **sayHi** method, in our case **Tinker**'s **sayHi** method. In our current example, compile-time binding is at work; so the compiler determines which **sayHi** to invoke by using **p**'s data type **TradesPerson\***. As a result, **TradesPerson::sayHi** is invoked even if **p** points to a **Tinker** object. ∎

## Name Hiding

Suppose that base class **B** has a non**virtual** method **m** and its derived class **D** also has a method **m**. **D**'s local method **D::m** is said to *hide* the inherited method **B::m**. Name hiding is particularly tricky if the derived class's method has a *different signature* than the base class's method of the same name.

**EXAMPLE 5.3.4.**   The program

```
#include <iostream>
using namespace std;
class B {
public:
    void m( int x ) { cout << x << endl; }
};

class D : public B {
public:
    void m() { cout << "Hi" << endl; }
};
```

```
int main() {
    D d1;
    d1.m();     // OK: D::m expects no arguments
    d1.m( 26 ); //***** ERROR: D::m expects no arguments
    return 0;
}
```

generates a fatal compile-time error because it tries to invoke **D**'s method **m** with a single argument. **D**'s base class **B** does have a method **m** that expects a single argument, and **D** inherits this method. The problem is that **D** has a method *with the same name*. Therefore, the local **D::m** *hides* the inherited **B::m**. To invoke the inherited **m** with an argument, we must amend the code to

```
d1.B::m( 26 ); // OK: explicitly call B::m
```

Name hiding can occur with **virtual** as well as non**virtual** methods. In effect, name hiding occurs with **virtual** methods whenever a derived class **virtual** method fails to override the base class **virtual** method.

**EXAMPLE 5.3.5.**   The program

```
#include <iostream>
using namespace std;
class B {
public:
    virtual void m( int x ) { cout << x << endl; }
};
class D : public B {
public:
    virtual void m() { cout << "Hi" << endl; }
};
int main() {
    D d1;
    d1.m();
    d1.m( 26 ); //***** ERROR: D's m takes no arguments
    return 0;
}
```

generates a fatal compile-time error. **D**'s local method **D::m**, which happens to be **virtual**, expects no arguments. **D** does inherit a **virtual** method **B::m**, and the inherited **B::m** does expect one argument. The problem is that **D**'s local **D::m** hides the inherited **B::m**. That the two methods happen to be **virtual** is irrelevant to the name hiding. One fix is to invoke the inherited **B::m** explicitly

```
d1.B::m( 26 ); // OK: B::m explicitly invoked
```

This solves the problem but represents bad programming practice. For polymorphism to occur, **B::m** and **D::m** must have the *same signature*, not just the same name.

Finally, it should be emphasized that the two **m**'s are *unrelated*, although each happens to be **virtual**. For polymorphism to occur with respect to base class **B** and derived class **D**, there must be a **virtual** method *with the same signature* in each class. In this example, the two **m**'s have two different signatures. Method **D::m** does *not* override **B::m** because **D::m** has a different signature. Instead, we have two unrelated **virtual** methods named **m**. ■

## Name Sharing in C++ Programming

The examples in this section illustrate some problems that can arise if functions share a name. Nonetheless, it is sometimes desirable for functions to share a name. The obvious cases are

- Top-level functions with overloaded names. This is a convenience to programmers, who then can use one name such as **print** to invoke many different **print** functions, that is, many functions whose *signatures* differ but whose name happens to be **print**. It is quite common to overload operators such as **<<** as top-level functions (see Chapter 6).

- Constructors with overloaded names. A class often has more than one constructor, which requires name overloading for the constructors.

- Nonconstructor methods of the same class with the same name. A class **C**, for example, might have three **print** methods for convenience. The motivation here is the same as in overloading top-level functions.

- Methods, especially **virtual** ones, in a hierarchy. For polymorphism to occur, the **virtual** methods must have the *same signature* and, therefore, the same name. In typical polymorphism, a derived class's local **virtual** method *overrides* a **virtual** method inherited from the base class. For overriding to occur, the methods must be **virtual** and have the *same signature*.

When functions in a hierarchy share a name but *not* a signature, name hiding becomes a danger. So we recommend that this type of name sharing be used with great caution, if at all.

---

### EXERCISES

1. Give an example of name overloading for top-level functions.

2. Given an example of name overloading for class constructors.

3. Is compile-time binding or run-time binding at work in name overloading?

4. Give an example of name hiding for non**virtual** methods.

5. Is compile-time binding or run-time binding at work in name sharing for non**virtual** methods?

6. Give an example of name overriding for **virtual** methods.

7. Is compile-time binding or run-time binding at work in name overriding for **virtual** methods?

**8.** Give an example of name hiding.

In Exercises 9 through 13, find all the errors, if any, and explain what is wrong. If there are no errors, show what is output.

**9.**
```cpp
#include <iostream>
using namespace std;
class A {  // base class
public:
  void m() { cout << "A::m" << endl; }
};
class Z : public A { // derived class
public:
  void m() { cout << "Z::m" << endl; }
};
int main() {
  A* p;
  p = new Z;
  p->m();
  return 0;
}
```

**10.**
```cpp
#include <iostream>
using namespace std;
class A {  // base class
public:
  virtual void m() { cout << "A::m" << endl; }
};
class Z : public A { // derived class
public:
  void m() { cout << "Z::m" << endl; }
};
int main() {
  A* p;
  p = new Z;
  p->m();
  return 0;
}
```

**11.**
```cpp
#include <iostream>
using namespace std;
class A {
public:
  virtual void m( double d ) { cout << d << endl; }
};
class Z : public A {
public:
  virtual void m() { cout << "foo" << endl; }
};
```

```cpp
int main() {
   A a1;
   a1.m();
   a1.m( 3.14 );
   return 0;
}
```

12. 
```cpp
#include <iostream>
using namespace std;
class A {
public:
   virtual void m( double d ) { cout << d << endl; }
};
class Z : public A {
public:
   virtual void m() { cout << "foo" << endl; }
};
int main() {
   A* p = new A;
   p->m();
   p->m( 3.14 );
   return 0;
}
```

13. 
```cpp
#include <iostream>
using namespace std;
class A {
public:
   virtual void m( int x ) { cout << x << endl; }
};
class Z : public A {
public:
   virtual void m() { cout << "baz" << endl; }
};
int main() {
   Z z1;
   z1.m();
   z1.A::m( 26 );
   return 0;
}
```

## 5.4 ABSTRACT BASE CLASSES

Consider the inheritance hierarchy

```
class B { // base class
public:
  virtual void m() { /*...*/ } // define m
};
class D1 : public B { // derived class
public:
  //... m could be--but need not be--overridden
};
class D2 : public B { // derived class
public:
  //... m could be--but need not be--overridden
};
```

with a base class **B** and two derived classes, **D1** and **D2**. The base class has a **virtual** method **m** that each derived class can override. Yet the derived classes **D1** and **D2** are *not required* to override method **m**. In object-oriented design, it is sometimes desirable to specify methods that classes such as **D1** and **D2** should define. Further, it is helpful if the language itself provides a construct to enforce this design decision.

A **shared interface** is a collection of methods that different classes must define, with each class defining the methods in ways appropriate to it (see Sections 1.2 and 1.4). Recall our example of a hierarchy with **Window** as a base class that represents a basic window and various derived classes such as **MenuWindow** that represent window subtypes (see Section 1.4). Suppose that the hierarchy's designer wants to ensure that each class in the hierarchy defines methods such as **display**, **close**, and **move**. C++'s **abstract base class** can be used to specify methods that any derived class must define if the class is to have objects instantiate it. An abstract base class thus can be used to specify a shared interface. An abstract base class has other uses as well. We begin with the syntax.

### Abstract Base Classes and Pure **virtual** Methods

An abstract base class is *abstract* in that no objects can instantiate it. Such a class can be used to specify **virtual** methods that any derived class *must* override in order to have objects instantiate the derived class. A class must meet one requirement to be an abstract base class:

- The class must have a **pure virtual** method.

A pure **virtual** method is one whose declaration ends with the special syntax **=0**.

> **EXAMPLE 5.4.1.** The code segment
>
> ```
> class ABC {  // Abstract Base Class
> public:
>   virtual void open() = 0;
> };
> ```

illustrates the special syntax used to declare a *pure* **virtual** method. The class declaration is for an abstract base class named **ABC** that has a single method, the pure **virtual** method named **open**. By making **open** pure **virtual**, we thereby make **ABC** an abstract base class. ∎

**EXAMPLE 5.4.2.** Given the definition for the abstract base class in Example 5.4.1, it is an error to define objects of type **ABC**:

```
class ABC {  // Abstract Base Class
public:
   virtual void open() = 0;
};
ABC obj; //***** ERROR: ABC is an abstract class
```
∎

Although an abstract base class cannot have objects instantiate it, such a class can have derived classes. A class derived from an abstract base class *must* override all of the base class's *pure* **virtual** methods; otherwise, the derived class itself becomes abstract and no objects can instantiate the derived class.

**EXAMPLE 5.4.3.** We derive two classes from the abstract base class **ABC** in Example 5.4.1:

```
class ABC { // Abstract Base Class
public:
   virtual void open() = 0;
};
class X : public ABC { // 1st derived class
public:
   virtual void open() { /*...*/ } // override open()
};
class Y : public ABC { // 2nd derived class
   //*** open is not overridden
};
ABC a1;  //***** ERROR: ABC is abstract
X   x1;  //***** Ok, X overrides open() and is not abstract
Y   y1;  //***** ERROR: Y is abstract--open() not defined
```

Class **X** overrides the pure **virtual** method inherited from the abstract base class **ABC**. Therefore, **X** is not abstract and may have objects instantiate it. By contrast, **Y** does not override the pure **virtual** method inherited from **ABC**. Therefore, **Y** becomes an abstract base class and cannot have objects instantiate it. ∎

One pure **virtual** method suffices to make a class an abstract base class. An abstract base class may have other methods that are not pure **virtual** or not even **virtual** at all. Further, an abstract base class may have data members. An abstract base class's members may be **private**, **protected**, or **public**.

**EXAMPLE 5.4.4.**   We amend Example 5.4.1

```
class ABC { // Abstract Base Class
public:
   ABC() { /*...*/ }                        // default constructor
   ABC( int x ) { /*...*/ }                 // convert constructor
   ~ABC() { /*...*/ }                        // destructor
   virtual void open() = 0;                  // pure virtual
   virtual void print() const { /*...*/ } // virtual
   int getCount() const { return n; }      // nonvirtual
private:
   int n; // data member
};
```

by having a mix of methods in **ABC** and by adding a data member. **ABC** remains abstract, however, because it still has the pure **virtual** method **open**. Therefore, no objects can instantiate **ABC**. Any class derived from **ABC** still must override **open** if the derived class is not to become abstract itself. However, a derived class can simply use the inherited versions of **print** and **getCount**.   ■

## Restrictions on Pure Functions

Only a **virtual** method can be pure. Neither a non**virtual** nor a top-level function can be declared pure **virtual**.

**EXAMPLE 5.4.5.**   The code segment

```
void f() = 0; //***** ERROR: not a virtual method
class C {
public:
   void open() = 0; //***** ERROR: not a virtual method
};
```

contains two errors because **f** is not a method at all and **open** is not a **virtual** method. Therefore, neither **f** nor **open** can be declared pure **virtual**.   ■

## Uses of Abstract Base Classes

Abstract base classes are useful for specifying pure **virtual** methods that any derived class must override in order to have objects instantiate the derived class. In this use, an abstract base class specifies a shared interface. The interface is shared by all classes derived from the abstract base class.

**EXAMPLE 5.4.6.**   In the inheritance hierarchy of Figure 5.4.1, the abstract base class **BasicFile** specifies three pure **virtual** methods that any derived class must override if the derived class is not to be abstract. Classes **InFile** and **OutFile** are derived from **BasicFile** and, in this sense, share the interface that **BasicFile** specifies as three pure **virtual** methods. The two derived classes define all three pure **virtual** methods declared in **BasicFile**, presumably in ways that are appropriate to each derived class.   ■

```
class BasicFile {   // Abstract Base Class
public:
  // methods that any derived class should override
  virtual void open() = 0;
  virtual void close() = 0;
  virtual void flush() = 0;
};
class InFile : public BasicFile {
public:
  virtual void open() { /*...*/ }   // definition
  virtual void close() { /*...*/ }  // definition
  virtual void flush() { /*...*/ }  // definition
};
class OutFile : public BasicFile {
public:
  virtual void open() { /*...*/ }   // definition
  virtual void close() { /*...*/ }  // definition
  virtual void flush() { /*...*/ }  // definition
};
```

**FIGURE 5.4.1** An abstract base class that specifies an interface shared by two derived classes.

Abstract base classes can be used to specify design requirements. For example, suppose that we are working on a large project involving many programmers, each of whom is responsible for several classes. During the project's design phase, we decide that each class should have two **public** methods: **listFields** lists the class's data members and data types and prints a brief explanation of the data member's role in the class, and **listMethods** lists the class's methods and prints a brief explanation of the functionality that the method provides. To enforce this design decision, we provide an abstract base class

```
class IIntrospect { // introspection interface
public:
  virtual void listFields() = 0;
  virtual void listMethods() = 0;
};
```

and require that *all* classes in the project be derived from **IIntrospect**. Any class derived from **IIntrospect** must override the two pure **virtual** methods in order to have objects instantiate it. In this way, we ensure that objects used in the project will have the methods **listFields** and **listMethods**. We pursue the point with a commercial example. By the way, because an abstract base class often has only **public** methods as members, it is common to use the keyword **struct** to declare an abstract base class.

## Microsoft's **IUnknown** Interface

Microsoft's COM (**C**omponent **O**bject **M**odel) is an infrastructure for assembling applications from prebuilt software components (see Chapter 9). For example, Microsoft itself provides a *Calendar* component that has an intuitive graphical interface for entering dates. This component might be plugged into an application that requires a user to enter, for example, a birth date. The user would enter a date on the calendar and then push a button to complete the operation. Under COM, a component must implement at least one interface, which is a list of functions that the component supports. At the C++ level, a COM interface is an abstract base class with pure **virtual** methods that the component must override. For example, Microsoft's calendar control implements an interface that includes functions such as **GetMonth** and **GetYear**, which can be used to get integer values that represent a date's month and year, respectively. COM requires that every interface be derived from **IUnknown**, a C++ abstract base class with three pure **virtual** methods:

- **QueryInterface**. This function supports navigation among multiple COM interfaces. Suppose that component *C* (e.g., the calendar) has two interfaces, *I1* and *I2*. For application *A* to use *C*, *A* must have access to one of the interfaces. Suppose that *A* has access to *I1*. Because *I1* must be derived from **IUnknown**, and because *C* implements *I1*, *A* can use the implementation of **QueryInterface**, as specified in *I1*, to gain access to *C*'s other interface, in this case *I2*. In general, **QueryInterface** allows a component's client to move among the component's interfaces, if the component supports multiple interfaces. Many COM components do implement multiple interfaces.
- **AddRef**. A key principle of component software is that a component's client (that is, an application using the component) should not be able to halt the component's execution. Instead, the component itself should keep a *count* of its clients and halt its own execution when the count is zero. This approach is known as **reference counting**. A COM component implements **AddRef** so that a client can increment the component's reference count. If the count ever equals zero, the component itself terminates its execution.
- **Release**. A component's client invokes this method to decrement the component's reference count.

Because COM components must implement at least one interface, and because *every* interface must be derived from **IUnknown**, every COM component must implement the three pure **virtual** methods in **IUnknown**. COM has other standard interfaces as well. To become proficient in COM is to become fluent in COM interfaces, that is, in the pure **virtual** methods specified in COM's abstract base classes.

## EXERCISES

1. What condition must a class meet to be an abstract base class?
2. Explain the error:

```
class A {
public:
   virtual void m() = 0;
private:
   int x;
};
A a1;
```

**3.** Explain the error:

```
class A {
public:
   void m() = 0;
private:
   int x;
};
```

**4.** Must every method in an abstract base class be pure **virtual**?

**5.** Explain the error:

```
struct A {
   virtual void m1() = 0;
   virtual void m2() = 0;
};
class Z : public A {
public:
   void m1() { cout << "Hi!" << endl; }
};
Z z1;
```

**6.** Suppose that **ABC** is an abstract base class and **z** is derived from it. What condition must **z** satisfy to be a nonabstract class, that is, a class that can have objects instantiate it?

**7.** Can an abstract base class have non**virtual** methods?

**8.** Can an abstract base class have data members?

## 5.5 RUN-TIME TYPE IDENTIFICATION

C++ supports **run-time type identification** (RTTI), which provides mechanisms to

- Check type conversions at run time.
- Determine an object's type at run time.
- Extend the RTTI provided by C++.

These mechanisms represent powerful and relatively advanced features of C++. We examine each of them in its own subsection.

### The `dynamic_cast` Operator

In C++ a legal *compile-time* cast still may result in a *run-time* error. This danger may be particularly acute when a cast involves pointers or references to *objects*. The **dynamic_cast** operator can be used to test, *at run time*, when a cast involving objects is problematic. We motivate the **dynamic_cast** operator and explain its syntax through a series of examples.

**EXAMPLE 5.5.1.**  Although a pointer to a *base class* can point, without explicit casting, to either a base class or a derived class object, the situation is quite different with a pointer to a *derived* class. In general, it is a bad idea for a derived class pointer to point to a base class object. Nonetheless, this can be done with *explicit* casting. In the code segment

```
class B {
  //...
};
class D : public B {
  //...
};
int main() {
  /* 1 */ D* p;        //*** pointer to derived class
  /* 2 */ p = new B; //***** ERROR: explicit cast needed
  /* 3 */ p = static_cast< D* >( new B ); // caution!
  //...
}
```

**p** is of type **D***, that is, a pointer to a derived class. It is therefore an error, in line 2, for **p** to point—without explicit casting—to a base class object. In line 3, we use a **static_cast** so that **p** can point to an object of the base class **B**.  ■

The **static_cast** in Example 5.5.1 is legal but dangerous. In particular, the cast may lead to a run-time error.

**EXAMPLE 5.5.2.**  We amend Example 5.5.1

```
class B {
public:
  void f() { } // Note: no method m
};
class D : public B {
public:
  void m() { } // not in base class
};
int main() {
  D* p;        //*** pointer to derived class
  p = static_cast< D* >( new B ); // caution!
  p->m(); //***** ERROR: there is no B::m!
  //...
}
```

by adding a method **m** to the derived class **D**. Base class **B** does *not* have a method named **m**. In **main**, the **static_cast** again allows **p** to point to a **B** object. There is no *compile-time* error from the method invocation

```
p->m();
```

because **p** is of type **D\*** and class **D** has the required method **m**. Nonetheless, a *run-time* error results because **p** points to a **B** object—that is, to an object that has no method **m**.

■

We can summarize the problem illustrated in Example 5.5.2 by saying that the **static_cast** does not ensure **type safety**. The cast is not type safe because the method invocation

```
p->m();
```

generates a run-time error, although it is syntactically legal. In more technical terms, **p**'s *declared* data type of **D\*** implies that **p** can be used to invoke the method **D::m**. The problem is that, at run time, **p** happens to point to a **B** object, which has no method **m**.

C++ provides the **dynamic_cast** operator to check, at run time, whether a cast is type safe. A **dynamic_cast** has the same basic syntax as a **static_cast**. However, a **dynamic_cast** is legal only on a **polymorphic type**, that is, on a class that has at least one **virtual** method.

**EXAMPLE 5.5.3.**  The code segment

```
class C {
  //... C has no virtual methods
};
class T {
  //...
};
int main() {
   dynamic_cast< T* >( new C ); //***** ERROR
   //...
}
```

contains an error because it applies a **dynamic_cast** to the nonpolymorphic type **C**. **C** is nonpolymorphic because it has no **virtual** methods. In the cast, it is irrelevant whether the *target* type **T** is polymorphic. The requirement is that the *source* type be polymorphic. We can eliminate the error by changing **C**'s declaration to

```
class C {
public:
   virtual void m() { }; //*** C is now polymorphic
};
```

■

The *target type* of a **dynamic_cast**, which is specified in angle brackets, must be a pointer or a reference. If **T** is a class, then **T\*** and **T&** are legal targets for a **dynamic_cast**, but **T** is not.

**EXAMPLE 5.5.4.**   The code segment

```
class A { // polymorphic type
  //... A has a virtual method
};
class T { // target class
  //...
};
int main() {
   A a1;
   dynamic_cast< T >( a1 ); //***** ERROR
   //...
}
```

contains an error because the target type is **T** rather than, for example, **T\*** or **T&**.   ■

**EXAMPLE 5.5.5.**   We now amend Example 5.5.2 by checking at run time whether it is safe for a **D\*** pointer to point to a **B** object. We add a **virtual** method to **B** to make the class a polymorphic type and, therefore, eligible for a **dynamic_cast**. In the code segment

```
class B {
public:
  virtual void f() { } // Note: no method m
};
class D : public B {
public:
  void m() { } // not in base class
};
int main() {
  D* p =  dynamic_cast< D* >( new B );
  if ( p ) // is the cast type-safe?
    p->m(); // if so, invoke p->m()
  else
    cerr << "Not safe for p to point to a B" << endl;
  //...
}
```

we initialize **p**, of type **D\***, to the value of a **dynamic_cast**. If **T** is a type and **Ptr** is a pointer to a polymorphic type, then the expression

```
dynamic_cast< T* >( Ptr )
```

evaluates to **Ptr**, if the cast is type safe, and to zero (**false**), if the cast is not type safe. In our example, the cast source is the expression **new B**, which evaluates to a non-**NULL** address if the **new** operation succeeds. So **p** would point to the dynamically allocated **B** object, if the **dynamic_cast** expression succeeded. If the cast expression failed, as it does in this case, then **p** is assigned **NULL** as its value.

The **dynamic_cast** evaluates to **NULL** (**false**) precisely because we are trying to have the *derived class* pointer **p** point to the *base class* object created by **new B**. By checking the result of the **dynamic_cast** in the **if** statement, we avoid the run-time error of Example 5.5.2. ∎

**EXAMPLE 5.5.6.**   The program in Figure 5.5.1 illustrates how a **dynamic_cast** might be used to determine at run time a parameter's data type. The function **printBookInfo** expects a pointer to the polymorphic type **Book**, which happens to be the base class of an inheritance hierarchy. **Textbook** is a derived class with a **printLevel** method that does *not* occur in either the base class or the other derived class, **PulpFiction**. After printing a **Book**'s title, **printBookInfo** uses a **dynamic_cast** to determine whether the parameter indeed points to a **Textbook**. If so, the **Textbook**'s level is printed. ∎

```
#include <iostream>
#include <string>
using namespace std;
class Book { // polymorphic type
public:
   Book( string t ) { title = t; }
   virtual void printTitle() const {
      cout << "Title: " << title << endl; }
private:
   Book(); // title required
   string title;
};
class Textbook : public Book {
public:
   Textbook( string t, int l ) : Book( t ), level( l ) { }
   void printTitle() const {
      cout << "Textbook ";
      Book::printTitle(); // defer to base class
   }
   void printLevel() const {
      cout << "Book level: " << level << endl; }
private:
   Textbook(); // title and level required
   int level;
};
```

**FIGURE 5.5.1** A program to illustrate a run-time check for type safety.

```
class PulpFiction : public Book {
public:
   PulpFiction( string t ) : Book( t ) { }
   void printTitle() const {
      cout << "Pulp ";
      Book::printTitle();
   }
private:
   PulpFiction(); // title required
};
void printBookInfo( Book* );
int main() {
   Book* ptr;
   int level;
   string title;
   int ans;
   cout << "Book's title? (no white space) ";
   cin >> title;
   do {
     cout << "1 == Textbook, 2 == PulpFiction " << endl;
     cin >> ans;
   } while ( ans < 1 || ans > 2 );
   if ( 1 == ans ) {
     cout << "Level? ";
     cin >> level;
     ptr = new Textbook( title, level );
   }
   else
     ptr = new PulpFiction( title );
   printBookInfo( ptr );
   return 0;
}
void printBookInfo( Book* bookPtr ) {
  bookPtr->printTitle(); // print title in any case
  Textbook* ptr = dynamic_cast< Textbook* >( bookPtr );
  if ( ptr ) // true if bookPtr points to a Textbook
    ptr->printLevel(); // type safe: ptr of type Textbook*
}
```

**FIGURE 5.5.1** Continued.

The program in Figure 5.5.1 can be improved by using polymorphism directly to print a **Textbook**'s level. If we revise **Textbook**'s declaration to

```
class Textbook : public Book {
public:
   Textbook( string t, int l ) : Book( t ), level( l ) { }
```

```
    void printTitle() const {
        cout << "Textbook ";
        Book::printTitle(); // defer to base class
        printLevel(); //**** invoke printLevel here
    }
    void printLevel() const {
        cout << "Book level: " << level << endl; }
private:
    Textbook(); // title and level required
    int level;
};
```

then **printBookInfo** can be simplified to

```
void printBookInfo( Book* bookPtr ) {
    bookPtr->printTitle(); // do it polymorphically
}
```

In general, polymorphism should be preferred over **dynamic_cast**s whenever either approach is possible. ∎

If the **Book-Textbook-PulpFiction** hierarchy were supplied by a vendor as part of a class library in binary form, we could not modify the underlying source code so that we then could use polymorphism instead of **dynamic_cast**s in our own code. In this case, making the program in Figure 5.5.1 type safe requires us to use constructs such as the **dynamic_cast**.

## The Rules for **dynamic_cast**s

The rules for **dynamic_cast**s are complex, especially in cases that involve multiple inheritance or casts to and from the type **void***. Here we examine the basic cases and, for simplicity, we express the rules in terms of pointers rather than references. In a single inheritance hierarchy, suppose that base class **B** is a polymorphic type and class **D** is derived from **B** directly or indirectly. Class **D** is also a polymorphic type through inheritance. In this case,

- The **dynamic_cast** from derived type **D*** to base type **B*** succeeds. This is known as an **upcast**.
- The **dynamic_cast** from base type **B*** to derived type **D*** fails. This is known as a **downcast**.

Now suppose that classes **A** and **Z** are polymorphic types but unrelated in that they do not occur in the same inheritance hierarchy. In this case,

- A **dynamic_cast** from **A*** to **Z*** fails.
- A **dynamic_cast** from **Z*** to **A*** fails.

In general, then, a dynamic upcast succeeds, whereas a dynamic downcast fails. Dynamic casts involving unrelated types other than **void*** also fail.

## Summary of `dynamic_cast` and `static_cast`

C++ provides different casts for different purposes. A **static_cast** can be applied to *any* type, polymorphic or not. A **dynamic_cast** can be applied only to a polymorphic type, and the target type of a **dynamic_cast** must be a pointer or a reference. In these respects, a **static_cast** is more basic and general than a **dynamic_cast**. However, only a **dynamic_cast** can be used to check at *run time* whether a conversion is type safe. In this respect, a **dynamic_cast** is more powerful than a **static_cast**.

## The `typeid` Operator

The **typeid** operator, which requires the header *typeinfo*, can be used to determine an expression's type. For instance, this operator can be used with C++'s built-in data types.

> **EXAMPLE 5.5.7.**  Given the definitions
>
> ```
> float x;
> long val;
> ```
>
> Figure 5.5.2 shows the values of several expressions that use the **typeid** operator.
> ■

| *Expression* | *Value* |
|---|---|
| `typeid( x ) == typeid( float )` | true |
| `typeid( x ) == typeid( double )` | false |
| `typeid( x ) == typeid( float* )` | false |
| `typeid( val ) == typeid( long )` | true |
| `typeid( val ) == typeid( short )` | false |
| `typeid( 5280 ) == typeid( int )` | true |
| `typeid( 9.218836E-9L ) == typeid( long double )` | true |

**FIGURE 5.5.2** Using the **typeid** operator to test built-in types.

The **typeid** operator returns a reference to an object in the system class **type_info** that describes a type. This operator may be applied either to type names, including class names, or to arbitrary C++ expressions. For example, in Figure 5.5.2 we apply the **typeid** operator to the built-in type name **float** and to the integer expression **5280**. In general, the **typeid** operator is invoked as

> **typeid(** *typename* **)**

or

> **typeid(** *expression* **)**

If the **typeid** operator is applied to the type *typename*, **typeid** returns a reference to a **type_info** object that represents *typename*. For example, if the **typeid** operator is applied to the class type **Task**, the operator returns a reference to a **type_info** object that represents a **Task**. If the **typeid** operator is applied to the expression *expression*, **typeid** returns a reference to a **type_info** object that represents the *expression*'s type. For example, if the **typeid** operator is applied to the **int** expression **5280**, the operator returns a reference to a **type_info** object that represents an **int**. The programmer does *not* need to know the details of the return type to use the **typeid** operator to compare types, as Figure 5.5.2 illustrates.

**EXAMPLE 5.5.8.** Given the **Book** hierarchy of Figure 5.5.1 and the definition

```
Book* bookPtr = new Textbook( "test", 1 );
```

Figure 5.5.3 shows the values of several more expressions that use the **typeid** operator.

| Expression | Value |
|---|---|
| typeid( bookPtr ) == typeid( Book* ) | true |
| typeid( *bookPtr ) == typeid( Book ) | false |
| typeid( bookPtr ) == typeid( Textbook* ) | false |
| typeid( *bookPtr ) == typeid( Textbook ) | true |

**FIGURE 5.5.3** Using the **typeid** operator to test class types.

The expressions in the figure require clarification. The value of the expression

```
typeid( bookPtr )
```

represents the type (**Book***) *declared* for **bookPtr**, *not* the type of object (**Textbook**) to which **bookPtr** points. For this reason, the first expression is true and the third expression is false. By contrast, the value of the expression

```
typeid( *bookPtr )
```

represents the type of object (**Textbook**) to which **bookPtr** points, *not* the declared data type of **bookPtr**. For this reason, the second expression is false and the last expression is true.

Recall that the base class **Book** is a polymorphic type and **bookPtr** is a pointer to that type. Accordingly, the system uses ***bookPtr**'s *run-time* type in evaluating the expression

```
typeid( *bookPtr ) == typeid( Textbook )
```

Because **bookPtr** indeed points to a **Textbook** object, the expression is true.

If **Book** were *not* a polymorphic type, the system would use **bookPtr**'s declared or *compile-time* type of **Book*** in evaluating the expression, which then would be false. In this case, the expression

```
typeid( *bookPtr ) == typeid( Book )
```

would be true despite the fact that **bookPtr** points to a **Textbook** object. ∎

## Extending RTTI

The programmer can extend C++'s run-time type identification. To do so, the programmer derives classes from the standard base class **type_info**, whose declaration occurs in the header *typeinfo*.

### EXERCISES

1. Explain the error:

```
class A {
public:
  void f() { }
};
class C {
public:
  void m() { }
};
int main() {
   A* p;
   p = dynamic_cast< A* >( new C );
   //...
}
```

2. Explain the error:

```
class A {
public:
  void f() { }
};
class C {
public:
  virtual void m() { }
};
int main() {
   A a1;
   C c1;
   a1 = dynamic_cast< A >( c1 );
   //...
}
```

3. What is a *polymorphic type*?

4. May a **static_cast** be applied to a nonpolymorphic type?

5. May a **dynamic_cast** be applied to a nonpolymorphic type?

6. Must the target type of a **static_cast** be a pointer or a reference?

7. Must the target type of a **dynamic_cast** be a pointer or a reference?

8. Must the target type of a **dynamic_cast** be a polymorphic type?

9. Explain when a cast is not *type safe*.

10. Give an example of a syntactically legal cast that is not type safe.

11. Can a **static_cast** be used at run time to ensure type safety?

12. Can the **typeid** operator be applied to built-in types?

13. Must the **typeid** operator be applied to polymorphic types?

The following exercises assume the class declarations

```
class B {
public:
   void b() { }
};
class C : public B {
public:
   void m() { }
};
class J : public B {
public:
   virtual void m() { }
};
```

and the definitions

```
B* p = new C;
B* q = new J;
```

Indicate whether each of the following expressions is **true** or **false**.

14. **typeid( p ) == typeid( B )**

15. **typeid( p ) == typeid( B* )**

16. **typeid( q ) == typeid( B* )**

17. **typeid( *p ) == typeid( B )**

18. **typeid( *q ) == typeid( B )**

19. **typeid( *p ) == typeid( C )**

20. **typeid( *q ) == typeid( J )**

## C++ POSTSCRIPT

## Strong and Weak Polymorphism

Some authors distinguish in C++ between *strong* and *weak* polymorphism. In this case, *strong* polymorphism refers to the run-time binding of overridden **virtual** methods. *Weak* polymorphism has two forms: overloading of top-level functions or methods, and name sharing among non**virtual** methods in a hierarchy. We use *polymorphism* to describe only the run-time binding of overridden **virtual** methods. We use *overloading*, *name sharing*, and other terms to describe C++ constructs that may resemble run-time binding but which, in fact, involve only compile-time binding.

## COMMON PROGRAMMING ERRORS

**1.** It is an error to declare a top-level function **virtual**:

```
virtual bool f(); //***** ERROR: f is not a method
```

Only *methods* can be **virtual**.

**2.** It is an error to declare a **static** method **virtual**:

```
class C {
public:
   virtual void m();        // ok, object method
   virtual static void s(); //***** ERROR: static method
};
```

**3.** If a **virtual** method is *defined outside* the class declaration, then the keyword **virtual** occurs in its declaration but not in its definition:

```
class C {
public:
   virtual void m1() { /*...*/ } // ok, decl + def
   virtual void m2();            // ok, declaration
};

//***** ERROR: virtual should not occur in a definition
//             outside the class declaration
virtual void C::m2() {
   //...
}
```

**4.** It is an error to declare any constructor **virtual**, although the destructor may be **virtual**:

```
class C {
public:
   virtual C();      //***** ERROR: constructor
   virtual C( int ); //***** ERROR: constructor
   virtual ~C();     // ok, destructor
};
```

**5.** It is bad programming practice not to **delete** a dynamically created object *before* the object is inaccessible:

```
class C {
   //...
};
void f() {
   C* p = new C; // dynamically create a C object
   //...            use it
} //****** ERROR: should delete the object!
```

Once control exits **f**, the object to which **p** points can no longer be accessed. Therefore, storage for this object ought to be freed:

```
void f() {
   C* p = new C; // dynamically create a C object
   //...           use it
   delete p;      // delete it
}
```

6. If a method hides an inherited method, then it is an error to try to invoke the inherited method without using its full name:

```
class A {
public:
   void m( int ) { /*...*/ } // takes 1 arg
};
class Z : public A {
public:
   void m() { /*...*/ }      // takes 0 args, hides A::m
};
int main() {
  Z z1;
  z1.m( -999 );     //***** ERROR: Z::m hides A::m
  z1.A::m( -999 ); // ok, full name
  z1.m();           // ok, local method
  //...
}
```

The error remains even if **m** is **virtual** because **A::m** and **Z::m** do not have the same signature.

7. It is an error to expect run-time binding of non**virtual** methods. In the code segment

```
class A {
public:
  void m() { cout << "A::m" << endl; }
};
class Z : public A {
public:
  void m() { cout << "Z::m" << endl; }
};
int main() {
  A* p = new Z; // ok, p points to Z object
  p->m();         // prints A::m, not Z::m
  //...
}
```

**m** is *not* **virtual**. Because compile-time binding is in effect, the call

```
p->m();
```

is to `A::m` since `p`'s data type is `A*`. It is irrelevant that `p` happens to point to a `Z` object. If we make `m` a **virtual** method

```
class A {
public:
  virtual void m() { cout << "A::m" << endl; }
};
```

then the output is `Z::m` because *run-time* binding is in effect and `p` points to a `Z` object.

8. It is an error to expect a derived class **virtual** method `D::m` to override a base class **virtual** method `B::m` if the two methods have *different* signatures. The code segment

```
class A {
public:
  virtual void m(); // base class virtual method
};
class Z : public A {
public:
  //***** Caution: Z::m hides A::m
  virtual void m( int ); // derived class virtual method
};
```

has two **virtual** methods named `m`, but `Z::m` does *not* override `A::m` because the two methods have different signatures. For useful polymorphism to occur, the **virtual** methods must have the same *signature*, not just the same name. In this example, the two **virtual** methods are completely unrelated. They simply happen to share a name.

9. It is an error to try to define objects that instantiate an abstract base class:

```
class ABC { // abstract base class
public:
  virtual void m() = 0; // pure virtual method
};
ABC a1; //***** ERROR: ABC is abstract
```

10. If a class `C` is derived from an abstract base class `ABC` and `C` does not override *all* of `ABC`'s pure **virtual** methods, then `C` is abstract and cannot have objects instantiate it:

```
class ABC { // abstract base class
public:
  virtual void m1() = 0; // pure virtual method
  virtual void m2() = 0; // pure virtual method
};
class C : public ABC {
public:
  virtual void m1() { /*...*/ } // override m1
  //*** m2 not overridden
};
C c1; //***** ERROR: C is abstract
```

11. A **dynamic_cast** may be applied only to a polymorphic type, that is, a class with at least one **virtual** method. Therefore, the following code segment is in error:

```
class C {
  //... no virtual methods
};
int main() {
   //***** ERROR: C is not polymorphic
   dynamic_cast< void* >( new C );
   //...
```

12. The *target type* of a **dynamic_cast** (that is, the expression in angle brackets) must be a *pointer* or a *reference*. Therefore, the following code segment is in error:

```
class C {
public:
   virtual void m() { }
};
class A {
  //...
};
int main() {
   C c1;
   //***** ERROR: target type must a pointer or reference
   A a1 = dynamic_cast< A >( c1 );
   //...
}
```

13. It is an error to expect the **typeid** operator to perform *run-time* type checking on nonpolymorphic types. Given the declarations and definitions

```
class Base {
  //... no virtual methods
};
class D1 : public Base { // D1 is polymorphic
public:
   virtual void m() { }
};
class D2 : public Base { // D2 is not polymorphic
public:
   void f() { }
};
Base* d1Ptr = new D1;
Base* d2Ptr = new D2;
```

the expression

```
typeid( *d1Ptr ) == typeid( D1 ) // true
```

is **true** but the expression

```
typeid( *d2Ptr ) == typeid( D2 ) // false
```

is **false**. Because **D1** is polymorphic, the system does *run-time type checking* to determine the **typeid** of **\*d1Ptr**. By contrast, **D2** is not polymorphic. The system therefore does *compile-time type checking* to determine the **typeid** of **\*d2Ptr**. The compile-time type of **\*d2Ptr** is **Base**, not **D2**.

## PROGRAMMING EXERCISES

**5.1.** Derive an additional class **SongAndDance** from class **Film** of Section 5.2. Add appropriate data members and methods, including overrides of the **virtual** methods for input and output. Implement a test client to test the hierarchy and, in particular, the overrides.

**5.2.** Revise the **intArray** hierarchy of Programming Exercise 4.4 by making the **print** method **virtual**. After revising the classes, write a test client for the hierarchy.

**5.3.** Implement a hierarchy with **Date** as the base class with a **virtual** method **print**. Derived classes are **ShortE**, **MediumDate**, and **LongDate**. **Date**'s **print** uses the format

```
10-1-1950
```

where 10 is the month (October), 1 is the day of the month, and 50 is the year 1950. **ShortE**'s **print** uses the **E**uropean format

```
1-10-1950
```

**MediumDate**'s **print** uses the format

```
Oct. 1, 1950
```

and **LongDate**'s **print** uses the format

```
October 1, 1950
```

Write a test client for the **Date** hierarchy to test the implementations of **print**.

**5.4.** Revise the **CardGame** hierarchy of Programming Exercise 4.5 by making the **deal** method **virtual**. After revising the classes, write a test client for the hierarchy.

**5.5.** Implement an index hierarchy with a base class **Entry** to represent entries in a book's index. The base class represents a basic index entry such as

```
quark, 234, 512, 901
```

A basic entry consists of a term such as **quark** followed by the page numbers on which the word occurs. Here are samples of other entry types that should be included in the hierarchy:

```
//*** Sample: proper name followed by pages
Gauss, Carl, 67, 69, 106

//*** Sample: entry with multiple subentries
topology, 46, 78-80
   map-coloring problems, 45-47
   Mordell's conjecture, 107

//*** Sample: entry with descriptive subentry
music, harmony in, 37
```

The hierarchy should have a polymorphic **format** method that correctly formats a particular entry type as the entry is printed. Write a test client that has an array of pointers to the base class **Entry**, with each pointer pointing to a particular type of entry. The output code segment might look like this:

```
// print index entries, correctly formatted
for ( int i = 0; i < n; i++ )
   entries[ i ]->format();
```

**5.6.** Revise the **Emp**loyee hierarchy of Programming Exercise 4.11 by implementing polymorphic **input** and **output** methods to handle reading data into data members and printing data members to the standard output (see Section 5.2). Implement a test client for the hierarchy.

**5.7.** Many object-oriented systems support **persistence**, which saves an application's objects in nonvolatile storage (e.g., a disk file) when the application is not running. Persistence is typically implemented through either a database or **serialization**, which saves a binary representation of an object to a sequential file. The name *serialization* underscores that an object's binary representation is written to a file in serial fashion, that is, one bit after the other. Serialization saves the object's *type*, which is the class to which it belongs, together with its members' values. Saving an object to a file is *serializing out*, and restoring an object from a file is *serializing in*. Create a class hierarchy with **Object** as an abstract base class and **serialize** as a pure **virtual** method. Classes derived from **Object** override **serialize** so that their objects can be serialized out and in. *Hint*: Provide **Object** with a data member **classID**, which uniquely identifies a class. Each derived class's constructors are then responsible for setting its **classID**, which can be used to identify objects during serialization. In particular, when an object is serialized in, the first *n* bytes are its **classID**. Once the **classID** is known, a call to the **new** operator can be used to create an object of the corresponding type. Data members can be saved and restored as bytes rather than as C++ data types such as **float**, **int**, and so forth.

**5.8.** Windows systems such as Motif and Windows NT are object-oriented. In such systems, there is a hierarchy of **Window** classes with appropriate methods such as **create**, **show**, **hide**, **move**, and **destroy** to manipulate particular types of **Window** objects. Simulate an object-oriented windows system by using simple console graphics. For example, the figure

represents a **SimpleWindow**, whereas

represents a **FramedWindow**. Implement a **Window** hierarchy with at least four derived classes. Classes in the hierarchy should implement an interface that consists of polymorphic methods to create, destroy, show, hide, move, and resize **Window** objects.

**5.9.** For the **Product** hierarchy of Programming Exercise 4.12, suppose that, once a month, the chain runs an application that contains the loop

```
for ( int i = 0; i < productCount; i++ )
    products[ i ]->adjustPrice();
```

where **products** is an array of pointers to the base class **Product**, which has a **virtual** method **adjustPrice**. The **virtual** method adjusts the price of each **Product** object depending on the corresponding class's **supply** and **demand** members. Derive at least 10 classes from **Product**, overriding the **adjustPrice** in each. Implement a test client that uses sample data to test the hierarchy.

**5.10.** The No Guarantees Dating Service (hereafter, NGDS) includes, for an extra charge, a breakup service in which NGDS generates a form letter to announce the breakup and handles any subsequent correspondence from the dumpee. The form letter is based on a personality profile that NGDS social scientists put together for each client. The personality categories are

- Normal.
- Slightly Neurotic.
- Passive/Aggressive.
- Comatose.
- Beavis or Butthead.
- Loose Cannon.
- Freddy.

Create an inheritance hierarchy to represent the personality profiles. The base class should have a pure **virtual** method called **dearJohn** that, when invoked, generates a breakup letter appropriate for the personality profile. Write a test client to generate letters for a mix of objects that belong to the different personality classes.

**5.11.** Implement a shape hierarchy with **Shape** as an abstract base class that has the pure **virtual** methods **draw** and **resize**. Derived classes should include **Point, Line, Circle, Triangle**, and **Rectangle**. Each derived class implements the **draw** method to draw an appropriate representation of an object in the class and the **resize** method to change an object's initial size. If you have access to a graphics package such as Visual C++, use the drawing capabilities provided; otherwise, use basic console graphics. Write a test client for the hierarchy.

**5.12.** Administrative software for computer networks provides various services that require **hosts**—that is, machines on the network—to be polled. A polled host typically responds with its network address and other pertinent information. Create a hierarchy with **Host** as the abstract base class with a pure **virtual** method **poll** whose declaration is

```
virtual HostInfo& poll() = 0;
```

The returned **HostInfo** reference contains pertinent information about a host such as its network address; its type (e.g., *applications server, file server, workstation, router, personal computer, print server*, etc.); most recent connect time to network; status (e.g., *active* or *idle*); and the like. Classes derived from **Host** are different types of host such as **Workstation, FileServer**, and so forth. Each class derived from **Host** overrides **poll** to return, as a **HostInfo** reference, appropriate information about itself. After creating the necessary hierarchy and auxiliary classes such as **HostInfo**, write a test client that includes a loop such as

```
for ( int i = 0; i < hostCount; i++ )
   printReport( hosts[ i ]->poll() );
```

**5.13.** For the **Vehicle** hierarchy of Programming Exercise 4.6, provide the **virtual** methods

- **start**, which outputs the steps in a recipe to start the **Vehicle** in question.

- **computeDepr**, which computes a **Vehicle**'s depreciation over **expectedLife**, which is a **Vehicle** data member that gives the expected life in years.

- **diagnose**, which tries to guide the user through a troubleshooting session by asking appropriate questions (e.g., *Does the engine turn over when the ignition is turned on?*).

**5.14.** Implement an **AbsCollection** abstract base class that specifies common operations on an abstract collection such as *add, delete, removeAll, enumerate, getCount, append* (from one abstract collection to another), *containsMember*, and *isEqual*. The abstract base class should also include an array of **int**s, which represents the objects in an abstract collection (see Programming Exercise 4.10). Derive classes such as **Set** (see Programming Exercise 3.12) and **Bag** (see Programming Exercise 3.13) from the abstract base class, and override all the inherited pure **virtual** methods in appropriate ways.

**5.15.** Implement a `PropSheet` abstract base class with the pure `virtual` method whose prototype is

```
virtual void listProps() = 0;
```

A derived class should override `listProps` to describe briefly, in messages to the standard output, what each of the class's data members represents and how these members may be accessed. For example, given the class

```
class Emp : public PropSheet {
public:
    void listProps() { /*...*/ }
    void setId( int n ) { id = n; }
    // other public methods
private:
    unsigned id;
    string   dept;
    // other data members
}
```

the override of `listProps` might print to the standard output messages such as

```
id:     Stores unique identification number.
            Must be set in constructor as unsigned.
            Read via getId().
            Not writable after construction.
dept:   Stores home department.
            Optionally set in constructor.
            Read via getDept().
            Written via setDept( string ).
```

Write a test client to demonstrate the override of `listProps` for at least three classes.

# CHAPTER
# 6

# OPERATOR OVERLOADING

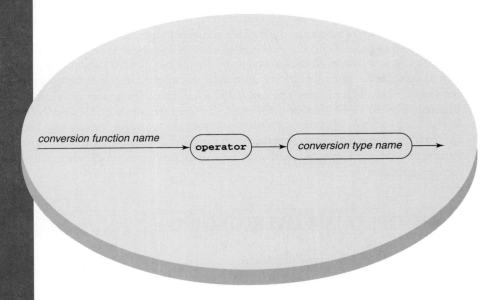

conversion function name → operator → conversion type name →

**6.1** Basic Operator Overloading

**6.2** Sample Application: A Complex Number Class

**6.3** Operator Overloading Using Top-Level Functions

**6.4** friend Functions

**6.5** Overloading the Input and Output Operators

**6.6** Overloading the Assignment Operator

**6.7** Overloading Some Special Operators

**6.8** Sample Application: An Associative Array

**6.9** Memory Management Operators

C++ Postscript

Common Programming Errors

Programming Exercises

**Overloading** refers to multiple meanings of the same name or symbol. An *overloaded function* (see Section 2.6) is a function with multiple definitions. In this chapter we discuss **operator overloading**, which refers to multiple definitions of operators such as **+**, **++**, and **[ ]**. These operators are overloaded by writing special kinds of functions.

Arithmetic operators such as **+** and **/** are overloaded in the C++ language. For example, the **/** operator may designate either integer division

```
2 / 3     // divide 2 by 3, which gives 0
```

or floating-point division

```
2.0 / 3.0     // divide 2.0 by 3.0, which gives 0.666667
```

Different algorithms are required to compute the two divisions even though **/** designates division in both cases. At the programmer level, it is convenient to have one symbol to designate division—whatever the type of the numbers to be divided.

The convenience of operator overloading extends from built-in types, such as **int** and **float**, to classes. For example, the system overloads the operator **>>** so that class objects such as **cin** can be used to read data. Similarly, the system overloads the operator **<<** so that class objects such as **cout** can be used to write data. The operators **>>** and **<<** were originally defined as the bitwise shift operators. Once overloaded, the same symbol, **>>**, can be used for input of many different types from the keyboard, from a file, and so on. Similarly, the same symbol, **<<**, can be used for output of many different types to the video display, to a file, and so on. In this chapter we will show how the programmer can overload the C++ operators for classes.

## 6.1 BASIC OPERATOR OVERLOADING

The following operators can be overloaded

| | | | | | | |
|---|---|---|---|---|---|---|
| new | new[ ] | | delete | | delete[ ] | |
| + | - | * | / | % | ^ | & |
| \| | ~ | ! | = | < | > | += |
| -= | *= | /= | %= | ^= | &= | \|= |
| << | >> | <<= | >>= | == | != | <= |
| >= | && | \|\| | ++ | -- | , | ->* |
| -> | ( ) | [ ] | | | | |

The operator **( )** is the function call operator, and **[ ]** is the subscript operator (see Section 6.7). Both the unary and binary forms of **+**, **-**, **\***, and **&** can be overloaded. Both the preincrement and postincrement forms of **++** and the predecrement and postdecrement forms of **--** can be overloaded (see Section 6.7). The member selector (**.**), member object selector (**.\***), scope resolution (**::**), and conditional (**?:**) operators can *not* be overloaded. Every overloaded operator in a base class, except the assignment operator (**=**), is inherited in a derived class.

If we want to overload the operator **+** for the class **C** so that we can add two **C** objects with the result being another **C** object, we can declare a method named **operator+** in the class **C**

```
class C {
public:
   C operator+( const C& ) const;
   //...
};
```

The method is implemented in the usual way

```
C C::operator+( const C& c ) const {
   //...
}
```

Following the usual syntax for invoking a method, **operator+** can be invoked as

```
C a, b, c;
a = b.operator+( c );
```

where **a**, **b**, and **c** are objects in the class **C**. Notice that since the result of the **+** operation is supposed to be a **C** object, this method properly returns type **C**. Because of the keyword **operator**, this method can, and normally would, be invoked as

```
a = b + c;
```

In the latter case, the meaning is clear; we add the **C** objects **b** and **c** to obtain another **C** object, which is then assigned to the **C** object **a**. Notice that in the declaration in the class **C**

```
C operator+( const C& ) const;
```

**operator+** has *one* parameter, even though **+** takes *two* operands. The first operand becomes the object whose method is invoked. In the statement

```
a = b + c;
```

**b**'s **operator+** method is invoked, which is clear in the alternative syntax

```
a = b.operator+( c );
```

The second operand **c** is passed as the argument to the method **operator+**, which accounts for the one parameter of type **const C&**. In general, if we use a method to overload a binary operator (i.e., an operator that takes two operands), the method has one parameter. If we use a method to overload a unary operator (i.e., an operator that takes one operand), the method has no parameters.

**EXAMPLE 6.1.1.** The code segment

```
class C {
public:
   C& operator=( const C& );
   C operator!();
   //...
};
```

shows how to declare operator overloads of the binary assignment operator **=** and the unary not operator **!**. ∎

**EXAMPLE 6.1.2.**   Consider an ordered-pair class

```
class OPair {
public:
   OPair( float f1 = 0.0, float f2 = 0.0 ) {
      p1 = f1;
      p2 = f2;
   }
   //...
private:
   float p1, p2;
};
```

Two **OPair** objects are equal if their **p1** members are equal and their **p2** members are equal. To overload the operator **==** to test for equality of **OPair**s, we write a method

```
operator==
```

The equality operator **==** is a binary operator that compares **OPair** objects. The first operand is the object on which **operator==** is invoked. The second operand becomes the sole argument to **operator==**. The result of the comparison is **true** or **false**, so **operator==** returns type **bool**. Thus, **operator==** can be declared in class **OPair** as

```
class OPair {
public:
   //...
   bool operator==( const OPair& ) const;
   //...
};
```

The two **const**s indicate that the overload will not change the two **OPair** objects that are compared. The first **const** indicates that the argument will not be changed, and the second indicates that the object on which **operator==** is invoked will not be changed.

The method may be implemented as

```
bool OPair::operator==( const OPair& s ) const {
   return p1 == s.p1 && p2 == s.p2;
}
```

The overloaded equality operator could be used in a context such as

```
OPair s1, s2;
//...
if ( s1 == s2 ) {
   //...
}
```

The expression **s1 == s2** is interpreted as

```
s1.operator==( s2 )
```

which therefore invokes the code for method **operator==**. If this method returns **true**, the expression **s1 == s2** thus evaluates to **true**, and the body of the **if** statement executes. If, on the other hand, the method returns **false**, the expression **s1 == s2** evaluates to **false**, and the body of the **if** statement does not execute.

The built-in meaning of **==** for integers and floating-point numbers is equality of numbers in the usual sense. By overloading **==** for the **OPair** class, we have extended this built-in meaning for numbers to ordered pairs so that the meaning of **==** for ordered pairs is equality of ordered pairs in the usual sense.  ■

## Operator Precedence and Syntax

Operator precedence and syntax cannot be changed through overloading. For example, the binary operator **||** always occurs *between* its two operands, whether built-in or overloaded; and **||** retains its original precedence even when overloaded.

**EXAMPLE 6.1.3.**   In the code segment

```
int main() {
   Complex c1, c2, c3, ans;
   //...
   ans = c1 + c2 * c3;
   //...
}
```

the expression

```
ans = c1 + c2 * c3;
```

is equivalent to

```
ans = c1 + ( c2 * c3 );
```

There is no way to change the precedence of the built-in operators **+** and **\*** so that, for example, **+** has a higher precedence than **\*** for the class **Complex**. Also, the *binary* operator **+** always occurs *between* its two operands. There is no way to overload the binary **+** so that it occurs either before or after its two operands. In a similar fashion, unary **+** always occurs *before* its operand, even if the operator is overloaded.  ■

If a built-in operator is unary, then all overloads of it remain unary. If a built-in operator is binary, then all overloads remain binary.

**EXAMPLE 6.1.4.**   The class declaration

```
class C {
public:
   C operator%(); // ***** ERROR: % is binary
   //...
};
```

contains an error. The operator **%** is *binary*, not *unary*, so when overloaded as a method must have *one* parameter.  ■

## EXERCISES

**1.** Explain the error:

```cpp
class Point {
   //...
   bool operator>( const Point& ) const;
   //...
};

bool Point:::>( const Point& s ) const {
   //...
}
```

**2.** Explain the error:

```cpp
class Point {
   //...
   bool operator>( const Point&, const Point& ) const;
   //...
};

bool Point::operator>( const Point& s1,
                       const Point& s2 ) const {
   //...
}
```

**3.** Explain the error:

```cpp
class Point {
   //...
   bool operator>( const Point& ) const;
   //...
};

bool Point::operator>( const Point& s ) {
   //...
}
```

**4.** Explain the error:

```cpp
class Point {
   //...
   int operator.( const Point& ) const;
   //...
};
int Point::operator.( const Point& s ) const {
   //...
}
```

**5.** Show a declaration of a method in class **Point** that overloads the operator **!**.

**6.** Overload the operator **!=** for the **OPair** class of Example 6.1.2. Show the declaration and write the definition.

## 6.2 SAMPLE APPLICATION: A COMPLEX NUMBER CLASS

### Problem

A *complex number* is a number of the form $z = a + bi$, where $a$ and $b$ are floating-point numbers. The symbol $i$ represents the square root of $-1$. The term $a$ is called the *real part* of $z$, and $b$ is called the *imaginary part* of $z$. Arithmetic operations on complex numbers are defined as follows:

$$(a + bi) + (c + di) = (a + c) + (b + d)i$$
$$(a + bi) - (c + di) = (a - c) + (b - d)i$$
$$(a + bi) \times (c + di) = (ac - bd) + (ad + bc)i$$
$$(a + bi)/(c + di) = (ac + bd)/(c^2 + d^2) + [(bc - ad)/(c^2 + d^2)]i$$

Implement a class that represents complex numbers and

- Overloads **+**, **-**, **\***, and **/** to support complex arithmetic.
- Contains a method **write** to output a complex number to the standard output.
- Provides a default constructor that sets the real and imaginary parts of the complex number to zero.
- Provides a one-parameter constructor that sets the real part of the complex number to the value passed and sets the imaginary part of the complex number to zero.
- Provides a two-parameter constructor that sets the real and imaginary parts of the complex number to the values passed.

### Sample Output

If **c1** represents the complex number $7.7 + 5.5i$ and **c2** represents the complex number $4.2 - 8.3i$, when the method **write** is used to print the sum, difference, product, and quotient of **c1** and **c2**, the output, suitably annotated, is

```
c1 + c2 = 11.9 + -2.8i
c1 - c2 = 3.5 + 13.8i
c1 * c2 = 77.99 + -40.81i
c1 / c2 = -0.153819 + 1.005547i
```

### Solution

We declare the class **Complex** with two **double** data members to represent the real and imaginary parts of a complex number. We overload the **Complex** operators using methods. Since each operator is a *binary* operator, as a method each has *one* parameter of type **Complex&**. Since the result of each operation is of type **Complex**, each method returns type **Complex**. For example, to overload **+**, we declare the method **operator+** as

```
Complex operator+( const Complex& ) const;
```

### C++ Implementation

```
class Complex {
public:
   Complex();                    // default
   Complex( double );            // real given
   Complex( double, double ); // both given

   void write() const;
   // operator methods
   Complex operator+( const Complex& ) const;
   Complex operator-( const Complex& ) const;
   Complex operator*( const Complex& ) const;
   Complex operator/( const Complex& ) const;
private:
   double real;
   double imag;
};

// default constructor
Complex::Complex() {
   real = imag = 0.0;
}

// constructor -- real given but not imag
Complex::Complex( double re ) {
   real = re;
   imag = 0.0;
}

// constructor -- real and imag given
Complex::Complex( double re, double im ) {
   real = re;
   imag = im;
}

void Complex::write() const {
   cout << real << " + " << imag << 'i';
}

// Complex + as binary operator
Complex Complex::operator+( const Complex& u ) const {
   Complex v( real + u.real,
              imag + u.imag );
   return v;
}
```

```
// Complex - as binary operator
Complex Complex::operator-( const Complex& u ) const {
   Complex v( real - u.real,
              imag - u.imag );
   return v;
}

// Complex * as binary operator
Complex Complex::operator*( const Complex& u ) const {
   Complex v( real * u.real - imag * u.imag,
              imag * u.real + real * u.imag );
   return v;
}

// Complex / as binary operator
Complex Complex::operator/( const Complex& u ) const {
   double abs_sq = u.real * u.real + u.imag * u.imag;
   Complex v( ( real * u.real + imag * u.imag ) / abs_sq,
              ( imag * u.real - real * u.imag ) / abs_sq );
   return v;
}
```

### Discussion

We declare two **double** data members: **real**, to represent the real part of a complex number, and **imag**, to represent the imaginary part of a complex number.

The class **Complex** has three constructors. The default constructor initializes the data members **real** and **imag** to 0.0. The one-parameter constructor initializes **real** to the value passed and **imag** to 0.0. The two-parameter constructor initializes **real** and **imag** to the values passed.

The three constructors could be combined into one by keeping only the two-parameter constructor and providing default values for the parameter in the declaration:

```
class Complex {
   //...
   Complex( double = 0.0, double = 0.0 );
   //...
};
```

The method **write** is implemented so that it outputs a **Complex** number in the form

*real part* **+** *imaginary part***i**

The implementation of each operator overload follows the same pattern. A **Complex** object is created and initialized using the two-parameter constructor. The values supplied are those given by the formulas for complex arithmetic. Then the object is returned. For example, the overload of**+**

```
Complex Complex::operator+( const Complex& u ) const {
   Complex v( real + u.real,
              imag + u.imag );
   return v;
}
```

defines a **Complex** object **v** and initializes its real part to

```
real + u.real
```

and its imaginary part to

```
imag + u.imag
```

because of the formula

$$(a + bi) + (c + di) = (a + c) + (b + d)i$$

for complex addition. For example, if **x1** and **x2** are **Complex** objects, the expression

```
x1 + x2
```

translates as

```
x1.operator+( x2 )
```

Thus when the code

```
Complex Complex::operator+( const Complex& u ) const {
    Complex v( real + u.real,
               imag + u.imag );
    return v;
}
```

executes, **real** and **imag** refer to **x1**'s real and imaginary parts, and **u.real** and **u.imag** refer to **x2**'s real and imaginary parts. Thus in **v**, we have **v.real** equal to **x1.real** + **x2.real** and **v.imag** equal to **x1.imag** + **x2.imag** as indicated by the definition of complex addition. The overload concludes by returning the object **v**. Incidentally, the overload could be written more simply as

```
Complex Complex::operator+( const Complex& u ) const {
    return Complex( real + u.real, imag + u.imag );
}
```

The function **main** shown in Figure 6.2.1 shows the **Complex** class in action. The output is

```
c1 + c2 = 11.9 + -2.8i
c1 - c2 = 3.5 + 13.8i
c1 * c2 = 77.99 + -40.81i
c1 / c2 = -0.153819 + 1.005547i
```

When a statement such as

```
c3 = c1 / c2;
```

executes, the appropriate overload (**operator/** in this case) is invoked. This overload defines a **Complex** object that represents the result of the operation. The execution of the statement concludes when the assignment operator copies the object returned by the overload into **c3**. When an object is copied by the assignment operator

```
obj1 = obj2;
```

```
int main() {
   Complex c1( 7.7, 5.5 );
   Complex c2( 4.2, -8.3 );
   Complex c3;

   c3 = c1 + c2;
   cout << "c1 + c2 = ";
   c3.write();
   cout << '\n';

   c3 = c1 - c2;
   cout << "c1 - c2 = ";
   c3.write();
   cout << '\n';

   c3 = c1 * c2;
   cout << "c1 * c2 = ";
   c3.write();
   cout << '\n';

   c3 = c1 / c2;
   cout << "c1 / c2 = ";
   c3.write();
   cout << '\n';
   return 0;
}
```

**FIGURE 6.2.1** The `Complex` class in action.

each of `obj2`'s data members is copied to the corresponding data member in `obj1`. (The action of the assignment operator can be changed because the assignment operator can itself be overloaded!) In this case, the values of the data members `real` and `imag` of the object defined by the overload are copied into `c3`'s `real` and `imag` data members. Thus `c3` represents the result of the arithmetic operation.

## EXERCISES

**1.** Could `operator+` be implemented so that its declaration is

```
Complex operator+( const Complex ) const;
```

Explain.

**2.** Could `operator+` be implemented so that its declaration is

```
Complex& operator+( const Complex& );
```

Explain.

3. The *conjugate* of the complex number $a + bi$ is $a - bi$. Overload ~ so that it returns the complex conjugate of the **Complex** object.

4. The *absolute value* of the complex number $a + bi$ is $\sqrt{a^2 + b^2}$. Overload **!** so that it returns the absolute value of the **Complex** object.

# 6.3 OPERATOR OVERLOADING USING TOP-LEVEL FUNCTIONS

An overloaded operator is a user-defined function that retains the convenience of operator syntax. In general, an overloaded operator must be either a method, as explained in Sections 6.1 and 6.2, or a top-level function, which is the subject of this section and the next. Except for the memory-management operators, **new**, **new[ ]**, **delete**, and **delete[ ]**, an operator that is overloaded as a top-level function must include a class object among its arguments. The operators **[ ]** (subscript operator), **=** (assignment operator), **()** (function call operator), and **->** (indirect selection operator) must be overloaded as methods.[†]

It makes sense to require that an operator such as **%** either be overloaded as a method or take at least one class object as an argument. Otherwise, in an expression such as

    x % y

where **x** and **y** are **int**s, the system could not distinguish between the built-in **%** and some user-defined overload of **%**. If **%** is overloaded either as a method or as a top-level operator function that takes a class object as an argument, the system can determine which **%** operator to invoke in a particular context.

To overload the operator **+** using a top-level function so that we can add two **C** objects with the result being another **C** object, we define a top-level function named **operator+**

    C operator+( const C& c1, const C& c2 ) {
       //...
    }

Notice that the class name and the scope resolution operator **::** do *not* appear in a top-level function overload—it is *not* a method. Notice also that both of the objects involved in the overload have names: **c1** and **c2**. When a binary operator is overloaded as a method, only the second object has an explicit name (see Section 6.2). Notice also that since the result of the **+** operation is a **C** object, this function returns type **C**.

Following the usual syntax for invoking a function, the top-level function overload can be invoked as

    a = operator+( b, c );

---

[†] Requiring these operators to be overloaded as methods ensures that the first operand is a class object; thus, expressions such as **9[ x ]** and **6.32 = x**, where **x** is a class object, cannot be introduced into a program.

where **a**, **b**, and **c** are objects in class **C**. Because of the keyword **operator**, this function can, and normally would, be invoked as

```
a = b + c;
```

The *top-level function* **operator+** has *two* parameters—the two **C** objects to add. Recall that when we overload **+** using a *method* in class **C**, the method has *one* parameter (see Section 6.1). If **+** is overloaded as a method, in the code segment

```
a = b + c;
```

the method is invoked on object **b**. The second operand **c** is passed to the method **operator+**. In general, if we use a method to overload a binary operator, the method has one parameter. If we use a top-level function to overload a binary operator, the function has two parameters, which correspond to the operator's two operands. Similarly, if we use a method to overload a unary operator, the method has no parameters. If we use a top-level function to overload a unary operator, the function has one parameter, which corresponds to the operator's single operand.

**EXAMPLE 6.3.1.**   The code segment

```
// ***** ERROR: neither a method nor a
// a function that takes a class argument
void operator%( float f1, float f2 ) {
  //...
}
```

contains an error because an overloaded operator either must be a class method or must take a class object as an argument. ∎

**EXAMPLE 6.3.2.**   The code segment

```
// ***** ERROR: [ ] must be overloaded as a method
void operator[ ]( int i, Point& s ) {
  //...
}
```

contains an error because the subscript operator [ ] must be overloaded as a method rather than as a top-level function. ∎

We have not yet indicated any advantage to overloading an operator as a top-level function rather than as a method. The next examples illustrate one advantage.

**EXAMPLE 6.3.3.** Consider a `main` function

```
int main() {
   Complex a, b( 4.3, -8.2);
   // OK: uses convert constructor
   a = b + 54.3;
   // ***** ERROR: first arg not a Complex object
   a = 54.3 + b;
   //...
}
```

that uses the `Complex` class of Section 6.2. The statement

```
a = b + 54.3;
```

is interpreted as

```
a = b.operator+( 54.3 );
```

There is no method `operator+` in class `Complex` that takes a floating-point argument, but there is a convert constructor

```
class Complex {
   //...
   // convert constructor converts double to Complex
   Complex( double );
   //...
};
```

that can convert a floating-point value to a `Complex` object. After the constructor converts `54.3` to a `Complex` object, the method `operator+`, which takes a `Complex` argument, executes. Thus the statement

```
a = b + 54.3;
```

executes properly. (This situation is similar to that in which an `int` and `double` are added, and the system converts the `int` to a `double` before performing the addition.) The statement

```
a = 54.3 + b;
```

is interpreted as

```
a = 54.3.operator+( b ); // ***** ERROR
```

Here an error results since the member operator cannot be applied to the nonobject `54.3`. Furthermore, the system does *not* convert `54.3` to an object so that the member operator can be applied. ∎

**EXAMPLE 6.3.4.** Suppose that **+** is overloaded as a top-level function for class **Complex**

```
Complex operator+( const Complex& c1, const Complex& c2 ) {
   //...
}
```

In the **main** function

```
int main() {
   Complex a, b( 4.3, -8.2);
   // OK: uses convert constructor
   a = b + 54.3;
   // OK: also uses convert constructor
   a = 54.3 + b;
   //...
}
```

both statements are now legal. When the first statement, which is interpreted as

```
a = operator+( b, 54.3 );
```

executes, the convert constructor converts **54.3** to a **Complex** object, after which the top-level function

```
Complex operator+( const Complex& c1, const Complex& c2 ) {
   //...
}
```

executes. Similarly, when the second statement, which is interpreted as

```
a = operator+( 54.3, b );
```

executes, the convert constructor converts **54.3** to a **Complex** object, after which the top-level overload function again executes. Here no member operator is used, so no error results from applying the member operator to a nonmember. Thus an advantage of using a top-level function rather than a method to overload a binary operator is that the two operands are treated in the same way by the system; either can be converted, if necessary. When a method is used to overload a binary operator, the first operand *must* be an object from the appropriate class.  ∎

Consider overloading **+** for the **Complex** class of Section 6.2 using a top-level function. The code might look like

```
Complex operator+( const Complex& t, const Complex& u ) {
    return Complex( t.real + u.real,
                    t.imag + u.imag );
}
```

However, this will *not* work because **real** and **imag** are **private** in class **Complex**, and **operator+** cannot access them. The problem can be solved in several ways. One possibility is to make **real** and **imag** **public** in class **Complex**; however, this violates the principle of hiding the implementation. Another possibility, which we implement in the next example, is to add **public** methods to class **Complex** that return the values of **real** and **imag**. A third possibility is to make **operator+** a **friend** of class **Complex**. If a function **f** is a **friend** of class **C**, **f** may access **C**'s **private** and **protected** members. We discuss this last technique in the next section.

**EXAMPLE 6.3.5.** We add **public** methods to the class **Complex** of Section 6.2 that return the values of **real** and **imag**, and overload the arithmetic operators using top-level functions (see Figure 6.3.1). The implementation of the constructors and method **write** is unchanged. ∎

## EXERCISES

1. Explain the error:

```
bool operator||( bool b1, bool b2 ) {
    //...
}
```

2. Explain the error:

```
class C {
    //...
};
bool operator&&( C& c ) {
    //...
}
```

3. Explain the error:

```
bool operator()( bool b1, bool b2, bool b3 ) {
    //...
}
```

4. Overload ~ using a top-level function so that it returns the complex conjugate of the **Complex** object.

```
class Complex {
public:
   Complex();                  // default
   Complex( double );          // real given
   Complex( double, double ); // both given
   void write() const;
   // added methods
   double get_real() const { return real; }
   double get_imag() const { return imag; }
private:
   double real;
   double imag;
};
// Complex + as top-level function
Complex operator+( const Complex& t, const Complex& u ) {
   return Complex( t.get_real() + u.get_real(),
                   t.get_imag() + u.get_imag() );
}
// Complex - as top-level function
Complex operator-( const Complex& t, const Complex& u ) {
   return Complex( t.get_real() - u.get_real(),
                   t.get_imag() - u.get_imag() );
}
// Complex * as top-level function
Complex operator*( const Complex& t, const Complex& u ) {
   return Complex( t.get_real() * u.get_real()
                   - t.get_imag() * u.get_imag(),
                   t.get_imag() * u.get_real()
                   + t.get_real() * u.get_imag() );
}
// Complex / as top-level function
Complex operator/( const Complex& t, const Complex& u ) {
   double abs_sq = u.get_real() * u.get_real()
                   + u.get_imag() * u.get_imag();
   return Complex( ( t.get_real() * u.get_real()
                     + t.get_imag() * u.get_imag() ) / abs_sq,
                   ( t.get_imag() * u.get_real()
                     - t.get_real() * u.get_imag() ) / abs_sq );
}
```

**FIGURE 6.3.1** Overloading the `Complex` arithmetic operators as top-level functions.

**5.** Overload ! using a top-level function so that it returns the absolute value of the `Complex` object.

6. Overload `==` for the `OPair` class of Example 6.1.2 using a top-level function. What changes, if any, would be required in the `OPair` class?

7. Overload `!=` for the `OPair` class of Example 6.1.2 using a top-level function. What changes, if any, would be required in the `OPair` class?

## 6.4 `friend` FUNCTIONS

A class's **private** members are accessible only to its methods and its **friend** functions. A class's **protected** members are accessible only to methods in its class hierarchy and its **friend** functions. To make a function **f** a **friend** of class **C**, we declare **f** within **C**'s declaration using the keyword **friend**:

```
class C {
   //...
   friend int f(); // friend function
   //...
};
```

Because **f** is *not* a method, the declaration serves only to give **f** access rights to **C**'s **private** and **protected** members; thus, the declaration may be placed within the **private**, **protected**, or **public** part of the declaration of class **C**. Because a **friend** function is not a **C** method, yet has access to **C**'s **private** and **protected** members, a **friend** function violates a strict interpretation of object-oriented principles. Accordingly, **friend** functions are controversial and open to misuse. We recommend using **friend** functions only in operator overloading.

**EXAMPLE 6.4.1.** In the previous section, we overloaded the arithmetic operators in the **Complex** class of Section 6.2 using top-level functions. We added **public** methods to access **Complex**'s **private** members so that these top-level functions could obtain the values of the **private** members.

Another way to overload the arithmetic operators in the **Complex** class as top-level functions is to make the top-level functions **friend**s of **Complex** (see Figure 6.4.1). As **friend**s, the top-level functions have access to **Complex**'s **private** members. The implementations of the constructors and method **write** are not shown because they are unchanged. ∎

An advantage of adding **public** methods to return the values of **private** and **protected** members needed by top-level overload functions rather than using **friend** functions is that **private** members remain visible only within the class and **protected** members remain visible only within the class hierarchy. A disadvantage is that the methods added to return the values of **private** or **protected** members may confuse and clutter the interface. Such methods may provide access to the client of mysterious values, particularly if such values are buried deep within the implementation. In such a situation, it is probably better to use **friend** functions and not muddle the interface. Of course, the whole issue of exposing **private** and **protected** members can be avoided if the overloads are

```
class Complex {
public:
    Complex();                // default
    Complex( double );        // real given
    Complex( double, double ); // both given

    void write() const;
    // friend functions
    friend Complex operator+( const Complex&, const Complex& );
    friend Complex operator-( const Complex&, const Complex& );
    friend Complex operator*( const Complex&, const Complex& );
    friend Complex operator/( const Complex&, const Complex& );
private:
    double real;
    double imag;
};

// Complex + as top-level friend
Complex operator+( const Complex& t, const Complex& u ) {
    return Complex( t.real + u.real,
                    t.imag + u.imag );
}

// Complex - as top-level friend
Complex operator-( const Complex& t, const Complex& u ) {
    return Complex( t.real - u.real,
                    t.imag - u.imag );
}

// Complex * as top-level friend
Complex operator*( const Complex& t, const Complex& u ) {
    return Complex( t.real * u.real - t.imag * u.imag,
                    t.imag * u.real + t.real * u.imag );
}
// Complex / as top-level friend
Complex operator/( const Complex& t, const Complex& u ) {
    double abs_sq = u.real * u.real + u.imag * u.imag;
    return Complex( (t.real * u.real + t.imag * u.imag)/abs_sq,
                    (t.imag * u.real - t.real * u.imag)/abs_sq);
}
```

**FIGURE 6.4.1** The `Complex` class with operators overloaded as top-level `friend` functions.

implemented using methods. In so doing, one gives up the advantage discussed in Example 6.3.4. Further, there are situations in which the overloads *must* be implemented using top-level functions (see Section 6.5).

## EXERCISES

1. Explain the error:

```cpp
class C {
public:
    //...
private:
    bool stored;
    //...
};

void operator!( C& c ) {
    c.stored = !c.stored;
}
```

2. Explain the error:

```cpp
class C {
public:
    //...
private:
    bool stored;
    friend void operator!( C& );
    //...
};
void operator!( C& c ) {
    stored = !stored;
}
```

3. Explain the error:

```cpp
class C {
public:
    //...
private:
    bool stored;
    friend void operator!( C& );
    //...
};

void C::operator!( C& c ) {
    c.stored = !c.stored;
}
```

4. Overload ~ using a top-level **friend** function so that it returns the complex conjugate of the **Complex** object.

5. Overload ! using a top-level **friend** function so that it returns the absolute value of the **Complex** object.

6. Overload == for the **OPair** class of Example 6.1.2 using a top-level **friend** function. What changes, if any, would be required in the **OPair** class?

7. Overload != for the **OPair** class of Example 6.1.2 using a top-level **friend** function. What changes, if any, would be required in the **OPair** class?

## 6.5 OVERLOADING THE INPUT AND OUTPUT OPERATORS

The system overloads the right-shift operator >> for formatted input of built-in types as a method in an appropriate system class. For example, if **i** is an **int**,

```
cin >> i
```

is interpreted as

```
cin.operator>>( i )
```

When this code executes, it reads and stores a value in **i**.

The operator >> can be further overloaded for user-defined types. The first operand of >> belongs to a system class (e.g., **istream**); therefore, if >> were overloaded as a method, it would have to be a method in a system class. To overload >> for a user-defined type, we should not modify the system class even if we could. Thus >> must be overloaded as a top-level function.

**EXAMPLE 6.5.1.** To overload >> to read two floating-point numbers, interpreted as a single complex number, into a **Complex** object (see Section 6.2), we could write a top-level function **operator>>**

```
istream& operator>>( istream& in, Complex& c ) {
   return in >> c.real >> c.imag;
}
```

Through inheritance (see Chapter 8), **istream** can be used to refer to input streams including **cin** and variables of type **ifstream**. The overloaded input operator could be used as

```
Complex c_obj;
cin >> c_obj;
```

The second statement

```
cin >> c_obj;
```

is equivalent to

```
operator>>( cin, c_obj );
```

and, when evaluated, is equivalent to

```
cin >> c_obj.real >> c_obj.imag;
```

Thus the statement does indeed read two floating-point numbers, interpreted as a single complex number, into the **Complex** object **c_obj**.

Both parameters are passed by reference. Input stream objects are always passed by reference because the system needs to update certain information about the stream in order to do input. The **Complex** object is passed by reference because we modify it; its data members are updated to the values read. The stream is returned so that we can chain input

```
Complex c1_obj, c2_obj;
cin >> c1_obj >> c2_obj;
```

just as we can for the built-in types.

As written, **operator>>** requires access to **Complex**'s **private** members. In order to provide this access, we make **operator>>** a **friend** of **Complex**

```
class Complex {
   //...
   friend istream& operator>>( istream&, Complex& );
   //...
};
```
■

Similarly, the system overloads the left-shift operator **<<** for formatted output of built-in types as a method in an appropriate system class. The operator **<<** can be further overloaded for user-defined types as a top-level function.

**EXAMPLE 6.5.2.**   To overload **<<** to output a **Complex** object, we would write a top-level function **operator<<**

```
ostream& operator<<( ostream& out, const Complex& c ) {
   return out << c.real << " + " << c.imag << 'i';
}
```

Similarly to **istream**, **ostream** can be used to refer to output streams including **cout** and variables of type **ofstream**. Since **operator<<** requires access to **Complex**'s **private** members, we would make **operator<<** a **friend** of **Complex**.   ■

## EXERCISES

1. Explain the error:

```
istream& operator>>( istream& in, Complex c ) {
   //...
}
```

2. Explain the error:

```
istream operator>>( istream in, Complex& c ) {
   //...
}
```

3. Show the declaration of the overload in Example 6.5.2 in the **Complex** class.

4. Use a **friend** function to overload **>>** to input an **OPair** object (see Example 6.1.2).

5. Use a **friend** function to overload **<<** to output an **OPair** object (see Example 6.1.2).

# 6.6 OVERLOADING THE ASSIGNMENT OPERATOR

The copy constructor (see Section 3.5) and the assignment operator are both used to copy one class object to another where the objects involved belong to the same class. The copy constructor copies a class object to a new object, whereas the assignment operator copies a class object to an already existing object.

The compiler provides a class with a *copy constructor* and an *assignment operator* if the class author does not provide a copy constructor or overload the assignment operator. The compiler-provided copy constructor and assignment operator copy each data member from the source to the corresponding data member in the target.

**EXAMPLE 6.6.1.**   In the code segment

```
class C {
public:
   void set_x( int i ) { x = i; }
   void dump() const { cout << x << '\n'; }
private:
   int x;
};
int main() {
  C c1, c2;
  c1.set_x( -999 );
  c1.dump();  // -999 is printed
  c2 = c1;    // compiler-supplied assignment operator
  c2.dump();  // -999 is printed
  //...
}
```

we do not overload the assignment operator for **c**. As the code segment in **main** shows, operations involving the assignment operator are still legal because the *compiler* furnishes an assignment operator. The compiler's version does a member-by-member copy of data members from the target to the source. For example, in the assignment

```
c2 = c1; // c2 is the target, c1 the source
```

the compiler's version of the assignment operator copies the value of **c1**'s data member **x** into **c2**'s data member **x**.  ∎

The class author typically defines a copy constructor and overloads the assignment operator for a class *whose data members include a pointer to dynamically allocated storage*.

In Section 3.5, we illustrated the danger of using the compiler's version of the copy constructor. A similar problem results if we use the compiler's version of the assignment operator.

**EXAMPLE 6.6.2.**    The program in Figure 6.6.1 provides a programmer-written copy constructor and overloads the assignment operator. The assignment

```
d2 = d1; // overloaded assignment operator
```

results in **d1.p** and **d2.p** pointing to different storage with the storage holding the same strings. We now look at the details.

Because the underlying functionality of the copy constructor and the assignment operator is so similar, we write a **private** method **copyIntoP** to provide the shared functionality.

The program's assignment operator

```
Namelist& Namelist::operator=( const Namelist& d ) {
   if ( this != &d )
      copyIntoP( d );
   return *this;
}
```

takes a single argument, a reference to a **Namelist** object. An assignment such as

```
d2 = d1; // d1 and d2 are Namelist objects
```

is equivalent to

```
d2.operator=( d1 );
```

In our overload of the assignment operator, we first check whether an object is being assigned to itself, for example:

```
d2 = d2; // assigning an object to itself
```

The pointer **this** points to the object whose method is being invoked. Therefore, in the assignment

```
d2 = d1;
```

**this** points to **d2**. So we check whether **this** points to the parameter

```
if ( this != &d ) // assigning an object to itself?
   copyIntoP( d ); // if not, proceed
```

before proceeding. If the object and the parameter differ, we invoke method **copyIn-toP** to allocate storage and copy the strings. Our overload of the assignment operator, unlike the compiler-supplied version, thus ensures that the target object and the source object have *their own copies* of the strings.

```
#include <iostream>
#include <string>
using namespace std;

class Namelist {
public:
   Namelist() : size( 0 ), p( 0 ) { }
   Namelist( const string [ ], int );
   Namelist( const Namelist& );
   Namelist& operator=( const Namelist& );
   void set( const string& s, int i ) { p[ i ] = s; }
   void set( const char* s, int i ) { p[ i ] = s; }
   void dump() const;
private:
   int size;
   string* p;
   void copyIntoP( const Namelist& );
};
Namelist::Namelist( const string s[ ], int si ) {
   p = new string[ size = si ];
   for ( int i = 0; i < size; i++ )
      p[ i ] = s[ i ];
}
Namelist::Namelist( const Namelist& d ) : p( 0 ) {
   copyIntoP( d );
}
Namelist& Namelist::operator=( const Namelist& d ) {
   if ( this != &d )
      copyIntoP( d );
   return *this;
}
```

**FIGURE 6.6.1** A program with a programmer-written copy constructor and an overloaded assignment operator.

```
void Namelist::copyIntoP( const Namelist& d ) {
   delete[ ] p;
   if ( d.p != 0 ) {
      p = new string[ size = d.size ];
      for ( int i = 0; i < size; i++ )
         p[ i ] = d.p[ i ];
   }
   else {
      p = 0;
      size = 0;
   }
}
void Namelist::dump() const {
   for ( int i = 0; i < size; i++ )
      cout << p[ i ] << '\n';
}
int main() {
   string list[ ] = { "Lab", "Husky", "Collie" };
   Namelist d1( list, 3 );
   d1.dump(); // Lab, Husky, Collie
   Namelist d2;
   d2 = d1; // overloaded assignment operator
   d2.dump(); // Lab, Husky, Collie
   d2.set( "Great Dane", 1 );
   d2.dump(); // Lab, Great Dane, Collie
   d1.dump(); // Lab, Husky, Collie
   return 0;
}
```

**FIGURE 6.6.1** Continued.

Our overload of the assignment operator returns a **Namelist** reference. The expression returned is **\*this**. Because **this** points to an object, we get the object itself by dereferencing **this**. For example, in the assignment

```
d2 = d1;
```

**operator=** returns a reference to **d2**. It is common for an overloaded assignment operator to return a reference to the object that invoked the operator. This practice allows assignments to be cascaded. For instance, the cascaded assignment

```
d3 = d2 = d1; // all Namelist objects
```

is equivalent to

```
d3.operator=( d2.operator=( d1 ) );
```

The call **d2.operator=( d1 )** returns a reference to **d2**, which then is the argument for the call of **d3.operator=**. ∎

## EXERCISES

1. If the class author does not provide an overload of the assignment operator, does the compiler provide one?

2. What is the output?

```
#include <iostream>
using namespace std;
class C {
public:
    C() { p = new int; }
    void set( int a ) { *p = a; }
    int get() const { return *p; }
private:
    int* p;
};
int main() {
  C c1, c2;
  c1.set( 1 );
  cout << c1.get() << '\n';
  c2 = c1;
  c2.set( -999 );
  cout << c1.get() << '\n';
  return 0;
}
```

3. When should a class author define a copy constructor and overload the assignment operator for the class?

4. An overload of the assignment operator

```
C& C::operator=( const C& c ) {
    // code to implement the overload
    return *this;
}
```

typically returns the object—**\*this**—by reference. Explain the reason for returning the object by reference.

5. What problems might arise if an overload of the assignment operator were written as in Exercise 4 except that we **return** the parameter **c** instead of **\*this**?

## 6.7 OVERLOADING SOME SPECIAL OPERATORS

In this section, we show how to overload some special operators: the subscript operator, [ ]; the function call operator, ( ); the increment and decrement operators, ++ and --; and the type conversion operator.

## Overloading the Subscript Operator

The subscript operator [ ] *must* be overloaded as a method. Its declaration typically looks like

```
class C {
  //...
  returntype& operator[ ]( paramtype );
  //...
  };
```

or

```
class C {
  //...
  const returntype& operator[ ]( paramtype ) const;
  //...
};
```

The first declaration can be used when the overloaded subscript operator modifies the object. The second declaration is used with a **const** object; in this case, the overloaded subscript operator can access, but *not* modify, the object.

If **c** is a **c** object, the expression

```
c[ i ]
```

is interpreted as

```
c.operator[ ]( i )
```

**EXAMPLE 6.7.1.** C++ does no checking for out-of-bounds indexes in arrays; however, by overloading the subscript operator, such checking can be added. The class **intArray** in Figure 6.7.1 implements an **int** array with bounds checking.

Because a non-default constructor is provided, the system does *not* generate a default constructor. For this reason, the user must provide an array size to the one-parameter constructor

```
intArray::intArray( int s ) {
  try {
    a = new int [ s ];
  }
  catch( bad_alloc ) {
    cerr << "Unable to allocate storage for intArray\n";
    throw;
  }
  size = s;
}
```

which attempts to allocate the requested storage. If the storage is successfully allocated, the constructor sets **size** to **s** and returns. If the storage cannot be allocated, the constructor prints a message and then re**throw**s the **bad_alloc** exception.

```
class intArray {
public:
    int& operator[ ]( int );
    const int& operator[ ]( int ) const;
    intArray( int s );
    int get_size() const { return size; }
private:
    int size;
    int* a;
};
int& intArray::operator[ ]( int i ) {
    if ( i < 0 || i >= size )
        throw string( "OutOfBounds" );
    return a[ i ];
}
const int& intArray::operator[ ]( int i ) const {
    if ( i < 0 || i >= size )
        throw string( "OutOfBounds" );
    return a[ i ];
}
intArray::intArray( int s ) {
    try {
        a = new int [ s ];
    }
    catch( bad_alloc ) {
        cerr << "Unable to allocate storage for intArray\n";
        throw;
    }
    size = s;
}
```

**FIGURE 6.7.1** Bounds checking by overloading the subscript operator.

The overloaded subscript operator that can be used to modify an object of type **intArray** is declared as

```
int& operator[ ]( int );
```

and the overloaded subscript operator that is used to access, but not modify, the object is declared as

```
const int& operator[ ]( int ) const;
```

The programmer uses the **int** parameter as an index into an ordinary array; that is, the programmer writes

```
arr[ i ]
```

where **arr** is an **intArray** object. The system interprets this to mean

```
arr.operator[ ]( i )
```

In either overload, if the index **i** is in bounds, the value **a[ i ]** is returned

```
if ( i < 0 || i >= size )
    throw string( "OutOfBounds" );
return a[ i ];
```

If the index is not in bounds, the overload throws an exception.

The non**const** overload returns an **int** reference so that if **arr** is an **intArray** object, **arr[ i ]** can be used on either side of an assignment expression

```
arr[ i ] = 8;
j = arr[ i ];
```

In particular, the first assignment statement modifies the data in the internal array **a**.

The **const** version of the overload returns a **const int** reference so that if **arr** is an **intArray** object, **arr[ i ]** must not be modified; for example,

```
j = arr[ i ];
```

is valid, but

```
arr[ i ] = 8;
```

is not valid.

The output of the following **main** function

```
int main() {
    intArray b( 5 );
    int i;
    try {
        for ( i = 0; i < b.get_size(); i++ )
            b[ i ] = 2 * i;
        for ( i = 0; i < 6; i++ )
            cout << b[ i ] << '\n';
    }
    catch ( string s ) {
        cerr << s << '\n';
        cerr << "i = " << i << '\n';
    }
    return 0;
}
```

is

```
0
2
4
6
8
OutOfBounds
i = 5
```

■

The **main** program of Example 6.7.1 would work correctly even if the **const** version of the overloaded subscript operator was not provided. However, a non**const** version of the overloaded subscript operator can never be applied to a **const** object. For this reason, both **const** and non**const** versions of the overloaded subscript operator are typically provided.

**EXAMPLE 6.7.2.**   The function

```
void print( const intArray& c ) {
   for ( int i = 0; i < c.get_size(); i++ )
      cout << c[ i ] << '\n';
}
```

prints the data in an **intArray** object (see Figure 6.7.1).  Because the parameter is marked **const**, only a **const** version of the overloaded subscript operator can be used. If the **const** version of the overloaded subscript operator is deleted from Figure 6.7.1, **print** will not compile.   ■

## Overloading the Function Call Operator

Like the subscript operator, the function call operator **()** *must* be overloaded as a method. Its declaration looks like

```
class C {

   //...

   returntype operator()( paramtypes );

   //...

};
```

where *paramtypes* is the list of parameter types separated by commas.  Suppose that there are two parameters; the first is of type **float**, and the second is of type **string**.  If **c** is a **C** object, **x** is a variable of type **float**, and **name** is of type **string**, the expression

```
c( x, name )
```

is interpreted as

```
c.operator()( x, name )
```

**EXAMPLE 6.7.3.**   The **intTwoArray** class in Figure 6.7.2 has the functionality of a two-dimensional array of **int** but also incorporates bounds checking. Instead of accessing the cells as **b[ i ][ j ]**, we overload the function call operator so that the cells are accessed as **b( i, j )**.

The user must provide the sizes of the dimensions of the array to the two-parameter constructor.  The first parameter gives the size of the first dimension, and the second parameter gives the size of the second dimension. The two-parameter constructor attempts to allocate the requested storage. If the storage is successfully allocated, the constructor sets **size1** to **s1** and **size2** to **s2** and returns.  The item at location **i,j**

```
class intTwoArray {
public:
    int& operator()( int, int );
    const int& operator()( int, int ) const;
    intTwoArray( int, int );
    int get_size1() const { return size1; }
    int get_size2() const { return size2; }
private:
    int size1;
    int size2;
    int* a;
};
int& intTwoArray::operator()( int i, int j ) {
    if ( i < 0 || i >= size1 )
        throw string( "FirstOutOfBounds" );
    if ( j < 0 || j >= size2 )
        throw string( "SecondOutOfBounds" );
    return a[ i * size2 + j ];
}
const int& intTwoArray::operator()( int i, int j ) const {
    if ( i < 0 || i >= size1 )
        throw string( "FirstOutOfBounds" );
    if ( j < 0 || j >= size2 )
        throw string( "SecondOutOfBounds" );
    return a[ i * size2 + j ];
}
intTwoArray::intTwoArray( int s1, int s2 ) {
    int size = s1 * s2;
    try {
        a = new int [ size ];
    }
    catch( bad_alloc ) {
        cerr << "Can't allocate storage for intTwoArray\n";
        throw;
    }
    size1 = s1;
    size2 = s2;
}
```

**FIGURE 6.7.2** Bounds checking by overloading the function call operator.

(from the user's point of view) is stored at cell **i * size2 + j** in the one-dimensional array **a** (see Figure 6.7.3). If the storage cannot be allocated, the constructor prints a message and then re**throw**s the **bad_alloc** exception.

The function call operator is overloaded in both **const** and non**const** versions for the same reason that the overloaded subscript operator is overloaded in both **const** and non**const** versions (see the preceding subsection). The overloaded function call operator is declared as

```
int& operator()( int, int );
```

and

```
const int& operator()( int, int ) const;
```

The programmer uses the **int** parameters as indexes into the two-dimensional array (from the user's point of view again); that is, the programmer writes

```
arr( i, j )
```

where **arr** is an **intTwoArray** object. The system interprets this to mean

```
arr.operator()( i, j )
```

The overloads are written so that, if the indexes are in bounds, the value

```
a[ i * size2 + j ]
```

is returned

```
if ( i < 0 || i >= size1 )
    throw string( "FirstOutOfBounds" );
if ( j < 0 || j >= size2 )
    throw string( "SecondOutOfBounds" );
return a[ i * size2 + j ];
```

If either index is not in bounds, the overloads throw an exception.

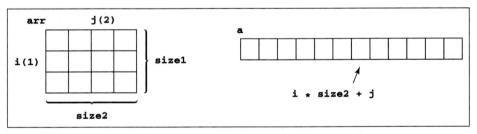

**FIGURE 6.7.3** Indexing from the user's point of view versus the actual implementation. The value of **size1** is 3, and the value of **size2** is 4. The user references **intTwoArray(1,2)**, which maps to **a[1 * 4 + 2]**.

The overloads return **int** references for exactly the same reason that the overloads of the subscript operator returned **int** references in Example 6.7.1.

The output of the **main** function of Figure 6.7.4 is

```
0 1 2 3
2 3 4 5
4 5 6 7
FirstOutOfBounds
```

■

```
int main() {
   intTwoArray b( 3, 4 );
   int i, j;
   for ( i = 0; i < b.get_size1(); i++ )
      for ( j = 0; j < b.get_size2(); j++ )
         b( i, j ) = 2 * i + j;
   for ( i = 0; i < b.get_size1(); i++ ) {
      for ( j = 0; j < b.get_size2(); j++ )
         cout << setw( 2 ) << b( i, j );
      cout << '\n';
   }
   try {
      cout << b( 4, 2 ) << '\n';
      cout << b( 2, 8 ) << '\n';
   }
   catch( string s ) {
      cerr << s << '\n';
   }
   return 0;
}
```

**FIGURE 6.7.4** A test driver for the overloaded function call operator of Figure 6.7.2.

## Overloading the Increment and Decrement Operators

The increment **++** and decrement **--** operators are among those that can be overloaded. Recall that each operator comes in a "pre" and "post" form:

```
int x = 6;
++x; // preincrement
x++; // postincrement
```

Accordingly, we can overload the preincrement, postincrement, predecrement, and post-decrement operators.

The declaration

```
operator++();
```

with no parameters overloads the preincrement operator, and the declaration

```
operator++( int );
```

with a single **int** parameter overloads the postincrement operator. (Similar comments apply to the decrement operator.) The **int** parameter in the postincrement form serves to distinguish it from the preincrement form. The parameter itself may be, but need not be, used.

**EXAMPLE 6.7.4.**  Class **Clock**, shown in Figure 6.7.5, overloads both the preincrement and postincrement operators so that they act on **Clock**s just as the built-in preincrement and postincrement operators act on numeric types such as **int**s. If **c** is a **Clock**, **c++** advances the time one minute. The value of the *expression* **c++** is the *original* **Clock**. Executing **++c** also advances the time one minute, but the value of the expression **++c** is the *updated* **Clock**.

The default constructor, which results from using the default values specified for all the parameters, sets the clock to 12:00 A.M. Method **tick** adds one minute to the **Clock** and then returns it.  Method **operator++()** overloads the preincrement operator. It advances the time one minute by invoking **tick** and returns the updated **Clock**.

```
class Clock {
public:
    Clock( int = 12, int = 0, int = 0 );
    Clock tick();
    friend ostream& operator<<( ostream&, const Clock& );
    Clock operator++();      // ++c
    Clock operator++( int ); // c++
private:
    int hour;
    int min;
    int ap; // 0 is AM, 1 is PM
};

Clock::Clock( int h, int m, int ap_flag ) {
    hour = h;
    min = m;
    ap = ap_flag;
}

Clock Clock::tick() {
    ++min;
    if ( min == 60 ) {
        hour++;
        min = 0;
    }
    if ( hour == 13 )
        hour = 1;
    if ( hour == 12 && min == 0 )
        ap = !ap;
    return *this;
}
```

**FIGURE 6.7.5** A **Clock** class with overloaded preincrement and postincrement operators.

```
Clock Clock::operator++() {
   return tick();
}

Clock Clock::operator++( int n ) {
   Clock c = *this;
   tick();
   return c;
}

ostream& operator<<( ostream& out, const Clock& c ) {
   out << setfill( '0' ) << setw( 2 ) << c.hour
       << ':' << setw( 2 ) << c.min;
   if ( c.ap )
      out << " PM";
   else
      out << " AM";
   return out;
}
```

**FIGURE 6.7.5** Continued.

Method **operator++( int )** overloads the postincrement operator. After saving the current **Clock**, referenced as **\*this**, in **c**, it advances the time one minute by invoking **tick** and returns **c**, the (unchanged) original **Clock**. The parameter **n** is not used; it serves only to distinguish the postincrement operator from the preincrement operator.

The left-shift operator is overloaded to output a **Clock**. It prints the time in the form

**xx:xx XX**

where **XX** is either **AM** or **PM**.

The output of the code

```
int main() {
   Clock c, d;
   c = d++;
   cout << "Clock c: " << c << '\n';
   cout << "Clock d: " << d << '\n';
   //...
}
```

is

```
Clock c: 12:00 AM
Clock d: 12:01 AM
```

The output of the code

```
int main() {
   Clock c, d;
   c = ++d;
   cout << "Clock c: " << c << '\n';
   cout << "Clock d: " << d << '\n';
   //...
}
```

is

```
Clock c: 12:01 AM
Clock d: 12:01 AM
```

■

## Type Conversions

Recall that a convert constructor for class **C** is a one-parameter constructor (not of type **C&**). If the parameter is of type *paramtype*, the convert constructor converts type *paramtype* to type **C**.

**EXAMPLE 6.7.5.**   In the code segment

```
class C {
   //...
   C( int ); // convert constructor
   //...
};
//...
int main() {
   int i = 8;
   C c;
   c = i;
   //...
}
```

in the statement

```
   c = i;
```

the convert constructor converts **i**, which is of type **int**, to type **C**, after which the converted result is assigned to **c**.                                                          ■

The convert constructor converts some other type to a class type. To convert a class type to some other type, the programmer can overload the type conversion operator. To convert class type **C** to *othertype*, the programmer writes a method whose declaration is

**operator** *othertype***();**

Note that the declaration does *not* include a return type, not even **void**. Nevertheless, the body of the method *must* contain a **return** statement to return the converted value.

**EXAMPLE 6.7.6.** We amend the `Clock` class (see Figure 6.7.5) by adding a conversion operator to convert the time of the clock to an integer

```
class Clock {
public:
   operator int();
   //...
};
Clock::operator int() {
   int time = hour;
   if ( time == 12 )
      time = 0;
   if ( ap == 1 )
      time += 12;
   time *= 100;
   time += min;
   return time;
}
```

The integer time is "military time," in which 1:00 P.M. becomes 1300, 2:00 P.M. becomes 1400, 12:00 A.M. becomes 0, and so on. For example, if the time is 8:34 A.M., the integer value is 834. If the time is 4:08 P.M., the integer value is 1608. As an example of the use of the conversion operator, the output of the code segment

```
Clock c( 8, 55, 1 );
int i;
i = c;
cout << i << '\n';
```

is

```
2055
```

■

**EXAMPLE 6.7.7.** The code segment

```
char next;
while ( cin >> next )
   cout << next;
```

copies the standard input to the standard output until end-of-file is reached (assuming that the flag is set for not skipping white space). The `while` condition must evaluate to an integer or pointer value. However, the expression

```
cin >> next
```

evaluates to an object. A type conversion operator handles the conversion to `void*`. If the value of the resulting pointer is zero, the condition is false; otherwise, the condition is true. ■

Despite their convenience, type conversion operators should be used with caution because the compiler, not the programmer, typically invokes a type conversion operator. The normal call to a type conversion operator is thus *hidden* from the programmer, who may not have anticipated all of the situations in which such an operator would be invoked.

## EXERCISES

1. If we overload the subscript operator, how many parameters does **operator[ ]** have?

2. If we overload the function call operator, how many parameters does **operator()** have?

3. Overload **>>** for input for the **intArray** class of Example 6.7.1. (The overload should input **get_size()** values.)

4. Overload **<<** for output for the **intArray** class of Example 6.7.1. (The overload should output **get_size()** values.)

5. Overload **>>** for input for the **intTwoArray** class of Example 6.7.3. (The overload should input **get_size1() * get_size2()** values.)

6. Overload **<<** for output for the **intTwoArray** class of Example 6.7.3. (The overload should output **get_size1() * get_size2()** values.)

7. Overload a non**const** version of the subscript operator for the **OPair** class of Example 6.1.2 so that, if **s** is an **OPair** object, **s[ 1 ]** is the value of the first member of the ordered pair, and **s[ 2 ]** is the value of the second member of the ordered pair. If the index is illegal, throw an exception.

8. Rewrite the class **intArray** of Example 6.7.1; replace the overloaded subscript operators with overloaded function call operators.

9. Write a copy constructor and overload the assignment operator for the **intArray** class of Example 6.7.1. After a copy, the target object and the source object should have their own copies of the data.

10. Write a copy constructor and overload the assignment operator for the **intTwoArray** class of Example 6.7.3. After a copy, the target object and the source object should have their own copies of the data.

11. Overload the preincrement operator for the **intArray** class of Example 6.7.1 so that 1 is added to each entry in the array. Return the updated **intArray** object.

12. Overload the postincrement operator for the **intArray** class of Example 6.7.1 so that 1 is added to each entry in the array. Return the original **intArray** object.

13. Overload the predecrement operator for the **intTwoArray** class of Example 6.7.3 so that 1 is subtracted from each entry in the array. Return the updated **intTwoArray** object.

14. Overload the postdecrement operator for the **intTwoArray** class of Example 6.7.3 so that 1 is subtracted from each entry in the array. Return the original **intTwoArray** object.

**15.** Explain the error:

```
class Point {
    //...
    char* operator char*();
    //...
};
```

**16.** Write a type conversion operator for the **OPair** class of Example 6.1.2 that converts **OPair** to **bool**. The conversion returns **false**, if both elements of the ordered pair are zero, and **true**, otherwise.

# 6.8 SAMPLE APPLICATION: AN ASSOCIATIVE ARRAY

### Problem

Create a dictionary class **Dict** that supports *word-definition* pairs, together with appropriate methods. In particular, the subscript operator should be overloaded so that if **d** is a **Dict** object, the following should be valid:

```
d[ "pixel" ] = "picture element";
```

Here **pixel** is defined as a **picture element**. An array that takes noninteger indexes is called an **associative array**. A statement such as

```
cout << d[ "pixel" ];
```

should print the definition of **pixel**, provided that **pixel** is in the dictionary. If it is not in the dictionary, a failure message should be printed.

### Sample Input/Output

The output from the **main** function of Figure 6.8.1 is

```
dump
residual fm defined as: incidental fm
pixel defined as: in a daffy state

dump
residual fm defined as: incidental fm
pixel defined as: picture element

lookup

residual fm defined as: incidental fm
pixie defined as: *** not in dictionary
pixel defined as: picture element
```

```
int main() {
   // Create a dictionary of word-definition pairs
   Dict d;
   // Add some pairs
   d[ "residual fm" ] = "incidental fm";
   d[ "pixel" ] = "in a daffy state";
   // Print all pairs in the dictionary.
   cout << "\n\ndump\n" << d;
   // Change definition of pixel
   d[ "pixel" ] = "picture element";
   // Print all pairs in the dictionary.
   cout << "\n\ndump\n" << d;
   // Look up some words
   cout << "\n\nlookup\n\n";
   cout << d[ "residual fm" ] << '\n';
   cout << d[ "pixie" ] << '\n';
   cout << d[ "pixel" ] << '\n';
   return 0;
}
```

**FIGURE 6.8.1** A test driver for the **Dict** class.

### Solution

We begin by implementing an auxiliary class **Entry** that holds a word, its definition, and a flag to show whether a word and its definition are stored. In addition, **Entry** has a default constructor to initialize the flag to **false**; methods to add a word and its definition, to test for a word match, and to get the flag; and overloads of the assignment operator to copy a string (**string** or C-style string), regarded as a definition, into an **Entry** object. An overload of **<<** to print the word and its definition is declared as a **friend** function.

The **Dict** class has a single data member—an array of **Entry** to store word-definition pairs—and overloads of the subscript operator. In addition, **Dict** declares an **enum** constant **MaxEntries**, which is used to define the array of **Entry**, and a **friend** overload of **<<** to print all of the entries in the dictionary.

The major challenge is to design overloads of the subscript operator. In an expression such as

```
d[ "pixel" ]
```

an overload must search the array of **Entry** for **pixel**. If it finds **pixel**, it returns the **Entry** cell in the array that contains **pixel**. Since **<<** is overloaded for output of **Entry** objects, we can use **<<** to output the entry:

```
cout << d[ "pixel" ];
```

If **pixel** is not found, an overload of the subscript operator must return a dummy **Entry** cell whose word is **pixel** and whose definition is

```
*** not in dictionary
```

Thus if **pixel** is not found, the output is

```
pixel defined as: *** not in dictionary
```

We use the first **Entry** cell that does not contain an actual definition for this purpose. We *always* reserve at least one extra cell for just this purpose.

Consider the situation when we enter a definition:

```
d[ "pixel" ] = "picture element";
```

Again an overload searches for the word **pixel**. Assuming that it is not found, it again returns the first unused **Entry** cell. Notice that this is exactly the right cell in which to add the new word-definition pair! Again the overload stores the word **pixel** and the definition

```
*** not in dictionary
```

in this cell. This time we want the assignment operator to replace

```
*** not in dictionary
```

by **picture element**. Since the left side of the assignment operator is of type **Entry**, we overload the assignment operator in class **Entry** to copy the definition **picture element** into the **Entry** cell and set the flag to indicate that a valid entry is now stored.

### C++ Implementation

```
class Entry {
public:
    Entry() { flag = false; }
    void add( const string&, const string& );
    bool match( const string& ) const;
    void operator=( const string& );
    void operator=( const char* );
    friend ostream& operator<<( ostream&, const Entry& );
    bool valid() const { return flag; }
private:
    string word;
    string def;
    bool flag;
};

void Entry::operator=( const string& str ) {
    def = str;
    flag = true;
}

void Entry::operator=( const char* str ) {
    def = str;
    flag = true;
}
```

```cpp
ostream& operator<<( ostream& out, const Entry& e ) {
   out << e.word << " defined as: "
       << e.def;
   return out;
}

void Entry::add( const string& w, const string& d ) {
   word = w;
   def = d;
}

bool Entry::match( const string& key ) const {
   return key == word;
}

class Dict {
public:
   enum { MaxEntries = 100 };
   friend ostream& operator<<( ostream&, const Dict& );
   Entry& operator[ ]( const string& );
   Entry& operator[ ]( const char* );
private:
   Entry entries[ MaxEntries + 1 ];
};

ostream& operator<<( ostream& out, const Dict& d ) {
   for ( int i = 0; i < MaxEntries; i++ )
      if ( d.entries[ i ].valid() )
         out << d.entries[ i ] << '\n';
   return out;
}

Entry& Dict::operator[ ]( const string& k ) {
   for ( int i = 0; i < MaxEntries && entries[ i ].valid(); i++ )
      if ( entries[ i ].match( k ) )
         return entries[ i ];
   string not_found = "*** not in dictionary";
   entries[ i ].add( k, not_found );
   return entries[ i ];
}

Entry& Dict::operator[ ]( const char* k ) {
   string s = k;
   return operator[ ]( s );
}
```

### *Discussion*

Class **Entry** has **string** data members to hold a word and its definition, and a **bool** member that is either **true**, to indicate that a word-definition pair is stored, or **false**, to indicate that a word-definition pair is not stored.

Class **Entry**'s default constructor sets **flag** to **false**. Method **add** copies a word and its definition into **word** and **def**. Method **match** checks whether the string passed matches **word** and returns **true** or **false** to signal the result.

Operator **<<** is overloaded for output as a **friend**, using the technique explained in Section 6.5. Overloads of the assignment operator copy the definition passed (either as a **string** or as a null-terminated array of **char**) and set **flag** to **true** to indicate that a valid entry has been stored.

Class **Dict** contains the data member **entries**, an array of **Entry** objects. The array is of size **MaxEntries + 1**, so it can hold up to **MaxEntries** actual entries; one cell is always reserved for a dummy cell to hold "not found" information as described in the preceding Solution subsection. The **Entry** default constructor initializes **flag** in each cell of the array to **false**.

Operator **<<** is also overloaded for output for the class **Dict**. It loops through all of the cells in the array **Entry**. Each cell that holds an actual word-definition pair is output using the overloaded **<<** operator for class **Entry**.

Overloads of the subscript operator check each valid entry for a match of the word **k** that is passed

```
for ( int i = 0; i < MaxEntries && entries[ i ].valid(); i++ )
    if ( entries[ i ].match( k ) )
        return entries[ i ];
```

If a match is found, it returns the matching **Entry** cell. The **Entry** cell is returned by reference, because it may be modified. For example if **pixel** is already in the dictionary, the statement

```
d[ "pixel" ] = "picture element";
```

modifies **pixel**'s definition.

If a match is not found, the overload stores the word that was passed and

```
*** not in dictionary
```

for use in a "not found" message and returns the **Entry** cell

```
string not_found = "*** not in dictionary";
entries[ i ].add( k, not_found );
return entries[ i ];
```

If a word-definition pair is being added to the dictionary

```
d[ "pixel" ] = "picture element";
```

execution of the statement is completed by an overload of the assignment operator in class **Entry**, which replaces

```
*** not in dictionary
```

by the actual definition (**picture element** in this case).

## EXERCISES

**1.** Could `operator=` be implemented so that its declaration is

```
void operator=( const string& ) const;
```

Explain.

**2.** Could `operator[ ]` be implemented so that its declaration is

```
Entry& operator[ ]( const string& ) const;
```

Explain.

**3.** Implement

```
void Dict::remove( const string& w )
```

which removes word **w** from the dictionary if **w** occurs there.

## 6.9 MEMORY MANAGEMENT OPERATORS

The memory management operators **new**, **new[ ]**, **delete**, and **delete[ ]** may be overloaded as either methods or top-level operator functions. Such overloading is useful when an application needs to take control of its own memory management. An embedded system (for example, a microprocessor system that regulates a refrigerator or an automobile engine) may have very limited memory resources that the application needs to manage directly. Some environments, such as Microsoft Windows, have memory management schemes that application programs are advised to follow, thus requiring direct memory management.

**EXAMPLE 6.9.1.**   The code segments

```
// overloaded as method in class C
void* C::operator new( size_t size ) {
  //...
}
```

and

```
// overloaded as top-level operator function
void* operator new( size_t size ) {
  //...
}
```

illustrate two overloads of the operator **new**. The overloaded **new** operators both return type **void***. In this example, each overloaded operator function expects a single argument of type **size_t**. A typical invocation of **C::new** would be

```
C* c1 = new C; // allocate a C object
```

The system uses the overloaded **C::new** operator. If such an operator were not defined, then the system would use the built-in **new** operator.  ■

The initial parameter in the overloaded **new** or **new[ ]** operator must be of type **size_t**. The value of this parameter is equal to the size in bytes of the object being created. (For **new[ ]**, it is equal to the size in bytes of *all* of the objects being created.) Other parameters are optional. In any case, an overload such as

```
void* C::new( void* ptr ) { // ***** ERROR: no size_t
  //...
}
```

contains an error because the first parameter is not of type **size_t**.

**EXAMPLE 6.9.2.**    The code segments

```
// overloaded as method
void C::operator delete( void* objPtr ) {
  //...
}
```

and

```
// overloaded as top-level function operator
void operator delete( void* objPtr ) {
  //...
}
```

illustrate two overloads of the **delete** operator. The operator returns **void** and its first parameter must be of type **void***, which points to the storage to be freed. A typical invocation of **C::delete** would be

```
C* c1 = new C;    // allocate
//...
delete c1;        // free
```

The system again uses the overloaded **delete** if one is present and the built-in **delete** otherwise.　■

The initial parameter in the overloaded **delete** or **delete[ ]** must be of type **void***, and either must return type **void**. Other parameters are optional.

Next we illustrate an overload of **new** as a method. The overloaded **new** allocates storage from a fixed pool available to the program.

**EXAMPLE 6.9.3.**    We define a **Frame** class, which represents data frames to be transmitted in a data communications application (see Figure 6.9.1). A **Frame** has data member **name**, which we use to trace the program's execution. Data member **data** holds **DataSize** bytes to be transmitted in a data communications application. All storage for **Frame**s comes from **framePool**, an array of **unsigned char** with size

```
MaxFrames * sizeof( Frame )
```

```cpp
const int MaxFrames = 4;
const int DataSize = 128;
class Frame {
public:
   Frame() { name = "NoName"; print(); }
   Frame( const char* n ) { name = n; print(); }
   Frame( const string& n ) { name = n; print(); }
   Frame( const string&, const void*, unsigned );
   void print() const;
   void* operator new( size_t );
private:
   string name;
   unsigned char data[ DataSize ];
};
Frame* allFrames = 0;   // no Frames yet
unsigned char framePool[ MaxFrames * sizeof( Frame ) ];
bool alloc[ MaxFrames ];
Frame::Frame( const string& n, const void* d,
              unsigned bsize ) {
   name = n;
   memcpy( data, d, bsize );
   print();
}
void Frame::print() const {
   cout << name << " created.\n";
}
void* Frame::operator new( size_t size ) {
   // allocating a new Frame?
   if ( size != sizeof( Frame ) )
      throw string( "Not a Frame" );
   // storage allocated yet?
   if ( allFrames == 0 ) {
      allFrames = reinterpret_cast<Frame*>(framePool);
      for ( int i = 0; i < MaxFrames; i++ )
         alloc[ i ] = false;
   }
   for ( int i = 0; i < MaxFrames; i++ )
      if ( !alloc[ i ] ) {
         alloc[ i ] = true;
         return allFrames + i;
      }
   throw string( "Out of Storage" );
   return 0;
}
```

**FIGURE 6.9.1** Overloading operator **new**.

Accordingly, **framePool** points to storage for up to **MaxFrames** objects of type **Frame**. The objects are allocated one at a time

```
Frame* f1 = new Frame( "f1" ); // allocate one
Frame* f2 = new Frame( "f2" ); // allocate another
```

The syntax for the overloaded **new** operator is the same as for the built-in **new** operator.

When a **Frame** object is created dynamically, the overloaded **new** operator allocates storage from **framePool** if any is available. The overloaded **new** begins by checking whether the size is correct for a **Frame**; if not, it throws an exception:

```
if ( size != sizeof( Frame ) )
    throw string( "Not a Frame" );
```

The first time **new** allocates storage from **framePool**, it sets **allFrames** to the start of the storage

```
allFrames = reinterpret_cast<Frame*>(framePool);
```

Since **framePool** is of type pointer to **unsigned char** and **allFrames** is of type pointer to **Frame**, a cast is required. The cast **reinterpret_cast** must be used because a pointer to one type is being cast to a pointer of a different type (see Section 2.4). Next **new** marks each position in the **framePool** array as available for allocation:

```
for ( int i = 0; i < MaxFrames; i++ )
    alloc[ i ] = false;
```

To allocate a **Frame**, **new** steps through the **alloc** array looking for an available **Frame**:

```
for ( int i = 0; i < MaxFrames; i++ )
    if ( !alloc[ i ] ) {
        alloc[ i ] = true;
        return allFrames + i;
    }
```

If **alloc[ i ]** is **false**, a **Frame** is available at position **i** in the **framePool** array. In this case, **new** marks this position as not available

```
alloc[ i ] = true;
```

and returns the address **allFrames + i** of the storage. If no more storage is available, **new** throws an exception:

```
throw string( "Out of Storage" );
```

The output of the **main** function of Figure 6.9.2 is

```
NoName created.
f1 created.
f2 created.
f3 created.
Out of Storage
```

```
int main() {
   Frame* a[ 5 ];
   string names[ 4 ] = { "f1", "f2", "f3", "f4" };
   try {
      a[ 0 ] = new Frame;
      for ( int i = 0; i < 4; i++ )
         a[ i + 1 ] = new Frame( names[ i ] );
   }
   catch( string s ) {
      cerr << s << '\n';
      exit( EXIT_FAILURE );
   }
   return 0;
}
```

**FIGURE 6.9.2**  A test client for the **Frame** class of Figure 6.9.1.


## EXERCISES

**1.** Assume that the **new** operator is overloaded for class **C1** but not for class **C2**. Explain which **new** operator is invoked in each case:

```
C1* c1 = new C1;
C2* c2 = new C2;
int* i1 = new int;
C1* cs = new C1[ 10 ];
```

**2.** Explain the error:

```
void* C::new( int howmany ) {
   //...
}
```

**3.** Explain the error:

```
void delete( char* ptr ) {
   //...
}
```

**4.** Is an overload of the **new** operator restricted to a single parameter?

**5.** Overload the **delete** operator for the class **Frame** of Figure 6.9.1.

**6.** Overload the **new[ ]** operator for the class **Frame** of Figure 6.9.1.

**7.** Overload the **delete[ ]** operator for the class **Frame** of Figure 6.9.1.

## C++ POSTSCRIPT

## friend Classes

A method in one class may be a **friend** in another class.

**EXAMPLE.** Class c

```
class F {
public:
    int f();
private:
    int adm;
};

class C {
public:
    int m();
    // F's method f is a friend of class C
    friend int F::f();
private:
    int adm;
};
```

declares the **friend** function **f**, which is a method in class **F**; thus, **f** can access **c**'s **private** data member **adm**. ∎

If *every* method in a class **F** is to be a **friend** of another class **C**, instead of individually declaring each method in **F**, we can declare **F** to be a **friend** class of **C**.

**EXAMPLE.** The code

```
class F {
    //...
};

class C {
    friend F;
    //...
};
```

makes **F** a **friend** of class **C**. As a result, any method in **F** has full access to all members of **C**, even **private** and **protected** ones. ∎

## COMMON PROGRAMMING ERRORS

**1.** It is an error to overload these operators:

| Operator | Purpose |
|---|---|
| **.** | Class member operator |
| **.\*** | Class member object selector operator |
| **: :** | Scope resolution operator |
| **? :** | Conditional operator |

Only the operators listed in Section 6.1 can be overloaded.

**2.** It is an error to assume that the assignment operator is inherited in a derived class. It is the *single* operator *not* inherited.

**3.** Except for the memory management operators **new**, **new[ ]**, **delete**, and **delete[ ]**, an operator must either be overloaded as a method or have at least one class object among its arguments. For example,

```
// ***** ERROR: neither a method nor a
// function that takes a class argument
int operator+( int num1, int num2 )  {
   //...
}
```

has an error because the overloaded operator is not a method and does not have a class object among its arguments.

**4.** It is an error to overload the subscript operator **[ ]** except as a method.

**5.** It is an error to overload the function call operator **()** except as a method.

**6.** It is an error to overload the assignment operator **=** except as a method.

**7.** It is an error to overload the class indirection operator **->** except as a method.

**8.** If a binary operator is overloaded as a method, it has *one* parameter. For example,

```
// ***** ERROR: + is binary
Complex Complex::operator+( const Complex& c1,
                           const Complex& c2 ) const {
   //...
}
```

contains an error because **+** is a binary operator. An expression such as

```
c1 + c2  // c1 and c2 are Complex
```

is shorthand for

```
c1.operator+( c2 )
```

Method **operator+** therefore should take one argument:

```
// ok
Complex Complex::operator+( const Complex& c ) const {
    //...
}
```

9. If a unary operator is overloaded as a method, except for the postincrement and post-decrement overloads, it has *no* parameters. For example,

```
// ***** ERROR: ! is binary
String String::operator!( String& s ) {
    //...
}
```

contains an error because **!** is a unary operator. An expression such as

```
!ss // ss is String object
```

is shorthand for

```
ss.operator!()
```

Method **operator!** therefore should take no arguments:

```
// ok
String String::operator!() {
    //...
}
```

10. If a binary operator is overloaded as a top-level function, it has *two* parameters. For example,

```
// ***** ERROR: + is binary
Complex operator+( const Complex& c ) {
    //...
}
```

contains an error because **+** is a binary operator. An expression such as

```
c1 + c2   // c1 and c2 are Complex
```

is shorthand for

```
operator+( c1, c2 )
```

The function **operator+** therefore should take two arguments:

```
// ok
Complex operator+( const Complex& c1,
                   const Complex& c2 ) {
    //...
}
```

**11.** If a unary operator is overloaded as a top-level function, it has *one* parameter. For example,

```
// ***** ERROR: ! is unary
String operator!() {
   //...
}
```

contains an error because **!** is a unary operator. An expression such as

```
!ss // ss is a String
```

is shorthand for

```
operator!( ss )
```

The function **operator!** therefore should take one argument:

```
// ok
String operator!( String& s ) {
   //...
}
```

**12.** A top-level function that overloads an operator for class **c** does not have access to **c**'s **private** or **protected** members unless it is a **friend** of **c**.

**13.** A top-level function—even a **friend**—is *not* a method. Thus it is an error to connect it to a class with the scope resolution operator:

```
class C {
   //...
   friend C operator+( const C&, const C& );
   //...
};

// ***** ERROR: operator+ not a method in class C
C C::operator+( const C& c1, const C& c2 ) {
   //...
}
```

The top-level function **operator+** is properly written as

```
// Correct
C operator+( const C& c1, const C& c2 ) {
   //...
}
```

**14.** When **>>** is overloaded for input, the class object *must* be passed by reference, because the data input are to be written into the object and *not* into a *copy* of the object. For this reason, the following is an error:

```
istream& operator>>( istream& in, Complex c ) {
   return in >> c.read >> c.imag;
}
```

The error is corrected by writing

```
istream& operator>>( istream& in, Complex& c ) {
    return in >> c.read >> c.imag;
}
```

15. The method declaration

```
operator++();
```

overloads the *preincrement* operator, not the postincrement operator. The method declaration

```
operator++( int );
```

overloads the *postincrement* operator. The **int** parameter serves to distinguish the two overloads. The parameter itself may be, but need not be, used. Similar statements apply to the predecrement and postdecrement operators.

16. It is an error to specify, in either a declaration or a definition, the return data type—even **void**—for a type conversion operator despite the fact that such an operator contains a **return** statement. For example,

```
// ***** ERROR: can't give return data type
char* String::operator char*() {
    //...
    return str;
}
```

17. It is an error to have the overloaded **new** or **new[ ]** operator return any value except **void***.

18. It is an error if the first argument to the overloaded **new** or **new[ ]** operator is not of type **size_t**. The overloaded operators may have additional arguments of any type, however.

19. It is an error to have the overloaded **delete** or **delete[ ]** operator return any value except **void**.

20. It is an error if the first argument to the overloaded **delete** or **delete[ ]** operator is not of type **void***. The overloaded operators may have additional arguments of any type, however.

## PROGRAMMING EXERCISES

**6.1.** Overload the equals (**==**), not equal (**!=**), unary minus (**-**), and right shift operator (**>>**) for the **Complex** class. Complex numbers $z_1 = a + bi$ and $z_2 = c + di$ are equal if and only if $a$ equals $c$ and $b$ equals $d$. If $z = a + bi$ is a complex number, $-z$ equals $-a - bi$. Overload the right shift operator for input.

**6.2.** Overload the function call operator to set the time for the **Clock** class of Example 6.7.4. The overload should behave similarly to the constructor. Also overload **==** and **!=** so that two **Clock**s can be compared. Two **Clock**s are equal if and only if they have the same time.

**6.3.** Overload the operator ˜ for the **Deck** class of Programming Exercise 3.6 so that if **d** is a **Deck**, ˜**d** (pronounced "twiddle dee") shuffles **d**. Also overload the **<<** operator for output of a **Deck**.

**6.4.** Overload **+** (union), **-** (difference), ***** (intersection), **<<** (output), **>>** (input), and the function call operator (to add an element) for the **Set** class of Programming Exercise 3.12.

**6.5.** Overload **+** (union), **<<** (output), **>>** (input), and the function call operator (to add an element) for the **Bag** class of Programming Exercise 3.13.

**6.6.** Overload the preincrement and postincrement **++** operators for the **Spaceship** class of Programming Exercise 3.14. The preincrement operator advances the time one unit, updates the **Spaceship**'s position, and returns the updated **Spaceship**. The postincrement operator advances the time one unit, updates the **Spaceship**'s position, and returns the original **Spaceship**.

**6.7.** Overload the operator **+** for the **LAN** (local area network) class of Programming Exercise 3.17. The code segment

```
LAN lan1, lan2, lan3;
//...
lan3 = lan1 + lan2;
```

makes **lan3** a **LAN** that includes **lan1** and **lan2** as subLANs. A combined **LAN** includes all of the nodes from the **LAN**s that it combines. However, its topology may differ from theirs because, for example, we might combine a *star* and a *bus* **LAN** into a new **LAN** with a hybrid topology.

**6.8.** Suppose that a class hierarchy has a **virtual** method **print**

```
class C {
    //...
    virtual void print( ostream& ) const;
    //...
};
```

that outputs **C**'s members to the stream **ostream**. Write *one* overload of **<<** so that the statement

```
out << p;
```

outputs **p**'s members to the stream **out**, where **p** is *any* object that belongs to a class in the hierarchy.

**6.9.** Suppose that **Matrix2** is a two-dimensional matrix class. Overload the subscript operator **[ ]** so that if **m** is a **Matrix2** object,

```
m[ i ][ j ]
```

references the cell in the **i**th row and **j**th column.

**6.10.** Implement a string class, similar to the class **string** of Section 2.5, with as much functionality of **string** as you can.

# CHAPTER

## 7

# TEMPLATES AND THE STANDARD TEMPLATE LIBRARY

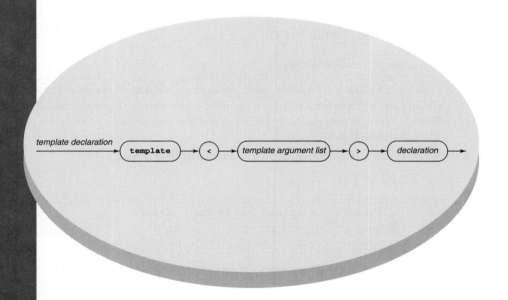

7.1 Template Basics

7.2 Sample Application: A Template Stack Class

7.3 The Standard Template Library

7.4 Sample Application: Stock Performance Reports

C++ Postscript

Common Programming Errors

Programming Exercises

**C**++ supports code reuse in different ways. For example, through inheritance a derived class is able to reuse a base class's members, in particular the inherited methods. This chapter examines template classes, another C++ mechanism for code reuse, and also introduces the Standard Template Library (STL), a powerful C++ library of template classes and functions.

## 7.1 TEMPLATE BASICS

Figure 7.1.1 creates an **intArray** class, which is a variant of the one in Section 6.7. We could build a separate **charArray** class, a separate **stringArray** class, and other separate classes modeled after **intArray**. C++ has a better way, however. We can write all the code for an **Array** class *only once* and then use this code to create **Array**s of *any data type*, built-in or user-defined. We do so by making **Array** a **template class**, that is, a class that is *not* data-type specific. A template class is created with at least one **class parameter**, a symbol that serves as a placeholder for a specific data type.

> **EXAMPLE 7.1.1.** The code in Figure 7.1.2 creates a template class **Array**. The declaration begins
>
> ```
> template< class T >
> class Array {
>  //...
> };
> ```
>
> **T** is the class parameter, which follows the keyword **class** or the keyword **typename** inside angle brackets; **class** and **typename** have the same meaning.[†] (**template** is also a C++ keyword.) Any legal C++ identifier can serve as a class parameter. In our class declaration, we place the **template header**
>
> ```
> template< class T >
> ```
>
> on a separate line only for readability. The declaration
>
> ```
> template< class T > class Array {
>  //...
> };
> ```
>
> is legal and equivalent to our original.
>
> In the template header, white space can occur between **template** and the left angle bracket **<**. The style
>
> ```
> template < class T > // legal
> ```

---

[†] The keyword **typename** is relatively new and may not be supported on all systems.

```
class intArray {
public:
   int& operator[ ]( int );
   const int& operator[ ]( int ) const;
   intArray( int );
  ~intArray();
   int get_size() const { return size; }
private:
   int* a;
   int size;
   intArray(); //*** for emphasis
   int dummy_val; // arbitrary value
};
int& intArray::operator[ ]( int i ) {
   if ( i < 0 || i >= size ) {
      cerr << "index " << i << " out of bounds: ";
      return dummy_val;
   }
   return a[ i ];
}
const int& intArray::operator[ ]( int i ) const {
   if ( i < 0 || i >= size ) {
      cerr << "index " << i << " out of bounds: ";
      return dummy_val;
   }
   return a[ i ];
}
intArray::intArray( int s ) {
   a = new int[ size = s ];
}
intArray::~intArray() {
   delete[ ] a;
}
```

**FIGURE 7.1.1** The class `intArray`.

is legal but uncommon. Inside the angle brackets, the only required white space is between **class** and the class parameter. So

```
template<class T>
```

is also legal.

Our parameterized **Array** constructor and the overloaded index operator are defined *outside* the class declaration, which requires that we repeat the template header

```
template< class T >
```

```
template< class T >
class Array {
public:
   T& operator[ ]( int );
   const T& operator[ ]( int ) const;
   Array( int );
  ~Array();
   int get_size() const { return size; }
private:
   T* a;
   int size;
   Array(); //*** for emphasis
   T dummy_val; // returned on bad index
};
template< class T >
T& Array< T >::operator[ ]( int i ) {
   if ( i < 0 || i >= size ) {
      cerr << "index " << i << " out of bounds: ";
      return dummy_val;
   }
   return a[ i ];
}
template< class T >
const T& Array< T >::operator[ ]( int i ) const {
   if ( i < 0 || i >= size ) {
      cerr << "index " << i << " out of bounds: ";
      return dummy_val;
   }
   return a[ i ];
}
template< class T >
Array< T >::Array( int s ) {
   a = new T[ size = s ];
}
template< class T >
Array< T >::~Array() {
   delete[ ] a;
}
// top-level overload of operator<<
template< class T >
ostream& operator<<(ostream& os, const Array< T >& ar) {
   for ( int i = 0; i < ar.get_size(); i++ )
     os << ar[ i ] << endl;
   return os;
}
```

**FIGURE 7.1.2** The template class `Array`.

in each definition. Further, there is new syntax for specifying the class to which the methods belong. For example, the definition of the convert constructor is

```
template< class T >
Array< T >::Array( int s ) {
   a = new T[ size = s ];
}
```

Because **Array** is a template class, the class name is **Array< T >**, where **T** is the class parameter in the template header. Therefore, **Array< T >** occurs to the left of the scope resolution operator **::** in the definition of the constructor and the overloaded index operator. The syntax is simpler if a method is defined *inside* the class declaration. Here, for instance, is how we would define the convert constructor inline:

```
template< class T >
class Array {
public:
   //...
   Array( int s ) {
      a = new T[ size = s ];
   }
   //...
};
```

A template class may have more than one class parameter, in which case the class parameters are separated by commas. The keyword **class** or **typename** must occur to the left of each class parameter.

**EXAMPLE 7.1.2.**   The declaration

```
template< class T1, class T2, class T3 >
class Sample {
public:
   T2 m( T3 p ) { /*...*/ } // expects a T3 arg, returns a T2
private:
   T1 x;  // var of type T1
};
```

illustrates the syntax for a template class with multiple class parameters.  ∎

# Template Instantiations

To use a template class, we specify a data type in angle brackets.

**EXAMPLE 7.1.3.**  Given the template class declaration in Figure 7.1.2, the code segment

```
Array< double > a1( 100 ); // Array of 100 doubles
```

defines **a1** as an **Array** of 100 **double**s. Object **a1**'s data type is

```
Array< double >
```

The syntax indicates that the data type **double** replaces the class parameter **T** in **Array**'s declaration. The compiler replaces occurrences of the class parameter **T** in **Array**'s declaration with **double**. For example, the compiler changes the declaration

```
T& operator[ ]( int ); // template version
```

to

```
double& operator[ ]( int ); // Array< double > version
```

The compiler likewise changes data member **a**'s declaration from

```
T* a; // template version
```

to

```
double* a; // Array< double > version
```

If we define object **a2** as

```
Array< string > a2( 50 );
```

then **a2**'s data type is

```
Array< string >
```

and the compiler replaces occurrences of the class parameter **T** in **Array**'s declaration with **string**. ∎

We refer to **Array< double >** and **Array< char >** as **template instantiations** or simply **instantiations** of the template class **Array< T >**, where **T** is the class parameter in the template header. The syntax for using a template instantiation is the same as the syntax for using an ordinary, nontemplate class.

**EXAMPLE 7.1.4.** The code segment

```
#include <iostream>
using namespace std;
// declaration of template class Array
int main() {
   Array< double > a1( 100 ); // array of 100 doubles
   a1[ 6 ] = 3.14;
   cout << a1[ 6 ] << endl;
   //...
}
```

creates a **double** instantiation of the template class **Array**. Once **a1** has been defined as an object of type **Array< double >**, we access its elements in the usual way. ∎

A template instantiation can be created with either a built-in or a user-defined data type.

**EXAMPLE 7.1.5.** Given the class declaration

```
class Task { // user-defined data type
  //...
};
```

we can create the **Array** instantiation

```
Array< Task > tasks( 500 ); // Task instantiation
```

and access **tasks**'s elements in the usual way. ∎

An object cannot belong to a template class but only to a template class instantiation. For example, given the template class declaration

```
template< class T >
class Array {
  //...
};
```

there cannot be an object whose type is **Array** or **Array< T >**, but there can be an object whose type is **Array< int >**. An object does not belong to a template class such as **Array** but rather to a template class instantiation such as **Array< char >**.

**EXAMPLE 7.1.6.** The code segment

```
template< class T >
class Array {
  //...
};
Array a0( 50 );         //***** ERROR: not an instantiation
Array< T > a1( 50 );    //***** ERROR: not an instantiation
template< class T >
Array< T > a2( 50 );    //***** ERROR: not an instantiation
Array< int > a3( 50 ); // ok, int instantiation
```

illustrates three invalid definitions involving a template class and one valid definition involving a template class **int** instantiation. ∎

## Template Classes in a Parameter List

A template class may occur as a data type in a parameter list. For example, the code in Figure 7.1.2 overloads the output operator at the top level:

```
template< class T >
ostream& operator<<( ostream& os, const Array< T >& ar ) {
   for ( int i = 0; i < ar.get_size(); i++ )
     os << ar[ i ] << endl;
   return os;
}
```

The operator's second argument is a reference to an **Array< T >**, where **T** is the class type in the template header.

**EXAMPLE 7.1.7.** Given the code in Figure 7.1.2, the program

```
#include <iostream>
using namespace std;
// Code from Figure 7.1.2 is here
int main() {
   Array< int > a( 3 );
   a[ 0 ] = 0; a[ 1 ] = 1; a[ 2 ] = 2;
   cout << a; // overloaded <<
   return 0;
}
```

prints

```
0
1
2
```

to the standard output. The **cout** statement uses an overload of the output operator whose second argument is an **Array< T >** reference. In this example, the compiler replaces occurrences of the class type **T** with **int** because **a**'s type is **Array< int >**. ∎

## Function-Style Parameters

A template class must have at least one class parameter, and it may have multiple class parameters. A template class also may have parameters that are not class parameters. These are informally called **function-style parameters**.[†] A template class may have any number of function-style parameters whose data types can be either built-in or user-defined. All parameters are separated by commas in the template header.

**EXAMPLE 7.1.8.** The declaration

```
template< class T, int X, float Y >
class Sample {
  //...
};
```

illustrates function-style parameters. Class parameter **T** comes first, followed by two function-style parameters separated by a comma: **int** parameter **X** and **float** parameter **Y**. ■

**EXAMPLE 7.1.9.** The code in Figure 7.1.3 amends the declaration for the template class **Array** by adding an **int** function-style parameter, which we name **S** for **S**ize. In the original code, we use a convert constructor to specify the size of an **Array**:

```
Array< double > a1( 10 ); // Array of 10 doubles
Array< char > a2( 50 );   // Array of 50 chars
```

In the amended code, we use the function-style parameter to do so:

```
Array< double, 10 > a1; // Array of 10 doubles
Array< char, 50 > a2;   // Array of 50 chars
```

The amended code therefore can use the default constructor instead of a convert constructor to allocate storage for the **Array**:

```
template< class T, int S >
Array< T, S >::Array() {
   a = new T[ size = S ];
}
```

Note that the template class's name is now

```
Array< T, S >
```

where **T** is the class parameter and **S** is a function-style parameter, both specified in the template header

```
template< class T, int S >
```
■

---

[†] The formal name for a *function-style parameter* is a *non-type template parameter*.

```
          template< class T, int S >
          class Array {
          public:
             T& operator[ ]( int );
             const T& operator[ ]( int ) const;
             Array();
            ~Array();
             int get_size() const { return size; }
          private:
             T* a;
             int size;
             T dummy_val;
          };
          template< class T, int S >
          T& Array< T, S >::operator[ ]( int i ) {
             if ( i < 0 || i >= size ) {
                cerr << "index " << i << " out of bounds: ";
                return dummy_val;
             }
             return a[ i ];
          }
          template< class T, int S >
          const T& Array< T, S >::operator[ ]( int i ) const {
             if ( i < 0 || i >= size ) {
                cerr << "index " << i << " out of bounds: ";
                return dummy_val;
             }
             return a[ i ];
          }
          template< class T, int S >
          Array< T, S >::Array() {
             a = new T[ size = S ];
          }
          template< class T, int S >
          Array< T, S >::~Array() {
             delete[ ] a;
          }
```

**FIGURE 7.1.3**  Template class **Array** with a function-style parameter.

**EXAMPLE 7.1.10.**  The code segment

```
       template< class T, int S >
       class A {
         //...
       };
```

```
A< float > a1; //***** ERROR: missing int value
```

contains an error because an instantiation of template class **A** requires

- A data type such as **float**, which is given.
- An **int** value, which is missing.

A correct definition is

```
A< float, 100 > a2; // ok, data type and int value given    ■
```

A template class is instantiated by replacing each class parameter in the template header with a data type and each function-style parameter in the template header with a value. For this reason, a template class is sometimes called a **parameterized class**. The **Array** class in Figure 7.1.3 is thus instantiated by replacing class parameter **T** with a data type such as **float** and function-style parameter **S** with a value such as 100.

## EXERCISES

1. What is a class parameter in a template class?

2. Explain the error:

```
template< T > class Queue {
  //...
};
```

3. May a template header have more than one class parameter?

4. Explain the error:

```
template< class T > class Queue {
public:
  Queue();
};
template< class T >
Queue::Queue() { /*...*/ }
```

5. Can a method in a template class be defined inline?

6. Explain the error:

```
template< class T > class Queue {
  //...
};
Queue< T > q1;
```

7. In a template class, what is a function-style parameter?

8. What is the difference between a template class and a template class instantiation?

**9.** Explain the error:

```
template< class T >
class Queue {
   //...
};
Queue< double > q1;
Queue< T > q2;
```

**10.** Explain the error:

```
template< class T >
class Queue {
   //...
};
Queue q1;
```

**11.** Explain the error:

```
template< class T, int Size >
class Queue {
   //...
};
Queue< double > q1;
```

# 7.2 SAMPLE APPLICATION: A TEMPLATE STACK CLASS

## *Problem*

Create a template **Stack** class to represent a **stack**, that is, a list of zero or more elements in which insertions and deletions occur at the same end (see Section 1.2). Implement methods to push elements onto a **Stack**, to pop them off a **Stack**, to inspect a **Stack**'s top element, to print a **Stack**'s contents, to determine whether a **Stack** is empty, and to determine whether a **Stack** is full. Make the **Stack** implementation robust so that standard stack operations do not lead to run-time errors.

## *Sample Output*

Given the input expression

```
(a + b) * (c + d)
```

the output for the test client in Figure 7.2.1 is

```
(d+c)*(b+a)
```

```
// #includes and Stack declaration
// (cctype must be #included for isspace)
int main() {
   const string prompt = "Enter an algebraic expression: ";
   const char lParen = '(';
   const char rParen = ')';
   Stack< char > s;
   string buf;
   //*** read fully parenthesized algebraic expression
   //      from standard input
   cout << prompt << endl;
   getline( cin, buf );
   // push characters in expression onto stack,
   // trimming white space
   for ( int i = 0; i < buf.length(); i++ )
     if ( !isspace( buf[ i ] ) )
       s.push( buf[ i ] );
   cout << "Original expression:   " << buf << endl;
   cout << "Expression in reverse: ";
   // pop characters from stack, exchanging left
   // parentheses for right parentheses and vice-versa
   while ( !s.empty() ) {
     char t = s.pop();
     if ( t == lParen )
       t = rParen;
     else if ( t == rParen )
       t = lParen;
     cout << t;
   }
   cout << endl;
   return 0;
}
```

**FIGURE 7.2.1** Test client for `Stack< char >`.

### Solution

Our template **Stack** class has the required class parameter but no function-style parameters.
The class has a default constructor that sets the **Stack**'s size to **DefaultStack**, currently
set at 50, and a convert constructor that sets the **Stack**'s size to a user-specified value.
Storage for **Stack** elements is dynamically allocated. The **Stack** destructor deallocates
the dynamically allocated storage. A **Stack**'s interface also includes methods to push and
pop **Stack** elements, to inspect the **Stack**'s top element without popping it, to check for
a full or an empty **Stack**, and to print the **Stack**'s contents. We also use assertions (see
Program Development section) to aid in testing **Stack** methods.

## C++ Implementation

```cpp
#include <iostream>
#include <string>
//#define NDEBUG //**** enable/disable assertions
#include <cassert>
using namespace std;
template< class T >
class Stack {
public:
   enum { DefaultStack = 50, EmptyStack = -1 };
   Stack();
   Stack( int );
   ~Stack();
   void push( const T& );
   T pop();
   T topNoPop() const;
   bool empty() const;
   bool full() const;
private:
   T* elements;
   int top;
   int size;
   void allocate() {
     elements = new T[ size ];
     top = EmptyStack;
   }
   void msg( const char* m ) const {
     cout << "*** " << m << " ***" << endl;
   }
   friend ostream& operator<<( ostream&, const Stack< T >& );
};

template< class T >
Stack< T >::Stack() {
   size = DefaultStack;
   allocate();
}

template< class T >
Stack< T >::Stack( int s ) {
   if ( s < 0 )        // negative size?
     s *= -1;
   else if ( 0 == s ) // zero size?
     s = DefaultStack;
   size = s;
   allocate();
}
```

```
template< class T >
Stack< T >::~Stack() {
   delete[ ] elements;
}

template< class T >
void Stack< T >::push( const T& e ) {
   assert( !full() );
   if ( !full() )
     elements[ ++top ] = e;
   else
     msg( "Stack full!" );
}

template< class T >
T Stack< T >::pop() {
   assert( !empty() );
   if ( !empty() )
     return elements[ top-- ];
   else {
     msg( "Stack empty!" );
     T dummy_value;
     return dummy_value; // return arbitrary value
   }
}

template< class T >
T Stack< T >::topNoPop() const {
   assert( top > EmptyStack );
   if ( !empty() )
     return elements[ top ];
   else {
     msg( "Stack empty!" );
     T dummy_value;
     return dummy_value;
   }
}

template< class T >
bool Stack< T >::empty() const {
   return top <= EmptyStack;
}

template< class T >
bool Stack< T >::full() const {
   return top + 1 >= size;
}
```

```
template< class T >
ostream& operator<<( ostream& os, const Stack< T >& s ) {
   s.msg( "Stack contents:" );
   int t = s.top;
   while ( t > s.EmptyStack )
     cout << s.elements[ t-- ] << endl;
   return os;
}
```

### Discussion

The template **Stack** class has two constructors so that **Stack** objects can be created in one of two ways. A definition such as

```
Stack< float > s1; // default constructor
```

invokes the default constructor, which sets the **Stack**'s size to **DefaultStack**, currently set at 10. A definition such as

```
Stack< unsigned > s2( 500 );
```

invokes the convert constructor, which sets the **Stack**'s size to 500. The **private** data member **size**, which stores the **Stack**'s size, serves as an argument to operator **new[ ]** to request storage for the **Stack**. The **private** method **allocate** does the work:

```
void allocate() {
   elements = new T[ size ];
   top = EmptyStack;
}
```

In the call to **new[ ]**

```
elements = new T[ size ];
```

**T** is the class parameter from the template header

```
template< class T >
```

When the user creates a **Stack** instantiation such as

```
Stack< double > s1;
```

the data type, in this case **double**, is substituted for **T**.

Data member **top** is used as an index into the array **elements**. The index is initialized to **EmptyStack**, the constant −1. Whenever an element is pushed onto the **Stack**, the preincremented **top** serves as the index in the array **elements** at which the new element is inserted:

```
template< class T >
void Stack< T >::push( const T& e ) {
   assert( !full() );
   if ( !full() )
     elements[ ++top ] = e;
   else
     msg( "Stack full!" );
}
```

When the first element is pushed onto the **Stack**, **top** is incremented from −1 to 0 and the element is inserted into **elements[ 0 ]**; the second element pushed onto the **Stack** is inserted into **elements[ 1 ]**; and so on. The **Stack** thus grows by incrementing the index **top**: from −1 to 0 to 1 to ... **size**−1. The Program Development section explains the **assert**, which is the first statement in **push**'s body.

When elements are popped off the **Stack**, **top** is decremented if the **Stack** is not empty:

```
template< class T >
T Stack< T >::pop() {
   assert( !empty() );
   if ( !empty() )
     return elements[ top-- ];
   else {
     msg( "Stack empty!" );
     T dummy_value;
     return dummy_value; // return arbitrary value
   }
}
```

Because **top** is the index of the element currently at the top of the **Stack**, we return

```
elements[ top-- ]
```

Recall that the value of the expression **top--** is **top**'s *current* value. Once the expression is evaluated, **top** is decremented. The **Stack** shrinks by decrementing **top**, whose maximum value is **size**−1 because this is the largest legal index into an array of **size** elements. If **top** is ever decremented to −1, the **Stack** is again empty.

Data member **size** also is used to test whether the **Stack** is full. The **public** method **full**

```
template< class T >
bool Stack< T >::full() const {
   return top + 1 >= size;
}
```

returns **true**, if the **Stack** is full, and **false**, if the **Stack** is not full. The method does so by doing a bounds check. Suppose that the **Stack**'s array, **elements**, has a **size** of 10. Legal indexes would then be 0, 1, ..., 9. The maximum value for index **top** therefore would be 9. Method **full** thus checks whether **top + 1** is greater than or equal to the array's **size**. If so, the **Stack** is full and no more elements should be pushed onto it. Index **top** is used to test whether the **Stack** is empty:

```
template< class T >
bool Stack< T >::empty() const {
   return top <= EmptyStack;
}
```

**EmptyStack** is −1, which is an illegal index into the array **elements**. So the checks for a full and an empty **Stack** are, in effect, bounds checks on the array **elements**.

We have two methods for accessing the **Stack**'s top element. Method **pop** returns the top element, if the **Stack** is not empty, and *changes* the **Stack** in the process: after the pop, the next element, if any, is in the top position. Our second method for accessing the **Stack**'s top element is **topNoPop**, which returns the **Stack**'s top element but leaves the **Stack** unchanged. This allows the user to inspect the **Stack**'s top element without removing it from the **Stack**. We say that **pop** is *destructive* because it changes the **Stack**, whereas **topNoPop** is *nondestructive* because it does not change the **Stack**. Method **dump** is also nondestructive. It prints the **Stack**'s elements, from top to bottom, to the standard output.

Finally, as a convenience, we overload the output operator as a top-level **friend**

```
template< class T >
ostream& operator<<( ostream& os, const Stack< T >& s ) {
    s.msg( "Stack contents:" );
    int t = s.top;
    while ( t > s.EmptyStack )
      cout << s.elements[ t-- ] << endl;
    return os;
}
```

so that a **Stack** can be printed to an output stream such as **cout**.

### Program Development

The **Stack** class is designed to be robust. For example, method **push** first tests whether the **Stack** has room before inserting an element into the **Stack**:

```
if ( !full() )               // enough room?
   elements[ top++ ] = e; // if so, insert element
```

Method **pop** tests whether the **Stack** has any elements before deleting the top one. These checks guard against array overflow and underflow, respectively, because the **Stack**'s implementation is an array of **size** elements. Further, the **empty** and **full** methods do checks beyond what may seem to be required. For example, **empty** checks whether index **top** is *less than* or equal to **EmptyStack**, the constant $-1$:

```
template< class T >
bool Stack< T >::empty() const {
    return top <= EmptyStack;
}
```

The **Stack** code as a whole ensures that **top** cannot be less than $-1$ because only **pop** decrements **top**, and **pop** always invokes **empty** before such a decrement. Nonetheless, as a precaution, **empty** checks whether **top**'s value is either less than or equal to $-1$. In similar fashion, **full** checks whether **top**+1 is either greater than or equal to the array's **size**.

Some other small measures guard against run-time errors. For example, the convert constructor checks whether the user-specified **Stack** size is either zero or a negative number. If the user specifies zero as the **Stack** size, the constructor uses **DefaultStack** as the size. If the user specifies a negative **Stack** size, the constructor converts the negative number to a positive one. These measures are well worth the small amount of code required.

# Assertions

An **assertion** is a condition that must be true at a specified point in a program's execution. If an assertion fails, the system halts the program's execution and reports the failure. Assertions can be used to ensure that, during execution, a program conforms to specification at selected points. Assertions are commonly used during application development as an aid to debugging. Once an application has been thoroughly debugged and is ready for release, the assertions are typically disabled.

C++ supports assertions with the **assert** macro, which requires that the header *cassert* be **#include**d. Method **push** has an assertion:

```
template< class T >
void Stack< T >::push( const T& e ) {
    assert( !full() ); //**** line 59 in source file
    //...
```

The statement

```
assert( !full() );
```

asserts that the **Stack** must be not full. On our system, an attempt to **push** an element onto a full **Stack** halts the program's execution and generates the error report

```
Assertion failed: !full(), file stack.cpp, line 59
```

The message is useful for debugging, as it indicates the line in the source file at which the assertion failed. Methods **pop** and **topNoPop** have similar **assert**s but ones that check whether the **Stack** is empty.

As these examples show, an **assert** expects an expression that evaluates to **true** or **false**. Relational expressions, logical expressions, and functions that return a **bool** are commonly used as **assert** expressions.

C++ assertions can be disabled easily. Our code contains the lines

```
//#define NDEBUG //**** enable/disable assertions
#include <cassert>
```

The **#define** of **NDEBUG** (**No DEBUG**) has been commented out. To disable our assertions, we place a **#define** of **NDEBUG** *above* the **#include** of *cassert*. So this change

```
#define NDEBUG //**** enable/disable assertions
#include <cassert>
```

*disables* the **assert**s in our code. We do not have to remove the **assert** statements themselves, which might be many in a large application.

Even with disabled assertions, the **Stack** class still performs checks to prevent run-time errors. For example, **pop**

```
template< class T >
T Stack< T >::pop() {
   assert( !empty() );
   if ( !empty() )                   // anything to pop?
     return elements[ top-- ]; // if so, pop element
   else {
     msg( "Stack empty!" );
     T dummy_value;
     return dummy_value; // return arbitrary value
   }
}
```

first checks whether the **Stack** is empty before removing an element from it. If the **Stack** is empty, **pop** returns **dummy_value**, an arbitrary value that satisfies the requirement that **pop** return an expression of the **Stack** instantiation's type (e.g., **int**). This is not as powerful a safeguard as an **assert**, but it does prevent our attempting to remove an element from an empty **Stack** if the **assert**s have been disabled.

## EXERCISES

1. What is the effect of changing the line

   ```
   //#define NDEBUG
   ```

   to

   ```
   #define NDEBUG
   ```

   in the application?

2. Write a sample client that pushes too many items onto a **Stack** under two conditions: first, with the assertions enabled; second, with the assertions disabled.

3. Explain why the method **pop** returns a dummy value if the **Stack** is empty.

4. What is the difference in behavior between **pop** and **topNoPop**?

5. Modify the **Stack** class so that **push** throws an exception if the **Stack** is full, and **pop** and **topNoPop** throw exceptions if the **Stack** is empty.

# 7.3 THE STANDARD TEMPLATE LIBRARY

The Standard Template Library (hereafter, STL) is part of the standard C++ library. STL has very powerful features in its own right, and it also promises to have significant impact on the organization of other C++ libraries (for example, Microsoft's ATL or *ActiveX T*emplate *L*ibrary). STL's template classes provide C++ with **data structures**, that is, high-level data types, such as stacks, together with appropriate operations on these high-level data types, such as *push*es and *pop*s.

## Containers, Algorithms, and Iterators

STL's three basic components are **containers**, **algorithms**, and **iterators**. An STL container is a collection of objects. Examples are vectors, stacks, queues, deques, lists, sets, and maps. In more formal language, an STL container is a data structure. An STL algorithm is a function for processing a container's contents. Examples are functions that copy, sort, search, merge, and permute containers. In more formal terms, an STL algorithm is a recipe or procedure for processing a data structure. An STL iterator is a mechanism for accessing the objects in a container one at a time. Suppose that we have a list of elements

$$L, A, Z, K, D, F$$

and need to search for element $K$. We could use an iterator to move through the list, element by element, so that $K$ could be compared one by one against the elements in the list. STL provides iterators to move through containers from front to back, from back to front, in either direction, and randomly. STL also has special iterators for input and output operations. STL iterators are a high-level alternative to the familiar looping constructs such as **for** and **while** loops. In any case, STL algorithms use iterators to process STL containers.

## Reasons for Using STL

STL containers, unlike C++ arrays, grow and shrink in size *automatically*. Suppose, for example, that an application needs to aggregate floating-point numbers but cannot anticipate beforehand exactly how many will need to be aggregated. The programmer might define an array with a presumably large enough size and then constantly check to ensure that the array does not overflow. This approach requires tedious, low-level programming that is prone to error. Instead, the programmer might dynamically allocate a **float** or **double** array; and, if the array fills, free it after copying the current entries and a candidate entry to a newly allocated array of larger size. This approach, too, is tedious and prone to error. Such problems are eliminated with STL containers, which grow automatically as elements are inserted and shrink automatically as elements are removed. STL thus contributes to programming ease, program robustness, and storage efficiency. Further, STL offers an assortment of containers (e.g., vectors, associative arrays, sets, stacks, queues) to meet application needs. STL also publicizes the time and storage complexity of its containers, which allows the programmer to make reasoned decisions about which type of container to use. We return to this topic shortly.

In addition to containers, STL provides built-in algorithms for processing them. Algorithms for sorting, searching, replacing, reversing, partitioning, and testing containers are provided. STL also supports powerful numeric algorithms. The algorithms are designed to be intuitive and easy to apply. Further, STL algorithms work on any appropriate container. For example, the **sort** algorithm can be used to sort a **vector**, a **deque**, or a **set**, which are three STL containers. Of particular interest are STL algorithms such as **for_each** and **copy**, which provide built-in iteration. Suppose, for example, that we want to double the value of each element in an aggregate. If the numbers are stored in, say, an STL **vector** of **int**s, and we have a function called **sq** that expects an **int** and returns its square, we can process the vector without any loops:

```
vector< int > v;
// fill up v with values
for_each( v.begin(), v.end(), sq ); // square each element
```

This code is easier to write and to understand than a C++ **while** loop that does the same work. The **copy** algorithm can be used to copy an aggregate—not only to another aggregate but also to a disk file. Similarly, the **copy** algorithm can be used to copy from an input file to an aggregate, such as a **vector**, or from an input file to an output file. Such flexibility is a hallmark of STL algorithms. Because STL algorithms such as **for_each** and **copy** are high level and have intuitive names, their use contributes to overall code clarity and correctness.

STL containers and algorithms are flexible and efficient because they use iterators. At the implementation level, an STL iterator behaves like a pointer. Yet an STL iterator is, at the same time, a high-level construct that allows the programmer to work with an iterator as if it were *not* a pointer.

**EXAMPLE 7.3.1.** The code segment

```
#include <vector>
#include <deque>
#include <algorithm>
using namespace std;
int main() {
  vector< int > v;
  deque< double > d;
  // fill v with integers, d with floating-points
  sort( v.begin(), v.end() );
  sort( d.begin(), d.end() );
  //...
}
```

illustrates the flexibility of an STL algorithm such as **sort**, which can be used to sort STL containers such as **deque**s and **vector**s. The **sort** algorithm does not need to know the type of container to be sorted but only where to start sorting, where to end, and how to sort (e.g., in ascending or descending order). The **deque** and **vector** methods **begin** and **end** return *iterators*, which mark the container's beginning and end. The **sort** algorithm uses such iterators in the process of moving elements into sorted order. By the way, ascending order is the default sort order; hence, the **deque** and the **vector** will be sorted in ascending order in this example. ∎

STL is **extensible**, which means that users can add new containers and new algorithms. STL algorithms can be used on built-in or user-defined containers. User-defined algorithms can be applied to built-in or user-defined containers. STL's efficiency, flexibility, ease of use, and extensibility should make it increasingly popular among C++ programmers.

The STL toolset is particularly advantageous in the development of large, complex applications. But to encourage experimentation with STL and to provide a quick reference for its main constructs, we illustrate STL tools with short programs that clarify basic syntax and operations. These short programs can be readily expanded and adapted. The Sample Application of Section 7.4 provides a realistic example of STL's power and elegance.

## Container Basics

STL has seven basic containers divided into two groups, sequential and associative (see Figure 7.3.1). The sequential containers **vector** and **deque** resemble arrays in that their elements can be accessed by position, for example, by using an index. For instance, if **v** is an STL **vector** of **int**s, then the statement

```
int x = v[ 2 ];
```

initializes **x** to the value of **v**'s third element. The **list** sequential container is a bidirectional linked list. Sequential containers also provide methods such as **begin** and **end** that can be used to access elements. For now we emphasize the similarities among the **vector**, **deque**, and **list** containers, although shortly we clarify how they differ.

| Container | Type | Description |
|---|---|---|
| **list** | Sequential | Bidirectional linked list of elements |
| **vector** | Sequential | Array that grows and shrinks as needed |
| **deque** | Sequential | Array with efficient insertions/deletions at either end |
| **set** | Associative | Collection of nonduplicate keys |
| **multiset** | Associative | A **set** with duplicates allowed |
| **map** | Associative | Collection of nonduplicate elements with access by key |
| **multimap** | Associative | A **map** with duplicates allowed |

**FIGURE 7.3.1** Basic STL Containers.

Elements in an associative container can be accessed by *key*, that is, by specifying a unique value of arbitrary data type such as a string. For example, if **m** is an STL map that stores a nation's gross national product as a floating-point number and uses the nation's name as a key, then the statement

```
float gnp = m[ "china" ];
```

initializes **gnp** to the floating-point value in **m** associated with the key **"china"**. An associative array (see Section 6.8) is thus an example of an associative container. STL associative containers are the **map**, the **multimap**, the **set**, and the **multiset**. For now, we emphasize the similarities among associative containers, although shortly we clarify how they differ. We introduce sequential and associative containers with a series of examples.

# Basic Sequential Containers: vector, deque, and list

**EXAMPLE 7.3.2.**    The program in Figure 7.3.2 shows the basic syntax and functionality of STL's template **vector** class. The program's output is

```
14
-999
57

57
```

The program first defines an **int** instantiation of the **vector** class. Note that no size is specified. A **vector** grows and shrinks automatically to meet its own storage needs, thus relieving the programmer of this obligation. This feature alone makes **vector**s superior to ordinary C++ arrays. It is common *not* to specify a **vector**'s initial size in its definition; however, this can be done. The definition

```
vector< double > d( 1000 );
```

defines a **vector** with an initial size of 1,000. The size still increases automatically if required. If a **vector** is created with an initial size, all of the cells are initialized to zero.

```
#include <iostream>
#include <vector>
using namespace std;
int main() {
  int i;
  vector< int > nums;
  nums.insert( nums.begin(), -999 ); // -999
  nums.insert( nums.begin(), 14 ) ;  // 14 -999
  nums.insert( nums.end(), 57 );     // 14 -999 57
  for ( i = 0; i < nums.size(); i++ )
    cout << nums[ i ] << endl; // 14 -999 57
  cout << endl;
  nums.erase( nums.begin() ); // -999 57
  nums.erase( nums.begin() ); // 57
  for ( i = 0; i < nums.size(); i++ )
    cout << nums[ i ] << endl; // 57
  return 0;
}
```

**FIGURE 7.3.2** The STL **vector** container.

A **vector** supports insertions at either end and provides the methods **begin** and **end** to access its beginning and its end, respectively. Each method returns a random-access iterator. The **begin** method returns an iterator that

- Points to a container's first element, if the container is not empty.
- Points just beyond the end of the container, if the container is empty.

The method **end** method returns an iterator that

- Points just beyond the end of the container.

Figure 7.3.3 illustrates with a **vector** that currently has three elements.

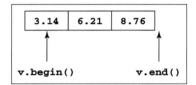

**FIGURE 7.3.3** Where the iterators returned by a **vector**'s **begin** and **end** methods point.

The **erase** method, like the **insert** method, can access either end of the **vector**. The **erase** method removes an element from the **vector**. The **size** method returns the **vector**'s current size. We are able to use the operator **[ ]** with the object **nums**

```
cout << nums[ i ] << endl;
```

because **vector** overloads **[ ]** so that it behaves the same for **vector**s as for ordinary arrays.

The header *vector* contains the declaration for the template **vector** class. We also have the using directive

```
using namespace std;
```

because **vector**, together with the other STL components, is in the **std** namespace. ■

At first glance, a **deque** seems almost indistinguishable from a **vector**. For the program in Figure 7.3.2, if we replace

```
#include <vector>
```

with

```
#include <deque>
```

and

```
vector< int > nums;
```

with

```
deque< int > nums;
```

the output is exactly the same. A **vector** and a **deque** differ in their underlying implementation, in particular with respect to insertions and deletions. For a **vector**, insertions at the *beginning* are less efficient than insertions at the *end*. Insertions at the end take about the same amount of time whether the **vector**'s size is 0, 100, or 100,000. Insertions at the beginning take an amount of time directly proportional to the **vector**'s size. For example, inserting at the beginning of a **vector** with 1,000 elements takes about 100 times longer than inserting into the beginning of a **vector** with 10 elements. The same rule holds for deletions in a **vector**. For this reason, **vector**s should be used only when insertions and deletions are typically done at the end. A **deque** is equally efficient whether insertions and deletions are done at the beginning or at the end. For example, insertions or deletions at the beginning of a **deque** take about the same amount of time, but typically *more* time than an insertion or deletion at the end of a **vector**, whether the **deque**'s size is 0, 100, or 100,000. For this reason, a **deque** is to be preferred over a **vector** if insertions and deletions typically need to be done at the beginning. After an example of a **list**, we summarize efficiency considerations for **vector**s, **deque**s, and **list**s.

**EXAMPLE 7.3.3.** The program in Figure 7.3.4 creates a list of **string**s

```
list< string > names;
```

After **insert**ing three strings at the **list**'s beginning and one at its end, we pass the list by reference to **dump**, which prints its contents to the standard output. Function **dump** provides a first look at iterators. All the STL containers have an associated iterator data type. For example, a container such as

```
list< int >
```

has the associated iterator types

```
list< int >::iterator
list< int >::const_iterator
```

The container

```
vector< double >
```

has the associated iterator types

```
vector< double >::iterator
vector< double >::const_iterator
```

The **const_iterator** is used if the iteration does not change any of the container's elements. In function **dump** we define a **const** iterator **it**, which is then used to traverse the **list** without changing any of its elements. After initializing **it** to the **list**'s beginning

```
it = l.begin(); // initialize iterator
```

we loop until reaching the **list**'s end

```
while ( it != l.end() )
```

```
#include <iostream>
#include <string>
#include <list>
using namespace std;
void dump( list< string >& );
int main() {
  list< string > names;
  // insert four names into a list
  names.insert( names.begin(), "Kamiko" );
  names.insert( names.end(), "Andre" );
  names.insert( names.begin(), "Chengwen" );
  names.insert( names.begin(), "Maria" );
  dump( names ); // Maria Chengwen Kamiko Andre
  names.reverse(); // reverse the list
  cout << endl;
  dump( names ); // Andre Kamiko Chengwen Maria
  return 0;
}
void dump( list< string >& l ) {
  list< const string >::const_iterator it; // list iterator
  // print list to standard output
  it = l.begin(); // initialize iterator
  while ( it != l.end() ) { // is iterator at the end?
    cout << *it << endl;
    it++; // increment iterator
  }
}
```

**FIGURE 7.3.4** The STL **list** container.

A container's **begin** and **end** methods return iterator values that mark the container's beginning and end, respectively. This allows us to loop safely without knowing how many elements happen to be in the **list**.

In each loop iteration, we print a **list** element to the standard output and increment the iterator **it** to access the next **list** element:

```
cout << *it << endl;
it++; // increment iterator
```

In the **cout** statement, we dereference the iterator—the expression is **\*it**. This suggests that an iterator is very much like a pointer. Indeed, an STL iterator can be viewed as a high-level pointer. The expression **it++** increments the iterator because the postincrement operator is overloaded for iterators. In **main** we then reverse the **list**

```
names.reverse();
```

and again **dump** it.

■

## Efficiency of vectors, deques, and lists

The **vector**, **deque**, and **list** are STL's three basic *sequential* containers. The three are alike in some respects. For example, each has an **insert** method for adding elements and an **erase** method for deleting them. They differ among themselves in other methods. For example, **[ ]** is overloaded for **vector**s and **deque**s, but not for **list**s. Another important difference among the three is the *efficiency*, in time and storage, associated with their common operations. Recall that inserting into the beginning of a **deque** requires about the same amount of time, regardless of whether the **deque** has, for example, 10 or 100 elements. By contrast, inserting at the beginning of a **vector** with 100 elements takes about 10 times longer than inserting at the beginning of a **vector** with 10 elements. We say that the time required to insert a **vector**'s beginning is **linear**, that is, directly proportional to the number of elements. For a **deque**, the time required to insert into the beginning is **constant**: it takes the same time to insert at the beginning of a **deque** with 100 elements as it does to insert at the beginning of a **deque** with 10 elements. By publicizing the efficiency of standard operations on its containers, STL supports intelligent decisions about which containers to use. For example, if our application requires insertions at the beginning and at the end, we might pick a **deque** over a **vector** for reasons of efficiency. Figure 7.3.5 summarizes the efficiency of standard operations on the three sequential containers.

| *Operation* | vector | deque | list |
|---|---|---|---|
| Insert/erase at beginning | Linear | Constant | Constant |
| Insert/erase at end | Constant | Constant | Constant |
| Insert/erase in middle | Linear | Linear | Constant |
| Access first element | Constant | Constant | Constant |
| Access last element | Constant | Constant | Constant |
| Access middle element | Constant | Constant | Linear |

**FIGURE 7.3.5** Time complexity of basic sequential container operations.

## Basic Associative Containers: set, multiset, map, and multimap

The four associative containers fall into two groups: sets and maps. A **set** is a collection of zero or more nonduplicate, unordered elements called *keys*. For example, the set

$$\{jobs, gates, ellison\}$$

contains three keys, which are last names of three computer moguls. A **map** is a collection of zero or more unordered pairs; in each pair, one element is a nonduplicate *key* and the other is a *value* associated with the key. For example, the map

$$\{(jobs, apple), (gates, microsoft), (ellison, oracle)\}$$

contains three pairs. In each pair, the first element such as *gates* is the key associated with a value such as *microsoft*. A **multiset** is a **set** that allows duplicate keys, and a **multimap** is a **map** that allows duplicate keys. To clarify basic functionality, we focus on **set** and **map**.

```
#include <iostream>
#include <set>
using namespace std;
int main() {
   set< int > s;
   s.insert( -999 );
   s.insert( 18 );
   s.insert( 321 );
   s.insert( -999 ); // not inserted -- duplicates not allowed
   set< int >::const_iterator it;
   it = s.begin();
   while ( it != s.end() )
     cout << *it++ << endl; // -999 18 321 in some order

   // prompt user for an integer
   int key;
   cout << "Enter an integer: ";
   cin >> key;
   it = s.find( key );
   if ( it == s.end() ) // not found
     cout << key << " is not in set." << endl;
   else
     cout << key << " is in set." << endl;
   return 0;
}
```

**FIGURE 7.3.6** The STL **set** container.

**EXAMPLE 7.3.4.** The program in Figure 7.3.6 illustrates the **set** container. The definition

```
set< int > s;
```

creates an **int** instantiation of the template **set** class. The **set** class overloads the **insert** method so that it can be invoked in similar fashion to a **vector**'s version

```
s.insert( s.begin(), 66 ); // insert at beginning
s.insert( s.end(), 99 );   // insert at end
```

or with no specified position

```
s.insert( 123 ); // insert somewhere
```

Whatever the overloaded version, **set**'s **insert** ensures that the set does not contain duplicates. Among other methods, **set** has **find**, which checks whether a **set** contains a specified key: if so, **find** returns an iterator that marks the key's occurrence in the **set**; if not, **find** returns the value of the **set**'s **end** method. The code segment

```
int key;
cout << "Enter an integer: ";
cin >> key;
it = s.find( key );
if ( it == s.end() ) // not found
  cout << key << " is not in set." << endl;
else
  cout << key << " is in set." << endl;
```

compares the value of **s.find( key )** against the value of **s.end()** to determine whether **s** contains a user-specified key.  ∎

An STL **map** is an **association list**, that is, a list that associates a key with a value. (For an array implementation of an association list, see Section 6.8.)

```
#include <iostream>
#include <string>
#include <map>
using namespace std;
int main() {
  map< string, int > m;
  m[ "zero" ]  = 0; m[ "one" ]   = 1;
  m[ "two" ]   = 2; m[ "three" ] = 3;
  m[ "four" ]  = 4; m[ "five" ]  = 5;
  m[ "six" ]   = 6; m[ "seven" ] = 7;
  m[ "eight" ] = 8; m[ "nine" ]  = 9;
  cout << m[ "three" ] << endl  // 3
       << m[ "five" ]  << endl  // 5
       << m[ "seven" ] << endl; // 7
  return 0;
}
```

**FIGURE 7.3.7**  The STL **map** container.

**EXAMPLE 7.3.5.**    The program in Figure 7.3.7 illustrates the **map** container. In **m**'s definition

```
map< string, int > m;
```

**string** and **int** are the data types of the key and the value, respectively.  For example, the string **"two"** is the key that can be used to store and then to look up the **int** value **2**. The **map** container, like all of the basic STL containers, has an **insert** method; but **map** also overloads **[ ]** so that it can be used both to insert new key/value pairs into the association list

```
m[ "zero" ] = 0;
```

and to search for elements in the association list

```
cout << m[ "zero" ] << endl; // prints 0
```

Because **map**s cannot contain duplicates, the effect of

```
m[ "one" ] = 1;
m[ "one" ] = -1; // cancels any previous association
```

is to associate the value **-1** with the key **one**.                                   ∎

## Container Adaptors

A container **adaptor** adapts a container to behave in a particular way. The three container adaptors are the **stack**, the **queue**, and the **priority_queue**. The **stack** adaptor creates a **LIFO** (**L**ast **I**n, **F**irst **O**ut) list. The **queue** adaptor creates a **FIFO** (**F**irst **I**n, **F**irst **O**ut) list. The **priority_queue** adaptor creates a queue whose elements are removed in some priority order. We illustrate container adaptors with two examples.

> **EXAMPLE 7.3.6.**   The program in Figure 7.3.8 amends the test client for our templated **Stack** class (see Figure 7.2.1). We replace our templated **Stack** class with STL's templated **stack** container. By default, an STL **stack** adapts a **deque**. So the definition
>
> ```
> stack< char > s;
> ```
>
> is equivalent to
>
> ```
> stack< char, deque< char > > s;
> ```
>
> We could force a **stack** to adapt a **vector** with the definition
>
> ```
> stack< char, vector< char > > s;
> ```
>
> The STL **stack**'s **top** returns the top element but without removing it. The STL **top** is thus equivalent to our **Stack**'s **topNoPop**. The STL **stack**'s **pop** removes the top element but has **void** as its return type. Our **Stack**'s **pop** removes the top element but also returns it.                                   ∎

> **EXAMPLE 7.3.7.**   The program in Figure 7.3.9 illustrates the **queue** adaptor. Like the **stack**, the **queue** adapts a **deque** by default. The **queue** also has **push** and **pop** methods for inserting and removing elements. The method **front** accesses the element at the front of the **queue**, which is why we use it for printing.                                   ∎

```
#include <iostream>
#include <stack>
#include <cctype>
using namespace std;
int main() {
   const string prompt = "Enter an algebraic expression: ";
   const char lParen = '(';
   const char rParen = ')';
   stack< char > s; //**** STL stack
   string buf;
   //*** read fully parenthesized algebraic expression
   //     from standard input
   cout << prompt << endl;
   getline( cin, buf );
   // push characters in expression onto stack,
   // trimming white space
   for ( int i = 0; i < buf.length(); i++ )
      if ( !isspace( buf[ i ] ) )
         s.push( buf[ i ] );
   cout << "Original expression:   " << buf << endl;
   cout << "Expression in reverse: ";
   // pop characters from stack, exchanging left
   // parentheses for right parentheses and vice-versa
   while ( !s.empty() ) {
      char t = s.top(); // get top element
      s.pop();              // remove it
      if ( t == lParen )
        t = rParen;
      else if ( t == rParen )
        t = lParen;
      cout << t;
   }
   cout << endl;
   return 0;
}
```

**FIGURE 7.3.8** The STL `stack` adaptor.

**EXAMPLE 7.3.8.**   The program in Figure 7.3.10 illustrates the `priority_queue` adaptor, which adapts a **vector** by default.

A priority queue removes its elements in a priority order. For example, a priority queue of integers might remove the integers in descending order by value. The `priority_queue` container thus ensures that a priority order is maintained during removals.

A `priority_queue` uses the familiar **push** for insertions and **pop** for deletions. The method **top** returns the next element without removing it. Our sample client inserts

```
#include <iostream>
#include <queue>
using namespace std;
int main() {
   queue< int > q; // == queue< int, deque< int > >
   q.push( 1 ); q.push( 3 ); q.push( 5 );
   q.push( 7 ); q.push( 11 ); q.push( 13 );
   // pop and print until queue is empty
   // output is 1 3 5 7 11 13
   while ( !q.empty() ) {
     cout << q.front() << endl; // returns integer
     q.pop(); // returns void
   }
   return 0;
}
```

**FIGURE 7.3.9** The STL **queue** adaptor.

**howMany** randomly generated integers, printing each to the standard output before it is inserted. After the insertions are completed, we print the **priority_queue**'s contents to confirm that the priority order is used in the course of deletions.

A sample run produced the output

```
8614
691
21890
3936
20054
369
3142
1191
*** Priority by value:
21890
20054
8614
3936
3142
1191
691
369
```

In effect, we use the **priority_queue** to sort the integers in descending order. ■

## Other Containers

The familiar **string** class and the **bitset** class qualify as containers in the STL sense. We illustrate with examples.

```
#include <iostream>
#include <functional>
#include <queue>
#include <cstdlib> // for rand and srand
#include <ctime>   // for time
using namespace std;
int main() {
   const int howMany = 8;
   int i;
   priority_queue< int > nums;
   srand( time( 0 ) ); // seed rand
   // insert howMany pseudorandom integers
   for ( i = 0; i < howMany; i++ ) {
     int next = rand();
     cout << next << endl;
     nums.push( next );
   }
   // now print the integers in priority order
   cout << "\n*** Priority by value:" << endl;
   for ( i = 0; i < howMany; i++ ) {
     cout << nums.top() << endl;
     nums.pop(); // remove element
   }
   return 0;
}
```

**FIGURE 7.3.10**  The `priority_queue` container adaptor.

**EXAMPLE 7.3.9.**    The program in Figure 7.3.11 uses STL algorithms such as `find`, `for_each`, and `random_shuffle` to manipulate a `string`. We clarify shortly how these algorithms work. For now, the point of interest is that a `string` qualifies as an STL container whose elements, `char`s, can be processed by using STL iterators and algorithms. In particular, note that a `string` object such as `s` has the `begin` and `end` methods of the standard STL containers. The header *algorithm* must be `#include`d to use the STL algorithms. On a sample run, the program's output was

```
s:              pele, the greatest ever
s in reverse: reve tsetaerg eht ,elep
'a' is the 14th char in: pele, the greatest ever
s after a random shuffle: ,eptgeer etsht evlreae
'a' is the 21th char in: ,eptgeer etsht evlreae
s sorted in ascending order:    ,aeeeeeeeghlprrstttv
```

■

A `bitset` is a sequence of binary digits such as `01010101`. The name `bitset` is unfortunate because a `bitset` is not a *set* in the mathematical sense. For one thing, a `bitset` may contain duplicate elements such as multiple `1`s, whereas a *set* in the mathematical

```
#include <iostream>
#include <string>
#include <algorithm>
using namespace std;
void printChar( char c ) {
    cout << c;
}
int main() {
    string s = "pele, the greatest ever";
    // print in original order and reverse
    cout << "s:             " << s << endl;
    cout << "s in reverse: ";
    for_each( s.rbegin(), s.rend(), printChar );
    cout << endl;
    // find the character 'a'
    char* where = find( s.begin(), s.end(), 'a' );
    cout << "'a' is the " << where - s.begin() + 1
         << "th char in: " << s << endl;
    // randomly shuffle the string
    random_shuffle( s.begin(), s.end() );
    cout << "s after a random shuffle: " << s << endl;
    // find 'a' again
    where = find( s.begin(), s.end(), 'a' );
    cout << "'a' is the " << where - s.begin() + 1
         << "th char in: " << s << endl;
    // sort the string in ascending order
    sort( s.begin(), s.end() );
    cout << "s sorted in ascending order: " << s << endl;
    return 0;
}
```

**FIGURE 7.3.11** A program that manipulates a `string` with STL algorithms.

sense must not contain duplicate elements. A `bitset` is really a sequence or string of bits; hence, `bitseq` or `bitstring` would be a better name.

A `bitset` can be used to represent an integer in binary. The code segment

```
#include <bitset>
using namespace std;
bitset< 8 > bs1;     // 8 bits
bitset< 128 > bs2;   // 128 bits
```

illustrates how `bitset`s of different sizes can be created. The `bitset`'s default constructor sets all bits to 0. The `bitset`s `bs1` and `bs2` thus consist of all zeros. The convert constructor

```
bitset( unsigned long n );
```

creates a **bitset** that represents **n** in binary. For example, the definition

```
bitset< 8 > bs( 9 );
```

creates the **bitset** whose value is **00001001**. Note that this parameterized constructor expects an *unsigned* integer.

The **bitset** class has methods, for example, to set specified bits to 0 or 1; to invert a specified bit or all bits at once; to test whether any bit is set to 0 or 1; to shift bits left or right; and to perform standard binary operations such as *and*, *or*, and *exclusive-or*. The class also has methods that convert a **bitset** to a **string** and to an **unsigned long** integer.

**EXAMPLE 7.3.10.**   The program in Figure 7.3.12 illustrates how the **bitset** class may be used to specify properties of a graphical object such as a window.

```
#include <iostream>
#include <bitset>
using namespace std;
const featureCount = 8;
const unsigned Framed    =  1; // 00000001 in binary
const unsigned Bordered  =  2; // 00000010 in binary
const unsigned StdMenu   =  4; // 00000100 in binary
const unsigned ToolBar   =  8; // 00001000 in binary
const unsigned StatusBar = 16; // 00010000 in binary
// constants for other Window features

class Window {
public:
   Window( const string& n, unsigned f ) {
      name = n;
      features = bitset< featureCount >( f );
      createWindow();
   }
   Window( const char* n, unsigned f ) {
      name = n;
      features = bitset< featureCount >( f );
      createWindow();
   }

private:
   // simulate window creation by printing features to
   // standard output
```

**FIGURE 7.3.12**  The **bitset** container.

```
      void createWindow() {
        cout << "\n*** Window features for " << name
             << " given bit mask " << features << ":" << endl;
        if ( features[ 0 ] ) // 1st bit set? (rightmost is 1st)
          cout << "\t" << "framed" << endl;
        if ( features[ 1 ] ) // 2nd bit set?
          cout << "\t" << "bordered" << endl;
        if ( features[ 2 ] ) // 3rd bit set?
          cout << "\t" << "with standard menu" << endl;
        if ( features[ 3 ] ) // 4th bit set?
          cout << "\t" << "with tool bar" << endl;
        if ( features[ 4 ] ) // 5th bit set?
          cout << "\t" << "with status bar" << endl;
      }
      string name;
      bitset< featureCount > features;
};
int main() {
  Window w1( "w1", Framed | ToolBar | StatusBar );
  Window w2( "w2", ToolBar | Framed | StatusBar );
  Window w3( "w3", Framed | StdMenu | StatusBar | ToolBar
                   | Bordered );
  return 0;
}
```

**FIGURE 7.3.12** Continued.

The program's output is

```
*** Window features for w1 given bit mask 00011001:
    framed
    with tool bar
    with status bar

*** Window features for w2 given bit mask 00011001:
    framed
    with tool bar
    with status bar

*** Window features for w3 given bit mask 00011111:
    framed
    bordered
    with standard menu
    with tool bar
    with status bar
```

We create a **Window** class to represent windows that have optional features such as a border, a title bar, and a standard menu. The programmer specifies the desired features by logically *or*ing integer constants that represent the features. For example, the integer 1 represents the **Framed** feature, whereas the integer 16 represents the **StatusBar** feature. Because the logical *or* operation is commutative, the integer constants that specify features may occur in arbitrary order. This explains why the **Window** objects **w1** and **w2** have the same features despite the fact that the features are not specified in the same order.

In a **bitset**, the operator **[ ]** is overloaded so that individual bits may be accessed through an index. If **b** is a **bitset** and **i** is a valid index, the expression

```
b[ i ]
```

converts to **true**, if the bit is 1, and **false**, if the bit is 0, whenever a boolean value is expected.  ∎

## Algorithms

STL has a rich assortment of algorithms for processing containers. The algorithms fall into standard categories: sorting and searching, numerical processing, set operations, copying, and so forth. Just as STL containers are implemented as template *classes*, so STL algorithms are implemented as template *functions*. Here, for example, is the prototype for STL's **reverse** algorithm:

```
template< class BidirectionalIterator > // template header
void reverse( BidirectionalIterator it1,    // iterator 1
              BidirectionalIterator it2 ); // iterator 2
```

Note that **reverse**'s two arguments are *iterators*, that is, **BidirectionalIterators**, which can traverse a container from either beginning to end or end to beginning. STL algorithms process a container by using iterators to traverse the container. Using iterators simplifies the algorithm implementation, for the algorithm does not require any container-specific information to process a container. Instead, the algorithm requires only the appropriate iterators. In different terms, an algorithm such as **reverse** cannot distinguish between, say, a **vector** and a **deque**. The algorithm works the same way on both: it uses iterators to access the container's elements so that these can be put in reverse order. We illustrate various STL algorithms with short examples. The goal is to highlight the processing power that these algorithms bring to STL containers.

**EXAMPLE 7.3.11.**   The program in Figure 7.3.13 illustrates four STL algorithms: **generate**, **replace_if**, **sort**, and **for_each**.

After defining an **int** vector with 10 elements

```
vector< int > v( 10 ); // vector of 10 elements
```

the program uses the **generate** algorithm to populate **v** with random integers:

```
generate( v.begin(), v.end(), rand );
```

The first two arguments are the iterators returned by the vector's **begin** and **end** methods, for we want to generate a random integer for each of **v**'s 10 elements. Because

```
#include <cstdlib>
#include <iostream>
#include <vector>
#include <algorithm> //*** for STL algorithms
using namespace std;

void dump( int i ) { cout << i << endl; }
bool odd( int i ) { return i % 2 != 0; }
bool comp( const int& i1, const int& i2 ) { return i1 > i2; }
int main() {
   vector< int > v( 10 ); // vector of 10 integers
   // fill with random ints
   generate( v.begin(), v.end(), rand );
   // replace odds with 0
   replace_if( v.begin(), v.end(), odd, 0 );
   // sort in descending order
   sort( v.begin(), v.end(), comp );
   for_each( v.begin(), v.end(), dump ); // print
   return 0;
}
```

**FIGURE 7.3.13** The STL algorithms `generate`, `replace_if`, `sort`, and `for_each`.

**v** is an **int** vector, **generate**'s third argument is a function that returns type **int**. In this case, the third argument is the library function **rand**, which returns a random integer.

After populating a **vector** with random integers, the program uses **replace_if** to replace odd integers with 0:

```
replace_if( v.begin(), v.end(), odd, 0 );
```

The first two arguments are again the two iterators returned by the vector's **begin** and **end** methods, for we want the replacements to occur from **v**'s beginning to its end. The third argument is a function's name, **odd**. This function tests whether its integer argument is odd. Because **v** is an **int** vector, the function **odd** expects an **int** parameter. The last argument 0 is the replace value to use if the test succeeds. This argument is also an **int** value precisely because **v** is an **int** vector. So **replace_if** invokes **odd** on each integer in **v**. If **odd** returns **true**, the integer is replaced by 0.

The program then sorts the vector in descending order:

```
sort( v.begin(), v.end(), comp ); // sort the vector
```

The first two arguments to **sort** are also the iterators returned by the vector's **begin** and **end** methods. The third argument is optional. If omitted, the vector would be sorted in *ascending* order, that is, in the order determined by the appropriate overload of **operator<**. Because **v** is an **int** vector, and **operator<** is defined for **int**s, we could sort **v** in ascending order simply by invoking **sort** with two arguments:

```
sort( v.begin(), v.end() ); // order by operator<
```

Because we want to sort **v** in descending order, we provide **sort** with a third argument, in this case the function **comp**'s name. This function takes two **int** references as arguments because **v** is an **int** vector, and it returns a **bool**. We return **true** if the first argument is greater than the second and **false** otherwise. This causes the **sort** algorithm to sort the vector in *descending* order.

To print the integers, the program uses **for_each** instead of a loop:

```
for_each( v.begin(), v.end(), dump ); // print it
```

The first two arguments are again the iterators returned by the vector's **begin** and **end** methods, for we again want to traverse the entire vector. The third argument is the name of a function, **dump**, to invoke on each of the vector's elements. Because **v** is an **int** vector, **dump** expects an **int** argument. Function **dump** prints its argument to the standard output.

The program has no loops. Algorithms such as **generate**, **for_each**, and **replace_if** have built-in iteration through their use of iterators. The iterators themselves are intuitive:

```
v.begin() // start at beginning
v.end()   // go to the end
```

The STL **sort** is easier to understand than **qsort**. For one thing, **sort** requires only two arguments to sort in ascending order. If a function's name is provided as the optional third argument, the function takes references rather than pointers to **void** as arguments.

Finally, we **#include** the header *algorithm*, which contains prototypes and supporting constructs for the STL algorithms. Other headers (e.g., *queue*) may **#include** *algorithm*. ∎

**EXAMPLE 7.3.12.** The program in Figure 7.3.14 shows that STL algorithms work on ordinary arrays. After defining the array **alph** and initializing it to a string consisting of 27 nonduplicate characters, the program randomly shuffles the array. Although **alph** is an ordinary array, it still may be passed to an STL algorithm such as **random_shuffle**. The algorithm **random_shuffle** expects two iterators as arguments: the first points to the beginning of the sequence to be shuffled, and the second points to the end of this sequence. Because an STL iterator behaves like a pointer, we can use the array's name **alph**, which points to the array's first element, as the first argument to **random_shuffle**. Because the array **alph** is a C-style string consisting of 27 characters and the null terminator, our second argument to **random_shuffle** is **alph + 27**, the address of the cell that holds the null terminator. This ensures that only the 27 string characters, and not the null terminator, will be shuffled.

After the random shuffle, we use the STL algorithm **nth_element** to place the sequence's **median element** in the sequence's middle position. In this example, which involves nonduplicate elements, the median element is the character **n** because the 13 characters **a**, **b**, . . . , **m** lexicographically precede **n**, and the 13 characters **o**, **p**, . . . , **}** lexicographically succeed **n**. In effect, **nth_element** places a specified element in the position it would occupy if the sequence were sorted in ascending order. However, **nth_element** does *not* necessarily sort the sequence. For example, a sample run produced the output

```
#include <iostream>
#include <algorithm>
using namespace std;
void print( const char*, char [ ], int );
int main() {
   const int len = 27;
   const int med = len / 2;

   // Print a sorted array of 27 nonduplicate characters
   char alph[ ] = "abcdefghijklmnopqrstuvwxyz{"; // 27
   print( "\n\nOriginal array:\n", alph, len );

   // Shuffle the array and print it.
   random_shuffle( alph, alph + len ); // shuffle the chars
   print( "\n\nAfter random_shuffle:\n", alph, len );

   // Arrange the array's elements so that the array cell
   // alph[ med ] holds the median character: all characters
   // less than alph[ med ] are to its left; all characters
   // greater than alph[ med ] are to its right.
   nth_element( alph, alph + med, alph + len );
   print( "\n\nAfter nth_element:\n", alph, len );
   print( "\n\t < median: ", alph, med );
   print( "\n\t   median: ", alph + med, 1 );
   print( "\n\t > median: ", alph + med + 1, len / 2 );

   cout << endl;
   return 0;
}
void print( const char* msg, char a[ ], int len ) {
  cout << msg;
  copy( a, a + len, ostream_iterator< char >( cout, " " ) );
}
```

**FIGURE 7.3.14** The STL algorithms `nth_element`, `random_shuffle`, and `copy`.

```
Original array:
a b c d e f g h i j k l m n o p q r s t u v w x y z {

After random_shuffle:
e t a r k m { l s y g q h o j x u z w p n b f d v c i

After nth_element:
e i a c d f b h g j k l m n o p q r s t u v { w z x y
        < median: e i a c d f b h g j k l m
          median: n
        > median: o p q r s t u v { w z x y
```

After the call to **nth_element**, the median element **n** is indeed in the middle position, but the sequence is not sorted.

The algorithm **nth_element** expects three random-access iterators as arguments. The first argument marks the beginning of the sequence; the second argument marks where in the sequence the specified element (that is, the **nth** element) is to be placed; and the last argument marks the end of the sequence. Because **alph** is an ordinary array, our arguments are the pointer values **alph**, **alph + 13**, and **alph + 27**.

Finally, the program uses the **copy** algorithm to print to the standard output:

```
copy( a, a + len, ostream_iterator< char >( cout, " " ) );
```

The algorithm's first two arguments mark where the **copy** is to begin and to end. The last argument is an **output iterator**, that is, a special STL iterator used to do output. (The parameter **a** has **alph** as its value.) Because **alph** consists of **char**acters, we use a **char** instantiation

```
ostream_iterator< char >
```

of **ostream_iterator**. The expression

```
ostream_iterator< char >( cout, " " )  // constructor call
```

invokes a parameterized constructor to create the iterator. The constructor's first argument is an output stream, in this case **cout**. The optional second argument specifies a separator for the items written to the output stream. In this example, a blank separates the characters. ∎

**EXAMPLE 7.3.13.** The program in Figure 7.3.15 populates a **vector** with the first 32 Fibonacci numbers and then copies the **vector** to a disk file and to the standard output. In the disk file, the numbers are separated by blanks; in the standard output, the numbers are separated by new lines. The program uses two **ostream_iterator**s:

```
ostream_iterator< int > outFileIt( outfile, " " );
ostream_iterator< int > stdOutIt( cout, "\n" );
```

We use one iterator associated with the standard output and a second iterator associated with a disk file. The iterator associated with the disk file uses blanks to separate the output, whereas the iterator associated with the standard input uses blanks. The iterators **outFileIt** and **stdOutIt** are **int** instantiations of the template class **ostream_iterator** because **fibs** is an **int** vector. We again use the **copy** algorithm with an output iterator as the third argument:

```
copy( fibs.begin(), fibs.end(), outFileIt );
copy( fibs.begin(), fibs.end(), stdOutIt );
```

This allows us to dispense with loops.

Our application writes the Fibonacci numbers in ascending order because this is the order in which they are added to the **vector**. It is straightforward to reverse this order. A **vector** has methods **rbegin** and **rend** (**r** stands for **r**everse) that could be used to print the **vector** in descending (that is, reverse) order:

```
copy( fibs.rbegin(), fibs.rend(), stdOutIt );
```

STL also provides input iterators for **copy**ing from input streams into containers such as **vector**s and **deque**s. ∎

```
#include <iostream>
#include <fstream>
#include <vector>
#include <algorithm>
using namespace std;
int main() {
   // populate vector with first 32 Fibonacci numbers
   vector< int > fibs( 32 );
   fibs[ 0 ] = fibs[ 1 ] = 1; // base cases
   for ( int i = 2; i < 32; i++ )
     fibs[ i ] = fibs[ i - 1 ] + fibs[ i - 2 ];
   // create output stream and iterator
   ofstream outfile( "output.dat" );
   ostream_iterator< int > outFileIt( outfile, " " );
   ostream_iterator< int > stdOutIt( cout, "\n" );
   // copy to output file and to standard output
   copy( fibs.begin(), fibs.end(), outFileIt );
   copy( fibs.begin(), fibs.end(), stdOutIt );
   return 0;
}
```

**FIGURE 7.3.15** The STL output iterator.

## Other STL Constructs

Containers and algorithms are the core parts of STL, and iterators are the means by which algorithms manipulate containers. STL has other constructs as well, which we describe briefly in this subsection.

A **function object** is a class object in which the function call operator is overloaded as a **public** method. An STL function object may be used instead of a function.

**EXAMPLE 7.3.14.** The program in Figure 7.3.13 has a **dump** function

```
void dump( int i ) { cout << i << endl; }
```

whose name is used as the third argument to the **for_each** algorithm

```
for_each( v.begin(), v.end(), dump );
```

Instead of this approach, we could create a function object

```
template< class T >
struct dumpIt {
   void operator()( T arg ) { cout << arg << endl; }
};
```

and then invoke the overloaded function call operator of an **int** instantiation:

```
for_each( v.begin(), v.end(), dumpIt< int >() ); // print
```

By the way, most STL programmers would create the **dumpIt** class with the keyword **struct** because the class's members then default to **public** (see Section 3.1); and the overloaded function call operator must be **public** for a function object to be used outside the class.  ∎

A **function adaptor** is a construct for building new function objects from already existing ones. A function adaptor is thus analogous to a container adaptor. There are function adaptors to negate a function object, to bind a constant to an argument in a function object's overloaded function call operator, to convert a function pointer to a function object, and to compose a new function object out of already existing ones.

```
#include <iostream>
#include <functional>
#include <algorithm>
using namespace std;
struct even : public unary_function< unsigned, bool > {
   bool operator()( unsigned n ) const { return n % 2 == 0; }
};
int main() {
   int a[ ] = { 1, 2, 3, 4, 5 };
   int n;
   n = count_if( a, a + 5, even() );
   cout << "a has " << n << " even integers." << endl;
   n = count_if( a, a + 5, not1( even() ) );
   cout << "a has " << n << " odd integers." << endl;
   return 0;
}
```

**FIGURE 7.3.16**  The STL function adaptor **not1**.

**EXAMPLE 7.3.15.**  The program in Figure 7.3.16 creates a function object **even** to test whether an integer is even. Function adaptors apply only to function objects that subclass one of two built-in STL function object types: **unary_function** and **binary_function**. Because **even** is a unary function, it subclasses **unary_function**. The first template parameter in **unary_function** is the argument type that the overloaded function call operator expects, in this case **unsigned**. The second template parameter is the operator's return type, in this case **bool**.

In the first call to the algorithm **count_if**, we pass **even** as the third argument. The algorithm uses this function object to test whether integers in array **a** are even, keeping count of the ones that are:

```
n = count_if( a, a + 5, even() );
```

The algorithm's return value is stored in **n**, which we then print to the standard output. In the second call to **count_if**, we negate **even** with the function adaptor **not1** (**1** stands for *unary*):

```
n = count_if( a, a + 5, not1( even() ) );
```

The return value is now the count of *odd* integers in **a**. To use function adaptors, the header file *functional* must be **#include**d. ■

An STL **allocator** is a template class that supports memory management. For example, a programmer working in a 16-bit PC environment could use STL allocators to adapt an application to one of the four standard PC memory models: small, compact, medium, and large. Programmers working in a UNIX, OS2, Apple, or Win32 environment typically can avoid allocators.

## EXERCISES

1. What is the difference between an STL container and an STL algorithm?
2. Explain the relationships among containers, algorithms, and iterators in STL.
3. What is the difference between a sequential and an associative container?
4. Suppose that you need a sequential container in which assertions and deletions must occur at either end. Would a **deque** or a **vector** be the more efficient container?
5. Are a **deque** and a **vector** equally efficient in inserting at the end?
6. What is the difference between a **set** and a **map**?
7. What is the difference between a **set** and a **multiset**?
8. Remove the line

   ```
   using namespace std;
   ```

   from the program in Figure 7.3.2 and try to compile the program.
9. Is [ ] overloaded for the **vector** class?
10. Is [ ] overloaded for the **list** class?
11. For a **list** container, are insertions at the beginning, in the middle, and at the end equally efficient?
12. Why do the **stack** and **queue** container adaptors adapt the **deque** rather than the **vector** by default?
13. Explain what a container adaptor does and give an example.
14. Run the program in Figure 7.3.13. Then change the line

    ```
    sort( v.begin(), v.end(), comp )
    ```

    to

    ```
    sort( v.begin(), v.end() );
    ```

    Recompile and run. How does the output differ between the two runs?
15. Explain what a function adaptor does and give an example.
16. What is an STL function object?
17. Can STL algorithms be used on ordinary C++ arrays?
18. STL provides algorithms such as **for_each** and **copy** that *discourage* the use of loops. What advantage does an algorithm such as **for_each** have over an ordinary C++ loop?
19. What advantage does an STL **vector** have over a C++ array?

# 7.4 SAMPLE APPLICATION: STOCK PERFORMANCE REPORTS

### Problem

Generate three reports on the daily performance of stocks for an exchange such as NAS-DAQ. The data come from a file of records in the format

$$< symbol > \quad < openingprice > \quad < closingprice > \quad < volume >$$

For example, the record

**MSFT 135.87 137.98 8301700**

represents information about Microsoft's stock, whose NASDAQ symbol is **MSFT**. For the day in question, Microsoft opened at $135.87 per share and closed at $137.98 per share, and 8,301,700 shares were traded. The data file is correctly formatted, but it contains an arbitrary number of unsorted records. After reading data from the file, generate three reports to the standard output. Each report lists the stock's symbol, its opening and closing price, its percentage of gain or loss during the day, and the volume of shares traded. The first report prints the stocks in *descending order by percentage of gain*. The second report prints the stocks in *ascending order by percentage of loss*. The third report prints the stocks in *descending order by volume*.

### Sample Input/Output

For the input file

```
BUTI    8.75    7.54   159000
ZTEC   39.54   39.23   100300
COHU   48.90   51.43   134900
TMXI    3.41    2.87   255000
ALCD   60.42   61.91   230000
EPEX   15.98   13.21    54000
MSFT  135.87  137.98  8301700
GMGC    2.76    2.81   129400
```

the output is

```
******* Gainers in descending order:
*** COHU
        % Changed:      5.17382
        Opening Price: 48.9
        Closing Price: 51.43
        Volume:         134900
*** ALCD
        % Changed:      2.46607
        Opening Price: 60.42
        Closing Price: 61.91
        Volume:         230000
```

```
*** GMGC
        % Changed:       1.81159
        Opening Price: 2.76
        Closing Price: 2.81
        Volume:          129400
*** MSFT
        % Changed:       1.55296
        Opening Price: 135.87
        Closing Price: 137.98
        Volume:          8301700
*** ZTEC
        % Changed:       -0.784016
        Opening Price: 39.54
        Closing Price: 39.23
        Volume:          100300
*** BUTI
        % Changed:       -13.8286
        Opening Price: 8.75
        Closing Price: 7.54
        Volume:          159000
*** TMXI
        % Changed:       -15.8358
        Opening Price: 3.41
        Closing Price: 2.87
        Volume:          255000
*** EPEX
        % Changed:       -17.3342
        Opening Price: 15.98
        Closing Price: 13.21
        Volume:          54000

******* Losers in ascending order:
*** EPEX
        % Changed:       -17.3342
        Opening Price: 15.98
        Closing Price: 13.21
        Volume:          54000
*** TMXI
        % Changed:       -15.8358
        Opening Price: 3.41
        Closing Price: 2.87
        Volume:          255000
*** BUTI
        % Changed:       -13.8286
        Opening Price: 8.75
        Closing Price: 7.54
        Volume:          159000
```

```
***  ZTEC
          % Changed:        -0.784016
          Opening Price: 39.54
          Closing Price: 39.23
          Volume:           100300
***  MSFT
          % Changed:        1.55296
          Opening Price: 135.87
          Closing Price: 137.98
          Volume:           8301700
***  GMGC
          % Changed:        1.81159
          Opening Price: 2.76
          Closing Price: 2.81
          Volume:           129400
***  ALCD
          % Changed:        2.46607
          Opening Price: 60.42
          Closing Price: 61.91
          Volume:           230000
***  COHU
          % Changed:        5.17382
          Opening Price: 48.9
          Closing Price: 51.43
          Volume:           134900

*******  Volume in descending order:
***  MSFT
          Volume:           8301700
          % Changed:        1.55296
          Opening Price: 135.87
          Closing Price: 137.98
***  TMXI
          Volume:           255000
          % Changed:        -15.8358
          Opening Price: 3.41
          Closing Price: 2.87
***  ALCD
          Volume:           230000
          % Changed:        2.46607
          Opening Price: 60.42
          Closing Price: 61.91
***  BUTI
          Volume:           159000
          % Changed:        -13.8286
          Opening Price: 8.75
          Closing Price: 7.54
```

```
*** COHU
        Volume:          134900
        % Changed:       5.17382
        Opening Price:   48.9
        Closing Price:   51.43
*** GMGC
        Volume:          129400
        % Changed:       1.81159
        Opening Price:   2.76
        Closing Price:   2.81
*** ZTEC
        Volume:          100300
        % Changed:       -0.784016
        Opening Price:   39.54
        Closing Price:   39.23
*** EPEX
        Volume:          54000
        % Changed:       -17.3342
        Opening Price:   15.98
        Closing Price:   13.21
```

### Solution

We create a class **Stock** to represent stocks as objects. The class has data members for the stock's symbol, its opening and closing price, the percentage of gain or loss during the day's trading, and the volume of stocks traded. The class interface consists of constructors to create **Stock** objects and other **public** methods to access data members. We use an STL **deque** container to hold the **Stock**s created from data in the input file. We use the STL **sort** algorithm to sort the **deque** twice:

- In descending order by percentage of gain.
- In descending order by volume.

After the first sort, we use the STL **for_each** algorithm to print the **deque**'s contents (that is, **Stock** objects) to the standard output. By printing the **deque** in regular order, we get the stocks in descending order by percentage of gain. By printing the **deque** in reverse order, we get the stocks in ascending order by percentage of loss. We then sort the **deque** in descending order by volume and print it again. We provide the appropriate STL function objects to handle comparisons used by the **sort** algorithm and to provide output functionality for the **for_each** algorithm.

### C++ Implementation

```cpp
#include <iostream>
#include <fstream>
#include <deque>
#include <algorithm>
#include <string>
using namespace std;
```

```cpp
//*** file names and miscellaneous globals
const string inFile = "stockData.dat";
const string Unknown = "????";

//*** objects generated from input records
class Stock {
public:
   Stock() {
      symbol = Unknown;
      open = close = gainLoss = volume = 0;
   }
   Stock( const string& s,        // symbol
          double o,               // opening price
          double c,               // closing price
          unsigned long v ) {  // volume traded
      symbol = s;
      open = o;
      close = c;
      volume = v;
      gainLoss = ( close - open ) / open;
   }
   const string& getSymbol() const {
      return symbol;
   }
   double getOpen() const {
      return open;
   }
   double getClose() const {
      return close;
   }
   unsigned long getVolume() const {
      return volume;
   }
   double getGainLoss() const {
      return gainLoss;
   }
private:
   string        symbol;
   double        open;     // opening price
   double        close;    // closing price
   double        gainLoss; // gain or loss fraction
   unsigned long volume;   // shares traded
};
```

```cpp
//*** Sort comparison: gains in descending order
struct winCmp {
   bool operator()( const Stock& s1, const Stock& s2 ) const  {
      return s1.getGainLoss() > s2.getGainLoss();
   }
};

//*** Sort comparison: volume in descending order
struct volCmp {
   bool operator()( const Stock& s1, const Stock& s2 ) const {
      return s1.getVolume() > s2.getVolume();
   }
};

//*** invoked by function objects to do output
void output( bool volFlag,
             const string& name,
             const char* openLabel, double open,
             const char* closeLabel, double close,
             const char* gainLabel, double gain,
             const char* volLabel, unsigned long vol ) {
   cout << "*** " << name << endl;
   if ( volFlag ) // if true, volume comes first
     cout << '\t' << volLabel << vol << endl;
   cout << '\t' << gainLabel  << gain  << endl
        << '\t' << openLabel  << open  << endl
        << '\t' << closeLabel << close << endl;
   if ( !volFlag ) // if false, volume comes last
     cout << '\t' << volLabel << vol << endl;
}

//*** Write Stocks sorted by gain-loss to standard output.
struct winPr {
   void operator()( const Stock& s ) const {
      output( false,
              s.getSymbol(),
              "Opening Price: ", s.getOpen(),
              "Closing Price: ", s.getClose(),
              "% Changed:     ", s.getGainLoss() * 100,
              "Volume:        ", s.getVolume() );
   }
};
```

```
//*** Write Stocks sorted by volume to standard output.
struct volPr {
   void operator()( const Stock& s ) const {
      output( true,
              s.getSymbol(),
              "Opening Price: ", s.getOpen(),
              "Closing Price: ", s.getClose(),
              "% Changed:      ", s.getGainLoss() * 100,
              "Volume:         ", s.getVolume() );
   }
};

void herald( const char* );
void input( deque< Stock >& );
int main() {
   deque< Stock > stocks;
   //*** Input stocks and separate into vectors for
   //    winners, losers, and break-evens.
   input( stocks );
   //*** Sort winners in descending order and output.
   herald( "Gainers in descending order: " );
   sort( stocks.begin(), stocks.end(), winCmp() );
   for_each( stocks.begin(), stocks.end(), winPr() );
   //*** Output losers in ascending order.
   herald( "Losers in ascending order: " );
   for_each( stocks.rbegin(), stocks.rend(), winPr() );
   //*** Sort volume in descending order and output
   herald( "Volume in descending order: " );
   sort( stocks.begin(), stocks.end(), volCmp() );
   for_each( stocks.begin(), stocks.end(), volPr() );
   return 0;
}

void input( deque< Stock >& d ) {
   string s;
   double o, c, v;
   ifstream input( inFile.c_str() );
   //*** Read data until end-of-file,
   // creating a Stock object per input record
   while ( input >> s >> o >> c >> v )
      d.insert( d.end(), Stock( s, o, c, v ) );
   input.close();
}

void herald( const char* s ) {
   cout << endl << "******* " << s << endl;
}
```

 ***Discussion***

By using an STL **deque** container and STL algorithms to process it, we are able to make the application's control structure relatively straightforward. After defining a **deque** to hold **Stock**s in **main**

```
deque< Stock > stocks;
```

we pass the **deque** to **input**, which reads data from an input file:

```
input( stocks );
```

The **deque** is passed *by reference* rather than by value because it is critical that the **deque** defined in **main**, and not a copy of this **deque**, hold the **Stock**s created from the input data. If the **deque** were passed by value, the **Stock**s would be entered into a *copy* of the **deque**; and **main** would be left with an empty **deque** to sort and output.

The function **input**

```
void input( deque< Stock >& d ) {
    string s;
    double o, c, v;
    ifstream input( inFile.c_str() );
    //*** Read data until end-of-file,
    // creating a Stock object per input record
    while ( input >> s >> o >> c >> v )
      d.insert( d.end(), Stock( s, o, c, v ) );
    input.close();
}
```

opens an **ifstream** and then uses a **while** loop to read data until end-of-file. The **deque** grows automatically to meet our storage requirements. We happen to insert at the **deque**'s end

```
d.insert( d.end(), Stock( s, o, c, v ) );
```

but it would be equally efficient to insert at the **deque**'s beginning. Recall that a **deque** does insertions at *either* end in constant time, whereas a **vector** does insertions at the end in constant time, but insertions at the beginning in *linear* time. A **deque** thus gives us flexibility for insertions without any penalty in efficiency, which is a major reason for our choosing it over a **vector** in this application. We insert a **Stock** by invoking the parameterized **Stock** constructor as the second argument to the **deque**'s **insert** method. By the way, the **while** loop in **input** is the only explicit loop in the application. All other looping is done implicitly by STL algorithms. This accounts for the application's relatively simple control structure.

When **input** returns, **main** invokes **sort** twice to sort the **Stock**s by percentage of gain and by volume. After the first sort, we use **for_each** to output the **deque** twice: first in regular order and then in reverse order. The code for the first sort is

```
sort( stocks.begin(), stocks.end(), winCmp() );
```

The first two arguments to **sort** specify where the sort is to begin and end, respectively. We use calls to the **deque** methods **begin** and **end** as these arguments. The third argument is the overloaded function call operator in the function object **winCmp**. Recall that a function object is a class object in which the function call operator is overloaded as a **public** method. Our definition

```
struct winCmp {
    bool operator()( const Stock& s1, const Stock& s2 ) const {
        return s1.getGainLoss() > s2.getGainLoss();
    }
};
```

uses the keyword **struct** rather than **class** because all members default to **public** when **struct** is used. This style is common in STL for defining function objects. In any case, the overloaded function call operator expects two references, in this case references to **Stock** objects. The **sort** algorithm is responsible for invoking the overloaded function call operator with the appropriate arguments, in this case two **Stock** objects that **sort** needs to compare in the course of sorting the **deque**. Because **winCmp** is used to sort the **Stock**s in *descending* order by their percentage of gain, we return the **bool**ean expression

```
s1.getGainLoss() > s2.getGainLoss()
```

So if **s1** has a greater gain than **s2**, we return **true**; otherwise, we return **false**. The **sort** algorithm uses the return value to order **Stock** objects as it sorts the **deque**.

After the first sort, we use **for_each**

```
for_each( stocks.begin(), stocks.end(), winPr() );
```

to print the **Stock**s to the standard output. Because the **deque** is now sorted in descending order by percentage of gain, the output is in this order. The first two arguments are the same as in the call to **sort**. The third argument is again a call to the overloaded function call operator in a function object, in this case **winPr**. The actual printing is handled by the top-level function **output**. After sorting by volume, we output a **Stock**'s volume first. After sorting by gain and loss, we output a **Stock**'s percentage of gain or loss first.

The second **for_each** statement

```
for_each( stocks.rbegin(), stocks.rend(), winPr() );
```

prints the **deque** in ascending order by percentage of loss. Because the **deque** is already sorted in descending order by percentage of gain, we simply print the **deque** in *reverse* order with calls to the methods **rbegin** and **rend** as the first two arguments to **for_each**. (The **r** stands for **r**everse.) Printing in reverse order is simpler and more efficient than sorting the **deque** again.

We use two separate function objects to handle the comparisons in the **sort**. This modular approach means that each function object's overloaded function call operator can consist of a single **return** statement. For output, we also have two function objects. The output for winners and losers share an overloaded function call operator in **winPr**, whereas the output for volume has its own overloaded function call operator in **volPr**.

Using STL for the application has two obvious benefits. First, the STL **deque** container grows dynamically to meet our storage requirements without forcing us to keep track of how many elements are inserted. Our input file is of an arbitrary size; hence, we cannot anticipate before reading the input data how many **Stock** objects the application requires. STL allows us to grow the **deque** as needed. Second, the STL **for_each** algorithm eliminates the need for output loops. Instead of using a **while** or a **for** loop to output the **Stock** objects, we use **for_each** to iterate through the **deque**, applying the appropriate overloaded output operator to each **Stock** object. The **deque** methods **begin**, **end**, **rbegin**, and **rend** allow us straightforwardly to output in either regular or reverse order. STL thus contributes to the application's overall simplicity, clarity, and robustness.

## C++ POSTSCRIPT

## Template Classes and Inheritance

A template class can be derived from a base class that is template or nontemplate. A template class or an instantiation of a template class can be a base class for a derived class that is template or nontemplate.

**EXAMPLE.**   The code segment

```
class B { // nontemplate base class
  //...
};

template< class T >
class TD : public B { // template derived class
  //...
};
```

illustrates the case in which the template class **TD** is derived from the nontemplate base class **B**. The code segment

```
template< class T >
class TB { // template base class
  //...
};

class D : public TB< int > { // derived class
  //...
};
```

illustrates the case in which nontemplate class **D** is derived from an **int** instantiation of the template class **TB**. The code segment

```
template< class T >
class TB { // template base class
  //...
};
```

```
template< class T >
class D : public TB< T > {
  //...
};
```

illustrates the case in which template class **D** is derived from template class **TB**. The template header must be included as part of **D**'s declaration because the class type **T** occurs in **D**'s declaration. ∎

Inheritance from STL template classes is also supported. For an example, see Figure 7.3.16.

## COMMON PROGRAMMING ERRORS

**1.** The template header uses *angle* brackets:

```
template{ class T } //***** ERROR: should be < class T >
class A {
  //...
};
template[ class T ] //***** ERROR: should be < class T >
class Z {
  //...
};
```

**2.** It is an error to omit the keyword **class** or **typename** when specifying a class parameter in a template's header:

```
template< T > //****** ERROR: keyword class missing
class C {
  //...
};
```

The correct syntax is

```
template< class T >
class C {
  //...
};
```

**3.** It is an error to omit the template header from a method definition that occurs *outside* the class declaration:

```
template< class T > class Array {
public:
  void m();  // declaration
  //...
};
//***** ERROR: template header missing
void Array< T >::m() { /*...*/ } // definition
```

The correct syntax is

```
template< class T >
class Array {
public:
  void m();  // declaration
  //...
};
template< class T >
void Array< T >::m() { /*...*/ } // definition
```

4. If a template class method is defined *outside* the class declaration, the class's name must occur, in template form, to the left of the scope resolution operator:

```
template< class T > class Array {
public:
  void m();  // declaration
  //...
};
//***** ERROR: should be Array< T >::m()
template< class T >
void Array::m() { /*...*/ }
```

5. It is an error for a template class not to have at least one class parameter:

```
template< int x > //***** ERROR: no class parameter
class C {
  //...
};
```

6. If a template header has multiple parameters, they must be separated by commas:

```
template< class T int x > //***** ERROR: no comma
class C {
  //...
};
```

7. Every function-style parameter's data type, built-in or user-defined, must be specified in the template header:

```
template< class T, x > //***** ERROR: no data type for x
class C {
  //...
};
```

**8.** It is an error to define objects that belong to a template class rather than to a template class *instantiation*:

```
template< class T >
class Array {
  //...
};
Array a1;             //***** ERROR: not an instantiation
Array< T > a2;        //***** ERROR: not an instantiation
template< class T >
Array< T > a3;        //***** ERROR: not an instantiation
Array< int > a4;      // ok
```

**9.** It is an error to use **assert**ions without an **#include** of the header *cassert* or *assert.h*.

**10.** It is an error to reference STL components without the appropriate **#include** directive, which uses the *new* C++ style. For example, to use a **vector**, we must **#include** the header *vector* (new style), not the header *vector.h* (old style).

## PROGRAMMING EXERCISES

**7.1.** Implement a template **Pair** class

```
template< class T1, class T2 >
class Pair {
public:
    // appropriate methods
private:
    T1 first;
    T2 second;
};
```

The class interface should include methods to create **Pair**s, to set and to get each element in the **Pair**, and to swap the elements so that, after the swap, the first element becomes the second and the second becomes the first.

**7.2.** Implement a template **Set** class (see Programming Exercise 3.12). Overload **+** (union), **–** (difference), **<<** (output), and **>>** (input).

**7.3.** Implement a template **Bag** class. A **bag** is like a set (see Programming Exercise 3.13) except that duplicates are allowed.

**7.4.** Implement a template **Queue** class, where a **queue** is a First **I**n, **F**irst **O**ut list of zero or more elements. Provide methods to insert and delete elements from a **Queue**, to check for full and empty **Queue**s, and to inspect a **Queue**'s front element without removing it. Name the insertion method **push** and the deletion method **pop** so that a **Queue**'s interface resembles a **Stack**'s interface (see Section 1.2). Use **assert**ions to promote systematic testing of **Queue** clients. Storage for **Queue** elements should be dynamically allocated.

**7.5.** Implement a template **Deque** class, where a **deque** is a list of zero or more elements that supports insertions and deletions at either end. Provide methods to insert and delete elements at either end (e.g., **push_front** and **push_back**), to check for full and empty **Deque**s, and to inspect a **Deque**'s front and rear elements without removing them. Use **assert**ions to promote systematic testing of **Deque** clients. Storage for **Deque** elements should be dynamically allocated.

**7.6.** Implement a template **ForwardIterator** class that supports iteration through the template **Array** class (see Figure 7.1.2). If the **Array**'s sequence of elements is $E_1, E_2, \ldots, E_n$, a **forward iterator** first selects $E_1$, then $E_2$, and so on. The iterator's interface consists of methods to associate it with a sequence, to **reset** it to the sequence's first element, to test whether it is at the end of the sequence, and to return the sequence's next element. The code segment

```
Array< float > f;          // Array instance
ForwardIterator< float> fi( f ); // ForwardIterator for f
// fill f with floating-point numbers
while ( fi.hasMoreElements() ) // iterate through f
  cout << fi.nextElement(); // return next f element
// fi is now at the end of the sequence
fi.reset(); // reset to f's first element
```

illustrates how a **ForwardIterator** might be initialized and used.

**7.7.** Implement a template **BackwardIterator** class that supports iteration through the template **Array** class (see Figure 7.1.2). If the **Array**'s sequence of elements is $E_1, E_2, \ldots, E_{n-1}, E_n$, a **backward iterator** first selects $E_n$, then $E_{n-1}$, and so on. This iterator shares an interface with the **ForwardIterator** (see Programming Exercise 7.6) with appropriate changes in behavior (e.g., a **BackwardIterator**'s **reset** method sets it to the sequence's last element rather than its first element).

**7.8.** Implement a template **RandomIterator** class for iteration through the template **Array** class (see Figure 7.1.2). A **random iterator** randomly selects an element from a sequence. A random iterator is guaranteed to select every element once before selecting any element twice. A **RandomIterator** shares an interface with the **ForwardIterator** (see Programming Exercise 7.6) with appropriate changes in behavior (e.g., a **RandomIterator**'s **reset** method resets it to a random element in the sequence).

**7.9.** Write a program that populates an STL container with $n$ randomly generated integers, where $n$ is a positive integer supplied by the user. Then keep a count $c$ of how many *more* integers must be randomly generated until each of the original $n$ integers is generated once again. Output a message that reports $n$ and $c$.

**7.10.** Write a program that tests the time complexity (see Figure 7.3.5) of STL **vector**s and **deque**s. In particular, test whether insertions and deletions at the beginning are more efficient for a **deque** than for a **vector** and whether insertions and deletions at the end are equally efficient for a **deque** and **vector**. The library functions **time** and **difftime** are useful for collecting timing data. The program

```
#include <ctime> //*** for time functions
#include <iostream>
#include <vector>
#include <algorithm>
```

```
using namespace std;
int main() {
   time_t start, finish;
   vector< int > v;
   // fill v with random integers
   start = time( 0 );   // set start time
   sort( v.begin(), v.end() ); // sort v
   finish = time( 0 );   // set finish time
   cout << difftime( finish, start ) << endl;
   return 0;
}
```

illustrates how **time** and **difftime** can be used to collect timing data.

**7.11.** Write a program that generates two sets of randomly generated integers. (Recall that a *set* must not have duplicate elements.) The sets need not be the same size. After sorting each set in descending order, merge them into an output file. The merged integers should likewise be sorted in descending order. The STL **merge** algorithm, whose prototype is

```
template< class InputIter1,
          class InputIter2,
          class OutputIter >
OutputIter merge( InputIter1 b1, // beginning of file 1
                  InputIter1 e1, // end of file 1
                  InputIter2 b2, // beginning of file 2
                  InputIter2 e2, // end of file 2
                  OutputIter o ); // output file
```

may be useful.

**7.12.** A World Wide Web site maintains a file of **hits**, that is, of visits to its site. The file has the format

```
<Visitor's IP Address> <day of year> <year>
```

where **IP** stands for Internet Protocol. Sample records are

```
140.192.16.8 34 1998
129.78.55.6 3 1999
140.192.34.6 35 1998
```

The file may hold duplicate records, which indicate multiple visits from the same visitor on the same day in the same year. A **visitor** is identified by an IP address. The file supports an interactive application that allows the user to

- List all visitors on a given day in any year.
- List all visitors on a given day in a given year.
- Count how many times a particular visitor has visited on a given day or in a given year.
- List the *n* most frequent visitors on a given day or in a given year, where *n* is a user-specified value.
- Print the file to the standard output sorted by either IP address, or day of year, or by year.

Write the application using whatever STL containers and algorithms seem appropriate. In particular, attempt to eliminate all loops (e.g., **for** or **while** loops) from the application.

**7.13.** Write a program that simulates shuffling a deck of cards and dealing a bridge hand. A bridge deal divides a 52-card deck into four hands of 13 cards each. The hands are labeled North, East, South, and West. A bridge deck has four suits: Clubs, Diamonds, Hearts, and Spades. In each suit, the cards are labeled Ace, King, Queen, Jack, 10, 9, . . . , 2. Major bridge tournaments play with computer-generated hands. *Hint*: See Figure 7.3.10.

**7.14.** Write a program that assigns faculty to courses for a given term. Each faculty member has a **teaching load**, which is the number of courses that the faculty member must teach in a given term. A faculty member expresses **preferences** for courses, which are numeric values that signal the faculty member's desire to teach a course. The preferences are integers 1, 2, . . . , *n*, with 1 as the highest preference. Courses have **priorities**, which are numeric values that determine the order in which the courses are assigned to faculty. Courses with a priority of 1 are scheduled first, those with a priority of 2 are scheduled second, and so on. Assume that faculty members and courses have unique identifiers (e.g., unique employee numbers for the faculty and unique course numbers for the courses). The course assignment application should use randomness to promote fairness. For example, if 10 courses have a priority of 1, the program should assign these courses to faculty in random order. If 20 faculty have a preference of 1 for a given course, the program should randomly select candidates from this pool in trying to assign the course. The program should reflect reasonable constraints. For example, a faculty member cannot teach two courses at the same time. If conflicts prevent a course from being assigned, it should be marked as *NotAssigned*. If a faculty member cannot be assigned courses equal to the teaching load, the faculty member should be marked as *UnderworkedAndOverpaid*.

**7.15.** Two statements in a computer program could be executed concurrently if the order of their serial execution is irrelevant. For example, consider the C++ statements

```
p = x + y; // statement 1
q = x * y; // statement 2
r = q - p; // statement 3
```

Statements 1 and 2 can be executed in either order—1 first and then 2, or 2 first and then 1—with the same result. However, statement 1 must be executed *before* statement 3 because statement 3 uses the value of **p** computed in statement 1. Conditions known as *Bernstein's conditions* can be used to determine whether two statements can be executed concurrently. Before stating Bernstein's conditions, we define two sets of variables. A statement's **write set** consists of variables whose values are changed when the statement executes, and its **read set** consists of variables whose values are unchanged when the statement executes. In a simple assignment statement such as

```
x = y;
```

the write set consists of the assignment's target **x**, and the read set consists of its source **y**. In our earlier example, statement 1's write set consists of **p** and its read set of **x** and **y**.

We now can state Bernstein's conditions for concurrent execution. Statements $S_1$ and $S_2$ can be executed concurrently if and only if they satisfy these conditions:

- The intersection of $S_1$'s read set and $S_2$'s write set is empty.
- The intersection of $S_2$'s read set and $S_1$'s write set is empty.
- The intersection of $S_1$'s write set and $S_2$'s write set is empty.

In our example, statement 1's write set is {**p**} and statement 3's read set is {**q**, **p**}. Their intersection is thus {**p**}, which is not empty. Therefore, statements 1 and 2 cannot be executed concurrently. Using either the **set** class of Programming Exercise 7.2 or the STL **set** container, write a program that prompts the user for two assignment statements that are read as character strings. After building the read and write sets for each statement, the program prints

1. The read and write sets of each statement.
2. The intersection sets specified in Bernstein's conditions.
3. A message about whether the statements can be executed concurrently.

# CHAPTER

# 8

# THE C++ INPUT/OUTPUT CLASS HIERARCHY

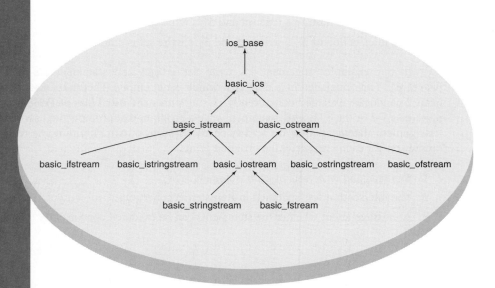

8.1 Overview

8.2 The Classes **ios_base** and **basic_ios**

8.3 The High-Level Input/Output Classes

8.4 Manipulators

8.5 The File Input/Output Classes

8.6 Sample Application: A Random Access File Class

8.7 The Character Stream Input/Output Classes

8.8 Sample Application: A High-Level Copy Function

8.9 The Buffer Classes

C++ Postscript

Common Programming Errors

Programming Exercises

**I**nput and output facilities are not part of the C++ language but instead are furnished through a class library. In this chapter, we explore this class library in detail.

The class hierarchy for C++'s input/output library is complex. We examine the hierarchy in detail for three reasons. First, this hierarchy illustrates the power available by combining polymorphism and multiple inheritance. Even programmers with no particular interest in the details of C++'s input/output hierarchy can learn important object-oriented design and coding lessons by attending to these details. Second, the input/output class hierarchy provides an excellent example of the use of templates. Third, through inheritance a programmer can extend the input/output classes (see Section 8.6). Such extensions require a clear understanding of the details of the classes.

The input/output class library has recently been extensively revised. We contrast the current version with the previous version in the C++ Postscript at the end of the chapter.

## 8.1 OVERVIEW

We begin by discussing the object-oriented design of the input/output class library. Object-oriented design begins by identifying objects and then defines operations (methods) appropriate to the objects. In C++ input and output, a central object is the **stream**, which is a sequence of bytes (see Figure 8.1.1). Operations on a stream include **reading from** and **writing to** the stream. A clean design can be achieved by having a common base class for two derived stream classes **basic_istream**, an input stream class, and **basic_ostream**, an output stream class. Although a single common base class could have been designed for **basic_istream** and **basic_ostream**, the current design has two common base classes (see Figure 8.1.2):

- **ios_base**, which provides a description of the stream *without regard* to the character set involved.

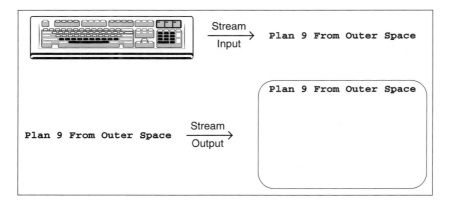

**FIGURE 8.1.1** Stream input/output.

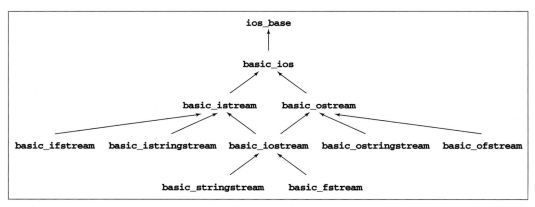

**FIGURE 8.1.2** The standard input/output hierarchy. Each class, except **ios_base**, is a template class.

- **basic_ios**, which provides a description of the stream *with regard* to the character set involved.

The derived classes **basic_istream** and **basic_ostream** inherit members from the common base classes **ios_base** and **basic_ios**. Many of the inherited *data members* represent attributes or features of a stream. One such inherited data member represents a stream's **format** attributes, for example, whether to left-justify output. Another inherited data member stores the number of digits of floating-point precision. Yet another inherited data member represents the status of operations on the stream, for example, whether end-of-file was encountered.

The derived classes **basic_istream** and **basic_ostream** add local members and operator overloads that are appropriately different for input and output stream, respectively. For example, class **basic_istream** adds methods for reading and moving around in the stream. Also, the right-shift operator **>>** is overloaded within **basic_istream** for reading the built-in types. Similarly, **basic_ostream** contains methods for writing and moving around in the stream. The left-shift operator **<<** is overloaded within **basic_ostream** for writing the built-in types.

Class **basic_iostream** is derived from both **basic_istream** and **basic_ostream** so that it inherits methods for both reading and writing a stream. Class **basic_iostream** has no additional data members and, except for a constructor and a destructor, it has no additional methods either.

The input/output class library provides for **buffered input/output**, in which data are not directly read or written but rather pass through intermediate storage (e.g., a character array) called a **buffer**.

**EXAMPLE 8.1.1.** Figure 8.1.3 depicts buffered output. When a request is received to write a character, the character is not written directly to the output stream but rather to the buffer. Periodically the buffer is written to the output stream. Writing the buffer is called **flushing** the buffer. A newline typically flushes the output buffer. ∎

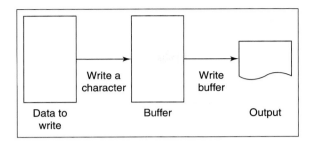

**FIGURE 8.1.3** Buffered output.

A buffer is another essential object in the class input/output library, and reading and writing the buffer are among the required operations. Various buffer classes (e.g., **basic_filebuf**, the file buffer class, and **basic_stringbuf**, the character stream buffer class) are derived from a common base class **basic_streambuf** (see Figure 8.1.4). These derived classes serve as interfaces to the actual sources and destinations of input and output. The base class **basic_streambuf** has methods (e.g., reading and writing the buffer) needed by both **basic_filebuf** and **basic_stringbuf**, which **basic_filebuf** and **basic_stringbuf** then obtain through inheritance.

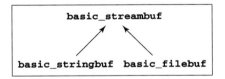

**FIGURE 8.1.4** The buffer classes. Each class is a template class.

Class **basic_streambuf** serves as a base class for deriving specialized stream buffer classes such as **basic_filebuf** and **basic_stringbuf**. It has methods for reading and writing the buffer and for moving around in the stream. These reading and writing methods are sometimes called *low-level input/output methods* because they provide direct access to the buffer. By contrast, the methods in the classes **basic_istream** and **basic_ostream** are called *high-level input/output methods* because they access the stream indirectly—by making calls to the low-level methods in the buffer classes.

Class **basic_streambuf** also contains the **virtual** methods **underflow**, which is responsible for dealing with an attempted read from an empty buffer, and **overflow**, which is responsible for dealing with an attempted write to a full buffer. A class derived from **basic_streambuf** overrides **underflow** and **overflow** so that action appropriate to the specific source or destination is taken. For example, when the buffer is full, **overflow** might ignore new writes or return an error flag, or, if the destination is a file, it might flush the buffer.

The class **basic_filebuf** contains constructors and methods for associating a **basic_filebuf** object with a file, and the class **basic_stringbuf** contains constructors and methods for handling arbitrary sequences of characters. Such sequences can be initialized from a **string** object and a copy of the character sequence can be made available as a **string** object. Both override **underflow** and **overflow**.

One reason that the buffer class hierarchy (Figure 8.1.4) is distinct from the stream class hierarchy (Figure 8.1.2) is to separate the high-level and low-level input/output methods. If these hierarchies were combined into a single hierarchy, some class would necessarily contain both high-level and low-level input/output methods.

Since **basic_ifstream** is derived from **basic_istream**, **basic_ifstream** inherits high-level input methods. It adds methods to open and close the file and a data member of type **basic_filebuf**.

Similarly, since **basic_ofstream** is derived from **basic_ostream**, **basic_of-stream** inherits high-level output methods. It too adds methods to open and close the file and a data member of type **basic_filebuf**.

Finally, since **basic_fstream** is derived from **basic_iostream**, **basic_fstream** inherits high-level input and output methods. It too adds methods to open and close the file and a data member of type **basic_filebuf**.

The **stringstream** classes (**basic_stringbuf**, **basic_istringstream**, **basic_ostringstream**, and **basic_stringstream**), which read and write character streams, are designed similarly to their **fstream** counterparts, which read and write files.

Since **basic_istringstream** is derived from **basic_istream**, **basic_istring-stream** inherits high-level, input methods. Similarly, since **basic_ostringstream** is derived from **basic_ostream**, **basic_ostringstream** inherits high-level, output methods. Finally, since **basic_stringstream** is derived from **basic_iostream**, **basic_stringstream** inherits high-level, input and output methods. Each of **basic_istringstream**, **basic_ostringstream**, and **basic_ostringstream** adds a method to provide a **string** object that is a copy of the internal buffer and a data member of type **basic_stringbuf**.

Figure 8.1.5 lists several input/output headers and briefly describes their purpose. Some of these headers **#include** others.

| Header | Partial Description |
|---|---|
| *iosfwd* | Contains forward declarations |
| *iostream* | Declares **cin**, **cout**, etc. |
| *ios* | Declares **ios_base** and **basic_ios** |
| *streambuf* | Declares **basic_streambuf** |
| *istream* | Declares **basic_istream** and **basic_iostream** |
| *ostream* | Declares **basic_ostream** |
| *iomanip* | Declares parameterized manipulators |
| *sstream* | Declares **basic_stringbuf** and the **stringstream** classes |
| *fstream* | Declares **basic_filebuf** and the **fstream** classes |

**FIGURE 8.1.5** Input/output headers and partial descriptions.

# Templates

In the standard input/output hierarchy, each class, except **ios_base**, is templated. For example, the declaration for **basic_ios** is

```
template<class charT, class traits = char_traits<charT>>
class basic_ios : public ios_base {
    //...
};
```

The parameter **charT** specifies the *type* to be used to represent a character, and **traits** specifies attributes of the character type. The character type can be either of the built-in types **char** or **wchar_t** (wide character) or a user-defined type. Examples of attributes of the character type are what the end-of-file character is (e.g., **EOF** for type **char**) and what it means for one character to be less than another. The familiar input/output types such as **istream** and **ofstream** are **typedef**s of the template input/output classes with **char** as the first template argument and, by default, **char_traits<char>** (the attributes of the character type **char**) as the second argument. For example, in header *iosfwd*, we find

```
typedef basic_ios<char> ios;
typedef basic_streambuf<char> streambuf;
typedef basic_istream<char> istream;
typedef basic_ostream<char> ostream;
typedef basic_iostream<char> iostream;
typedef basic_filebuf<char> filebuf;
typedef basic_ifstream<char> ifstream;
typedef basic_ofstream<char> ofstream;
typedef basic_fstream<char> fstream;
typedef basic_stringbuf<char> stringbuf;
typedef basic_istringstream<char> istringstream;
typedef basic_ostringstream<char> ostringstream;
typedef basic_stringstream<char> stringstream;
```

The header *iosfwd* also includes similar **typedef**s for **w_char** with a **w** prefixed to the corresponding **char** name, for example,

```
typedef basic_ios<wchar_t> wios;
```

The standard input/output hierarchy is headed by two classes: the nontemplated class **ios_base**, which provides a description of the stream independent of the character set, and the templated class **basic_ios**, which provides a description of the stream that involves the character set (see Figure 8.1.2). The reason for splitting the basic functionality into two classes is to minimize the size of the executable code (code compiled from a nontemplate class is usually smaller than that compiled from a template class).

## EXERCISES

1. Print the headers *iostream*, *fstream*, and *sstream*, and identify the data members and methods referred to in this section.

2. The C++ input/output class hierarchy assumes the stream model for input and output. Give an example of input or output for which some other model might be more suitable.

3. Argue that *any* input or output can be viewed as a stream.

4. Suggest how an input/output class hierarchy might be organized in the absence of multiple inheritance.

5. How are the buffer classes connected to the classes that use them (e.g., `basic_ifstream`, `basic_stringstream`)?

6. Why not replace class `basic_ofstream` with a class derived from `basic_ostream` and `basic_filebuf`?

## 8.2 THE CLASSES `ios_base` AND `basic_ios`

The standard input/output hierarchy is headed by two classes: `ios_base`, which provides a description of the stream independent of the character set, and `basic_ios`, which provides a description of the stream that involves the character set. We discuss `ios_base` and then `basic_ios`.

### `ios_base`

Except for the buffer classes, `ios_base`

```
namespace std {
  class ios_base {
  //...
  };
}
```

is a direct or indirect base class for all of the standard input/output classes, (see Figure 8.1.2).

Class `ios_base` declares several *bitmask* types. The underlying type used is implementation-dependent, but it can be an integer type. For example, `ios_base` declares `fmtflags` as a bitmask type that is used to specify format information. Several constants of this type are defined (see Figure 8.2.1), and bitwise *and* and *or* of such constants is supported to combine attributes. Methods to read, set, and clear format flags are given in Figure 8.2.2. In addition, `ios_base` has methods `precision` and `width`. When invoked with no arguments, each returns the current precision or width. When invoked with an argument, each sets the precision or width to the value passed and returns the old precision or width. Many of the same effects can be obtained by using manipulators (see Section 8.4).

| Name | Description |
|---|---|
| **boolalpha** | Read and write **bool**s as **true** and **false** |
| **dec** | Read and write in decimal |
| **fixed** | Use fixed notation for floating-point numbers: **d.ddd** |
| **hex** | Read and write in hexadecimal |
| **internal** | Padding after sign or base flag |
| **left** | Left-justify |
| **oct** | Read and write in octal |
| **right** | Right-justify |
| **scientific** | Use scientific notation for floating-point numbers: **d.dddEdd** |
| **showbase** | Use base indicator on output |
| **showpoint** | Put in a decimal point |
| **showpos** | Use + with nonnegative integers |
| **skipws** | Skip white space |
| **unitbuf** | Flush any stream after write |
| **uppercase** | Use uppercase letters on hex output |
| **adjustfield** | Value must be **left**, **right**, or **internal** |
| **basefield** | Value must be **dec**, **oct**, or **hex** |
| **floatfield** | Value must be **scientific** or **fixed** |

**FIGURE 8.2.1** Format flags.

**EXAMPLE 8.2.1.**   Because **cout** is an object of type **basic_ostream**, a class indirectly inherited from **ios_base**, we may apply the methods of Figure 8.2.2 to **cout**. The statement

```
ios_base::fmtflags old_flags =
                    cout.flags( ios_base::left
                              | ios_base::hex
                              | ios_base::showpoint
                              | ios_base::uppercase
                              | ios_base::fixed );
```

saves the old flags in **old_flags** and formats the standard output as left-justify output, print integers in hexadecimal, show the decimal point, print hexadecimal output using uppercase letters, and print floating-point output as **dd.dddddd**.   ■

**EXAMPLE 8.2.2.**   The method **setf**, with one argument, sets the specified format flags without changing the other flags. For example, the statement

```
cout.setf( ios_base::showbase );
```

| *Method* | *Purpose* |
|---|---|
| `flags()` | Return format flags |
| `flags( val )` | Set the format flags to the value passed and return the old flags |
| `setf( val )` | Set specified flags and return the old flags |
| `setf( val, ios_base::basefield )` | Set integer base to **val** and return the old flags. **val** is **ios_base::dec**, **ios_base::oct**, or **ios_base::hex**. |
| `setf( val, ios_base::adjustfield )` | Set left or right justification and return the old flags. **val** is **ios_base::left** or **ios_base::right**. |
| `setf( ios_base::internal, ios_base::adjustfield )` | Put fill character between sign and value and return the old flags |
| `setf( ios_base::scientific, ios_base::floatfield )` | Set scientific notation and return the old flags |
| `setf( ios_base::fixed, ios_base::floatfield )` | Set fixed notation and return the old flags |
| `setf( 0, ios_base::floatfield )` | Set default notation and return the old flags |
| `unsetf( val )` | Clear specified flags and return the old flags |

**FIGURE 8.2.2**  Methods to read, set, and clear the format flags.

causes subsequent output to show the integer base; that is, octal integers will be printed with a leading zero, hexadecimal integers will be printed with a leading **0x**, and decimal integers will be printed in the usual way. The preceding statement is equivalent to

```
cout.flags( cout.flags() | ios_base::showbase );
```

**EXAMPLE 8.2.3.**   Example 8.2.2 shows how **setf** can be used to change the format when only a single flag is involved.  The situation is more complex when several flags are involved.  For example, to format integer output as hexadecimal, the **hex** bit must be set and the **dec** and **oct** bits cleared.  To simplify changing the format when several flags are involved, **setf** can take a second argument.  For example, output can be formatted as decimal, hexadecimal, or octal by using **ios_base::basefield** as the second argument to **setf**.  The output from the code segment

```
cout.setf( ios_base::hex, ios_base::basefield );
cout << "Hex: " << 168 << '\n';
cout.setf( ios_base::oct, ios_base::basefield );
cout << "Octal: " << 168 << '\n';
```

is

```
Hex: a8
Octal: 250
```

**EXAMPLE 8.2.4.**   We can modify the code of Example 8.2.3 so that the output shows the base, and uppercase letters are used on hexadecimal output:

```
cout.setf( ios_base::showbase | ios_base::uppercase );
cout.setf( ios_base::hex, ios_base::basefield );
cout << "Hex: " << 168 << '\n';
cout.setf( ios_base::oct, ios_base::basefield );
cout << "Octal: " << 168 << '\n';
```

The output is now

```
Hex: 0XA8
Octal: 0250
```

**EXAMPLE 8.2.5.**   We can left- or right-justify output by using **ios_base::adjust-field** as the second argument to **setf**.  The output from the code segment

```
cout.width( 6 );
cout << -100 << '\n'; // default is right-justify
cout.width( 6 );
cout.setf( ios_base::left, ios_base::adjustfield );
cout << -100 << '\n';
cout.width( 6 );
cout.setf( ios_base::right, ios_base::adjustfield );
cout << -100 << '\n';
// width reverts to 0 (default)
cout.setf( ios_base::right, ios_base::adjustfield );
cout << -100 << '\n';
```

is

```
     -100
 -100
   -100
 -100
```

■

**EXAMPLE 8.2.6.** Another option that can be used with **ios_base::adjust-field** is **ios_base::internal**, which uses the fill character to pad between the sign and the value. For example, the output from the following code segment

```
cout.width( 6 );
cout.setf( ios_base::internal, ios_base::adjustfield );
cout << setfill( '0' ) << -100 << '\n';
```

is

```
-00100
```

■

**EXAMPLE 8.2.7.** Floating-point output can be formatted in fixed or scientific notation by using **ios_base::floatfield** as the second argument to **setf**. The output from the code segment

```
const float log10_pi = .497149872;
cout.setf( ios_base::scientific, ios_base::floatfield );
cout << log10_pi << '\n';
cout.setf( ios_base::fixed, ios_base::floatfield );
cout << log10_pi << '\n';
```

on our system is

```
4.971499e-001
0.497150
```

The default precision is six. Thus, in the first line of output, six digits are printed to the right of the decimal point. Notice that the value is rounded. In the second line of output, the sixth digit to the right of the decimal point is zero and, by default, is not printed. (Trailing zeros can be printed by setting the **ios_base::showpoint** flag.) Again, the value is rounded. ■

**EXAMPLE 8.2.8.** The method **unsetf** always takes only one argument. It clears the specified flags. For example, the statement

```
cin.unsetf( ios_base::skipws );
```

clears the **skipws** flag so that white space is *not* skipped. (The default is to skip white space.) An equivalent statement using method **flags** is

```
cin.flags( cin.flags() & ~ios_base::skipws );
```

■

The stream status flags defined in **ios_base** are described in Figure 8.2.3. Methods to access and modify the stream state are provided in **basic_ios**.

| Name | If Set |
|------|--------|
| **badbit** | Bad input or output source |
| **eofbit** | End of stream on input |
| **failbit** | Failure to read input or failure to produce expected output |
| **goodbit** | Input or output OK (the constant zero) |

**FIGURE 8.2.3** Stream status flags.

Flags defined in **ios_base** to describe the status of an open stream are listed in Figure 8.2.4. Methods to access and modify the stream state are provided in **basic_ios**.

| Name | If Set |
|------|--------|
| **app** | Open for appending |
| **ate** | Open and move to end of stream |
| **binary** | Read and write as a binary stream |
| **in** | Open for input |
| **out** | Open for output |
| **trunc** | Discard stream if it already exists |

**FIGURE 8.2.4** Flags to describe the status of an open stream.

**EXAMPLE 8.2.9.** The class **ofstream** has a constructor whose first argument is a file name (see Section 8.5) and whose second argument is *or*ed with **ios_base::out** (to open the file for output) after which it becomes the initial mode. Thus

```
ofstream fout( "out.dat", ios_base::app );
```

creates an **ofstream** object associated with the file *out.dat*, which is opened for appending (writing at the end of the file). ∎

Class **ios_base** declares an **enum** to give names to flag bits to indicate how to seek (move) in the stream as shown in Figure 8.2.5. These flags are used in classes indirectly derived from **ios_base** (see Section 8.3).

**EXAMPLE 8.2.10.** The method **seekp** is defined in the output class **basic_ostream** (see Section 8.3). One form of **seekp** has two arguments: the first is an offset, and the second is the direction. If **out** is an object in class **basic_ostream**, the expression

```
out.seekp( 10, ios_base::cur )
```

moves the current position in the stream 10 bytes forward. ∎

| Name | Purpose |
|------|---------|
| **beg** | Seek from the beginning |
| **cur** | Seek from the current position |
| **end** | Seek from the end |

**FIGURE 8.2.5** Seek flags.

Class **ios_base** contains a **static** method **sync_with_stdio** that synchronizes the C++ input/output with the standard C input/output functions. Any time the C and C++ input/output libraries are intermixed, the method **sync_with_stdio** should be invoked

```
ios_base::sync_with_stdio();
```

before doing any input or output.

## basic_ios

Class **basic_ios** is a template class derived from **ios_base**:

```
namespace std {
   template <class charT, class traits = char_traits<charT>>
   class basic_ios : public ios_base {
   //...
   };
}
```

Figure 8.2.6 lists several methods contained in **basic_ios** to read, set, and clear the stream status flags.

**EXAMPLE 8.2.11.** The statement

```
ios_base::iostate cur_state = cin.rdstate();
```

saves the current state for the standard input in **cur_state**. The type **iostate** is a bitmask type. ∎

**EXAMPLE 8.2.12.** The code segment

```
int i;
do {
   cin >> i;
   if ( !cin.eof() )
      cout << i << '\n';
} while ( !cin.eof() );
```

| Method | Effect |
|---|---|
| rdstate() | Returns the stream state |
| clear( val ) | Sets the stream state to the value passed. If no argument, sets stream state to 0 (goodbit). |
| setstate( val ) | Sets specified flags in the stream state |
| good() | Returns true if stream state is zero; otherwise, returns false |
| eof() | Returns true if eofbit is set; otherwise, returns false |
| fail() | Returns true if failbit or badbit is set; otherwise, returns false |
| bad() | Returns true if badbit is set; otherwise, returns false |

**FIGURE 8.2.6** Methods to read, set, and clear the stream status flags.

echoes integers in the standard input to the standard output, one per line. (We assume that a newline follows the last integer in the input.) An attempted read beyond the end of the stream is required to set **eofbit**. Thus, the following code segment that attempts to echo integers in the standard input to the standard output is *not* correct; an extra line is printed:

```
int i;
// ***** ERROR: extra line is printed
while ( !cin.eof() ) {
   cin >> i; // eof bit set here
   cout << i << '\n';
}
```

**EXAMPLE 8.2.13.** On many systems, a control character (e.g., control-D in UNIX and control-Z in DOS) is interpreted as end-of-file. To receive additional input after an end-of-file signal from the standard input, some systems require the end-of-file flag to be cleared. The statement

```
cin.clear();
```

clears all of the standard input status flags, including the end-of-file flag.

Class **basic_ios** overloads the not operator **!** and provides a conversion from **basic_ios** to **void***. The declarations are

```
template <class charT, class traits = char_traits<charT>>
class basic_ios : public ios_base {
   //...
   operator void*() const;
   bool operator!() const;
   //...
};
```

The value of **operator void*()** is zero (false) if **failbit** or **badbit** is set; otherwise, the value is nonzero (true). Similarly, the overloaded not operator returns **true** if **failbit** or **badbit** is set; otherwise, it returns **false**.

**EXAMPLE 8.2.14.**   In the code

```
if ( cin ) { // standard input ok?
   // process input
}
```

if **failbit** or **badbit** is set on the standard input, **cin** is converted to zero (false) and we do not process input. Otherwise, **cin** is converted to nonzero (true) and we process the input.                                                                              ■

Class **ios_base** has a method **fill**. When **fill** is invoked with no argument, it returns the current fill character. When it is invoked with an argument, it sets the fill character to the value passed and returns the old fill character. When invoked with an argument, it has the same effect as the manipulator **setfill** (see Section 8.4).

**EXAMPLE 8.2.15.**   The code

```
basic_ios::char_type old_fill = cout.fill( '0' );
// write to standard output
cout.fill( old_fill );
```

changes the fill character to zero and saves the old fill character in **old_fill**. After writing to the standard output, it restores the original fill character. A **typedef** makes **char_type** a synonym for the character type used (e.g., **char**).                               ■

## Exceptions

If an error occurs on input or output, one or more of the bit flags in Figure 8.2.3 is set. A check for an error can be made using one of the methods in Figure 8.2.6 or one of the overloads: **operator void*()** or **operator()**.

**EXAMPLE 8.2.16.** The code segment

```
cout << "Boola, boola!\n";
if ( cout.fail() ) {
   cerr << "Output operation failed\n";
   //...
}
```

writes a string to the standard output and then checks whether the operation failed.

■

The method **exceptions** in **basic_ios** can be used to require that certain input/output conditions throw exceptions. When the argument is **eofbit**, **badbit**, **failbit**, or a combination of these bits using operator | (or), if an error of the type specified occurs, an exception of type **ios_base::failure** is thrown. The argument **goodbit** can be used to deactivate throwing input/output exceptions. If **exceptions** is invoked with no arguments, it returns the current input/output status flags.

**EXAMPLE 8.2.17.** Example 8.2.16 can be rewritten using exceptions as

```
try {
   cout.exceptions( ios_base::failbit );
   cout << "Boola, boola!\n";
}
catch( ios_base::failure ) {
   cerr << "Output operation failed\n";
   //...
}
```

■

An advantage of using exceptions rather than checking flags to test for input/output errors is that *all* exceptions specified can be tested by putting the code to be checked in a **try** block. If flags are used to check for the same exceptions, an **if** statement would have to follow every input/output operation.

## EXERCISES

1. Write an expression whose value is **true** if **cout**'s **eofbit** is set, and **false** if **cout**'s **eofbit** is not set.

2. Write a statement that clears **cout**'s **eofbit** and does not change any other status bit.

3. Explain how the expression **!cin** is evaluated in the code

```
if ( !cin ) {
   //...
}
```

4. Write a statement to create an object **flout** of type **ofstream**, where **flout** is associated with the file *data.dat*, which is opened as a binary file.

5. Write a statement that moves the current position in the file associated with the object **fout** in class **ostream** 10 bytes from the end of the file.

6. Write a statement that formats the standard output as follows: skip white space, right justify, use decimal conversion, use + with positive integers, and use fixed notation for floating-point numbers.

7. Use the method **setf** to set the **showpoint** flag on the standard output.

8. Using only the method **flags**, set the **showpoint** flag on the standard output. Do not change any other format flag.

9. Use the method **unsetf** to clear the **showpoint** flag on the standard output.

10. Using only the method **flags**, clear the **showpoint** flag on the standard output. Do not change any other format flags.

11. Use the method **setf** to set the integer base to octal on the standard output.

12. Using only the method **flags**, set the **oct** flag, and clear the **dec** and **hex** flags on the standard output.

13. Use the method **setf** to restore the default notation for floating-point output on the standard output.

14. What is the output?

```
cout.setf( ios_base::showpos );
cout.setf( ios_base::left, ios_base::adjustfield );
cout.fill( 'X' );
cout.width( 6 );
cout << 66;
cout.width( 6 );
cout << 66 << 66 << 66 << '\n';
```

15. What is the output?

```
cout.setf( ios_base::hex, ios_base::basefield );
cout.setf( ios_base::showbase | ios_base::uppercase );
cout.setf( ios_base::left, ios_base::adjustfield );
cout.fill( '$' );
cout.width( 6 );
cout << 66;
cout.width( 6 );
cout << 66 << 66 << 66 << '\n';
```

**16.** What is the output?

```
cout.setf( ios_base::showpoint );
cout.setf( ios_base::left, ios_base::adjustfield );
cout.setf( ios_base::fixed, ios_base::floatfield );
cout.precision( 4 );
float x = 8.72;
cout.width( 8 );
cout << x;
cout.width( 8 );
cout << x << x << x << '\n';
```

**17.** Why is method **fill** defined in **basic_ios** and not in **ios_base**?

## 8.3 THE HIGH-LEVEL INPUT/OUTPUT CLASSES

In this section we discuss the classes **basic_istream**, **basic_ostream**, and **basic_iostream**, which provide a high-level interface to input and output.

### basic_istream

Class **basic_istream** is a template class derived from **basic_ios**

```
namespace std {
   template <class charT, class traits = char_traits<charT>>
   class basic_istream
         : virtual public basic_ios<charT, traits> {
   //...
   };
}
```

and provides high-level methods for input streams.

The method **get** is overloaded and so can be invoked in various ways. When the version of **get** with the declaration

```
basic_istream<charT, traits>& get( char_type& c );
```

is invoked, the next character, white space or not, is read into **c**, and **get** returns the (updated) stream that invoked it. If there is no character to read, **failbit** is set.

When the version of **get** with the declaration

```
int_type get();
```

is invoked, the next character in the stream, white space or not, is returned, or if no characters remain to be read, **get** returns an end-of-file flag appropriate to the character type being used and sets **failbit**. If **char** is the character type, the end-of-file flag is **EOF**. This version of **get** resembles the C function **fgetc**. A **typedef** makes **int_type** a synonym for some integer type (e.g., **long**).

**EXAMPLE 8.3.1.** The code segment

```
int c;
while ( ( c = cin.get() ) != EOF )
   cout << c;
```

copies the standard input to the standard output.                                  ■

The method **getline** whose declaration is

```
basic_istream<charT, traits>& getline( char_type* b,
                                       streamsize s,
                                       char_type d );
```

expects three arguments: an array **b** into which to write characters, an integer value **s** that
bounds the number of characters, and an end-of-line marker **d**. If the end-of-line marker
is omitted, it defaults to a newline. The value of **s** should be equal to the length of the
character array **b**. A **typedef** makes **streamsize** a synonym for some integer type. The
method **getline** reads characters until it

- Reaches end-of-file
- Encounters an end-of-line marker
- Stores **s** − 1 characters

whichever happens first. If end-of-file is reached, **eofbit** is set. If **s** − 1 characters are
stored, **failbit** is set. After it stops reading, **getline** adds a null terminator to the array
to make a C-style string and returns the stream that invoked it. If **getline** stops reading
because it encounters an end-of-line marker, **getline** does *not* store the marker in the array
but rather discards it. Note that **getline** never reads more than **s** − 1 characters. If the
array's size **s** is the same as **getline**'s second argument, array overflow cannot occur.

**EXAMPLE 8.3.2.** The program

```
#include <iostream>
#include <fstream>
using namespace std;

const int BuffSize = 133;

int main() {
   ifstream in;
   ofstream out;
   char buff[ BuffSize ];
   in.open( "infile.dat" );
   out.open( "outfile.dat" );
   while ( in.getline( buff, BuffSize ) )
      out << buff << "\n\n";
   return 0;
}
```

writes a double-spaced version of the file *infile.dat* to the file *outfile.dat*.              ■

The method **read** whose declaration is

```
basic_istream<charT, traits>& read( char_type* a,
                                     streamsize n );
```

reads characters and stores them in the array **a** until **n** characters are read or end-of-file occurs. If end-of-file occurs, **failbit** is set. No terminator character such as a newline is used, and no null terminator is placed in the array **a**. The method **read**, which is used to read binary data, returns the stream that invoked it. A **typedef** makes **streamsize** a synonym for some integer type. The method **gcount** can be used to determine the number of characters actually read. The method **read** resembles the C function **fread**.

The method **peek** whose declaration is

```
int_type peek();
```

returns the next character from the stream but does not remove it from the stream. If no characters remain to be read, **peek** returns end-of-file (**EOF** for type **char**).

The method **putback** whose declaration is

```
basic_istream<charT, traits>& putback( char_type c );
```

returns the character **c** to the stream. The method **putback** returns the stream that invoked it. It resembles the C function **ungetc**.

The method **ignore** whose declaration is

```
basic_istream<charT, traits>& ignore( int count = 1,
                                       int_type stop );
```

removes **count** characters from the stream, or all characters until end-of-file, or all characters from the stream up to and including **stop**, whichever comes first. If a value is not specified for **stop**, it defaults to end-of-file. The removed characters are not stored but simply discarded. The method **ignore** returns the stream that invoked it.

The method **gcount** whose declaration is

```
streamsize gcount() const;
```

returns the number of characters read by the last unformatted input method.

There are separate stream position markers—one for input and one for output. The methods **seekg** and **tellg** set and read the position within the input stream (**g** in **seekg** stands for "get"). The output stream class **basic_ostream** has methods **seekp** and **tellp** to set and read the position within the output stream (**p** in **seekp** and **tellp** stands for "put"). These methods resemble the C functions **fseek** and **ftell**.

There are two versions of **seekg**. The first, whose declaration is

```
basic_istream<charT, traits>& seekg( off_type off,
                                      ios_base::seek_dir dir );
```

moves the input stream position marker **off** bytes from **dir**, which must be one of the following: **ios_base::beg** (from the beginning of the stream), **ios_base::cur** (from the current position), or **ios_base::end** (from the end of the stream). A **typedef** makes **off_type** a synonym for an integer type. The method **seekg** returns the stream that invoked it. When this version of **seekg** is used with a file, the file should be opened as a binary file.

The method **tellg** whose declaration is

```
pos_type tellg();
```

returns the location of the input stream position marker. A **typedef** makes **pos_type** a synonym for an integer type.

The version of **seekg** whose declaration is

```
basic_istream<charT, traits>& seekg( pos_type pos );
```

sets the input stream position marker to location **pos** as returned by **tellg**. When this version of **seekg** is used with a file, it is *not* necessary to open the file as a binary file.

The class **basic_istream** overloads the right-shift operator for formatted input of built-in types. A typical declaration is

```
basic_istream<charT, traits>& operator>>( int& );
```

Here an **int** is read into a variable passed by reference, after which the stream is returned.

**EXAMPLE 8.3.3.**   Because **operator>>** returns the stream, **>>** can be chained:

```
cin >> i >> j;
```

Because **>>** associates from the left, first the expression

```
cin >> i
```

is evaluated. An integer is read into **i** and the expression is replaced by its value, the updated stream. This updated stream then acts on **j**

```
cin >> j
```

and an integer is read into **j**.                                                                              ■

Among the types handled by **>>** are

| | |
|---|---|
| **bool&** | **int&** |
| **signed char*** | **unsigned int&** |
| **unsigned char*** | **long&** |
| **charT*** | **unsigned long&** |
| **signed char&** | **float&** |
| **unsigned char&** | **double&** |
| **charT&** | **long double&** |
| **short&** | **void*&** |
| **unsigned short&** | |

The type **charT** is the template parameter for the character type used (e.g., **char**). The type **void*&** is used to read an address. The **char*** and **charT*** types are used to store a string in a character array. A null terminator is added to make a C-style string.

When **>>** is used for input, the default action is to skip white space, even for type **char** (unlike **scanf** in C).

**EXAMPLE 8.3.4.** The type `char&` is used to read one character. For the input

```
x     y     z
```

the code segment

```
char c;
while ( cin >> c )
   cout << c;
cout << '\n';
```

prints

```
xyz
```

since white space is skipped. ∎

The type `char*` is used with `>>` to read a C-style string. If the field width is zero (the default), white space is skipped, after which all non-white space characters up to the next white space character are read and stored. If the width is set to **n**, white space is skipped, after which all non-white space characters up to the next white space character, or **n - 1** characters, whichever occurs first, are read and stored. In either case, a null terminator is added.

**EXAMPLE 8.3.5.** The code segment

```
char a[ 80 ];
cin.width( 80 );
cin >> a;
```

avoids overflow in the array **a**. ∎

The skip white space option can be disabled by clearing the `skipws` flag.

**EXAMPLE 8.3.6.** The following code echoes the standard input to the standard output:

```
char c;
// clear skip white space flag
cin.unsetf( ios_base::skipws );
while ( cin >> c )
   cout << c;
cout << '\n';
```
∎

For integer types, if the first non-white space character is not a digit or a sign, `failbit` is set and no further data can be read until `failbit` is cleared. Similarly, for floating-point types, if the first non-white space character is not a digit, a sign, or a decimal point, `failbit` is also set and no further data can be read until `failbit` is cleared.

**EXAMPLE 8.3.7.** The program in Figure 8.3.1 accepts integer input and echoes it in hexadecimal. If the input is not an integer, a message is printed and the user is prompted to reenter the item. ∎

```
int main() {
   int val;
   bool ok;
   string line;
   cout << hex;
   for ( ; ; ) {
      cout << "Enter an integer (negative to quit): ";
      ok = true;
      cin >> val; // if val illegal, cin converted to false
      if ( !cin ) {
         cout << "Bad input. Redo.\n";
         cin.clear(); // clear state so input can be read
         getline( cin, line ); // read and dump bad input
         ok = false;
      }
      if ( ok )
         if ( val < 0 )
            break;
         else
            cout << val << '\n';
   }
   return 0;
}
```

**FIGURE 8.3.1** A program that accepts integer input and echoes it in hexadecimal. If the input is not an integer, a message is printed and the user is prompted to reenter the item.

## basic_ostream

Class **basic_ostream** is a template class derived from **basic_ios**

```
namespace std {
   template <class charT, class traits = char_traits<charT>>
   class basic_ostream :
         virtual public basic_ios<charT, traits> {
   //...
   };
}
```

and provides high-level methods for output streams.

The method **put** whose declaration is

```
basic_ostream<charT, traits>& put( char_type );
```

writes the character passed to the output stream. The method **put** returns the (updated) stream that invoked it. It resembles the C function **fputc**.

**EXAMPLE 8.3.8.** Given the definition

```
char c = '$';
```

the statements

```
cout << c;
```

and

```
cout.put( c );
```

are equivalent.    ■

The method **write** whose declaration is

```
basic_ostream<charT, traits>& write( const char_type* a,
                                     streamsize m );
```

writes **m** characters from the array **a** to the output stream. If the operation fails, **badbit** is set. The method **write**, which is used to write binary data, returns the stream that invoked it. It resembles the C function **fwrite**.

The methods **seekp** and **tellp** whose declarations are

```
basic_ostream<charT, traits>& seekp( pos_type );
basic_ostream<charT, traits>& seekp( off_type,
                                     ios_base::seek_dir );
pos_type tellp();
```

set and read the output stream file position marker. They behave similarly to their **basic_istream** counterparts **seekg** and **tellg**.

When the version

```
basic_ostream<charT, traits>& seekp( off_type,
                                     ios_base::seek_dir );
```

is used with a file, the file should be opened as a binary file. The version

```
basic_ostream<charT, traits>& seekp( pos_type );
```

should take as an argument a value returned by **tellp**. When this latter version is used with a file, it is *not* necessary to open the file as a binary file.

The method **flush** whose declaration is

```
basic_ostream<charT, traits>& flush();
```

flushes the buffer. The method **flush** returns the stream that invoked it. It resembles the C function **fflush**.

The class **basic_ostream** overloads the left-shift operator for formatted output. A typical declaration is

```
basic_ostream<charT, traits>& operator<<( short );
```

Here a **short** is written, after which the stream is returned.

Among the types handled by **<<** are

| | |
|---|---|
| **bool** | **short** |
| **const signed char\*** | **unsigned short** |
| **const unsigned char\*** | **long** |
| **const char\*** | **unsigned long** |
| **const charT\*** | **float** |
| **signed char** | **double** |
| **unsigned char** | **long double** |
| **char** | **void\*** |
| **charT** | |

The type **charT** is the template parameter for the character type used (e.g., **char**). The type **void\*** is used to write an address. The **char\*** and **charT\*** types are used to write a null-terminated, C-style string to the output stream.

**EXAMPLE 8.3.9.**   On our system, the code

```
float x = 146.25;
cout << "x = " << x << "\n&x = "
    << static_cast<void*>(&x) << '\n';
```

printed

```
x = 146.25
&x = 0012FF7C
```

∎

## basic_iostream

Class **basic_iostream** is publicly inherited from both **basic_istream** and **basic_ostream**. Its *entire* declaration is

```
namespace std {
  template <class charT, class traits = char_traits<charT>>
  class basic_iostream :
    public basic_istream<charT, traits>,
    public basic_ostream<charT, traits> {
  public:
    explicit basic_iostream( basic_streambuf<charT, traits>* );
    virtual ~basic_iostream();
  };
}
```

Thus class **basic_iostream** provides high-level methods for input/output streams.

## EXERCISES

1. Why is **basic_ios** a **virtual** base class for **basic_istream**?

2. Write a statement that reads the next 100 bytes from the standard input (white space or not) and stores them in the **char** array **a**.

3. Write a statement that reads and discards the next 100 bytes from the standard input (white space or not).

4. What is the output?

```
cin.ignore( 50 );
cout << cin.gcount() << '\n';
```

Assume that the standard input is **abcde** (with **e** as the last character). Tell which character would next be read after each sequence of statements in Exercises 5–9 is executed.

5. `cin.seekg( 1, ios_base::beg );`

6. `cin.seekg( -1, ios_base::end );`

7. `cin.seekg( 2 );`
   `cin.seekg( 1, ios_base::cur );`

8. `cin.seekg( -2, ios_base::end );`
   `cin.seekg( 1, ios_base::cur );`

9. `cin.seekg( 1, ios_base::beg );`
   `p = cin.tellp();`
   `cin.seekg( -2, ios_base::end );`
   `cin.seekg( p );`

10. Write a code segment that reads strings, delimited by single quotes, from the standard input until end-of-file and stores them in an array of **string**. *Example*: If the input is

    ```
    'Marty Kalin'    'Don Knuth'
    ```

    **Marty Kalin** would be read and stored as the first string and **Don Knuth** would be read and stored as the second string. Assume that there are no errors in the input.

11. Write a code segment that reads lines (terminated by **'\n'**) from the standard input and stores them in an array of **string**. Reading stops when a line containing only **'\n'** is encountered. This newline is removed from the standard input but is not stored. *Example*: If the input is

    ```
    Marty Kalin
    Don Knuth

    Grace Slick
    ```

    the strings **Marty Kalin** and **Don Knuth** would be read and stored. The file position marker would be on **G** in **Grace Slick**. Assume that the standard input begins with a nonblank line.

12. Write a statement to write 50 characters from the **char** array **a** to the standard output.

## 8.4 MANIPULATORS

We introduced manipulators in Section 2.2; here, we look at them in detail.

A **manipulator** is a function that either directly or indirectly modifies a stream. For example, the system manipulator **hex** causes subsequent input or output to be hexadecimal. A manipulator is used with the overloaded input operator **>>** or the overloaded output operator **<<**. For example,

```
int i = 10;
cout << hex << i << '\n';
```

prints the value 10 in hexadecimal.

Several manipulators with arguments are predefined (see Figure 8.4.1). To use predefined manipulators with arguments, include *iomanip*.

| Manipulator | Acts On | Purpose |
|---|---|---|
| `setbase( int n )` | `basic_ostream` | Set integer base to **n** (0 means default) |
| `setfill( char_type c )` | `basic_ostream` | Set fill character to **c** |
| `setprecision( int n )` | `basic_ostream` | Set precision to **n** |
| `setw( int n )` | `basic_ostream` | Set field width to **n** |
| `setiosflags( mask )` | `ios_base` | Set specified format bits |
| `resetiosflags( mask )` | `ios_base` | Clear specified format bits |

**FIGURE 8.4.1** Manipulators with arguments defined in *iomanip*.

**EXAMPLE 8.4.1.**   We can rewrite Example 8.2.5 in which the output shows the base, and uppercase letters are used on hexadecimal output as

```
cout << setiosflags( ios_base::showbase
                | ios_base::uppercase )
     << hex << "Hex: " << 168 << '\n'
     << oct << "Octal: " << 168 << '\n';
```
■

We use the terminology *manipulator with no arguments* to refer to manipulators such as **hex** or **endl** because, *when used with* **<<** *or* **>>**, these manipulators appear without arguments. Here is an example:

```
cout << endl;
```

In this example, the overloaded **<<** operator invokes the manipulator **endl** and, at this time, **endl** *is passed an argument* and performs its modifications to the stream.

Consider how we might implement a manipulator such as **endl** with no arguments. Because **endl** modifies the output stream **basic_ostream**, it should take an argument of type **basic_ostream&** and return an argument of type **basic_ostream&**. Now consider a statement such as

```
cout << endl;
```

where **endl** is referenced. The name of a function by itself is of type *pointer to function*; thus, **endl** is of type "pointer to a function with one argument of type **basic_ostream&** that returns type **basic_ostream&**."

Because the statement

```
cout << endl;
```

is equivalent to

```
cout.operator<<( endl );
```

we need an overload of **operator<<** that takes this type of argument: "pointer to a function with one argument of type **basic_ostream&** that returns type **basic_ostream&**." Fortunately for our needs, class **basic_ostream** contains the following declaration:

```
basic_ostream<charT, traits>&
   operator<<( basic_ostream<charT, traits>&
      ( *f )( basic_ostream<charT, traits>& ) );
```

The argument **f** to **operator<<** is of type "pointer to a function with one argument of type **basic_ostream&** that returns type **basic_ostream&**." In practice, **f** is a pointer to a manipulator. The method **operator<<** simply invokes the manipulator to which **f** points:

```
template <class charT, class traits>
basic_ostream<charT, traits>&
   basic_ostream<charT, traits>::operator<<(
                     basic_ostream& ( *f )( basic_ostream& ) ) {
   return f( *this );
}
```

**EXAMPLE 8.4.2.**   For the special case of **ostream**, the manipulator **endl** might be written as

```
ostream& endl( ostream& os ) {
   os << '\n';
   return os.flush();
}
```

When the statement

```
cout << endl;
```

is executed, **operator<<** is invoked as

```
cout.operator<<( endl );
```

The body of **operator<<**

```
return f( *this );
```

is equivalent to

```
return endl( cout );
```

which in turn is equivalent to

```
cout << '\n';
return cout.flush();
```

Using the technique illustrated in Example 8.4.2, it is possible to write our own manipulators.

**EXAMPLE 8.4.3.**   The manipulator

```
ostream& bell( ostream& os ) {
   return os << "\a";
}
```

rings the bell. It could be used as

```
cout << bell;
```

Consider writing a manipulator that takes an argument. Suppose, for example, that we want a manipulator **bell( n )** that rings the bell **n** times. Such a manipulator could be invoked as

```
cout << bell( 10 );
```

Because the function call operator has greater precedence than **<<**, when this statement executes, the function **bell** is invoked with argument 10, after which **operator<<** is invoked as

```
operator<<( cout, val );
```

where *val* is the value returned by **bell**.

So that the compiler can unambiguously choose the correct version of **operator<<** to invoke, the type of the value returned by **bell** must be different from the type of argument expected by all of the other versions of **operator<<**. The trick is to define a class for use with manipulators and to have a manipulator return an object in this class. The returned object is then responsible for invoking some function that actually modifies the stream. We illustrate with the **bell** example.

The argument to the manipulator **bell** is of type **int**, but other manipulators might have different types of arguments. For this reason, the class for use with manipulators is a parameterized class; the parameter type matches the type of the argument to the manipulator. The templates for these classes are implementation-specified, but they are normally declared in *iomanip*. We illustrate how to write a manipulator that takes an argument by writing the manipulator **bell( n )** that rings the bell **n** times.

**EXAMPLE 8.4.4.**    The header *iomanip* normally includes a class **omanip** similar to the following that facilitates writing one-argument manipulators

```
template< class Typ,
          class charT,
          class traits = char_traits<charT> >
struct omanip {
   Typ n;
   void ( *f )( basic_ostream<charT, traits>&, Typ );
   omanip( void ( *f1 )( basic_ostream<charT, traits>&, Typ ),
                        Typ n1 ) : f( f1 ), n( n1 ) { }
};
```

and the overload of **<<**

```
template<class charT, class traits, class Typ>
basic_ostream<charT, traits>&
 operator<<( basic_ostream<charT, traits>& os,
             const omanip<Typ, charT>& sman ) {
   ( sman.f )( os, sman.n );
   return os;
}
```

The parameterized type **Typ** describes the type of the manipulator's argument. In our case, the type is **int**.

The constructor has two parameters: the first **f1** is a pointer to a secondary function that actually modifies the stream, and the second **n1** is the argument to **f1**. The constructor simply initializes the members to the arguments passed to it. The function **operator<<** invokes the function that modifies the stream.

We can write the secondary bell ringer function as

```
void bell_ringer( ostream& os, int n ) {
   for ( int i = 0; i < n; i++ )
      os << "\a";
}
```

and the **bell** manipulator as

```
omanip< int, char > bell( int n ) {
   return omanip< int, char >( bell_ringer, n );
}
```

The **bell** manipulator can be invoked as

```
cout << bell( 10 );
```

which is equivalent to

```
operator<<( cout, bell( 10 ) );
```

Because **cout** belongs to **basic_ostream<char>** and **bell** returns type

```
omanip< int, char >
```

the correct version of **<<** is invoked. When the expression

```
omanip< int, char >( bell_ringer, n )
```

in **bell** is evaluated, the constructor for **omanip< int, char >** is invoked, and an object *temp* of type **omanip< int, char >** comes into existence. The constructor initializes **f** to **bell_ringer** and **n** to 10. The function **bell** then returns *temp*, which becomes the second argument to **operator<<**.

When **operator<<** executes with arguments **cout** and *temp*, it invokes **bell_ringer** as

```
bell_ringer( cout, 10 )
```

and returns the output stream **cout**. Thus the bell is rung 10 times and the updated **cout** is returned. ∎

Although our examples in this section have dealt with **basic_ostream**, similar techniques can be used to write manipulators for **basic_istream**.

## EXERCISES

1. Write a statement to clear the **showpoint** flag on **cout**. Use a manipulator.
2. Write a statement to set the fill character on **cout** to **'0'**. Use a manipulator.
3. Provide an implementation of the manipulator **ws** that skips white space in the input.
4. Provide an implementation of the manipulator **hex**. *Hint*: This manipulator takes an **ios_base&** argument and returns type **ios_base&**.
5. Write a manipulator **scien** that sets scientific notation for floating-point numbers on **ostream**.
6. Write a manipulator **tab** that writes a tab in **ostream**.
7. Provide an implementation of the manipulator **setfill**.
8. Provide an implementation of the manipulator **resetiosflags**.
9. Write a manipulator **setoff( off_type n )** that sets the file position marker in **istream** to **n**.
10. Write a manipulator **skipline( int n )** that writes **n** newlines to **ostream** and then flushes the stream.
11. Explain the difference between a manipulator and a method.

## 8.5 THE FILE INPUT/OUTPUT CLASSES

The classes

```
basic_filebuf  basic_ofstream  basic_ifstream  basic_fstream
```

are declared in *fstream*. They provide a high-level interface to file input and output. Class **basic_filebuf** provides buffered access to files. We discuss this class in detail in Section 8.9.

## `basic_ofstream`

Class **basic_ofstream** is a template class derived from **basic_ostream**

```
namespace std {
   template <class charT, class traits = char_traits<charT>>
   class basic_ofstream : public basic_ostream<charT, traits> {
   //...
   };
}
```

and contains constructors and methods to associate output files with **basic_ofstream** objects. The class **basic_ofstream** inherits methods from **basic_ostream** to write and move within files.

The default constructor is used when a **basic_ofstream** object is created, but a file is not attached to the object.

The constructor with declaration

```
explicit basic_ofstream( const char* filename,
                         ios_base::openmode mode
                         = ios_base::out );
```

is used to associate a **basic_ofstream** object with the file **filename**, which is opened in mode **mode**. The type **openmode** is a bitmask type. The default mode is output. If a mode is specified, it is automatically *or*ed by the constructor with **ios_base::out**. If the file cannot be opened, the **failbit** is set.

**EXAMPLE 8.5.1.** The statement

```
ofstream fout( "data.out" );
```

opens the file *data.out* for output and creates an **ofstream** object **fout** associated with this file. (Recall that **ofstream** is a synonym for **basic_ofstream<char>**.)

∎

Recall (see Section 8.2) that a **basic_ios** object can be used as a condition in a statement. Since **ofstream** is indirectly derived from **basic_ios**, an **ofstream** object can be used as a condition.

**EXAMPLE 8.5.2.** The code

```
ofstream fout( "data.out" );
if ( !fout )
   cerr << "Can't open data.out\n";
```

attempts to open the file *data.out* for output. If the file cannot be opened, an error message is written to the standard error.

∎

The **ofstream** method **open**

```
void open( const char* filename,
           ios_base::openmode mode = ios_base::out );
```

opens the file **filename** in mode **mode** and associates it with an already existing **basic_ofstream** object. The default mode is output. If a mode is specified, it is automatically *or*ed with **ios_base::out**. If the file cannot be opened, the **failbit** is set.

**EXAMPLE 8.5.3.**   The code segment

```
ofstream fout;
fout.open( "data.out" );
```

has the same effect as that of Example 8.5.1. The file *data.out* is opened for output and the **ofstream** object **fout** is associated with this file.   ∎

The **ofstream** method **is_open**

```
bool is_open();
```

returns **true** if the file is open, and **false** if the file is not open.

**EXAMPLE 8.5.4.**   The code segment of Example 8.5.2 may be rewritten using method **is_open** as

```
ofstream fout( "data.out" );
if ( !fout.is_open() )
   cerr << "Can't open data.out\n";
```
   ∎

The method **close** closes the file, if any, attached to the **ofstream** object.

**EXAMPLE 8.5.5.**   The file *data.dat* associated with the **ofstream** object **fout** of Example 8.5.4 may be closed with the statement

```
fout.close();
```
   ∎

# basic_ifstream

Class **basic_ifstream** is a template class derived from **basic_istream**

```
namespace std {
   template <class charT, class traits = char_traits<charT>>
   class basic_ifstream : public basic_istream<charT, traits> {
   //...
   };
}
```

and contains constructors and methods to associate output files with **basic_ifstream** objects. The class **basic_ifstream** inherits methods from **basic_istream** to write and move within files.

The default constructor is used when a **basic_ifstream** object is created, but a file is not attached to the object.

The constructor with declaration

```
explicit basic_ifstream( const char* filename,
                         ios_base::openmode mode
                         = ios_base::in );
```

is used to associate a **basic_ifstream** object with the file **filename**, which is opened in mode **mode**. The default mode is input. If a mode is specified, it is automatically *or*ed by the constructor with **ios_base::in**. If the file cannot be opened, the **failbit** is set.

**EXAMPLE 8.5.6.**    The statement

```
ifstream fin( "data.in" );
```

opens the file *data.in* for input and creates an **ifstream** object **fin** associated with this file. (Recall that **ifstream** is a synonym for **basic_ifstream<char>**.)    ■

Since **ifstream** is indirectly derived from **basic_ios**, an **ifstream** object can be used as a condition.

**EXAMPLE 8.5.7.**    The code segment

```
ifstream fin( "data.in" );
if ( !fin )
   cerr << "Can't open data.in\n";
```

attempts to open the file *data.in* for input. If the file cannot be opened, an error message is written to the standard error.    ■

The **ifstream** method **open**

```
void open( const char* filename,
           ios_base::openmode mode = ios_base::in );
```

opens the file **filename** in mode **mode** and associates it with an already existing **basic_ifstream** object. The default mode is input. If a mode is specified, it is automatically *or*ed with **ios_base::in**. If the file cannot be opened, the **failbit** is set.

**EXAMPLE 8.5.8.**    The code segment

```
ifstream fin;
fin.open( "data.in" );
```

has the same effect as that of Example 8.5.6. The file *data.in* is opened for input and the **ifstream** object **fin** is associated with this file.    ■

The methods **is_open** and **close** behave similarly to the corresponding methods in **basic_ofstream**.

## basic_fstream

Class **basic_fstream** is a template class derived from **basic_iostream**

```
namespace std {
   template <class charT, class traits = char_traits<charT>>
   class basic_fstream : public basic_iostream<charT, traits> {
   //...
   };
}
```

and contains constructors and methods to associate files (input or output or both) with **basic_fstream** objects. The class **basic_fstream** inherits methods from **basic_iostream** to write and move within files.

The default constructor is used when a **basic_fstream** object is created, but a file is not attached to the object.

The constructor with declaration

```
explicit basic_fstream( const char* filename,
                        ios_base::openmode mode
                          = ios_base::in | ios_base::out );
```

is used to associate a **basic_fstream** object with the file **filename**, which is opened in mode **mode**. The default mode is input and output. If the file cannot be opened, the **failbit** is set.

**EXAMPLE 8.5.9.** The statement

```
fstream finout( "data.txt" );
```

opens the file *data.txt* for input and output and creates an **fstream** object **finout** associated with this file. (Recall that **fstream** is a synonym for **basic_fstream<char>**.)
∎

Since **fstream** is indirectly derived from **basic_ios**, an **fstream** object can be used as a condition.

**EXAMPLE 8.5.10.** The code segment

```
fstream finout( "data.txt" );
if ( !finout )
   cerr << "Can't open data.txt\n";
```

attempts to open the file *data.txt* for input and output. If the file cannot be opened, an error message is written to the standard error.
∎

The method **open**

```
void open( const char* filename,
          ios_base::openmode mode
              = ios_base::in | ios_base::out );
```

opens the file **filename** in mode **mode** and associates it with an already existing **basic_fstream** object. The default mode is input and output. If the file cannot be opened, **failbit** is set.

**EXAMPLE 8.5.11.**    The code segment

```
fstream finout;
finout.open( "data.txt" );
```

has the same effect as that of Example 8.5.9. The file *data.txt* is opened for input and output and the **fstream** object **finout** is associated with this file.                     ■

The methods **is_open** and **close** behave similarly to the corresponding methods in **basic_ofstream** and **basic_ifstream**.

## EXERCISES

1. Write two statements. The first statement creates an **ifstream** object **fin**. The second statement opens the file *weather.in* and associates it with **fin**.

2. Write two statements. The first statement creates an **ofstream** object **fout**. The second statement opens the file *news.out* for appending and associates it with **fout**.

3. Write one statement that creates an **fstream** object **finout** associated with the binary file *stars.dat*, which is opened for input and output.

4. Since we could open a file for input and output with the statement

```
ifstream finout( "data.dat", ios_base::out );
```

why do we need class **fstream**?

5. The following code attempts to open the file *data.dat* for input, do some processing, close it, reopen it for output, and then do more processing. What is the error?

```
// open file for reading
ifstream f( "data.dat" );
// process
f.close();
// open file for writing
ofstream f( "data.dat" );
// process
```

6. Correct the error in Exercise 5.

7. Write a complete program that copies files in the order listed on the command line (the first file—the executable—is skipped) to the standard output. Files that cannot be opened for reading are ignored. (This program is similar to the UNIX utility **cat**.)

# 8.6 SAMPLE APPLICATION: A RANDOM ACCESS FILE CLASS

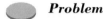 *Problem*

A **random access file** is a file in which we can access records in any order whatsoever and not necessarily in physical order. We implement a random access file class that allows the user to create and use a random access file. In particular, the user can add a record, find a record, or remove a record.

In our implementation, the data read and written are *binary data* so that *any* kind of data can be stored and retrieved from the file. The user can directly manipulate the binary data, or a class could be created as an interface to the binary data.

*Sample Input/Output*

The following sample input/output shows the random access file class in action. We first create a new file. Although the random access file class allows records and keys of any size, the records here are five bytes long to simplify the example. The first three bytes make up the key.

```
New file (Y/N)? y

[A]dd
[F]ind
[R]emove
[Q]uit? a
Which record to add? 125xx
Record added

[A]dd
[F]ind
[R]emove
[Q]uit? f

Key? 125
Record found: 125xx

[A]dd
[F]ind
[R]emove
[Q]uit? f
Key? 130
Record not found

[A]dd
[F]ind
[R]emove
[Q]uit? r
Key? 125
Record removed
```

```
[A]dd
[F]ind
[R]emove
[Q]uit? f
Key? 125
Record not found

[A]dd
[F]ind
[R]emove
[Q]uit? q
```

### Solution

We use a **relative file**, that is, a file in which a record's **relative address** (as opposed to its *physical* address) is its position in the file: first, second, . . . . Given a key, we can translate it into a relative address. Once we have the relative address, we can determine approximately where the record is located in the file, find it quickly, and then access it. A relative file is thus analogous to an array. Just as each of the array's elements has a position relative to the first, so each element in a relative file has a position relative to the first.

The records in a relative file are stored contiguously following the file header, whose purpose we will explain later. The first byte of a record, which is not part of the logical record, holds a status flag that indicates whether a record is stored (**T** for "taken"), whether a record was stored but deleted (**D** for "deleted"), or whether a record was never stored (**F** for "free"). The remaining bytes store the key and the rest of the record. If, as in the sample input/output, the logical records are five bytes, the file appears as in Figure 8.6.1, assuming a 256-byte header.

| File | Header... | T150aaF | | T167bb... |
|---|---|---|---|---|
| | ↑ | ↑ | ↑ | ↑ |
| Byte | 0 | 256 | 262 | 268 |
| Relative address | | 0 | 1 | 2 |

**FIGURE 8.6.1** A relative file.

To access a record, we define a **hash function** $h$ that, given a key, produces a relative storage address:

$$h(\,key\,) \; = \; \text{Record's relative address}$$

Although there are many different ways to define hash functions, our implementation uses the division-remainder method. We define the hash function $h$ by the rule

$$h(\,key\,) \; = \; key \,\%\, divisor$$

where the modulus operator % yields the remainder after dividing *key* by *divisor*. For example, if *key* is 134 and *divisor* is 13, the record's relative address is 4. If *divisor* is $n$, the relative addresses range from 0 through $n - 1$.

When two distinct keys hash to the same relative storage address, we say that a **collision** occurs. For example, if our hash function is

$$h(\ key\ )\ =\ key\ \%\ 13$$

we have

$$h(\ 134\ )\ =\ 4\ =\ h(\ 147\ )$$

There is a collision: the keys 134 and 147 map to the same relative address.

Any hashing system must provide a **collision resolution policy**—a way of handling collisions. Our collision resolution policy is called **linear probing**. When a collision occurs, we simply move to the next highest relative address (with the first record position assumed to follow the last record position). For example, if we insert the keys 42, 6, 31, and 14 in the relative file with relative addresses 0 through 12 using the hash function $h(\ key\ ) = key\ \%\ 13$, we obtain the situation shown in Figure 8.6.2. Now suppose that we insert the key 135. Because

$$h(\ 135\ )\ =\ 5\ =\ h(\ 31\ )$$

a collision occurs. Using linear probing, we insert 135 in the next highest unoccupied spot, 7. We obtain the situation shown in Figure 8.6.3.

| | | 14 | | 42 | | 31 | 6 | | | | | | |
|---|---|---|---|---|---|---|---|---|---|---|---|---|---|
| Relative address: | 0 | 1 | 2 | 3 | 4 | 5 | 6 | 7 | 8 | 9 | 10 | 11 | 12 |

**FIGURE 8.6.2** Inserting in a relative file.

| | | 14 | | 42 | | 31 | 6 | 135 | | | | | |
|---|---|---|---|---|---|---|---|---|---|---|---|---|---|
| Relative address: | 0 | 1 | 2 | 3 | 4 | 5 | 6 | 7 | 8 | 9 | 10 | 11 | 12 |

**FIGURE 8.6.3** Resolving a collision in a relative file.

Divisors should be chosen to minimize collisions. Research and experience show that divisors with no small prime factors do reasonably well at avoiding collisions. Avoiding collisions requires more than a good divisor, however. As more and more records are added to a relative file, collisions become more likely. A file's **load factor**, defined as

$$\text{load factor} \; = \; \frac{\text{number of records in file}}{\text{file's maximum capacity}}$$

is the percentage of occupied cells. Research and experience show that a relative file's load factor should not exceed 70 to 80 percent.

To delete a record, we mark it **D** (deleted) rather than physically delete it.

When we search for a record with a given key $k$, we first hash to relative address *addr* = $k \% divisor$, where *divisor* is the number of slots in the file. If the record at relative address *addr* has status **T** (taken), we check whether this record has key $k$. If so, the search terminates successfully; otherwise, we continue the search by checking the record at relative address

$$(\, addr + 1 \,) \% \, divisor$$

If the record at relative address *addr* has status **F** (free), the search terminates unsuccessfully since, if the record were present, we would have found it before reaching the free slot. If the record at relative address *addr* has status **D** (deleted), we must continue the search by checking the record at relative address

$$(\, addr + 1 \,) \% \, divisor$$

since the record we are searching for may have been inserted before the record at address *addr* was deleted and would thus be found after further probing.

Distinguishing between free and deleted slots usually allows us to terminate the search for a nonexistent record before searching the entire file.

### C++ Implementation

```
#include <iostream>
#include <cstdio>
#include <fstream>
#include <cstring>
#include <cstdlib>
#include <cctype>
using namespace std;

const int header_size = 256;
const char Taken = 'T';
const char Free = 'F';
const char Deleted = 'D';
```

```
class frandom : public fstream {
public:
    frandom();
    frandom( const char* ); // open existing file
    frandom( const char*, int, int, int ); // open new file
    ~frandom();
    void open( const char* ); // open existing file
    void open( const char*, int, int, int ); // open new file
    void close();
    long get_slots() const { return slots; }
    long get_record_size() const { return record_size; }
    long get_key_size() const { return key_size; }
    long get_total_bytes() const { return total_bytes; }
    long get_no_records() const { return no_records; }
    bool add_record( const char* );
    bool find_record( char* );
    bool remove_record( const char* );
private:
    long slots;
    long record_size; // includes 1-byte flag
    long key_size;
    long total_bytes;
    long no_records; // no of records stored
    long loc_address; // computed by locate
    char* buffer; // holds one record
    char* stored_key; // holds one key
    long get_address( const char* ) const;
    bool locate( const char* );
};

frandom::~frandom() {
    if ( is_open() ) {
        delete [ ] stored_key;
        delete [ ] buffer;
        char buff[ header_size ];
        for ( int i = 0; i < header_size; i++ )
            buff[ i ] = ' ';
```

```
        sprintf( buff, "%ld %ld %ld %ld",
                slots, record_size,
                key_size, no_records );
        seekp( 0, ios_base::beg );
        write( buff, header_size );
    }
}

frandom::frandom() : fstream() {
    buffer = stored_key = 0;
    slots = record_size = key_size = 0;
    total_bytes = no_records = 0;
}

frandom::frandom( const char* filename ) : fstream() {
    buffer = stored_key = 0;
    open( filename );
}

frandom::frandom( const char* filename,
                    int sl,
                    int actual_record_size,
                    int ks ) : fstream() {
    buffer = stored_key = 0;
    open( filename, sl, actual_record_size, ks );
}

// open an existing file
void frandom::open( const char* filename ) {
    fstream::open( filename,
                    ios_base::in |
                    ios_base::out |
                    ios_base::binary );
    if ( is_open() ) {
        char buff[ header_size ];
        read( buff, header_size );
        sscanf( buff, "%ld%ld%ld%ld",
                &slots, &record_size, &key_size,
                &no_records );
```

```
        total_bytes = slots * record_size + header_size;
        // get_address needs \0
        stored_key = new char [ key_size + 1 ];
        buffer = new char [ record_size ];
    }
}

// open a new file
void frandom::open( const char* filename,
                    int sl,
                    int actual_record_size,
                    int ks ) {
    fstream::open( filename,
                   ios_base::in |
                   ios_base::out |
                   ios_base::binary );
    // if open succeeds, file already exists
    if ( is_open() ) {
        setstate( ios_base::failbit );
        fstream::close();
        return;
    }

    // file does not exist; create it
    fstream::open( filename, ios_base::out | ios_base::binary );
    if ( is_open() )
        fstream::close();
    // file created; now open it for input and output
    fstream::open( filename,
                   ios_base::in |
                   ios_base::out |
                   ios_base::binary );

    if ( is_open() ) {
        clear(); // clear failbit flag set by open failure
        char buff[ header_size ];
        slots = sl;
        record_size = actual_record_size + 1;
        key_size = ks;
        total_bytes = slots * record_size + header_size;
        no_records = 0;
    }
```

```
      // get_address needs \0
      stored_key = new char [ key_size + 1 ];
      for ( int i = 0; i < header_size; i++ )
         buff[ i ] = ' ';
      sprintf( buff, "%ld %ld %ld %ld",
               slots, record_size,
               key_size, no_records );
      write( buff, header_size );
      buffer = new char [ record_size ];
      for ( i = 1; i < record_size; i++ )
         buffer[ i ] = ' ';
      buffer[ 0 ] = Free;
      for ( i = 0; i < slots; i++ )
         write( buffer, record_size );
   }
}

// hash function
long frandom::get_address( const char* key ) const {
   memcpy( stored_key, key, key_size );
   stored_key[ key_size ] = '\0';
   return ( atol( stored_key ) % slots )
            * record_size + header_size;
}

// locate searches for a record with the specified key.
// If successful, locate returns true.
// If unsuccessful, locate returns false.
// locate sets data member loc_address to the address
// of the record if the record is found.  This
// address can be then used by find_record
// or remove_record.
//
// If the record is not found, locate sets loc_address
// to the first D or F slot encountered in its search
// for the record.  This address can be used by add_record.
// If there is no D or F slot (full file), locate sets
// loc_address to the hash address of key.
bool frandom::locate( const char* key ) {
   // address = current offset in file
   // start_address = hash offset in file
   // unocc_address = first D slot in file
   //              = start_address, if no D slot
   long address, start_address, unocc_address;
```

```
    // delete_flag = false, if no D slot is found
    //             = true, if D slot is found
    int delete_flag = false;

    address = get_address( key );
    unocc_address = start_address = address;
    do {
       seekg( address, ios_base::beg );
       switch( get() ) {
       case Deleted:
          if ( !delete_flag ) {
             unocc_address = address;
             delete_flag = true;
          }
          break;
       case Free:
          loc_address = delete_flag ? unocc_address : address;
      return false;
       case Taken:
          seekg( address + 1, ios_base::beg );
          read( stored_key, key_size );
          if ( memcmp( key, stored_key, key_size ) == 0 ) {
             loc_address = address;
             return true;
          }
          break;
       }
       address += record_size;
       if ( address >= total_bytes )
          address = header_size;
    } while ( address != start_address );

    loc_address = unocc_address;
    return false;
}

bool frandom::add_record( const char* record ) {
    if ( no_records >= slots || locate( record ) )
       return false;
```

```cpp
        seekp( loc_address, ios_base::beg );
        write( &Taken, 1 );
        write( record, record_size - 1 );
        no_records++;
        return true;
}


bool frandom::find_record( char* record ) {
    if ( locate( record ) ) {
        seekg( loc_address + 1, ios_base::beg );
        read( record, record_size - 1 );
        return true;
    }
    else
        return false;
}


bool frandom::remove_record( const char* key ) {
    if ( locate( key ) ) {
        --no_records;
        seekp( loc_address, ios_base::beg );
        write( &Deleted, 1 );
        return true;
    }
    else
        return false;
}


void frandom::close() {
    if ( is_open() ) {
        delete [ ] stored_key;
        delete [ ] buffer;
        char buff[ header_size ];
        for ( int i = 0; i < header_size; i++ )
            buff[ i ] = ' ';
```

```
        sprintf( buff, "%ld %ld %ld %ld",
                  slots, record_size,
                  key_size, no_records );
        seekp( 0, ios_base::beg );
        write( buff, header_size );
        fstream::close();
    }
}


int main() {
    char b[ 10 ], c;

    frandom finout;

    cout << "New file (Y/N)? ";
    cin >> c;
    if ( toupper( c ) == 'Y' ) {
        finout.open( "data.dat", 15, 5, 3 );
        if ( !finout ) {
            cerr << "Couldn't open file\n";
            return EXIT_FAILURE;
        }
    }
    else {
        finout.open( "data.dat" );
        if ( !finout ) {
            cerr << "Couldn't open file\n";
            return EXIT_FAILURE;
        }
    }
```

```
   do {
      cout << "\n\n[A]dd\n[F]ind\n[R]emove\n[Q]uit? ";
      cin >> c;
      switch ( toupper( c ) ) {
      case 'A':
         cout << "Which record to add? ";
         cin >> b;
         if ( finout.add_record( b ) )
            cout << "Record added\n";
         else
            cout << "Record not added\n";
         break;
      case 'F':
         cout << "Key? ";
         cin >> b;
         if ( finout.find_record( b ) ) {
            b[ 5 ] = '\0';
            cout << "Record found: " << b << '\n';
         }
         else
            cout << "Record not found\n";
         break;
      case 'R':
         cout << "Key? ";
         cin >> b;
         if ( finout.remove_record( b ) )
            cout << "Record removed\n";
         else
            cout << "Record not removed\n";
         break;
      case 'Q':
         break;
      default:
         cout << "Illegal choice\n";
         break;
      }
   } while ( toupper( c ) != 'Q' );

   return 0;
}
```

### *Discussion*

We derive our random access file class from the system input/output file class **fstream**:

```
class frandom : public fstream {
   //...
};
```

We provide constructors, with behavior similar to those in the base class **fstream**, for associating a random access file with an **frandom** object. We also provide methods for associating a random access file with an already existing **frandom** object; a destructor; methods for adding, finding, and removing records; and methods for obtaining information about the file (e.g., the number of slots, the record size, etc.).

The data members of **frandom** and their purposes are listed in Figure 8.6.4. The first 256 bytes of the file are reserved as a *header* for the file. The values of **slots**, **record_size**, **key_size**, and **no_records**, in this order, are stored in the file header.

| *Member* | *Purpose* |
|---|---|
| **slots** | Number of slots. |
| **record_size** | Actual record size + 1 (for flag). |
| **key_size** | Size of key. |
| **total_bytes** | **slots * record_size** |
| **no_records** | Number of records stored. |
| **loc_address** | Set by method **locate**. **loc_address** is where a record was found or where a record can be stored. |
| **buffer** | Storage for one record. |
| **stored_key** | Storage for one key plus null terminator. |

**FIGURE 8.6.4** Data members of **frandom**.

The default constructor

```
frandom::frandom() : fstream() {
   //...
}
```

invokes the base class constructor and initializes certain members to zero. The default constructor does not associate a file with an **frandom** object. If an **frandom** object is created with the default constructor, the method **open** could be used to open a file and associate it with the **frandom** object.

The constructor

```
frandom::frandom( const char* filename,
                  int sl,
                  int actual_record_size,
                  int ks ) : fstream() {
   //...
}
```

creates an **frandom** object and associates the new file **filename** with it. The constructor sets **buffer** and **stored_key** to zero and then opens the file using method **open**.

Method **open**

```
void frandom::open( const char* filename ) (
                  int sl,
                  int actual_record_size,
                  int ks ) {
   //...
}
```

opens a new file by using the method **open** from **fstream**

```
fstream::open( filename,
               ios_base::in |
               ios_base::out |
               ios_base::binary );
```

We assume that if the file already exists, **open** succeeds. This is an error because we are supposed to be opening a *new* file. In this case, we set the **failbit** to indicate an error, close the file, and return:

```
setstate( ios_base::failbit );
fstream::close();
return;
```

If the open fails, we then create a new file:

```
fstream::open( filename, ios_base::out | ios_base::binary );
```

We then close it and reopen it for input and output:

```
if ( is_open() )
   fstream::close();
fstream::open( filename,
               ios_base::in |
               ios_base::out |
               ios_base::binary );
```

The file is opened as a binary file for input and output, thus allowing any kind of data to be read and written.

If the file is opened

```
if ( is_open() ) {
```

we first clear the **failbit** flag that was set by the **open** statement that failed. We then initialize data members, allocate storage, write the file header, and initialize the file.

We first allocate storage for the header

```
char buff[ header_size ];
```

and initialize **slots**, **record_size**, **key_size**, **total_bytes**, and **no_records**. We then allocate storage for the key:

```
stored_key = new char [ key_size + 1 ];
```

Next we place the text for the header in **buff** and then write the header to the file:

```
for ( int i = 0; i < header_size; i++ )
   buff[ i ] = ' ';
sprintf( buff, "%ld %ld %ld %ld",
         slots, record_size,
         key_size, no_records );
write( buff, header_size );
```

Instead of using the C function **sprintf**, we could use class **ostringstream** (see Section 8.7). Many C++ programmers use **sprintf** because it is easier to use than **ostringstream**.

We then create storage for a record and write **slots Free** records to the file:

```
buffer = new char [ record_size ];
for ( i = 1; i < record_size; i++ )
   buffer[ i ] = ' ';
buffer[ 0 ] = Free;
for ( i = 0; i < slots; i++ )
   write( buffer, record_size );
```

We use the methods **read** and **write** throughout since their purpose is to read and write binary data.

The constructor

```
frandom::frandom( const char* filename ) : fstream() {
   //...
}
```

creates an **frandom** object and associates an existing file **filename** with it. The constructor sets **buffer** and **stored_key** to zero and then opens the file using method **open**.

Method **open**

```
void frandom::open( const char* filename ) {
   //...
}
```

opens an existing file by using the method **open** from **fstream**

```
fstream::open( filename,
               ios_base::in |
               ios_base::out |
               ios_base::binary );
```

The file is opened as a binary file for input and output. We assume that if the file does not exist, **open** fails.

If the file is opened, we create storage for the header, read the header, initialize **slots**, **record_size**, **key_size**, **total_bytes**, and **no_records**:

```
char buff[ header_size ];
read( buff, header_size );
sscanf( buff, "%ld%ld%ld%ld",
        &slots, &record_size, &key_size,
        &no_records );
total_bytes = slots * record_size + header_size;
```

Instead of using the C function **sscanf**, we could use class **istringstream** (see Section 8.7). Many C++ programmers use **sscanf** because it is easier to use than **istringstream**.

We conclude by creating storage for a key and a record:

```
stored_key = new char [ key_size + 1 ];
buffer = new char [ record_size ];
```

The destructor checks whether a file is open. If a file is open, it **delete**s the dynamically allocated storage for the key and record and writes an updated header to the file:

```
if ( is_open() ) {
   delete [ ] stored_key;
   delete [ ] buffer;
   char buff[ header_size ];
   for ( int i = 0; i < header_size; i++ )
      buff[ i ] = ' ';
   sprintf( buff, "%ld %ld %ld %ld",
            slots, record_size,
            key_size, no_records );
   seekp( 0, ios_base::beg );
   write( buff, header_size );
}
```

The file is closed when the destructor executes since the destructor implicitly invokes **basic_filebuf**'s destructor, which closes the file.

The method **close** works similarly to the destructor. It adds a call to **fstream**'s method **close** to close the file:

```
fstream::close();
```

The **protected** method **locate** is used to search for a record. It is used by the **public** methods **add_record**, **find_record**, and **remove_record**.

First **locate** initializes **delete_flag** to **false**:

```
int delete_flag = false;
```

The flag **delete_flag** is reset to **true** if **locate** encounters a **D** (delete) slot. A **D** slot could be used by **add_record** to store a record.

Next **locate** calls the hash function **get_address**:

```
address = get_address( key );
```

This value is then copied into **unocc_address** and **start_address**:

```
unocc_address = start_address = address;
```

The value of **start_address** is never changed. It is used to check whether all slots in the file have been examined and to terminate the loop if all slots have been examined:

```
do {
   //...
} while ( address != start_address );
```

The variable **unocc_address** is used to save the first occurrence of a **D** slot.

In the loop, **locate** seeks to **address**

```
seekg( address, ios_base::beg );
```

and reads the first byte

```
switch( get() ) {
```

If this slot is **D** and this is the first occurrence of a **D** slot, the address of this slot is saved and **delete_flag** is changed to **true**:

```
case Deleted:
   if ( !delete_flag ) {
      unocc_address = address;
      delete_flag = true;
   }
   break;
```

Then the search continues.

If this slot is **F** (free), **loc_address** is set to the first occurrence of an **F** or **D** slot

```
case Free:
   loc_address = delete_flag ? unocc_address : address;
   return false;
```

and **false** is returned to signal an unsuccessful search. If **locate** was called by **add_record**, **add_record** will insert the new record at address **loc_address**.

If this slot is **T** (taken), **locate** reads the record and checks whether it is has the desired key:

```
case Taken:
   seekg( address + 1, ios_base::beg );
   read( stored_key, key_size );
   if ( memcmp( key, stored_key, key_size ) == 0 ) {
      loc_address = address;
      return true;
   }
   break;
```

If the key matches, **loc_address** is set to the address of the record and **true** is returned to signal a successful search. If **locate** was called by **find_record**, **find_record** will store the record at address **loc_address**. If **locate** was called by **delete_record**, **delete_record** will change the flag to **D** at address **loc_address**.

If the record was not found and an **F** slot did not terminate the search, **address** is updated to the next slot and the search continues:

```
address += record_size;
if ( address >= total_bytes )
   address = header_size;
```

If all the slots are searched, **loc_address** is set to **unocc_address**, and **locate** returns **false**.

The method **add_record** checks whether all slots are filled and, if so, it returns **false**; it also returns **false** if there is already a record stored with the given key:

```
if ( no_record >= slots || locate( record ) )
   return false;
```

Duplicate keys are not allowed.

If **locate** cannot find a record with the given key, **add_record** stores the record at **loc_address** (computed by **locate**), updates **no_records**, and returns **true**:

```
seekp( loc_address, ios_base::beg );
write( &Taken, 1 );
write( record, record_size - 1 );
no_records++;
return true;
```

The method **find_record** calls **locate**. If **locate** finds the record, **find_record** copies it at the address passed and returns **true**; otherwise, **find_record** simply returns **false**:

```
if ( locate( record ) ) {
   seekg( loc_address + 1, ios_base::beg );
   read( record, record_size - 1 );
   return true;
}
else
   return false;
```

The method **remove_record** calls **locate**. If **locate** finds the record, **remove_record** updates **no_records**, flags the record as **D**, and returns **true**; otherwise, **remove_record** simply returns **false**:

```
if ( locate( key ) ) {
   --no_records;
   seekp( loc_address, ios_base::beg );
   write( &Deleted, 1 );
   return true;
}
else
   return false;
```

The function **main** creates an **frandom** object (using the default constructor):

```
frandom finout;
```

The user is then asked whether a new or existing file is to be opened:

```
cout << "New file (Y/N)? ";
```

If a new file is to be opened, the version of **open** for new files is invoked. An attempt is made to open the new file *data.dat* with 15 slots, 5-byte records, and 3-byte keys:

```
finout.open( "data.dat", 15, 5, 3 );
```

If the file cannot be opened, a message is printed and the program is terminated:

```
if ( !finout ) {
   cerr << "Couldn't open file\n";
   exit( EXIT_FAILURE );
}
```

(Recall that this version of **open** was written so that opening the file would fail if the file already exists.)

If an existing file is to be opened, the version of **open** for existing files is invoked. An attempt is made to open the existing file *data.dat*:

```
finout.open( "data.dat" );
```

As in the previous code, if the file cannot be opened, a message is printed and the program is terminated. (Recall that this version of **open** was written so that opening the file would fail if the file did not already exist.) A loop then allows the user to repeatedly add, find, or remove records.

# 8.7 THE CHARACTER STREAM INPUT/OUTPUT CLASSES

The classes

| | |
|---|---|
| **basic_stringbuf** | **basic_ostringstream** |
| **basic_istringstream** | **basic_stringstream** |

are declared in *sstream*. They provide a high-level interface to character stream input and output in much the same way that their counterparts, the **basic_fstream** classes, provide a high-level interface to file input and output. Class **basic_stringbuf** provides buffered access to character streams. The system-supplied buffers are dynamic; they grow and shrink as needed. We discuss **basic_stringbuf** in detail in Section 8.9.

## basic_ostringstream

The class **basic_ostringstream** is used to write characters to an internal buffer that can be copied to a **basic_string**. It performs somewhat the same functionality as the C function **sprintf**. Class **basic_ostringstream** is a template class derived from **basic_ostream**

```
namespace std {
  template <class charT,
            class traits = char_traits<charT>,
            class Allocator = allocator<charT>>
  class basic_ostringstream : public basic_ostream<charT, traits> {
  //...
  };
}
```

The third **template** parameter, **Allocator**, is an allocator used by the **basic_string** class. Class **basic_ostringstream** inherits methods from **basic_ostream** to write and move within the internal buffer.

The constructor with declaration

```
explicit basic_ostringstream( ios_base::openmode
                                  = ios_base::out );
```

is used when a **basic_ostringstream** object is created but a **basic_string** is not copied to the internal buffer.

**EXAMPLE 8.7.1.** The statement

```
ostringstream sout;
```

defines the **ostringstream** object **sout**. The internal buffer is not initialized. (Recall that **ostringstream** is a synonym for **basic_ostringstream<char>**.)  ■

The constructor with declaration

```
explicit basic_ostringstream(
        const basic_string<charT, traits, Allocator>& s,
        ios_base::openmode = ios_base::out );
```

is used to initialize the internal buffer to **s**.

> **EXAMPLE 8.7.2.**   The statement
>
> ```
> string name = "Monica";
> ostringstream sout( name );
> ```
>
> creates an **ostringstream** object **sout** and initializes **sout**'s internal buffer to *Monica*.   ■

The version

```
basic_string<charT, traits, Allocator> str() const;
```

of method **str** returns a **basic_string** that is a copy of the internal buffer.

> **EXAMPLE 8.7.3.**   The output from the code
>
> ```
> int i = 6;
> ostringstream sout;
> sout << "Santa Claus Conquers " << i << " Martians";
> string s = sout.str();
> cout << s << '\n';
> ```
>
> is
>
> ```
> Santa Claus Conquers 6 Martians
> ```
>                                                                         ■

The version

```
void str( const basic_string<charT, traits, Allocator>& s );
```

of method **str** replaces the internal buffer's contents with **s**.

## basic_istringstream

The class **basic_istringstream** is used to read characters from an internal buffer. The buffer can be copied to a **basic_string**. The class performs somewhat the same functionality as the C function **sscanf**. Class **basic_istringstream** is a template class derived from **basic_istream**

```
namespace std {
  template <class charT,
            class traits = char_traits<charT>,
            class Allocator = allocator<charT>>
  class basic_istringstream
        : public basic_istream<charT, traits> {
  //...
  };
}
```

Class **basic_istringstream** inherits methods from **basic_istream** to read and move within the internal buffer.

The constructor with declaration

```
explicit basic_istringstream( ios_base::openmode
                            = ios_base::in );
```

is used when a **basic_istringstream** object is created but a **basic_string** is not copied to the internal buffer.

**EXAMPLE 8.7.4.** The statement

```
istringstream sin;
```

defines the **istringstream** object **sin**. The internal buffer is not initialized. (Recall that **istringstream** is a synonym for **basic_istringstream<char>**.) ■

The constructor with declaration

```
explicit basic_istringstream(
    const basic_string<charT, traits, Allocator>& s,
    ios_base::openmode = ios_base::in );
```

is used to initialize the internal buffer to **s**.

**EXAMPLE 8.7.5.** The statement

```
float x;
string val = "37.805";
istringstream sin( val );
sin >> x;
cout << "x = " << val << '\n';
```

creates an **istringstream** object **sin** and initializes **sin**'s internal buffer to 37.805. The statement

```
sin >> x;
```

reads the value 37.805 from **sin** into **x**. Thus the output is

```
x = 37.805
```
■

**EXAMPLE 8.7.6.** The output from the code

```
char c;
string s = "abcde";
istringstream sin( s );
while ( sin >> c )
   cout << "Input succeeded.  c = " << c << '\n';
cout << "at end of string\n";
```

is

```
Input succeeded.  c = a
Input succeeded.  c = b
Input succeeded.  c = c
Input succeeded.  c = d
Input succeeded.  c = e
at end of string                                    ■
```

Class **basic_istringstream** has two versions of **str** that behave similarly to those in **basic_ostringstream**.

## basic_stringstream

The class **basic_stringstream** is used to read and write an internal buffer that can be copied to a **basic_string**. Class **basic_stringstream** is a template class derived from **basic_iostream**

```
namespace std {
  template <class charT,
            class traits = char_traits<charT>,
            class Allocator = allocator<charT>>
  class basic_stringstream
        : public basic_iostream<charT, traits> {
  //...
  };
}
```

Class **basic_stringstream** inherits methods from **basic_iostream** to read, write, and move within the internal buffer.

The constructor with declaration

```
explicit basic_stringstream( ios_base::openmode
                              = ios_base::in | ios_base::out );
```

is used when a **basic_stringstream** object is created but a **basic_string** is not copied to the internal buffer.

The constructor with declaration

```
explicit basic_stringstream(
      const basic_string<charT, traits, Allocator>& s,
      ios_base::openmode = ios_base::in | ios_base::out );
```

is used to initialize the internal buffer to **s**.

Class **basic_stringstream** has two versions of **str** that behave similarly to those in **basic_ostringstream** and **basic_istringstream**.

## EXERCISES

**1.** Use an **ostringstream** object to convert a **long** value to a **string**.

2. Use an **istringstream** object to convert a **string** that represents a **long double** value to type **long double**.

3. A **string** contains

    ```
    s "..." "..."
    ```

    Use an appropriate object from this section to place the characters between the first pair of double quotes in the **string first** and the characters between the second pair of double quotes in the **string second**.

4. Rewrite the code involving **sscanf** and **sprintf** in the random file class of Section 8.6 using **stringstream** classes.

# 8.8 SAMPLE APPLICATION: A HIGH-LEVEL COPY FUNCTION

## *Problem*

Write a template function that copies from an arbitrary **basic_istream** object to an arbitrary **basic_ostream** object.

## *Solution*

We copy character by character using the overloaded **>>** and **<<** operators. We must be careful to change the default from "skip white space" to "do not skip white space," because we want to copy all of the characters—white space or not. Before returning from the function, we restore the format flags. After presenting the C++ implementation, we give several examples using classes discussed in this chapter.

## *C++ Implementation*

```
#include <iostream>
using namespace std;

// copy from basic_istream to basic_ostream
template< class charT, class traits>
void copy( basic_istream<charT, traits>& in,
           basic_ostream<charT, traits>& out ) {
   charT c;
   ios_base::iostate fl;
   // don't skip white space
   // save old flags in fl to restore at end
   fl = in.flags();
   in.unsetf( ios_base::skipws );
   while ( in >> c )
      out << c;
   // restore flags
   in.flags( fl );
}
```

### *Discussion*

We present several **main** programs to show how **copy** can be used to copy one object to another when the objects are in classes derived from **basic_istream** and **basic_ostream**.

The following code copies the standard input to the standard output:

```
#include <iostream>
using namespace std;

template<class charT, class traits>
void copy( basic_istream<charT, traits>& in,
           basic_ostream<charT, traits>& out );

int main() {
   copy( cin, cout );
   return 0;
}
```

The next code copies from the file *data.in* to the file *data.out*:

```
#include <iostream>
#include <fstream>
using namespace std;

template<class charT, class traits>
void copy( basic_istream<charT, traits>& in,
           basic_ostream<charT, traits>& out );

int main() {
   ifstream fin( "data.in" );
   ofstream fout( "data.out" );
   copy( fin, fout );
   return 0;
}
```

The last code copies a **string** to the file *data.out*:

```
#include <iostream>
#include <fstream>
#include <sstream>
using namespace std;

template<class charT, class traits>
void copy( basic_istream<charT, traits>& in,
           basic_ostream<charT, traits>& out );

int main() {
   string s = "Junior G-Men of the Air";
   istringstream sin( s );
   ofstream fout( "data.out" );
   copy( sin, fout );
   return 0;
}
```

## EXERCISES

1. Write a **main** function that copies a file to an **ostringstream** object.

2. Write a **main** function that copies an **istringstream** object to the standard output.

3. Write a **main** function that copies a file to the standard error.

4. Write a high-level nontemplate copy function that converts each lowercase character to an uppercase character and passes non-lowercase characters unchanged.

5. Write a high-level nontemplate copy function that replaces each tab character by the appropriate number of spaces. The copy function should have a third parameter that describes the tab setting (e.g., if this parameter is 3, the tabs are set at columns 4, 7, 10, . . . , where column 1 is the first column).

# 8.9 THE BUFFER CLASSES

The classes

### basic_streambuf   basic_filebuf   basic_stringbuf

provide support for the programmer to manipulate buffers. Class **basic_streambuf** is declared in *streambuf*; **basic_filebuf** is declared in *fstream*; and **basic_stringbuf** is declared in *sstream*. Class **basic_streambuf** is a base class for the classes that actually create storage to use as buffers. It has methods for moving around in buffers and for reading from and writing to buffers. Class **basic_filebuf**, which is derived from **basic_streambuf**, provides buffered access to files. Class **basic_stringbuf**, which is also derived from **basic_streambuf**, provides buffered access to character streams. The high-level classes discussed previously in this chapter make use of these buffer classes and provide a transparent user interface to the buffer classes. For this reason, many programmers never directly use these buffer classes.

## basic_streambuf

Class **basic_streambuf** is the base buffer class. The default constructor, which is **protected**, is the only constructor. Class **basic_streambuf** serves as a base class for other buffer classes; **basic_streambuf** objects are not to be created.

The **public** method

```
basic_streambuf<char_type, traits>*
    pubsetbuf( char_type* buff, streamsize len );
```

invokes the **protected** method

```
virtual basic_streambuf<char_type, traits>*
    setbuf( char_type* buff, streamsize len );
```

which is to be overridden in each class derived from **basic_streambuf**. If **bobj** is an object in a class **buff** derived from **basic_streambuf** and **buff** overrides **setbuf**,

```
bobj.pubsetbuf( b, l );
```

invokes **pubsetbuf**, which is inherited from **basic_streambuf**. The effect is to invoke **buff**'s **setbuf** because **setbuf** is **virtual**. Each overridden **setbuf** specifies a character array and its size to use as a buffer.

Most other methods in **basic_streambuf** work similarly to **pubsetbuf**; that is, most methods invoke a **virtual**, **protected** member that is overridden in each derived class.

The method

```
streamsize in_avail();
```

invokes a **protected** member that returns the number of characters remaining in the input buffer.

The method

```
int_type sbumpc();
```

invokes a **protected** member that returns the current character in the input buffer and advances the buffer position marker, which designates the character to read or write, one byte. If **sbumpc** fails (e.g., we are at the end of the file), it returns end-of-file (**EOF** for type **char**). This low-level method resembles the high-level method **get** in class **basic_istream**.

The method

```
int_type sgetc();
```

invokes a **protected** member that returns the next character in the buffer. The buffer position marker is unchanged. If **sgetc** fails, it returns end-of-file. This low-level method resembles the high-level method **peek** in class **basic_istream**.

The method

```
streamsize sgetn( char_type* store, streamsize n );
```

invokes a **protected** member that returns the next **n** characters from the buffer and stores them in **store**. It returns the number of characters actually retrieved. The buffer position marker is moved the number of bytes retrieved. This low-level method resembles the high-level method **read** in class **basic_istream**.

The method

```
int_type snextc();
```

invokes a **protected** member that advances the buffer position marker one byte and returns the character in the buffer. If **snextc** fails, it returns end-of-file.

The method

```
int_type sputbackc( char_type c );
```

invokes a **protected** member that returns the character **c** to the buffer. The value returned by **sputbackc** is end-of-file on error. This low-level method resembles the high-level method **putback** in class **basic_istream**.

The method

```
int_type sputc( char_type c );
```

writes the character **c** to the output buffer. It returns end-of-file on error. This low-level method resembles the high-level method **put** in class **basic_ostream**.

The method

```
streamsize sputn( const char_type* store, streamsize n );
```

invokes a **protected** member that writes **n** characters, beginning at address **store**, into the buffer. It returns the number of characters actually placed into the buffer. This low-level method resembles the high-level method **write** in class **basic_ostream**.

The method

```
pos_type pubseekoff( off_type off,
                     ios_base::seek_dir dir,
                     ios_base::openmode pt
                       = ios_base::in | ios_base::out );
```

invokes a **protected** member that moves the input or output stream position marker (or both) **off** bytes from **dir**, which must be one of the following: **ios_base::beg** (from the beginning of the stream), **ios_base::cur** (from the current position), or **ios_base::end** (from the end of the stream). If **pt** is **ios_base::in**, the input marker is moved; if **pt** is **ios_base::out**, the output marker is moved; and if **pt** is

```
ios_base::in | ios_base::out
```

both markers are moved.

The method

```
pos_type pubseekpos( pos_type off,
                     ios_base::openmode pt
                       = ios_base::in | ios_base::out );
```

invokes a **protected** member that moves the input or output stream position marker (or both) to position **off**. As in method **pubseekoff**, the second argument determines which markers are moved. The low-level methods **pubseekoff** and **pubseekpos** resemble the high-level methods **seekg** and **seekp** in classes **basic_istream** and **basic_ostream**.

We defer examples to the next subsections, which consider the derived classes **basic_filebuf** and **basic_stringbuf**, as it is these classes that provide the facilities for associating buffer objects with files and character streams.

## basic_filebuf

Class **basic_filebuf** is a template class derived from **basic_streambuf**:

```
namespace std {
  template <class charT, class traits = char_traits<charT>>
  class basic_filebuf : public basic_streambuf<charT, traits> {
    //...
  };
}
```

It provides buffered access to files.

The default constructor creates a **basic_filebuf** object that is not associated with any file.

The method **open**

```
basic_filebuf<charT, traits>* open( const char* filename,
                                    ios_base::openmode mode );
```

opens the file **filename** in mode **mode** and associates it with the **basic_filebuf** object.

### EXAMPLE 8.9.1.    The code

```
filebuf fin;
fin.open( "data.in", ios_base::in )
```

creates the **filebuf** object **fin** (**filebuf** is a **typedef** for **basic_filebuf<char>**). It then opens the file *data.in* for input and associates this file with the object **fin**.    ■

The overridden method **setbuf**

```
basic_streambuf<charT, traits>*
   setbuf( char_type* b, streamsize len );
```

establishes the array **b** as the buffer for the **basic_filebuf** object. It is invoked by the member **pubsetbuf** inherited from **basic_streambuf**.

### EXAMPLE 8.9.2.    The code

```
filebuf fout;
char b[ 256 ];
fout.open( "data.out", ios_base::out );
fout.pubsetbuf( b, sizeof( b ) );
```

creates the **filebuf** object **fout**. It next opens the file *data.out* for output and associates this file with the object **fout**. It then establishes the array **b** as the buffer for **fout**. Output to *data.out* takes place through the buffer **b**.    ■

### EXAMPLE 8.9.3.    The following program copies file *data.in* to *data.out*:

```
#include <fstream>
using namespace std;

const int buffsize = 256;
```

```
int main() {
   char inbuff[ buffsize ], outbuff[ buffsize ];
   filebuf fin, fout;
   int c;
   fin.open( "data.in", ios_base::in );
   fin.pubsetbuf( inbuff, sizeof( inbuff ) );
   fout.open( "data.out", ios_base::out );
   fout.pubsetbuf( outbuff, sizeof( outbuff ) );
   c = fin.sgetc();
   while ( c != EOF ) {
      fout.sputc( c );
      c = fin.snextc();
   }
   return 0;
}
```

After setting up the buffers **inbuff** and **outbuff** and opening the files, we read a character from the input buffer **inbuff**, but the input buffer position marker does not move:

```
c = fin.sgetc();
```

If we are not at the end of the file, we enter the body of the **while** loop. We write one character to the output buffer **outbuff** and move one byte in the input buffer and return that character:

```
fout.sputc( c );
c = fin.snextc();
```

We continue until all of the characters have been read from the input file.  ∎

The method

```
basic_filebuf<charT, traits>* close();
```

closes the file associated with the **basic_filebuf** object and flushes the buffer. The destructor also closes the file and flushes the buffer.

**EXAMPLE 8.9.4.**   When the program of Example 8.9.3 terminates, the destructor is automatically called for **fin** and **fout**. The destructor closes the files. The destructor for **fout** flushes the output buffer; that is, data still in the output buffer but not yet written to the file are now written to the file.  ∎

The **protected** methods **overflow** and **underflow** take action when the buffer is full or empty. The method

```
virtual int_type overflow( int_type stop );
```

flushes the buffer. More precisely, it writes all of the data in the buffer, up to but not including **stop**, to the destination file. The default value of **stop** is end-of-file (**EOF** for type **char**).

The method

```
virtual int_type underflow();
```

reads data from the source file into the buffer.

**EXAMPLE 8.9.5.** In this example, we look more closely at what happens when the program of Example 8.9.3 executes. For the purposes of illustration, we assume that **buffsize** is 8, rather than 256.

When we first execute

```
c = fin.sgetc();
```

the input buffer is empty, so method **underflow** is invoked and the input buffer is filled (see Figure 8.9.1).

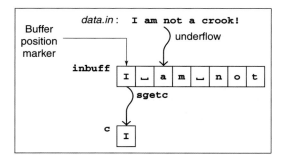

**FIGURE 8.9.1** Result of invoking **fin.sgetc()**.

Next we execute

```
fout.sputc( c );
```

and **c** is written to the output buffer (see Figure 8.9.2).

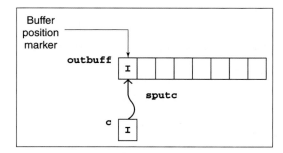

**FIGURE 8.9.2** First call of **fout.sputc( c )**.

We then execute

```
c = fin.snextc();
```

and the next character in the input buffer is read (see Figure 8.9.3).

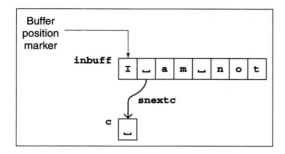

**FIGURE 8.9.3** First call of `fin.snextc()`.

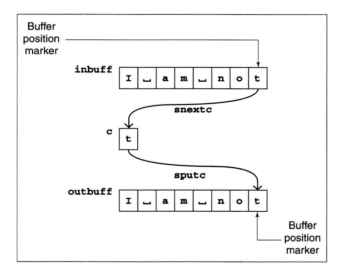

**FIGURE 8.9.4** Full buffers.

Figure 8.9.4 shows the situation somewhat later—just after we execute

```
fout.sputc( c );
```

for the eighth time. At this point, both the input and output buffers are full. When we next execute

```
c = fin.snextc();
```

no characters are available in the input buffer, so method **underflow** is invoked and the input buffer is refilled (see Figure 8.9.5).

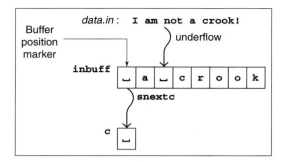

**FIGURE 8.9.5** Refilling the input buffer the first time.

Next we execute

```
fout.sputc( c );
```

Since the output buffer is full, the method **overflow** is invoked and the output buffer is flushed (see Figure 8.9.6).

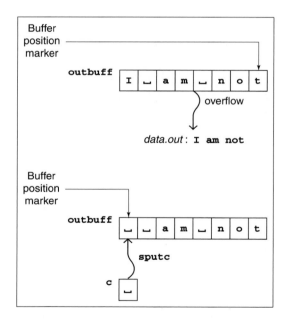

**FIGURE 8.9.6** Flushing the output buffer the first time.

Figure 8.9.7 shows the situation when the statement

```
c = fin.snextc();
```

is executed and the last character **!** is read; underflow again occurs. Next

```
fout.sputc( c );
```

is executed; overflow occurs and the output buffer is flushed (see Figure 8.9.8).

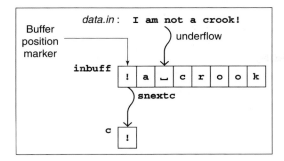

**FIGURE 8.9.7** Refilling the input buffer the last time.

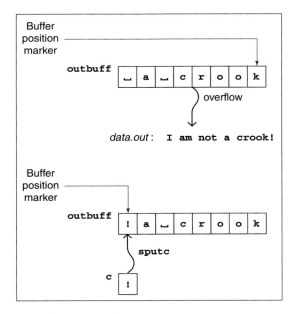

**FIGURE 8.9.8** Flushing the output buffer the second time.

When we next execute

```
c = fin.snextc();
```

since we are at the end of the file, **snextc** returns **EOF** and the **while** loop terminates. When the program terminates and the destructor for **fout** is called, the output buffer is flushed and the last character (**!**) is written to the file *data.out* (see Figure 8.9.9).

If the program terminated without the destructor for **fout** being called, the output buffer would not be flushed the last time and *data.out* would contain

```
I am not a crook
```

For example, the destructor would *not* be called if the program terminated with a call to **exit**:

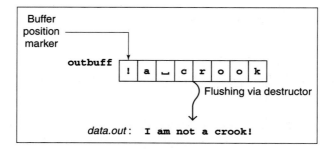

**FIGURE 8.9.9** The result of the destructor flushing the output buffer.

```
int main() {
   //...
   while ( c != EOF ) {
      fout.sputc( c );
      c = fin.snextc();
   }
   exit( EXIT_SUCCESS );
}
```

■

The method

```
bool is_open() const;
```

returns **true** if the file is open and **false** if the file is not open.

## basic_stringbuf

Class **basic_stringbuf** is a template class derived from **basic_streambuf**:

```
namespace std {
   template <class charT,
             class traits = char_traits<charT>,
             class Allocator = allocator<charT>>
   class basic_stringbuf
       : public basic_streambuf<charT, traits> {
     //...
   };
}
```

Class **Allocator** is used by **basic_string**. Class **basic_stringbuf** provides buffered access to character streams.

The constructor

```
explicit basic_stringbuf( ios_base::openmode mode =
                          ios_base::in | ios_base::out );
```

In the previous version of C++, classes **istream_withassign**, **ostream_with-assign**, and **iostream_withassign** were derived from **istream**, **ostream**, and **iostream**, respectively. These **withassign** classes permitted assignment and copying of input/output objects. Because allowing such assignments and copies is difficult to implement and use, the **withassign** classes were eliminated. Copying of objects belonging to **istream**, **ostream**, and **iostream** and their template counterparts has *never* been allowed.

The **stringstream** classes replace **strstream** classes. The principal difference between these classes is that the **strstream** classes used **char** array buffers and permitted direct access to these buffers, whereas the **stringstream** classes use dynamic buffers and direct access to these buffers is not allowed. Instead, method **str** can be used to obtain a copy of the buffer as a **string** object.

A minor change in the new version of C++ is that file descriptors are no longer supported.

## COMMON PROGRAMMING ERRORS

1. It is an error to attempt to use any of the input/output classes or any of the system manipulators with no parameters (e.g., **endl**) without including at least one of the input/output headers (e.g., *iostream*).

2. It is an error to attempt to use any of the file input/output classes without including the header *fstream*.

3. It is an error to attempt to use any of the character stream input/output classes without including the header *sstream*.

4. It is an error to attempt to use any of the system manipulators with parameters (e.g., **setfill**) without including the header *iomanip*.

5. The flag **ios_base::eofbit** is set by attempting to read beyond the end of the file. Simply reading the last byte does *not* set **ios_base::eofbit**. For this reason, the following code that attempts to echo integers in the standard input to the standard output is incorrect; an extra line is printed:

```
int i;
// ***** ERROR: extra line is printed
while ( !cin.eof() ) {
   cin >> i;
   cout << i << '\n';
}
```

A correct version is

```
int i;
do {
   cin >> i;
   if ( !cin.eof() )
      cout << i << '\n';
} while ( !cin.eof() );
```

**6.** The method **flags** with one argument in class **ios_base** sets the format flags to the value passed, whereas method **setf**, also in class **ios_base**, sets *specified* flags without changing the other flags. For example,

```
cout.flags( ios_base::showpoint );
```

sets the flag that causes floating-point numbers to be printed with the decimal point and *clears all other format flags*. The statement

```
cout.setf( ios_base::showpoint );
```

also sets the flag that causes floating-point numbers to be printed with the decimal point but does *not* modify any other format flag. In many applications, **setf** is more useful than **flags**.

**7.** When the versions

```
basic_istream<charT, traits>& seekg(
   off_type off, ios_base::seek_dir dir );
basic_ostream<charT, traits>& seekp(
   off_type off, ios_base::seek_dir dir );
```

are used with files, the files should be opened as **binary** files. These methods may not work properly if they are used with files that were not opened in **binary** mode.

When the versions of methods **seekg** and **seekp** whose declarations are

```
basic_istream<charT, traits>& seekg( pos_type pos );
basic_ostream<charT, traits>& seekg( pos_type pos );
```

are used with files, the files can be opened as **binary** or non-**binary** files. The argument should be a value returned by **tellg** (for **seekg**) or **tellp** (for **seekp**).

**8.** When the overloaded operator **>>** is used to read a string and the field width is set to $n \neq 0$, do *not* assume that the next $n$ characters, white space or not, are read and stored. The default action is to skip white space and then read and store all non-white space characters up to the next white space character, or $n - 1$ characters, whichever occurs first. A null terminator is always added. As examples, if the standard input is

   ⊔ ⊔ ⊔**Pepper**

the code

```
char a[ 10 ];
cin >> setw( 6 ) >> a;
```

reads and stores

   **Peppe**

followed by ′**\0**′ in the array **a**. If the standard input is

   ⊔ ⊔ ⊔**Dr⊔Pepper**

the code

```
char a[ 10 ];
cin >> setw( 6 ) >> a;
```

reads and stores

```
Dr
```

followed by `'\0'` in the array **a**.

9. The code for a manipulator *must* return the modified stream. For this reason,

```
void bell( ostream& os ) {
    // ***** ERROR: Must return the stream
    os << "\a";
}
```

is an error. A correct version is

```
ostream& bell( ostream& os ) {
    return os << "\a";
}
```

10. The method **sgetc** in class **basic_streambuf** returns the next character in the buffer but does *not* change the buffer position marker. For this reason,

```
filebuf fin, fout;
//...
// ***** ERROR: Infinite loop
while ( ( c = fin.sgetc() ) != EOF )
    fout.sputc( c );
```

is an infinite loop. See Example 8.9.3 for a correct version.

11. The output file buffer is *not* flushed if the file is not closed. The file may be closed explicitly by using the method **close** or passively by the destructor.

## PROGRAMMING EXERCISES

**8.1.** Modify the random access file class of Section 8.6 in the following manner. Add another field to the header, which flags the file as a random access file, by writing **RA** in the first two bytes of the header. When an existing file is opened, this flag is checked. If the file is the wrong type, it is closed and an error condition is set.

**8.2.** Provide implementations of **flags**, **setf**, and **unsetf** (see Section 8.2).

**8.3.** Write a class **imanip**, similar to **omanip** of Example 8.4.4, and an overload of **>>** that could be used to write one-argument manipulators for **basic_istream**.

**8.4.** Derive a **sequential file** class from **fstream** (see Section 8.5).

**8.5.** Derive an **indexed file** class from **fstream** (see Section 8.5). The underlying data structure should be a **B-tree** [see, e.g., S. Sahni, *Data Structures and Applications in C++*, (Boston: WCB/McGraw Hill, 1998)]. The indexed file class should allow the following operations:

- Direct access to a record through the key.
- Sequential reads.
- Adding, deleting, or updating records.

**8.6.** Develop a class that serves as an interface to the **frandom** class of Section 8.6. The class should contain a pointer to another class that describes a record. The record must contain a member of type **string**, which serves as the key.

**8.7.** Install assertions in the **frandom** class (see Section 8.6).

**8.8.** Write a high-level (in the sense of Section 8.8) encryption function based on Huffman codes [see, e.g., R. Johnsonbaugh, *Discrete Mathematics*, 4th ed., (Upper Saddle River, N.J.: Prentice Hall, 1997)].

**8.9.** Rewrite the **frandom** class (see Section 8.6) using buffer classes directly.

**8.10.** Derive a class **scrn_out** from **ostream** that provides output in specified colors to specified parts of the screen.

**8.11.** Revise class **frandom** of Section 8.6 so that it is a template class:

```
template<class charT, class traits = char_traits<charT>>
class basic_frandom : public basic_fstream<charT, traits> {
    //...
};
```

The statement

```
typedef basic_frandom<char> frandom;
```

should create a class equivalent to **frandom**.

# CHAPTER

# 9

# OBJECT-ORIENTED PROGRAMMING IN THE MICROSOFT FOUNDATION CLASSES

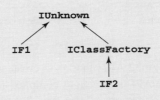

9.1 Windows Programming in MFC

9.2 The Document/View Architecture in MFC

9.3 Sample Application: Document Serialization

9.4 The Common Object Model

9.5 Sample Application: An Automation Server and Controller

C++ Postscript

Programming Exercises

**M**icrosoft's family of operating systems includes Windows 98 and Windows NT, which are two implementations of the **Win32 system**. (The *32* underscores that Win32 is a so-called 32-bit system, that is, a system in which the address size is 32 bits.) An applications programmer can interact with the Win32 system through the Win32 Applications Programmer Interface (API).[†] The Win32 API comprises thousands of C functions, divided into various groups. For example, there are Win32 API functions for graphics, networking, database, and interapplication communication. Many Win32 API functions are complicated. For example,

```
HWND CreateWindow(
    LPCTSTR lpClassName,    /* registered class name */
    LPCTSTR lpWindowName,   /* window name */
    DWORD dwStyle,          /* window style */
    int x,                  /* horizontal position */
    int y,                  /* vertical position */
    int nWidth,             /* window width */
    int nHeight,            /* window height */
    HWND hWndParent,        /* parent or owner window */
    HMENU hMenu,            /* menu or child-window id */
    HANDLE hInstance,       /* application instance */
    LPVOID lpParam          /* window-creation data */
);
```

is the declaration for a Win32 API function to create a window.

Because the Win32 API is large and complex, Microsoft provides a C++ library of classes that *wrap* the C functions of the Win32 API, the Microsoft Foundation Classes (MFC). The methods encapsulated in MFC classes ultimately invoke C functions in the Win32 API. However, it is normally far easier to write Win32 applications in MFC than directly in the Win32 API. In summary, the Win32 API is a collection of C *function* libraries, whereas MFC is a C++ *class* library in which several *hundred* C++ classes wrap the *thousands* of functions in the Win32 API.

Support for MFC is available in several products. One such product is Microsoft's own Visual C++ (hereafter, VC++), which is an **i**ntegrated **d**evelopment **e**nvironment (IDE) that includes compilers and linkers, code generators, search and browse utilities, project management utilities, debuggers, and other utilities for applications development. The code generators can be particularly helpful. For example, they can be used to create a minimal Windows application that compiles, links, and runs without a single line of code from the applications programmer. Just as MFC hides from the applications programmer many complicated details in the Win32 API, so an IDE such as VC++ hides from the applications programmer many complicated details in MFC. Programmers who work in MFC typically take full advantage of an IDE such as VC++.

---

[†] For ease of reference, the C++ Postscript at the end of the chapter summarizes some acronyms associated with MFC (the Microsoft Foundation Classes).

This chapter introduces object-oriented programming in MFC. Because MFC itself is quite large and complicated, we focus on two dominant issues in object-oriented programming:

- **Persistence**—the mechanism for saving an object together with its state, that is, the values of its data members.
- **Interface registration**—the mechanism for exposing to client applications the methods that deliver a server application's services.

MFC supports both mechanisms in powerful ways. We illustrate with two sample applications. Our applications are built in VC++ and exploit its code-generation powers in particular. Our homepage

```
http://condor.depaul.edu/~mkalin
```

includes a step-by-step description of how the code generators were used. We begin with an overview of Windows programming in MFC.

## 9.1 WINDOWS PROGRAMMING IN MFC

Modern windows systems, such as Microsoft's Win32 or Motif under UNIX, employ an **event-driven programming model**. In this model, an application typically has a graphical user interface (GUI). A user can interact with the application through its GUI, for example, through mouse clicks on an application window or selections from an application menu. A user-generated action such as a mouse click is an **event**. The system queues up such events and then **dispatches** them to procedures known as **event handlers**. An event handler is a callback procedure, that is, a procedure that the programmer writes but the system invokes ("calls back"). Although many events are user-generated, others may be system-generated. For example, if the system shuts down, it typically generates events that any currently executing application may need to handle. The general process in which the system queues up events and later dispatches them to event handlers is known as the **event loop**. Figure 9.1.1 illustrates what an event loop might look like at the code level.

When an event-driven application begins execution, it usually enters an **initialization phase** for setting graphical features, such as fonts and colors, and traditional processing, such as reading command-line arguments and opening files for input and output. Once the initialization phase ends, the application enters its event loop where the application waits for the system to notify it that some event has occurred. Such notification occurs when the system dispatches an event to the application's appropriate callback procedure, which then handles the event. For example, the application might wait for the user to click a mouse in a particular region of the application's GUI. The system notifies the application of such a click by invoking a callback provided by the application to signal this event. A callback then does whatever processing is appropriate for handling the event.

The event-driven programming model has obvious implications for how an applications programmer works. Much of the applications programmer's own code may consist of callbacks. A callback is often a *pure callback*, that is, a function invoked *exclusively* by the system as it dispatches an application's events. An applications programmer may write many pure callbacks, which are never invoked in the programmer's *own* code. This callback-

```
while ( theApp.isRunning() ) { // theApp is the application
   Event e = nextEvent();       // get next Event from the queue
   unsigned id = e.getId();     // getId returns Event's integer
id
   switch( id ) {
   case Event_SingleMouseClick:
      theApp.handleSingleMouseClick( e );
      break;
   case Event_DoubleMouseClick:
      theApp.handleDoubleMouseClick( e );
      break;
   case Event_ButtonPush:
      theApp.handleButtonPush( e );
      break;
   //... other events
   default:
      ignoreEvent( e );
      break;
   } //*** end switch
} //*** end while( theApp.isRunning() )
```

**FIGURE 9.1.1** A main event loop for the application `theApp`.

style of coding is among the first skills to be mastered for applications programming in a modern windows environment.

## Code Generators for MFC Programming

VC++ provides two main code generators, or **wizards**, that correspond roughly to the initialization and event-loop phases of a windows application. The first generator, the **AppWizard**, generates code to set up the appropriate interface between the application and the Win32 API. This wizard generates class declarations that serve as appropriate wrappers for Win32 API library functions. The wizard also provides code for special types of initialization, for example, reading command-line arguments or interfacing with packages for network programming. The AppWizard normally is used once per application, at the very start. The programmer directs the wizard by selecting options from a series of screens. This wizard can create boilerplate code for different types of Windows applications: stand-alone executable programs (with file extension *exe*), dynamic link libraries (with file extension *dll*), and so forth. In addition to generating code, the AppWizard provides various tools for managing an application. The wizard creates a **project**, which consists of headers (with file extension *h*), implementation files (with file extension *cpp*), a graphics resource file (with file extension *rc*), and various other files. Once a project has been created, other VC++ wizards and utilities help to manage the project and its component files.

The second major code generator, the **ClassWizard**, can be used to create boilerplate code for callback functions. This wizard allows the programmer to map a particular type of event, such as a single click on a specific button, to a callback procedure. The ClassWizard suggests a name for the callback (typically beginning with the term *On*) and provides the appropriate parameters and return value. For example, the ClassWizard generated the boilerplate code

```
void CDateCDlg::OnButton1()
{
    // TODO: Add your control notification handler code here
}
```

as the callback for a button click in an application for which the AppWizard generated the class **CDateCDlg** (see Section 9.5). The ClassWizard also can be used to create classes that correspond to GUI elements (for example, dialog windows) and to populate classes with data members. After running the AppWizard once, the programmer then runs the ClassWizard as often as needed to give the application its required event-handling functionality. Finally, the ClassWizard has some specialized uses in interapplication communication (see Section 9.5).

## EXERCISES

1. What does GUI stand for?
2. What does MFC stand for?
3. What does API stand for?
4. What does IDE stand for?
5. Does the Win32 API consist of C functions or C++ classes?
6. Explain the relationship between the Win32 API and MFC.
7. What purpose does a callback function serve in the event-driven programming model?
8. What is a *pure callback*?
9. Give an example of a Win32 operating system.
10. Can MFC be used independently of VC++?
11. What is a *wizard* in VC++?
12. In VC++, a callback's name typically begins with *On*, for instance, *OnButton1*. What does the *On* emphasize about the callback?

## 9.2 THE DOCUMENT/VIEW ARCHITECTURE IN MFC

A stand-alone application under VC++ has two main subtypes: the document/view application and the dialog-based application. In Section 9.5, we illustrate a dialog-based application. In this section, we focus on document/view applications.

A document/view application falls under MFC's **document/view architecture**. The document/view architecture is central to Microsoft's own system and applications software. For example, Window's familiar cut-and-paste utility is based ultimately on this architecture. Document sharing among applications—such as embedding an Excel spreadsheet in a Word document—also builds upon the document/view architecture. Microsoft's document/view architecture derives from Smalltalk's similar architecture. In the Smalltalk architecture, an application has three principal parts:

- The **model**. The model comprises the application's data. For example, a weather forecasting application's model might consist of data about barometric pressures, temperatures, humidities, wind velocities, and the like. The model also would presumably include the forecasts themselves. In general, a model consists of data structured to meet the application's objectives.

- The **view**. The view comprises the user's interface to the model; or, the view presents the model to the user, typically through graphics. For example, the view for a weather forecasting application might use graphical representations such as bar charts or video clips to display the model.

- The **controller**. The controller handles interactions between the view and the model. In particular, the controller is responsible for handling events generated through the application's view. The controller typically has callbacks to handle user-generated events such as mouse clicks and menu selections. The callbacks, in turn, may make appropriate changes to the application's model, which then require a redrawing of the application's view. For example, a user might use a mouse click to signal that a weather forecast is to focus on a particular region of the country. Such a click would cause the model to be updated appropriately, which then would require that the corresponding graphics in the view be updated as well.

In Microsoft's document/view architecture, the document closely resembles the Smalltalk model, but Microsoft's view integrates Smalltalk's view and controller. In the document/architecture, for example, callbacks occur in the application's view class rather than in a separate controller class.

MFC supports two subtypes of document/view applications. The first subtype is the single **d**ocument **i**nterface (SDI) application. In an SDI application, there is only *one* document and, therefore, only one view required. This view typically occurs in a single framed window. The second subtype is the **m**ultiple **d**ocument **i**nterface (MDI) application. An MDI application may have more than one document, each of which requires its own view; each view, in turn, occurs in its own framed window, which is a child of the application's parent framed window. For simplicity, we begin with a discussion of SDI applications.

When the AppWizard first creates an SDI application, it generates four boilerplate classes derived from MFC classes. In MFC, *all* inheritance is **public** and single. Classes generated by wizards therefore use only **public**, single inheritance. Assuming that the project is named *Proj1*, the classes are

- **CProj1App**, which is derived from MFC's **CWndApp**. This class has data members and methods that can interact with the system in ways that 0are appropriate for a *windows* application. This class handles application initialization. The programmer often does not change this class.

- **CProj1Doc**, which is derived from MFC's **CDocument**. This class represents the application's document, that is, its data. The programmer typically adds data members and methods to this class so that the class can represent and manipulate the application's data.

- **CProj1View**, which is derived from MFC's **CView**. This class represents the application's view and its controller. To handle events, the programmer typically adds callbacks (directly or through the ClassWizard) to this class. Also, the programmer normally adds to the body of at least the **OnDraw** callback, which is responsible for presenting the application's view of its document in the framed window. A boilerplate **OnDraw** is generated by the AppWizard.

- **CMainFrame**, which is derived from MFC's **CFrameWnd**. This class represents the framed window used, in an SDI application, to hold the application's view of its document. The programmer often does not change this class.

**EXAMPLE 9.2.1.**    **F** igure 9.2.1 shows the AppWizard's declaration for the document class in an SDI application named *Proj1*. Figure 9.2.2 shows the AppWizard's declaration of the view class in the same application.    ∎

```
class CProj1Doc : public CDocument
{
protected: // create from serialization only
    CProj1Doc();
    DECLARE_DYNCREATE(CProj1Doc)
// Attributes
public:
// Operations
public:
// Overrides
    // ClassWizard generated virtual function overrides
    //{{AFX_VIRTUAL(CProj1Doc)
    public:
    virtual BOOL OnNewDocument();
    virtual void Serialize(CArchive& ar);
    //}}AFX_VIRTUAL
// Implementation
public:
    virtual ~CProj1Doc();
#ifdef _DEBUG
    virtual void AssertValid() const;
    virtual void Dump(CDumpContext& dc) const;
#endif
protected:
// Generated message map functions
protected:
    //{{AFX_MSG(CProj1Doc)
        // NOTE - the ClassWizard will add and remove member
        //     functions here.
        //     DO NOT EDIT what you see in these blocks of
        //     generated code !
    //}}AFX_MSG
    DECLARE_MESSAGE_MAP()
};
```

**FIGURE 9.2.1** The AppWizard's declaration for the document class in application *Proj1*.

```
class CProj1View : public CView
{
protected: // create from serialization only
    CProj1View();
    DECLARE_DYNCREATE(CProj1View)
// Attributes
public:
    CProj1Doc* GetDocument();
// Operations
public:
// Overrides
    // ClassWizard generated virtual function overrides
    //{{AFX_VIRTUAL(CProj1View)
    public:
    virtual void OnDraw(CDC* pDC);   // overridden for this view
    virtual BOOL PreCreateWindow(CREATESTRUCT& cs);
    protected:
    virtual BOOL OnPreparePrinting(CPrintInfo* pInfo);
    virtual void OnBeginPrinting(CDC* pDC, CPrintInfo* pInfo);
    virtual void OnEndPrinting(CDC* pDC, CPrintInfo* pInfo);
    //}}AFX_VIRTUAL
// Implementation
public:
    virtual ~CProj1View();
#ifdef _DEBUG
    virtual void AssertValid() const;
    virtual void Dump(CDumpContext& dc) const;
#endif
protected:
// Generated message map functions
protected:
    //{{AFX_MSG(CProj1View)
        // NOTE - the ClassWizard will add and remove member
        //      functions here.
        //      DO NOT EDIT what you see in these blocks of
        //      generated code !
    //}}AFX_MSG
    DECLARE_MESSAGE_MAP()
};
```

**FIGURE 9.2.2** The AppWizard's declaration of the view class in application *Proj1*.

## Document Serialization

Figure 9.2.1 includes a declaration for a **CProj1Doc**'s polymorphic **Serialize** method, which takes a reference to a **CArchive** object as its single argument. Recall that **CProj1Doc** is the AppWizard's boilerplate class derived from MFC's **CDocument**, which in turn is derived indirectly from MFC's **CObject**. Figure 9.2.3 depicts the inheritance relationships. By the way, the class between **CDocument** and **CObject** is **CCmdTarget**, the wrapper class for any server application. The class's name alludes to the fact that a server is an application that acts as the target of commands from client applications. Of interest here is that **CObject**, which occurs as the top base class in MFC's single-inheritance hierarchy, has **Serialize** as a **virtual** method. Therefore, every class derived from **CObject** can override **Serialize**, whose purpose is to implement **object persistence**, that is, to save an object—including the values of its data members—in a standard binary format. In object-oriented jargon, we talk about *serializing an object out* (that is, writing it to a file) and *serializing an object in* (that is, reading it from a file to which it was earlier written). The **CArchive** argument to **Serialize** is an intermediary between the application and the file involved in serialization. For example, when an application serializes an object out, the application writes to the **CArchive** object using the overloaded **<<** operator. The **CArchive** object, in turn, deals with the underlying file used to save the object. The **CArchive** argument to **Serialize** simplifies the coding required to serialize an object out and in.

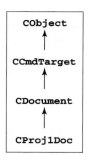

**FIGURE 9.2.3** Inheritance relationships among **CObject**, **CDocument**, and **CProj1Doc**.

In a document/view application, it is appropriate that only the *document* can be serialized. After all, the document is the application's data encapsulated in a **CDocument**-derived object. An application's document could, of course, include information about its view. For example, suppose that we want our application's view to occur in a framed window with a width of 300 device units and a height of 600 device units. Assume, further, that our document has the appropriate data members:

```
class CProj1Doc : public CDocument {
//...
private:
    unsigned long width, height;
};
```

Our **Serialize** might then be drafted as follows:

```
void CProj1Doc::Serialize(CArchive& ar)
{
    //*** jk: invoke base class method
    CDocument::Serialize( ar );
    //*** CArchive knows whether we're
    //     serializing in or out
    if (ar.IsStoring()) //*** serializing out
    {
        // TODO: add storing code here
        ar << width << height; //*** jk
    }
    else                     //*** serializing in
    {
        // TODO: add loading code here
        ar >> width >> height; //*** jk
    }
}
```

We comment **jk** to highlight what we, rather than the VC++ wizards, have written.

Objects in the MFC's **CObject** hierarchy are *self-serializing* in that the appropriate overload of **Serialize** is part of each class in this hierarchy. The programmer obviously should leverage this built-in serialization. In the next section, we illustrate built-in serialization with a sample application in which we rely *exclusively* on MFC's built-in serialization. One point still needs to be stated however: to be serializable under MFC, an object's class must have at least a *default* constructor. When the object is serialized in, its default constructor is automatically invoked as a standard part of object construction.

## EXERCISES

1. What is a model in the Smalltalk sense?

2. What is a view in the Smalltalk sense?

3. What is a controller in the Smalltalk sense?

4. How does the MFC document/view pair relate to the Smalltalk model/view/controller triple?

5. Explain the relationship between persistence and serialization.

6. What general role does an MFC **CArchive** play in MFC serialization?

7. In the main MFC inheritance hierarchy, what is the ultimate base class?

8. What is the difference between an SDI and an MDI document/view application?

9. Does MFC use any **private** inheritance?

10. Does MFC use any multiple inheritance?

# 9.3 SAMPLE APPLICATION: DOCUMENT SERIALIZATION

### Problem

Write an application under MFC's document/view architecture and implement document serialization where the document is a vector of geometric figures. The document's view should use the appropriate graphics to display the document's contents. In particular, the view should offer a graphical depiction of each document figure. For instance, a document triangle could be represented graphically as a colored triangular figure. For flexibility, use an MDI (multiple document interface) application under MFC's document/view architecture. An MDI application is more flexible than an SDI application in that the former can contain and display multiple documents simultaneously. Each document's view occurs in its own framed window.

### Sample Output

Figure 9.3.1 shows a sample document and its view.

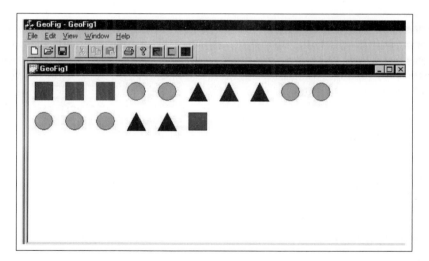

**FIGURE 9.3.1** A sample document and its view.

### Solution

We rely upon built-in MFC support for serialization. In particular, we use MFC's **CTyped-PtrArray** to store pointers to each document figure, which is an object belonging to a class (e.g., **Triangle**) derived from MFC's **CObject**. A **CTypedPtrArray** is self-serializing in that it serializes its own size and contents and invokes the **Serialize** method of the objects to which its own elements point. Because our document's geometric figures belong to classes derived from **CObject**, these figures themselves are self-serializing. Each object stores its own *data type*, that is, the class to which it belongs. Because an object's default constructor is invoked automatically when the object is serialized in, we rely upon the different constructors to do appropriate initialization, for example, to determine the object's color when displayed in the document's view. By leveraging MFC's own support for serialization, we minimize the serialization code that we have to write.

## C++ Implementation

The complete project is available from the homepage

```
http://condor.depaul.edu/~mkalin
```

The listing here consists of code that we added to the project together with important segments of wizard-generated code.

```cpp
//**************** Begin Figure.h
//**** jk: header for our CFigure class
//**** all code in this header is ours
#define CFigure_DEFINED //*** jk: to avoid multiple includes
class CFigure : public CObject { //*** jk: derived from CObject
public:
    DECLARE_SERIAL( CFigure ) // VC++ macro for serialization
    CFigure();
    virtual ~CFigure();
    virtual void Serialize( CArchive& ar );
    virtual void Draw( CDC*, const CRect& );
    virtual COLORREF GetColor();
protected:
    CBrush* brushPtr;
    void DeleteBrush();
    void CreateBrush( CBrush**, const COLORREF& );
    unsigned x, y; // display coordinates
};

class CRectangle : public CFigure {
public:
    DECLARE_SERIAL( CRectangle )
    CRectangle();
    ~CRectangle();
    virtual void Serialize( CArchive& ar );
    virtual void Draw( CDC*, const CRect& );
    virtual COLORREF GetColor();
};

class CTriangle : public CFigure {
public:
    DECLARE_SERIAL( CTriangle )
    CTriangle();
    ~CTriangle();
    virtual void Serialize( CArchive& ar );
    virtual void Draw( CDC*, const CRect& );
    virtual COLORREF GetColor();
};
```

```
class CCircle : public CFigure {
public:
   DECLARE_SERIAL( CCircle )
   CCircle();
  ~CCircle();
   virtual void Serialize( CArchive& ar );
   virtual void Draw( CDC*, const CRect& );
   virtual COLORREF GetColor();
};
//*************** End Figure.h

//**************** Begin Figure.cpp
//**** jk: implementation class for our CFigure class
// All code in this implementation file is ours.
#ifndef CFigure_DEFINED
#include "Figure.h"
#endif
//*** jk: VC++ macros to implement serialization
// Format is: <class>, <parent>, <version>
IMPLEMENT_SERIAL( CFigure, CObject, 1 )
IMPLEMENT_SERIAL( CRectangle, CFigure, 1 )
IMPLEMENT_SERIAL( CCircle, CFigure, 1 )
IMPLEMENT_SERIAL( CTriangle, CFigure, 1 )
//*** jk: constructors, destructor, and other
// methods use the TRACE macro, which is allows
// printf-style formatting.  TRACE is enabled when
// the VC++ target is a "debug" rather than a "release."
CFigure::CFigure() {
   TRACE( _T( "CFigure()\n" ) );
}
CFigure::~CFigure() {
   TRACE( _T( "~CFigure()\n" ) );
}
void CFigure::Serialize( CArchive& ar ) {
   CObject::Serialize( ar );
   TRACE( _T( "CFigure::Serialize\n" ) );
}
COLORREF CFigure::GetColor() {
   return RGB( 0, 0, 0 ); // black
}
void CFigure::Draw( CDC* pDC, const CRect& r ) {
   // empty body: available for later development
}
void CFigure::CreateBrush( CBrush** p, const COLORREF& c ) {
   *p = new CBrush( c );
}
```

```cpp
void CFigure::DeleteBrush() {
   brushPtr->DeleteObject();
   delete brushPtr;
}
CRectangle::CRectangle() {
   CreateBrush( &brushPtr, GetColor() );
   TRACE( _T( "CRectangle()\n" ) );
}
CRectangle::~CRectangle() {
   DeleteBrush();
   TRACE( _T( "~CRectangle()\n" ) );
}
void CRectangle::Serialize( CArchive& ar ) {
   CFigure::Serialize( ar );
   TRACE( _T( "CRectangle::Serialize\n" ) );
}
COLORREF CRectangle::GetColor() {
   return RGB( 255, 0 , 0 ); // red
}
void CRectangle::Draw( CDC* pDC, const CRect& r ) {
    pDC->SelectObject( brushPtr );
    pDC->Rectangle( r.TopLeft().x, r.TopLeft().y,
                    r.BottomRight().x, r.BottomRight().y );
}
CCircle::CCircle() {
   CreateBrush( &brushPtr, GetColor() );
   TRACE( _T( "CCircle()\n" ) );
}
CCircle::~CCircle() {
   DeleteBrush();
   TRACE( _T( "~CCircle()\n" ) );
}
void CCircle::Serialize( CArchive& ar ) {
   CFigure::Serialize( ar );
   TRACE( _T( "CCircle::Serialize\n" ) );
}
COLORREF CCircle::GetColor() {
   return RGB( 0, 255, 0 ); // green
}
void CCircle::Draw( CDC* pDC, const CRect& r ) {
   pDC->SelectObject( brushPtr );
   pDC->Ellipse( r.TopLeft().x, r.TopLeft().y,
                 r.BottomRight().x, r.BottomRight().y );
}
```

```
CTriangle::CTriangle() {
   CreateBrush( &brushPtr, GetColor() );
   TRACE( _T( "CTriangle()\n" ) );
}
CTriangle::~CTriangle() {
   DeleteBrush();
   TRACE( _T( "~CTriangle()\mn" ) );
}
void CTriangle::Serialize( CArchive& ar ) {
   CFigure::Serialize( ar );
   TRACE( _T( "CTriangle::Serialize\n" ) );
}
COLORREF CTriangle::GetColor() {
   return RGB( 0, 0, 255 ); // blue
}
void CTriangle::Draw( CDC* pDC, const CRect& r ) {
   pDC->SelectObject( brushPtr );
   CPoint pts[ ] =
      { CPoint( r.TopLeft().x + r.Width() / 2, r.TopLeft().y ),
        CPoint( r.TopLeft().x, r.TopLeft().y + r.Height() ),
        CPoint( r.BottomRight().x, r.BottomRight().y ) };
   pDC->Polygon( pts, 3 );
}
//*************** End Figure.cpp

//*************** Begin GeoFigDoc.h
//**** jk: header for the Document class
#include <afxtempl.h>    //*** jk: for CTypedPtrArray
#ifndef CFigure_DEFINED
#include "Figure.h"  //*** jk: header for our CFigure class
#endif
class CGeoFigDoc : public CDocument
{
protected: // create from serialization only
   CGeoFigDoc();
   DECLARE_DYNCREATE(CGeoFigDoc)
   // Attributes
public:
   // Operations
public:
   // Overrides
   // ClassWizard generated virtual function overrides
   //{{AFX_VIRTUAL(CGeoFigDoc)
```

```
public:
    virtual BOOL OnNewDocument();
    virtual void Serialize(CArchive& ar);
    virtual void DeleteContents();
    //}}AFX_VIRTUAL
public:
    //*** jk: accessor for the private figures, a CTypedPtrArray
    // whose elements are pointers to our CFigure objects
    CTypedPtrArray< CObArray, CFigure* >& GetFigures() {
        return figures;
    }
private:
    //*** jk: array of pointers to our CFigure objects
    CTypedPtrArray< CObArray, CFigure* > figures;
};
//*************** End GeoFigDoc.h

//*************** Begin GeoFigDoc.cpp
//**** implementation file for the Document class
// CGeoFigDoc construction/destruction
CGeoFigDoc::CGeoFigDoc()
{
    // TODO: add one-time construction code here
}

CGeoFigDoc::~CGeoFigDoc()
{
}
//*** jk: delete CFigures before closing document
void CGeoFigDoc::DeleteContents() {
    for ( int i = 0; i < figures.GetSize(); i++ )
        delete figures[ i ];
    CDocument::DeleteContents();
}
BOOL CGeoFigDoc::OnNewDocument()
{
    if (!CDocument::OnNewDocument())
      return FALSE;
    // TODO: add reinitialization code here
    // (SDI documents will reuse this document)
    //*** jk: set the document's title, which appears in window
    SetTitle( "Drawing and Serializing Geometric Figures" );
    return TRUE;
}
```

```
void CGeoFigDoc::Serialize(CArchive& ar)
{
   if (ar.IsStoring())
   {
      // TODO: add storing code here
   }
   else
   {
      // TODO: add loading code here
   }
   //*** jk: a CTypedPtrArray is "self-serializing":
   // It will invoke the Serialize for each object
   // pointed to.  The CArchive knows whether
   // we're serializing "in" or "out."
   figures.Serialize( ar );
}


//*** jk: add a CFigure to the array,
// mark the document as modified, and
// force a redrawing of all open documents
// in their respective views
void CGeoFigDoc::AddFigure( CFigure* f ) {
   figures.Add( f );
   SetModifiedFlag();
   UpdateAllViews( 0 ); // 0 == NULL == all views
}
//*************** End GeoFigDoc.cpp


//*************** Begin GeoFigView.h
//**** jk: header for the View class
class CGeoFigView : public CView
{
protected: // create from serialization only
   CGeoFigView();
   DECLARE_DYNCREATE(CGeoFigView)
// Attributes
public:
   CGeoFigDoc* GetDocument(); // for View to get Document
```

```
// Operations
public:
// Overrides
    // ClassWizard generated virtual function overrides
    //{{AFX_VIRTUAL(CGeoFigView)
public:
    virtual void OnDraw(CDC* pDC); // overridden
    virtual BOOL PreCreateWindow(CREATESTRUCT& cs);
protected:
    virtual BOOL OnPreparePrinting(CPrintInfo* pInfo);
    virtual void OnBeginPrinting(CDC* pDC, CPrintInfo* pInfo);
    virtual void OnEndPrinting(CDC* pDC, CPrintInfo* pInfo);
//}}AFX_VIRTUAL
protected:
// Generated message map functions
//*** jk: these are callbacks for menu items and toolbar buttons
//*** afx_msg is a VC++ keyword that signals (1) that the
//      corresponding method behaves polymorphically but (2) that
//      VC++ is using a systems of macros rather than the vtable
//      proper to implement the polymorphism.  In effect,
//      "afx_msg" means "polymorphic but without vtable
//      "overhead." VC++ builds a "message map" to achieve
//      polymorphic behavior without the vtable.
protected:
    //{{AFX_MSG(CGeoFigView)
    afx_msg void OnFileInstructions();
    afx_msg void OnFileRectangle();
    afx_msg void OnFileTriangle();
    afx_msg void OnFileCircle();
    afx_msg void OnFiguresRectangle();
    afx_msg void OnFiguresCircle();
    afx_msg void OnFiguresTriangle();
    //}}AFX_MSG
    DECLARE_MESSAGE_MAP()
};
//*************** End GeoFigView.h

//*************** Begin GeoFigView.cpp
//**** jk: implementation file for the View class
// VC++ "message map" used instead of vtable to
// support polymorphic callbacks
```

```
BEGIN_MESSAGE_MAP(CGeoFigView, CView)
    //{{AFX_MSG_MAP(CGeoFigView)
    ON_COMMAND(ID_FILE_RECTANGLE, OnFileRectangle)
    ON_COMMAND(ID_FILE_TRIANGLE, OnFileTriangle)
    ON_COMMAND(ID_FILE_CIRCLE, OnFileCircle)
    ON_COMMAND(ID_FIGURES_RECTANGLE, OnFiguresRectangle)
    ON_COMMAND(ID_FIGURES_CIRCLE, OnFiguresCircle)
    ON_COMMAND(ID_FIGURES_TRIANGLE, OnFiguresTriangle)
    //}}AFX_MSG_MAP
    // Standard printing commands
    ON_COMMAND(ID_FILE_PRINT, CView::OnFilePrint)
    ON_COMMAND(ID_FILE_PRINT_DIRECT, CView::OnFilePrint)
    ON_COMMAND(ID_FILE_PRINT_PREVIEW, CView::OnFilePrintPreview)
END_MESSAGE_MAP()
CGeoFigView::CGeoFigView()
{
    // TODO: add construction code here
}
CGeoFigView::~CGeoFigView()
{
}
//*** jk: we add to the wizard boilerplate in order to draw
// our document in an appropriate fashion
void CGeoFigView::OnDraw(CDC* pDC)
{
    CGeoFigDoc* pDoc = GetDocument();
    ASSERT_VALID(pDoc);
    // TODO: add draw code for native data here
    int xOrig = 10,
        x = xOrig, y = 10,
        w = 30, h = 30,
        xOff = w + 20,
        yOff = h + 20,
        figsPerRow = 12;
    for ( int i = 0; i < pDoc->GetFigures().GetSize(); i++ ) {
      CRect r( x, y, x + w, y + h );
      pDoc->GetFigures()[ i ]->Draw( pDC, r );
      if ( 0 == ((i + 1) % figsPerRow) ) {
        x = xOrig;
        y += yOff;
      }
      else
        x += xOff;
    }
}
```

```
CGeoFigDoc* CGeoFigView::GetDocument()
{
    ASSERT(m_pDocument->IsKindOf(RUNTIME_CLASS(CGeoFigDoc)));
    return (CGeoFigDoc*)m_pDocument;
}
//*** jk: our callbacks for menu and button selections.  Stub
// is created by ClassWizard.  We then fill in the details.
// The callbacks that begin "OnFile" are for menu choices;
// the ones that begin "OnFigures" are for toolbar buttons.
// The toolbar button callbacks simply invoke the corresponding
// menu callback to ensure identical behavior.
void CGeoFigView::OnFileRectangle()
{
    // TODO: Add your command handler code here
    GetDocument()->AddFigure( new CRectangle() );
}
void CGeoFigView::OnFileTriangle()
{
    // TODO: Add your command handler code here
    GetDocument()->AddFigure( new CTriangle() );
}
void CGeoFigView::OnFileCircle()
{
    // TODO: Add your command handler code here
    GetDocument()->AddFigure( new CCircle() );
}
void CGeoFigView::OnFiguresRectangle()
{
    // TODO: Add your command handler code here
    OnFileRectangle();
}
void CGeoFigView::OnFiguresCircle()
{
    // TODO: Add your command handler code here
    OnFileCircle();
}
void CGeoFigView::OnFiguresTriangle()
{
    // TODO: Add your command handler code here
    OnFileTriangle();
}
//*************** End GeoFigView.cpp
```

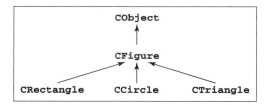

**FIGURE 9.3.2** The `CFigure` hierarchy.

### Discussion

Our application is designed to leverage, first, the serialization built into the MFC classes derived from **CObject** and, second, the built-in interplay between a project's document and its view. In particular, our **CFigure** hierarchy (see Figure 9.3.2) is derived from **CObject** so that **CFigure**s—**CRectangle**s, **CTriangle**s, and **CCircle**s—can be made self-serializing. The **CFigure** class

```
class CFigure : public CObject {
public:
    DECLARE_SERIAL( CFigure ) // macro for serialization
    CFigure();
    virtual ~CFigure();
    virtual void Serialize( CArchive& ar );
    virtual void Draw( CDC*, const CRect& );
    virtual COLORREF GetColor();
protected:
    CBrush* brushPtr;
    void DeleteBrush();
    void CreateBrush( CBrush**, const COLORREF& );
    unsigned x, y; // display coordinates
};
```

includes the VC++ **DECLARE_SERIAL** parameterized macro, which takes a class tag as its argument. This macro occurs in the header (*.h*) file and its companion macro **IMPLE-MENT_SERIAL** occurs in the corresponding implementation (*.cpp*) file. Together the macros signal the compiler that the class in question supports serialization for its objects. **CFigure**'s exposed methods include a **virtual** destructor and three other **virtual** methods:

- An override of **Serialize** inherited from **CObject**. In our case, the override merely prints a message that the object in question is being serialized. To serialize **CFigure**s, we do not need any code of our own in the overrides of **Serialize** within the **CFigure** hierarchy.

- A **Draw** method overridden in the classes derived from **CFigure**. Each such class knows how to draw an object in the class. For example, **CTriangle**'s override is responsible for drawing a triangle rather than, say, a circle.

- A **GetColor** method overridden in the classes derived from **CFigure**. Each such class returns the color appropriate to the object.

The two **protected** methods, which are nonpolymorphic, allocate and free graphics resources, in particular, an MFC **CBrush** object used for coloring the **CFigure**s. The three classes derived from **CFigure** use the inherited **CreateBrush** with a **COLORREF** parameter, which represents a particular color:

```
void CFigure::CreateBrush( CBrush** p, const COLORREF& c ) {
    *p = new CBrush( c );
}
```

In our implementation, all objects in a given class happen to have the same color. For instance, all **CRectangle**s are red. Because **CreateBrush** is not **static**, our implementation makes it possible for each object to have its own color (see Programming Exercise 9.1). Each derived class also has a polymorphic destructor that frees the storage for the **CBrush** by invoking the inherited **DeleteBrush**. Here, for example, is the **CRectangle** destructor along with **CFigure::DeleteBrush**

```
void CFigure::DeleteBrush() { //*** our method
    brushPtr->DeleteObject();   //*** MFC method
    delete brushPtr;
}
CRectangle::~CRectangle() {
    DeleteBrush();
    TRACE( _T( "~CRectangle()\n" ) );
}
```

VC++ provides the **TRACE** macro, which allows **printf**-style formatting and is used for debugging. VC++ applications have a **target**, which may be either a *Debug* or a *Release* target. For *Debug* targets, the **TRACE** macro prints messages in the VC++ IDE's debug window. The macro **_T** can convert ASCII characters to Unicode characters.

Class **CFigure** and each derived class has a *default* constructor, which is required for serializing objects in the class. When an object is serialized *in*, the system automatically invokes the appropriate default constructor to create the object. For example, when a **CTriangle** is serialized in, the system invokes the **CTriangle** default constructor to construct the **CTriangle** object.

Recall that an MFC view class combines the Smalltalk view and controller. Accordingly, our project's view class is responsible for drawing our document and handling user-generated events. To draw a document, which in our project consists of none or more **CFigure**s, we add to the wizard's **OnDraw** callback:

```
void CGeoFigView::OnDraw(CDC* pDC)
{
    CGeoFigDoc* pDoc = GetDocument();
    ASSERT_VALID(pDoc);
    // TODO: add draw code for native data here
    int xOrig = 10,
        x = xOrig, y = 10,
        w = 30, h = 30,
        xOff = w + 20,
        yOff = h + 20,
        figsPerRow = 12;
    for ( int i = 0; i < pDoc->GetFigures().GetSize(); i++ ) {
      CRect r( x, y, x + w, y + h );
      pDoc->GetFigures()[ i ]->Draw( pDC, r );
      if ( 0 == ((i + 1) % figsPerRow) ) {
        x = xOrig;
        y += yOff;
      }
      else
        x += xOff;
    }
}
```

The wizard generates the **TODO** comment and the two lines above it. **GetDocument** is a **public** method by which the view gets a pointer to its document. VC++'s **ASSERT_VALID** macro extends the functionality of the standard C++ **assert**. In particular, the **ASSERT_VALID**macro does some type checking to ensure that **pDoc** indeed points to a project document. Our code draws a document's **CFigure**s in as many rows as required, with **figsPerRow** figures in each row. In the **for** loop, we get the size of the vector that holds pointers to **CFigure**s and then polymorphically invoke the **Draw** method of each **CFigure**. The polymorphic **Draw** expects two arguments: the first is **OnDraw**'s pointer to an MFC **CDC**, which contains members for manipulating a **device context**. In general, all drawing in a windows system occurs within a device context that determines, for example, the width of drawn lines or the font of drawn characters. The second argument to **Draw** is an MFC **CRect**angle that bounds the **CFigure**. These bounding triangles have the same width and height, thus ensuring that the **CFigure**s contained therein have the same sizes. The **CRect**s differ from one another only in their horizontal and/or vertical coordinates.

Our view handles two types of user-generated events: menu selections and button pushes. There are menu selections and buttons to create instances of each class derived from **CFigure**. The effect of selecting, for example, **Rectangle** from the menu is the same as pushing the button labeled **R** on the project window's toolbar. We use the ClassWizard to generate the boilerplate callbacks. Here, for example, are the callbacks for a **CTriangle**:

```
void CGeoFigView::OnFileTriangle()   //*** menu selection
{
   // TODO: Add your command handler code here
   GetDocument()->AddFigure( new CTriangle() );
}

void CGeoFigView::OnFiguresTriangle() //*** button push
{
   // TODO: Add your command handler code here
   OnFileTriangle();
}
```

The callback for the button push simply invokes the callback for the corresponding menu selection to ensure that each user action has the same effect. In either case, our document's **AddFigure** is invoked to insert a pointer to a new **CFigure** into our vector of figures.

Our contribution to the wizard's document boilerplate consists of one **private** data member and two **public** methods. Method **AddFigure** is used to add a new **CFigure** to **figures**, which is a vector of MFC type **CTypedPtrArray**. A **CTypedPtrArray** is similar in style and function to an STL vector. There are two template arguments:

```
CTypedPtrArray< CObArray, CFigure* > figures; //*** jk
```

The first is the MFC type **CObArray**, which is one of two possible base classes for a **CTypedPtrArray**; the other possibility is **CPtrArray**. The second template argument is **CFigure\***, which indicates that the vector will hold pointers to **CFigure** objects. Because **figures** is **private**, we provide the **public** method **GetFigures**, which returns a reference to **figures**.

A **CTypedPtrArray** is self-serializing in that it serializes its own data type as template class instantiation, its size (number of elements), and its contents. The last item needs clarification. The vector's contents are pointers. What is serialized out is *not* the value of each pointer but rather its polymorphic type. For example, if the vector's first element were a pointer to a **CRectangle**, then the data type **CRectangle\*** would be serialized out. To illustrate how the serialization works, consider the case in which **figures** holds three pointers: the first points to a **CRectangle**, the second to a **CCircle**, and the third to a **CTriangle**. Of course, any combination of pointers to **CFigures** is possible. When **figures** serializes out, it saves its own data type (**a CTypedPtrArray** with pointers to **CFigure**s), its size (3), and the types of its pointer contents (**CRectangle\***, **CCircle\***, and **CTriangle\***). When **figures** is serialized in, it allocates storage for three **CFigure** pointers and the corresponding objects, storage for which is allocated dynamically as part of serializing in. The first element in **figures** then points to a **CRectangle**, the second to a **CCircle**, and the third to a **CTriangle**. During the serializing in, each object's default constructor is invoked in constructing the object. Because serializing in changes the project's document—indeed, creates a *new* document from a binary file—the process automatically notifies the document's view that the document needs to be (re)drawn. Our own **AddFigure** indicates the underlying MFC calls:

```
void CGeoFigDoc::AddFigure( CFigure* f ) {
    figures.Add( f );   //*** CTypedPtrArray method
    SetModifiedFlag(); //*** MFC
    UpdateAllViews( 0 ); //*** MFC, 0 == all views
}
```

The document's inherited **SetModifiedFlag** method signals that the document has been changed. Invoking method **UpdateAllViews** forces a redrawing of the document's view. During serializing in, these calls are provided as part of the underlying process. Recall that the actual drawing occurs in the view's **OnDraw** callback. In our implementation, this view callback first determines the size of a **figure** and then invokes a polymorphic **Draw** method for each figure in the vector. After serializing in, **OnDraw** is automatically invoked.

Because MFC provides so much support for serialization, our own coding effort is a single line in the document's **Serialize**:

```
figures.Serialize( ar );
```

We invoke the **CTypedPtrArray**'s own **Serialize** method, passing it the **CArchive** reference passed to our own boilerplate **Serialize**. The **CArchive** knows whether the serialization is in or out. The rest, then, is automatic—and quite powerful.

## EXERCISES

1. What advantage results from deriving our **CFigure** hierarchy from MFC's **CObject**?

2. Does the **DECLARE_SERIAL** macro appear in a header or implementation file?

3. Does the **IMPLEMENT_SERIAL** macro appear in a header or implementation file?

4. Why is it appropriate for the **Serialize** method to be polymorphic?

5. What role does the default constructor play for a class whose objects can be serialized?

6. What is a device context?

7. What does our application store in the document's **CTypedPtrArray**?

8. Explain the sense in which a **CTypedPtrArray** is *self-serializing*.

## 9.4 THE COMMON OBJECT MODEL

Microsoft's Common Object Model (hereafter, COM) is an infrastructure for interapplication communication on a single machine. The Distributed Common Object Model (DCOM) extends this infrastructure for interapplication communication across machines. For simplicity, we focus on COM.

COM leverages and integrates four powerful technologies:

- Remote Procedure Call (RPC), in particular the version developed as part of the Distributed Computing Environment (DCE) initiative. DCE is a family of technologies meant to support platform-independent, robust, and sophisticated distributed systems. Major vendors such as the former Digital Equipment Corporation and IBM, together with universities such as MIT, developed DCE in general and its RPC in particular. Under RPC, an application on one machine can invoke a function that executes in an application running on another machine. RPC also can be used *locally*, that is, in cases where the function's invoking and executing applications occur on the *same* machine.

- Serialization. In an RPC environment, a function invoked on one machine (the client) is executed on another machine (the server). If the function has arguments and a return value, the arguments must be passed from the client to the server, and the return value must be passed from the server to the client. Serialization is an underlying mechanism. Arguments are serialized out by the client and in by the server; the return value is serialized out by the server and in by the client. If serialization can be used in this fashion across machines, it obviously can be used on the same machine.

- The C++ vtable. At the implementation level, the vtable is a mechanism through which an application can access pointers to functions. The vtable's standard use is *within* an application, but the underlying mechanism can be extended so that one application can access pointers to functions that execute in another application.

- The object-oriented distinction between interface and implementation. An object in the object-oriented sense is a *server* whose services are typically exposed as high-level, public methods. An object's implementation, which is hidden, typically consists of private data members and low-level functions. The object itself can be seen as the **back end** of its exposed interface, that is, as the hidden server that supports an exposed interface. Under COM, a client application gains access to an interface; a corresponding COM server is *any* application (on the same machine) that exposes and supports the interface.

COM applications fall within a client/server rather than a peer-to-peer architecture. In a particular COM pairing, one application is the server and the other is the client. If the server serves up *documents*, the client is known as a **container**. If the server serves up arbitrary functionality that the client can invoke, the client is known as an **automation controller**. We pursue these distinctions in a later subsection. Under COM in general, however, a client application requests services from a server application. To do so, the client requires access to at least one interface that the server exposes and supports. A server exposes an interface through the system **registry**, which is a database of servers together with the interfaces that they support. Registry entries have a unique 128-bit, specially formatted identifier known internationally as a Universally Unique IDentifier (UUID). Microsoft has its own subcategories of UUID. For example, a server has a CLSID (**CLaSs IDentifier**). Note that Microsoft thereby pursues the object-oriented theme that a class is a server. Because a given client may request services from multiple servers, each server appears to the client as a **component** of the client application. A server application is thus a potential component in some other application. A client application practices code reuse by using servers as its very own components. Seen in this light, COM is an infrastructure that allows server applications to behave as reusable components of client applications.

## Changeable Servers and Unchangeable Interfaces

Under COM, a server is basically the back end of one or more registered interfaces. Figure 9.4.1 depicts a server **s** that exposes two interfaces, **IF1** and **IF2**. Suppose that **s** is buggy, inefficient, or otherwise defective. Suppose, further, that client **c** uses **s** as a component in that **c** invokes functions from both **IF1** and **IF2**. Client **c** does *not* require **s** in particular; rather, **c** requires that *some server or other* support the interfaces **IF1** and **IF2**. Suppose, for example, that **s** is removed from the local machine but that two other applications happen to support the interfaces that **c** requires (see Figure 9.4.2). Under COM, **c** is not tied to a particular server such as **s**; instead, **c** is tied to *interfaces*. The underlying components (servers) that support interfaces may come and go; the interfaces themselves, once published, must not change under this model. If **c** relies upon interfaces **IF1** and **IF2**, then nothing in these interfaces should ever change because a change would require that **c** itself change. Under COM, therefore, stability requires that an interface published in the registry be unchangeable. The back ends to such interfaces—the servers that support them—may change as often as required. The key point for the client is that there be *some server or other* that supports all of the published interfaces on which the client relies. A server such as **s** is free to support *new* interfaces, even interfaces that combine the functionality of **IF1** and **IF2**. Nonetheless, the vendor responsible for publishing **IF1** and **IF2** in the registry is responsible for ensuring that these interfaces are forever supported by some combination of servers.

**FIGURE 9.4.1** A component that exposes two interfaces.

**FIGURE 9.4.2** Two components that together expose the two interfaces of Figure 9.4.1.

## The Interface Hierarchy

COM interfaces fall within a hierarchy whose ultimate base class is **IUnknown** (see Section 5.4). Class **IUnknown** is an abstract base class with three pure **virtual** methods: **QueryInterface**, which allows a client to navigate among a component's interfaces given access to any one of them; **AddRef**, which allows a client to increment an interface's reference count and thereby signal that the underlying component has one more active client; and **Release**, which allows a client to decrement the interface's reference count and thereby signal that the underlying component has one fewer active client. In general, a server stops executing when the reference counts for all of its exposed interfaces equal zero. This condition occurs when the server has no clients because a client requires access to a server interface.

To be a COM server, an application must expose through the registry at least one interface; and any such interface must be derived from **IUnknown**. An interface may be derived directly or indirectly from **IUnknown**. Figure 9.4.3 depicts the situation in which **IF1** is derived directly from **IUnknown**, whereas **IF2** is derived indirectly from **IUnknown**.

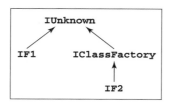

**FIGURE 9.4.3** COM interfaces derived directly and indirectly from **IUnknown**.

Accordingly, every COM server must implement the three pure **virtual** methods in **IUnknown**. Of course, a typical COM server implements many other functions besides the pure **virtual** methods listed in **IUnknown**. A server that implemented only the three methods in **IUnknown** would not be useful.

## The **IDispatch** Interface

In a strict sense, a COM interface enables a client application to access a server function through a vtable lookup. A vtable thus mediates between a client and a server. This makes sense if the client and server are both written in, say, C++ because the vtable is central to the language's implementation. In principle, however, a component might be written in *any* language and its client might be written in some *other* language. For example, it is common under Windows for a Visual Basic client to request services from a C or C++ server. Visual Basic, particularly in its early versions, was not equipped to handle vtable lookups. Microsoft therefore supports what is called the **IDispatch** interface as a flexible alternative to a COM interface in the strict sense. It should be emphasized, however, that COM in the loose sense includes all interface mechanisms through which a client requests services from a component. The distinction between COM interfaces and **IDispatch** continues to blur as COM evolves. Nonetheless, we now clarify **IDispatch** to illustrate its flexibility and to prepare for our sample COM application.

**IDispatch** has several methods, the central one of which is **Invoke**. Method **Invoke** has counterparts in other languages such as Lisp and Java. In effect, **Invoke** is a method that invokes other methods by name. Suppose, for example, that a server exposes COM interface **IF1**, which includes function **f** that expects no arguments. If a client has a pointer **ptrIF1** to this interface, it could invoke **f** using the standard syntax

```
ptrIF1->f()
```

By contrast, if the client has a pointer `ptrID` to an `IDispatch` interface, `f` could be invoked by name

```
ptrID->Invoke( "f", NULL ) // NULL == no arguments for f
```

For emphasis, we have taken liberties with the details. For instance, `Invoke` actually uses an integer identifier rather than a string to invoke a function. Another `IDispatch` method maps a function's name to this integer identifier. Nonetheless, the example underscores that `Invoke` serves as a generic function invoker. Method `Invoke` is thus very flexible, as it can be used to invoke any interface method for which it has the integer identifier, which in turn can be obtained from the function's name. `Invoke` is likewise inefficient, as it requires that the function's name first be mapped to an identifier, which is then passed to `Invoke`, which then invokes the corresponding function. These steps take time. A single vtable lookup is more efficient.

It is increasingly common for a COM server to support a **dual interface**, that is, both an `IDispatch` and a vtable interface. Recent versions of Visual Basic and VC++ allow clients to use vtable interfaces even though, at the syntax level, such clients may appear to use `IDispatch`. The distinction between a strict COM interface and `IDispatch` is becoming increasingly transparent to the applications programmer. The programmer typically enjoys the syntactic flexibility of `IDispatch` with the underlying efficiency of vtable lookups.

## Types of COM Applications

What COM applications have in common is their interaction with other applications within a client/server architecture. One of the interacting applications is a client, whereas the other is a server. The applications themselves may be any mix of stand-alone processes (files with an *exe* extension) and dynamic link libraries (called DLLs because they are files with a *dll* or comparable extension). For example, the client might be a stand-alone application (that is, a process) but the server might be a DLL. (Microsoft calls DLL servers *in-process servers* to underscore that they execute within the client's process space. A stand-alone server is sometimes called an *out-of-process server*.) A client/server pair might both be DLLs, running in some other application's process space.

COM clients and servers have special names that emphasize their roles. A client for a document server is known as a **container**. For example, when an Excel spreadsheet is embedded in a Word document, Excel acts as a document server and Word as a container. The Word document that contains the Excel document is a **compound document**. If a Visual Basic application invokes Excel functions, Excel is an **automation server** and the Visual Basic application is an **automation controller**, that is, a client that controls Excel by invoking functions exposed in some Excel-supported interface. An ActiveX control is a DLL server with a built-in **property sheet** that allows visual editing of whatever properties or features the control exposes. An ActiveX control also has built-in mechanisms for communicating with its client. An automation server, by contrast, has no such mechanisms for communicating with its controller. ActiveX controls can be written within MFC or within a special **A**ctiveX **T**emplate **L**ibrary (ATL). ATL is modeled on the standard C++ STL. ATL relies heavily on powerful template classes and clever operator overloading. As a relatively small and specialized library, it has advantages over MFC. At present, however, VC++ has better wizard support for MFC than for ATL.

## VC++ Support for COM

COM is complex in its details; but language systems such as Visual Basic, Visual J++ (Java), and VC++ hide most of the complexity from the applications programmer. In VC++, for example, the AppWizard generates the COM initialization code or either a client or a server. The ClassWizard plays different roles for a COM server and client. On the server side, the ClassWizard generates the required code to create, expose, and register the server's interface methods. On the client side, this wizard generates C++ code that implements a server's exposed methods. (Recall that the server need not be written in VC++.) The ClassWizard on the client side generates such C++ code from a **type library**, which is a binary file created by a wizard on the server side. On the client side, the ClassWizard imports the type library into the client's project and then uses the type library to generate the VC++ code required to invoke the methods exposed in the server's interfaces. The type library is a binary representation of an RPC **idl** file (interface **d**efinition **l**anguage file). Figure 9.4.4 shows the idl file generated on the server side in the next section's sample COM application. In the idl file, a VC++ wizard generates a UUID for the server and provides integer identifiers for the methods exposed in the server's interface. In Figure 9.4.4, the exposed methods are **ShowCalendar** and **GetDate**. The idl file also indicates that the server's default interface is an **IDispatch** interface, which is standard for an automation server. What is not evident from the idl file is that the server actually supports a dual interface, which the client ClassWizard can use by generating VC++ code from an imported type library.

On the server side, the ClassWizard uses an industry-standard RPC utility known as an **idl compiler** to generate a binary representation of an idl file. This binary file is the type library, which then can be imported by a client-side wizard to generate language-specific code. For example, a VC++ wizard would use a type library to generate VC++ code. A Java wizard would generate Java code from the same type library. Conceptually, the type library and the underlying idl file contain the same information about the server. The main difference is that type library is binary, whereas the idl file is text.

## COM and OLE

COM is a work in progress, and Microsoft frequently changes the terminology. These frequent changes can be confusing at the code and the documentation level. Many COM classes begin with **Co** for COM; others include the term **Ole**. Early in COM's history, Microsoft drew a relatively sharp distinction between COM as the infrastructure for inter-application communication and OLE as a collection of built-in services that used COM. (OLE originally stood for **O**bject **L**inking and **E**mbedding.) For example, document sharing would be an OLE service in this sense. An automation server or client would be other examples of OLE in the old sense. Recently, however, Microsoft has begun to broaden the meaning of COM so that the distinction between the infrastructure and the built-in services has weakened. Microsoft is not always consistent in its usage. Nonetheless, we follow their more recent lead by using COM as an umbrella term that now covers both the infrastructure and the built-in services supported by this infrastructure. In short, we use COM to cover COM and OLE.

```
[ uuid(7CC34B6E-5D99-11D2-8050-00609714E9AC), version(1.0) ]
library DateS
{
    importlib("stdole32.tlb");
    //  Primary dispatch interface for CDateSDoc
    [ uuid(7CC34B6F-5D99-11D2-8050-00609714E9AC) ]
    dispinterface IDateS
    {
        properties:
        // NOTE - ClassWizard will maintain property
        //     information here.
        //     Use extreme caution when editing this section.
        //{{AFX_ODL_PROP(CDateSDlgAutoProxy)
        //}}AFX_ODL_PROP
        methods:
        // NOTE - ClassWizard will maintain method information
        //     here.
        //     Use extreme caution when editing this section.
        //{{AFX_ODL_METHOD(CDateSDlgAutoProxy)
            [id(1)] void ShowCalendar();
            [id(2)] DATE GetDate();
        //}}AFX_ODL_METHOD
    };
    //  Class information for CDateSDoc
    [ uuid(7CC34B6D-5D99-11D2-8050-00609714E9AC) ]
    coclass DateS
    {
        [default] dispinterface IDateS;
    };
};
```

**FIGURE 9.4.4** An idl file for a server.

## EXERCISES

1. What does COM stand for?

2. What does DCOM stand for?

3. What is the basic difference between COM and DCOM?

4. What does OLE stand for?

5. What is the traditional distinction between COM and OLE?

6. What does DCE RPC stand for?

7. How is DCE RPC related to COM?

8. What role does serialization play in COM?

9. What general role does the vtable play in COM?

10. How is the object-oriented distinction between interface and implementation adapted in COM?

11. What does DLL stand for?

12. Is COM based on a client/server architecture?

13. Must a COM server be a process, that is, a stand-alone application as opposed to a DLL?

14. What is a *component* in the COM sense?

15. What does Microsoft mean by an *in-process server*?

16. What does UUID stand for?

17. What is the system *registry*?

18. Under Windows, is a registered interface supposed to change?

19. Under Windows, is an interface's back end allowed to change?

20. What is `IUnknown`?

21. If `IF1` is a COM interface, what is its ultimate base class?

22. What is the main difference between an `IDispatch` interface and a COM interface in the strict sense?

23. What does idl stand for?

24. What information does an idl file provide?

25. What is the chief difference between an idl file and its companion type library?

26. Under COM document sharing, what is the client called?

27. Under COM automation, what is the client called?

28. Is an ActiveX control an in-process or out-of-process server?

## 9.5 SAMPLE APPLICATION: AN AUTOMATION SERVER AND CONTROLLER

 *Problem*

Write a COM server that can run either stand-alone or under the control of an automation client, that is, a *controller*. The server should expose two methods in a registered interface:

- `ShowCalendar`, which displays an ActiveX calendar control embedded in a dialog window. The user can manipulate the calendar directly by selecting, for example, the first Friday in January, 2000, also known as *fearsome Friday*.

- `GetDate`, which returns to the client the date displayed on the calendar.

The server, when run under client control, should terminate automatically when it no longer has clients.

### Sample Output

Figure 9.5.1 shows the server and its controller.

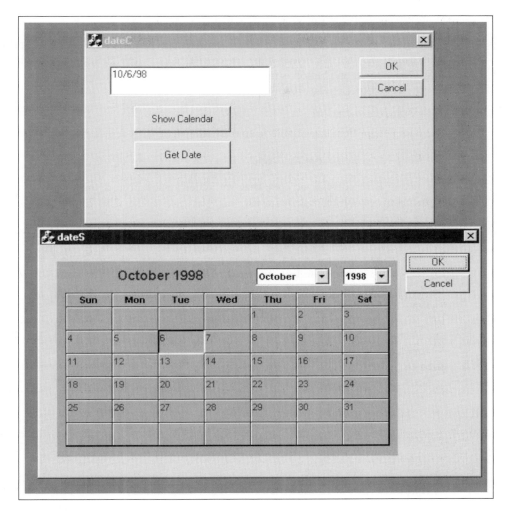

**FIGURE 9.5.1**  The date server and a controller.

### Solution

Our server is a dialog-based application that can run either stand-alone or in response to a client's request for its services. The server embeds an ActiveX control, which is a dynamic link library (DLL) that supports visual editing of its exposed properties. For example, a user can manipulate our ActiveX calendar control's font, foreground and background features, and other properties through a special-purpose dialog known as a **property sheet** that comes bundled with the ActiveX control. The calendar control is itself an example of a COM component, which Microsoft provides as part of its Access database. This component can be embedded in applications outside Access, as our server illustrates. In stand-alone mode, our server's principal role is to display the calendar so that users can manipulate this control visually. In effect, our dialog-based server is likewise a client to the ActiveX control embedded in it.

Our client is also a dialog-based application to which we add a text box and two buttons. Pushing one of the buttons causes the server to display the ActiveX calendar. Pushing the other causes the date displayed on the server's calendar control to appear in the client's text box. Once the second button is pushed, the client releases its interface to the server. If the server has no other clients, it halts execution.

## C++ Implementation

The complete project is available from the homepage

> `http://condor.depaul.edu/~mkalin`

The listing here consists of code that we added to the project together with important segments of wizard-generated code.

```
//**************** Begin Calendar.h
//********** The server
//**** wizard-generated header and implementation files for
//      ActiveX calendar control
//** header
class CCalendar : public CWnd
{
protected:
    DECLARE_DYNCREATE(CCalendar)
public:
    CLSID const& GetClsid()
    {
        static CLSID const clsid
            = { 0x8e27c92b, 0x1264, 0x101c,
                { 0x8a, 0x2f, 0x4, 0x2, 0x24, 0x0, 0x9c, 0x2 } };
        return clsid;
    }
    virtual BOOL Create(LPCTSTR lpszClassName,
                        LPCTSTR lpszWindowName, DWORD dwStyle,
                        const RECT& rect,
                        CWnd* pParentWnd, UINT nID,
                        CCreateContext* pContext = NULL)
            return CreateControl(GetClsid(),
                                 lpszWindowName,
                                 dwStyle,
                                 rect,
                                 pParentWnd,
                                 nID);
    }
//...
```

```
// Operations
public:
   unsigned long GetBackColor();
   void SetBackColor(unsigned long newValue);
   short GetDay();
   void SetDay(short nNewValue);
   //...
   short GetMonth();
   void SetMonth(short nNewValue);
   short GetMonthLength();
   void SetMonthLength(short nNewValue);
   //...
   VARIANT GetValue();
   void SetValue(const VARIANT& newValue);
   BOOL GetValueIsNull();
   void SetValueIsNull(BOOL bNewValue);
   short GetYear();
   void SetYear(short nNewValue);
   void NextDay();
   //...
   void PreviousYear();
   void Refresh();
   void Today();
   void AboutBox();
};
//*************** End Calendar.h

//*************** Begin Calendar.cpp
//** selections from implementation file
short CCalendar::GetYear()
{
   short result;
   InvokeHelper(0xf, DISPATCH_PROPERTYGET, VT_I2,
               (void*)&result, NULL);
   return result;
}
void CCalendar::SetYear(short nNewValue)
{
   static BYTE parms[] = VTS_I2;
   InvokeHelper(0xf, DISPATCH_PROPERTYPUT, VT_EMPTY, NULL,
               parms, nNewValue);
}
void CCalendar::PreviousDay()
{
   InvokeHelper(0x1a, DISPATCH_METHOD, VT_EMPTY, NULL, NULL);
}
```

```
void CCalendar::Today()
{
    InvokeHelper(0x1e, DISPATCH_METHOD, VT_EMPTY, NULL, NULL);
}
VARIANT CCalendar::GetValue()
{
    VARIANT result;
    InvokeHelper(0xc, DISPATCH_PROPERTYGET, VT_VARIANT,
                 (void*)&result, NULL);
    return result;
}
//*************** End Calendar.cpp


//*************** Begin DateSDlg.h
//**** header for server's main dialog
class CDateSDlg : public CDialog
{
    DECLARE_DYNAMIC(CDateSDlg);
    friend class CDateSDlgAutoProxy;
// Construction
public:
    CDateSDlg(CWnd* pParent = NULL);
Dlg(CWnd*
    virtual ~CDateSDlg();
// Dialog Data
    //{{AFX_DATA(CDateSDlg)
    enum { IDD = IDD_DATES_DIALOG };
    CCalendar m_cal; //*** jk: added through ClassWizard
    //}}AFX_DATA
    // ClassWizard generated virtual function overrides
    //{{AFX_VIRTUAL(CDateSDlg)
protected:
    virtual void DoDataExchange(CDataExchange* pDX); // DDX/DDV
    //}}AFX_VIRTUAL
```

```
// Implementation
protected:
    CDateSDlgAutoProxy* m_pAutoProxy;
    HICON m_hIcon;
    BOOL CanExit();
    // Generated message map functions
    //{{AFX_MSG(CDateSDlg)
    virtual BOOL OnInitDialog();
    afx_msg void OnPaint();
    afx_msg HCURSOR OnQueryDragIcon();
    afx_msg void OnClose();
    virtual void OnOK();
    virtual void OnCancel();
    //}}AFX_MSG
    DECLARE_MESSAGE_MAP()
};
//*************** End DateSDlg.h

//*************** Begin DateSDlg.cpp
//**** selections from implementation file for server's
//      main dialog
//*** jk: IDC_CALENDAR1 is VC++'s identifier for the
// gui component embedded in our dialog.  m_cal is the
// data member that represents the ActiveX control.  This
// wizard method exchanges data between the data member and
// the gui component
void CDateSDlg::DoDataExchange(CDataExchange* pDX)
{
    CDialog::DoDataExchange(pDX);
    //{{AFX_DATA_MAP(CDateSDlg)
    DDX_Control(pDX, IDC_CALENDAR1, m_cal);
    //}}AFX_DATA_MAP
}
//***** selections from header for the proxy class
//  the represents our server as a COM component
class CDateSDlgAutoProxy : public CCmdTarget
{
    DECLARE_DYNCREATE(CDateSDlgAutoProxy)
    CDateSDlgAutoProxy();
// Attributes
public:
```

```
g* m_pDi
protected:
    // Generated message map functions
    //{{AFX_MSG(CDateSDlgAutoProxy)
        // NOTE - the ClassWizard will add and
        // remove member functions here.
    //}}AFX_MSG
    DECLARE_MESSAGE_MAP()
    DECLARE_OLECREATE(CDateSDlgAutoProxy)
    // Generated OLE dispatch map functions
    //{{AFX_DISPATCH(CDateSDlgAutoProxy)
      afx_msg void ShowCalendar(); //*** jk: exposed method 1
      afx_msg DATE GetDate();      //*** jk: exposed method 2
    //}}AFX_DISPATCH
    DECLARE_DISPATCH_MAP()
    DECLARE_INTERFACE_MAP()
};
//*************** End DateSDlgAutoProxy.h

//*************** Begin DateSDlgAutoProxy.cpp
//**** selections from implementation for the proxy class
//*** jk: having a client invoke this method forces the
//    server to execute and show the calendar.
void CDateSDlgAutoProxy::ShowCalendar()
{
    // TODO: Add your dispatch handler code here
}
//*** jk: this method gets the date from the ActiveX
//    calendar control and returns it as a COM type
//** m_cal is our data member representing the
//    calendar; GetValue is an exposed calendar method
DATE CDateSDlgAutoProxy::GetDate()
{
    // TODO: Add your dispatch handler code here
    return COleDateTime( m_pDialog->m_cal.GetValue() );
    //return (DATE) 0; //*** jk: boilerplate from wizard
}
//********** end of server
//*************** End DateSDlg.cpp
```

```
//**************** Begin DateS.h
//********** The client
//**** wizard's header from server's type library
class IDateS : public COleDispatchDriver
{
public:
    IDateS() {}
() {}     // Calls COleDispatchDr
    IDateS(LPDISPATCH pDispatch) :
          COleDispatchDriver(pDispatch) {}
    IDateS(const IDateS& dispatchSrc) :
          COleDispatchDriver(dispatchSrc) {}
// Attributes
public:
// Operations
public:
    void ShowCalendar(); //*** jk: server's 1st exposed method
    DATE GetDate();      //*** jk: server's 2nd exposed method
};
//**************** End DateS.h

//**************** Begin DateS.cpp
//**** implementation file from server's type library
void IDateS::ShowCalendar()
{
    InvokeHelper(0x1, DISPATCH_METHOD, VT_EMPTY, NULL, NULL);
}
DATE IDateS::GetDate()
{
    DATE result;
    InvokeHelper(0x2, DISPATCH_METHOD, VT_DATE,
               (void*)&result, NULL);
    return result;
}
//**************** End DateS.cpp

//**************** Begin DateC.cpp
//**** InitInstance in our client's main implementation file
BOOL CDateCApp::InitInstance()
```

```cpp
{
   // Initialize OLE libraries
   if (!AfxOleInit())
   {
      AfxMessageBox(IDP_OLE_INIT_FAILED);
      return FALSE;
   }
   AfxEnableControlContainer();
   // Parse the command line to see if launched as OLE server
   if (RunEmbedded() || RunAutomated())
   {
      // Register all OLE server (factories) as running.
      COleTemplateServer::RegisterAll();
   }
   else
   {
      // When a server application is launched stand-alone,
      // it is a good idea to update the system registry
      // in case it has been damaged.
      COleObjectFactory::UpdateRegistryAll();
   }
   CDateCDlg dlg;
   m_pMainWnd = &dlg;
   int nResponse = dlg.DoModal();
   if (nResponse == IDOK)
   {
      // TODO: Place code here to handle when the dialog is
      //  dismissed with OK
   }
   else if (nResponse == IDCANCEL)
   {
      // TODO: Place code here to handle when the dialog is
      //  dismissed with Cancel
   }
   // Since the dialog has been closed, return FALSE so
   // that we exit the application, rather than start
   // the application's message pump.
   //*** jk: invoked when client dialog is closed
   dlg.checkRelease();
   return FALSE;
}
//*************** End DateC.cpp
```

```
//*************** Begin DateCDlg.cpp
//**** our callbacks for the two buttons that invoke the
//      methods exposed by the server
#include "dates.h" //*** jk: header for server
IDateS id;          //*** jk: interface class & object
bool dispatchExists = false; //*** jk: flag for internal use
//*** jk: ensure that IDispatch interface is
// released before the client (this) is destroyed
// ** Invoked from InitInstance in the application
// file (dateC.cpp) after the client dialog is closed;
// also invoked from OnButton2 below.
void CDateCDlg::checkRelease() {
   if ( dispatchExists ) {
     id.ReleaseDispatch();
     dispatchExists = false;
   }
}
//*** jk: callback for a click on the Show Calendar
// button.  Create an IDispatch interface to the server
// and force the server's execution by invoking a method
// in that interface, namely, ShowCalendar().  Turn off
// "automatic" release of the interface, which forces
// the calendar to remain open so that the user can
// specify a date.
void CDateCDlg::OnButton1()
{
   // TODO: Add your control notification handler code here
   if ( !dispatchExists ) {
     id.CreateDispatch( "dateS.Application" );
     id.ShowCalendar();
     dispatchExists = true;
   }
}
//*** jk: callback for a click on the Get Date button.
// Get the date from the server by invoking the
// interface's GetDate method.  Release the interface
// (hence, the server) and format the date to display
// in the client's text box.
// m_date is a data member that represents the client's
// text box
```

```
void CDateCDlg::OnButton2()
{
   // TODO: Add your control notification handler code here
   if ( !dispatchExists ) //*** jk: server interface created?
     return;                      //*** jk: if not, exit
   COleDateTime dt = id.GetDate(); // gets date from server
   checkRelease();                 // releases
   m_date = dt.Format();        // from return type to CString
   //*** jk: false means "write from m_date to the text box"
   //          true means "read from text box into m_date"
   UpdateData( false ); //*** jk: forces data exchange
}
//**************** End DateCDlg.cpp
```

### Discussion

We begin with the server, which can run either stand-alone or under the control of a client. The server's main GUI consists of a dialog window that a wizard generates with two buttons, one labeled **OK** and the other labeled **Cancel**. Pushing either button terminates the server. We used the ClassWizard to embed an ActiveX calendar control in the server dialog (see Figure 9.5.1). ActiveX controls come with a built-in type library, from which the ClassWizard generates a C++ header and implementation file. The header is, in effect, the programmer's documentation for manipulating the calendar through C++ code. For example, **CCalendar** has a **GetDay** method that returns the displayed day of the month as an integer. The companion method **SetDay** takes an integer argument such as 26, which sets the day of the displayed month to the 26th. Of interest to our client is **GetValue**, which returns the calendar's current value—month, day, and year—as a **VARIANT**. A **VARIANT** is an all-purpose structure that allows clients and servers written in different languages (e.g., Visual Basic and VC++) to communicate. MFC has various functions and macros for manipulating **VARIANT**s, one of which we discuss in the client section. Each time the server runs stand-alone, its initialization code ensures that the server is properly registered as a COM object. The server registers two methods that clients can invoke: **ShowCalendar**, which has an empty body but whose invocation forces the server to execute and its embedded calendar to be displayed; and **GetDate**, which returns the calendar's displayed date as the COM data type **DATE**, a subtype of **VARIANT**. In stand-alone mode, the server displays the calendar, which the user can manipulate, for example, by selecting an arbitrary year, month, or day of the month.

On the server side, wizard code is responsible for generating the idl files required for the type library, which is generated automatically whenever the application is built. Wizard code also ensures proper server registration and initialization. Our contribution consists of embedding the calendar control in the server's dialog window. We do so through VC++'s Resource Editor. The homepage documentation provides details. We then used the ClassWizard to create a data member that represents the calendar control and to expose the server methods. The wizard walked us through specification of method names, arguments, and return values. The server is clearly the simpler of the two applications to create.

The client, like the server, is a dialog-based application. The client application has two related parts. The first is the local GUI. We use the Resource Editor to create two buttons and a text box, and the ClassWizard to generate boilerplate callbacks for the two buttons. We also had the ClassWizard create a data member to represent the text box.

The client's second part is more complicated, for it involves building an interface to the server. The ClassWizard again plays a decisive role. We use this wizard to create a VC++ class from the server's type library. The wizard generates a header and an implementation file. The header is again, in effect, the programmer's documentation:

```
class IDateS : public COleDispatchDriver
{
public:
    IDateS() {}
    IDateS(LPDISPATCH pDispatch) :
            COleDispatchDriver(pDispatch) {}
    IDateS(const IDateS& dispatchSrc) :
            COleDispatchDriver(dispatchSrc) {}
// Attributes
public:
// Operations
public:
    void ShowCalendar(); //*** jk: 1st exposed method
    DATE GetDate();      //*** jk: 2nd exposed method
};
```

Because the server's type library occurs in a project called **DateS**, the wizard names the interface class **IDateS**. This class derives from **COleDispatchDriver**, which supports an **IDispatch** interface to the server. The programmer's first task is to create an object of type **IDateS**. Our object **id** happens to be an **extern** variable for convenience, but a variable of any storage class would do. Class **IDateS** lists two **public** methods, which correspond to the methods exposed and registered by the server. We now can summarize what, in general, the programmer does with this wizard-generated class:

- Creates an object of type **IDateS**. In our case, the object is **id**.

- Invokes the object's **CreateDispatch** method, passing it the server's *name*. In our case, we invoke the method with the name **dateS.Application**, which is the name under which the server is registered. A server wizard creates this name by concatenating the server's project name **dateS** with **Application**. We could use a CLSID (UUID) instead of a name to identify the server.

- Invokes the appropriate **public** methods encapsulated in the object. In our case, we invoke **id**'s **ShowCalendar** method to display the calendar and **GetDate** to retrieve the displayed date, which the user can set by manipulating the server's embedded ActiveX calendar control. We use an object of the COM data type **COleDateTime** to store the returned **DATE** type. Class **COleDateTime** has a convenient **Format** method to produce an MFC **CString** representation of a COM date. (Class **CString** is similar to the standard C++ **string**.)

## The Challenge of Reference Counting

A critical part of coding the client is to ensure that the reference counting works correctly. Recall how a server, under client control, knows when it can stop executing. The server exposes interfaces, each of which has a reference count that indicates how many clients are currently using the interface. If a server has *any* interface with a reference count greater than zero, the server must continue executing. So the server can stop executing only when the reference count for every interface is zero, thus indicating that the server no longer has clients. Mistakes in reference counts are notorious in modern desktop software and are chiefly responsible for the *Dracula applications* that refuse to die even when they no longer have actual clients. A major challenge on the client side is to ensure that the reference counting is done correctly. By the way, ATL uses operator overloading to ensure that reference counting is done correctly—and behind the scenes so that the programmer need not bother with it.

Our case is relatively simple in that the date server has a single interface and, on the client side, we create a single object **id** to represent the interface. The call

```
id.CreateDispatch( "dateS.Application" );
```

automatically increments the reference count. When **id**'s destructor is invoked, it calls the companion method **ReleaseDispatch**, which decrements the reference count, in this case to zero. However, **id** is **extern** so that it is destroyed only when the client application itself stops executing. In this case, it is unclear whether **id**'s destructor will, in fact, be executed. Our first concern is thus to ensure that **ReleaseDispatch** is invoked when the client stops executing. We therefore wrote a method

```
void CDateCDlg::checkRelease() {
   if ( dispatchExists ) {
     id.ReleaseDispatch();
     dispatchExists = false;
   }
}
```

that checks whether the interface is still active and, if so, invokes **ReleaseDispatch**. We invoke **checkRelease** from our callback for the **Get Date** button. Once the displayed date has been retrieved from the server, our client releases the interface to the server, which in turn allows the server to stop executing. Method **checkRelease** is also invoked from our client's **InitInstance** method, which occurs in the file *dateC.cpp*. Method **InitInstance** opens the client's main dialog window and exits only when the dialog window is closed through the user's having clicked the **OK** or the **Cancel** button. So, to be safe, we place a call to **checkRelease** right before **InitInstance** exits.

### EXERCISES

1. Is our application's server an in-process or out-of-process server?
2. What is a **VARIANT**?
3. The ActiveX calendar control exposes the method **GetValue**, which returns a **VARIANT**. What does the **VARIANT** represent in this case?

**4.** What is the relationship between the **VARIANT** and **DATE** data types?

**5.** On the client side, the ClassWizard generates a class from the server's type library. In our case, the class is **IDateS**. Explain why the wizard begins the class name with **I**.

**6.** How is the wizard-generated **IDateS** class used in our own code on the client side?

**7.** From what MFC class is **IDateS** derived?

**8.** Explain reference counting.

**9.** Does a call to **CreateDispatch** increment a reference count?

**10.** What is the purpose of **ReleaseDispatch**?

## C++ POSTSCRIPT

## Acronyms Used in Chapter 9

| Acronym | Meaning |
|---------|---------|
| API | Applications Programmer Interface |
| ATL | ActiveX Template Library |
| CLSID | CLaSs IDentifier |
| COM | Component Object Model |
| DCE | Distributed Computing Environment |
| DCOM | Distributed Component Object Model |
| DLL | Dynamic Link Library |
| GUI | Graphical User Interface |
| IDE | Integrated Development Environment |
| IDL | Interface Definition Language |
| MDI | Multiple Document Interface |
| MFC | Microsoft Foundation Classes |
| OLE | Object Linking and Embedding |
| RPC | Remote Procedure Call |
| SDI | Single Document Interface |
| UUID | Universally Unique IDentifier |
| VC++ | Visual C++ |
| Win32 | Windows 32-Bit Operating System |

## PROGRAMMING EXERCISES

**9.1.** Extend the document serialization application of Section 9.3 by randomly assigning a color to each object created. At present, each **CTriangle** has the *same* color; in the extension, individual **CTriangle**s could have different colors. When a document is serialized out, the colors of its component objects should be saved as well so that the objects can be serialized in with the same colors. *Hint*: Create an array of **RGB** values and randomly select an element from this array as the object's color.

**9.2.** Extend Programming Exercise 9.1 as follows:

- Add a callback to the view to handle mouse clicks on the displayed objects. If the user clicks on any displayed object, the callback is invoked.

- The callback invokes a polymorphic **Explain** method, which displays a text message about the type of figure clicked on. For instance, if a click occurs on a **CCircle**, the message gives a brief geometric explanation of a circle. The message may appear in the document's view or, even better, in a separate dialog window.

*Hint*: Any drawing that occurs in a view occurs within a device context. The **OnDraw** callback's **CDC** argument exposes methods such as **TextOut** for drawing *text* in a view. Dialog windows can embed controls such as labels, which are suitable for messages. The application's **AboutBox** dialog, accessible from the VC++ Resource Editor, illustrates the basic idea.

**9.3.** Use the AppWizard to create a *document server* application that has the same functionality as Programming Exercise 9.2. The application should be a *full server* so that it can run stand-alone or under client control. Running the server just once in stand-alone mode automatically registers it so that client applications, such as Microsoft Word, can embed documents from the server. A list of documents available for embedding can be obtained on the client side by selecting the *Insert* button from the client's toolbar. An embedded document can be edited from within the container, which automatically provides the appropriate choices under the *Edit* button on the toolbar. *Hint*: Transforming Programming Exercise 9.2 into a document server requires, in effect, one click in the AppWizard phase. The document, view, and related files can then be copied from the original application to the document server application. Further, Microsoft Word is a suitable container for any document server. Run Word and insert a document such as an Excel spreadsheet to illustrate the possibilities.

**9.4.** Write a document/view application in which the document tracks a student's academic history. The document consists of *records*, one per course taken. A record, in turn, would track such information as the course identifier, its name, the instructor, the term in which the course was taken, whether the course was required or an elective, and the grade received. The document can hold indefinitely many records. The view displays the document in an appropriate fashion. For example, if there are too many records to display at once, the view should provide scrolling or comparable support. *Hint*: The document could be a vector of **CDocument**-derived objects, each representing an academic record. Because **CDocument** falls under **CObject**, **CDocument**s have built-in serialization. Record fields could be represented as **CString**s. Although **CString**

is not derived from **CObject**, the operators **<<** and **>>** are overloaded to allow **CString**s to be written to and read from a **CArchive**.

**9.5.** Extend the COM sample application of Section 9.5 by providing the client with a third button labeled **Set Date**. When this button is pushed, the date specified as text in the client text box is displayed on the server's embedded calendar control. *Hint*: The ActiveX calendar control has *get* and *set* pairs of exposed methods. For example, the current application uses **GetValue**, which returns a **VARIANT**. The companion **SetValue** expects a **VARIANT** argument. MFC classes such as **COleDateTime** provide utility methods to convert **VARIANT**s to **CString**s and **CString**s to **VARIANT**s. Also, the calendar control has methods such as **SetYear** that expect **short** integers as arguments. So the control's displayed date could be set by separately setting the day of the month, the month, and the year.

**9.6.** Amend the COM application of Section 9.5 by making the server an *in-process* server, that is, a DLL. *Hint*: Because a DLL cannot run stand-alone, the server cannot be registered automatically simply by executing it stand-alone. However, VC++ provides tools for such registration. The main difference between the stand-alone and in-process versions of the server has to do with registration and, of course, testing.

**9.7.** Create a login server as a dialog-based, DLL application. The server's GUI consists of the standard **OK** and **Cancel** buttons together with two labeled text boxes: one for the user to enter a *user name* and the other for the user to enter a *password*. For security, the echo character for the password text box should be **\***, not the actual character typed. The login server exposes four registered methods for clients:

- **Login**. Invoking this method causes the login server to load and its GUI to be displayed.

- **Release**. Invoking this method allows the login server to unload if it has no other clients. In any case, the client that invokes this method ends the login session.

- **GetUserName**. Invoking this method retrieves the user name.

- **GetPassword**. Invoking this method retrieves the password.

The client is responsible for validating the user name and the password, presumably with a database or comparable lookup.

**9.8.** Write an MFC application that integrates Programming Exercises 9.2 and 9.7. Before the user can add geometric figures to the document of Programming Exercise 9.2, a login session is required. The login dialog should appear automatically whenever the user starts the figures application or serializes in a figures document.

**9.9.** Write a dialog-based application with a GUI that allows a system administrator to enter names and passwords for users. The names and passwords should be stored in a binary file rather than a text file. The application has a button **Test** that, when pushed, runs the login server of Programming Exercise 9.7. The **Test** button allows the system administrator to run tests on sample user names and passwords. *Hint*: MFC serialization uses **CArchive**s as a convenient way to write to and read from binary files.

**9.10.** Write a dialog-based application to which a text box, a label, and a button are added. The user enters a candidate server's name in the text box (e.g., `GeoFig.Application`). When the user pushes the button, the application looks in the registry to map the name to a CLSID, which is then displayed as the label. If the registry search fails, the label displays an appropriate error message. *Hint*: MFC has various utility classes and methods for getting registry information. Under VC++ *Help*, do a search on *registry*.

# APPENDIX

# A

# ASCII TABLE

**Table A.1** ASCII Codes

| Decimal | Hexadecimal | Octal | Standard Function |
|---------|-------------|-------|-------------------|
| 0 | 00 | 000 | NUL (Null) |
| 1 | 01 | 001 | SOH (Start of heading) |
| 2 | 02 | 002 | STX (Start of text) |
| 3 | 03 | 003 | ETX (End of text) |
| 4 | 04 | 004 | EOT (End of transmission) |
| 5 | 05 | 005 | ENQ (Enquiry) |
| 6 | 06 | 006 | ACK (Acknowledge) |
| 7 | 07 | 007 | BEL (Ring bell) |
| 8 | 08 | 010 | BS (Backspace) |
| 9 | 09 | 011 | HT (Horizontal tab) |
| 10 | 0A | 012 | LF (Line feed) |
| 11 | 0B | 013 | VT (Vertical tab) |
| 12 | 0C | 014 | FF (Form feed) |
| 13 | 0D | 015 | CR (Carriage return) |
| 14 | 0E | 016 | SO (Shift out) |
| 15 | 0F | 017 | SI (Shift in) |
| 16 | 10 | 020 | DLE (Data link escape) |
| 17 | 11 | 021 | DC1 (Device control 1) |
| 18 | 12 | 022 | DC2 (Device control 2) |
| 19 | 13 | 023 | DC3 (Device control 3) |
| 20 | 14 | 024 | DC4 (Device control 4) |
| 21 | 15 | 025 | NAK (Negative acknowledge) |
| 22 | 16 | 026 | SYN (Synchronous idle) |
| 23 | 17 | 027 | ETB (End of transmission block) |
| 24 | 18 | 030 | CAN (Cancel) |
| 25 | 19 | 031 | EM (End of medium) |

**Table A.1** ASCII Codes (Continued)

| Decimal | Hexadecimal | Octal | Standard Function |
|---|---|---|---|
| 26 | 1A | 032 | SUB (Substitute) |
| 27 | 1B | 033 | ESC (Escape) |
| 28 | 1C | 034 | FS (File separator) |
| 29 | 1D | 035 | GS (Group separator) |
| 30 | 1E | 036 | RS (Record separator) |
| 31 | 1F | 037 | US (Unit separator) |
| 32 | 20 | 040 | SP (Space) |
| 33 | 21 | 041 | ! |
| 34 | 22 | 042 | " |
| 35 | 23 | 043 | # |
| 36 | 24 | 044 | $ |
| 37 | 25 | 045 | % |
| 38 | 26 | 046 | & |
| 39 | 27 | 047 | '(Single quote) |
| 40 | 28 | 050 | ( |
| 41 | 29 | 051 | ) |
| 42 | 2A | 052 | * |
| 43 | 2B | 053 | + |
| 44 | 2C | 054 | , (Comma) |
| 45 | 2D | 055 | - (Hyphen) |
| 46 | 2E | 056 | . |
| 47 | 2F | 057 | / |
| 48 | 30 | 060 | 0 |
| 49 | 31 | 061 | 1 |
| 50 | 32 | 062 | 2 |
| 51 | 33 | 063 | 3 |
| 52 | 34 | 064 | 4 |
| 53 | 35 | 065 | 5 |
| 54 | 36 | 066 | 6 |
| 55 | 37 | 067 | 7 |
| 56 | 38 | 070 | 8 |
| 57 | 39 | 071 | 9 |
| 58 | 3A | 072 | : |
| 59 | 3B | 073 | ; |
| 60 | 3C | 074 | < |
| 61 | 3D | 075 | = |
| 62 | 3E | 076 | > |
| 63 | 3F | 077 | ? |
| 64 | 40 | 100 | @ |
| 65 | 41 | 101 | A |
| 66 | 42 | 102 | B |

**Table A.1** ASCII Codes (Continued)

| Decimal | Hexadecimal | Octal | Standard Function |
|---------|-------------|-------|-------------------|
| 67 | 43 | 103 | C |
| 68 | 44 | 104 | D |
| 69 | 45 | 105 | E |
| 70 | 46 | 106 | F |
| 71 | 47 | 107 | G |
| 72 | 48 | 110 | H |
| 73 | 49 | 111 | I |
| 74 | 4A | 112 | J |
| 75 | 4B | 113 | K |
| 76 | 4C | 114 | L |
| 77 | 4D | 115 | M |
| 78 | 4E | 116 | N |
| 79 | 4F | 117 | O |
| 80 | 50 | 120 | P |
| 81 | 51 | 121 | Q |
| 82 | 52 | 122 | R |
| 83 | 53 | 123 | S |
| 84 | 54 | 124 | T |
| 85 | 55 | 125 | U |
| 86 | 56 | 126 | V |
| 87 | 57 | 127 | W |
| 88 | 58 | 130 | X |
| 89 | 59 | 131 | Y |
| 90 | 5A | 132 | Z |
| 91 | 5B | 133 | [ |
| 92 | 5C | 134 | \ |
| 93 | 5D | 135 | ] |
| 94 | 5E | 136 | ^ |
| 95 | 5F | 137 | _ (Underscore) |
| 96 | 60 | 140 | ' (Grave accent) |
| 97 | 61 | 141 | a |
| 98 | 62 | 142 | b |
| 99 | 63 | 143 | c |
| 100 | 64 | 144 | d |
| 101 | 65 | 145 | e |
| 102 | 66 | 146 | f |
| 103 | 67 | 147 | g |
| 104 | 68 | 150 | h |
| 105 | 69 | 151 | i |
| 106 | 6A | 152 | j |
| 107 | 6B | 153 | k |

**Table A.1** ASCII Codes (Continued)

| Decimal | Hexadecimal | Octal | Standard Function |
|---------|-------------|-------|-------------------|
| 108 | 6C | 154 | l |
| 109 | 6D | 155 | m |
| 110 | 6E | 156 | n |
| 111 | 6F | 157 | o |
| 112 | 70 | 160 | p |
| 113 | 71 | 161 | q |
| 114 | 72 | 162 | r |
| 115 | 73 | 163 | s |
| 116 | 74 | 164 | t |
| 117 | 75 | 165 | u |
| 118 | 76 | 166 | v |
| 119 | 77 | 167 | w |
| 120 | 78 | 170 | x |
| 121 | 79 | 171 | y |
| 122 | 7A | 172 | z |
| 123 | 7B | 173 | { |
| 124 | 7C | 174 | \| |
| 125 | 7D | 175 | } |
| 126 | 7E | 176 | ~ |
| 127 | 7F | 177 | DEL (Delete) |

## Type and Conversion Functions

| | |
|---|---|
| `atof` | Convert string to **double** |
| `atoi` | Convert string to **int** |
| `atol` | Convert string to **long** |
| `isalnum` | Alphanumeric? |
| `isalpha` | Alphabetic character? |
| `iscntrl` | Control character? |
| `isdigit` | Decimal digit? |
| `isgraph` | Nonblank, printable character? |
| `islower` | Lowercase character? |
| `isprint` | Printable character? |
| `ispunct` | Punctuation character? |
| `isspace` | Space character? |
| `isupper` | Uppercase character? |
| `isxdigit` | Hexadecimal character? |
| `tolower` | Convert from uppercase to lowercase |
| `toupper` | Convert from lowercase to uppercase |

## Selected STL Algorithms

| | |
|---|---|
| `binary_search` | Search for a key |
| `copy` | Copy a range |
| `copy_backward` | Copy a range backwards |
| `count` | Count occurrences of a value |
| `count_if` | Count elements that satisfy a predicate |
| `equal` | Test whether ranges are the same |
| `equal_range` | Find insertion positions that maintain sorted order |
| `fill` | Fill a range with a value |
| `fill_n` | Fill first $n$ positions with a value |
| `find` | Find a key |
| `find_if` | Find a key that satisfies a predicate |
| `for_each` | Invoke a function on each element |
| `generate` | Generate values through function calls |
| `generate_n` | Generate values through $n$ function calls |
| `inplace_merge` | Merge consecutive ranges |
| `lower_bound` | Find lowest insertion position that maintains sorted order |
| `merge` | Merge sorted ranges |
| `mismatch` | Find mismatched elements in two ranges |
| `next_permutation` | Generate successor permutation |
| `nth_element` | Place the $n$th smallest element in its sorted position |

## Selected STL Algorithms cont.

| | |
|---|---|
| `partial_sort` | Sort a subrange |
| `partial_sort_copy` | Copying version of `partial_sort` |
| `partition` | Partition a range |
| `prev_permutation` | Generate predecessor permutation |
| `random_shuffle` | Randomly reorder a range |
| `remove` | Remove a specified value |
| `remove_copy` | Copying version of `remove` |
| `remove_copy_if` | Copying version of `remove_if` |
| `remove_if` | Remove elements that satisfy a predicate |
| `replace` | Replace a specified value with a new value |
| `replace_copy` | Copying version of replace |
| `replace_copy_if` | Copying version of `replace_if` |
| `replace_if` | Replace elements that satisfy a predicate |
| `reverse` | Reverse a range |
| `reverse_copy` | Copying version of `reverse` |
| `search` | Search for a specified subrange |
| `sort` | Sort a range |
| `stable_partition` | Stable version of `partition` |
| `stable_sort` | Stable version of `sort` |
| `swap` | Swap two values |
| `swap_ranges` | Swap values pairwise in two ranges |
| `transform` | Transform a range by invoking a function on each element |
| `unique` | Remove consecutive duplicates |
| `unique_copy` | Copying version of `unique` |
| `upper_bound` | Find highest insertion position that maintains sorted order |

## String Functions

| | |
|---|---|
| `c_str` | Convert to C-style string |
| `erase` | Remove substring |
| `find` | Find first substring from left |
| `find_first_of` | Find first character in a given set |
| `find_first_not_of` | Find first character not in a given set |
| `insert` | Insert string |
| `length` | Return length of string |
| `replace` | Replace a substring |
| `rfind` | Find first substring from right |
| `substr` | Return substring |
| `swap` | Swap strings |

| Miscellaneous Functions | |
|---|---|
| **abort** | Cause abnormal program termination |
| **bsearch** | Binary search |
| **difftime** | Compute difference between times |
| **exit** | Terminate program |
| **qsort** | Quicksort |
| **set_terminate** | Specify function for **terminate** to call |
| **set_unexpected** | Specify function for **unexpected** to call |
| **system** | Execute a command |
| **terminate** | End because of exception handling error |
| **time** | Find time |
| **unexpected** | Called when illegal **throw** specification |

We now list the functions and class methods alphabetically. Class methods are designated as such and the class to which each belongs is specified. Each description consists of the file to include, the function's declaration, and a few sentences that describe what the function does. All character codes are given in ASCII.

## abort

```
#include <cstdlib>
void abort();
```

Causes abnormal program termination. The status "unsuccessful termination" is returned to the invoking process.

## abs

```
#include <cstdlib>
int abs( int x );
long abs( long x );
float abs( float x );
double abs( double x );
long double abs( long double x );
```

Returns the absolute value of **x**.

## acos

```
#include <cmath>
float acos( float real );
double acos( double real );
long double acos( long double real );
```

Returns the arccosine (in radians) of **real**. The value returned is between 0 and $\pi$.

## asin

```
#include <cmath>
float asin( float real );
double asin( double real );
long double asin( long double real );
```

Returns the arcsine (in radians) of **real**. The value returned is between $-\frac{\pi}{2}$ and $\frac{\pi}{2}$.

## atan

```
#include <cmath>
float atan( float real );
double atan( double real );
long double atan( long double real );
```

Returns the arctangent (in radians) of **real**. The value returned is between $-\frac{\pi}{2}$ and $\frac{\pi}{2}$.

## atof

```
#include <cstdlib>
double atof( const char* s );
```

Converts a real number, represented as a null-terminated array of **char**, to **double**. It returns the converted number; **s** consists of optional tabs and spaces followed by an optional sign followed by digits followed by an optional decimal point followed by an optional exponent. The optional exponent is **e** or **E** followed by an integer. See also **atoi** and **atol**.

## atoi

```
#include <cstdlib>
int atoi( const char* s );
```

Converts an integer, represented as a null-terminated array of **char**, to **int**. It returns the converted number; **s** consists of optional tabs and spaces followed by an optional sign followed by digits. See also **atof** and **atol**.

## atol

```
#include <cstdlib>
long atol( const char* s );
```

Converts an integer, represented as a null-terminated array of **char**, to **long**. It returns the converted number; **s** consists of optional tabs and spaces followed by an optional sign followed by digits. See also **atof** and **atoi**.

## bad

```
#include <iostream>
bool basic_ios::bad() const;
```

Returns **true** if **badbit** is set; otherwise, returns **false**.

## binary_search

```
#include <algorithm>
template< class ForwardIt, class T >
bool binary_search( ForwardIt first, ForwardIt last,
                    const T& value );
template< class ForwardIt, class T, class Compare >
bool binary_search( ForwardIt first, ForwardIt last,
                    const T& value, Compare comp );
```

The STL algorithm **binary_search** searches the range **[first, last)**, returning **true**, if **value** is found, and **false**, if **value** is not found. The range must be sorted according to **<** in the first version and the comparison function in the second version. The algorithm's time complexity is logarithmic.

## bsearch

```
#include <cstdlib>
void* bsearch( const void* key,
               void* start,
               size_t no_elts,
               size_t size_elt,
               int ( *cmp ) ( const void*, const void* ) );
```

Searches for **\*key** in a sorted array of size **no_elts** whose initial cell is at address **start**. The parameter **size_elt** is the size in bytes of one cell of the array. The parameter **cmp** is a pointer to a function that compares **\*key** and an element in the array and returns an integer to signal the result of the comparison. The first argument to the comparison function **\*cmp** is **key** and the second is a pointer to an item in the array. The value of the expression **\*cmp( \*first, \*second )** is negative if **\*first** precedes **\*second** in the sorted order; **\*cmp( \*first, \*second )** is zero if **\*first** is equal to **\*second**; and **\*cmp( \*first, \*second )** is positive if **\*first** follows **\*second** in the sorted order. If **\*key** is in the array, **bsearch** returns a pointer to a cell containing **\*key**; if **\*key** is not in the array, **bsearch** returns zero.

## ceil

```
#include <cmath>
float ceil( float real );
double ceil( double real );
long double ceil( long double real );
```

Returns the least integer (as a floating-point value) greater than or equal to **real**.

## clear

```
#include <iostream>
void basic_ios::clear( iostate st = goodbit );
```

Changes stream state to **st**.

## close

```
#include <fstream>
void basic_ifstream::close();
void basic_ofstream::close();
void basic_fstream::close();
```

Closes the file, if any, attached to the object.

## copy

```
#include <algorithm>
template< class InputIt, class OutputIt >
OutputIt copy( InputIt first1, InputIt last1, OutputIt first2 );
```

The STL algorithm **copy** copies **[first1, last1)** to **[first2, last2)**, where

```
    last2 == first2 + (last1 - first1)
```

The copy proceeds from **first1** through **last1 - 1** and returns **last2**. The algorithm's time complexity is linear. See also **copy_backward**.

## copy_backward

```
#include <algorithm>
template< class BidirectionalIt1, class BirdirectionalIt2 >
BidirectionalIt2 copy_backward( BidirectionalIt1 first1,
                                BidirectionalIt1 last1,
                                BidirectionalIt2 last2 );
```

The STL algorithm **copy_backward** copies **[first1, last1)** to **[first2, last2)** where

    first2 == last2 - (last1 - first1)

in reverse order, that is, from **last1 - 1** through **first1**. The algorithm returns **last2**. The algorithm's time complexity is linear.  See also **copy**.

## cos

```
#include <cmath>
float cos( float real );
double cos( double real );
long double cos( long double real );
```

Returns the cosine of **real**; **real** must be in radians.

## cosh

```
#include <cmath>
float cosh( float real );
double cosh( double real );
long double cosh( long double real );
```

Returns the hyperbolic cosine of **real**.

## count

```
#include <algorithm>
template< class InputIt, class T >
iterator_traits< InputIt >::difference_type
   count( InputIt first, InputIt last, const T& value );
```

The STL algorithm **count** returns the number of elements in the range **[first, last)** that equal **value**.  Comparisons are made with **==**.  The algorithm's time complexity is linear.  See also **count_if**.

## count_if

```
#include <algorithm>
template< class InputIt, class Pred >
iterator_traits< InputIt >::difference_type
   count_if( InputIt first, InputIt last, Pred p );
```

The STL algorithm **count_if** returns the number of elements in the range [**first, last**) that satisfy the predicate **p**. The algorithm's time complexity is linear. See also **count**.

## c_str

```
#include <string>
const charT* basic_string::c_str() const;
```

Returns a pointer to the first element in a null-terminated array of **charT** that is a copy of the string.

## difftime

```
#include <ctime>
double difftime( time_t end, time_t begin );
```

Returns the difference (**end** − **begin**), in seconds, between the times **end** and **begin**. See also **time**.

## eof

```
#include <iostream>
bool basic_ios::eof() const;
```

Returns **true** if a read was attempted past the end of the file; otherwise, returns **false**.

## equal

```
#include <algorithm>
template< class InputIt1, class InputIt2 >
bool equal( InputIt1 first1, InputIt1 last1, InputIt2 first2 );
template< class InputIt1, class InputIt2,
          class BinaryPred >
bool equal( InputIt1 first1, InputIt1 last1, InputIt2 first2,
            BinaryPred bp );
```

The STL algorithm **equal** tests whether the range **[first1, last1)** contains the same elements in the same order as the range that begins at **first2**. If so, **equal** returns **true**; if not, it returns **false**. In the first version, comparisons are made with **==**. In the second version, comparisons are made with the binary predicate **bp**. The algorithm's time complexity is linear.

## equal_range

```
#include <algorithm>
template< class ForwardIt, class T >
pair< ForwardIt, ForwardIt >
         equal_range( ForwardIt first, ForwardIt last,
                       const T& value );
template< class ForwardIt, class T, class Compare >
pair< ForwardIt, ForwardIt >
         equal_range( ForwardIt first, ForwardIt last,
                       const T& value, Compare comp );
```

The **equal_range** algorithm returns, as a pair, the iterators that **lower_bound** and **upper_bound**, respectively, would return. The range must be sorted according to **<** in the first version and the comparison function in the second version. The algorithm's time complexity is logarithmic. See also **lower_bound** and **upper_bound**.

## erase

```
#include <string>
basic_string<charT,traits,Allocator>&
    basic_string::erase( size_type p = 0, size_type n = max );
```

(**max** is the maximum value of type **size_type**.) **erase** throws an **out_of_range** exception if **p** > **length()**. If no exception is thrown, **erase** computes *len* as the minimum of **n** and **length()** − **p**. It then deletes the substring of length *len* beginning at index **p**. It returns **\*this**.

## exit

```
#include <cstdlib>
void exit( int status_value );
```

Terminates the program and sends the value **status_value** to the invoking process (operating system, another program, etc.). The constants **EXIT_SUCCESS** and **EXIT_FAILURE**, defined in *cstdlib*, may be used as arguments to **exit** to indicate successful or unsuccessful termination. Zero also indicates successful termination. The function **exit** flushes all buffers and closes all open files.

# exp

```
#include <cmath>
float exp( float real );
double exp( double real );
long double exp( long double real );
```

Returns $e^{\text{real}}$, where $e$ (2.71828...) is the base of the natural logarithm. See also **pow**.

# fail

```
#include <iostream>
bool basic_ios::fail() const;
```

Returns **true** if **failbit** or **badbit** is set; otherwise, returns **false**.

# fill (basic_ios)

```
#include <iostream>
char_type basic_ios::fill() const;
char_type basic_ios::fill( char_type fill_char );
```

The first version returns the current fill character. The second version changes the fill character to **fill_char** and returns the old fill character.

# fill (STL)

```
#include <algorithm>
template< class ForwardIt, class T >
void fill( ForwardIt first, ForwardIt last, const T& value );
```

The STL algorithm **fill** fills the range **[first, last)** with **value**. The algorithm's time complexity is linear. See also **fill_n**.

# fill_n

```
#include <algorithm>
template< class OutputIt, class Size, class T >
void fill_n( OutputIt first, Size n, const T& value );
```

The STL algorithm **fill_n** fills the range **[first, first + n)** with **value**. The algorithm's time complexity is linear. See also **fill**.

# find (STL)

```
#include <algorithm>
template< class InputIt, class T >
InputIt find( InputIt first, InputIt last, const T& value );
```

The STL algorithm **find** traverses the range **[first, last)** and returns the first iterator **it** such that **\*it == value**. The iterator **last** is returned if the search fails. The algorithm's time complexity is linear. See also **find_if**.

# find (string)

```
#include <string>
size_type
    basic_string::find(
        const basic_string<charT,traits,Allocator>& s,
        size_type p = 0 ) const;
size_type
    basic_string::find( const charT* s,
        size_type p, size_type n ) const;
size_type
    basic_string::find( const charT* s, size_type p = 0 ) const;
size_type
    basic_string::find( charT c, size_type p = 0 ) const;
```

In the first version, if **s** is a substring of **\*this** at index **p** or higher, **find** returns the smallest index $\geq$ **p** where **s** begins. If **s** is not found, **find** returns **max**, the maximum value of type **size_type**.

The second version returns

```
find( basic_string<charT,traits,Allocator>( s, n ), p )
```

The third version returns

```
find( basic_string<charT,traits,Allocator>( s ), p )
```

The fourth version returns

```
find( basic_string<charT,traits,Allocator>( 1, c ), p )
```

# find_first_of

```
#include <string>
size_type
    basic_string::find_first_of(
        const basic_string<charT,traits,Allocator>& s,
        size_type p = 0 ) const;
size_type
    basic_string::find_first_of( const charT* s,
                                 size_type p,
                                 size_type n ) const;
size_type
    basic_string::find_first_of( const charT* s,
                                 size_type p = 0 ) const;
size_type
    basic_string::find_first_of( charT c,
                                 size_type p = 0 ) const;
```

The first version returns the index of the first character in **\*this** that is also in **s**; if unsuccessful, it returns **max**, the maximum value of type **size_type**.

The second version returns

```
find_first_of( basic_string<charT,traits,Allocator>( s, n ), p )
```

The third version returns

```
find_first_of( basic_string<charT,traits,Allocator>( s ), p )
```

The fourth version returns

```
find_first_of( basic_string<charT,traits,Allocator>( 1, c ), p )
```

# find_first_not_of

```
#include <string>
size_type
    basic_string::find_first_not_of(
        const basic_string<charT,traits,Allocator>& s,
        size_type p = 0 ) const;
size_type
    basic_string::find_first_not_of( const charT* s,
                                     size_type p,
                                     size_type n ) const;
size_type
    basic_string::find_first_not_of( const charT* s,
                                     size_type p = 0 ) const;
size_type
    basic_string::find_first_not_of( charT c,
                                     size_type p = 0 ) const;
```

The first version returns the index of the first character in **\*this** that is not in **s**; if unsuccessful, it returns **max**, the maximum value of type **size_type**.

The second version returns

```
find_first_not_of( basic_string<charT,traits,Allocator>( s, n ), p )
```

The third version returns

```
find_first_not_of( basic_string<charT,traits,Allocator>( s ), p )
```

The fourth version returns

```
find_first_not_of( basic_string<charT,traits,Allocator>( 1, c ), p )
```

# find_if

```
#include <algorithm>
template< class InputIt, class Pred >
InputIt find_if( InputIt first, InputIt last, Pred p );
```

The STL algorithm **find_if** returns the first iterator **it** such that **p( \*it )** is true. The iterator **last** is returned if the search fails. The algorithm's time complexity is linear. See also **find**.

# flags

```
#include <iostream>
fmtflags ios_base::flags() const;
fmtflags ios_base::flags( fmtflags new_flags );
```

The first version returns the current format flags. The second version changes the format flags to **new_flags** and returns the old flags.

# floor

```
#include <cmath>
float floor( float real );
double floor( double real );
long double floor( long double real );
```

Returns the greatest integer (as a floating-point value) less than or equal to **real**.

# flush

```
#include <iostream>
basic_ostream& basic_ostream::flush();
```

Flushes the output buffer and returns the updated stream.

## for_each

```
#include <algorithm>
template< class InputIt, class Func >
Func for_each( InputIt first, InputIt last, Func f );
```

The STL algorithm **for_each** applies the function **f** exactly once to each element in the range [**first, last**) by dereferencing each iterator in this range. Function **f** should not alter the elements accessed through the dereferenced iterators. Any value that **f** returns is ignored and **for_each** returns **f**. The algorithm's time complexity is linear.

## gcount

```
#include <iostream>
streamsize basic_istream::gcount() const;
```

Returns the number of characters last read.

## generate

```
#include <algorithm>
template< class ForwardIt, class Generator >
void generate( ForwardIt first, ForwardIt last, Generator g );
```

The STL algorithm **generate** fills the range [**first, last**) with the values generated by **last - first** invocations of the function or function object **g**. The algorithm's time complexity is linear. See also **generate_n**.

## generate_n

```
#include <algorithm>
template< class OutputIt, class Size, class Generator >
void generate_n( OutputIt first, Size n, Generator g );
```

The STL algorithm **generate_n** algorithm fills the range of size **n**, beginning at **first**, with the values generated by **n** successive invocations of **g**. The algorithm's time complexity is linear. See also **generate**.

## get

```
#include <iostream>
basic_istream<charT,traits>&
    basic_istream::get( char_type* buff,
                        streamsize n );
basic_istream<charT,traits>&
    basic_istream::get( char_type* buff,
                        streamsize n,
                        char_type stop );
basic_istream<charT,traits>&
    basic_istream::get( char_type& c );
```

In the first version, characters are read from the stream into the array **buff** until a newline is encountered, until end-of-file, or until **n** - **1** characters have been read into **buff**, whichever happens first. The newline character is *not* placed in the array **buff**, nor is it removed from the stream. The method **get** adds a null terminator **'\0'**.

The second version is like the first, except that newline is replaced by **stop**.

In the third version, the next character, white space or not, is read into **c**.

In all versions, **get** returns the updated stream.

## getline

```
#include <string>
basic_istream<charT,traits>&
    getline( basic_istream<charT,traits>& in,
             basic_string<charT,traits,Allocator>& str,
             charT stop );
basic_istream<charT,traits>&
    getline( basic_istream<charT,traits>& in,
             basic_string<charT,traits,Allocator>& str );
```

In the first version, characters are read from the stream **in** into the **string str** until end-of-file, until **stop** is encountered, or until **str**'s capacity is reached, whichever happens first. The character **stop** is *not* placed into **str**, but it is removed from the stream. If no characters are read, **failbit** is set. The updated stream is returned.

The second version is like the first except that **stop** is replaced by newline.

## good

```
#include <iostream>
bool basic_ios::good() const;
```

Returns **true** if the stream state is zero; otherwise, returns **false**.

## ignore

```
#include <iostream>
istream<charT,traits>&
    basic_istream::ignore( int count = 1,
                           int_type stop = traits::eof() );
```

Removes **count** characters from the stream, all characters from the stream up to **stop**, or all characters until end-of-file, whichever happens first. The removed characters are not stored, but discarded. It returns the updated stream.

## inplace_merge

```
#include <algorithm>
template< class BidirectionalIt >
void inplace_merge( BidirectionalIt first,
                    BidirectionalIt mid,
                    BidirectionalIt last );
template< class BidirectionalIt, class Compare >
void inplace_merge( BidirectionalIt first,
                    BidirectionalIt mid,
                    BidirectionalIt last,
                    Compare comp );
```

The STL algorithm **inplace_merge** merges in place the two sorted consecutive ranges **[first, mid)** and **[mid, last)**. The merge is stable in that, for equivalent elements in the two ranges, the elements in the first range always precede the elements in the second range. The first version of **inplace_merge** uses **<** for element comparisons and the second version uses a **comp**arison function. With sufficient memory, the algorithm's time complexity is linear. See also **merge**.

## insert

```
#include <string>
basic_string<charT,traits,Allocator>&
   basic_string::insert(
      size_type p1,
      const basic_string<charT,traits,Allocator>& s,
      size_type p2,
      size_type n );
basic_string<charT,traits,Allocator>&
   basic_string::insert(
      size_type p,
      const basic_string<charT,traits,Allocator>& s );
```

```
basic_string<charT,traits,Allocator>&
   basic_string::insert( size_type p,
                         const charT* s,
                         size_type n );
basic_string<charT,traits,Allocator>&
   basic_string::insert( size_type p, const charT* s );
basic_string<charT,traits,Allocator>&
   basic_string::insert( size_type p, size_type n, charT c );
```

The first version throws an **out_of_range** exception if **p1** > **length()** or **p2** > **s.length()**. It computes *len* as the minimum of **n** and **s.length()** − **p2** and throws an exception of type **length_error** if **length()** ≥ **max** − *len*, where **max** is the maximum value of type **size_type**. If no exception is thrown, it inserts the *len* characters beginning at index **p2** in **s** into **\*this** beginning at index **p1**. It returns **\*this**.

The second version returns

```
insert( p, s, 0, max )
```

The third version returns

```
insert( p, basic_string<charT,traits,Allocator>( s, n ) )
```

The fourth version returns

```
insert( p, basic_string<charT,traits,Allocator>( s ) )
```

The fifth version returns

```
insert( p, basic_string<charT,traits,Allocator>( n, c ) )
```

## isalnum

```
#include <cctype>
int isalnum( int character );
```

Returns a nonzero integer if **character** is an alphanumeric character (**'a'** through **'z'**, **'A'** through **'Z'**, or **'0'** through **'9'**); otherwise, it returns 0.

## isalpha

```
#include <cctype>
int isalpha( int character );
```

Returns a nonzero integer if **character** is an alphabetic character (**'a'** through **'z'** or **'A'** through **'Z'**); otherwise, it returns 0.

# iscntrl

```
#include <cctype>
int iscntrl( int character );
```

Returns a nonzero integer if **character** is a control character (integer value decimal 127 or less than decimal 32); otherwise, it returns 0.

# isdigit

```
#include <cctype>
int isdigit( int character );
```

Returns a nonzero integer if **character** is a decimal digit (`'0'` through `'9'`); otherwise, it returns 0.

# isgraph

```
#include <cctype>
int isgraph( int character );
```

Returns a nonzero integer if **character** is a nonblank printing character (integer value greater than or equal to decimal 33 and less than or equal to decimal 126); otherwise, it returns 0.

# islower

```
#include <cctype>
int islower( int character );
```

Returns a nonzero integer if **character** is a lowercase character (`'a'` through `'z'`); otherwise, it returns 0.

# isprint

```
#include <cctype>
int isprint( int character );
```

Returns a nonzero integer if **character** is a printable character (integer value greater than or equal to decimal 32 and less than or equal to decimal 126); otherwise, it returns 0.

## ispunct

```
#include <cctype>
int ispunct( int character );
```

Returns a nonzero integer if **character** is a punctuation character (integer value decimal 127 or integer value less than decimal 33); otherwise, it returns 0.

## isspace

```
#include <cctype>
int isspace( int character );
```

Returns a nonzero integer if **character** is a space character (space, tab, carriage return, form feed, vertical tab, or newline—decimal 32 or greater than decimal 8 and less than decimal 14); otherwise, it returns 0.

## isupper

```
#include <cctype>
int isupper( int character );
```

Returns a nonzero integer if **character** is an uppercase character (**'A'** through **'Z'**); otherwise, it returns 0.

## isxdigit

```
#include <cctype>
int isxdigit( int character );
```

Returns a nonzero integer if **character** is a hexadecimal digit (**'0'** through **'9'**, **'a'** through **'f'**, or **'A'** through **'F'**); otherwise, it returns 0.

## length

```
#include <string>
size_type basic_string::length() const;
```

Returns the length of the string.

## log

```
#include <cmath>
float log( float real );
double log( double real );
long double log( long double real );
```

Returns the natural logarithm (log to the base *e*) of **real**.

## log10

```
#include <cmath>
float log10( float real );
double log10( double real );
long double log10( long double real );
```

Returns the logarithm to the base 10 of **real**.

## lower_bound

```
#include <algorithm>
template< class ForwardIt, class T >
ForwardIt lower_bound( ForwardIt first, ForwardIt last,
                       const T& value );
template< class ForwardIt, class T, class Compare >
ForwardIt lower_bound( ForwardIt first, ForwardIt last,
                       const T& value, Compare comp );
```

The STL algorithm **lower_bound** returns an iterator pointing to the *first* position in the range **[first, last)** into which **value** may be inserted while maintaining sorted order. The range must be sorted according to **<** in the first version and the **comp**arison function in the second version. The algorithm's time complexity is logarithmic. See also **upper_bound** and **equal_range**.

## merge

```
#include <algorithm>
template< class InputIt1, class InputIt2, class OutputIt >
OutputIt merge( InputIt1 first1, InputIt1 last1,
                InputIt2 first2, InputIt2 last2,
                OutputIt result );
template< class InputIt1, class InputIt2, class OutputIt,
          class Compare >
OutputIt merge( InputIt1 first1, InputIt1 last1,
                InputIt2 first2, InputIt2 last2,
                OutputIt result, Compare comp );
```

The STL algorithm **merge** merges two sorted ranges **[first1, last1)** and **[first2, last2)** into the range **[result, result + n)**, where **n** is the total number of elements in the two ranges to be merged. The merge is stable in that, for equivalent elements in the two ranges, the elements in the first range always precede the elements in the second range. The algorithm returns **result + n**. The first version of **merge** uses **<** for element comparisons and the second version uses a **comp**arison function. With sufficient memory, the algorithm's time complexity is linear. See also **inplace_merge**.

## mismatch

```
#include <algorithm>
template< class InputIt1, InputIt2 >
pair< InputIt1, InputIt2 >
   mismatch( InputIt1 first1, InputIt1 last1, InputIt2 first2 );
template< class InputIt1, InputIt2, class BinaryPred >
pair< InputIt1, InputIt2 >
   mismatch( InputIt1 first1, InputIt1 last1,
             InputIt2 first2, BinaryPred bp );
```

The STL algorithm **mismatch** compares corresponding pairs of elements from two ranges and returns the first mismatched pair. In the first version, **==** is used for comparisons. In the second version, a binary predicate is used for comparisons. The algorithm's time complexity is linear.

## next_permutation

```
#include <algorithm>
template< class BidirectionalIt >
bool next_permutation( BidirectionalIt first,
                       BidirectionalIt last );
template< class BidirectionalIt, class Compare >
bool next_permutation( BidirectionalIt first,
                       BidirectionalIt last,
                       Compare comp );
```

The STL algorithm **next_permutation** produces a distinct permutation of a sequence. For a sequence of $n$ elements, $n!$ successive applications of **next_permutation** produce all permutations of the $n$ elements. A strict weak ordering of elements, given by **<** or a **comp**arison function, is required. Under this ordering, the first permutation is the one in which all elements are in ascending order and the last permutation is the one in which all elements are in descending order. If **next_permutation** can permute a sequence into its successor in the lexicographical ordering of permutations, the algorithm returns **true**; otherwise, **next_permutation** transforms the sequence into the first permutation and returns **false**. The algorithm's time complexity is linear. See also **prev_permutation**.

## nth_element

```
#include <algorithm>
template< class RandomAccessIt >
void nth_element( RandomAccessIt first,
                  RandomAccessIt pos,
                  RandomAccessIt last );
template< class RandomAccessIt, class Compare >
void nth_element( RandomAccessIt first,
                  RandomAccessIt pos,
                  RandomAccessIt last,
                  Compare comp );
```

The STL algorithm **nth_element** places an element at position **pos** so that it is in the position it would occupy if the entire range were sorted. Furthermore, any element to the left of position **pos** is less than or equal to any element to the right of position **pos**. In the first version of the algorithm, < is used for element comparisons; in the second version, **comp** is used for element comparisons. The algorithm's time complexity is linear in the average case.

## open

```
#include <fstream>
void basic_ofstream::open( const char* filename,
        ios_base::openmode mode
        = ios_base::out | ios_base::trunc );
void basic_ifstream::open( const char* filename,
        ios_base::openmode mode
        = ios_base::in );
void basic_fstream::open( const char* filename,
        ios_base::openmode mode
        = ios_base::in | ios_base::out );
```

Opens the file **filename** in mode **mode** and associates it with an already existing object.

## partial_sort

```
#include <algorithm>
template< class RandomAccessIt >
void partial_sort( RandomAccessIt first, RandomAccessIt mid,
                   RandomAccessIt last );
template< class RandomAccessIt, class Compare >
void partial_sort( RandomAccessIt first, RandomAccessIt mid,
                   RandomAccessIt last, Compare comp );
```

If $k$ is **mid - first**, the STL algorithm **partial_sort** places in **[first, mid)** the $k$ elements in sorted order that would appear there if the entire range **[first, last)** were sorted. The **partial_sort** algorithm has copying versions that do not modify the original sequence (see **partial_sort_copy**). The first version of **partial_sort** uses **<** to compare elements, and the second version uses a **comp**arison predicate. The algorithm's time complexity is $n \log k$ in the average case, where $n$ is **last - first** and $k$ is **mid - first**. See also **sort** and **stable_sort**.

# partial_sort_copy

```
#include <algorithm>
template< class InputIt, class RandomAccessIt >
RandomAccessIt partial_sort_copy( InputIt first, InputIt last,
                                  RandomAccessIt rFirst,
                                  RandomAccessIt rLast );
template< class InputIt, class RandomAccessIt, class Compare >
RandomAccessIt partial_sort_copy( InputIt first, InputIt last,
                                  RandomAccessIt rFirst,
                                  RandomAccessIt rLast,
                                  Compare comp );
```

Let $k$ = **first - last** and $m$ = **rLast - rFirst**. If $m < k$, the STL algorithm **partial_sort_copy** places the elements in sorted order that would appear in **[first, first + m)** if **[first, last)** were sorted. In this case, **rLast** is returned. If $m \geq k$, the algorithm puts the elements from **[first, last)** into **[rFirst, rLast)** in sorted order. In this case, **rFirst** + $k$ is returned. The first version uses **<** to compare elements, and the second version uses a **comp**arison predicate. The algorithm's time complexity is $k \log n$, where $n = \min\{k, m\}$. See also **partial_sort**, **sort**, and **stable_sort**.

# partition

```
#include <algorithm>
template< class BidirectionalIt, class Pred >
BidirectionalIt partition( BidirectionalIt first,
                           BidirectionalIt last,
                           Pred p );
```

The STL algorithm **partition** places elements in the range **[first, last)** that satisfy predicate **p** before elements in this range that do not satisfy **p**. The algorithm returns an iterator **it** such that elements in the range **[first, it)** satisfy **p** but elements in the range **[it, last)** do not satisfy **p**. The **partition** algorithm is not stable; that is, it need not preserve relative order among elements. The algorithm's time complexity is linear. See also **stable_partition**.

## peek

```
#include <iostream>
int_type basic_istream::peek();
```

Returns, but does not remove, the next character from the stream. If no characters remain to be read, it returns end-of-file.

## pow

```
#include <cmath>
float pow( float real1, float real2 );
float pow( float real1, int real2 );
double pow( double real1, double real2 );
double pow( double real1, int real2 );
long double pow( long double real1, long double real2 );
long double pow( long double real1, int real2 );
```

Returns $real1^{real2}$. An error occurs if **real1** is negative and **real2** is not an integer. See also **exp**.

## precision

```
#include <iostream>
streamsize ios_base::precision() const;
streamsize ios_base::precision( streamsize new_prec );
```

The first version returns the current precision. The second version changes the precision to **new_prec** and returns the old precision.

## prev_permutation

```
#include <algorithm>
template< class BidirectionalIt >
bool prev_permutation( BidirectionalIt first,
                       BidirectionalIt last );
template< class BidirectionalIt, class Compare >
bool prev_permutation( BidirectionalIt first,
                       BidirectionalIt last,
                       Compare comp );
```

The STL algorithm **prev_permutation** produces a distinct permutation of a sequence. For a sequence of *n* elements, *n*! successive applications of **prev_permutation** produce all permutations of the *n* elements. A strict weak ordering of elements, given by **<** or a comparison function, is required. Under this ordering, the first permutation is the one in which all elements are in ascending order and the last permutation is the one in which all elements are in descending order. If **prev_permutation** can permute a sequence into its predecessor in the lexicographical ordering of permutations, the algorithm returns **true**; otherwise, **prev_permutation** transforms the sequence into the last permutation and returns **false**. The algorithm's time complexity is linear. See also **next_permutation**.

## put

```
#include <iostream>
basic_ostream<charT,traits>& basic_ostream::put( char_type c );
```

Writes **c** to the output stream and returns the updated stream.

## putback

```
#include <iostream>
basic_istream<charT,traits>&
    basic_istream::putback( char_type c );
```

Puts the character **c** back into the stream and returns the updated stream.

## qsort

```
#include <cstdlib>
void qsort( void* start, size_t no_elts, size_t size_elt,
            int ( *cmp ) ( const void*, const void* ) );
```

Sorts an array of size **no_elts** whose initial cell is at address **start**. The parameter **size_elt** is the **sizeof** one cell. The parameter **cmp** is a pointer to a function that compares two elements whose data type is the same as that of the array and returns an integer to signal the result of the comparison. The arguments to the comparison function **\*cmp** are pointers to the two items to be compared. The value of the expression **\*cmp( \*first, \*second )** is negative if **\*first** precedes **\*second** in the sorted order; **\*cmp( \*first, \*second )** is zero if **\*first** is equal to **\*second**; and **\*cmp( \*first, \*second )** is positive if **\*first** follows **\*second** in the sorted order.

## rand

```
#include <cstdlib>
int rand();
```

Returns a pseudorandom integer in the range 0 to **RAND_MAX** (a constant defined in *cstdlib*). See also **srand**.

## random_shuffle

```
#include <algorithm>
template< class RandomAccessIt >
void random_shuffle( RandomAccessIt first, RandomAccessIt last );
template< class RandomAccessIt, class RandomNumberGen >
void random_shuffle( RandomAccessIt first, RandomAccessIt last,
                     RandomNumberGen& g );
```

The STL algorithm **random_shuffle** randomly reorders the elements in the range **[first, last)** by using a function such as **rand** that generates pseudorandom numbers. The permutations produced by **random_shuffle** are approximately uniformly distributed. The second version takes a particular random number-generating function **g**. The algorithm's time complexity is linear.

## rdbuf

```
#include <iostream>
basic_streambuf<charT,traits>* basic_ios::rdbuf() const;
basic_streambuf<charT,traits>*
    basic_ios::rdbuf( basic_streambuf<charT,traits>* buff ) const;
```

The first version returns a pointer to the **basic_streambuf** buffer object associated with the stream. The second version sets the internal buffer pointer to the value passed, calls **clear()**, and returns the previous pointer's value.

## rdstate

```
#include <iostream>
iostate basic_ios::rdstate() const;
```

Returns the stream state.

## read

```
#include <iostream>
basic_istream<charT,traits>&
    basic_istream::read( char_type* buff, streamsize n );
```

Reads **n** characters into **buff** and returns the updated stream.

## remove

```
#include <algorithm>
template< class ForwardIt, class T >
ForwardIt remove( ForwardIt first, ForwardIt last,
                  const T& value );
```

The STL algorithm **remove** removes from the range **[first, last)** every element equal to **value** and returns the beyond-the-end location of the resulting sequence, that is, the sequence with all occurrences of **value** removed.  The algorithm is *stable*; that is, any elements that remain after the removals are in the same relative order as before the removals.  The algorithm's time complexity is linear.  See also **remove_if**, **remove_copy**, and **remove_copy_if**.

## remove_copy

```
#include <algorithm>
template< class InputIt, class OutputIt, class T >
OutputIt remove_copy( InputIt first, InputIt last,
                      OutputIt result, const T& value );
```

The STL algorithm **remove_copy** copies the range **[first, last)**, with every element equal to **value** removed, to **result**.  The algorithm returns the beyond-the-end location of the **result**ing sequence to which the elements are copied. The algorithm is *stable*; that is, any elements that remain after the removals are in the same relative order as before the removals.  The algorithm's time complexity is linear.  See also **remove**, **remove_if**, and **remove_copy_if**.

## remove_copy_if

```
#include <algorithm>
template< class InputIt, class OutputIt, class Pred >
OutputIt remove_copy_if( InputIt first, InputIt last,
                         OutputIt result, Pred p );
```

The STL algorithm **remove_copy_if** copies the range **[first, last)**, with every element that satisfies **p** removed, to **result**.  The algorithm returns the beyond-the-end location of the **result**ing sequence to which the elements are copied.  The algorithm is *stable*; that is, any elements that remain after the removals are in the same relative order as before the removals. The algorithm's time complexity is linear.  See also **remove**, **remove_if**, and **remove_copy**.

## remove_if

```
#include <algorithm>
template< class ForwardIt, class Pred >
ForwardIt remove_if( ForwardIt first, ForwardIt last, Pred p );
```

The STL algorithm **remove_if** removes from the range **[first, last)** every element that satisfies the predicate **p** and returns the beyond-the-end location of the resulting sequence. The algorithm is *stable*; that is, any elements that remain after the removals are in the same relative order as before the removals. The algorithm's time complexity is linear. See also **remove**, **remove_copy**, and **remove_copy_if**.

## replace (STL)

```
#include <algorithm>
template< class ForwardIt, class T >
void replace( ForwardIt first, ForwardIt last,
              const T& old, const T& new );
```

The STL algorithm **replace** replaces with **new** every occurrence of **old** in the range **[first, last)**. The algorithm's time complexity is linear. See also **replace_if**, **replace_copy**, and **replace_copy_if**.

## replace (string)

```
#include <string>
basic_string<charT,traits,Allocator>&
    basic_string::replace( size_type p1, size_type n1,
        const basic_string<charT,traits,Allocator>& s,
        size_type p2, size_type n2 );
basic_string<charT,traits,Allocator>&
    basic_string::replace( size_type p, size_type n,
        const basic_string<charT,traits,Allocator>& s );
basic_string<charT,traits,Allocator>&
    basic_string::replace( size_type p, size_type n1,
        const charT* s, size_type n2 );
basic_string<charT,traits,Allocator>&
    basic_string::replace( size_type p, size_type n,
        const charT* s );
basic_string<charT,traits,Allocator>&
    basic_string::replace( size_type p, size_type n1,
        size_type n2, charT c );
```

The first version throws an **out_of_range** exception if **p1** > **length()** or **p2** > **s.length()**. It then computes *len1* as the minimum of **n1** and **length()** − **p1**, and *len2* as the minimum of **n2** and **s.length()** − **p2**. It throws a **length_error** exception if **s.length()** − *len1* ≥ **max** − *len2*, where **max** is the maximum value of type **size_type**. If no exception is thrown, it replaces the substring in **\*this** beginning at index **p1** of length *len1* with the substring in **s** beginning at index **p2** of length *len2*. It returns **\*this**.

The second version returns

```
replace( p, n, s, 0, max )
```

The third version returns

```
replace( p, n1, basic_string<charT,traits,Allocator>( s, n2 ) )
```

The fourth version returns

```
replace( p, n, basic_string<charT,traits,Allocator>( s ) )
```

The fifth version returns

```
replace( p, n1, basic_string<charT,traits,Allocator>( n2, c ) )
```

# replace_copy

```
#include <algorithm>
template< class InputIt, class OutputIt, class T >
OutputIt replace_copy( InputIt first, InputIt last,
                       OutputIt result,
                       const T& old, const T& new );
```

The STL algorithm **replace_copy** copies the range **[first, last)** to **result** with every occurrence of **old** replaced by **new**. The algorithm returns the beyond-the-end location of the **result**ing sequence. The algorithm's time complexity is linear. See also **replace**, **replace_if**, and **replace_copy_if**.

# replace_copy_if

```
#include <algorithm>
template< class It, class OutputIt, class Pred, class T >
OutputIt replace_copy_if( It first, It last,
                          OutputIt result,
                          Pred p, const T& new );
```

The STL algorithm **replace_copy_if** copies the range **[first, last)** to **result**, replacing with **new** every element that satisfies **p**. The algorithm returns the beyond-the-end location of the **result**ing sequence. The algorithm's time complexity is linear. See also **replace**, **replace_if**, and **replace_copy**.

## replace_if

```
#include <algorithm>
template< class ForwardIt, class Pred, class T >
void replace_if( ForwardIt first, ForwardIt last,
                 Pred p, const T& new );
```

The STL algorithm **replace_if** replaces with **new** every element in the range **[first, last)** that satisfies the predicate **p**. The algorithm's time complexity is linear. See also **replace**, **replace_copy**, and **replace_copy_if**.

## reverse

```
#include <algorithm>
template< class BidirectionalIt >
void reverse( BidirectionalIt first, BidirectionalIt last );
```

The STL algorithm **reverse** reverses the relative order of the elements in the range **[first, last)**. The algorithm's time complexity is linear. See also **reverse_copy**.

## reverse_copy

```
#include <algorithm>
template< class BidirectionalIt, class OutputIt >
OutputIt reverse_copy( BidirectionalIt first,
                       BidirectionalIt last,
                       OutputIt result );
```

The STL algorithm **reverse_copy** reverses the relative order of the elements in the range **[first, last)** and copies the reversed elements into a new range that begins at **result**, returning the past-the-end iterator **result + n**, where **n** is **last - first**. The original range is unmodified. The algorithm's time complexity is linear. See also **reverse**.

## rfind

```
#include <string>
size_type
    basic_string::rfind(
        const basic_string<charT,traits,Allocator>& s,
        size_type p = max ) const;
size_type
    basic_string::rfind( const charT* s,
        size_type p, size_type n ) const;
size_type
    basic_string::rfind( const charT* s, size_type p = max ) const;
size_type
    basic_string::rfind( charT c, size_type p = max ) const;
```

**max** is the maximum value of type **size_type**. In the first version, if **s** is a substring of ***this** at index **p** or lower, **rfind** returns the greatest index $\leq$ **p** where **s** begins. If **s** is not found, **rfind** returns **max**.

The second version returns

```
rfind( basic_string<charT,traits,Allocator>( s, n ), p )
```

The third version returns

```
rfind( basic_string<charT,traits,Allocator>( s ), p )
```

The fourth version returns

```
rfind( basic_string<charT,traits,Allocator>( 1, c ), p )
```

## search

```
#include <algorithm>
template< class ForwardIt1, class ForwardIt2 >
ForwardIt1 search( ForwardIt1 first1, ForwardIt1 last1,
                   ForwardIt2 first2, ForwardIt2 last2 );
template< class ForwardIt1, class ForwardIt2,
          class BinaryPred >
ForwardIt1 search( ForwardIt1 first1, ForwardIt1 last1,
                   ForwardIt2 first2, ForwardIt2 last2,
                   BinaryPred p );
```

The STL algorithm **search** tests whether the sequence in the second range **[first2, last2)** is a subsequence of the first range **[first1, last1)**. If so, an iterator that points to the start of the subsequence in the first range is returned; otherwise, **last1** is returned. In the first version, comparisons are made with **==**. In the second version, comparisons are made with the binary predicate **p**. The algorithm's time complexity is linear in the average case and quadratic in the worst case.

## seekg

```
#include <iostream>
basic_istream<charT,traits>&
    basic_istream::seekg( off_type& off, ios_base::seekdir dir );
basic_istream<charT,traits>&
    basic_istream::seekg( pos_type pos );
```

The first version moves the input stream position marker **off** bytes from **dir**, which must be one of **ios_base::beg** (from the beginning of the stream), **ios_base::cur** (from the current position), or **ios_base::end** (from the end of the stream). The second version sets the input stream position marker to location **pos**, which should be a value returned by **tellg**. It returns the updated stream.

## seekp

```
#include <iostream>
basic_ostream<charT,traits>&
    basic_ostream::seekp( off_type& off, ios_base::seekdir dir );
basic_ostream<charT,traits>&
    basic_ostream::seekp( pos_type pos );
```

The first version moves the output stream position marker **off** bytes from **dir**, which must be one of **ios_base::beg** (from the beginning of the stream), **ios_base::cur** (from the current position), or **ios_base::end** (from the end of the stream). The second version sets the output stream position marker to location **pos**, which should be a value returned by **tellp**. It returns the updated stream.

## setf

```
#include <iostream>
fmtflags ios_base::setf( fmtflags spec_flags );
fmtflags ios_base::setf( fmtflags spec_flags, fmtflags mask );
```

The first version sets the format flags specified by **spec_flags**. The second version clears the flags specified by **mask** and sets the flags specified by **spec_flags & mask**. Both versions return the previous format flags.

## set_terminate

```
#include <exception>
terminate_handler set_terminate( terminate_handler h ) throw();
```

Sets **h** as the handler function for terminating exception processing. It returns the function previously specified.

## set_unexpected

```
#include <exception>
unexpected_handler
    set_unexpected( unexpected_handler u ) throw();
```

Sets **u** as the unexpected handler. It returns the function previously specified.

## sin

```
#include <cmath>
float sin( float real );
double sin( double real );
long double sin( long double real );
```

Returns the sine of **real**, which must be in radians.

## sinh

```
#include <cmath>
float sinh( float real );
double sinh( double real );
long double sinh( long double real );
```

Returns the hyperbolic sine of **real**.

## sort

```
#include <algorithm>
template< class RandomAccessIt >
void sort( RandomAccessIt first, RandomAccessIt last );
template< class RandomAccessIt, class Compare >
void sort( RandomAccessIt first, RandomAccessIt last,
          Compare comp );
```

The STL algorithm **sort** sorts elements in the range **[first, last)**. The first version uses **<** to compare elements, whereas the second version uses a comparison predicate. The algorithm's time complexity is $n \log n$ in the average case, where $n$ is the length of the sequence to be sorted. See also **partial_sort** and **stable_sort**.

## sqrt

```
#include <cmath>
float sqrt( float real );
double sqrt( double real );
long double sqrt( long double real );
```

Returns the square root of **real**.

## srand

```
#include <cstdlib>
void srand( unsigned int seed );
```

Seeds the random number generator. Calling **srand** with **seed** equal to 1 is equivalent to calling the random number function **rand** without first invoking **srand**. See also **rand**.

## stable_partition

```
#include <algorithm>
template< class BidirectionalIt, class Pred >
BidirectionalIt stable_partition( BidirectionalIt first,
                                   BidirectionalIt last,
                                   Pred p );
```

The STL algorithm **stable_partition** places elements in the range **[first, last)** that satisfy predicate **p** before elements in this range that do not satisfy **p**. The algorithm returns an iterator **it** such that elements in the range **[first, it)** satisfy **p** but elements in the range **[it, last)** do not satisfy **p**. The algorithm preserves relative order within the two partition groups. The time complexity for **stable_partition** is linear if there is sufficient memory. See also **partition**.

## stable_sort

```
#include <algorithm>
template< class RandomAccessIt >
void stable_sort( RandomAccessIt first, RandomAccessIt last );
template< class RandomAccessIt, class Compare >
void stable_sort( RandomAccessIt first, RandomAccessIt last,
                  Compare comp );
```

The STL algorithm **stable_sort** sorts elements in the range **[first, last)** and preserves the relative order of equivalent elements. The first version uses **<** to compare elements, and the second version uses a comparison predicate. The algorithm's time complexity is $n \log n$ if there is sufficient memory ($n$ is the length of the sequence to be sorted). See also **sort** and **partial_sort**.

## str

```
#include <sstream>
basic_string<charT,traits,Allocator>
     basic_ostringstream::str() const;
basic_string<charT,traits,Allocator>
     basic_istringstream::str() const;
basic_string<charT,traits,Allocator>
     basic_stringstream::str() const;
```

Returns a **basic_string**, which is a copy of the **stringstream** object's contents.

## substr

```
#include <string>
basic_string<charT,traits,Allocator>
    basic_string::substr( size_type p = 0,
                          size_type n = max ) const;
```

**max** is the maximum value of type **size_type**. **substr** throws an exception of type **out_of_range** if **p** > **length()**. If no exception is thrown, it computes *len* as the minimum of **n** and **length()** − **p**. It then returns the substring beginning at index **p** of length *len*.

## swap (STL)

```
#include <algorithm>
template< class T >
void swap( T& x, T& y );
```

The STL algorithm **swap** exchanges the values of **x** and **y**. The algorithm's time complexity is constant. See also **swap_ranges**.

## swap (string)

```
#include <string>
void basic_string::swap( basic_string<charT,traits,Allocator>& s );
```

Swaps the two strings.

## swap_ranges

```
#include <algorithm>
template< class ForwardIt1, class ForwardIt2 >
ForwardIt2 swap_ranges( ForwardIt1 first1, ForwardIt1 last1,
                        ForwardIt2 first2 );
```

The STL algorithm **swap_ranges** invokes the algorithm **swap** on pairs of corresponding elements, one each from the ranges **[first1, last1)** and **[first2, first2 + n)**, where **n** is **last1 - first1**. The algorithm returns the iterator **first2 + n**. The algorithm's time complexity is linear. See also **swap**.

## sync_with_stdio

```
#include <iostream>
static void ios_base::sync_with_stdio();
```

Synchronizes the C++ input/output with the standard C input/output functions. Anytime the C and C++ input/output libraries are intermixed, the method **sync_with_stdio** should be invoked before doing any input or output.

## system

```
#include <cstdlib>
int system( const char* s );
```

Executes the command **s**. The value returned is implementation dependent. (The value returned usually indicates the exit status of the command executed.)

## tan

```
#include <cmath>
float tan( float real );
double tan( double real );
long double tan( long double real );
```

Returns the tangent of **real**, which must be in radians.

## tanh

```
#include <cmath>
float tanh( float real );
double tanh( double real );
long double tanh( long double real );
```

Returns the hyperbolic tangent of **real**.

## tellg

```
#include <iostream>
pos_type basic_istream::tellg();
```

Returns the location of the input stream position marker.

## tellp

```
#include <iostream>
pos_type basic_ostream::tellp();
```

Returns the location of the output stream position marker.

## terminate

```
#include <exception>
void terminate();
```

The function **terminate** is called when there is an error in the exception handling mechanism (e.g., a handler is missing for a thrown exception). The function **terminate**, in turn, calls the function most recently specified by **set_terminate**.

## time

```
#include <ctime>
time_t time( time_t* storage );
```

Returns the time (typically measured in seconds elapsed since midnight, January 1, 1970 GMT). If **storage** is not equal to zero, **time** stores the current time at address **storage**. See also **difftime**.

## tolower

```
#include <cctype>
int tolower( int character );
```

Converts **character** from uppercase to lowercase and returns the converted value. If **character** is not **'A'** through **'Z'**, **tolower** returns **character**.

## toupper

```
#include <cctype>
int toupper( int character );
```

Converts **character** from lowercase to uppercase and returns the converted value. If **character** is not **'a'** through **'z'**, **toupper** returns **character**.

## transform

```
#include <algorithm>
template< class InputIt, class OutputIt, class UnaryOp >
OutputIt transform( InputIt first, InputIt last, OutputIt result,
                    UnaryOp uop );
template< class InputIt1, class InputIt2, class OutputIt,
          class BinaryOp >
OutputIt transform( InputIt first1, InputIt last1,
                    InputIt2 first2, OutputIt result,
                    BinaryOp bop );
```

The STL algorithm **transform** transforms a sequence by applying to each element a function that changes the element. The first version applies the unary function **uop** to each element in the range **[first, last)**. The second version applies the binary function **bop** to pairs of elements. The pairs are corresponding elements in the ranges **[first1, last1)** and **[first2, first2 + n)**, where **n** is **last1 - first1**. In both cases, the resulting sequence starts at **result** and the end-of-sequence iterator **result + n** is returned. The algorithm's time complexity is linear.

## unexpected

```
#include <exception>
void unexpected();
```

When a function throws an exception not specified in its **throw** specification, **unexpected** is called. The function **unexpected**, in turn, calls the function most recently specified by **set_unexpected** or a default handler if no function was specified by **set_unexpected**.

## unique

```
#include <algorithm>
template< class ForwardIt >
ForwardIt unique( ForwardIt first, ForwardIt last );
template< class ForwardIt, class BinaryPred >
ForwardIt unique( ForwardIt first, ForwardIt last,
                  BinaryPred bp );
```

The STL algorithm **unique** eliminates consecutive duplicates from the range **[first, last)**. An element is a *consecutive duplicate* if it equals an element to its immediate right. Accordingly, **unique** should be applied to a sorted sequence to ensure that all duplicates are consecutive duplicates. The first version of **unique** checks for equality using **==**, whereas the second version uses the binary predicate **bp**. The algorithm's time complexity is linear. See also **unique_copy**.

## unique_copy

```
#include <algorithm>
template< class InputIt, class OutputIt >
OutputIt unique_copy( InputIt first, InputIt last,
                      OutputIt result );
template< class InputIt, class OutputIt, class BinaryPred >
OutputIt unique_copy( InputIt first, InputIt last,
                      OutputIt result, BinaryPred bp );
```

The STL algorithm **unique_copy** copies the range **[first, last)** to **result**, eliminating consecutive duplicates. An element is a *consecutive duplicate* if it equals an element to its immediate right. Accordingly, **unique** should be applied to a sorted sequence to ensure that all duplicates are consecutive duplicates. The first version checks for equality using **==**, whereas the second version uses the binary predicate **bp**. Both versions return the end of the **result**ing range. The algorithm's time complexity is linear. See also **unique**.

## unsetf

```
#include <iostream>
void ios_base::unsetf( fmtflags spec_flags );
```

Clears specified flags **spec_flags**.

## upper_bound

```
#include <algorithm>
template< class ForwardIt, class T >
ForwardIt upper_bound( ForwardIt first, ForwardIt last,
                       const T& value );
template< class ForwardIt, class T, class Compare >
ForwardIt upper_bound( ForwardIt first, ForwardIt last,
                       const T& value, Compare comp );
```

The STL algorithm **upper_bound** returns an iterator pointing to the *last* position in the range **[first, last)** into which **value** may be inserted while maintaining sorted order. The range must be sorted according to **<** in the first version and the **comp**arison function in the second version. The algorithm's time complexity is logarithmic. See also **lower_bound** and **equal_range**.

## width

```
#include <iostream>
streamsize ios_base::width() const;
streamsize ios_base::width( streamsize new_width );
```

The first version returns the field width. The second version changes the field width to **new_width** and returns the old field width.

## write

```
#include <iostream>
basic_ostream<charT,traits>&
    basic_ostream::write( const char_type* buff, streamsize n );
```

Writes **n** characters from the array **buff** to the output stream. It returns the updated stream.

# HINTS AND SOLUTIONS TO ODD-NUMBERED EXERCISES

## Section 1.1

1. A program module is a part of a program that can be designed, coded, and tested separately.

3. A class

5. Cascading changes are changes that are transmitted from one procedure to its subprocedures, from those subprocedures to their subprocedures, and so on.

7. Software maintenance deals with the testing, debugging, and upgrading of software systems.

9. A data type

11. As procedures

13. A *CardDeck HasA Card*.

15. *Jack Nicholson belongs to* the class *Actors*.

## Section 1.2

1. A function member

3. The private data members and methods that support the public interface

5. A class's implementation is private in that it is hidden from the user.

7. Yes

9. Yes

11. A data type that exposes in its public interface only high-level operations and hides all low-level implementation details

13. Let $n$ denote the number of elements on the *Stack*, $a$ denote the number of pushes, and $d$ denote the number of pops. When a *Stack* is first created, it has no elements, and no pushes or pops have occurred; thus, at this time

$$n = a - d$$

Thereafter, if an item is pushed on the *Stack*, $n$ and $a$ both increase by one. Therefore we still have $n = a - d$. If an item is popped from the *Stack*, $n$ and $d$ both decrease by one. Therefore we still have $n = a - d$.

## Section 1.3

1. A class **c** provides services to a client. The client requests services from **c** by invoking one of its methods.

3. Information hiding conceals the data members from the client; thus the client accesses the server's data member indirectly—through the server's methods. Information hiding makes servers easy for clients to use and promotes robustness.

5. Invoking a method is characterized as sending a message to the object.

7. High-level methods are used by the server to conceal the *low-level* implementation details. High-level methods are easier to use, easier to understand, and more intuitive than low-level details.

## Section 1.4

1. Class *SortedList* might be inherited from class *List*.

3. Yes

5. A child class overrides a method in a parent class if it provides its own definition of the method.

7. Suppose that class *D* is inherited from class *BC* and that *D* and *BC* each have a method named *get*. Suppose further that when the statement

$$p->get();$$

executes, the system invokes *D*'s *get* if *p* points to a *D* object, but invokes *BC*'s *get* if *p* points to a *BC* object. In this case, method *get* is said to be polymorphic.

## Section 1.5

1. Declarations

3. No

5. No

7. A container is a component that holds other components. A container provides the infrastructure for components to communicate with one another.

9. A component implements the functionality exposed in its interfaces and, in this sense, is the back end implementation of these interfaces.

11. No

## Section 2.1

1. Namespaces can be used to avoid name conflicts.

3. Because of the using declaration

```
using foo:showDate;
```

the statement

```
showDate( 23 );
```

refers to **foo**'s **showDate**. Since **foo**'s **showDate** expects two **int** arguments, an error results.

5. The *namespace* is **myLib**; **Baz** is a *function*.

7. *cmath*

# Section 2.2

1. ```
cin >> i >> x;
```

3. ```
cout << setw( 12 );
```

5. ```
cout << setprecision( 0 );
```

7. ```
cout << right << showpos;
```

9. ```
#include <iostream>
#include <iomanip>
using namespace std;
int main() {
   char c;
   int count = 0;
   cin >> noskipws;
   cout << hex << setfill( '0' );;
   while ( cin >> c ) {
      // new-style casts are discussed in ~.4
      cout << setw( 2 ) << ( int ) c;
      if ( ++count == 25 ) {
         cout << '\n';
         count = 0;
      }
      else
         cout << ' ';
   }
   return 0;
}
```

# Section 2.3

1. ```
#include <iostream>
#include <fstream>
#include <cstdlib>
using namespace std;
```

```cpp
int main() {
    ifstream in;
    ofstream out;
    int yard;
    in.open( "yard.in" );
    if ( !in ) {
        cout << "Unable to open yard.in\n";
        exit( 0 );
    }
    out.open( "length.out" );
    if ( !out ) {
        cout << "Unable to open length.out\n";
        exit( 0 );
    }
    while ( in >> yard ) {
        out << yard << " yards\n";
        out << "    = " << yard * 3 << " feet\n";
        out << "    = " << yard * 36 << " inches\n";
    }
    in.close();
    out.close();
    return 0;
}
```

## Section 2.4

1. `static_cast<double>(val)`

3. `good_jobs j1, j2;`

5. Because the scope of **i**, which is defined in the first **for** loop, *is* the first **for** loop, **i** is undefined in the second and third **for** loops.

## Section 2.5

1. `string t1 = "David Letterman", t2 = "";`

3. `#include <fstream>`
   `#include <string>`
   `using namespace std;`

```
int main() {
    string line[ 1000 ];
    int count;
    ifstream in;
    in.open( "text.in" );
    ofstream out;
    out.open( "text.out" );
    for ( count = 0;
            count < 1000 && getline( in, line[ count ] );
            count++ )
        ;
    in.close();
    for ( int i = count - 1; i >= 0; i-- )
        out << line[ i ] << '\n';
    out.close();
    return 0;
}
```

5. The statement

   ```
   s2 = s1;
   ```

   is incorrect. The array name **s2** is a constant and cannot have any value assigned to it.

7. The code is correct. The output is

   ```
   C++ is great fun!
   ```

9. The code is correct. The output is

   ```
   at fun
   ```

   The value of **"C++ is great fun"** is the address of the first character **c**. The value of **'\n'** is 10, the ASCII code for the newline character. Thus the value of the expression

   ```
   "C++ is great fun" + '\n'
   ```

   is the address of the character **a**. Therefore the string **"at fun"** is stored in **s**.

11. The code is correct. The output is

    ```
    Charles
    ```

13. The code is correct. The output is

    ```
    Charles
    ```

15. The code is correct. The output is

    ```
    Charles Foster Kane
    ```

17. The code is correct. The output is

    ```
    Windows 98
    ```

19. The code is correct. The output is

    **WINDOWS 95**

21. The code is correct. The output is

    **6**

23. The code is correct. The output is

    **4294967295**

25. The code is correct. The output is

    **8**

27. The code is correct. The output is

    **8**

29. The code is correct. The output is

    **6**

31. The code is correct. The output is

    **4**

33. The code is correct. The output is

    **not less than or equal**

35. The code is correct. The output is

    **not equal**

    The values of the expressions **"John Beresford Tipton"** and **"John Bear"** are the addresses of the first characters in the strings, which are not equal.

## Section 2.6

1. Portable

3. The definition is incorrect because no return type is specified.

5. Portable. The definition is equivalent to

    ```
    int main() {
        //...
    }
    ```

7. **p.x = 5**
   **p.y = -12**

9. **\*p.x = 4**
   **\*p.y = -11**

11. The **ofstream** variable should be passed by reference. The correct definition is

```
void print( ofstream& fp, int i ) {
    fp << i << '\n';
}
```

13.
```
void print( char c ) {
    cout << static_cast< int >( c );
}
```

15. The statement

```
print( 10 );
```

is ambiguous. It could invoke

```
void print( int count, int i = 0 ) {
    //...
}
```

with **count** equal to 10 and **i** equal to 0, or it could invoke

```
void print( int count, const char* s = "Beavis" ) {
    //...
}
```

with **count** equal to 10 and **s** equal to **"Beavis"**.

## Section 2.7

1. **dbl_ptr new double;**

3. **delete dbl_ptr;**

5. **int** `**` **ptr;**

7. After the line

```
int response;
```

insert the following lines

```
cout << "\nAdd another? (1 == yes, 0 == no): ";
cin >> response;
if ( response == 0 )
    return 0;
```

## Section 2.8

1.
```
string s;
int i, j;
//...
try {
    s.erase( i, j );
}
catch( out_of_range ) {
    cerr << "erase: out of range...aborting\n";
    exit( EXIT_FAILURE );
}
```

3.
```
int* ptr;
//...
try {
    ptr = new int[ 500 ];
}
catch( bad_alloc ) {
    cerr << "new[ ]: unable to allocate storage...aborting\n";
    exit( EXIT_FAILURE );
}
```

5. If a function throws an exception but has no **catch**er to handle it, the system handles the exception by invoking the function **unexpected**. In effect, **unexpected** is the default handler for exceptions not caught by user-supplied **catch** blocks. The function **unexpected** typically prints an error message and aborts the program.

## Section 3.1

1. A class declaration must end with a semicolon.

3. **private**

5. **private**

7. Yes

9. If a method is defined outside the class declaration, the class name must be included. The correct definition is

```
float Circus::getHeadCount() {
    // function body
}
```

11.
```
class Person {
public:
    inline unsigned getAge();
    // other members
};
```

## Section 3.2

1. The **stack** methods all have very short bodies.

## Section 3.3

1. Because an object passed or returned by value must be copied and the object copied may be large, the result may be an inefficient use of storage and time. Also, passing and returning an object by reference is easier, at the syntax level, than passing and returning a pointer to an object.

3. In the definition

   ```
   void f( C& c ) { /* ... */ }
   ```

   **f** is allowed to change **c**'s data members. In the definition

   ```
   void f( const C& c ) { /* ... */ }
   ```

   **f** is *not* allowed to change **c**'s data members.

5. A **const** method may *not* invoke a non**const** method. The **const** in

   ```
   void set( string s) const { setAux( s ); }
   ```

   states that **set** will not change the values of any data members. Since the method **setAux** is not marked **const**, it may, and in fact does, change the values of data members.

## Section 3.4

1. The **TimeStamp** class packages, in an object-oriented style, the functionality already available in the C procedural library described by the header **ctime**.

3. The **TimeStamp** class encapsulates the functionality of the C library described in the header *ctime*.

5. The **extract** method is a low-level method meant to be invoked only by high-level methods within the class such as **getMonth**, which are **public**. The **extract** method is therefore **private**.

## Section 3.5

1. The class name is **C** (uppercase), not **c** (lowercase). So the default constructor is **C()**, not **c()**. The technical error is that **c()** must return a value because it is not a constructor or destructor.

3. Yes, and this is common.

5. No

7. Because the default constructor is **private**, it cannot be invoked in a nonmethod such as **main**. In **main**, the statement

   ```
   K k1;
   ```

   therefore causes an error by trying to invoke the default constructor.

9. The copy constructor expects a *reference* to an object of the class type. The correct declaration is

   ```
   class R {
   public:
      R( R& arg ); // ok, a reference to R
   };
   ```

11. 
```
class Person {
public:
   Person( Person& p ) {
     // method body
   }
   // other members
};
Person foo;
Person fooTwin( foo ); // clone foo
```

13. 
```
1
-999
```

15. A convert constructor is a one-parameter constructor other than the copy constructor. The name indicates that the convert constructor converts an argument of some type into an object of the class type. For example, we could provide the **TimeStamp** class with a constructor **TimeStamp( time_t )** that converts a **time_t** value into a **TimeStamp** object.

17. No. The convert constructor converts the **int** 999 into a **C** object that is passed to **g**.

19. A **const** variable, including a data member, cannot be the target of an assignment operation. The **const**ant **c** must be initialized in the constructor's initialization section; it cannot be assigned a value in the constructor's body.

21. Only constructors have initialization sections. Therefore, **f** cannot initialize **c** in its header.

23. 
```
1 created
2 created
3 created
3 destroyed
2 destroyed
1 destroyed
```

## Section 3.6

1. If an **ofstream** is opened in **out** mode for an already existing file, the file's contents are first deleted and writing then begins at the beginning of the file. In our sample application, each invocation of **logToFile** would first delete the records written during all previous invocations. Therefore, the log file at any time would contain records about one object at most.

## Section 3.7

1. For an *object data member* of, for example, type **int**, there is one **int** cell per object. So each object has its own **int** cell. For a *class data member* of the same type, there is *one* cell shared by all objects.

3. The **static** data member **x** is declared but not defined. It must be defined outside all blocks:

```
int C::x; // define static data member
```

5. 1
   2
   3

# Section 3.8

1. Because a pointer rather than a reference to a **c** object is passed to **g**, the correct syntax is

```
p->m();
```

3. The member selector operator **.** is used exclusively with objects and object references.

# Section 4.1

1.

3. Data members that might be added are **boss**, **dept**, and **salary**. Methods to get and set the added data members might be added.

# Section 4.2

1. Two: **y** is local to **B** and **x** is inherited from **A**.

3. *R*
  ↑
  *Q*
  ↑
  *P*

# Section 4.4

1. We explain with an example. In the hierarchy

```
class Base {
public:
    void m() { /* ... */ }
protected:
    int pro;
private:
    int pri;
};
class Derived : public Base {
  // Derived's local members
};
```

**Derived** inherits **pro** and **pri** from **Base**. Because **pri** is **private** in **Base**, it cannot be accessed by any of **Derived**'s local methods. (However, the **m** that **Derived** inherits from **Base** can access **pri**.) Because **pro** is **protected** in **Base**, it can be accessed by any of **Derived**'s local methods.

3. An advantage of **protected** members is that they are accessible throughout an inheritance hierarchy yet inaccessible outside the inheritance hierarchy. In this way, **protected** members provide information hiding from the point of view of clients outside the inheritance hierarchy. At the same time, **protected** members compromise information hiding in that they are visible beyond the class in which they are declared. In general, **protected** data should be avoided. Data that might be **protected** can usually be made **private** and made accessible by **protected** accessors. Using **private** data members promotes data hiding. There are other advantages as well. For example, a class with **private** data members and **protected** accessors can be completely reimplemented without disturbing the interface, that is, the **protected** and **public** member functions.

5. Because **A**'s member **set_x** is **protected**, it is visible only within **A** and classes derived from **A**. In particular, this **protected** member is not visible in **main**.

7. 
```
void DC::init( int n1, int n2, int n3 ) {
    set1( n1 );
    set2( n2 );
    num3 = n3;
}
```

## Section 4.5

1. Base class **BC** has a convert constructor, but no *default* constructor. Therefore, derived class **DC**'s constructor must invoke **BC**'s convert constructor in its header. A better solution would be to provide **BC** with a default constructor, in which case **DC**'s constructor would not be forced to invoke explicitly a **BC** constructor.

3. 
```
BC constructor
BC constructor
DC1 constructor
BC constructor
DC1 constructor
DC2 constructor
DC2 destructor
DC1 destructor
BC destructor
DC1 destructor
BC destructor
BC destructor
```

5. No

7. No

9. No

11. 
```
class Singer : public Human {
public:
    Singer() : Human() { }
    Singer( int c ) : Human( c ) { }
    void set_range( int i ) { range = i; }
    int get_range() { return range; }
private:
    int range; // 0 = soprano, 1 = alto, etc.
};
class PopSinger : public Singer {
public:
    PopSinger() : Singer() { }
    PopSinger( int c ) : Singer( c ) { }
    void set_loudness( long double i ) { loudness = i; }
    int get_loudness() { return loudness; }
private:
    long double loudness;
};
```

## Section 4.7

1. Single inheritance is used to specialize or refine a class, whereas multiple inheritance is used to combine classes.

3. 
```
void R::assign( int xx, int yy, int aa, int bb ) {
    x = xx;
    y = yy;
    a = aa;
    b = bb;
}
```

5. One

## Section 5.1

1. A function's entry point is the starting memory address at which the executable code in its body begins.

3. (1) An inheritance hierarchy. (2) A pointer or reference to a base class that points to an object in the hierarchy. (3) Use of the pointer or reference to invoke an overridden **virtual** method.

5. Only a method can be **virtual**, and **hi** is not a method.

7. Yes

9. If a derived class redefines a **virtual** method, the derived class is said to *override* the method.

11. The storage penalty is the size of the vtable. The time penalty is the time required to do vtable lookups when **virtual** methods are invoked.

13. Yes

15. A constructor cannot be **virtual**.

## Section 5.2

1. Because the invocation of **input** is no longer polymorphic, **Film::input** is called each time the statement

   ```
   films[ next++ ]->input( fin );
   ```

   executes in **readInput**'s loop. Similarly, each time the statement

   ```
   films[ i ]->output();
   ```

   executes in **main**, **Film::output** is called. This is all right only if the data file contains only **Film** records.

## Section 5.3

1. Here is an overloading at the top level of a **print** function:

   ```
   void print( unsigned n ) { /* ... */ }
   void print( char c ) { /* ... */ }
   void print( double n1, double n2 ) { /* ... */ }
   ```

3. Compile-time binding

5. Compile-time binding

7. Run-time binding

9. **A::m**

11. The statement

    ```
    a1.m(); //****** ERROR: missing argument
    ```

    is in error because **A::m** expects a **double** argument.

13. **baz**
    **26**

## Section 5.4

1. It must contain a pure **virtual** method.

3. Only for a **virtual** method can we use the special = **0** syntax, and **m** is not **virtual**.

5. Class **z** is abstract because it does not override **m2**. It is thus an error to define a **z** object such as **z1**.

7. Yes

## Section 5.5

1. It is illegal to apply **dynamic_cast** to a nonpolymorphic type (**C** in this case). Class **C** is nonpolymorphic because it has no **virtual** methods.

3. A polymorphic type is a class with at least one **virtual** method.

5. No

7. Yes

9. A cast is not type safe when it is syntactically valid but may generate a run-time error.

11. No

13. No

15. **true**

17. **true**

19. **false**

## Section 6.1

1. The overload definition's header is missing the keyword **operator**. The header should be

```
bool Point::operator>( const Point& s ) const
```

3. The declaration

```
bool operator>( const Point& ) const;
```

does not match the definition header

```
bool Point::operator>( const Point& s )
```

because the latter is missing **const** after the parameter list.

5. ```
class Point {
public:
   bool operator!();
   //...
};
```

## Section 6.2

1. Yes. When the object is passed by value, the copied object's data members are not changed.

3. ```
Complex Complex::operator~() const {
   return Complex( real, -imag );
}
```

## Section 6.3

1. This attempted top-level overload of || takes two **bool** arguments and, therefore, is indistinguishable from the built-in binary operator. At least one of the arguments must be of a class type.

3. The operator () must be overloaded as a class *method*; it cannot be overloaded as a top-level function.

5. 
```
#include <cmath> // for sqrt
double operator!( const Complex& c ) {
    return sqrt( c.get_real() * c.get_real() +
                 c.get_imag() * c.get_imag() );
}
```

7. The overload may be written

```
bool operator!=( const OPair& a, const OPair& b ) {
    return a.get1() != b.get1() || a.get2() != b.get2();
}
```

provided **public** methods **get1** and **get2** are added to the **OPair** class as follows

```
class OPair {
public:
    float get1() { return p1; }
    float get2() { return p2; }
    //...
};
```

## Section 6.4

1. **c** data member **stored** is **private** and, therefore, inaccessible to the top-level overload of the operator !, which is not a **friend** of **c**.

3. The operator ! is declared a **friend** of **c** but then defined as if it were a **c** method. The correct definition is

```
void operator!( C& c ) {
    c.stored = !c.stored;
}
```

5. 
```
#include <cmath> // for sqrt
double operator!( const Complex& c ) {
    return sqrt( c.real() * c.real() +
                 c.imag() * c.imag() );
}
```

7. The overload may be written

```
bool operator!=( const OPair& a, const OPair& b ) {
    return a.p1 != b.p1 || a.p2 != b.p2;
}
```

provided that `operator!=` is made a **friend** of class `OPair`:

```
class OPair {
    //...
    friend bool operator!=( const OPair& a, const OPair& b );
    //...
};
```

## Section 6.5

1. The overloaded input operator `>>` changes its second argument, a `Complex` object. Therefore, the `Complex` object should not be passed by value but rather by reference.

3. 
```
class Complex {
    //...
    friend ostream& operator<<( ostream&, const Complex& );
    //...
};
```

5. 
```
class OPair {
    //...
    friend ostream& operator<<( ostream&, const OPair& );
    //...
};
ostream& operator<<( ostream& os, const OPair& s ) {
    return os << s.p1 << "  " << s.p2;
}
```

## Section 6.6

1. Yes

3. The class author typically defines a copy constructor and overloads the assignment operator for a class whose data members include a pointer to dynamically allocated storage.

5. The object **c**, being the right operand of the assignment operator, could be a temporary object. For example, in the assignment

```
c1 = c2 + c3;
```

the system creates an unnamed temporary object to hold the result of the operation **c2 + c3**. This temporary object is then passed to the overloaded assignment operator. The problem is that, when the assignment operator finishes executing and returns a reference to the temporary object, the temporary object no longer exists.

## Section 6.7

1. One

3. 
```
istream& operator>>( istream& is, intArray& a ) {
    for ( int i = 0; i < a.get_size(); i++ )
        is >> a[ i ];
    return is;
}
```

5.
```cpp
istream& operator>>( istream& is, intTwoArray& a ) {
    for ( int i = 0; i < a.get_size1(); i++ )
      for ( int j = 0; j < a.get_size2(); j++ )
        is >> a( i, j );
    return is;
}
```

7.
```cpp
class OPair {
public:
    float& operator[ ]( int );
    //...
};
float& OPair::operator[ ]( int i ) {
    if ( i == 1 )
        return p1:
    if ( i == 2 )
        return p2;
    throw string( "IllegalIndex" );
    return 0.0;
}
```

9.
```cpp
class intArray {
public:
    intArray( const intArray& );
    intArray& operator=( const intArray& );
    //...
private:
    void copyIntoA( const intArray& );
    //...
};
void intArray::copyIntoA( const intArray& d ) {
    delete[ ] a;
    try {
        a = new int[ size = d.size ];
    }
    catch( bad_alloc ) {
        cerr<< "Unable to allocate storage for intArray\n";
        throw;
    }
    for ( int i = 0; i < size; i++ )
        a[ i ] = d.a[ i ];
}
intArray::intArray( const intArray& d ) : a( 0 ) {
    copyIntoA( d );
}
```

```
intArray& intArray::operator=( const intArray& d ) {
    if ( this != &d )
        copyIntoA( d );
    return *this;
}
```

11. 
```
intArray& intArray::operator++() {
    for ( int i = 0; i < size; i++ )
        ++a[ i ];
    return *this;
}
```

13. 
```
intTwoArray& intTwoArray::operator--() {
    for ( int i = 0; i < size1; i++ )
        for ( int j = 0; j < size2; j++ )
            --a[ i * size2 + j ];
    return *this;
}
```

15. No return type may be specified in overloading a type conversion operator. The correct declaration is

```
operator char*();
```

## Section 6.8

1. No, because the overloaded assignment operator changes an **Entry**'s definition
3. We first add **del** as follows

```
class Entry {
    //...
    void del() { flag = false; }
    //...
};
```

Now **remove** may be written as

```
void Dict::remove( const string& w ) {
    int i, j;
    for ( i = 0; i < MaxEntries; i++ )
        if ( entries[ i ].valid() && entries[ i ].match( w ) )
            break;
    if ( i == MaxEntries ) // not found
        return;
    for (j = i+1;j < MaxEntries && entries[ j ].valid();j++)
        entries[ j - 1 ] = entries[ j ];
    entries[ j - 1 ].del();
}
```

## Section 6.9

1. 
```
C1* c1 = new C1;        // overloaded new for C1
C2* c2 = new C2;        // top-level system new
int* i1 = new int;      // top-level system new
C1* cs = new C1[ 10 ];  // top-level system new[ ]
```

3. The first argument to an overloaded **delete** must be of type **void\***.

5. 
```
void Frame::operator delete( void* adr ) {
   // compute index of Frame to delete
   int i = static_cast<unsigned char*>(adr) - framePool;
   i /= sizeof( Frame );
   alloc[ i ] = false;
}
```

7. We assume that a global array **how_many** is added whose value is set by **new[ ]**; **how_many[ i ]** is the number of contiguous **Frame**s allocated by **new[ ]** beginning at index **i** in the **framePool** array.

```
void Frame::operator delete[ ]( void* adr ) {
   // compute index of first Frame to delete
   int i = static_cast<unsigned char*>(adr) - framePool;
   i /= sizeof( Frame );
   // delete how_many[ i ] Frames
   for ( int j = 0; j < how_many[ i ]; j++ )
      alloc[ i + j ] = false;
}
```

## Section 7.1

1. A class parameter is a user-selected symbol introduced in the template header by the keyword **class** or **typename**. The parameter represents a generic type for which the compiler substitutes an actual data type, built-in or user-defined, when a template class instantiation is created. In the code segment

```
template< class T >
class C {
  //...
};
```

**T** is a class parameter.

3. Yes

5. Yes

7. A function-style parameter is a user-selected symbol introduced in the template header by a data type, built-in or user-defined, rather than by the keyword **class** or **typename**. In the code segment

```
template< class T, double d >
class Z {
  //...
};
```

**d** is a function-style parameter of type **double**.

9. Objects can be created only for *instantiations* of a template class. The definition

```
Queue< T > q2; //***** ERROR: not a template instantiation
```

is therefore an error.

11. If a template class has function-style parameters, values for these must be provided in a template instantiation. The statement

```
Queue< double > q1; //*** ERROR: no function-style argument
```

can be corrected as

```
Queue< double, 100 > q1; // OK, function-style arg given
```

## Section 7.2

1. All the **assert**s are disabled.

3. **pop** returns a **Stack** element. If the **Stack** is empty, **pop** returns a dummy value—not on the **Stack** but of the same type as a **Stack** element—to satisfy this requirement.

5.
```
template< class T >
void Stack< T >::push( const T& e ) {
    assert( !full() );
    if ( !full() )
        elements[ ++top ] = e;
    else
        throw string( "Full stack" );
}
template< class T >
T Stack< T >::pop() {
    assert( !empty() );
    if ( !empty() )
        return elements[ top-- ];
    else {
        throw string( "Empty stack" );
        T dummy_value;
        return dummy_value;
    }
}
template< class T >
T Stack< T >::topNoPop() const {
    assert( !empty() );
    if ( !empty() )
        return elements[ top ];
    else {
        throw string( "Empty stack" );
        T dummy_value;
        return dummy_value;
    }
}
```

## Section 7.3

1. An STL container is a templated data structure, whereas an STL algorithm is a templated function that processes an STL container, for example, by sorting it.

3. A sequential container such as a **vector** resembles a C++ array in that its elements are typically accessed by position. In an associative container such as a **map**, the elements are typically accessed through keys, that is, identifying values.

5. Yes

7. A **multiset** can contain duplicate key values, whereas a **set** cannot.

9. Yes

11. No

13. A container adaptor adapts a basic container such as a **deque** so that the basic container behaves in some special way. For example, the **stack** adaptor can be used to adapt a **deque** so that it behaves like a stack, with **push**es, **pop**s, and other stack-appropriate methods.

15. A function adaptor adapts an STL function object so that the STL function behaves in a special way. For example, the program in Figure 7.3.16 uses the function adaptor **not1** to invert our function object **even** so that

   ```
   not1( even( n ) ); // n is an unsigned int
   ```

   returns **false**, if **n** is even, and **true**, if **n** is odd.

17. Yes

19. The user need not specify the size of an STL **vector**, whose size grows and shrinks automatically to meet storage needs. Also, a **vector** has built-in methods such as **begin**, **end**, **rbegin**, and **rend** to reference its beginning and end. This safeguards against underflow and overflow.

## Section 8.1

3. Any data set can ultimately be encoded as a string of bits and so is a stream.

5. A class such as **basic_ifstream** contains a buffer object (an object of type **basic_filebuf** for class **basic_ifstream**).

## Section 8.2

1. `cout.eof()`

3. The not operator (**!**) is overloaded so that the value of the expression **!cin** is converted to a pointer. (If the pointer value is zero, the expression is false; otherwise, the expression is true.)

5. `fout.seekp( -10, ios_base::end );`

7. `cout.setf( ios_base::showpoint );`

9. `cout.unsetf( ios_base::showpoint );`

11. `cout.setf( ios_base::oct, ios_base::basefield );`

13. `cout.setf( 0, ios_base::floatfield );`

15. `0X42$$0X42$$0X420X42`

17. The behavior of `fill` depends on the character set. Since class `ios_base` deals the part of the stream *independent* of the character set and `basic_ios` deals the part of the stream that *involves* the character set, `fill` is properly a member of `basic_ios`.

## Section 8.3

1. `basic_ios` is a **virtual** base class for `basic_istream` so that the members inherited from `basic_ios` will be passed on only one time to classes derived from `basic_istream`. If `basic_ios` were *not* a **virtual** base class for `basic_istream`, `basic_iostream` and classes derived from it would receive two copies of each member of `basic_ios`.

3. `cin.ignore( 100 );`

5. `b`

7. `d`

9. `b`

11.
```
string a[ MAX_NO_STRINGS ];
int i = -1;
do {
   getline( cin, a[ ++i ] );
} while ( a[ i ] != "" );
```

## Section 8.4

1. `cout << resetiosflags( ios_base::showpoint );`

3.
```
istream& ws( istream& is ) {
   int c;
   while ( ( c = is.get() ) != EOF && isspace( c ) )
      ;
   if ( c != EOF )
      is.putback( c );
   return is;
}
```

5.
```
ostream& scien( ostream& os ) {
   os.setf( ios_base::scientific, ios_base::floatfield );
   return os;
}
```

7.
```
void set_filler( ostream& os, char c ) {
   os.fill( c );
}
omanip< char, char > setfill( char c ) {
   return omanip< char, char >( set_filler, c );
}
```

9. We assume a template class **imanip** that is the input counterpart of the output class **omanip**.

```
void seto( istream& is, ios::off_type n ) {
    is.seekg( n, ios_base::beg );
}
imanip< ios::off_type, char > setoff( ios::off_type n ) {
    return imanip< ios::off_type, char >( seto, n );
}
```

11. A manipulator is a *top-level* function that "manipulates" an object in a class using the overloaded input (>>) or output (<<) operator. A manipulator can be added without modifying the class. A method is part of a class. It too can manipulate an object using the overloaded input or output operator in the class to which it belongs; however, adding such a method means modifying the class, which may not be convenient or even possible if the class is provided by a library.

## Section 8.5

1. ```
   ifstream fin;
   fin.open( "weather.in" );
   ```

3. ```
   fstream finout( "stars.dat", ios_base::in
                                 | ios_base::out
                                 | ios_base::binary );
   ```

5. It is illegal to have two definitions of the same variable in the same scope.

7. ```
   #include <fstream>
   using namespace std;
   int main( int c, char** argv ) {
       char c;
       ifstream fin;
       for ( int i = 1; i < c; i++ ) {
           fin.open( argv[ i ], ios_base::binary );
           if ( fin )
               while ( fin.get( c ) )
                   cout.put( c );
           fin.close();
       }
       return 0;
   }
   ```

## Section 8.7

1. ```
   string val;
   long x = 1098694772;
   ostringstream sout;
   sout << x;
   val = sout.str();
   ```

3. 
```
string buff;
//...
// assume buff now contains s "..." "..."
string first, second;
char c;
istringstream sin( buff );
// discard s and double quotes
sin >> c >> c;
// read first and discard next double quotes
getline( sin, first, "" );
// discard next double quotes
sin >> c;
// read second and discard last double quotes
getline( sin, second, "" );
```

## Section 8.8

1. 
```
#include <fstream>
#include <sstream>
using namespace std;
int main() {
    ifstream fin( "data.in" );
    ostringstream sout;
    copy( fin, sout );
    return 0;
}
```

3. 
```
#include <iostream>
#include <fstream>
using namespace std;
int main() {
    ifstream fin( "data.in" );
    copy( fin, cerr );
    return 0;
}
```

```
5. void copy( istream& in, ostream& out, int tabsize ) {
      char c;
      int i;
      ios_base::iostate fl = in.flags();
      in.unsetf( ios_base::skipws );
      int count = 0, i, numb;
      while ( in >> c )
         if ( c == '\t' ) {
            numb = tabsize - ( count % tabsize );
            for ( i = 0; i < numb; i++ )
               out << ' ';
            count += numb;
         }
         else {
            count++;
            out << c;
            if ( c == '\n' )
               count = 0;
         }
      in.flags( fl );
   }
```

## Section 8.9

```
1. filebuf finout;
   char b[ 256 ];
   finout.open( "balance.dat", ios_base::in | ios_base::out );
   finout.pubsetbuf( b, sizeof( b ) );
```

## Section 9.1

1. Graphical user interface

3. Applications programmer interface

5. C functions

7. A callback does whatever processing is appropriate for handling an event.

9. Windows NT

11. A code generator

## Section 9.2

1. The model comprises the application's data.

3. The controller handles interactions between the view and the model.

5. "Object persistence" refers to saving an object. "Serializing an object out" means to save an object by writing it to a file. "Serializing an object in" means to restore an object by reading it from a file.

7. `CObject`

9. No

## Section 9.3

1. By deriving the **CFigure** hierarchy from **CObject**, **CFigure**s can be made self-serializing.

3. In an implementation file

5. When an object is serialized in, the system automatically invokes the appropriate default constructor to create the object.

7. Pointers to objects in our **CFigure** hierarchy

## Section 9.4

1. Component object model

3. COM is an infrastructure for interapplication communication on a single machine, whereas DCOM extends this infrastructure across machines.

5. COM was originally the infrastructure for interapplication communication and OLE was a collection of built-in services that used COM.

7. COM uses DCE RPC, which allows an application running on one machine to invoke a function that executes in an application running on the same or a different machine.

9. The vtable's underlying mechanism can be extended so that one application can access pointers to functions that execute in another application.

11. Dynamic link library

13. No

15. An in-process server executes within the client's process space.

17. The system registry is a database of servers together with the interfaces that they support.

19. Yes

21. **IUnknown**

23. Interface definition language

25. The type library is a binary representation of an RPC idl file.

27. A controller

## Section 9.5

1. An out-of-process server

3. The **VARIANT** represents the calendar's value, that is, its month, day, and year.

5. The **I** stands for *interface*.

7. **COleDispatchDriver**

9. Yes

# INDEX

## A

**abort** 535

**abs** 535

Abstract base class 17, 260, 261, 278
  as an interface 18
  uses for 262

Abstract collection 283

Abstract data type 5, 6
  and class 5
  and procedural languages 8
  and robustness 7
  and string 9

**acos** 535

Active Template Library (ATL) 359, 507

ActiveX control 507

Adaptor of STL containers 370

**AddRef** in **IUnknown** 264

**adjustfield** 409

Adjusting access in inheritance 181

**algorithm** 379

Algorithm, STL 360, 377

Allocator 457, 472
  STL 384

Anonymous **enum** 41

Anonymous enumerated type 41

Anonymous **union** 78

API (Application Programmer's Interface) 480

**app** 413

Application Programmer's Interface (API) 480

AppWizard 482

Architecture, document/view 483

Argument, default 63

ASCII table 527

**asin** 536

**assert** 353, 358

Assertion 77, 358

Assignment operator (**=**)
  and copy constructor 129
  overloading 129, 307
  **string** 47

Associative array sample application 324

Association list and STL **map** 369

Asynchronous exception 77

**atan** 536

**ate** 413

ATL (Active Template Library) 359, 507

**atof** 536

**atoi** 536

**atol** 536

Attribute of an object 3

**auto** 113

Automation controller in MFC 504, 507

Automation server and controller sample application 510

## B

B-tree 477
Backward iterator 398
**bad** 415, 537
**bad_alloc** 75
**badbit** 413
Bag, and set 171
Base class 176
   abstract 260, 261, 278
   **virtual** 218
**basefield** 409
**basic_filebuf** 405, 465
**basic_fstream** 406, 436
**basic_ifstream** 406, 434
**basic_ios** 404, 407, 414
**basic_iostream** 404, 426
**basic_istream** 403, 404, 419
**basic_istringstream** 406, 458
**basic_ofstream** 406, 433
**basic_ostream** 403, 404, 424
**basic_ostringstream** 406, 457
**basic_streambuf** 405, 463
**basic_stringbuf** 405, 406, 472
**basic_stringstream** 406, 460
**beg** 414
Berstein's conditions 401
**binary** 413
**binary_function** 383
**binary_search** 537
Binding
   compile-time 231, 252, 275
   run-time 230, 231, 232, 252, 275
   run-time and vtable 236
Bitmask 408
**bitset** 372
Booch, G. 4
**bool** 40
**boolalpha** 41, 409
**bsearch** 537
Buffer 404
   classes 463

flushing 404
Buffered input/output 404
Bug 3

## C

C 2
C++ and object-oriented programming
   99
C-style string 116, 125, 150
   and **const char\*** 116
   versus **string** 116
Call by reference 58
Callback 481, 501
**calloc**, versus **new[ ]** 139
**CArchive** in MFC 487
Carroll, L. 96
Cascading changes 3
*cassert* 353, 358
Cast 38
   **const_cast** 39
   **dynamic_cast** 40
   **reinterpret_cast** 40
   **static_cast** 38, 266
**cin** 28
**class** 100, 103, 342, 344, 395
   contrasted with **struct** 103
Class 3, 99
   and abstract data type 5
   base 176
   buffer 463
   as a collection of objects 3
   constructors and destructor 124
   as a data type 3, 4, 99
   declaration 99, 100, 107, 161, 162
   derived 176
   efficiency and robustness 112
   **friend** 334
   hierarchy 177
   identifier in MFC 504
   indirection operator (**->**) 101,
      159, 167, 168

Class (*continued*)
  and information hiding  5
  inheritance  176
  members versus instance members
    151
  method, defining  104
  and object  4
  parameter  341, 344
  relationships among  4
  scope  103, 129
  subclass  4, 176
  superclass  176
  tag  99
  template  341
  as thin wrapper  120
Class declaration  99, 100, 107, 161, 162
  public and private regions  101
ClassWizard  482
**clear**  415, 538
Client  9, 10, 12, 101, 112
Client/Server Model  9
**close**  37, 434, 436, 437, 467, 538
CLSID, in MFC  504
**CObject**, in MFC  487
Code generator  482
Code reuse  12
Collision  440
Collision resolution policy  440
  linear probing  440
COM (Component Object Model)  263,
  264, 503
Comment  22
Comparison, **string**  53
Compile-time binding  231, 252, 275
Complex number  291
  imaginary part  291
  operations on  291
  real part  291
Complex number class sample applica-
  tion  291
Component  17, 20, 504

as a back-end server  20
and container  19
and information hiding  17
and interface  17, 19
Component Object Model (COM)  263,
  264, 503
Compound document  507
Concatenation, **string**  48
**const**  40, 101, 113, 114, 139
  data member  165
  method  114, 115, 168
  parameter  113
**const_cast**  39
**const_iterator**  365
**const** method  114
  as read-only  115
Constant  40
Constructor  124, 125, 165
  convert  129, 136, 137, 149
  copy  129, 130, 131, 132, 134
  default  125, 127, 128, 129, 163
  defined inline  126
  initializer  138
  inline  126
  and operators **new** and **new[ ]**  139
  overloading  125
  parameterized  125, 129
  private  128
  restricting object creation  127
  and robustness  125
  under inheritance  195
Container  19
  adaptor  370
  associative  363, 367
  efficiency of  367
  in MFC  504
  sequential  363
  STL  360, 362
Controller in Smalltalk and MFC  484
Convert constructor  129, 136, 149
  and implicit type conversion  137

Copy constructor 129, 130, 131, 132, 134, 135
  and assignment operator 129
  and compiler 129
  and disabling pass and return by value 135
  and dynamic storage 129
  and passing and returning by value 135
  when to define 129, 132
**copy** 361, 538
**copy_backward** 539
**cos** 539
**cosh** 539
**count** 539
**count_if** 383, 540
**cout** 28
*csignal* 77
**ctime** 119, 120, 121, 122
Ctor initializer 138
**CTypedPtrArray** 489, 502
**cur** 414
**c_str** 45, 540

**D**

Data member 4
Data structure 359
Data type 3
  abstract 5
  built-in 5
  class as example of 99
  primitive 5
Database 171
DCE (Distributed Computing Environment) 504
DCOM (Distributed Common Object Model) 503
Debugging 3
**dec** 30, 409
Declaration
  of a class 99, 100, 161, 162, 163
  of a function 18, 101
  of a method 101
  versus definition of a method 105
Decomposition of a problem 2
Decrement operator (--), overloading 318
Default argument 63
Default class scope 103
Default constructor 125, 127, 129, 163
  and arrays 127
  public 128
  and serialization in MFC 488
Defining **static** data members 153
Definition
  of a function 18
  of an object 100
  variable 42
  versus declaration of a method 105
**delete** 70, 140
  overloading 329
Deque 170
**deque** 361, 362, 363
Derived class 176
Design
  object-oriented 3, 4, 5
  top-down 2, 3
Destructor 124, 125, 139, 140, 164, 165
  and constructor 141
  under inheritance 202
  **virtual** 237, 238, 239, 499
Difference of two sets 171
**difftime** 146, 399, 540
Direct inheritance 183
Distributed Common Object Model (DCOM) 503
Distributed Computing Environment (DCE) 504
DLL (Dynamic Link Library) 511
Document, compound 507
Document serialization 486

Document serialization sample application 489
Document server 524
Document view architecture 483
Downcast 271
Dynamic Link Library (DLL) 511
Dynamic storage and copy constructor 129
**dynamic_cast** 40, 265, 267, 268, 271, 279
  and **NULL** 269
  versus **static_cast** 272

### E

Efficiency
  for classes 112
  of STL containers 367
Encapsulation 6, 8, 9
**end** 414
**endl** 29, 428
Entry point 230, 236
**enum** 41
Enumerated type 41
  anonymous 41
**EOF** 407
**eof** 415, 540
**eofbit** 413, 415
**equal** 540
**equal_range** 541
**erase** 48, 74, 541
Event handler 481
Event loop 481
Event-driven programming model 481
Exception 73
  asynchronous 77
  catching 73
  input/output 416
  rethrowing 76
  synchronous 77
  throwing 73
  **try** block 73

**exceptions** 417
**exit** 541
**EXIT_FAILURE** 75
**exp** 542
**explicit** 137
Extensibility, STL 361

### F

**fail** 415, 542
**failbit** 413
**failure** 417
**false** 40
Feature of an object 3
Feigenbaum, M. 95
Fibonacci numbers 381
Field 4
FIFO (First In First Out) 370
File 35
  **close** 37
  indexed 477
  load factor 441
  **open** 36
  random access 438
  relative 439
  sequential 477
  testing open 37
**filebuf** 407
**fill** 416, 542
**fill_n** 542
**find** 51, 543
**find_first_not_of** 544
**find_first_of** 52, 544
**find_if** 545
First In First Out (FIFO) 370
**fixed** 33, 409
**flags** 410, 545
**floatfield** 409
**floor** 545
**flush** 425, 545
Flushing the buffer 404

**fmtflags** 408

Format 404

 flags 409

Forward iterator 398

**for_each** 361, 378, 546

Foundations of object-oriented programming 99

**friend** 102

 class 334

 function 302

*fstream* 35, 406, 407, 432, 463

Function 2, 56

 adaptor 383

 call by reference 58

 call operator (**()**), overloading 315

 declaration 18

 default argument 63

 definition 18

 **friend** 302

 hash 439

 inline 62

 **main** 47

 member 4

 object 382

 overload 64

 prototype 56

 return by reference 59

 return type 22

 signature 65

Function-style parameter 348, 349, 396

Functional decomposition 2


## G

**gcount** 421, 546

**generate** 377, 546

**generate_n** 546

**get** 419, 547

**getline** 10, 46, 420, 547

Gillman, L. 96

**good** 415, 547

**goodbit** 413


## H

Hash function 439

Header

 file 107

 standard 22, 26

**hex** 30, 409, 428

Hiding, name 252, 255, 256, 277

Hierarchy, inheritance 13, 14

High-level copy function sample application 461

High-level input/output classes 419


## I

IDE (Integrated Development Environment) 480

**IDispatch** 506

IDL (Interface Definition Language) 508

IDL compiler 508

**ifstream** 35, 407

**ignore** 421, 548

Imperative language 2

Implementation 5, 8, 9, 19, 100

 file 107

 and information hiding 7

Implicit type conversion 137

 and convert constructor 137

**in** 413

**in_avail** 464

Increment operator (**++**), overloading 318

Indexed file 477

Indirect inheritance 183

Information hiding 5, 7, 8, 9, 10, 17 100, 104

 and class 5

 and component 17

 and implementation 7

Inheritance  12, 176
 adjusting access  181
 constructors under  195
 destructors under  202
 direct  183
 hierarchy  13, 14
 indirect  183
 in MFC  484
 multiple  13, 216
 name hiding  182
 and polymorphism  12
 private  221
 private member in  180
 protected  221
 protected member in  190
 public  178
 public member in  178
 single  13
 and template class  394
 of virtual methods  235
Initializer, constructor  138
**inline**  105, 106, 163
 constructor  126
 function  62
**inplace_merge**  548
Input, polymorphic  244, 250, 251
Input operator (**>>**)  28
Input/output  27
 buffered  404
 class library  403
 exception  416
 hierarchy  404
 high-level classes  419
 operators (**>>**, **<<**), overloading  305
 stream  27
**insert**  49, 75, 548
Insertion into a **vector** and a **deque**  365
**int_type**  419
Integer as abstract data type  8

Integrated Development Environment (IDE)  480
Interface  5, 6, 8, 12, 17, 18, 19, 20, 100, 101, 104, 109, 117, 505
 and abstract base class  18
 and component  17, 19
 **IDispatch**  506
 and reference counting  522
 registration  481
 shared  260
Interface Definition Language (IDL)  508
**internal**  409
International Standard Book Number (ISBN)  169
Intersection of two sets  171
*iomanip*  406, 428, 431
**ios**  406, 407, 474
**ios_base**  403, 407, 408
*iosfwd*  406, 407
**iostate**  414
*iostream*  25, 28, 406, 407
**iostream_withassign**  475
**is_open**  434, 436, 437
**isalnum**  549
**isalpha**  549
ISBN (International Standard Book Number)  169
**iscntrl**  550
**isdigit**  550
**isgraph**  550
**islower**  550
**isprint**  550
**ispunct**  551
**isspace**  551
**istream**  406, 407
**istream_withassign**  475
**istringstream**  407
**isupper**  551
**isxdigit**  551
Iterator

Iterator (*continued*)
backward 398
forward 398
input 381
output 381
random 398
in STL 360, 365, 377
**IUnknown** 263, 264, 505

## J

Java 17
Johnsonbaugh, R. 478

## K

Keyword list 78

## L

LAN (Local Area Network) 172
Language
object-oriented 4
procedural 4
Last In First Out (LIFO) 7
Leakey, Mary 3, 4
**left** 33, 409
**length** 45, 551
Let's Make a Deal 95
LIFO (Last In First Out) list 7
Linear probing 440
**list** 362, 363
Load factor of a file 441
Local area network (LAN) 172
**log** 552
**log10** 552
**lower_bound** 552

## M

**main** 2, 47
return statement in 47
Maintenance, software 3

**malloc** versus **new** 139
Manipulator 29, 428
user-written 429
**map**
and association list 369
STL 362, 367
MDI (Multiple Document Interface)
484
Member
class versus instance 151
initialization 163
Member selector operator (**.**) 101, 1(
157, 159
and object reference 167
Member selector operators (**.***, **->***)
79
Memory management operators (**new**,
**delete**),
overloading 329
**merge** 399, 552
Message passing 9, 10
and method invocation 10
Method 4, 8, 104
class versus instance 166
**const** 114, 115, 168
declaration 101, 106
declaration as **virtual** 234
declaration versus definition 10
defining versus declaring 105,
and **friend** functions 102
invocation 10
overloading 116
polymorphic 14
read-only 115
signature 13
versus top-level function
**virtual** 231, 233, 235
with **static** variables
MFC (Microsoft Founda′
20, 240, 480
Microsoft 263, 480

Microsoft Foundation Classes (MFC) 20, 240, 480

**mismatch** 553

Model in Smalltalk and MFC 483

Module 2, 4

Monty Hall puzzle 95

Motif 481

**multimap** 362, 367

Multiple Document Interface (MDI) 484

Multiple inheritance 13, 216

   access 217

**multiset** 362, 367

# N

Name

   hiding 182, 252, 255, 256, 277

   overriding 252, 253

   overriding versus overloading 252

Namespace 22

   **std** 22, 25, 364

   unnamed 78

   using declaration 23

   using directive 25

**NDEBUG** 353

**new** 70, 75, 139, 159

   **bad_alloc** 75

   and constructors 139

   overloading 329

   versus **malloc** 139

**new[ ]** 139, 159

   and constructors 139

   versus **calloc** 139

**next_permutation** 553

**noboolalpha** 41

**noshowpoint** 34

**noshowpos** 34

**noskipws** 34

**not1** 383

**nth_element** 379, 554

**NULL**, and **dynamic_cast** 269

Null terminator 9

# O

Object 3, 99

   and class 4

   copying 113

   creation, restricting through constructors 127

   definition 100, 107

   as parameters 4

   persistence 487

   pointer to 157, 158

   reference 167

   relationship to classes 4

Object-oriented design 3, 4, 5

Object-oriented language 2, 4, 9

Object-oriented programming 3, 4, 5, 99

   in C++ 99, 112

   and information hiding 6

   and problem complexity 16

**oct** 30, 409

**ofstream** 35, 146, 150, 407

Object Linking and Embedding (OLE) 508

OLE (Object Linking and Embedding) 508

**omanip** 431

**open** 36, 434, 435, 437, 466, 554

**openmode** 433

**operator** 286

Operator

   overload 286

   precedence 24, 289

Operator overloading 286

   assignment operator 307

   decrement operator 318

   **delete** 329

   function call operator 315

   increment operator 318

   input/output operators 305

   memory management operators 329

Operator overloading (*continued*)
   **new** 329
   subscript operator 312
   type conversion operator 321
   using **friend** functions 302
   using top-level functions 296
**ostream** 406, 407
**ostream_withassign** 475
**ostringstream** 407
**out** 413
Output, polymorphic 245, 250, 251
Output operator (**<<**) 28
**out_of_range** 74
**overflow** 405, 467
Overload 116, 252, 275, 286
   constructor 125
   function 64
   operator 286
Override 14, 236, 241, 252, 253, 275
   and polymorphism 14

**P**

Pair 174
Parameter, **const** 113
Parameterized constructor 125, 129
**partial_sort** 554
**partial_sort_copy** 555
**partition** 555
Pascal 2
Pass and return by value, disabling
   135
Passing and returning by reference
   113
Paulos, J. A. 95
**peek** 421, 556
Persistence 481
   and serialization 281, 487
Pointer
   constant **this** 159
   to object 157, 158
Polymorphic type 267, 268, 269

Polymorphism 12, 13, 14, 16, 177
   231, 232, 244, 245
   and inheritance 12
   for input and output 244, 245, 2.
   251
   and override 14
   and recursion 14
   requirements for 231, 233
   and run-time binding 230, 231
   strong versus weak 275
Pop 7
**pow** 556
Precedence of operators 24, 289
**precision** 408, 556
**prev_permutation** 556
Primitive data type 5
**priority_queue** 370
**private** 6, 100, 102, 103
   inheritance 221
   member in inheritance 180
Problem 2
   complexity 16
   decomposition 2
Procedural language 2, 4
   and abstract data types 8
Procedural library 120
Programming, object-oriented 4
Project in Visual C++ 482
Property of an object 3
Property sheet 507, 511
**protected** 100, 103, 500
   inheritance 221
   member in inheritance 190
Prototype 56
**public** 6, 100, 103
   member in inheritance 178
   scope 5, 103
**pubseekoff** 465
**pubseekpos** 465
**pubsetbuf** 463
Pure virtual method 260, 261

Pure virtual method (*continued*)
  restrictions 262
Push 7
**put** 424, 557
**putback** 421, 557

## Q

**qsort** 557
  versus STL **sort** 379
**QueryInterface** in **IUnknown** 264
Queue 170, 397
**queue** 370

## R

**rand** 557
Random access file 438
Random access file class sample
    application 438
Random iterator 398
**random_shuffle** 373, 379, 558
**rdbuf** 558
**rdstate** 415, 558
**read** 421, 558
Recursion and polymorphism 14, 15, 16
Reference 57, 113
  call by 58
  counting 522
  to an object 167
  passing and returning by 113, 114
  return by 59
  versus values 113
Registry 504
Regular expression 173
**reinterpret_cast** 40
Relationship
  *belongs to* 4, 5
  and classes 4
  *has a* 4, 5
  *instance of* 4
  *is a* 4, 5

Relative address 439
Relative file 439
**Release** in **IUnknown** 264
Remote Procedure Call (RPC) 504
**remove** 559
**remove_copy** 559
**remove_copy_if** 559
**remove_if** 559
**replace** 49, 75, 560
**replace_copy** 561
**replace_copy_if** 561
**replace_if** 378, 562
**resetiosflags** 428
Rethrowing an exception 76
Return by reference 59, 113
Returning by value, disabling 135
**reverse** 562
**reverse_copy** 562
**rfind** 52, 562
**right** 33, 409
Robustness 10, 125
  and abstract data type 7
  for classes 112
  and constructors 125
RPC (Remote Procedure Call) 504
RTTI (Run-Time Type Identification)
    265
  extending 274
Rumbaugh, J. 4
Run-time binding 230, 231, 232, 252,
    275
  and vtable 236
Run-Time Type Identification (RTTI)
    265
  extending 274

## S

Sahni, S. 477
Sample application
  associative aray 324

Sample application (*continued*)
automation server and controller 510
complex number class 291
document serialization 489
high-level copy function 461
random access file class 438
sequence hierarchy 205
stack class 109
stock performance reports 385
task class 145
template stack class 351
time stamp class 117
tracking films 185
tracking films revisited 242
**sbumpc** 464
Schedule 172
**scientific** 33, 409
Scope 103
class 103
public 103
Scope resolution operator (**::**) 16, 23, 105
**search** 563
**seekg** 421, 563
**seekp** 413, 421, 425, 564
Self-serialization in MFC 488, 502
Semaphore 170
Sequence 205
sorted 205
Sequence hierarchy sample application 205
Sequential file 477
Serialization 281
in MFC 486, 499
Server 9, 10
and automation controller 505
Set 170
**set** 362, 367
**set_terminate** 564
**set_unexpected** 564

**setbase** 428
**setbuf** 463, 466, 473
**setf** 409, 410, 564
**setfill** 32, 428
**setiosflags** 428
**setprecision** 32, 428
**setstate** 415
**setw** 29, 31, 428
**sgetc** 464, 467
**sgetn** 464
Shared interface 260
**showbase** 409
**showpoint** 33, 409
**showpos** 409
Signal 77
Signature 13, 65, 257
method 278
**sin** 565
Single inheritance 13
**sinh** 565
**sizeof** 153
**skipws** 409
Smalltalk 484
**snextc** 464, 467
Software maintenance 3
Software system 3
**sort** 360, 378, 565
Sorted sequence 205
**sputbackc** 464
**sputc** 464
**sputn** 465
**sqrt** 565
**srand** 566
*sstream* 406, 457, 463
**stable_partition** 566
**stable_sort** 566
Stack class sample application 109
Stack 7, 8, 109, 110, 112, 125, 126
as abstract data type 7
checking for empty and full 111
initialization 110

Stack (*continued*)
    interface  110
    push and pop  111
    template version  351, 355
    top  111
**stack**  370
Stack class sample application  109
Standard header  22, 26
Standard Template Library (STL)  359
Starting address of a function  230
**static**  152, 154, 155, 166
    defining member  153
    method, and **this**  160
    variables defined inside methods
        155
**static_cast**  38, 266
    and type safety  267
    versus **dynamic_cast**  272
**std**  22, 25, 364
STL (Standard Template Library)  359
    algorithm  360, 377
    container  360, 362
    extensibility  361
    function object  382
    iterator  360, 377
    reasons for using  360
Stock performance reports sample
    application  385
**str**  458, 460, 473, 566
Stream  403
Stream input/output  27
Stream status flags  413
**streambuf**  406, 407, 463
**streamsize**  420, 421
**string**  9, 10, 11, 44
    and abstract data type  9
    assignment  47
    **c_str**  45, 540
    comparison  53
    concatenation  48
    conversion to C-style string  45

**erase**  48, 74, 541
**find**  51, 543
**find_first_of**  52, 544
**getline**  46
**insert**  49, 75, 548
**length**  45, 551
reading and writing  45
**replace**  49, 75, 560
**rfind**  52, 562
and STL  372
**substr**  51, 75, 567
**swap**  50, 567
variable  45
versus C-style string  116
**stringbuf**  407
**stringstream**  407
**strstream** classes  475
**struct**  43, 100, 103
    contrasted with **class**  103
Structure  43
Subclass  4, 13, 176
Subproblem  2
Subscript operator ([ ]), overloading
    312
**substr**  51, 75, 567
Superclass  176
**swap**  50, 567
**swap_ranges**  567
Symbol table  173
Synchronous exception  77
**sync_with_stdio**  34, 414, 568
**system**  568

## T

Tag  99
**tan**  568
**tanh**  568
Task class sample application  145
**tellg**  421, 568
**tellp**  421, 425, 569

Template 341, 342, 346, 350
   class 341
   function-style parameters 348
   header 341
   and inheritance 394
   input/output classes 407
   instantiation 345, 346, 350
   in a parameter list 347
Template stack class sample application
   351
**terminate** 569
Test client 109, 112, 123, 146
Testing 3
Thin wrapper 120
**this** 159, 160
   as a constant 168
**throw** 73
Throwing an exception 73
   rethrow 76
Time stamp, and Task class 146
Time stamp class sample application
   117
**time** 119, 120, 399, 569
**time_t** 120
**tolower** 569
Top-down design 2
Top-down functional decomposition
   2, 5
**toupper** 569
Tracking films revisited sample application 242
Tracking films sample application 185
**traits** 407
**transform** 570
**true** 40
**trunc** 413
**try** block 73
Type conversion operator, overloading
   321
**type_info** 272, 273, 274
Type library in MFC 508

Type safety 267, 272
**typeid** 272, 273, 279
**typename** 341, 344, 395

**U**

**unary_function** 383
**underflow** 405, 468
**unexpected** 76, 570
Union
   anonymous 78
   of two sets 171
**unique** 570
**unique_copy** 571
**unitbuf** 409
Universally Unique Identifier (UUI
   504
Unnamed namespace 78
**unsetf** 410, 571
Upcast 271
**upper_bound** 571
**uppercase** 409
Using declaration 23
Using directive 25
Utility class 117
UUID (Universally Unique Identifie
   504

**V**

Variable
   definition 42
   **string** 45
**VARIANT** in MFC 520
**vector** 361, 362, 363
View in Smalltalk and MFC 484
**virtual** 18
   base class 218
   destructor 237, 238, 239, 499
   method 231, 233, 235, 236, 254, 2:
   and method declaration 234
   overriding 236, 241

**virtual** (*continued*)
   pure 260, 261, 262
   and **static** 240
Visual C++ 480
   code generators 482
   project 482
Vtable 236, 241, 504

## W

**wchar_t** 407

**width** 408, 571
Win32 system 480
Wizards as code generators 482
World Wide Web 399
Wrapper 120
**write** 425, 572

## Y

Y2K 10, 11
Year 2000 10, 11

# LICENSE AGREEMENT AND LIMITED WARRANTY

READ THE FOLLOWING TERMS AND CONDITIONS CAREFULLY BEFORE OPENING THIS CD PACKAGE, *OBJECT-ORIENTED PROGRAMMING IN C++, SECOND EDITION*. THIS LEGAL DOCUMENT IS AN AGREEMENT BETWEEN YOU AND PRENTICE-HALL, INC. (THE "COMPANY"). BY OPENING THIS SEALED CD PACKAGE, YOU ARE AGREEING TO BE BOUND BY THESE TERMS AND CONDITIONS. IF YOU DO NOT AGREE WITH THESE TERMS AND CONDITIONS, DO NOT OPEN THE CD PACKAGE. PROMPTLY RETURN THE UNOPENED CD PACKAGE AND ALL ACCOMPANYING ITEMS TO THE PLACE YOU OBTAINED THEM FOR A FULL REFUND OF ANY SUMS YOU HAVE PAID.

1. **GRANT OF LICENSE:** In consideration of your purchase of this book, and your agreement to abide by the terms and conditions of this Agreement, the Company grants to you a nonexclusive right to use and display the copy of the enclosed software program (hereinafter the "SOFTWARE") on a single computer (i.e., with a single CPU) at a single location so long as you comply with the terms of this Agreement. The Company reserves all rights not expressly granted to you under this Agreement.

2. **OWNERSHIP OF SOFTWARE:** You own only the magnetic or physical media (the enclosed CD) on which the SOFTWARE is recorded or fixed, but the Company and the software developers retain all the rights, title, and ownership to the SOFTWARE recorded on the original CD copy(ies) and all subsequent copies of the SOFTWARE, regardless of the form or media on which the original or other copies may exist. This license is not a sale of the original SOFTWARE or any copy to you.

3. **COPY RESTRICTIONS:** This SOFTWARE and the accompanying printed materials and user manual (the "Documentation") are the subject of copyright. The individual programs on the CD are copyrighted by the authors of each program. Some of the programs on the CD include separate licensing agreements. If you intend to use one of these programs, you must read and follow its accompanying license agreement. You may <u>not</u> copy the Documentation or the SOFTWARE, except that you may make a single copy of the SOFTWARE for backup or archival purposes only. You may be held legally responsible for any copying or copyright infringement which is caused or encouraged by your failure to abide by the terms of this restriction.

4. **USE RESTRICTIONS:** You may <u>not</u> network the SOFTWARE or otherwise use it on more than one computer or computer terminal at the same time. You may physically transfer the SOFTWARE from one computer to another provided that the SOFTWARE is used on only one computer at a time. You may <u>not</u> distribute copies of the SOFTWARE or Documentation to others. You may <u>not</u> reverse engineer, disassemble, decompile, modify, adapt, translate, or create derivative works based on the SOFTWARE or the Documentation without the prior written consent of the Company.

5. **TRANSFER RESTRICTIONS:** The enclosed SOFTWARE is licensed only to you and may <u>not</u> be transferred to any one else without the prior written consent of the Company. Any unauthorized transfer of the SOFTWARE shall result in the immediate termination of this Agreement.

6. **TERMINATION:** This license is effective until terminated. This license will terminate automatically without notice from the Company and become null and void if you fail to comply with any provisions or limitations of this license. Upon termination, you shall destroy the Documentation and all copies of the SOFTWARE. All provisions of this Agreement as to warranties, limitation of liability, remedies or damages, and our ownership rights shall survive termination.

7. **MISCELLANEOUS:** This Agreement shall be construed in accordance with the laws of the United States of America and the State of New York and shall benefit the Company, its affiliates, and assignees.

8. **LIMITED WARRANTY AND DISCLAIMER OF WARRANTY:** The Company warrants that the SOFTWARE, when properly used in accordance with the Documentation, will operate in substantial conformity with the description of the SOFTWARE set forth in the Documentation. The

Company does not warrant that the SOFTWARE will meet your requirements or that the operation of the SOFTWARE will be uninterrupted or error-free. The Company warrants that the media on which the SOFTWARE is delivered shall be free from defects in materials and workmanship under normal use for a period of thirty (30) days from the date of your purchase. Your only remedy and the Company's only obligation under these limited warranties is, at the Company's option, return of the warranted item for a refund of any amounts paid by you or replacement of the item. Any replacement of SOFTWARE or media under the warranties shall not extend the original warranty period. The limited warranty set forth above shall not apply to any SOFTWARE which the Company determines in good faith has been subject to misuse, neglect, improper installation, repair, alteration, or damage by you. EXCEPT FOR THE EXPRESSED WARRANTIES SET FORTH ABOVE, THE COMPANY DISCLAIMS ALL WARRANTIES, EXPRESS OR IMPLIED, INCLUDING WITHOUT LIMITATION, THE IMPLIED WARRANTIES OF MERCHANTABILITY AND FITNESS FOR A PARTICULAR PURPOSE. EXCEPT FOR THE EXPRESS WARRANTY SET FORTH ABOVE, THE COMPANY DOES NOT WARRANT, GUARANTEE, OR MAKE ANY REPRESENTATION REGARDING THE USE OR THE RESULTS OF THE USE OF THE SOFTWARE IN TERMS OF ITS CORRECTNESS, ACCURACY, RELIABILITY, CURRENTNESS, OR OTHERWISE.

IN NO EVENT, SHALL THE COMPANY OR ITS EMPLOYEES, AGENTS, SUPPLIERS, OR CONTRACTORS BE LIABLE FOR ANY INCIDENTAL, INDIRECT, SPECIAL, OR CONSEQUENTIAL DAMAGES ARISING OUT OF OR IN CONNECTION WITH THE LICENSE GRANTED UNDER THIS AGREEMENT, OR FOR LOSS OF USE, LOSS OF DATA, LOSS OF INCOME OR PROFIT, OR OTHER LOSSES, SUSTAINED AS A RESULT OF INJURY TO ANY PERSON, OR LOSS OF OR DAMAGE TO PROPERTY, OR CLAIMS OF THIRD PARTIES, EVEN IF THE COMPANY OR AN AUTHORIZED REPRESENTATIVE OF THE COMPANY HAS BEEN ADVISED OF THE POSSIBILITY OF SUCH DAMAGES. IN NO EVENT SHALL LIABILITY OF THE COMPANY FOR DAMAGES WITH RESPECT TO THE SOFTWARE EXCEED THE AMOUNTS ACTUALLY PAID BY YOU, IF ANY, FOR THE SOFTWARE.

SOME JURISDICTIONS DO NOT ALLOW THE LIMITATION OF IMPLIED WARRANTIES OR LIABILITY FOR INCIDENTAL, INDIRECT, SPECIAL, OR CONSEQUENTIAL DAMAGES, SO THE ABOVE LIMITATIONS MAY NOT ALWAYS APPLY. THE WARRANTIES IN THIS AGREEMENT GIVE YOU SPECIFIC LEGAL RIGHTS AND YOU MAY ALSO HAVE OTHER RIGHTS WHICH VARY IN ACCORDANCE WITH LOCAL LAW.

ACKNOWLEDGMENT

YOU ACKNOWLEDGE THAT YOU HAVE READ THIS AGREEMENT, UNDERSTAND IT, AND AGREE TO BE BOUND BY ITS TERMS AND CONDITIONS. YOU ALSO AGREE THAT THIS AGREEMENT IS THE COMPLETE AND EXCLUSIVE STATEMENT OF THE AGREEMENT BETWEEN YOU AND THE COMPANY AND SUPERSEDES ALL PROPOSALS OR PRIOR AGREEMENTS, ORAL, OR WRITTEN, AND ANY OTHER COMMUNICATIONS BETWEEN YOU AND THE COMPANY OR ANY REPRESENTATIVE OF THE COMPANY RELATING TO THE SUBJECT MATTER OF THIS AGREEMENT.

Should you have any questions concerning this Agreement or if you wish to contact the Company for any reason, please contact in writing at the address below.

Robin Short

Prentice Hall PTR

One Lake Street

Upper Saddle River, New Jersey 07458

# END-USER LICENSE AGREEMENT FOR MICROSOFT SOFTWARE

IMPORTANT—READ CAREFULLY: This Microsoft End-User License Agreement ("EULA") is a legal agreement between you (either an individual or a single entity) and Microsoft Corporation for the Microsoft software product identified above, which includes computer software and may include associated media, printed materials, and "online" or electronic documentation ("SOFTWARE PRODUCT"). The SOFTWARE PRODUCT also includes any updates and supplements to the original SOFTWARE PRODUCT provided to you by Microsoft. By installing, copying, downloading, accessing or otherwise using the SOFTWARE PRODUCT, you agree to be bound by the terms of this EULA. If you do not agree to the terms of this EULA, do not install , copy , or otherwise use the SOFTWARE PRODUCT.

## SOFTWARE PRODUCT LICENSE

The SOFTWARE PRODUCT is protected by copyright laws and international copyright treaties, as well as other intellectual property laws and treaties. The SOFTWARE PRODUCT is licensed, not sold.

**1. GRANT OF LICENSE.** This EULA grants you the following rights:

**1.1    License Grant. Microsoft grants to you as an individual, a personal nonexclusive license to make and use copies of the SOFTWARE PRODUCT for the sole purposes of evaluating  and learning how to use the SOFTWARE PRODUCT, as may be instructed in accompanying publications or documentation.  You may install the software on an unlimited number of computers provided that you are the only individual using the SOFTWARE PRODUCT.**

1.2    **Academic Use.** You must be a "Qualified Educational User" to use the SOFTWARE PRODUCT in the manner described in this section. To determine whether you are a Qualified Educational User, please contact the Microsoft Sales Information Center/One Microsoft Way/Redmond, WA 98052-6399 or the Microsoft subsidiary serving your country.  If you are a Qualified Educational User, you may either:

(i)    exercise the rights granted in Section 1.1, OR

(ii)    if you intend to use the SOFTWARE PRODUCT solely for instructional purposes in connection with a class or other educational program, this EULA grants you the following alternative license models:

(A)    Per Computer Model.  For every valid license you have acquired for the SOFTWARE PRODUCT, you may install a single copy of the SOFTWARE PRODUCT on a single computer for access and use by an unlimited number of student end users at your educational institution, provided that all such end users comply with all other terms of this EULA, OR

(B)    Per License Model. If you have multiple licenses for the SOFTWARE PRODUCT, then at any time you may have as many copies of the SOFTWARE PRODUCT in use as you have licenses, provided that such use is limited to student or faculty end users at your educational institution and provided that all such end users comply with all other terms of this EULA.  For purposes of this subsection, the SOFTWARE PRODUCT is "in use" on a computer when it is loaded into the temporary memory (i.e., RAM) or installed into the permanent memory (e.g., hard disk, CD ROM, or other storage device) of that computer, except that a copy installed on a network server for the sole purpose of distribution to other computers is not "in use".  If the anticipated number of users of the SOFTWARE PRODUCT will exceed the number of applicable licenses, then you must have a reasonable mechanism or process in place to ensure that the number of persons using the SOFTWARE PRODUCT concurrently does not exceed the number of licenses.

**2. DESCRIPTION OF OTHER RIGHTS AND LIMITATIONS.**

- **Limitations on Reverse Engineering, Decompilation, and Disassembly.** You may not reverse engineer, decompile, or disassemble the SOFTWARE PRODUCT, except and only to the extent that such activity is expressly permitted by applicable law notwithstanding this limitation.

- **Separation of Components.** The SOFTWARE PRODUCT is licensed as a single product. Its component parts may not be separated for use on more than one computer.

- **Rental.** You may not rent, lease or lend the SOFTWARE PRODUCT.

- **Trademarks.** This EULA does not grant you any rights in connection with any trademarks or service marks of Microsoft.

- **Software Transfer.** The initial user of the SOFTWARE PRODUCT may make a one-time permanent transfer of this EULA and SOFTWARE PRODUCT only directly to an end user. This transfer must include all of the SOFTWARE PRODUCT (including all component parts, the media and printed materials, any upgrades, this EULA, and, if applicable, the Certificate of Authenticity). Such transfer may not be by way of consignment or any other indirect transfer. The transferee of such one-time transfer must agree to comply with the terms of this EULA, including the obligation not to further transfer this EULA and SOFTWARE PRODUCT.

- **No Support.** Microsoft shall have no obligation to provide any product support for the SOFTWARE PRODUCT.

- **Termination.** Without prejudice to any other rights, Microsoft may terminate this EULA if you fail to comply with the terms and conditions of this EULA. In such event, you must destroy all copies of the SOFTWARE PRODUCT and all of its component parts.

3. **COPYRIGHT.** All title and intellectual property rights in and to the SOFTWARE PRODUCT (including but not limited to any images, photographs, animations, video, audio, music, text, and "applets" incorporated into the SOFTWARE PRODUCT), the accompanying printed materials, and any copies of the SOFTWARE PRODUCT are owned by Microsoft or its suppliers. All title and intellectual property rights in and to the content which may be accessed through use of the SOFTWARE PRODUCT is the property of the respective content owner and may be protected by applicable copyright or other intellectual property laws and treaties. This EULA grants you no rights to use such content. All rights not expressly granted are reserved by Microsoft.

4. **BACKUP COPY.** After installation of one copy of the SOFTWARE PRODUCT pursuant to this EULA, you may keep the original media on which the SOFTWARE PRODUCT was provided by Microsoft solely for backup or archival purposes. If the original media is required to use the SOFTWARE PRODUCT on the COMPUTER, you may make one copy of the SOFTWARE PRODUCT solely for backup or archival purposes. Except as expressly provided in this EULA, you may not otherwise make copies of the SOFTWARE PRODUCT or the printed materials accompanying the SOFTWARE PRODUCT.

5. **U.S. GOVERNMENT RESTRICTED RIGHTS.** The SOFTWARE PRODUCT and documentation are provided with RESTRICTED RIGHTS. Use, duplication, or disclosure by the Government is subject to restrictions as set forth in subparagraph (c)(1)(ii) of the Rights in Technical Data and Computer Software clause at DFARS 252.227-7013 or subparagraphs (c)(1) and (2) of the Commercial Computer Software—Restricted Rights at 48 CFR 52.227-19, as applicable. Manufacturer is Microsoft Corporation/One Microsoft Way/Redmond, WA 98052-6399.

6. **EXPORT RESTRICTIONS.** You agree that you will not export or re-export the SOFTWARE PRODUCT, any part thereof, or any process or service that is the direct product of the SOFTWARE PRODUCT (the foregoing collectively referred to as the "Restricted Components"), to any country, person, entity or end user subject to U.S. export restrictions. You specifically agree not to export or re-export any of the Restricted Components (i) to any country to which the U.S. has embargoed or restricted the export of goods or services, which currently include, but are not necessarily limited to Cuba, Iran, Iraq, Libya, North Korea, Sudan and Syria, or to any national of any such country, wherever located, who intends to transmit or transport the Restricted Components back to such country; (ii) to any end-user who you know or have reason to know will utilize the Restricted Components in the design, development or production of nuclear, chemical or biological weapons; or (iii) to any end-user who has been prohibited from participating in U.S. export transactions by any federal agency of the U.S. government. You warrant and represent that neither the BXA nor any other U.S. federal agency has suspended, revoked, or denied your export privileges.

7. **NOTE ON JAVA SUPPORT.** THE SOFTWARE PRODUCT MAY CONTAIN SUPPORT FOR PROGRAMS WRITTEN IN JAVA. JAVA TECHNOLOGY IS NOT FAULT TOLERANT AND IS NOT DESIGNED, MANUFACTURED, OR INTENDED FOR USE OR RESALE AS ON-LINE CONTROL EQUIPMENT IN HAZARDOUS ENVIRONMENTS REQUIRING FAIL-SAFE PERFORMANCE, SUCH AS IN THE OPERATION OF NUCLEAR FACILITIES, AIRCRAFT NAVIGATION OR COMMUNICATION SYSTEMS, AIR TRAFFIC CONTROL, DIRECT LIFE SUPPORT MACHINES, OR WEAPONS SYSTEMS, IN WHICH THE FAILURE OF JAVA TECHNOLOGY COULD LEAD DIRECTLY TO DEATH, PERSONAL INJURY, OR SEVERE PHYSICAL OR ENVIRONMENTAL DAMAGE.

**MISCELLANEOUS**

If you acquired this product in the United States, this EULA is governed by the laws of the State of Washington.

If you acquired this product in Canada, this EULA is governed by the laws of the Province of Ontario, Canada. Each of the parties hereto irrevocably attorns to the jurisdiction of the courts of the Province of Ontario and further agrees to

commence any litigation which may arise hereunder in the courts located in the Judicial District of York, Province of Ontario.

If this product was acquired outside the United States, then local law may apply.

Should you have any questions concerning this EULA, or if you desire to contact Microsoft for any reason, please contact Microsoft, or write: Microsoft Sales Information Center/One Microsoft Way/Redmond, WA 98052-6399.

## LIMITED WARRANTY

**LIMITED WARRANTY.** Microsoft warrants that (a) the SOFTWARE PRODUCT will perform substantially in accordance with the accompanying written materials for a period of ninety (90) days from the date of receipt, and (b) any Support Services provided by Microsoft shall be substantially as described in applicable written materials provided to you by Microsoft, and Microsoft support engineers will make commercially reasonable efforts to solve any problem. To the extent allowed by applicable law, implied warranties on the SOFTWARE PRODUCT, if any, are limited to ninety (90) days. Some states/jurisdictions do not allow limitations on duration of an implied warranty, so the above limitation may not apply to you.

**CUSTOMER REMEDIES.** Microsoft's and its suppliers' entire liability and your exclusive remedy shall be, at Microsoft's option, either (a) return of the price paid, if any, or (b) repair or replacement of the SOFTWARE PRODUCT that does not meet Microsoft's Limited Warranty and that is returned to Microsoft with a copy of your receipt. This Limited Warranty is void if failure of the SOFTWARE PRODUCT has resulted from accident, abuse, or misapplication. Any replacement SOFTWARE PRODUCT will be warranted for the remainder of the original warranty period or thirty (30) days, whichever is longer. Outside the United States, neither these remedies nor any product support services offered by Microsoft are available without proof of purchase from an authorized international source.

**NO OTHER WARRANTIES. TO THE MAXIMUM EXTENT PERMITTED BY APPLICABLE LAW, MICROSOFT AND ITS SUPPLIERS DISCLAIM ALL OTHER WARRANTIES AND CONDITIONS, EITHER EXPRESS OR IMPLIED, INCLUDING, BUT NOT LIMITED TO, IMPLIED WARRANTIES OR CONDITIONS OF MERCHANTABILITY, FITNESS FOR A PARTICULAR PURPOSE, TITLE AND NON-INFRINGEMENT, WITH REGARD TO THE SOFTWARE PRODUCT, AND THE PROVISION OF OR FAILURE TO PROVIDE SUPPORT SERVICES. THIS LIMITED WARRANTY GIVES YOU SPECIFIC LEGAL RIGHTS. YOU MAY HAVE OTHERS, WHICH VARY FROM STATE/JURISDICTION TO STATE/JURISDICTION.**

**LIMITATION OF LIABILITY. TO THE MAXIMUM EXTENT PERMITTED BY APPLICABLE LAW, IN NO EVENT SHALL MICROSOFT OR ITS SUPPLIERS BE LIABLE FOR ANY SPECIAL, INCIDENTAL, INDIRECT, OR CONSEQUENTIAL DAMAGES WHATSOEVER (INCLUDING, WITHOUT LIMITATION, DAMAGES FOR LOSS OF BUSINESS PROFITS, BUSINESS INTERRUPTION, LOSS OF BUSINESS INFORMATION, OR ANY OTHER PECUNIARY LOSS) ARISING OUT OF THE USE OF OR INABILITY TO USE THE SOFTWARE PRODUCT OR THE FAILURE TO PROVIDE SUPPORT SERVICES, EVEN IF MICROSOFT HAS BEEN ADVISED OF THE POSSIBILITY OF SUCH DAMAGES. IN ANY CASE, MICROSOFT'S ENTIRE LIABILITY UNDER ANY PROVISION OF THIS EULA SHALL BE LIMITED TO THE GREATER OF THE AMOUNT ACTUALLY PAID BY YOU FOR THE SOFTWARE PRODUCT OR U.S.$5.00; PROVIDED, HOWEVER, IF YOU HAVE ENTERED INTO A MICROSOFT SUPPORT SERVICES AGREEMENT, MICROSOFT'S ENTIRE LIABILITY REGARDING SUPPORT SERVICES SHALL BE GOVERNED BY THE TERMS OF THAT AGREEMENT. BECAUSE SOME STATES/JURISDICTIONS DO NOT ALLOW THE EXCLUSION OR LIMITATION OF LIABILITY, THE ABOVE LIMITATION MAY NOT APPLY TO YOU.**

**Si vous avez acquis votre produit Microsoft au CANADA, la garantie limitée suivante vous concerne :**

## GARANTIE LIMITÉE

**GARANTIE LIMITÉE** — Microsoft garantit que (a) la performance du LOGICIEL sera substantiellement en conformité avec la documentation qui accompagne le LOGICIEL, pour une période de quatre-vingt-dix (90) jours à compter de la date de réception; et (b) tout support technique fourni par Microsoft sera substantiellement en conformité avec toute documentation afférente fournie par Microsoft et que les membres du support technique de Microsoft feront des efforts raisonnables pour résoudre toute difficulté technique découlant de l'utilisation du LOGICIEL. Certaines juridictions ne permettent pas de limiter dans le temps l'application de la présente garantie. Aussi, la limite stipulée ci-haut pourrait ne pas s'appliquer dans votre cas. Dans la mesure permise par la loi, toute garantie implicite portant sur le LOGICIEL, le cas échéant, est limitée à une période de quatre-vingt-dix (90) jours.

**RECOURS DU CLIENT** — La seule obligation de Microsoft et de ses fournisseurs et votre recours exclusif seront, au choix de Microsoft, soit (a) le remboursement du prix payé, si applicable, ou (b) la réparation ou le remplacement du LOGICIEL qui n'est pas conforme à la Garantie Limitée de Microsoft et qui est retourné à Microsoft avec une copie de votre reçu. Cette Garantie Limitée est nulle si le défaut du LOGICIEL est causé par un accident, un traitement abusif ou une mauvaise application. Tout LOGICIEL

de remplacement sera garanti pour le reste de la période de garantie initiale ou pour trente (30) jours, selon la plus longue de ces périodes. A l'extérieur des Etats-Unis, aucun de ces recours non plus que le support technique offert par Microsoft ne sont disponibles sans une preuve d'achat provenant d'une source autorisée.

**AUCUNE AUTRE GARANTIE — DANS LA MESURE PREVUE PAR LA LOI, MICROSOFT ET SES FOURNISSEURS EXCLUENT TOUTE AUTRE GARANTIE OU CONDITION, EXPRESSE OU IMPLICITE, Y COMPRIS MAIS NE SE LIMITANT PAS AUX GARANTIES OU CONDITIONS IMPLICITES DU CARACTERE ADEQUAT POUR LA COMMERCIALISATION OU UN USAGE PARTICULIER EN CE QUI CONCERNE LE LOGICIEL OU CONCERNANT LE TITRE, L'ABSENCE DE CONTREFAÅON DUDIT LOGICIEL, ET TOUTE DOCUMENTATION ECRITE QUI L'ACCOMPAGNE, AINSI QUE POUR TOUTE DISPOSITION CONCERNANT LE SUPORT TECHNIQUE OU LA FAÅON DONT CELUI-CI A ETE RENDU. CETTE GARANTIE LIMITEE VOUS ACCORDE DES DROITS JURIDIQUES SPECIFIQUES.**

**PAS DE RESPONSABILITE POUR LES DOMMAGES INDIRECTS — MICROSOFT OU SES FOURNISSEURS NE SERONT PAS RESPONSABLES, EN AUCUNE CIRCONSTANCE, POUR TOUT DOMMAGE SPECIAL, INCIDENT, INDIRECT, OU CONSEQUENT QUEL QU'IL SOIT (Y COMPRIS, SANS LIMITATION, LES DOMMAGES ENTRAINES PAR LA PERTE DE BENEFICES, L'INTERRUPTION DES ACTIVITES, LA PERTE D'INFORMATION OU TOUTE AUTRE PERTE PECUNIAIRE) DECOULANT DE OU RELIE A LA LICENCE D'ACCES DU CLIENTET CE, MEME SI MICROSOFT A ETE AVISEE DE LA POSSIBILITE DE TELS DOMMAGES. LA RESPONSABILITE DE MICROSOFT EN VERTU DE TOUTE DISPOSITION DE CETTE CONVENTION NE POURRA EN AUCUN TEMPS EXCEDER LE PLUS ELEVE ENTRE I) LE MONTANT EFFECTIVEMENT PAYE PAR VOUS POUR LA LICENCE D'ACCES DU CLIENT OU II) U.S.$5.00. ADVENANT QUE VOUS AYEZ CONTRACTE PAR ENTENTE DISTINCTE AVEC MICROSOFT POUR UN SUPPORT TECHNIQUE ETENDU, VOUS SEREZ LIE PAR LES TERMES D' UNE TELLE ENTENTE.**

La présente Convention est régie par les lois en vigeur dans ela province d'Ontario, Canada. Chacune des parties à la présente reconnaît irrévocablement la compétence des tribunaux de la province d'Ontario et consent à instituer tout litige qui pourrait découler de la présente auprès des tribunaux situés dans le district judiciaire de York, province d'Ontario.

Au cas où vous auriez des questions concernant cette licence ou que vous désiriez vous mettre en rapport avec Microsoft pour quelque raison que ce soit, veuillez contacter la succursale Microsoft desservant votre pays, dont l'adresse est fournie dans ce produit, ou écrire à: Microsoft Sales Information Center, One Microsoft Way, Redmond, Washington 98052-6399

| Manipulator | Effect |
|---|---|
| boolalpha | Input or output **bool**s as **true** and **false** |
| noboolalpha | Input or output **bool**s as 1 (true) and 0 (false) |
| dec | Input or output in decimal |
| endl | Write newline and flush output stream |
| fixed | Use fixed notation for floating-point numbers: **d.ddd** |
| flush | Flush output stream |
| hex | Input or output in hexadecimal |
| left | Left-justify |
| oct | Input or output in octal |
| right | Right-justify |
| scientific | Use scientific notation for floating-point numbers: **d.dddEdd** |
| setfill( c ) | Make **c** the fill character |
| setprecision( n ) | Set floating-point precision to **n** |
| setw( n ) | Set field width to **n** |
| showpoint | Always print decimal point and trailing zeros |
| noshowpoint | Don't print trailing zeros. Drop decimal point, if possible. |
| showpos | Use + with nonnegative numbers |
| noshowpos | Don't use + with nonnegative numbers |
| skipws | Skip white space before input |
| noskipws | Don't skip white space before input |
| ws | Remove white space |